CRIME AND PUNISHMENT

CRIME AND

An
Introduction
to
Criminology

PUNISHMENT

Harry E. Allen
Paul C. Friday
Julian B. Roebuck
Edward Sagarin

THE FREE PRESS

A Division of Macmillan Publishing Co., Inc.

NEW YORK

Collier Macmillan Publishers

LONDON

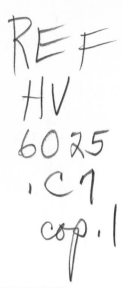
Copyright © 1981 by THE FREE PRESS
A Division of Macmillan Publishing Co., Inc.

THE FREE PRESS
A Division of Macmillan Publishing Co., Inc.
866 Third Avenue, New York, N. Y. 10022

Collier Macmillan Canada, Ltd.

Library of Congress Catalog Card Number: 80-69715

Printed in the United States of America

printing number
2 3 4 5 6 7 8 9 10

Library of Congress Cataloging in Publication Data
Main entry under title:

Crime and punishment.

   Includes bibliographies and indexes.
   1. Crime and criminals.   2. Criminal justice,
Administration of.   3. Corrections.   I. Allen,
Harry E.
HV6025.C7   364   80-69715
ISBN 0-02-900460-8   AACR2

Contents

Criminal Justice: Prevention and Control of Crime

Corrections, Rehabilitation, Resocialization

Directions and Outlook

Preface

With a literature already too large for any one person to digest and so much of it excellent beyond dispute, we add still another text to those now available, and do so with explanation rather than apology.

Our book differs in origin and development from all the others in that it is multiauthored, not in the sense of being a reader or collection, but rather in that the four of us (with some aid from others, to be acknowledged shortly) have participated in a joint effort in writing it, in reading and criticizing each other's work, and in rewriting until a single unified book was ready to emerge. We hope that our writing has been enriched by this cooperative enterprise, a task that at times seemed formidable to the point of being discouraging but in the end produced something that no one of us could have done by himself.

Further, it was felt that this work would be aided by the variety in background and experience of the four authors, all criminologists. We span more than a generation in age, and received our education in four different universities, studying in America and abroad. We represent both in our origins and in current and recent locales of our teaching posts four different sections of the country: the Northeast, the Midwest, the Far West, and the South. And in previous writings and research we have focused on different aspects of crime, justice, and corrections.

A single criminology text cannot hope to encompass the vast store of knowledge accumulated over the years that one would like to pass down to young people obtaining an education in this field. But it was our hope to handle some aspects of this subject matter in a manner that might prove particularly helpful to professor and student alike. Among other features, we have sought to present the following:

1. A discussion of crime as a concept—a discussion that accepts the usefulness of a legal definition without accepting the righteousness of it and

that avoids the error of making crime synonymous with all law-breaking (which turns the traffic violator or litterer into a criminal).

2. An elaboration of crime statistics that embodies a recognition of the inherent difficulties of amassing accurate and reliable data and acknowledges the value of the data being gathered in the United States without dismissing the critics of the present system.

3. An overview of theories of crime that would give students an indication of a body of relevant research (both in support of and in opposition to many of the approaches), and that, although based largely (as most criminological theories are) on studies of youthful delinquents, would be made germane to adult crime.

4. Studies of major criminal behavior systems, to indicate for various types of crime such relevant information as legal aspects, criminal careers, correspondence between legitimate and illegitimate behavior, and nature of societal reaction.

5. A view of political crime that sees it as behavior conducted both by the government (or its agents and employees) and by opponents of the government, neither of which should be dismissed or glorified for ideological reasons.

6. A discussion of white-collar crime that shows its pervasiveness and its dangers, without ignoring the very real and immediate danger of crime committed by robbers, burglars, and others of whom the public appears to be so frightened.

7. A look at victims and victimology—probably the most recent emphasis in criminology: what does such a type of study tell us, where does it lead, what are its dangers?

8. A brief examination of some elementary precepts of the criminal justice system, the nature of the process of arrest, trial, sentencing, the rationale behind the maze of rules governing courtroom procedures.

9. An exposition on crime prevention: the problem of environmental defense and the danger that prevention may lead only to displacement, in which the offenders turn to another part of town or another type of offense.

10. An introduction to American police systems; the diverse models, the struggle for police professionalization, and the problem of police corruption.

11. A summary of recent thinking in the field of corrections: the new debate over capital punishment and experiments with shock imprisonment, work furloughs, educational furloughs, flat or determinate sentencing, and more parole or less, or even its abolition altogether.

12. Finally, a few words—daring for anyone to write—on what the immediate future appears to hold in store for crime and criminology.

If we have succeeded to at least a small extent in bringing some of these often neglected facets into our criminology text, we shall be pleased and feel a sense of gratification. But we reached out far, our tasks were many, and we offer the final product with humility.

It is with humility, too, that we have appropriated our title from not one but two great works of the past. The short book by Cesare Beccaria that appeared in 1764, translated into English under the title *Essay on Crimes and Punishments*, was followed about a century later by Dostoevsky's classic novel. Probably no modern work on this subject has been so influential as Beccaria's or so profound as Dostoevsky's. We owe them our thanks, then, for the title, but also for much more than that.

We owe thanks to others, too. Originally this was planned as a six-author collaboration, but two of the original writers, deeply involved in other work, found it impossible to continue the collaboration. Nonetheless, they contributed not only in the planning of the book but by writing material that we have used herein (sometimes with changes, for which they are not responsible) and criticizing various parts of the manuscript. We thank both of them: Thomas Reppetto, professor of law and police science at John Jay College of Criminal Justice and president of the Citizen's Crime Commission of New York, and Donal E. J. MacNamara, also professor of law and police science at John Jay and author, consultant, researcher, activist, and council and committee member for more projects than we can list. To these should be added many names of people who have looked over all or part of the manuscript, or with whom various aspects have been discussed. Among them, we single out particularly Robert J. Kelly of Brooklyn College.

And finally there is Gladys Topkis of The Free Press. We hope, for the sake of the fields of criminology and sociology and other disciplines, that her unique abilities continue to work their magic on many more books by and for the academic community.

Now, having paid our debts and explained our intentions, we place the book in your hands.

THE AUTHORS

PART I

Crime: Its Nature and Scope

Defining Crime, the Criminal, and Criminology

Criminology can be defined as the study of crime. As for crime, everyone knows what it is; information about it reaches the public through newspapers, television programs, films, and novels. Some of us have accumulated experience with crime by having ourselves been victims or knowing others who have been victims, some by being offenders (or at least defendants) or knowing such individuals, and others by being occupationally concerned with prevention of crime or supervision of people found guilty of violating the law. Nevertheless, both laymen and professionals would be hard-pressed to offer a wholly satisfactory definition of crime, a word frequently used and a phenomenon often encountered. For purposes of scholarly study —specifically, the amassing of reliable statistics, development of explanations and theories, and preparation of sound public policy—a definition more exact than the mental images held by the public is essential.

Crime is apparently widespread nowadays, although it is difficult to be certain of this without knowing what is meant by the term. It affects our daily lives, and reaches into the highest political circles in America and abroad. Social scientists seek to know the conditions under which crime increases; the characteristics of offenders and victims; why some acts are illegal and others are not. For these and other important purposes, one must again ask: What is crime? How is the term defined?

The distinguished scientist Karl Pearson (1937: 11)[1] stated, "The classification of facts and the formation of absolute judgments upon the basis of this classification . . . essentially sum up the *aim and method of modern science*" (emphasis in original). Classification is a procedure by which some items in

Toward a Definition of Crime

1. References cited within the text will be found in a separate section at the end of each part. Dates given in the citations are those of the most recent edition, not necessarily the year of first publication.

3

the world of reality are brought together under a single heading—although they may be dissimilar in all respects save one. Science aims to find patterns among the apparently unique, to group into a single class or category those objects that are in some way similar and to exclude those that do not qualify —after which the attributes of the members of the category that has been formed are investigated. The boundaries of the category are drawn: this is the process of classification. The category is given a symbolic label: this is the process of naming. In general terms, a common attribute of all members of the class is described: this is the process of definition.

By this process, some phenomena are separated from others to which they might be linked by common sense, custom, or language; and some instances are brought together that might have been overlooked had a definition not been available. A definition is important because it enables us to know whether the conclusions drawn from the observation or investigation of several experiences can be properly applied to other phenomena that have not been studied. Can researchers studying homicide, bribery, and automobile theft draw some general conclusions concerning crime as an abstraction, and if so are these conclusions applicable, for example, to prostitution, public drunkenness, traffic violations, and treason? The answer to this question requires a definition of crime, knowledge that all of the examples studied fall within the definition, and a determination of whether the examples still unstudied fall within its boundaries.

Let us start with simple definitions. Thorsten Sellin (1931a: 564) refers to crime as "any form of conduct which is forbidden by the law under pain of some punishment." Paul Tappan (1960: 10), along similar lines, writes, "Crime is an intentional act or omission in violation of criminal law." Most scholars—though not all—then proceed to exempt from their definition events forbidden by law but too insignificant to be considered criminal offenses. Thus, Tappan would distinguish between lesser violations, such as vagrancy, and criminal acts, "thereby avoiding the unnecessary attribution of criminal status to individuals who offer little or no real threat to the safety of the community" (Tappan, 1960: 19). But it may well be that Tappan is really making a distinction between the *behavior*—which after all is commonly deemed criminal if it is against the law—and the *status* of individuals—who are not seen and treated as criminals when their violations are of a minor nature.

We suggest, as a working definition, that *crime is any form of conduct forbidden by law and for which authorized government personnel can inflict punishment, when those violations carry relatively severe penalties and provoke moral outrage against the offenders.*

TWO VISIONS OF CRIME

The definition we offer is a legalistic one, and although at times it may prove troublesome to the user, because it introduces boundary lines between criminal and other behavior that are not as sharply drawn as might be desired, it is a definition that, we believe, reflects the thinking of most American and European criminologists. Most, but not all. For essentially there are two approaches to a definition of crime: the legalistic, which we have adopted with some modifications, and the social.

The legalistic approach defines crime as conduct forbidden in the penal codes. It has been criticized because it implies agreement on the part of criminologists with the authorities who make the laws and acceptance of the statements of authorities on what is and what is not criminal. Such a criticism, we believe, is entirely unwarranted. Max Weber (1967) pointed out that to say that an act is within the law is not to say that it is good or bad.[2] By extension, to say that an act is illegal—a crime—is not to say that it is bad or *ought* to be considered a crime. While there is considerable agreement that certain types of behavior are crimes and ought to be punishable as such, there is disagreement as to other types. In many parts of the United States and elsewhere in the world, for example, people have been sentenced to long prison terms for possession of marijuana, and it seems to us illogical to refuse to conceptualize as criminal an act for which people are arrested, tried in a court of law, and sent to prison simply because one does not approve of the illegalization and imprisonment process. In a legalistic definition, crime is not inherently a social evil. Many crimes are indeed evil acts, in our view and that of almost the entire populace, but the concept of evilness is a moral judgment that people hold and frequently share, whereas crime has an objective existence outside the judgment of the beholders.

Some scholars would abandon the legalistic approach to crime altogether and define crime in terms of an antisocial act (see, for example, Schwendinger and Schwendinger, 1970). They argue that a type of behavior harmful to society as a whole and to many of its individual members is not less criminal because a small, powerful group or even a larger oppressive one has found it in its interests to permit such acts to go unpunished. Sellin (1931a: 564), however, rejects such a view: "Crime," he writes, "is a legal concept, although some writers have used the term indiscriminately to denote antisocial, immoral, or sinful behavior." Consider, by contrast, the view of the well-known Italian criminologist Raffaele Garofalo, who concludes:

> The element of immorality requisite before a harmful act can be regarded as criminal by public opinion is the injury to so much of the moral sense as is represented by one or the other of the elementary altruistic sentiments of *pity* and *probity*. Moreover, the injury must wound these sentiments not in their superior and finer degrees, but in the average measure in which they are possessed by a community—a measure which is indispensable for the adaptation of the individual to society [emphasis in original]. [Garofalo, 1968: 33–34]

Garofalo notwithstanding, to include under the rubric of crime any type of conduct of which we disapprove, which annoys us, or which we deem immoral or antisocial, but which is not illegal, would appear to be a serious dilution of the concept of crime.

Is poverty amid plenty a crime? Is the failure to pass laws against pollution a crime? Is it a crime that American tax laws have been formulated in such a way that many people with annual incomes of a million dollars or more do not have to pay any income tax whatsoever? As examples of social injustice, these situations certainly deserve the attention of scholars and the public. Perhaps it can even be said that in the opinion of large numbers of

2. The statement is made by Max Rheinstein in his "Introduction" to *Max Weber on Law in Economy and Society* (New York: Simon and Schuster, 1967), pp. lvi–lvii.

people they ought to be considered crimes. This would mean that they should be illegal and punishable, and that agitation along that line is desirable. It is important, however, to make a distinction between legal and illegal outrageous acts, for without such a distinction study of the criminalization process would not be possible, nor could one understand those power structures that criminalize certain forms of behavior but not others that are equally antisocial or dangerous.

Furthermore, crime is conduct, not condition. That is, it requires one or more individuals who are responsible for the conduct. It is not useful to say that garbage on the street is a crime. If there is crime here at all, it would have to be in the act of placing the garbage on the street, the failure of persons with the responsibility of removing it to do so, or the taking of bribes or use of extortion resulting in garbage-filled streets. Poverty cannot be a crime, but it would be possible to criminalize (i.e., make illegal) those actions that are responsible for poverty. This distinction between condition and conduct may appear to be technical, but it is extremely significant; without the concept of conduct there cannot be culpable individuals and a process of arrest, trial, and punishment or exoneration.

CRIME AS BREACH OF LAW

Crime, then, consists of acts that violate laws promulgated by a government having the power to enforce its legal dicta. Law is one form of what is called social control—a term encompassing all kinds of pressure upon individuals to do what is customarily considered the right thing in a given society. Ronald Akers (1965) notes that laws are external, formal, and negative. By this he means that the pressures come from outside the individual, not from an internalized conscience or sense of right and wrong; that the rules are stated explicitly— which ordinarily means in writing; and that laws declare what one may *not* do, not what one *may* do.[3] In modern societies, Akers suggests, norms are also laws "if sanctions are applied for their violation by a legally constituted court set up by the political state." He concludes with a broader definition (1965: 306) that might apply to both primitive and modern societies: "A social norm is law if its breach is met by physical force or the threat of physical force in a socially approved and regular way by a socially authorized third person."

There are, however, some problems with this interesting definition. It would eliminate from law the rule that is unenforced, even though it has been passed by a legislative body and is part of a penal code, because the breach is not met by a threat of sanctions in a regular way. There are also questions that might be raised with regard to unpopular laws; for example, was physical force or its threat *socially* approved when applied to those buying and selling alcoholic beverages when this activity was illegal in the United States during the Prohibition era?

---

3. Some will find a semantic problem with this concept—that laws are negative and do not prescribe what one may do—since laws often prescribe what one *must* do, as in filing an income tax return or, in some countries, casting a vote. But here the law is still essentially negative, in the definition of Akers, because it provides penalties for *not* doing what is prescribed.

Other scholars have defined law with a greater emphasis on social consensus and obedience. Thus, J. Roland Pennock writes that law may be defined as a body or system of rules of human conduct

> that the bulk of the members of a given political community recognize as binding upon all its members—this recognition being induced by certain factors such as general obedience to the rule, the organization of sanctions for its enforcement and of procedures for its interpretation and application, and a general conviction of the rightness of the rule (or of the end it is apparently designed to promote), especially when this conviction is reinforced by the knowledge that others believe it right or at least act in accordance with it. [Pennock, 1964: 378]

Another view stresses the *functions* of the criminal law. The Wolfenden Report (on homosexuality and prostitution in Britain) emphasizes the need

> to preserve public order and decency, to protect the citizen from what is offensive or injurious, and to provide sufficient safeguards against exploitation and corruption of others, particularly those who are specially vulnerable because they are young, weak in body or mind, inexperienced, or in a state of special physical, official or economic dependence. [Wolfenden, 1963: 9–10]

Laws, however, do not always perform these functions; nevertheless they remain laws, and conduct that violates them is criminal. The above, then, is a statement not so much of what law is as of what it ought to be. It suggests not what conduct is criminal, but what a society ought to use as criteria in declaring some acts to be crimes and others, by omission from the penal codes, noncriminal or legal.

The legalistic approach to a definition of crime has led some people simply to define crime—usually cynically, as if to dismiss it as undefinable or emphasize that it is defined by power groups controlling the government—as whatever the criminal law says it is. The cynics notwithstanding, this is an accurate statement—although it tells us little or nothing about the type of behavior proscribed by the criminal law.

This definition of crime as being what the criminal law says it is was summarized with all its apparent shortcomings and tautologies by Lord Atkin (quoted by J. E. Williams in the UNESCO *Dictionary of the Social Sciences*). Atkin wrote:

> The domain of criminal jurisprudence can only be ascertained by examining what acts at any particular period are declared by the State to be crimes, and the only common nature they will be found to possess is that they are prohibited by the State and those who commit them are punished. [Williams, 1964: 147]

If crime is what the criminal law says it is, then, in the view of some people, without criminal law there would be no crime. Hence criminal law is the cause of crime. This argument was stated quite baldly, and taken rather seriously, by two scholars, Jerome Michael and Mortimer J. Adler (1933: 5): "If crime is merely an instance of conduct which is proscribed by the criminal code it follows that the criminal law is the *formal* cause of crime" (emphasis added). But there is no logic in this contention. The authors themselves go on

7

to say that they do not mean that the law produces the behavior, but even in the "formal" sense law is not the cause of crime: it is the codification by which governmental bodies officially declare that certain forms of behavior will be regarded as crime. It would be more accurate to say that crime is the cause of criminal law than the converse.

At most, criminal law causes certain types of behavior to be officially labeled as crime and reacted to by authorities in the officially designated and accepted manner, but the act itself—whether homicide, robbery, or whatever—would take place without criminal law, probably with greater frequency. Along these lines one is reminded of the statement of Emile Durkheim (1964), the great French sociologist, that an act does not outrage the public because it is a crime, it is a crime because it outrages the public. This important observation deserves some modification, for there are acts that first become crimes and as a result of government and social pressure then begin to outrage the population (as with pornography or blasphemy), but Durkheim's formulation nonetheless is a succinct observation on the relationship between crime and public attitudes.

Individual types of crime are defined in the penal codes, but crime itself is not. The definitions in the penal codes are necessary in order to guard against the harassment and imprisonment of individuals on charges so vague and poorly defined that the person might not have known that what he was doing was against the law.

CRIME AS OFFENSE AGAINST THE STATE

The victim of a crime can be an individual or group of individuals, as in robbery; a corporation, as in many instances of larceny; the public at large, as in consumer fraud; a municipality, as in bribery; or the nation, as in treason. However, crime is always conceptualized as having been committed against society in general, symbolized by the nation or the state.[4] The victim of all crime is society as a whole, although there is usually a more specific victim involved. The government through its criminal laws codifies society's moral demands upon the individual, makes them specific, defines them in detail, and declares what punishments shall befall those who violate them. It may decide—in the twentieth century in the United States and elsewhere there has been a movement in this direction—that some of these moral demands are private and personal matters in which a person has a right to depart from the morality of the surrounding society, community, or peer group without government interference or sanctions. Except in instances of self-defense, the state has the sole and exclusive right to take action against the

4. There is a problem here with the use of the word "state." This usually refers to sovereign governing authority in a society or a group of societies constituting a country or what today is more frequently called a nation (although there may be many nationalities within the one nation). However, in the United States the term "state" is also used to designate one of the fifty quasi-autonomous governmental bodies that together constitute the nation or republic. When the statement is made that crime is an offense against the state, on an abstract and philosophical level (and cross-culturally) this refers to the central sovereign power in a society and the people of that entire society. In the United States, where most crimes are defined and prosecuted by each of the fifty states, the statement means that the criminal act would be against the society as a whole in its abstract sense, and technically against the individual state, such as Delaware, California, or Texas.

perpetrator or suspect. The state as victim is symbolized by the words that appear on an indictment: A case is tried as the State of Alabama v. John Doe, The People v. Robert Roe, United States v. Jane Doe. The name of the individual who says he or she was robbed or kidnapped and who made the official complaint does not appear in the title of the case.

In this view, it is the state—the political arm of the society—that has been offended. What separates crime from the vast category of civil hurt and civil wrong, known in law as torts, is that with crime the state is presented as the victim. Some dismiss this as a legal fiction. Indeed the burgeoning field of victimology largely ignores it, concentrating on real people who have been victimized. It is mainly in such matters as public disorder and public drunkenness—crimes only in the most marginal sense of the word—or espionage and treason, where the intended hurt is to the nation, that one can easily conceptualize the society as victim.

But in law a crime is said to injure the society as a whole, its ability to function and protect its members. The society alone has as an entity the right to retaliate, and this it does in modern times through its government institutions. Sometimes an apprehended offender will offer to make restitution. Inasmuch as people who have been illegally deprived of money or property are often more interested in recovering their assets than in sending the guilty person to prison, restitution may be accepted and the complaint not pursued. There may not even be a record of an arrest, certainly not of a conviction. Nonetheless, restitution does not restore the situation to the point existing before the crime. To use a legal phrase that has found its way into everyday speech, it cannot make the victim whole because society is the victim. On the other hand, an offer of restitution may be rejected, and a person awaiting trial released on bail. If bail is high, he may remain in jail, costing the victimized society money not only for his upkeep but perhaps for that of his family as well; if he can borrow the money to get out on bail, he must return it, and further thievery while awaiting trial is sometimes the easiest available method.

Because the state is the victim, a person who has been robbed or assaulted cannot take revenge upon the predator, and friends and family of a murdered individual do not have the legal right to seek revenge. The right of retaliation and infliction of punishment is lodged exclusively with the state or its authorized agents; they have a monopoly on legitimate use of such power.

The principle that forbids taking the law into one's own hands is violated in practice with a frequency that varies with time and place. There has been a long tradition of such retaliatory action in some European countries, particularly Sicily and other areas of Italy, where a group of people for many decades has acted as a sort of shadow government, taking effective action against violators of their code, but without official and open government approval and without indictments, trials, and opportunities for defense. In the United States, bloody feuds were at one time not uncommon between families and family-like groups. Except when such retaliations occurred in connection with gang wars or organized crime activities, American courts and juries have tended to be lenient. However, on a formal level, personal and familial retaliation is completely unacceptable under modern concepts of criminal law, not only because it so easily lends itself to abuse, but because it violates the principle of the state as victim.

This concept has also led to the movement—already successful in many jurisdictions—to legalize certain hitherto illegal forms of activity that have come to be called victimless crimes. These are sometimes defined as acts that do not victimize society. If there is a personal victim involved, he or she is an adult who is participating consensually. While there is a social interest in diminishing the incidence of murder, rape, burglary, and bribery, many have questioned whether any harm is done society by private consensual homosexual relations or gambling. The same argument has been extended to suicide—namely, that a person has the right to decide whether or not to continue living, and that a negative answer to Hamlet's question—to be, or not to be—is not injurious to society. Others have claimed that prostitution and drug use are victimless crimes (Schur, 1965) and that these acts are "not the law's business" (Geis, 1979).

CRIME AND UNJUST LAW

Two types of violations of law take place in response to laws that individual dissidents or sectors of the populace consider unjust, laws which they disobey—they contend—as a matter of conscience or as a last resort to further a cause. These are more or less divisible into *nonviolent civil disobedience* and *violent politically directed protest*.

Refusal to abide by certain laws because of conscience was the basis of the movement against the British in India led by Mahatma Gandhi. Later, this type of civil disobedience was dramatically brought to the attention of the world by Martin Luther King in his struggle for desegregation and other civil rights for racial minorities in America. Daniel Berrigan and other antiwar protesters practiced civil disobedience during the Vietnam War, and Andrei Sakharov and various dissidents have resorted to similar strategies in the Soviet Union. If the acts that these people committed were in violation of the laws of the nation in which they took place, it would seem more useful in criminology and social science generally to conceptualize them as political crime (a subject discussed in greater detail later in this book) than to state that they were not crimes because the laws were unjust.

In contrast to nonviolent civil disobedience, many people in almost all parts of the world have from time to time planned or committed illegal violent acts for what they considered the advancement of a proper cause. These include, among many others, violence against black people and others by the Ku Klux Klan and similar groups in the United States; radical bombings during the 1960s in America; violence in Palestine by the Irgun and Stern group prior to 1948, and in Israel by Palestinians in later years; and diverse acts by various national minorities, dissidents, political separatists, slave rebels, and irredentists, in Northern Ireland, Yugoslavia, Iran, Puerto Rico, and elsewhere.

Are these acts crimes? Some people would answer that they not only are crimes but are always wrong, never justified. Others would define the acts as crimes if they personally oppose the group's goals and as necessary protest if they do not. The "freedom fighter" to one group is the "terrorist" to another.

The relationship between crime and the concept of righteousness is illustrated in Stephen Vincent Benét's narrative poem *John Brown's Body.* Mrs. Ellyat asks her husband, Will, if John Brown will be hanged for leading the raid on Harper's Ferry; when he replies in the affirmative, his son utters a protest, to which he says, "They have the right, my son,/He broke the law."

The poem continues, in a few lines that capture the relationship between crime, law, and justice:

> "But, Will! You don't believe—"
> A little spark lit Mr. Ellyat's eyes.
> "I didn't say I thought that he was wrong.
> I said they had the right to hang the man,
> But they'll hang slavery with him."

Mrs. Ellyat responds,

> "I prayed for him in church last Sunday, Will.
> I pray for him at home here every night.
> I don't know—I don't care—what laws he broke.
> I know that he was right."[5]

To deny that an act is a crime because of the motives of the actor introduces a fuzziness into the entire concept, making it difficult for a social science to develop crime statistics, typologies, theories, and research on motives, attitudes, or any other aspect of law-breaking. It would reduce the considerable element of objectivity with which crime can be studied and assessed, for crime would then be measured according to the values of individuals and groups in the society. (By contrast, much can be learned about the dissatisfactions of people by focusing only on deeds that are evil in intention and motivation, separating these from acts committed for purposes that the perpetrator considers a social good.)

A somewhat more complicated problem emerges when groups within a society challenge the legitimacy of the governing bodies that declare some acts to be criminal. Some persons go further than stating that the law is wrong and breaking it is socially desirable; they aver that the law does not really exist because it was not promulgated by a body representative of the society. In a situation in which an opposition becomes so powerful that one can speak of civil war within a country, one might meaningfully deny that violation of the law by persons engaged in the civil war constitutes crime. So long as there is effective de facto control within a territory, the challenge to

---

5. From Rosemary and Stephen Vincent Benét, *A Book of Americans* (New York: Holt, Rinehart and Winston, 1927). Copyright © 1927, 1928, by Stephen Vincent Benét. Copyright © renewed 1955, 1956, by Rosemary Carr Benét. Reprinted by permission of Brandt & Brandt. The quotations are from *John Brown's Body* by Stephen Vincent Benét.

legitimacy may be more a tactical or propaganda ploy than a serious effort to redefine permanently the nature of a particular criminal act.

The problem with approaching unjust laws and the crimes committed in defiance of them largely derives from a widespread tendency to make crime synonymous with evil. Once the distinction between crime and evil is made, it should not be difficult to define some acts of law-breaking as good and others as bad while still regarding both types as criminal.

NUREMBERG AND LEGAL CRIMINALITY

At one end of the spectrum are acts that most of us regard as inherently evil and yet do not violate any laws of a country; in fact they may be committed by the national leaders themselves or with their knowledge, approval, or connivance. Those who define such acts as crime—crimes against humanity, in some instances ethnocide or genocide—rely on a concept of "natural law," by which is meant that in the very nature of society and humanity there is a law of social order, of social contract, that goes beyond man-made law and is merely supplemented by it.

In retrospect, the kidnapping and enslavement of Africans would, in this view, be termed crime, although it was not against the laws of Britain or the colonies at the time when it occurred. And after the abolition of slave-kidnapping, slavery itself remained legal in the United States until the ratification of the Thirteenth Amendment following the Civil War.[6] As slavery was legal, and with no government apparatus or authorized personnel that could arrest, prosecute, and punish the slavetraders and slaveholders, most criminologists prefer to classify the slavery not as crime but as social outrage, condemning it and those who condoned it all the more because it was not illegal. Such criminologists prefer to confine the study of crime to acts illegal in the jurisdiction in which they are or were perpetrated.

This controversy arose in a dramatic manner after World War II, when some surviving leaders of the defeated German and Japanese governments were tried in the highly publicized war crimes trials. The most famous of these trials took place in Nuremberg, where a special tribunal was set up by the four leading allies. A deliberate effort was made to follow generally accepted criminal court procedures, as the allies sought to establish that the German leaders were being tried, not for having lost the war, but for a variety of crimes against humanity. It was contended at Nuremberg (Jackson, 1946)—and later in the Eichmann trial by the Israeli prosecutor, Gideon Hausner (1966)—that some acts are so blatantly evil that they are crimes even when not so defined by governmental authorities; further, that failure to define them as crimes may itself be a symbol of the criminality of the leaders of a government.

The Nuremberg principles have been widely debated; their ramifications could lead us astray from our current task of defining crime. Suffice it to say

6. Bruce Franklin (1978) contends that the Thirteenth Amendment did not altogether abolish slavery, but merely made it illegal except if the victim had been convicted of a crime. To return a former slave to servitude, it was necessary only to arrest him, convict him of vagrancy or anything else, and sentence him to a long term of involuntary servitude. (For a brilliant historical review of the relationship of slavery to punishment, see Sellin [1976].)

that efforts are proceeding to establish an international code for criminal law, but the United Nations has not become—and is unlikely to become in the near future—a sovereign world power with coercive ability to enforce international law. There can be no enforcement of such a code unless the government in a given society so decides, and it is most unlikely that any government would make such a decision against itself or its own leaders. Trials by other persons such as took place at Nuremberg can be imagined only when there is complete defeat and unconditional surrender and when it is politically, militarily, and diplomatically wise, in the view of the victorious, to prosecute.

During the war in Vietnam, some European intellectuals such as Bertrand Russell, Jean-Paul Sartre, and Gunnar Myrdal, with the support of some antiwar partisans in the United States, set up a "people's court"—without governmental sanction or power—to indict American political and military authorities for what they contended were war crimes. Although the purpose of the trial was to expose American participation as indefensible and hence "criminal," the actual charges made in the trial concerned violations of the Geneva Convention regarding prisoners of war, violations of American military law, and similar acts. However, even the Geneva Convention can hardly be considered penal law or violations of it crimes, without a governmental authority that has the willingness and power to enforce, coerce, and punish.

The Nuremberg trials and similar ones were based on the concept that crimes are divisible into two categories. Some acts are *mala in se*—that is, evil in and of themselves; the criminal code simply records that fact and makes provision for punishment, but their inherent evilness, including criminality, is in no way dissipated if the code fails to record them as crimes. Other illegal acts are called *mala prohibita*—evil only because prohibited by the penal code or by a government authority.

After the Nazi regime, with its reign of terror, its concentration camps, its holocaust, it may have been socially desirable for Western societies to undertake a great retribution, with punishment meted out to those leaders responsible for the atrocities. To include such government-sponsored acts under the heading of crime, however, would appear both to dilute the concept of crime and to deprive it of whatever exactness and specificity it contains, while at the same time diverting struggles against oppressive regimes into legalistic channels.

One of the problems encountered in the legalistic definition of crime is that modern law offers a large array of minor edicts and bureaucratic orders, reinforced by the power of the state, violations of which will bring forth sanctions enforced by coercion. When such laws are violated, it is difficult and not very useful to conceptualize the law-breaking act as crime. What separates these laws from others is that the offenses are purely administrative in nature; they carry no moral force and incite no moral outrage. They are the most extreme examples of *mala prohibita*. Minor offenses that break the law

MINOR INFRACTIONS AND OFFENSES

13

but are difficult to think of as crimes include, for example, many traffic violations, having a pet without a license, building a fence where it is not permitted, or being intoxicated in public.

Some sociologists, such as H. Laurence Ross (1960–61), take an ultralegalistic view: all violations of the law are crimes. (However, Ross would separate from other crimes minor offenses that do not outrage the public and are widely committed without great pangs of conscience or stigma against the offender, and would call these "folk crime.") The advantage of including all law violations as crime is that it handles as a single entity major and minor offenses, the process by which an act becomes a violation, the mechanisms for apprehending and dealing with the violator, the system for penalties and sanctions, the effects of punishment as deterrence, and other aspects of the study of crime.

If Ross's concept of folk crime were adopted, it would still be necessary to have a separate term and field of study for those acts that become major social problems, to which there is a hostile public reaction, a sense of victimization, strong conflict between the accused and the larger society, and other aspects of what is generally called crime. To identify crime totally with law violation and make one concept out of the two, rather than see crime as a very important aspect of law violation, does violence to the manner in which the term is used in everyday life as well as in legal, political, and scholarly circles. It would make it necessary to create a new word in order to express views and direct studies toward what is generally understood as crime. In short, double parking, having an unlicensed pet, or sending in one's income tax return three days late do not make one a criminal, and these acts are not crimes even though they violate the law.

The late Paul Tappan (1960), a foremost criminologist and a lawyer, suggested that this conceptual distinction is being handled in many jurisdictions, particularly in the United States, by placing minor or administrative law-breaking acts into a noncriminal category—variously called offenses, violations, or infractions—as distinct from acts specified in the penal codes. Tappan also pointed out that for the most part such law-breaking activities are in violation of ordinances of a city or county rather than state or federal government, and that when the latter they were usually in violation of an administrative rule rather than a law passed by a legislature.

Tappan's aim, to separate crime from administrative violations, was realistic, but neither his terminology nor criteria are particularly useful. One could stipulate that the term "violation" should be restricted to minor law-breaking acts, but it is hardly possible to speak of major criminal activities as other than violations of the law. There is an entire literature on criminals as offenders, and only confusion would develop if the term "offense" were to be restricted to noncriminal violations. "Infraction," however, might serve as the heading for a useful category.

Crime by its nature, we contend, has serious moral connotations; lacking such, it would usually not qualify as crime. One can point to crime despite the difficulty of formulating a definition; and in pointing to it, one would not include jaywalking or littering.

"Crime is a legal term," writes Daniel Glaser (1978b: 155), "that in its broadest usage denotes any behavior for which a court may lawfully impose punishment." Only when an act violates the law as promulgated by a government, and that government has authorized a court of law to be set up to determine the facts of the case and the punishment, if any, for the transgressor, can there be crime.

Although crimes are violations of the rules and norms of a society, not all such violations can be fruitfully conceptualized as crime. Such rules can be laid down by employers, schools, clubs, cliques, underworld gangs, voluntary associations, powerful members of a family, or almost any other social groups or organizations. Violations of these rules can result in punishment, including expulsion, ostracism, discharge, murder of the violator, the spanking of a child, or a ban on viewing television for a period of time. These punishments can be legal or illegal, but in no instance are they sanctioned by an authority set up by the government and legitimately empowered to carry them out.

Only when the violation is against a law set forth by a government in power, rather than against a widely held norm or the rules of a union, employer, or club, can there be crime. For there must be, as Glaser states, a court having a legal monopoly to mete out punishment. As an example, it is criminal—against the law—for an employee to steal from an employer, or vice versa, but it would be only against the rules and not a crime for the worker to fail to call in when ill, even though there might be severe punishment in the form of discharge.

This distinction between crime and rule violation extends even to government bodies. The authority to pass laws—the violations of which are treated as crime—is assigned only to certain specified units of the governmental apparatus. A police department might rule that its employees have to carry a gun while off duty and outside their homes, and it can discharge violators, but it cannot prosecute those violators as criminals. Thus, in arriving at a definition of crime, it is inadequate to rely merely on the distinction between government bodies and other groups whose rules are broken.

One often speaks of the "law" of the family, club, gang, or underworld. In a criminal organization, it would be a serious violation to give information to the authorities, but the organization that sets forth this "law" is not an authorized law-making body, the group that punishes the informer is not a court, and the act itself is thus not a crime.

Sometimes, however, norms or rules are so powerful in their effect on people that violations come to be considered synonymous with crime. For many people, they would be considered sin. However, crime and sin are not synonymous terms, and could not be except in a complete theocracy. In a small and probably preliterate society there may be no other law except that of a religious order, which is not distinguished from the political order. In ancient Israel—when the Jews were not dispersed and not residents, citizens, or wanderers in other lands where there may have been a secular government—the Ten Commandments probably were considered law, and their violation both sin and crime. A similar situation, in which the two are interchangeable, would be somewhat more difficult to locate in the modern world, although examples of the merging of sin and crime into a single concept might be cited in colonial Massachusetts and modern Iran after the overthrow of the Shah.

CRIME AS ABSTRACTION AND SPECIFIC ACT

Some of the confusion over the definition of crime centers on the question of identifying an individual act, rather than a type of act, as criminal. Our definition, intended to be legalistic but modified to incorporate the idea that there must be some sense of public outrage involved as well as illegal conduct, is meant to describe the behavior itself; we are not concerned with motivation, responsibility, or adjudication of an individual act as a crime.

However, some acts become crimes in the legal sense only when intent or malice can be demonstrated. Others require determination of responsibility on the part of the perpetrator.

It is a tenet of Anglo-American law that a crime can be committed only by a person with the mental capacity to understand the nature of the wrong being done. When this capacity is found, the offender is said to be capable of *mens rea*, or guilty intent. For reasons of youth, confused mental state, provocation, or coercion, a person committing an act that would otherwise be deemed criminal might not be judged guilty of a crime. A child under an age that has variously been placed at from seven to eighteen, depending on the jurisdiction and the nature of the offense, commits in legal terms a delinquent act, and sometimes no more than an accident, when the same act would be a crime if committed by an adult.

Since the mid-nineteenth century, as a result of the McNaughtan case in England, insanity has been a defense against a criminal charge (Goldstein, 1970; Moran, 1981). By and large, accident is likewise a defense, with the person liable under civil rather than criminal law, but this becomes a less than clear area when such crimes as negligent homicide or criminal endangerment are considered or when certain illegal acts are carried out under the influence of alcohol.

Some legal scholars would prefer to place the issues that we have discussed above in a slightly different perspective leading to a slightly different definition. They would say that an unlawful act committed by someone suffering from insanity (or who is so young as to be judged a delinquent and not a criminal) is nonetheless a crime, but the person perpetrating that act is excused from criminal responsibility. This view is reflected in the wording of a law that finds a person not guilty by reason of insanity, without stating that the act was not a crime.

Definitions often need modifications. They are frequently too general, broad, and vague to permit precise understanding of what events fall within their scope and what do not. In our definition of crime (see p. 4), we would add that a given event is a crime only if committed by a person of sufficient maturity and sanity so that, in the jurisdiction involved, he is deemed capable of criminal behavior, and only if the behavior proved upon subsequent investigation not to be the result of noncriminal negligence or accident.

This is a general guideline; it is not intended to answer the question whether a specific act ought properly to be labeled a crime. This would not be as important for definition as for criminal statistics (see Chapter 2), and courtroom procedures and the administration of justice (see Chapter 16), but it has been confused with the problem of definition and warrants some elaboration here.

WHEN CAN AN ACT BE CALLED A CRIME?

On the face of it, there seems to be no problem in knowing whether an occurrence is criminal. In most instances in which people are victims of crime, or in which such events are reported to the police, the fact of crime is not in doubt. People who return from a vacation to find their home vandalized and material goods removed do not need a decision by police or courts to validate that there was a crime. However, subsequent investigation may determine that the home was broken into by children below the age of criminal responsibility, or by someone with a long record of institutionalization in mental hospitals and previously judged insane.

In another instance there may be doubt whether there was crime because of the inability to determine whether a person died by suicide, murder, or accident, and again the classification of the act as crime, or the failure to do so, can leave a sense of dissatisfaction and uncertainty. In still another example, a jury may find a defendant not guilty of a charge of bribery. The jury is not saying that the bribery did not occur, but rather that the defendant is not legally guilty because the prosecution did not demonstrate his guilt beyond a reasonable doubt. Classification of the event as a crime is again uncertain.

A report of a crime to the police may be false for many reasons: misunderstanding, lack of sufficient knowledge of the circumstances, a motivation of revenge, a desire to collect insurance, or inadequate knowledge of the law, among others. For statistical purposes, these instances may be insufficient in number to change the public's perception of the extent of crime, and it is generally believed among criminologists that such instances are outweighed overall by the underreporting of crime (see Chapter 2). For definitional purposes, however, one must ask whether an act can be considered a crime before there has been a trial and a determination of guilt. To answer this question, we contend that it would not be useful to define as crime only those illegal events for which an individual has been tried and found guilty. Such a category—consisting of crimes known and solved, for which persons have been apprehended and their guilt either admitted or determined—is a perfectly logical one for study, but is a subdivision of the larger field of crime itself. Although there is usually considerable doubt about any specific event until the circumstances have been aired in court, this need not affect the general definition. There are known and unknown crimes—the latter including those unknown to anyone but the perpetrator—and to declare that a course of conduct is not criminal until known would be equivalent to saying that it is the fact of its becoming public knowledge that makes it criminal. Unknown crime, unreported crime, undetected crime, unpunished crime—

these are all significant categories, and to banish them from a definition of crime would distort our understanding of the phenomenon of unlawful behavior. Although only a legally authorized body can determine that a specific crime has occurred, crime still occurs independently of the official verdicts of authorities. The discovery by police, prosecutors, or public has consequences, but does not create the act.

Crime is a general category, and as a generalization it can be defined without the certainty of knowing whether a given act falls within its boundaries. A crime occurs whether or not anyone but the perpetrator is aware of it, although the consequences for the offender may be minimal if it is not known. Discovery does not create the crime but creates the situation in which the act can be identified, counted, and reacted to as crime. The crime is an objective fact with consequences, albeit different ones depending on whether or not the crime becomes known and the perpetrator is brought to trial and found guilty.

Almost all types of crime permit the possibility of a finding that the law has not actually been violated. A jury may find that a man accused of rape actually had consensual sexual relations with the woman, as was the contention of the defense in Giles-Johnson. A defendant in a murder case may state that he committed the act but did it in self-defense, as the defendants successfully claimed in Sweet, defended by Clarence Darrow; or the defendant may plead that he was temporarily insane, as a white policeman did, with acceptance by the jury, in the unprovoked killing of a black adolescent in New York City in the 1970s. And what a prosecutor may charge was a swindle might be defended as advertising puffery carried out in good faith.

Whether or not there was a crime remains an objective issue that researchers, investigative journalists, criminologists, criminal investigators, or others might determine for their own purposes, although they may be restrained from making such information public by libel laws protecting persons not found guilty in a criminal trial.

On Defining the Criminal

Much controversy has surrounded the formulaton of a definition of the term "criminal." To a large extent, this debate has stemmed from the exchange between Edwin Sutherland (1945) and Paul Tappan (1947), following Sutherland's efforts to create public indignation over white-collar crime. If violations of the rules of regulatory agencies are crimes, as Sutherland contended, then are the offenders not criminals? Tappan argued that only someone convicted of a crime before an authorized court of law can be termed a criminal.

In a simplistic way, one can say that a criminal is one who commits a crime. Such a definition, however, makes no distinction between the one-time and the habitual offender, and thus makes no provision for the temporary application of the label of criminal. It does not take into account the difference between the convicted criminal, the fugitive, and the individual whose crime is known only to himself. Nor does it provide a guideline for the classification of someone believed by prosecutors, police, and researchers to be guilty but found not guilty by a court of law (for example, Lizzie Borden, well-known defendant widely believed guilty in a case in which she was accused and exonerated of murdering her father and stepmother).

In some respects, of course, the definition of criminal depends on the definition of crime. George Vold (1979), for example, defines crime to include all law-breaking acts including traffic violations. Note, however, where this leads Vold in his claim that there is no such entity as a criminal personality and that it is meaningless to look for abnormality of any type in the investigation of crime:

> The general implications of this entire discussion [of crime committed by people who are considered to be normal, law-abiding citizens] should be clear and inescapable. The theory of crime as consisting primarily of ordinary, everyday learned behavior of normal people has its principal reason for being, as well as its principal type of supporting data, in the overall frequency and distribution of facts known about those individuals who become involved in criminality. They include a considerable part of the total population: every economic and social class, every race and nationality, every political party, and every religious denomination. Just as it makes little sense in political discussion to try to convict an entire people of treason, so in criminology, it is meaningless to look for abnormality—biological, psychological, economic, or social—as the explanation of behavior that includes individuals in every segment and group, and of such a large and constantly changing part of the total population. [Vold, 1979: 247]

Although we reject the idea that it is meaningful to describe as criminal the traffic-law violator and to dismiss on that basis any effort to look for "abnormality" as the explanation of criminality, there are other, better reasons for which the term criminal might not be useful. Daniel Glaser (1978a: 120), for example, suggests that such words as burglar, rapist, and thief can be pernicious as identifying labels, because they tend to categorize large numbers of diverse people as if they were identical. This is even more true of the general label of criminal.

Some criminologists have contended that self-report questionnaire studies—particularly among youths, including those of middle- and upper-class backgrounds—indicate that almost all young people have at one time or another committed at least one offense that is indictable under the criminal codes (Porterfield, 1946). From this, it is argued that such terms as delinquent and criminal could be applied to such a large proportion of the population that they would lose their significance, no longer serving to separate some people from others. Some would argue that the term criminal should either be abandoned or else confined to persons committing extremely serious crimes or making a lifelong career of crime.

To return to Tappan's controversy with Sutherland, Tappan presents what he calls the juristic view:

> Only those are criminal who have been adjudicated as such by the courts. . . . In studying the offender there can be no presumption that arrested, arraigned, indicted, or prosecuted persons are criminals unless they also be held guilty beyond a reasonable doubt of a particular offense. Even less than the unconvicted suspect can those individuals be considered criminal who have violated no law.

19

Only those are criminals who have been selected by a clear substantive and a careful adjective law,[7] such as obtains in our courts. The unconvicted offenders of whom the criminologists may wish to take cognizance are an important but unselected group; it has no specific membership presently ascertainable. [Tappan, 1947: 100]

In a footnote to this passage, Tappan adds:

The unconvicted suspect cannot be known as a violator of the law; to assume him so would be in derogation of our most basic political and ethical philosophies. In empirical research it would be quite inaccurate, obviously, to study all suspects or defendants as criminals. [Tappan, 1947: 100]

Most criminologists would agree that, for legal and social purposes and for protection of the rights of a suspect, no one ought to be declared a criminal until found guilty of a specific crime. Even then, there is a possibility that one day he or she will be exonerated. Convicted people have been exculpated after spending years in prison, after being granted a new trial, some have been pardoned posthumously, after being executed. Even under Tappan's strict definition some people would wrongly fall under the classification of being criminal—that is, innocent men and women convicted of crimes.

One is left with the feeling that in the view of Tappan there is no criminal if there has not been an indictment and a verdict of guilt. There are then, if one interprets his statement correctly, no unknown and unapprehended criminals. Yet it is common knowledge that there are unsolved crimes, and apparently there were people who committed them—but one is admonished here not to call such persons criminals.

The difficulty with this line of reasoning is not beyond solution. It would be an abrogation of the rights of an individual to treat him as guilty when he had not had a fair trial or had not been found guilty in an authorized court of law. But for purposes of understanding the nature of criminals, their behavior, their age, sex, and other traits and attributes, to confine a study only to those found guilty in a court of law would be indefensible. It would be bad research and bad criminology.

Criminals, in short, are those who commit the acts that we call crimes. A specific criminal is an individual who has been judged by an authorized court as having committed a specific act, which act constitutes behavior that we call crime.

Criminology and the Criminologist

We opened this text with the statement that criminology can be defined as the study of crime. More accurately, criminology is a systematic, scientific pursuit of a body of knowledge concerning crime. In that sense it is like other areas of the behavioral and social sciences, and different from social philosophy, social thought, and investigative journalism—insightful and profound

7. Adjective law is law governing rules of evidence and procedure.

as these often are—in its systematization of both knowledge and the pursuit of it.

Edwin Sutherland has offered what remains a more or less acceptable definition of criminology, one that is quoted with approval by Wolfgang and Ferracuti:

> Criminology is the body of knowledge regarding crime as a social phenomenon. It includes within its scope the process of making laws, of breaking laws, and of reacting toward the breaking of laws. . . . The objective of criminology is the development of a body of general and verified principles and other types of knowledge regarding this process of law, crime, and treatment. [Wolfgang and Ferracuti, 1967: 19]

To this definition, Wolfgang and Ferracuti append a note that "the term criminology should be used to designate a body of *scientific* knowledge about crime" (emphasis in original).

Some might raise the question whether criminology is the body of knowledge on the phenomenon of crime or the study of it. Thorsten Sellin (1938: 3) suggests that the term be used to designate both "the body of scientific knowledge and the deliberate pursuit of such knowledge."

The field of criminology overlaps with criminal law, forensic psychiatry, political science, and other disciplines. The internal logic of the field of study, as well as tradition and common agreement, have established certain areas that are covered by criminology, although there are *aspects* to many of them that fall outside criminology as such. We suggest that criminology might be said to encompass the following:

1. The process by which certain types of behavior are criminalized—that is, made illegal—whether by legislative or administrative action.
2. Social control—the process by which formal and informal measures are taken in a society to control the activities of people so that criminal law is not violated.
3. Preventive measures of an environmental or ecological nature taken in a society or community to diminish the opportunities, likelihood, or temptations for criminal behavior.
4. Criminal behavior: the settings, statistics on incidence and frequency, modus operandi, and consequences.
5. Criminogenesis: the factors present in individuals, groups, or a society that make law-breaking more likely or less so; the social-structural components of a society that induce or reduce crime.
6. The offender: who commits crimes, why, and with what rationalizations.
7. The police: their roles, duties, privileges, and responsibilities; their place in the social control apparatus and in the prevention of crime and apprehension of offenders.

8. The criminal justice system: the roles of prosecutors, judges, juries, and defense counsel; the "rules of the game" for determining innocence or guilt of the accused.[8]

9. Penology or corrections: the nature of punishment imposed upon the guilty offender, including probation, parole, fines, incarceration, corporal and capital punishment, exile, and others; also reform and rehabilitation, and the efficacy of punishment as deterrence.

10. Victimology: the study of the victims of crime, their relationship if any to offenders; victim-proneness, victim restitution, and other aspects of victimization.

CRIMINOLOGY AS A SUBDISCIPLINE AND AS AN INTERDISCIPLINARY FIELD

In Italy and other European nations criminology has its roots in medicine, biology, and psychiatry, while in Germany it was primarily a subdiscipline of the study of criminal law or jurisprudence. In the United States it has largely but not exclusively become an area of specialization within sociology, taught by people whose major training and orientation has been sociological to students whose other areas of interest and investigation are sociological.

The relationship of criminology to sociology has an inherent logic (although possibly no more than would a relationship to psychology). Sociology is the study of human societies and human social behavior. This includes rules of behavior, norms, laws, and social expectations, and hence would logically include a study of the violations of those norms, measures taken to prevent those violations, and punishments inflicted—both formally and informally—on offenders. This, in short, is criminology, or at least becomes criminology when the norms under discussion have been codified in criminal law.

Nevertheless, a body of knowledge about crime has been generated that is often no more closely interwoven with sociology than with political science or psychiatry, and certainly no more so than with the philosophy of criminal law. While many of the foremost American criminologists have been trained in sociology, others have had their primary training in psychiatry, public administration, criminal law, anthropology, or political science.[9]

Most American universities have not found it fruitful to create a school or department of criminology.[10] However, although criminology does not seem to have flourished as an area of study administratively independent of

8. The terms "criminal justice" or "administration of criminal justice" sometimes include the study of police and corrections; some are using "criminal justice" as synonymous with "criminology." We prefer to limit the concept of criminal justice to one phase of criminology—namely, the handling of persons accused of crime in a court of law.

9. Edwin Sutherland, often regarded as the dean of American criminologists, was a president of the American Sociological Association. At this writing, of the past seventeen presidents of the American Society of Criminology, eleven have been sociologists, two professors of criminal law, three public administration specialists, and one a psychiatrist.

10. As of 1979, the State University of New York at Albany, Florida State University, and the John Jay College of Criminal Justice (part of the City University of New York) were among the few senior colleges having such schools or departments. The University of California at Berkeley had abandoned its criminology school after many years. Other colleges that have separate entities—often called criminal justice departments, divisions, or schools—are concentrating on training in police science and public administration rather than in criminology as we have here defined it.

others (particularly sociology), as a research pursuit it has led an independent existence in the United States, with several hundred research centers.

The body of knowledge embraced by criminology is so vast, its interests and investigations so broad, that the input of numerous types of training into the study of crime is not only inevitable but highly desirable. Understanding the criminalization process requires study of criminal law; the motivation of the offender, an insight into psychiatry; the handling of the accused by police, a grasp of public administration and political science; the corrections system, an understanding not only of the inmate subculture, a sociological phenomenon, but of the psychology of adaptation and the workings of treatment modalities.

Criminology would thus best emerge as an interdisciplinary field of study. The interdisciplinary field can take on essentially two forms: (1) cooperation among people trained in different areas of thought, having different orientations, outlooks, and bodies of knowledge, and exchanging views, ideas, information, and influencing each other; or (2) the emergence of a new discipline, combining those aspects of biology, psychology, political science, sociology, criminal law, legal philosophy, public administration, ethics, and even architecture, among others, that are most germane to an understanding of crime. The first can be conceived of as cooperation, the second as integration.

THEORETICAL AND APPLIED CRIMINOLOGY

Division between theory and application in the behavioral sciences is almost invariably artificial. While it is possible to speak of a special area of "theoretical criminology" or "criminological theory," this refers to that subsection of the discipline involved in the generation of explanations for behavior, patterns of conduct, and events. It is not meant to contrast with "practical" or "applied" criminology.

There is, in fact, no "applied criminology," in the sense of the use of information generated by criminological research for crime prevention, apprehension, or treatment. Criminological theory or research might in fact be applied in these ways, but the objective of criminology is not such use but the development of a body of knowledge about crime.

Criminology might further be distinguished from criminalistics. The latter has as its objective the *solving* of crimes, including the apprehension of suspects and the gathering of information for trial. Criminology seeks to gather somewhat similar information, but not for the purpose of solving crimes; its purpose is to accumulate information about crime as a phenomenon.

Who, then, is the criminologist? Unlike the physician and the lawyer, the criminologist is not licensed. There is no legal determination that one person is entitled to use that description of himself while another is not. Unlike the policeman, taxi driver, and numerous others, the criminologist is not easily defined by his employment: he does not have a descriptive word for himself by virtue of having a job that uses that word in its job title or description.

The criminologist is anyone whose pursuit is the study of crime and the accumulation of knowledge about it. Although the detective is involved in the solution of crimes, the policeman in preventing crimes and apprehending offenders, the judge in deciding important questions about evidence concerning crimes, the offender in planning and carrying out the criminal behavior, and the probation officer in handling and advising people put under supervision, none of these people is a criminologist, none is engaged in criminology. All, of course, have knowledge about crime, and in some instances their intimate knowledge may be greater than that of the criminologist and may be fortified with experience and insights.

It is not so much the difference in training that distinguishes the ballistics expert, policeman, parole officer, or prison warden from the criminologist: it is the difference in objective. These people are not engaged in the scientific development of knowledge about crime, and it is likely that their goals of crime prevention, apprehension, control and rehabilitation not only might take precedence over the development of a systematic literature scientifically accumulated but would sometimes clash with that aim.

This is not to imply that criminology necessarily lacks social value. It is useful and can be even more so; it is possible that much human suffering could be alleviated were criminology to be put to use by government authorities and administrators. However, the task of science is study, research, and the gathering of knowledge. One hopes that the knowledge will be put to use, but that is another problem, for other people to solve.

People of varied training and in numerous occupations who have contact with crime can supply information vital to criminologists. In turn, they can receive assistance by drawing upon the general propositions that criminologists may develop. At times the criminologist's pursuit of knowledge and the practitioner's experience may converge, not only in a cooperative effort but even within the same person. The policeman, corrections officer, lawyer, or ex-convict may receive formal training in criminology, and the criminologist may even receive practical experience by becoming a policeman, prison warden, judge, or criminal. But the corrections officer trained in criminology, for example, goes about the work with the objective of handling, classifying, treating, perhaps subduing, and sometimes mollifying prisoners, and the same could be said of the therapist in a prison setting. They are not engaged in the goal of systematically building a body of knowledge, although as a consequence of their other goals that may be a byproduct. The fact that they possess a great deal of information about crime does not turn them into criminologists, any more than it would turn the offender or ex-convict into one. Criminology, in sum, is a scientific study and a scientifically gathered set of propositions, theories, and generalizations, and the facts upon which they are based.

Crime
Statistics

Ever since the first scientific studies of crime, there has been unceasing interest in accumulating accurate statistical data on illegal events, offenders, and, more recently, victims. Scholars, administrative officials, police personnel, correctional practitioners, others associated with government, journalists, and of course the lay public have demonstrated a fascination with crime statistics. This is not hard to understand. People want to know as much as possible about an aspect of life that constitutes a danger to them personally, or to the community or larger society of which they are a part, and that contains a potential for interfering with the normal pursuit of their needs and pleasures.

Data on crime, for those engaged in the scientific study of this phenomenon, offer information from which theories can be built, revised, or discarded. For the government official or advisor, statistics can establish a basis for policy-making. From data, knowledge can be derived about the fluctuations in various types of crime according to economic trends, unemployment, poverty or affluence, and demographic change in a neighborhood or nation. Statistics can provide information on offenders—age, education, family life, previous criminal history, and an almost endless number of other variables; on victims, so that one can understand the differential vulnerability to being victimized; and on the relative efficacy of various environmental preventive and defense measures. Only statistical analysis can determine whether changes in police procedure, term of prison sentence, parole and probation, and diverse rehabilitative programs affect the total crime scene.

This is not to say, as some ultraquantitative criminologists might suggest, that no other information is reliable except that which can be put in numbers. Criminology can develop insights through participant-observation studies of policemen, criminals, victims, judges, court officers, bystanders, and others.[1] Criminology can utilize biographical and autobiographical accounts and self-report surveys, although these must be read with the realization that they may well be self-serving, boastful, and rationalizing, and may depart from truth for other reasons (Sutherland, 1937; Klockars, 1974). Also useful can be detailed investigation into one or a few case histories, utilizing the "own story" technique or psychological biographies (Evans, 1966). One can gain understanding of crime by the perusal of fiction, such as Dostoevsky's *Crime and Punishment* or Faulkner's *Sanctuary* (see Sagarin, 1981), particularly fiction produced by ex-convicts (see Franklin, 1978). In short, the techniques are numerous, but none can replace quantitative studies; rather, they complement statistics, providing insights that illuminate the minds and motivations of participants in the interaction, whether they be criminals, victims, the public, or government personnel. Qualitative investigations are essential, but without hard data are insufficient in a field of study that aspires to be scientific.

Statistics on crime are important as correctives of public impressions and as warnings to the public to be particularly prudent under especially dangerous circumstances. Without statistical data, the public is probably heavily influenced by personal experience, haphazard impressions, and the news media, which play a major part in building its image of crime. In the competition for readers and viewers the media may sensationalize, distort, select, and discard, giving a warped view that can best be corrected by sound statistics. Crime, particularly when it is violent, outrageous, or bizarre, gets a great deal of time and space on airwaves and newsprint; its absence does not.

Marvin Wolfgang (1963) has summarized the major reasons for the accumulation of accurate crime statistics. In addition to some of the points raised above, Wolfgang finds that such information is needed to determine the extent of population involvement in crime, provide data for testing hypotheses about the causes of crime, and measure the degree of enforceability of various types of legal norms.

Few would argue with the proposition that reliable statistics on crime and criminals are valuable. However, some criminologists question the accuracy of the available information and challenge the proposition that such data, granted their shortcomings, are better than none at all.

Historical Background

The development of official statistics on crime has roots in European sociology, criminal law, criminology, and penology. The Belgian social scientist Adolphe Quetelet (b. 1796–d. 1874) believed that hard facts were available and could be obtained, and that the progress of social science would be possible only with the accumulation of data. Emile Durkheim (1951) sought to develop his theories of suicide—and by extension theories of society and social cohesion—on the basis of study of data, thus producing a major work in the

1. See, as one type of this vast literature, a collection edited by Peter Manning and John van Maanen (1978) appropriately entitled *Policing: A View from the Streets.*

history of sociology.[2] In nineteenth-century Italy, France, and England, criminologists attempted to gather crime statistics, albeit with crude measuring devices, and the once popular field of criminal anthropology was partially based on such data. Much of the work on the Continent, however, involved information only about the criminals themselves, specifically known, convicted, and incarcerated ones, rather than about the incidence, relative frequency, and types of crime, and was centered around the issue whether there are biological differences between criminals and other sectors of the population (see Goring, 1972). Data on juvenile delinquents and criminals continued to be amassed in the United States and elsewhere during the early decades of this century, particularly by Earnest Hooton (1939) and Sheldon and Eleanor Glueck (1950). Their work was often assailed, but the attacks were based on alleged errors in their methodology and conclusions and were not meant to deny the value of data-gathering itself.[3]

In the late 1920s and 1930s, both predating and contemporaneous with the work of Hooton and the Gluecks, interest in the accumulation of reliable data on crime was mounting in the United States. During the presidency of Herbert Hoover, the National Commission on Law Observance and Enforcement issued its *Report on Criminal Statistics* (discussed by Audrey Davies, 1931). The commission noted that municipalities were falsifying their records, a problem that would continue to plague American government officials for decades to come:

> The basic reports are made by persons and under conditions which involve varying degrees of guarantees of their accuracy and reliability. Indeed, the significant fact that the cities are beginning to use these reports in order to advertise their freedom from crime as compared to other municipalities suggests at once a difficulty under which the voluntary system of gathering police statistics for national purposes must labor. [*Report*, p. 13, quoted by Davies, 1931: 363]

Soon after the issuance of this report, Thorsten Sellin (1931b) addressed himself to the problem of the development of a crime index. Sellin indicated that newspapers and even scholarly journals were publishing reports of putative increases or decreases in crime based on such a doubtful index as fluctuation in the number of commitments to penal institutions. Unless we have a reliable crime index, wrote Sellin,

> it is impossible to make conclusive studies of the relationship of crime fluctuations or trends to fluctuations or trends in other social phenomena, such as changes in the rate of social mobility, changes in the biological composition of social groups, or in their economic or political life. Furthermore, a crime index is necessary in order that the effects of deliberate policies of social reform, particularly in the field of crime treatment or prevention, may be gauged. [Sellin, 1931b: 336]

In Europe, interest in a crime index was developing at the same time as in the United States. However, the Finnish criminologist V. Verkko stated in

2. Jack Douglas (1967), however, has challenged some of Durkheim's premises for accepting the official data; particularly he has shown the importance of definition in statistical studies.

3. See the discussion of this work in Chapter 4, in the section dealing with biological predisposition to crime (pp. 74–79).

1930 that only a few crimes can furnish data for such an index. Taking note of this, Sellin pointed out that certain crimes have a low degree of "reportability or detectability," and gave some of the reasons for this: the acts are of a private nature, the victim is anxious to avoid publicity, there is inconvenience to the victim in complaining and in pursuit of prosecution, and the offense is not regarded as serious in public opinion. Since such events compose the major part of recorded criminality, Sellin writes,

> it is obvious that a crime index must be based on the recorded crime rates of only a few selected offenses which are considered as greatly injurious to social welfare, and at the same time public in nature, and of such a kind that they induce the fullest possible cooperation between the victim and those interested in him, and the agency of law enforcement. [Sellin, 1931b: 339]

At this point, Sellin contends—in what has become a generally accepted concept in criminal statistics—that the greater the distance of the procedure of reporting from the criminal event itself, the less reliable the data. This means that "crimes known to the police" furnish the best data for a crime index as contrasted with arrests, convictions, or incarcerations.

Accurate and Inaccurate Information

Some types of information with regard to crime may be quite accurate while others can only be educated guesses. The most accurate is usually information on the number of prisoners confined at any one time. Not all countries provide such figures or collect them with care, and sometimes they are deliberately distorted (particularly in the case of political offenders). In the United States, *National Prisoner Statistics* (1977, 1978) is issued annually by the United States Department of Justice, and although at one time it gave information only on prisoners held in federal prisons (who constitute a minority of the incarcerated), it is today a compilation on both federal and state prisons.[4] It discloses the number of prisoners tabulated as of January 1 of each year; new admissions, discharges, deaths, and escapes during the year; and prisoners in confinement on December 31. This is broken down according to jurisdiction (federal or individual state), with further breakdown by sex, age, race, and other characteristics. When this information is translated into rates (i.e., total number of prisoners or number of a given age or sex category in a given state as a percentage of the total state population, usually expressed as prisoners per 100,000), then the figures can be meaningfully compared with those of previous years or with those of another state.

Even such data—cited here only to illustrate the possibility of a highly accurate count—are less than exact and can be misinterpreted. To them one must add the inmates of municipal or county jails, which on any one day are estimated to contain half as many incarcerated persons as are in state and federal penitentiaries combined. Although some of these persons are

4. Most of the remaining discussion in this and the following chapter will place emphasis on the American scene.

overnight detainees or may even be in jail for only an hour or two until released by a bail bondsman, others are there long enough to be counted meaningfully as part of the American prison population.[5] One might also add juvenile detention inmates, illegal aliens detained for deportation, military prisoners, deserters held for the military authorities, confined material witnesses, and persons who are incarcerated unwillingly in mental hospitals for crimes of which they have been accused, having been declared unable to stand trial because of alleged mental incompetence.

There are, then, difficulties in arriving at an accurate figure; but they can largely be overcome. An extremely reliable, though less than perfectly exact, figure can be obtained for those held in jails and military prisons, as well as (with greater difficulty) for minors in various detention centers or industrial schools (which have been called prisons by the United States Supreme Court). A fairly close approximation of those incarcerated in mental hospitals for crimes of which they have been accused can also be computed. Further, if one omits the figures for inmates of mental hospitals, military prisoners, those in juvenile detention centers and local lockups—all of which might be less exact than the figures for the federal and state prison population—the latter can be accepted and analyzed for what they are, without comparing them with information that might include other categories.[6]

Prisoner statistics represent one end of a scale: they are the most accurate and most reliable figures that can be obtained, but they are not figures on the totality of crime and, in fact, as Sellin warned, they are so far removed from the event as to be among the least reliable as an indication of who does what illegal acts. They give important information, but only on offenders convicted and incarcerated during a given period of time.[7] It is doubtful that the prisoner sample reflects the actual criminal population in terms of age, race, physical and psychological attributes, types of crimes committed, or other characteristics. In fact, it probably does not even reflect accurately a cross section of those convicted or incarcerated. It is entirely possible—and one must remain skeptical in looking at such information— that of those committing crimes, the apprehended differ from persons never arrested and, of those apprehended, the proportion brought to trial may differ in traits and characteristics (as age, race, sex, social class) from those never tried. The convicted in turn may well be dissimilar from those not found guilty, in some major respects other than the probable guilt of the former and the probable innocence of the latter. Among those found guilty, there may be differences between those sent to prison and others granted suspended sentences, probation, or fines. Finally, the prison inmates at a given moment may be unrepresentative of all those incarcerated over a peri-

5. In penology, the word "jail" is usually employed to denote a local lockup, under the administration of town, city, or county; the word "prison" refers to a state or federal institution, which generally receives persons only after they have been found guilty of a crime.

6. Closely related to jail and prison statistics would be data on parole and probation. Information on parolees is relatively accurate and complete, but probation statistics are far less reliable. (Probation and parole are discussed in Chapter 24.)

7. Among other reasons not to use the prisoner statistics as an indication of fluctuation in crime is that they reflect the state of prison construction. When more prisons are built there are more prisoners, whether crime has decreased or increased.

od of time in state and federal facilities, because of distortion caused by differential lengths of sentences and discretionary and often arbitrary parole decisions, as well as prison suicides, homicides, and escapes.[8]

If such difficulties face the criminologist in dealing with statistics on prisoners, they multiply many times in dealing with crimes themselves, which by their nature are not as "countable" as prisoners. Nevertheless, they are not beyond the realm of statistical study. It is true that for some crimes only the vaguest estimate of incidence is possible: examples include bribery, pimping, election fixing, tax and business frauds, and blackmail. There is, however, a vast area where statistics are compiled that, though constantly challenged as inaccurate, give some indication of having a close and rather constant relationship to events. Such is the case for homicide, burglary, automobile theft, and some other crimes. Yet, even for these serious felonies, exactness cannot be attained.

Vested Interests and Statistical Manipulation

There are vested interests involved in reports of crime-rate fluctuations, which can be produced by manipulation or by special interpretation, giving a distorted image. Influential persons or groups may look with favor on reports of high crime rates, used to demonstrate, for example, a need for increased police budgets, the ineffectiveness of some special program to combat crime and the urgency for the substitution of another program, a desire to aid one side in a political campaign, or perhaps to impress people that they need house locks, bicycle chains, burglar-alarm systems, insurance, and other items and services connected with the prevention and detection of crimes and restitution or compensation to victims.

On the other hand, political officeholders, police officials, corrections officers, educators, rehabilitative personnel, and even architects, city planners, and sometimes realtors might have an interest in showing crime to be lower in one area than another or reduced over a period of time. In similar fashion, persons on different sides in political, religious, racial, and ethnic disputes may be motivated to collect quite different crime data, publish the material selectively, and interpret it self-servingly.

This is not to suggest fraud in statistical manipulation. Such fraud is possible and has been known, but in all likelihood it plays a small part in the total distortion. The point is, rather, that data *can be* collected, arranged, developed, manipulated, interpreted, or presented in such manner as to show a greater or lesser incidence of crime. Furthermore, even where there is no suppression or distortion, data that might point to a certain conclusion can be selectively chosen and presented out of context, in order to give an impression unobtainable if all known facts were impartially revealed.

According to John Kitsuse and Aaron Cicourel, the persons and agencies producing crime rates have considerable discretion as to whether they report, whom they report, and how they classify those reported:

8. All of the variables mentioned above—except for the small number of suicides, homicides, and escapes—can seriously distort the findings of a researcher who confuses the prison with the criminal population. For an interesting analysis of how race, age, and sex affect whether a shoplifter goes to prison, see Cameron, 1964.

For example, with reference to the rates of delinquency reported by the police department, we would ask: What are the criteria that the police personnel use to identify and process a youth as "incorrigible," "sex offender," "vandal," etc.? The criteria of such categories are vague enough to include a wide range of behaviors which in turn may be produced by various "sources and contexts" within the social structure. [Kitsuse and Cicourel, 1963: 136]

There are accommodations in the conviction processes as well as elsewhere in the official handling of offenses and offenders that distort statistics, as shown in this statement, cited by Kitsuse and Cicourel from a work by Donald J. Newman (1962) and documented by the American Bar Foundation:

Some offenders are excluded [from the official statistics] because they are not processed even though known to be guilty (e.g., drug addicts, prostitutes, and gamblers are often hired by the police or coerced by them to help apprehend other offenders), and the practice of relabeling offenses and reducing sentences because of insufficient evidence, "deals," and tricks (e.g., telling the defendant or his lawyer that because the offender "seems like a decent person" the charge will be reduced from a felony to a misdemeanor, when in fact the prosecution finds there is insufficient evidence for either charge). These accommodations may occur at the time of arrest, or during prior or subsequent investigation of crimes, filing of complaints, adjudication, sentencing and post-sentencing relations with authorities, and so on. [Kitsuse and Cicourel, 1963: 138]

That the same behavior will be handled and classified differently when committed by persons of different social classes, neighborhoods, ethnic and racial identities, and even appearance seems to be beyond doubt (Cameron, 1964). This may be a more difficult problem in delinquency than in adult crime statistics,[9] and greater for some adult offenses than others.

When there is accommodation in the legal process by a guilty plea to a lesser offense, the latter is usually placed in the crime statistics. There may be errors in two directions here: (1) some of these defendants might have been acquitted had they been given trials (this is probably more true of the poor than of others), and (2) some of these defendants—probably a greater number—may have been guilty of a much more serious crime than the one for which they plea-bargained.

William Chambliss and Richard Nagasawa made a study along these lines of official delinquency figures for black, white, and Japanese youths, and came to the conclusion that such data "may tell us a good deal about the activities of agencies responsible for generating statistics, but they tell us very little about the distribution of criminal or delinquent activities in the population" (1969: 76–77). They found that official and self-reported rates of delinquency fail to show correlation for the different nationality groups. Demeanor, bias, extent to which youths of different groups are under careful surveillance: all have to be accounted for.

9. While it is important to have good statistics on such a phenomenon as juvenile delinquency—including figures on so vague a term as "incorrigibility"—note that this issue is outside the scope of our definition of crime.

In both of these studies (Kitsuse and Cicourel, 1963; Chambliss and Nagasawa, 1969), the issue is not falsification so much as it is discretion on the part of police and the exercise of that discretion as a reflection of various biases. Donald J. Black (1970: 734) raises an interesting point when he looks at the data on crime rates as social facts in themselves rather than material to be evaluated for accuracy or reliability. These rates, Black argues, "are an aspect of social organization and cannot, sociologically, be wrong." He continues:

> Rates of known crimes do not perfectly reflect the volume of citizen complaints. A complaint must be given official status in a formal written report before it can enter police statistics, and the report by no means automatically follows receipt of the complaint by the police. . . . The decision to give official status to a crime ordinarily is an outcome of face-to-face interaction between the police and the complainant rather than a programmed police response to a bureaucratic or legal formula. . . . The police discriminate against blue-collar citizens who feloniously offend white-collar citizens by being comparatively lenient in the investigation of felonies committed by one blue-collar citizen against another. In this instance the legal system listens more attentively to the claims of higher-status citizens. The pattern is recorded in the crime rate. [Black, 1970: 735–736, 746]

In addition, there is false reporting of crime by police. Sophia Robison, in a careful critique of American crime statistics, notes failure on the part of police officers to accept complaints or report them accurately, causing distortion in statistics:

> In Philadelphia during the interval between 1951 and 1953 the local reports showed a 70 percent increase in serious offenses. This apparent increase in the number of crimes was not the result of an invasion of the city by criminals; it was the consequence of a failure in 1951 of one police district in the center of the city to include 5,000 complaints in its report. On the basis of the revised reports, the actual increase was found to be 30 percent for the three-year period. [Robison, 1966: 1035–1036]

It is generally believed that this type of distortion diminished during the 1970s, but it did not completely disappear. In New York City, the chief of police noted that during the first three months of 1972 there had been a decline of 28.3 percent in recorded robberies, including holdups, muggings, and some kinds of purse snatches (see *New York Times*, 1972). However, interviews with 755 victims of crimes that had been classified as larcenies, a lesser offense, showed that almost 5 percent of the acts should have been recorded as robberies. In this instance, we have misclassification rather than complete suppression of data.

How great is the influence of such manipulation on total statistical reliability? The New York police chief mentioned above indicated a belief that deliberate misclassification of crime uncovered by the department "would have only a small effect on the total number of reported robberies" and would not affect the trends being shown at the time. He further noted that for more serious crimes such as murder and rape the downgrading into a lesser serious offense could not be greatly influenced by the police, since such downgrading occurs in plea bargaining and at other points in the criminal justice system.

Unreported crime (including undiscovered and unobserved as well as undisclosed acts), not distortion, suppression, and misclassification by vested interests, may be the biggest single factor in producing crime data of an unreliable nature. Although there is some overreporting of crime (due to insurance fraud, revenge, racism, political chicanery, psychopathological paranoia, and honest error), this is probably relatively minor compared with the underreported sector.

Manuel López-Rey (1970) offers an extensive discussion and analysis of unknown, undetected, and unreported criminality, and warns particularly against the use of reports by victims. Yet it is upon just such self-reports by those who stated that they had been victimized that considerable reliance has been placed in recent years in an effort to correct the official figures, based as they are on illegal behavior known to the police.

Where does this leave the criminologist in pursuit of the dark figure of unreported crime? To start, we would divide that category into three parts: (1) crimes unknown except to the perpetrator; (2) crimes with victims, known to those victims and perhaps others, but not reported to the police; and (3) consensual victimless crimes. Inasmuch as only the first two are factors of importance in the study of significant offenses, the victimless crimes will not be considered here.

The Dark Figure of Unreported Crime

To speak of crime as unknown to anyone at all would probably be a contradiction. A person violating the penal law is said to have committed a crime only if he had evil intent (or *mens rea*); hence, he must be of sufficiently sound mind to know that he had perpetrated the act and to know that it was wrong, for otherwise the act would usually not be defined as a crime.[10] Unknown crimes, then, are illegal acts known only to the offender or offenders, no one else. These include a wide variety of offenses, covering roughly three groups: (1) crimes against a large impersonal entity, ranging from the society as a whole to corporations and organizations; (2) crimes in which the sole victim has been killed; and (3) crimes against individuals who are unaware that a criminal act has been perpetrated against them.

UNKNOWN CRIMES

Impersonal Structures as Victim. Where there are no specific persons victimized, but only the society as a whole or some corporate body, the criminal act may never be revealed. Treason and espionage can remain unknown except to the perpetrators and the authorities to whom they report in another

10. This issue is more complex than stated here. Some crimes do not require evil intent; others do not require intent to commit the specific crime charged. For example, vehicular homicide and drunken driving may have no evil intent; and homicide by arson can be charged in the death of a victim whose presence on the premises deliberately set afire was wholly unknown to the arsonist, who did not intend to commit murder.

country. Crimes by corporation executives are probably seldom revealed: these can include illegal price-fixing, fraud, and bribery (Sutherland, 1949; Geis and Meier, 1977). Offical statistics offer no clue to the frequency of such acts, the number of persons involved, the amount of money and gifts illegally exchanged, or the social consequences. Only the number of persons accused, investigated, indicted, brought to trial, found guilty, or incarcerated can be determined, and there is no reason to believe that fluctuation in such minimal figures reflects real increases or decreases in these white-collar felonies; it is more likely due to chance, journalistic investigation, serendipitous findings, political fallings out, better or poorer official surveillance, activities of pressure groups, and such forces (see Geis, 1974). A combination of journalistic and social scientific investigation might indicate the extent and trends for such crimes, but the findings could hardly be reduced to reliable numerical data.

The Deceased as Victim.   Homicide may go unreported because it is unknown to any living person except the perpetrator. Thousands of people disappear in the United States every year; some of them are reported missing, while other disappearances are not noted at all, even by family or friends. Some of these missing persons have been murdered and their bodies never found. Although the corpses of a few missing persons may eventually surface, there is still no indication of how many remain permanently undiscovered and are never recorded as victims of murder.

In four instances in the United States over a short span of years, bodies were discovered a considerable time after the apparent murders took place. Several Arkansas prisoners, in all likelihood murder victims, had been buried without official death notices, and the corpses later exhumed by a criminologist who had come in as warden (Murton and Hyams, 1969). More than a score of dead bodies of migrant farm laborers were found in a California grave, for which a labor contractor was eventually convicted of murder; the motive, according to the prosecution, was to avoid payment of the meager wages to these migrants, some of whom were derelicts seeking to earn enough money for the next bottle of wine and who were evidently without family. Finally, numerous young males were killed in two unrelated and apparently sadistic homosexual sprees, in Texas and Illinois. Mass murders are more likely to be detected than individual murders—in fact, in all four cases it is difficult to understand that no alarm led to an investigation of even a single missing individual. One or two bodies might be hidden for long periods, or a single person might be missing forever, without the events finding their way into the statistics on homicide.[11]

11. For those interested in pursuing this lugubrious subject, there is a fascinating and copious literature. Fiction, of course, has many examples of murders known only to the living offenders. The situation is handled as macabre comedy in the play *Arsenic and Old Lace* (Kesselring, 1941). For one such episode from history, see *Murder at Harvard* (Thomson, 1971), in which a professor murdered a man to whom he owed money and who was pressing him for repayment, and then successfully hid his body for a long time. Eventually the body was found; the professor was brought to trial and was hanged (a fate to which not even a professor should be subjected). In the Christie case in England, reported in *Ten Rillington Place* (Kennedy, 1961), the bodies of several murdered females were found long after their deaths, and in fact after an innocent man,

Probably just as common, if not more so, are murders in which the victims are reported to have expired from natural causes or an accident or suicide. Murder is sometimes followed by arson, in the hope, usually unsuccessful, of burning the body so that the fact of a deliberate slaying cannot be established. Many of these crimes may be intrafamilial murders. Because of their expert training in the circumstances leading up to death, it is possible that physicians have committed more than their proportionate share of murders.

The Unknowing Victim.   A living victim is not always aware that a crime has been perpetrated against him. Sometimes money or goods are stolen and not missed for a long time, if ever, or the victim believes they have been mislaid or lost. An automobile might be taken for a ''joyride'' and then returned undamaged to its original place; a person's name might be removed from a list of those who have passed an examination; a will naming someone as beneficiary might be destroyed, making a previous will, which omits this beneficiary entirely or gives him or her a lesser amount, legally binding. A few such events become known, but one can only speculate on how often such crime occurs without ever coming to the knowledge of the victim. Fraud is a crime of which the victim is frequently unaware; landlords, storekeepers, and corporations large and small often victimize tenants and customers. The surviving members of a family may not know that they have been victimized when valuables, including money, are stolen from the clothing or premises of one who has just died.

Most crimes are known to the victim—and to others such as family, friends, and witnesses—as well as to the offender. Nevertheless, they do not become part of criminal statistics in significant numbers because they are never reported to the police. Among major reasons for failing to report a crime to the police, the following can be cited:

KNOWN BUT UNREPORTED CRIME

1. The victim believes that this is a minor matter that can be handled without police intervention, that it can be ignored, or that he or she can take some measures against reoccurrence. An example of this would be the rifling of one's mailbox—a serious federal offense, yet seldom reported to authorities.
2. The victim fears retaliation or revenge if the crime is reported, and does not believe this can be done without the source of information becoming known. This would be true in cases of extortion, matters involving organized crime, many instances of forcible rape, and even robbery and burglary.

Timothy Evans, had been sent to the gallows for a different murder committed by the same Christie who had slain the then undiscovered victims. Finally, as we write, almost a half century has passed since the disappearance of a prominent New York political figure, Judge Force Crater, and it is unlikely that the public will ever know whether he was murdered, committed suicide, changed his identity, or met some other fate. Nor are the fate and whereabouts of Jimmy Hoffa known several years after his disappearance. Thus are homicide statistics less than perfect.

3. The victim fears that an arrest would expose some facet of life that would preferably be kept concealed. This is at the very heart of the crime of blackmail.

4. The victim may fear being stigmatized for simply having been a victim. This has been widely publicized as a reason for failure to report rape; it may also apply in confidence games and other types of fraud.

5. The victim believes that the police will not be able to accomplish anything in the way of recovery of stolen goods or even finding the offender. If there has been a theft, the victim is often interested only in restitution, and, thinking that eventuality to be remote, decides it is not worth the trouble to inform the police.

6. As part of negotiations for restitution, the victim may agree not to make a formal complaint to the police. This is not infrequent in cases of embezzlement.

7. The victim believes that an arrest may result in numerous trips to court at a great expenditure of time that he can ill afford, and that such visits will not be arranged to suit his convenience but that of the defendant, his attorney, and others involved in the case.

8. The victim may not want to establish a reputation for being the center or target for certain types of victimization, lest this result in further crime of a similar nature.

9. The victim suspects (or knows) that the offender is a relative or "friend" of the family. This is especially true in cases of incest—by definition an intrafamilial relationship—and in forcible and statutory rape and theft for the purpose of purchasing drugs.

10. The victim is a child, and the parents are unwilling to expose him or her to the anticipated trauma of a courtroom experience. Although this is more obviously an issue in cases of child molestation and incest (see Mc-Caghy, 1966; Bender and Blau, 1937; Finkelhor, 1979; MacNamara and Sagarin, 1977), it can be a factor in nonsexual crimes as well.

11. The victim is part of a subculture in which it is against the code of normative behavior to inform the police. In such a group, the normative response to victimization is usually private or group retaliation. This is true of some Italian-American (particularly Sicilian-American) subcultural groups, and is expressed in the concept of *omertà* (which refers to the resistance to providing information to the authorities).

12. There is a general distrust of the police by the victims, whether for ideological reasons (as would be the case with antiwar and other youth demonstrators during the 1970s), because of the victims' own involvement in other illegal acts (particularly in the drug scene), or because there is a history of conflict between the police and the racial and ethnic groups to which the victims belong (as would be found in the instance of blacks, Hispanics, and others).

13. The victim may be part of an ethnic group (true of Jewish, Chinese, and Gypsy groups and others in the United States) that prefers to handle its intraethnic crime without public knowledge and hence without police intervention.

14. The victim has either been involved in ancillary crime or believes himself otherwise vulnerable should there be a police or tax investigation. Stolen cash may not be reported because the victim cannot easily explain how he himself came into possession of the money without exposing himself to possible arrest.

15. The event itself might have been willingly and consensually indulged in by all the parties involved, who see it not as an antisocial act but as a private matter. This is, in short, what is meant by the concept of the crime without a victim.

Slightly counterbalancing all this is the fact that the victim is not always the sole source for the police to become knowledgeable of a crime. The police can and do discover crimes by their own efforts. However, crimes reported to police by victims or their families make up the bulk of official crime statistics.

How widespread is the failure to report crime will vary with the nature of the offense, its seriousness, and the sophistication and vulnerability of the victim. With some types of crimes only the number of arrests is recorded, and there is no reason to believe that this is an indication of the incidence of these events. To compare the number of arrests for prostitution from one year or state to another is not to compare the number of people engaged in sex for sale. However, for some other illegal acts official figures are generally given as the number of offenses *known* to the police, rather than just those for which an arrest is made. Although the percentage of unreported crime has for some time generally been believed to be high, many criminologists and law enforcement officials were still shocked when the results of victimization research surveys were disclosed. In these surveys—conducted primarily by interviewing members of households in carefully defined census tracts—the respondents reported that they or members of their families had been victimized during a single year about two to three times more frequently than official figures suggested.

Some criminologists have challenged the accuracy of criminal victimization studies, claiming that the public tends to exaggerate the degree, extent, and frequency of victimization when interrogated under the circumstances of a study. James Levine (1976) suggests, for example, that people do not recall time frames with accuracy, are not aware of legal definitions and may report a simple assault as an attempted rape, want to please the interrogator (apparently receptive to reports of victimization) and hence redefine incidents that have occurred so that they fit into crime categories, and generate exaggeratedly high figures in other ways as well.

There is some overreporting of crime, but there is general agreement that the official crime figures released in the United States each year reflect an underestimation of the total number of crimes committed. The major problems, then, are, (1) Approximately how accurate are the official data? (2) How can they be improved? (3) What elements or sectors of these statistics are relatively reliable? (4) Can these figures be compared for different time periods and geographic areas and for age, sex, race, and other social variables, and still give meaningful results?

Uniform Crime Reports

For more than half a century, the Federal Bureau of Investigation has been gathering data on crime and releasing this information, at first twice a year and later annually. Inasmuch as violations of state criminal codes constitute the overwhelming bulk of law-breaking in America, this information has to be obtained by voluntary reporting from agencies not under federal jurisdiction. Nevertheless, by 1976 the FBI reports were covering 96 percent of the population of the country. This coverage was higher for urban centers, and there has been an increase in this already high figure since that time. This series, officially called *Crime in the United States* (followed by the year for which the statistics are given) and also known as FBI Uniform Crime Reports (UCR), had but recently made its appearance when the distinguished criminologist Thorsten Sellin (1931b) remarked that the American crime statistics were probably the most unreliable in the Western world. It is unlikely that this would be said today, and it might even be argued that they surpass in accuracy the statistics released by other Western countries, except the United Kingdom (including Scotland and Wales), Ireland, and the Scandinavian nations.

The annual edition of *Crime in the United States* generally appears some eight to ten months after the end of the year for which it reports the data. The Uniform Crime Reports have been severely criticized; some of the criticisms may have led to improvements in the gathering of information. Marvin Wolfgang wrote a brief history of the UCR in which he quoted from Adolphe Quetelet, who in 1833 had warned:

> I do not fear to say that everything we possess on statistics of crimes and misdemeanors would be of no utility if we did not tacitly assume that there exists a nearly invariable relationship between offenses known and adjudicated and the total sum of offenses committed. [Wolfgang, 1963: 713]

The continued use of UCR is based on just such a tacit and often explicit, although difficult to verify, assumption.

But this assumption has been challenged. Soon after the appearance of UCR, Sam Bass Warner (1931), writing in the *Harvard Law Review*, questioned whether, given their inaccuracy, the statistics were not worse than none at all. He pointed out that crime reporting was anything but uniform, and that crimes known to the police at the precinct level and deliberately not reported were a major source of distortion.

INDEX CRIMES The FBI, in order to emerge with a single figure that could be used as an index of criminality and determine fluctuations over time and regional variations in the United States, segregates eight crimes (there were seven until 1980, when arson was added to the list). These are known as the "index crimes." The total of these eight crimes, in proportion to the population of the United States, is the single figure used to construct an index of crime. The index crimes, in addition to arson, are homicide and nonnegligent manslaughter, forcible rape, robbery, aggravated assault, burglary, larceny-theft, and motor vehicle theft. Manslaughter by negligence and statutory rape were included in the index in early FBI statistics but later dropped.

38

These statistics are gathered in accordance with instructions in a manual which defines the crimes, so that some uniformity might be obtained. With the exception of homicide, an attempt to commit a crime is generally classified as if the crime had been committed. In crimes against the person (homicide, rape, assault, and robbery), the number of victims is counted, with each victim constituting a separate crime.[12] For the other index crimes —crimes against property (burglary, arson, larceny-theft, and motor vehicle theft)—each event is counted singly, regardless of the number of victims or offenders.

Index crimes are often called "serious crimes," and not infrequently index crime has been equated with crime as a whole. The eight index offenses were chosen with the end in mind of creating a single figure that would serve as a numerical indicator of overall serious criminality. For this purpose, it was deemed desirable to include only offenses which have *all* of the following characteristics: (1) they are serious; (2) they occur with sufficient frequency to be usable for statistical purposes; and (3) there is reason to believe that a reliably constant although approximate relationship exists between the number of events known to the police and the number of such crimes that actually occur.

Thus, kidnapping meets the first and third criteria but not the second. To include an event that occurs in America some 50 to 100 times a year would not be statistically meaningful, although one could include it under aggravated assault. If there was one kidnapping during the year in Kansas and two in Nebraska, it would not add to our knowledge of crime to speak of a 100 percent increase in one state as compared with the other. Blackmail and extortion meet the first and second criteria but not the third and are thus not useful for the construction of an index. Statutory rape, by which is meant voluntary sexual relations between an adult male and a female under the legal age of consent but not legally identified as a child, does not meet the first and third criteria although it undoubtedly meets the second (in this respect it is the very reverse of kidnapping).

One criticism frequently made of UCR is that any single crime index, desirable as it might be, is inherently misleading. An index of wages or purchasing power, in which a base year is taken as 100, may present many difficulties in construction and reliability, but it is possible to arrive at one single figure that becomes useful and informative. Suppose, on the other hand, that in two years or regions the distribution of index crimes is as shown in Table 2-1. One would say that time or place B had only about four-fifths (or a little under 80 percent) as much "serious crime" as (or, more exactly, had a crime index figure some 20 percent lower than) time or place A, assuming that the total populations of A and B are the same.

IS AN INDEX INHERENTLY MISLEADING?

12. Robbery is generally defined as a theft from a person by means of force, threat of force, or putting the victim in fear, and thus can be classified as a crime against the person or property, although it is officially listed as against the person. Inasmuch as the term "crimes against the person" is interchangeably called "violent crimes" or "crimes of violence," the placing of robbery in this category has an importance in the presentation of the total crime picture in America. For the UCR definitions of the index crimes, see pp. 44–45.

Crime	Time or Place A	Time or Place B
Homicide	200	300
Forcible rape	600	900
Robbery	4,100	3,800
Aggravated assault	5,100	4,000
Burglary	300,000	250,000
Larceny-theft	600,000	450,000
Automobile theft	10,000	11,000
Arson	5,000	5,000
Totals	925,000	725,000

TABLE 2-1 Hypothetical Changes in Index Crimes

However, an examination of the data shows how misleading the overall index figure can be. Although the total of all index crime in B is considerably smaller than in A, there is 50 percent more murder and rape in B than in A. Under such circumstances, is it meaningful to speak of a reduction in crime as expressed by a single index? Can one add automobile thefts, forcible rapes, and murders together with the five other types of event and get something that comes to a significant total figure of crime?

Sometimes this problem is handled by adding to the one figure for the total crime index two subsidiary figures to show what has occurred in offenses against the person and those against property. Thus, for example, the public can be alerted, as can criminologists and government officials, to the fact that there has been an increase in crimes against the person although there has at the same time been a general decrease in all index crimes. However, in the case in Table 2-1 even this would not remedy the situation, for A shows 10,000 crimes against the person and B only 9,000, despite the lead in murder and forcible rape with B.

Some criminologists might contend that this is a straw-man issue, as individual crimes are not likely to change selectively from time to time and place to place but rather follow the general trends of serious crime and violence and of accuracy in crime reporting. However, while the hypothetical figures we have given do demonstrate more dramatic changes than would ordinarily be found, similar discrepancies between the trends in index crimes, on a smaller scale, are not rare. The fact is that during the decade of the 1970s, motor vehicle theft went up nearly 18 percent in absolute numbers and its rate per total population rose 9 percent, while for other index crimes in this period, the increases in the absolute number of offenses and rates per population were a minimum of 34 and 23 percent respectively for homicide and a high of 100 and 84 percent for rape. Nevertheless, automobile theft contributes about 9 percent to the entire index, while murder and rape combined contribute 0.8 percent. (See Table 3-3, p. 56, for these figures.)

Some criminologists and other interested persons, particularly government administrators, propose to deal with the statistical problem of the unequal seriousness of various crimes by abolishing the idea of a single crime index and even that of "index crimes." Whatever merit this proposal might have had in the past, the abolition of the index would serve no purpose today. Journalists and politicians would then work with the raw data and create their own figures, using Uniform Crime Reports as model. Such new indexes, while not having the official imprimatur of the government, would nonetheless be widely disseminated and would only aggravate an already difficult situation. Without precedent and with no accountability, such persons could add new offenses to an index and drop old ones as required by the exigencies of the moment. If one wanted to prove that crime had decreased, one could choose figures documenting this trend, even if they included prostitution and public drunkenness; for increases, the opposite selective manipulation and mechanism could be used.

It would appear that the crime index system, as used by the FBI, is suitable for sensing fluctuation and variation in crime, although great care is required in explaining what the figures are and what they mean, and work remains to be done toward improving the reliability and the accuracy of the data. The FBI itself issues a strong caveat in each annual edition of Uniform Crime Reports, warning against misinterpretation and misuse of the data, and particularly against making invidious comparisons. For example, in presentating the data for 1979 the FBI states, "Care should be exercised in any direct data comparisons with statistics in prior issues of *Crime in the United States.* Changes in the crime level may have been due in part to improved reporting or records procedures, redefinition of reporting areas, or other variables" (Uniform Crime Reports, 1980: 4).

A WEIGHTED INDEX

One very complex proposal for establishing a more reliable index of crime involves a system of weighting, modeled after the pioneer work done on the measurement of juvenile delinquency by Thorsten Sellin and Marvin Wolfgang (1964). In their work, a crime is analyzed to determine its seriousness, taking into consideration such factors, among others, as bodily harm and use of weapons by the offenders, A homicide is given the greatest weight (it is "worth" 26 points); forcible rape is assigned 10 points, to be increased by 2 if a weapon is used for intimidation. There are descending numbers until one reaches automobile theft and petty larceny without injury to the victim and intimidation, scored as 2 points and 1 respectively.

It is possible that such a weighted index could be agreed upon in the future, but it entails many difficulties. It is unlikely that general consensus could be reached on the "value" of one type of crime as compared with another. Within a given criminal category the amount of injury suffered, degree of fear, presence or absence of mitigating factors—all could differ considerably. Statisticians could not be expected to study each event to assign it the deserved weight, and police officials could hardly be expected to report in detail every offense, although a random sample might suffice. The task of obtaining accurate reports from precinct and police headquarters is challenging enough; to burden personnel reporting to the FBI with the job of gathering details on each event, stating whether there was a weapon and describing injuries suffered, is hardly practical in a country in which more than twelve million index crimes are reported in a single year.

A review of the major proposals for weighting was made by Michael Hindelang (1974), who concluded that the weighting of offenses among index crimes would not "markedly alter the rankings of states and counties which are produced when an unweighted scheme is used."

We would suggest that weighting is more useful for criminological investigation than for official reporting of crime. Scholars can themselves devise a system of relative values and do a sampling of crimes in order to determine, with seriousness taken into account, whether, where, and to what extent crime is on the increase.

THE CRIME CLOCK

A less serious objection may be raised to the manner of presentation of some of the crime data, particularly what has become known as the "crime clock." Such a clock, as reproduced in Figure 2-1, shows, for example, that one murder takes place in the United States every 24 minutes, one forcible rape every 7 minutes, and one motor vehicle theft every 29 seconds; an index offense of some type occurs every 3 seconds.

It is possible that such clocks increase fear and panic without increasing insight, care, and prudence.[13] One could just as well show a calendar or a diagram indicating that the chances are about five million to one that a given citizen will *not* be killed on a certain day; that the possibilities of being killed on the highway during a given year are two to three times as great as being slain by a homicidal offender; that if one lived for one thousand years, at the present rate of murder (as shown by the statistics but not presented in the clock), the odds against being victimized in a murder would be more than one hundred to one.

However, objections to crime clocks and the other methods of presenting crime data to the public raise important questions of policy and public relations but are not germane to the larger issues of the accuracy, reliability, and value of the data.

VEHICULAR THEFT: A PROBLEM IN CATEGORIZATION

One of the index crimes is vehicular theft. This could logically be placed in the more general category of larceny or grand larceny—defined as the theft of money, object, or property above a certain value (generally set at fifty dollars). But the large number of thefts of automobiles, the near-accuracy of the reports, the fact that cars are individually registered and usually insured would appear to make it worthwhile to show this item separately on crime statistics.

Some contend that the category of automobile theft covers two widely divergent types of behavior: (1) joyride theft, a sort of unauthorized borrowing without malice but without consent in which the automobile is sometimes returned near the area from which it had been taken, usually in an unharmed state; and (2) theft for purposes of sale, stripping for profit, or use in the commission of another crime. Peter Lejins (1966) suggested to the International Association of Chiefs of Police that a distinction be made between these two types of event, but this proposal was rejected by those in charge of

---

13. This is not to deny the accuracy of the clock on its own terms; nor is it claimed that it exaggerates the incidence of the offenses. If one is to believe the victimization surveys, the clock underestimates all offenses, particularly rape, and possibly murder as well.

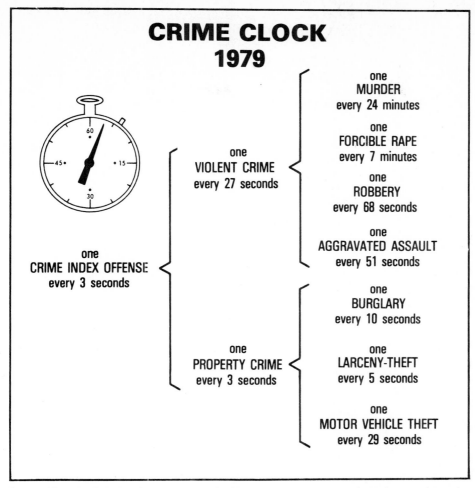

CRIME CLOCK
1979

one
CRIME INDEX OFFENSE
every 3 seconds

one
VIOLENT CRIME
every 27 seconds

one
MURDER
every 24 minutes

one
FORCIBLE RAPE
every 7 minutes

one
ROBBERY
every 68 seconds

one
AGGRAVATED ASSAULT
every 51 seconds

one
PROPERTY CRIME
every 3 seconds

one
BURGLARY
every 10 seconds

one
LARCENY-THEFT
every 5 seconds

one
MOTOR VEHICLE THEFT
every 29 seconds

The crime clock should be viewed with care. Being the most aggregate representation of UCR data, it is designed to convey the annual reported crime experience by showing the relative frequency of occurrence of the Index Offenses. This mode of display should not be taken to imply a regularity in the commission of the Part I Offenses; rather, it represents the annual ratio of crime to fixed time intervals.

FIGURE 2-1

SOURCE: Uniform Crime Reports, 1980, p. 5.

crime statistics "on the grounds that separating the offense of joyriding from auto theft would diminish the deterrent effect on potential violators" (Lejins, 1966: 1024). We do not find this a good scientific reason for the refusal to make the distinction; data should not be classified in one manner rather than another because of the effects categorization may produce on behavior. In fact, every distinction, if it can be validly made, is added information for the user of crime statistics. A more important objection might be the difficulty of determining which of the two categories a particular theft falls into, the additional burdens on those keeping records at the precinct or police level and reporting them to the FBI, and the overloading of those assigned the task of compiling crime statistics with added detail, which might reduce their accuracy rather than add to it or deflect energy from other and more valuable activities.

VARIATIONS AMONG JURISDICTIONS Inasmuch as each of the fifty states has jurisdiction over all of the crimes that are part of the index and the state penal codes define the crimes, there can be major discrepancies in the definitions, leading to inconsistencies in classification.[14]

Everyone may know what burglary means, but whether a given act falls within that category depends on the definition in the penal code of the state in which the event occurs and the accumulation of interpretations there since passage of the law. As a result, an act may be reported as burglary in one state and as larceny in another.

The FBI seeks to diminish the effect of such differences by offering succinct descriptions of each index crime. These are not and cannot be identical to the definitions in the state penal codes, and only the latter hold in court (except if the crime falls within the federal jurisdiction, in which case the federal law, not the FBI definition, prevails). But these descriptions are excellent presentations of what is meant by each of the index categories, and are given below:

MURDER AND NONNEGLIGENT MANSLAUGHTER.   Murder and nonnegligent manslaughter, as defined in the Uniform Crime Reporting Program, is the willful (nonnegligent) killing of one human being by another.

The classification of this offense, as in all other Crime Index offenses, is based solely on police investigation as opposed to the determination of a court, medical examiner, coroner, jury, or other judicial body. Not included in the count for this offense classification are deaths caused by negligence, suicide, or accident; justifiable homicides, which are the killings of felons by law enforcement officers in the line of duty or by private citizens; and attempts to murder or assaults to murder, which are scored as aggravated assaults.

FORCIBLE RAPE.   Forcible rape, as defined in the Program, is the carnal knowledge of a female forcibly and against her will. Assaults or attempts to commit rape by force or threat of force are also included; however, statutory rape (without force) and other sex offenses are not included in this category.

ROBBERY.   Robbery is the taking or attempting to take anything of value from the care, custody, or control of a person or persons by force or threat of force or violence and/or by putting the victim in fear.

AGGRAVATED ASSAULT.   Aggravated assault is an unlawful attack by one person upon another for the purpose of inflicting severe or aggravated bodily

14. The federal Criminal Code applies only in restricted circumstances, such as crimes of an interstate character and those against federal property, among others. There are also military codes and special codes for the District of Columbia. This results in a total of more than fifty sets of definitions.

injury. This type of assault is usually accompanied by the use of a weapon or by means likely to produce death or great bodily harm. Attempts are included since it is not necessary that an injury result when a gun, knife, or other weapon is used which could and probably would result in serious personal injury if the crime were successfully completed.

BURGLARY.   The Uniform Crime Reporting Program defines burglary as the unlawful entry of a structure to commit a felony or theft. The use of force to gain entry is not required to classify an offense as burglary. Burglary in this Program is categorized into three subclassifications: forcible entry, unlawful entry where no force is used, and attempted forcible entry.

LARCENY-THEFT.   Larceny-theft is the unlawful taking, carrying, leading, or riding away of property from the possession or constructive possession of another. It includes crimes such as shoplifting, pocket-picking, purse-snatching, thefts from motor vehicles, thefts of motor vehicle parts and accessories, bicycle thefts, etc., in which no use of force, violence, or fraud occurs. In the Uniform Crime Reporting Program, this crime category does not include embezzlement, "con" games, forgery, and worthless checks. Motor vehicle theft is also excluded from this category for crime reporting purposes inasmuch as it is a separate Crime Index offense.

ARSON.   Arson is defined by the Uniform Crime Reporting Program as any willful or malicious burning or attempt to burn, with or without intent to defraud, a dwelling, public building, motor vehicle or aircraft, personal property of another, etc. Only fires determined through investigation to have been willfully or maliciously set are classified as arsons. Fires of suspicious or unknown origins are excluded.[15]

MOTOR VEHICLE THEFT.   In Uniform Crime Reporting, motor vehicle theft is defined as the theft or attempted theft of a motor vehicle. This definition excludes the taking of a motor vehicle for temporary use by those persons having lawful access. [Uniform Crime Reports (*Crime in the United States*), 1980]

These official definitions notwithstanding, local police units of necessity find it more convenient to follow the legal definitions and classifications of their own states. With more than twelve million index crimes known to the police nationwide each year, it can hardly be expected that for each individual event authorities will make a study to determine whether there is a discrepancy between the FBI classification and that of the state penal law.

One can exaggerate the effects of this problem. There are differences from one state to another, but essentially the definitions have a great deal in common, so that interjurisdictional distinctions do not make a major contribution to error in Uniform Crime Reports. Furthermore, under the impact of geographic mobility and ease of communication, state penal codes have

15. The words "of another" may cause some confusion. It is criminal to burn one's own personal property only if it is with intent to defraud. Arson is committed if a person burns his own dwelling; a dwelling is not personal property but real property, and the words "of another" in this definition are meant to refer only to personal property.

been moving in the direction of greater consistency with one another. At the same time, various decisions of the United States Supreme Court have increasingly made the Constitution applicable to what were formerly state matters, and the effective work of the American Law Institute (1962) in suggesting a Model Penal Code has also contributed to a decline in differences between the states.[16]

MULTIPLE OFFENSES, OFFENDERS, AND VICTIMS

Perhaps the single most serious problem affecting the validity and reliability of the data in Uniform Crime Reports—other than the dark figure of unknown and unreported illegal conduct—is the issue of multiplicity: when a single event occurs actually as a series of simultaneous or continuous crimes, embodies many different crimes or the same crime occurring several times, is committed by many offenders, or has more than one victim.

In the UCR method of reporting, only one offense is reported when many have taken place as part of a single event. The crime reported is the most serious in a hierarchy that peaks with murder, continues with forcible rape, and goes down to the least serious of the index crimes, automobile theft. Many have objected to this system as concealing a number of serious (if lesser) index crimes, and also as assigning the same weight to an event that may have consisted of only one crime and to another that in fact consisted of several. Along this line, Sellin and Wolfgang (1964: 294) write, "By counting only one offense when several are conjoined, it provides only a partial enumeration of the specific criminal offenses known to the police, and by equating all offenses which carry the same legal label, differences in the degree of seriousness of offenses within any given category are concealed." Sellin and Wolfgang would instead take into account "each violation of the law occurring during an event" (p. 297) as well as numerous aggravating factors (mentioned above in discussion of weighting, pp. 41–42).

The problem of handling multiple offenses is illustrated by the following newspaper item, quoted here in full, with names removed:

GRAND RAPIDS, MICH., Dec. 2 (UPI)—_____, a prison fugitive, was convicted tonight of kidnapping a 59-year-old woman and keeping her hostage for eight days during which, she testified, he repeatedly raped her.

The jury of seven women and five men took 38 minutes to find the 22-year-old Lansing man guilty of kidnapping _____ of Marquette, wife of _____, a former Northern Michigan University vice president, from their summer cottage on August 25.

Mr. _____ was also convicted of taking a stolen car across state lines.

Mrs. _____, a small, slightly built woman, testified that Mr. _____ repeatedly raped her during eight terror-filled days of captivity and left her in severe, crippling pain for days. [*New York Times*, 1977: 10]

16. Inconsistency of definition is only one aspect of a wider problem that makes international comparison of crime rates frustrating—often valueless, or at least misleading. However, multiple jurisdictions within one country exist nowhere to the extent that they do in the United States. Only Australia has diverse penal codes in one nation. In most other countries a federal penal code prevails for the entire country, covering all criminal conduct.

The defendant was here found guilty of two crimes, kidnapping and taking a stolen car across state lines. Both are federal crimes, and it is doubtful, in the light of the severe sentence that a kidnapping charge generally brings, that it was intended to try him on the charges of inflicting bodily harm (assault), rape, or stealing an automobile. If only the most severe crime—in the legal sense—is recorded, it is kidnapping, which is not an index crime. If all alleged illegal acts are recorded, statisticians would have to decide whether each rape constitutes a separate offense and determine how many such offenses occurred.

Many serious crimes involve the use of stolen automobiles, illegal possession of guns, and resisting arrest in addition to the robbery or burglary that apparently motivated the offender. Rape during the commission of another felony makes up a considerable portion of the total number of rapes, according to the studies of Menachem Amir (1971). However, such an event would be listed as rape, and thus the burglary would be statistically concealed; similarly, rape followed by murder would be listed as murder and the rape concealed. The problem here, in the opinion of many criminologists, is that as a result the UCR seriously underestimates the total incidence of index crime. The UCR authorities, on the other hand, contend that any other method of reporting would be unwieldy and unlikely to result in consistency and uniformity.

Sophia Robison (1966: 104), in a trenchant and early critique of UCR, refers with disdain to the method of reporting only the most serious offense and omitting all others. "It should be evident that this procedure may easily obscure the severity of the criminal behavior, as does the process in some jurisdictions of persuading defendants to plead guilty to a lesser offense in situations where several criminal acts were committed."[17]

REPLIES TO THE CRITICS

The Uniform Crime Reports have had their defenders. Peter Lejins contends that in the United States there are three difficulties in compiling crime statistics distinct from the hurdles and impediments encountered anywhere in the world:

> First, the absence of a central authority to require cooperation in any kind of national program results in complete dependence upon voluntary participation for all contributions. . . . Second, since a potential contributor of data to the national program does not have complete control over the entire law enforcement system in his own locality, but only of a segment, he very often cannot secure uniform data because the rest of the local units cannot be modified, either by him or by the national program, so as to provide comparable information. . . . Third, the divergence of views on the value of various kinds of data and their usefulness for law enforcement which exists among the personnel of law enforcement systems is apt to cripple the needed voluntary cooperation. [Lejins, 1966: 1012–1013]

17. Enormous statistical difficulties arise in this circumstance—when a more serious crime known to the police is reduced to a lesser one for purposes of plea bargaining. Statistics can and should reflect the offense as known to police. Plea bargaining in the criminal justice system is discussed in some detail in Chapter 18.

Lejins takes note of the distortions caused by unreported serious crime, and finds in addition that certain offenses are not channeled through the police, but are handled by federal commissioners, prosecutors, marshals, and others, thus never finding their way, ironically enough, into federal statistics derived from police sources.

However, on the question of multiple offenses during a single event, Lejins concedes considerable merit to the argument that a serious error is committed when, for example, a particular act is reported as murder, and the accompanying robbery and auto theft are completely omitted, but he states that the alternative of listing all the offenses would present great difficulties. He cites a hypothetical case in which the police chase and catch the driver of a stolen car. During the chase the driver goes through fifteen red lights, exceeds the speed limit in five different speed zones, makes five unauthorized left turns, and fails to signal at ten intersections. "Although such itemized accounts are occasionally presented by the police in court," writes Lejins, "it is highly questionable whether thirty-five moving traffic violations should be reported" (1966: 1021–1022).

So where does this leave us? Lejins concludes that both extremes—reporting only one offense or reporting all—are less than altogether desirable. One of the ways this could be handled—although it would entail no small amount of difficulty—would be to record all index crimes known to the police but record only arrests or convictions for non-index crimes. Thus, a man who steals a car, burglarizes a house, and apprehends a woman therein and rapes and murders her would be accounting for four index crimes, not one. This type of record-keeping would provide a more accurate picture of crime in the United States than the one that now obtains.

Some Tentative Conclusions

It has become a national sport among criminologists to take pot shots at Uniform Crime Reports. That UCR leaves much room for improvement cannot be denied. However, the key question is whether the statistics give a sufficiently accurate image of the nature and scope of crime to be worth their compilation and publication. Are they accurate enough to be usable for studies of fluctuations from one time period to another and one geographic area to another?

In order to test the accuracy of UCR on homicide, Michael Hindelang (1974) compared the FBI data with information supplied by the Center for Health Statistics of the Department of Health, Education and Welfare. Despite some discrepancies between the definitions used by the two agencies, he found remarkable similarities, first by showing comparisons nationally over the thirty-five-year period from 1935 to 1970, and then by taking state-by-state comparisons for one year, 1968. However, these favorable results, pointing to the accuracy of UCR, may derive from the fact that Hindelang here dealt with one of the most accurate figures in the tabulation of crimes known to the police—namely, murder—and the reliability of this figure may in no way reflect similar reliability for rape, burglary, or grand larceny.

Moreover, the UCR and HEW data may conceal the same dark figure of unknown homicides.

Some years earlier, Donald Cressey (1957) wrote, "The general statistics on crime are among the most unsatisfactory of all social statistics." Since not all or even most crimes are reported to the police, those that are constitute at best only an index, Cressey maintained, which fails because it does not "maintain a constant ratio with the true rate, whatever it may be." Cressey listed five principal reasons why the figure on crimes known to the police is not an adequate index of crime: (1) The number known to the police is much smaller than the number committed. (2) The police may be recording only a proportion of all the crimes known to them. (3) The ratio of crimes committed to those reported and recorded differs with the nature of the offense. (4) There is variation in the definition and classification of the behavior as crime in different jurisdictions. (5) It would be more meaningful to have reports of crime as rates rather than absolute numbers.

The first of these problems remains. Probably the second has been reduced in importance. As for the third, Cressey cites statutory rape as an example, but that is no longer an index crime, and while the third objection has considerable merit it is not a major problem in comparing rates and noting fluctuations among the index crimes. On the fourth objection, it is unlikely that any index crimes would not be criminal offenses in any jurisdiction, although this is true of many other non-index crimes. Finally, along the lines of Cressey's suggestion, the fifth objection has been met and the index is being increasingly reported in terms of crime rates.

Criminologist and legal scholar Paul Tappan (1960: 64) noted that the FBI was successful during the 1950s in making its coverage more complete and uniform. He concluded, "So far as major felonies are concerned, useful comparisons can be made from year to year and from state to state. Significant changes in rates and trends can be traced in part, at least, to their sources."

Since these words were written the situation has no doubt improved further; those who felt in 1960 that these were words of deserved praise would no doubt feel now that this is even more the case. Others are less enthusiastic, believing that improvement is still necessary before such confidence can be placed in the FBI statistics and sound theory or policy formulated from them. The fact is that, as we write, the entire UCR system is under review, and a much more comprehensive, informative, and, we hope, accurate system of criminal statistics is likely to emerge in the United States before the end of the century.

The Extent, Impact, and Cost of Crime in the United States

Although traditionally the major interest in crime statistics for criminologists is probably in fluctuations that permit comparisons between time periods and geographic areas and in data that identify offenders and victims according to age, sex, ethnicity, and other variables, the public and the policy-makers are primarily concerned with the extent, nature, impact, and cost of crime.

In some respects the cost of crime is beyond calculation because it involves pain and suffering, fear, and changes in life-style, which cannot be expressed in dollars. In crimes against the person it is possible to count the events, show approximately how many murders, forcible rapes, assaults, and robberies have taken place, and even describe the degree and nature of the injuries in some detail. But these events involve suffering, trauma, grief, and long-term harm to victims and families. The presence of crime and the fear of crime, whether rooted in reality or in exaggeration, has an impact on how people shop and visit, whether they go for a stroll or bicycle ride, where they live, and even what type of employment they will choose or refuse. Nonetheless, in some respects crime can be reduced to numbers, and these should be presented in such a way as to give an accurate picture, regardless of whether this leads to undue alarm or unjustified complacency.

As this book is being written, an estimate of the cost nationwide of the criminal justice system for the year 1976 has been made available. It appears here as Table 3–1. It will be seen that the total expenditure amounts to a little under $20 billion. (Compare this with some $11.7 billion in 1972.) Further study shows the percentage of this sum spent by federal, state, and local governments for the police, judiciary, and other services.

At first glance, a cost of almost $20 billion appears incredibly high, especially since more than half of it must be borne by municipal and county governments, which have the poorest taxing powers and whose residents already suffer from high taxation and fiscal crises. On the other hand, one might note that the apparently staggering sum amounts to less than $100 per person per year, far less than is spent on health care, education of the young, and other vital needs.

However, the figures are both misleadingly high and low. They are "too high" in part because a considerable portion of the time and service of local police is not devoted to crime control at all. The police answer sick call emergencies, look for lost children, assist persons in trouble, give directions, handle traffic, aid firefighters, and perform countless other tasks that would have to be done and paid for even if there were no crime. (Note that the cost of local police amounts to almost $8 billion—more than 39 percent of the total of all expenditures in the United States for criminal justice activities.)

On the other hand, the total dollar amount represents only the cost of prevention and handling of crime and criminals by government agencies. It constitutes but a small portion of the real cost of crime. Private citizens and corporate groups purchase gates, locks, fences, and other devices exclusively used for the prevention of crime; employ private security forces; install burglar-alarm systems in stores, homes, and automobiles; repair goods and property such as motor vehicles injured by vandalism, malicious mischief, or some other illegal activity; pay medical expenses for those injured in crime; insure against theft, fire (including criminally set fire), and other loss due to crime—and this does not exhaust the list of costs that must be added to those directly incurred by federal, state, and local governments.

Crimes against the Person

The greatest impact of crime is to be found in death and physical and psychological injury caused by homicide, forcible rape, assault, drunken driving, and many other acts. We have noted that the crime-victimization studies carried out in the mid-1960s and since indicated that victims and families of victims reported to interviewers considerably greater victimization than was reflected in the official statistics of Uniform Crime Reports. Homicide was an exception. In fact, UCR reported a greater number of victims and a higher rate than did the victimization studies, in the areas of murder and manslaughter, although the differences were not large. In Table 3–2, the crime rates according to UCR and according to criminal victimization studies are compared. It will be seen that the rate of forcible rape attested to in the victimization studies but not reported to the police was greater than for any other crime against the person, which substantiates the widely held view that there has been great reluctance to report that crime because of the stigma attached to being a victim.

Crime figures are given in the form of offenses and rates per population. The latter are computed on the basis of the number of criminal events per

TABLE 3-1
Expenditure for Criminal Justice Activities (by type of activity and expenditure, and level of government, United States, fiscal year 1976)

(Dollar amounts in thousands)

Type of activity and expenditure	Total	Level of government					
		Federal[a]		State		Local[b]	
		Amount	Percent	Amount	Percent	Amount	Percent
Total criminal justice system[c]	$19,681,409	$3,322,073	X	$5,986,650	X	$12,068,308	X
Direct expenditure	19,681,409	2,450,229	12.5	5,204,226	26.4	12,026,954	61.1
Intergovernmental expenditure	(c)	871,844	X	782,424	X	133,855	X
Police protection[c]	11,028,244	1,615,714	X	1,789,471	X	7,723,588	X
Direct expenditure	11,028,244	1,611,640	14.6	1,696,460	15.4	7,720,144	70.0
Intergovernmental expenditure	(c)	4,074	X	93,011	X	59,390	X
Judicial[c]	2,428,472	219,445	X	663,068	X	1,633,645	X
Direct expenditure	2,428,472	219,445	9.0	585,151	24.1	1,623,876	66.9
Intergovernmental expenditure	(c)	0	X	77,917	X	18,123	X
Legal services and prosecution[c]	1,047,929	149,402	X	253,591	X	653,502	X
Direct expenditure	1,047,929	149,402	14.3	247,723	23.6	650,804	62.1
Intergovernmental expenditure	(c)	0	X	5,868	X	3,142	X

Public defense[c]	331,102	103,718	X	78,622	X	157,364	X
Direct expenditure	331,102	103,718	31.3	70,139	21.2	157,245	47.5
Intergovernmental expenditure	(c)	0	X	8,483	X	1,279	X
Corrections[c]	4,385,512	285,973	X	2,589,609	X	1,678,879	X
Direct expenditure	4,385,512	256,352	5.9	2,474,783	56.4	1,654,377	37.7
Intergovernmental expenditure	(c)	29,621	X	114,826	X	49,547	X
Other criminal justice[c]	460,150	947,821	X	612,289	X	221,329	X
Direct expenditure	460,150	109,672	23.8	129,970	28.3	220,508	47.9
Intergovernmental expenditure	(c)	838,149	X	482,319	X	2,374	X

NOTE: The survey of expenditure and employment is conducted annually through the joint efforts of the Law Enforcement Assistance Administration and the U.S. Bureau of the Census. In general, six categories of activity are covered: police protection, judicial, legal services and prosecution, public defense, corrections, and other. Data are also collected for each of three levels of government: Federal, State, and local. Local government coverage includes all county governments, all municipalities having a 1970 population of 10,000 or more, and a sample of the remaining cities and townships under 10,000 population. The survey panel was comprised, therefore, of the Federal Government, the 50 State governments, and 9,045 local governments (3,042 county governments, 4,305 municipalities, and 1,697 townships).

Because all State and county governments were surveyed, data relating to them are not subject to sampling error (i.e., variations that might result if a different sample were used). However, data reported for local governments are estimates that are subject to sampling error. Local government estimates are accurate (at the 95 percent level of confidence) to within three-quarters of 1 percent of the totals that would have been expected if all local governments were surveyed (Source, p. 17). Field compilation and mail canvass methods were used to obtain the data reported and were supplemented by reference to a variety of published government documents such as budgets, financial statements, and audit reports. Expenditure data are generally for the fiscal year ending June 30, 1976 for the Federal Government and all States except New York (Mar. 31, 1976), Texas (Aug. 31, 1976), and Alabama (Sept. 30, 1976). Employment data are for October 1976, for all levels of government.

[a]Federal Government data are for the fiscal period beginning July 1, 1975 and ending June 30, 1976. Data for the transition quarter from July 1, 1976 to Sept. 30, 1976 are displayed separately in Table 4A of the Source.

[b]Local governments data are estimates subject to sampling variation; see Source for data limitations.

[c]The total line for each sector, and for the total criminal justice system, excludes duplicative intergovernmental expenditure amounts. This was done to avoid the artificial inflation that would result if an intergovernmental expenditure amount for one government is tabulated and then counted again when the recipient government(s) ultimately expend(s) that amount. The intergovernmental expenditure lines are not totaled for the same reason.

SOURCE: U.S. Department of Justice, Law Enforcement Assistance Administration and U.S. Bureau of the Census, *Expenditure and Employment Data for the Criminal Justice System 1976* (Washington, D.C.: Government Printing Office, 1978), p. 23, Table 2.

TABLE 3-2
Comparison of National Opinion Research Center Survey and UCR Rates

			(Per 100,000 population)
Index crimes	NORC survey 1965–66	UCR rate for individuals 1965[a]	UCR rate for individuals and organizations 1965[a]
Willful homicide	3.0	5.1	5.1
Forcible rape	42.5	11.6	11.6
Robbery	94.0	61.4	61.4
Aggravated assault	218.3	106.6	106.6
Burglary	949.1	299.6	605.3
Larceny ($50 and over)	606.5	267.4	393.3
Motor vehicle theft	206.2	226.0	251.0
Total violence	357.8	184.7	184.7
Total property	1,761.8	793.0	1,249.6

[a]"Uniform Crime Reports," 1965, p. 51. The UCR national totals do not distinguish crimes committed against individuals or households from those committed against businesses or other organizations. The UCR rate for individuals is the published national rate adjusted to eliminate burglaries, larcenies, and vehicle thefts not committed against individuals or households. No adjustment was made for robbery.

SOURCE: President's Commission on Law Enforcement and Administration of Justice, *The Challenge of Crime in a Free Society* (Washington, D.C.: Government Printing Office, 1967), p. 21.

100,000 persons. With all crimes against the person in the United States taken into account, it was found that in 1979 there were approximately 1,178,000 such events reported to or known by the police.[1] For the decade of the seventies, this is an increase in violent crime of just under 60 percent in absolute numbers and almost 48 percent in rate. In Table 3–3, the numbers and rates of index offenses are shown, including both violent and property crimes, for each year of the decade.

In the total crime index, using absolute numbers, a perusal of Table 3–3 indicates that there was stabilization for the period from 1975 through 1978, with a considerable jump in 1979, and the same is true of rates. When the breakdown between violent and property crime is made, the stabilization for property crimes, both in absolute figures and rates, was even more dramatic—in fact, there were slight decreases—but again the trend abruptly stopped in 1979.

If there is an assumption that the rate of unreported crime is somewhat constant in proportion to total crime, and if one accepts the figures obtained through victimization studies, then the estimated rate for offenses against the person rises from a little more than 535 per 100,000 population (based on UCR index crimes) to approximately 1,000. However, the official rate for forcible rape, which is shown in Table 3–3 as 34.5 for 1979—a rise of 84.4 percent over a decade—would have to be tripled to take into account the results of unofficial victimization surveys. Even this tripled figure, which goes

1. This includes only *index* crimes against the person (homicide and nonnegligent manslaughter, forcible rape, assault, and robbery). There are many other crimes against the person, such as child molestation, not included in the index and hence not counted as part of the figure mentioned here.

over 100 (indicating that there is one forcible rape during the year for every 1,000 persons) is no doubt misleading, for it is based on the total population of the nation, not just of females, and by definition only sexual assaults on females are counted as rape in the UCR. To obtain a realistic rate, one would have at least to double it, inasmuch as females constitute a little more than half of the total population. If one were to recompute the rate figures to take into account the most vulnerable years (from ages fifteen to forty), the risk of rape for females becomes extraordinarily high, and ascends sharply with lower social class, inner-city residence, and identification as a member of a minority group.

However, one of the problems in looking at fluctuations is that they may be distorted over time by improvements in crime statistics and by the larger percentage of reporting by victims, thus changing ratios of reported to total crimes committed. One is hard pressed, for example, to believe that the feminist movement had no effect on reducing the fear of reporting rape during the 1970s. Duncan Chappell (1976), who has studied this problem, reports a belief, based on his own research and that of others, that by 1975 about one-half of all forcible rapes were being reported, compared to a little more than one-fourth in 1965–66. It is, however, difficult to reconcile these statements with the statistics, because they lead to the conclusion that during the decade of the 1970s there was a great increase in violent crime while the actual number of rapes remained practically unchanged.

The single crime that attracts the greatest attention from media and public is homicide. By definition, it does not include death caused by negligence, suicide, accident, by a police officer in the line of duty, or in self-defense, nor does it include unsuccessfully attempted murder (counted as aggravated assault). Homicide rates are often compared for different countries, and such comparisons generally show the United States rate to be considerably lower than the rates for Latin American nations and higher than those for the nations of Western Europe. Table 3-4 gives such rates for some selected nations; however, these statistics were compiled in the early 1960s, and since then the rate in the United States has increased considerably, probably at a swifter pace than in Europe.

To return to Table 3-3, homicide in America rose during the 1970s by 34 percent in numbers of persons killed, and by 22.8 percent in rate. In 1979 the victims of murder totaled 21,460, according to official reports. As with forcible rape, the vulnerability rate (the possibility that an individual will be victimized, taking into consideration numerous factors) differs sharply for homicide when such variables as age, race, sex, and social class are taken into account.

Crimes against Property

When one adds the figures for crimes against property to those for crimes against the person in 1979 one finds that the total—the more than twelve million index crimes reported to the police—yields a crime victimization rate of about 5.5 percent, meaning that one person in eighteen could expect to be victimized in this period. This victimization rate is far understated, not

TABLE 3-3
Index of Crime,
United States,
1970–1979

Population[a]	Crime[b] Index total	Modified[c] Crime Index total	Violent[d] crime	Property[d] crime	Murder and non-negligent man-slaughter	Forcible rape	Robbery	Aggra-vated assault	Burglary	Larceny–theft	Motor vehicle theft	Arson[c]
Number of offenses:												
1970–203,235,298	8,098,000		738,820	7,359,200	16,000	37,990	349,860	334,970	2,205,000	4,225,800	928,400	
1971–206,212,000	8,588,200		816,500	7,771,700	17,780	42,260	387,700	368,700	2,399,300	4,424,200	948,200	
1972–208,230,000	8,248,800		834,900	7,413,900	18,670	46,850	376,290	393,090	2,375,500	4,151,200	887,200	
1973–209,851,000	8,718,100		875,910	7,842,200	19,640	51,400	384,220	420,650	2,565,500	4,347,900	928,800	
1974–211,392,000	10,253,400		974,720	9,278,700	20,710	55,400	442,400	456,210	3,039,200	5,262,500	977,100	
1975–213,124,000	11,256,600		1,026,280	10,230,300	20,510	56,090	464,970	484,710	3,252,100	5,977,700	1,000,500	
1976–214,659,000	11,304,800		986,580	10,318,200	18,780	56,730	420,210	490,850	3,089,800	6,270,800	957,600	
1977–216,332,000	10,935,800		1,009,500	9,926,200	19,120	63,020	404,850	522,510	3,052,200	5,905,700	968,400	
1978–218,059,000	11,141,300		1,061,830	10,079,500	19,560	67,130	417,040	558,100	3,104,500	5,983,400	991,600	
1979–220,099,000	12,152,700		1,178,540	10,974,200	21,460	75,990	466,880	614,210	3,299,500	6,577,500	1,097,200	
Rate per 100,000 inhabitants[e]												
1970	3,984.5		363.5	3,621.0	7.9	18.7	172.1	164.8	1,084.9	2,079.3	456.8	
1971	4,164.7		396.0	3,768.8	8.6	20.5	188.0	178.8	1,163.5	2,145.5	459.8	
1972	3,961.4		401.0	3,560.4	9.0	22.5	180.7	188.8	1,140.8	1,993.6	426.1	
1973	4,154.4		417.4	3,737.0	9.4	24.5	183.1	200.5	1,222.5	2,071.9	442.6	
1974	4,850.4		461.1	4,389.3	9.8	26.2	209.3	215.8	1,437.7	2,489.5	462.2	
1975	5,281.7		481.5	4,800.2	9.6	26.3	218.2	227.4	1,525.9	2,804.8	469.4	
1976	5,266.4		459.6	4,806.8	8.8	26.4	195.8	228.7	1,439.4	2,921.3	446.1	
1977	5,055.1		466.6	4,588.4	8.8	29.1	187.1	241.5	1,410.9	2,729.9	447.6	
1978	5,109.3		486.9	4,622.4	9.0	30.8	191.3	255.9	1,423.7	2,743.9	454.7	
1979	5,521.5		535.5	4,986.0	9.7	34.5	212.1	279.1	1,499.1	2,988.4	498.5	

aPopulations are Bureau of Census provisional estimates as of July 1, except April 1, 1970, census.

bDue to rounding, the offenses may not add to totals.

cThe collection of statistics on arson, a newly established Index offense, was begun in 1979. However, summary statistics are not yet available for inclusion in this table.

dViolent crimes are offenses of murder, forcible rape, robbery, and aggravated assault. Property crimes are offenses of burglary, larceny–theft, and motor vehicle theft. Data are not included for the property crime of arson.

eCrime rates calculated prior to rounding number of offenses.

SOURCE: Uniform Crime Reports, 1980, p. 41.

| (Per 100,000 population) | | | TABLE 3-4 |
Country	Rate	Year reported	Homicide Rates for Selected Countries
Colombia	36.5	1962	
Mexico	31.9	1960	
South Africa	21.8	1960	
United States	4.8	1962	
Japan	1.5	1962	
France	1.5	1962	
Canada	1.4	1962	
Federal Republic of Germany	1.2	1961	
England/Wales	.7	1962	
Ireland	.4	1962	

SOURCE: "Demographic Yearbook," 15th issue, United Nations Publication, 1963, pp. 594–611.

only because of unreported crimes and serious crimes not in the index, but because some offenses victimize an entire family. Burglary of a home victimizes every resident, and even robbery of a person on the street may victimize that individual's spouse and children in the most direct manner.

How much does this cost the individuals who sustain the losses? A study made for the President's Commission on Law Enforcement and Administration of Justice (1967) indicated that the average cost to individuals suffering losses from property crimes amounted to some $2,000 in one year, as computed in the early 1960s. This is a net loss, after deductions for recovery; it is shown in Table 3-5. No later official estimates are available, but inflation alone would probably account for a sizable increase during the years that followed.

TABLE 3-5 Estimated Losses to Individuals from Property Crimes, by Offense

| Offense | Average loss in dollars | | | National loss (in millions of dollars) |
	Gross loss[a]	Recovered[a]	Net loss[a]	
Robbery	274	4	271	49.4
Burglary	191	20	170	312.7
Larceny $50 and over	160	51	109	128.1
Auto theft	1,141	982	159	63.5
Larceny under $50	21	6	15	42.4
Malicious mischief	120	18	102	209.8
Forgery and counterfeiting	323[b]	. . . .	323[b]	26.2[b]
Consumer fraud	99	20	78	18.3
Other fraud (bad checks, swindling, etc.)	906	150	756	368.8

[a]Detail may not add to total due to rounding.

[b]There were only 9 instances in which losses from forgery and counterfeiting were reported.

SOURCE: National Opinion Research Center survey.

Perhaps the best estimate of the overall economic impact of crime—which includes the cost of law enforcement and administration of justice, police, and corrections in addition to economic loss to victims—was that made by the President's Commission (1967), and is shown in Figure 3-1.

While some of the large crime costs shown in Figure 3-1 may involve crimes defined as victimless—which many criminologists and laymen believe do not require accounting for in this type of survey (such as the $7 billion for gambling)—this is balanced somewhat by the lack of any reliable estimates for other types of crime. Of fraud, for example—which is particularly important socially because the victim, as in so many other crimes, is usually the person least able to sustain a loss—the President's Commission writes:

> It has sometimes been asserted that this is the most common of all offenses. It seems clear that it is a very widespread offense and that the amounts involved are substantial.
>
> While there are many estimates regarding various kinds of fraud, they are often based on very limited information. Estimating criminal fraud is particularly difficult because the line dividing it from civil fraud is that of criminal intent. The fragmentation of agencies dealing with fraud also makes estimation difficult. . . .
>
> Studies also indicate sizable losses to the public from fraudulent solicitations for charities (as much as $150 million in some years) and from frauds involving credit cards ($20 million annually). Phony land promotion schemes, defective TV tubes, fraudulent insurance claims, worthless life insurance, fraudulent bankruptcies, improper debt consolidations, home study rackets, and numerous other schemes all cause the public inestimable losses. Losses to businesses and individuals from check frauds and bad checks also run into the millions.
>
> Particularly disturbing is the impact of fraud upon the poor or those who live on the margin of poverty. . . . What few studies there are indicate the disastrous impact this kind of fraud can often have. In one study of 500 households in four low-income housing projects, more than two of every five families reported being cheated or exploited by sellers or finance companies. [President's Commission, 1967: 49–50]

Hidden Economic Costs of Crime

It is not only a part of our tax dollar that pays for crime, not only the part of our purchasing dollar lost when our pockets are literally and figuratively picked by ordinary and extraordinary criminals—individuals and corporations—it is the part of our purchasing dollar that buys goods and services as well. How great the cost is cannot be calculated, but it enters into our rent when we pay for bribery and extortion and into each object we buy in a store when we pay for embezzlement by personnel; bribes by industrial concerns; illegal lobbying, bonding, and investigation of employees; management and employee theft of merchandise and supplies; store losses through hijacking and burglaries; insurance of various kinds against such eventualities; alarms and other security systems; private police and detective forces; and shoplifting. In some stores this may add as much as 10 percent to the cost of purchases. The greatest burden of this cost falls upon the poor because so much of their income goes for direct purchases from stores, and of course the burden falls upon the honest, who must pay for the delicts of the

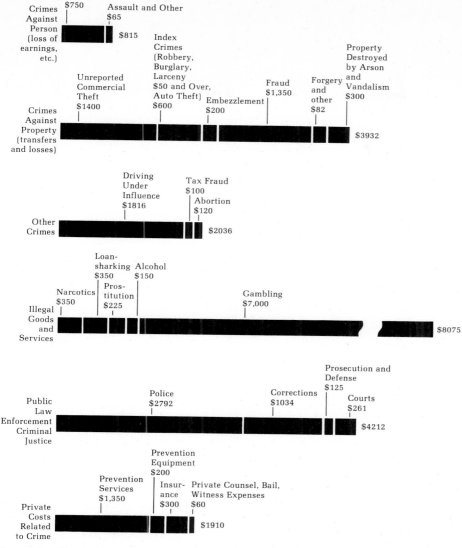

**FIGURE 3-1
Economic Impact of
Crimes and Related Ex-
penditures (estimated
in millions of dollars)**

SOURCE: President's Commission on Law Enforcement and Administration of Justice, 1967.

dishonest. In some rare cases this type of cost has contributed to the bankruptcy of a store or, somewhat more frequently, to its closing.

There can be only vague estimates of the total value of goods and merchandise stolen or money passing hands illegally during a single year. The greatest dollar amounts of such crimes occur in the white-collar area, and this is where the reporting of crime is most deficient. A single embezzlement may involve millions of dollars, whereas there are few burglaries and robberies (including bank holdups) that bring such sums to the thieves. While a Medicare fraud may result in someone's illegally obtaining one or two hundred dollars, it is more often part of a continuing enterprise, and by the time the perpetrators are apprehended (if ever), the sums may come to hundreds of thousands of dollars. This is equally true of nursing home frauds, where money is stolen not only from government agencies but from the elderly and their families.

All this seems to add up to an unmistakable and irrefutable conclusion that crime in the United States is widespread and costly, more so than in most other parts of the world—and indications are that it is not small there. Nevertheless, the United States is a relatively rich country, with a per capita income higher than in most places in the world, so that the per capita economic cost of crime cannot logically be compared with that of nations abroad. However, the amount spent or earned in illegal ways is probably disproportionately high in America; the cost of crime here is probably a higher portion of a family's purchasing power than in most other parts of the world. Still, even this can be a somewhat misleading statement, for crime may effect a greater hardship on poverty-stricken people with a per capita income only a tiny proportion of that in the United States. For such people, it is intolerable to lose anything at all to crime.

Public Response and the Cost of Crime

One of the consequences of crime is fear. Whether generated from personal experience or media discussion, whether justified or exaggerated, the fear of crime affects both the thoughts and actions of many people. Most personal response to the fear of crime involves some form of social withdrawal, such as restricting movement, refusing to talk with strangers, or moving to a new location.

In essence, such fear tends to erode social solidarity. Fear of crime is in many ways a fear of strangers, and withdrawal from strangers to avoid victimization creates a breakdown in informal social-control mechanisms. That is to say, such social isolation and aloofness, the unwillingness of people to become involved, may actually reduce informal surveillance, keep people off the streets, and thus make the streets "safer" for criminals. By moving away from or otherwise avoiding potentially high-crime areas, law-abiding people increase the proportion of criminals to victims in those areas and hence increase the chances that someone may successfully engage in crime without detection. Thus, a type of self-fulfilling prophecy is generated: fear of crime leads to social actions of withdrawal which actually increase the probabilities of crime.

The public's idea of appropriate governmental response to crime is focused more on criminals than on the causes of crime itself. There is strong popular belief that extremely harsh penalties deter crime. As a result, public pressure has been exerted on legislatures and courts to "get tough." However, long prison sentences, elimination of the possibilities of parole, and doubling or tripling of prison terms for repeat offenders are responses to crime that may actually reinforce the causes of crime and increase, not decrease, its incidence. Data have not shown that harsh penalties actually deter, and it has been demonstrated that prisons in many ways breed crime. In the long run, the "lock 'em up" philosophy may cost the society more in terms of both financial and human resources.

Even more significant than the financial and personal losses resulting from the strong reaction to and fear of crime is the contribution that crime and the public response to it may make to the erosion of civil liberties. Fear of crime can precipitate a willingness by the public to surrender its own rights and freedom of movement in order to limit the opportunities for criminal behavior and increase those for apprehension. Fear of political terrorism or other activism, for example, may lead to the support of search-and-seizure powers that would otherwise have been considered inappropriate and vigorously opposed by American citizens, or the support for widespread wiretaps, surveillance, and infiltration into social and political groups espousing unpopular causes. Fear of looting may result in support of curfews for juveniles and sometimes adults and even of the establishment of temporary martial law.

Many people may acquiesce in governmental intrusions into their privacy or restrictions on their freedoms in order to prevent serious crime from occurring. With very few voices of protest, the public willingly consents to searches of airline passengers to avoid hijacking. The current debate over gun control revolves around attempts by the government to limit the freedom to possess arms and to restrict the availability of weapons that may be used to perpetrate crimes. In these and many other instances, the matter for concern is not the immediate one of the search of airline passengers or restriction on ownership of weapons: it is whether further searches of homes and offices, further restrictions on what we may possess will continue as crime takes its toll in public fear and fright. Americans pay for crime in the form of some erosion of civil liberties; if they successfully resist this erosion, they pay for the continued civil liberties in increased fear of crime and increased crime itself.

Arrests for Index and Other Crimes

For index crimes, the FBI offers statistics both on the illegal events known to the police and the number of people arrested. For all other crimes, the statistics for the year show only the number arrested for each type of offense. If the arrest figures omit a great deal of serious crime because for some offenses—such as fraud and embezzlement—there are so few arrests, they are also inflated because they include so much trivial and victimless crime.

As Table 3-6 shows, there were slightly more than ten million arrests in the United States in 1979, for other than traffic offenses, as compared with less than half that figure in 1972. Dealing only with the 1979 data, one finds that of these arrests, 2,326,000 were for index crimes, indicating that fewer than one out of five index crimes reported to the police resulted in an arrest. This extremely low rate is almost entirely traceable to the large number of burglaries and larcenies, which result in relatively few arrests.[2]

Once the index crimes are put aside, the only official information on the perpetration of crime comes through arrest data rather than reports to the police. When minor offenses, victimless crimes, and nuisance matters are

2. Sometimes two or more persons are arrested for a single crime. Hence, there would be a slight distortion if one were to take the number of arrests for index crimes as an exact percentage of the total number of such events reported.

TABLE 3-6
Total Estimated
Arrests,[a] United
States, 1979

TOTAL[b]	10,205,800		
Murder and nonnegligent		Drug abuse violations	558,600
manslaughter	19,590	Opium or cocaine and their	
Forcible rape	31,470	derivatives	68,100
Robbery	140,640	Marijuana	391,600
Aggravated assault	276,000	Synthetic or manufactured drugs	18,400
Burglary	503,600	Other–dangerous nonnarcotic	
Larceny–theft	1,181,500	drugs	80,400
Motor vehicle theft	154,500		
Arson	19,800	Gambling	54,800
Violent crime	467,700	Bookmaking	4,600
Property crime[c]	1,859,200	Numbers and lottery	7,500
		All other gambling	42,700
Crime Index total[c]	2,326,900	Offenses against family and children	57,400
Other assaults	485,500	Driving under the influence	1,324,800
Forgery and counterfeiting	76,400	Liquor laws	416,200
Fraud	261,900	Drunkenness	1,172,700
Embezzlement	8,600	Disorderly conduct	765,500
Stolen property; buying, receiving,		Vagrancy	37,200
possessing	115,800	All other offenses (except traffic)	1,716,600
Vandalism	257,300	Suspicion (not included in total)	19,600
Weapons; carrying, possessing, etc.	164,200	Curfew and loitering law violations	84,100
Prostitution and commercialized vice	89,400	Runaways	164,400
Sex offenses (except forcible rape			
and prostitution)	67,400		

[a]Arrest totals based on all reporting agencies and estimates for unreported areas.
[b]Because of rounding, items may not add to totals.
[c]Includes arson, a newly established Index offense in 1979.

SOURCE: Uniform Crime Reports, 1980, p. 188.

eliminated from this list, the arrest records decline considerably.[3] Thus, prostitution, commercialized vice, and other sex offenses except forcible rape; gambling; offenses against family and children; violations of liquor laws other than driving while intoxicated; public drunkenness; marijuana offenses; disorderly conduct; vagrancy, curfew, and loitering-law violations; and runaways account for three and one-third million of the ten million arrests. This is a considerable proportion (over 40 percent) of all arrests for non-index crimes. A huge figure is also given for "all other offenses" except traffic violations. This is a catch-all category that can include items trivial and significant; only a cross-sectional study of such arrests could disclose how serious are the crimes for which almost two million people are recorded as arrested in a single year.

3. Some of the arrests for minor offenses may conceal serious crimes, but this is in no way revealed by the official data.

For many reasons, then, it is difficult to judge the meaning of the arrest figures in terms of the extent or cost of crime in the United States. One can dismiss the drunkenness figure, which is substantial (more than one million), thus making a sharp reduction, if one wishes to use the arrests as an indicator either of criminality or of law enforcement. But it is hard to know what to do about offenses against family and children: they may involve nonpayment of support, or they may involve the battered-wife or battered-child syndrome.

The arrest records are social facts in themselves, as Donald Black (1970) has said about all official crime records. They indicate who is being arrested: the age groups, sex, race, and other characteristics and social variables. Finally, they offer an opportunity to follow statistically what happens to the offender from apprehension to adjudication of the case. A study of the available statistics also reveals what happens after conviction, the number of persons on parole and on probation, and other related information.[4]

Decriminalization of certain crimes will of course diminish arrests; in the cases of drunkenness, prostitution, marijuana use, and some other offenses there are compelling arguments for it, as there are for lifting all criminal sanctions against adult consensual sex such as fornication, adultery, sodomy, and even—in the opinion of some criminologists—incest. Following decriminalization of any or all of these types of behavior, however, the amount of major crime is relatively unaffected, although a new and dramatically lower arrest figure would be recorded. (Drunkenness alone, if it ceased to be a cause for arrest, would result in such a precipitate drop in official arrest data.)

Not only would decriminalization have no serious effect on the reality of crime, it would not accomplish anything in terms of freeing police for other duties. The intoxicated are often arrested to give them a place to sleep and, ideally, a bath and warm meal, as well as to remove the unsightly from public places. Unless public drunkenness were to diminish for some unexpected and inexplicable reason, the intoxicated persons would still require care, whether at the hands of police, social workers, paraprofessionals, or special service workers created for this task.

What emerges from the study of official and unofficial data, victimization reports, and other sources? Leaving aside the fact that little is known about the extent of white-collar and certain other crimes, the following can be stated with confidence:

The Total Crime Scene: Capsule Summary

1. There is a major crime problem in the United States.
2. Every year, about one out of eighteen persons in the United States is the direct victim of a reported index crime. This victimization figure increases substantially if one adds multiple victimization for burglaries

4. For further discussion of what happens to offenders after arrest, see Chapters 18 and 19, on the administration of justice.

and some other crimes and makes some rough estimate of unreported crime.

3. The amount and rate of crime in the United States rose very rapidly in the first half of the 1970s, beginning to level off shortly thereafter, only to rise again at the end of the decade.

4. Crime is extremely costly in terms of pain and suffering as well as money, and fear of crime is widespread and affects many aspects of the quality of life.

5. Crime involves large numbers of perpetrators and offenders. It extends into all social classes, racial and religious groups, both sexes, and into younger and older parts of the populace than was formerly the case.

The victims of crime are all of us, and in the eyes of many crime constitutes a major social problem. It is in the hope of learning more about this phenomenon that one pursues study and research in criminology.

References for Part

AKERS, RONALD L. "Toward a Comparative Definition of Law." *Journal of Criminal Law, Criminology and Police Science*, 1965, 56: 301–306.

AMERICAN LAW INSTITUTE. *Model Penal Code*. Philadelphia: American Law Institute, 1962.

AMIR, MENACHEM. *Patterns in Forcible Rape*. Chicago: University of Chicago Press, 1971.

BENDER, LAURETTA, and ABRAM BLAU. "The Reaction of Children to Sexual Relations with Adults." *American Journal of Orthopsychiatry*, 1937, 7: 500–518.

BLACK, DONALD J. "Production of Crime Rates." *American Sociological Review*, 1970, 35: 733–748.

CAMERON, MARY OWEN. *The Booster and the Snitch*. New York: Free Press, 1964.

CHAMBLISS, WILLIAM J., and RICHARD H. NAGASAWA. "On the Validity of Official Statistics: A Comparative Study of White, Black, and Japanese High-School Boys." *Journal of Research in Crime and Delinquency*, 1969, 6: 71–77.

CHAPPELL, DUNCAN. "Forcible Rape and the Criminal Justice System: Surveying Present Practices and Projecting Future Trends." In Marcia J. Walker and Stanley L. Brodsky, eds., *Sexual Assault: The Victim and the Rapist*, pp. 9–22. Lexington, Mass.: Lexington Books, 1976.

CRESSEY, DONALD R. "The State of Criminal Statistics." *National Probation & Parole Association Journal*, 1957, 3: 230–241.

Crime in the United States. See Uniform Crime Reports.

DAVIES, AUDREY M. "Criminal Statistics and the National Commission's Report." *Journal of Criminal Law and Criminology*, 1931, 22: 357–374.

DOUGLAS, JACK D. *The Social Meanings of Suicide*. Princeton: Princeton University Press, 1967.

DURKHEIM, EMILE. *Suicide: A Study in Sociology*. New York: Free Press, 1951. (First published, in French, in 1897.)

_____. *The Division of Labor in Society*. New York: Free Press, 1964. (First published, in French, in 1893; in English in 1933.)

EVANS, JEAN. *Three Men: An Experiment in the Biography of Emotion*. New York: Vintage, 1966. (First published in 1950.)

FEDERAL BUREAU OF INVESTIGATION. See Uniform Crime Reports.

FINKELHOR, DAVID. *Sexually Victimized Children*. New York: Free Press, 1979.

Franklin, H. Bruce. *The Victim as Criminal and Artist: Literature from the American Prison*. New York: Oxford University Press, 1978.

Garofalo, Raffaele. *Criminology*. Montclair, N.J.: Patterson Smith, 1968. (First published, in Italian, in 1885; in English in 1914.)

Geis, Gilbert. "Upperworld Crime." In Abraham S. Blumberg, ed., *Current Perspectives on Criminal Behavior*, pp. 114–137. New York: Knopf, 1974.

_____. *Not the Law's Business: An Examination of Homosexuality, Abortion, Prostitution, Narcotics and Gambling in the United States*. 2nd ed. New York: Schocken Books, 1979. (First published in 1972.)

Geis, Gilbert, and Robert F. Meier, eds. *White-Collar Crime: Offenses in Business, Politics, and the Professions*. New York: Free Press, 1977.

Glaser, Daniel. *Crime in Our Changing Society*. New York: Holt, Rinehart and Winston, 1978a.

_____. "Deviance, Crime, Alienation, and Anomie." In Edward Sagarin, ed., *Sociology: The Basic Concepts*, pp. 151–171. New York: Holt, Rinehart and Winston, 1978b.

Glueck, Sheldon, and Eleanor Glueck. *Unraveling Juvenile Delinquency*. Cambridge, Mass.: Harvard University Press (for The Commonwealth Fund), 1950.

Goldstein, Abraham. *The Insanity Defense*. New Haven: Yale University Press, 1970.

Goring, Charles. *The English Convict: A Statistical Study*. Montclair, N.J.: Patterson Smith, 1972. (First published in England in 1913.)

Hausner, Gideon. *Justice in Jerusalem*. New York: Harper and Row, 1966.

Hindelang, Michael J. "The Uniform Crime Reports Revisited." *Journal of Criminal Justice*, 1974, 2: 1–17.

Hooton, Earnest A. *Crime and the Man*. Cambridge, Mass.: Harvard University Press, 1939.

Jackson, Robert H. *The Case against the Nazi War Criminals: Opening Statements for the United States of America*. New York: Knopf, 1946.

Kennedy, Ludovic. *Ten Rillington Place*. New York: Simon and Schuster, 1961.

Kesselring, Joseph. *Arsenic and Old Lace*. New York: Random House, 1941.

Kitsuse, John I., and Aaron V. Cicourel. "A Note on the Uses of Official Statistics." *Social Problems*, 1963, 11: 131–139.

Klockars, Carl B. *The Professional Fence*. New York: Free Press, 1974.

Lejins, Peter P. "Uniform Crime Reports." *Michigan Law Review*, 1966, 64: 1011–1030.

Levine, James P. "The Potential for Crime Overreporting in Criminal Victimization Surveys." *Criminology*, 1976, 14: 307–330.

López-Rey, Manuel. *Crime: An Analytical Appraisal*. New York: Praeger, 1970.

MacNamara, Donal E. J., and Edward Sagarin. *Sex, Crime, and the Law*. New York: Free Press, 1977.

Manning, Peter K., and John van Maanen, eds. *Policing: A View from the Streets*. Santa Monica, Cal.: Goodyear, 1978.

McCaghy, Charles H. "Child Molesters: A Study of Their Careers as Deviants." Ph.D. dissertation, University of Wisconsin, 1966. Excerpted in Marshall B. Clinard and Richard Quinney, *Criminal Behavior Systems: A Typology*, pp. 75–88. New York: Holt, Rinehart and Winston, 1967.

Michael, Jerome, and Mortimer J. Adler. *Crime, Law, and Social Science*. New York: Harcourt, Brace, 1933.

Moran, Richard. *Knowing Right from Wrong: The Insanity Defense of Daniel McNaughtan*. New York: Free Press, 1981.

Murton, Tom, and Joe Hyams. *Accomplices to the Crime: The Arkansas Prison Scandal*. New York: Grove Press, 1969.

National Prisoner Statistics. Washington, D.C.: U.S. Department of Justice, 1977, 1978.

NEWMAN, DONALD J. "The Effects of Accommodations in Justice Administration on Criminal Statistics." *Sociology and Social Research,* 1962, 46: 144–155.

New York Times, May 15, 1972.

New York Times, December 3, 1977.

PEARSON, KARL. *The Grammar of Science.* London: J.M. Dent, 1937. (First published in 1892.)

PENNOCK, J. ROLAND. "Law." In Julius Gould and William L. Kolb, eds., *A Dictionary of the Social Sciences,* pp. 378–380. Compiled under the auspices of UNESCO. New York: Free Press, 1964.

PORTERFIELD, AUSTIN L. *Youth in Trouble.* Fort Worth, Tex.: Leo Potishman Foundation, 1946.

PRESIDENT'S COMMISSION ON LAW ENFORCEMENT AND ADMINISTRATION OF JUSTICE. *Crime and Its Impact: An Assessment.* Washington, D.C.: Government Printing Office, 1967.

ROBISON, SOPHIA M. "A Critical Review of the Uniform Crime Reports." *Michigan Law Review,* 1966, 64: 1031–1054.

ROSS, H. LAURENCE. "Traffic Law Violation: A Folk Crime." *Social Problems,* 1960–61, 8: 231–241.

SAGARIN, EDWARD. *Raskolnikov and Others: Literary Images of Crime, Punishment, Redemption and Atonement.* New York: St. Martin's Press, 1981.

SCHUR, EDWIN M. *Crimes without Victims: Deviant Behavior and Public Policy—Abortion, Homosexuality and Drug Addiction.* Englewood Cliffs, N.J.: Prentice-Hall, 1965.

SCHWENDINGER, HERMAN, and JULIA SCHWENDINGER. "Defenders of Order or Guardians of Human Rights?" *Issues in Criminology,* 1970, 5: 123–157.

SELLIN, THORSTEN. "Crime." In *Encyclopaedia of the Social Sciences,* vol. 4, pp. 563–569. New York: Macmillan, 1931a.

_____. "The Basis of a Crime Index." *Journal of Criminal Law and Criminology,* 1931b, 22: 335–356.

_____. *Culture Conflict and Crime.* Social Science Research Council, Bulletin 41. New York, 1938.

_____. *Slavery and the Penal System.* New York: Elsevier, 1976.

SELLIN, THORSTEN, and MARVIN E. WOLFGANG. *The Measurement of Delinquency.* New York: Wiley, 1964.

SUTHERLAND, EDWIN H. *The Professional Thief.* Chicago: University of Chicago Press, 1937.

_____. "Is 'White-Collar Crime' Crime?" *American Sociological Review,* 1945, 19: 132–139. Reprinted in Geis and Meier, 1977.

_____. *White Collar Crime.* New York: Dryden, 1949.

TAPPAN, PAUL W. "Who Is the Criminal?" *American Sociological Review,* 1947, 12: 96–102. Reprinted in Geis and Meier, 1977.

_____. *Crime, Justice and Correction.* New York: McGraw-Hill, 1960.

THOMSON, HELEN. *Murder at Harvard.* Boston: Houghton Mifflin, 1971.

UNIFORM CRIME REPORTS. *Crime in the United States, 1979.* Washington, D.C.: Federal Bureau of Investigation, 1980. (Published annually.)

VOLD, GEORGE B. *Theoretical Criminology.* 2nd ed., revised by Thomas J. Bernard. New York: Oxford University Press, 1979. (First published in 1958.)

WARNER, SAM BASS. "Crimes Known to the Police—An Index of Crime?" *Harvard Law Review,* 1931, 45: 307–334.

WEBER, MAX. *Max Weber on Law in Economy and Society.* New York: Simon and Schuster, 1967.

WILLIAMS, J. E. HALL. "Crime." In Julius Gould and William L. Kolb, eds., *A Dictionary of the Social Sciences*, pp. 147–148. Compiled under the auspices of UNESCO. New York: Free Press, 1964.

WOLFENDEN, JOHN, et al. *Report of the Committee on Homosexual Offenses and Prostitution* (known as The Wolfenden Report.) New York: Stein & Day, 1963. (Originally published in England in 1957.)

WOLFGANG, MARVIN E. "Uniform Crime Reports: A Critical Appraisal." *University of Pennsylvania Law Review*, 1963, 111: 708–738.

WOLFGANG, MARVIN E., and FRANCO FERRACUTI. *The Subculture of Violence: Towards an Integrated Theory in Criminology*. London: Tavistock, 1967.

PART II

Theories
and Explanations

The Development of Criminological Theory

All science depends upon theory as a way of understanding, explaining, and predicting aspects of the phenomena with which it deals. Theory is the cornerstone of science; it is the foundation upon which an interpretation of the world is made and upon which research is predicated. It is important in the social sciences in understanding the dynamics of a phenomenon: why it occurs; why it manifests itself in a specific form; what its relationships are to society as a whole, to other people, and to social institutions and culture. Science needs theory, and, to be useful, theory should provide clarity in its effort to answer questions and make generalizations.

In the past, the search for criminological theory has focused on attempts to elaborate the "causes" of crime—sometimes referred to as its etiology. According to Donald Newman (1966), this has been the major thrust of the work of sociologists as reflected in criminology textbooks, and it has clearly been the concern of criminologists from the dawn of the effort to study crime scientifically.

The emphasis on causation has its historical roots in the attempts of early criminologists to emulate the methods and assumptions of the natural and physical sciences. The natural, physical world appeared to operate on the basis of universal laws, and it was assumed that there were underlying causes for the existence of all phenomena. It was believed that the social order must operate under similar laws, and that the objective of social science was to discover them.

Early Theories of Crime

Intense interest in crime predates any efforts to establish it as a subject for scientific investigation. Considerable concern with criminal behavior is manifested in the Homeric epics and other writings that have come down to us from classical Greece, in the works of scientists of the Middle Ages, and in Shakespeare, among many other Renaissance figures. The primary approach of attempts to explain crime in the long period from the dawn of history until the eighteenth-century Enlightenment seems to have been imbued with a spirit of demonology. That is, a superempirical power or spirit was invoked to explain behavior that grossly violated the prevailing rules of society. Primitive and preliterate societies believed that such spirits infused everything—this is termed animism—and that if they could be controlled at all, this could be accomplished through magic.

The criminal was believed by many to be "possessed by the devil." To exorcise the demon required some powerful, magical, ritualistic procedure. A related view was of the devil as tempter, seducing the weak-willed into a life of evil. During both the Middle Ages and Renaissance in Europe as well as the early colonial period in America, supernatural explanations were dominant, and they resulted in the excesses of the Inquisition and witchhunts, often applied against political and religious dissidents who were conveniently labeled transgressors. Even in the modern United States, with its strong tradition of separation of church and state and its highly secularized society, the theocratic tradition survives in such a ceremony as having the witness swear in court with a hand on the Bible.

Demonology eventually fell into disfavor, for it did not explain behavior so much as renounce the possibility of explanation, and it failed to serve as a successful guideline for those attempting to formulate social policy with regard to crime.

For all of the dominance of demonism in these early periods, explanations based on the perceivable physical world were not unknown. Both the Phoenicians and the ancient Greeks had some empirical explanations for social behavior, and Hippocrates as early as 460 B.C. suggested a physiological basis for thinking. The Romans developed a philosophy of natural law in which penalties and rights were seen as arising out of nature or at least out of the nature of society.

In the ascendancy of Christianity, ambiguities and antithetical principles developed. While still clinging to demonology, particularly in the approach to mental disorder, Christians put forth the belief that individuals, not demons, are responsible for their social transgressions. The idea of individual responsibility for both social and antisocial acts (the latter termed sins) became embedded in ecclesiastical and criminal law. During the Renaissance, with its this-worldly rather than other-wordly orientation, there was a rise in naturalism, but the theocratic influence persisted.

Three basic perspectives and orientations emerged from early naturalism, each emphasizing a different element of humanity and each ultimately generating a perspective on the causes of crime: (1) the belief that people basically are rational, which served as a frame of reference for *classical thought*; (2) the belief that each person is primarily a biological organism, the perspective of the *positivists* and the *constitutionalists*; and (3) the belief that each such person is an interacting unit with culture, the basis for *socio-cultural* theories. To these can be added a fourth perspective, combining elements of the second and third with a view of the individual as an often irrational being motivated by an unconscious, the basis for the psychoanalytic approach. Elements of these frames of reference can be seen in theories that developed during the last two centuries and that continue to be promulgated and defended to this day.

The Classical School

The so-called preclassical period in criminology, lasting from primitive times up to the period of the Enlightenment, gave way to the classical school, which was ushered in by the influential Cesare Beccaria (b.1738–d.1794). Hermann Mannheim (1972: 3), himself a towering figure in twentieth-century criminology and a chronicler of the discipline, writes that the publication of Beccaria's work was one of the most momentous events in the history of modern criminology.

Beccaria was not yet out of his twenties when in 1764 he published his *Essay on Crimes and Punishments*, one of the most significant landmarks in the history of criminology. He placed the origin of criminal behavior in the mind of the offender, a rational human being endowed with free will. The thrust of his argument and of the entire classical school of criminology, of which he was the first and probably most eminent leader, was based on the prevailing Enlightenment philosophy, which placed great stress on the rational facilities and faculties of the human being.[1] Fundamentally, the classicists believed that criminals made choices based on a utilitarian hedonistic philosophy—that is, out of a desire to minimize pain and maximize pleasure derived from their actions. The "cause" of crime, therefore, was viewed as residing in the rational processes of the individual rather than in the immortal soul or in some supernatural spirit possessing it.

For the classicists, motives other than the search for pleasure were ignored or at least considered unimportant, since all people were seen to have free will and were in this sense alike in their responsibility for their actions. The means of dealing with crime subsequently rested on the identification and prescription of specific punishments for specific illegal acts. Beccaria urged that punishment be prompt, certain, and equal for all offenders guilty of committing the same offense. Punishment was conceived of in terms of deterrence.

The British utilitarians, particularly Jeremy Bentham (b.1748–d.1832), further developed the approach of Beccaria. Bentham stressed motivation, ethics, and social reform. In a manner not unlike that of Beccaria, he suggested that in their actions all persons, being rational, make a calculation of the anticipated pleasure of behavior balanced against the anticipated pain; crime results when pleasure for violation of the law outweighs pain in this calculation. Bentham (1973) proposed a "penal pharmacy" whereby each offense would incur a prescribed penalty. Inherent in this philosophy was the notion that certainty of punishment deters the would-be offender, a leg-

1. For a discussion of Beccaria see Vold (1979) and Monachesi (1972).

acy which to this day dominates a considerable portion of the criminal codes. The emphasis was on the crime, not the criminal, and distinguished between crimes, not the nature or circumstances of the offenders.

The Neo-classical Period

Some problems became evident in the application of classical principles. It was found that while punishments may be applied rationally and systematically, individuals respond differently to the same penalty. The hedonistic principle was vulnerable in that it was unable to account for individual differences in reaction to anticipated pleasure and pain. Further, the doctrine of free will came to be challenged, in that it did not take into account extenuating circumstances contributing to the diminution of free will.

Several modifications of classical theory were therefore introduced, and their proponents became known as the neoclassical school. They believed that freedom of will could be affected by pathology, incompetence, insanity, or other conditions. There were mitigating events that interfered with the free will, it was contended: these could be physical, environmental (sociocultural), or mental (psychological). Along this line, children were believed to have only limited responsibility for their actions, in spite of the doctrine of free will, and the same was true of mental defectives or "lunatics." It followed, then, that under neoclassical principles, judges were to be accorded discretion in order to assess and account for special situations surrounding an individual offender and the offenses for which that person had been found guilty.

The Positivist School

LOMBROSO AND HIS FOLLOWERS

If criminology in the modern sense of the word can be traced to Cesare Beccaria, it is with another Italian, about a century later, that the *scientific* study of crime causation can be said to have begun. Although Cesare Lombroso (b.1835–d.1909) is frequently associated with theories of the biological origins of criminal behavior, his contributions were in fact far wider than that:

1. Lombroso recognized the inadequacy of the prevailing methods used to discover the causes of criminal conduct, and was among the first to focus attention on the individual offender. He helped shift the focus from metaphysical, legal, and juristic abstraction as a basis for criminological study to scientific investigation of the offender and the conditions under which he or she commits crime. In short, he advocated the study of the criminal rather than the crime. He stressed the individualization of treatment.

2. Lombroso attempted to apply a scientific approach to his data; that is, he utilized measurements and statistical methods—albeit crude ones by

present-day criteria—in the analysis of anthropological, social, and economic data. He also employed the method of control-group comparison—e.g., he compared prisoner groups with civilian, certain criminal types with other criminal types, prostitutes and other female offenders with women not involved in such activities. He used in his comparisons of female groups such variables as height, age, weight, and what today would be termed socioeconomic status.

3. In a crude fashion Lombroso engaged in multiple-factor analysis in his search for "positive facts."

4. Lombroso made the first attempt to establish a criminal psychopathology. Contemporary endocrinological, psychiatric, and biological studies reflect his indirect influence.

5. Lombroso made use of typological methods in classifying criminals.

6. Lombroso employed clinical methods in his efforts to study personality factors—e.g., he described the persistent criminal in terms strikingly similar to the modern psychopathic personality syndrome. On the other hand, his indication of a relationship between epilepsy and violent crime did not prove productive in the study of criminality.

7. Finally, Lombroso exemplified scholarly resilience by modifying his theory and methodology in the light of findings of his critics. He also challenged his critics to test his ideas by controlled investigations of criminals and noncriminals.[2]

Lombroso's name is today most frequently associated with his work on the biological makeup of the offender. A physician by profession, he was influenced by the positivism of the natural and physical sciences and by contemporary theories on the origin and evolution of species, as well as by the biological ambience surrounding the European intellectual world in the decades following the publication of Darwin's *Origin of Species* in 1859. That Lombroso was the founder of the positivist school of criminology is hardly disputed.

Lombroso conceived of some criminals as having physical characteristics that distinguished them from other people. He reached this conclusion after studying thousands of incarcerated criminals—measuring, photographing, performing autopsies, and carefully recording his observations. In keeping with the evolutionary doctrine of his day, Lombroso suggested that criminals constituted an atavistic form of homo sapiens, a throwback to apelike ancestors on the evolutionary scale. To Lombroso, some criminals were physically and psychologically "retarded" and consequently incapable of adapting to advanced social orders. These unfortunates, however, constituted only the "born criminals"—individuals destined by their biological inferiority to perform antisocial acts. Not all of Lombroso's criminals fit into this category. Some were insane, imbeciles, idiots, or epileptics (the latter were still widely associated with criminality, an association since discarded). Others were what Lombroso called "criminaloid," individuals who

2. For a discussion of Lombroso, see Wolfgang (1972), Lindesmith and Levin (1937), and Vold (1979). For his own writings in translation, see Lombroso (1968) and Lombroso-Ferrero (1972).

by physical and psychological constitution were predisposed to crime but not destined to commit it; they could easily fall into a life of crime, under conditions favorable thereto.

A major problem with Lombroso's studies was his sample selection. Most of the criminals he examined were Sicilians, and he failed to contrast them in physical characteristics with other (law-abiding) people from the same area; rather, his comparison group was the Italian population as a whole. Later criminologists would contend that the criminal behavior of Lombroso's sample was related not to anatomy and physiology but rather to a sociocultural background conducive to law-breaking. In the early years of the twentieth century, a British penologist, Charles Goring (1972), working with sophisticated statistical techniques, tested Lombroso's theory by comparing three thousand inmates of British prisons with one thousand Cambridge University students. The results were inconclusive, although they tended to be more unfavorable than favorable to the physiological approach (see Driver, 1972). Actually, a charge can be made against Goring that was later to be hurled against those who, conducting similar studies, reached the opposite conclusion: namely, that inmates are not necessarily representative of offenders and that university students are not a cross section of the male population (this was particularly true in England at the time).

In later years, the emphasis of Lombroso was somewhat modified by his most distinguished students, Enrico Ferri (b.1856–d.1929) and Raffaele Garofalo (b.1852–d.1934). The latter placed greater stress on the environmental and circumstantial conditions surrounding the criminal; neither, however, ever relinquished the belief in genetic inferiority manifested in physiological and anatomic characteristics.

According to Ferri, crime was caused by a large number of factors, including the physical—such as race, sex, climate; anthropological—age, organic and physiological conditions; and social—population density, customs, industrialization, political and economic conditions. Ferri proposed a classification of offenders that encompassed the born criminal, the insane criminal, the occasional criminal, the habitual criminal, and the criminal by passion. These labels by themselves largely depict the vision of criminality held by Ferri. Thus, the born criminal had a disposition toward serious offenses through heredity. The insane was quite obviously affected by a major mental disorder. The occasional criminal (the majority of offenders were in this group) was the product of unfortunate family and social circumstances. The habitual criminal acquired the habit because of ineffective social measures for the prevention and repression of crime. There were two types of criminal by passion: one had a chronic mental state that could lead to the offense, and the other an explosive emotional state.

MODERN CRIMINAL ANTHROPOLOGY: ENTER HOOTON

The concern with physical bases for crime did not end with Lombroso, his students, or Goring, but continued to receive a considerable amount of support both in Europe and in America. Adherents of the approach saw evidence that Freud, despite his major emphasis on early childhood training, leaned in the direction of assigning importance to a person's basic "constitution" as affecting to some extent a lifetime of behavior. The distinguished American anthropologist Earnest Hooton (1939) conducted an extensive study of the relationship between inherited physical characteristics and antisocial behavior. Holding race and ethnicity constant (that is, comparing only groups of the same ethnic and racial ancestries), Hooton collected information on 13,873 male criminals and 3,023 civilians (using the latter as controls), and concluded that habitual criminals are "hopeless constitutional inferiors" who on no account should be allowed to breed (1939: 392).

Hooton's findings for the most part were greeted with suspicion if not vigorous opposition. A major criticism of his work, as of that of his predecessors, centers on his sampling procedures. That prisoners are probably a representative sample not of criminals but only of those who have been caught is a problem in all such studies, and not one easy to solve. More serious was the unrepresentative nature of Hooton's control group of civilians (noncriminals), who had not been selected at random.

BODY-TYPE THEORIES

The biological approach to crime received impetus from the work of William Sheldon and collaborators (1949), who concluded that there was a relationship between certain physical characteristics, or basic body types, and temperament. Revising a system suggested in Germany a few years earlier by Ernest Kretschmer (1926), Sheldon identified essentially four types of people by their body builds, which he found to be inborn, constitutional, and not subject to change.

That Sheldon's diagnostic terminology was impressionistic at points, thus creating problems for a replication of his study, is undeniable. This error Sheldon shares with many diagnosticians. But he did attempt to define some of his psychiatric categories. As for his "scoring techniques," to use his own term, they were disappointing, but he was attempting quantification at a time when few of his colleagues and peers had embraced the idea of scaling attitudes, beliefs, opinions, and behavior that existed on a continuum.

Many critics claimed that the magnitude of the correlations between body build and temperament may have reflected the strength of the investigator's preconceptions rather than an actual association between physique and temperament. In answer to this criticism, Sheldon stated that the temperament ratings were made first and that the body type ratings were highly objective, thus somewhat reducing the likelihood that one contaminated or prejudiced the other.

In a scathing review of Sheldon's work, S. L. Washburn (1951) ended with the warning, "I hope that all will recognize it for what it is, the New Phrenology in which the bumps of the buttocks take the place of the bumps of the skull."

LATER BIOLOGICAL AND BIOSOCIAL ORIENTATIONS

However, not all social scientists were equally unimpressed. Shortly after the work of Sheldon appeared, a matched-sample study was undertaken by Sheldon Glueck and Eleanor Glueck (1950, 1956), who found about 60 percent of their delinquents as against 31 percent of the nondelinquents to fit into one of William Sheldon's body types (a muscular group that he referred to as mesomorphs). The Gluecks drew no causal inference from the data, though they indicated some evidence that mesomorphic children are more likely to become delinquent, since by definition they are relatively uninhibited and may be more likely than others to conduct themselves in a manner defined as delinquent. The Gluecks strongly advocated what has been called a multiple-factor or eclectic approach; they emphasized that physique is only one factor that, in conjunction with other forces, can explain delinquency. What confuses the problem of causality, if one accepts the findings of the Gluecks, is that while mesomorphs seem to be disproportionately overrepresented among delinquents, they are also found in large numbers among energetic social leaders and in other roles requiring a great deal of physical activity. In short, the mesomorphs tend to veer toward physicality, not necessarily toward antisocial behavior.

Upon examination of the data of the Gluecks, Hermann Mannheim and Leslie Wilkins (1955) concluded that no specific combination of character, physique, and temperament permits any prediction as to delinquency. Although the sample used by the Gluecks was better than that used by most of the previous researchers, it was not representative of delinquents; in addition, it was charged that placing them into a category based on physical characteristics (the somatotyping process) is itself a difficult and imprecise task that suffers from vagueness (Cortés, 1972).

The overall assessment of constitution and delinquency is not one of cause and effect. Constitution, including physical type, is likely to be a matter more of proclivity than of cause; that is, persons of different muscularity, energy level, and body build will tend to select (or be selected for) types of activity in which these traits are assets. Furthermore, some contend—Sheldon notwithstanding—that constitution is not unalterable, so the effect is not one of either heredity or environment but one of heredity *and* environment. (Of course, constitution is unalterable if only the unalterable component of a person is defined as that individual's constitution, but that begs the larger question.)

Although Lombroso (1968) later discarded a great deal of his biological determinism, and many subsequent constitutional theories have been faulted, the early Italian research in this field is of lasting importance, insofar as its general assumptions are reflected in the contemporary reemergence of biosocial orientations. One variant is the attention directed to the relationship of genetic and chromosomal anomalies with crime. Some recent studies have pointed to a causal link between the presence in some males of an extra Y or "male-producing" chromosome, designated as the XYY syndrome (XX is the normal female combination, XY the normal male), but much of this work has since been discarded. At this point in the controversy, the XYY as a distinct criminal type is regarded by many to be a myth (Fox, 1971).

The middle and late 1970s saw a resurgence of biological theory in the study of human behavior and the emergence of what has come to be called sociobiology (Wilson, 1975; van den Berghe, 1978). In the area of crime, very sophisticated studies conducted in Denmark, the United States, and elsewhere have pointed to some evidence of biological predisposition (see particularly Mednick and Christiansen, 1977). In Copenhagen, boys who had been adopted at birth were followed through to their teenage years and later. Those with criminal biological parents became delinquents in significantly larger proportions than those whose biological parents had not had criminal records. (The fact of parental criminality was unknown to the boys.)

Few scientists are today ready to return to the concept of the born criminal with a destiny of damnation upon him, but few are willing to deny the possibility that there are inborn predilections toward hyperactivity, super-aggressiveness, self-destructiveness, inability to exercise control, and impulsivity and compulsivity, traits that under some conditions may lead to criminality more frequently than with persons lacking these traits and exposed to essentially the same environment (for an excellent review of this subject, see Shah and Roth, 1974).

*Psychoanalytic
Explanations*

Darwin's writings provided the intellectual climate for the positivist school of criminology. Somewhat later, the psychoanalytic theories of Sigmund Freud (b.1856–d.1939) made an independent and lasting impact on the direction of criminological thinking. According to this school of thought the primary cause or explanation of criminal behavior is found in the unconscious. The human being, in the image of Freud, is essentially antirational. The mind itself is an interaction or resolution of rational and irrational forces. Within the mind is a buried reservoir of unconscious, instinctual animal impulses— the id—which seek immediate gratification and strive after pleasure. The id operates on the hedonistic principle. But, denying Beccaria's proposition that choice is rational, psychoanalysts argue that the maximization of pleasure will manifest itself unless controlled by the conscious reality principle through the ego. In the ego, the id impulses meet the socially accepted, civilized aspect of the human being. The id and ego are often in conflict, and the resolution of the conflict—the sense of morality, remorse, or guilt—arises out of the development of the superego, or conscience. Conscience is partly unconscious and partly conscious, and is derived from cultural definitions of conduct.

Basically, the id is the biological component of personality, the ego the psychological component, and the superego the social component. In the image postulated by Freud, these three elements do not operate mechanistically, but they do follow set principles: the id is the pleasure principle, the ego the reality principle, and the superego the morality principle. The three usually work together in harmony to produce behavior that is both normal and normative. When they do not, the result is abnormality, deviance, or crime, among other manifestations. Psychoanalytic theory interprets the causes of crime to lie in a deficiency in ego or superego development, which in turn creates an inability to control the innate primitive criminal drives (the id). In individuals who, because of deficient development, possess little capacity to repress their instincts the id dominates, and criminality may result (see Friedlander, 1947).

Instincts clearly play a major role in the Freudian system. Freud defines instinct as an innate psychological representation of an inner somatic source of excitation. This means that the body has basic demands or needs which take on psychological expression. Hunger, for example, is physiologically a need and psychologically a wish for food. The psychological desire acts as the motivating force behind behavior. Instincts, then, are the propelling factors of personality, since they are the drive that brings forth the behavior. Instincts are part of the id—which itself does not exist as a physically real entity but is simply the term used to describe the innate animalistic drive toward immediate gratification. When the instinctual needs of individuals are not gratified by sex, food, or other objects or activities, they may be satisfied by various substitutes: some vicarious, some symbolic, some displacing the original object because of its inaccessibility or because it is forbidden by the conscience (in the form of the superego).

In a sense, then, the psychoanalytic view of the unconscious corresponds to the physiological determinism of the positivists. In both systems, little freedom of choice or will is allowed. In both, all people are seen as born with potential and even a predilection to be criminal, but the noncriminal as having successfully repressed the innate, natural impulses.

Many criticisms have been leveled at the psychoanalytic orientation (Clinard and Meier, 1979; Hook, 1959; Rachman, 1963), but foremost is the criticism that it is laden with symbolism (Salter, 1963: 75–76) that cannot be measured or validated, and hence it is more speculative than scientific. Description of the unconscious mental state rests on insight, intuition, conjecture, and projection. Deviant behavior is psychoanalytically seen as an indicator of unrepressed impulses, while at the same time as the consequence of such repression. The mental state is assumed from observable behavior, yet there is no independently measurable or analyzable indicator of that mental condition save what it hopes to explain (Hakeem, 1958). In addition, psychoanalytic studies generally have employed only legally or medically classified deviants and have rarely made comparisons with normative control groups. While the cases studied may be "classic" examples of the theory, opponents insist that the conclusions are not generalizable beyond the cases used and therefore provide little utility in understanding the problems of crime in society. At best, in this point of view, a Freudian approach can account for only a few crimes, particularly those of a bizarre nature (see MacNamara and Sagarin, 1977).

Freudians see the struggle between id and ego as manifesting itself in the personality traits of the individual. It has been suggested that while one cannot measure directly the id-ego relationship, personality manifestation is a way of discerning what characteristics may predispose a person to crime. If this is true, one could expect criminal types to be clearly distinguishable from all other types. Research directed at this particular point, however, has been less than conclusive. Karl Schuessler and Donald Cressey (1950) evaluated 113 studies dealing with personality and criminality and found such an overlap in traits that they considered it "practically impossible" to predict individual criminality from personality-test scores. The biggest confusion has arisen over the inability to distinguish the normal from the abnormal personality except in very extreme cases. In fact, no one knows precisely what a "normal" personality is; some forms of extreme abnormality do not seem to be difficult to discern, but the diagnostic labels may still be controversial (such as in cases labeled manic depression or paranoia).

The original Freudian emphasis on the unrepressed id as a causal explanation of criminality has received considerable support from believers, but little from attempts to demonstrate its utility as a theory. The debate between proponents and antagonists of Freudianism has blurred the importance of certain aspects of the theory, such as the source of the development of ego and superego. (The id does not require similar explanation, as it is inborn and given.) Freud suggested that the ego, being the reality principle, evolved as the id was confronted with the spectrum of social expectations. Close examination of this theory reveals the importance of forces outside the individual—social norms, roles, expectations.

Many of Freud's early associates, collaborators, and disciples differed with him in important respects. For example, Carl Jung (b.1875–d.1961) stressed the "collective unconscious" and the heritage of cultural aspects of society as they impinge on the personality development of individuals. Alfred Adler (b.1870–d.1927) emphasized the desire to belong to groups and attain status within them, an idea later developed in detail by many modern sociologists working in crime and delinquency, including James Short, Albert Cohen, Richard Cloward, Lloyd Ohlin, and particularly Edwin Sutherland with his theory of differential association.

While recognition has been given to the significance of social and environmental conditions, they have never played a major role in psychoanalytic explanations of crime. Early family experiences have been the major external forces recognized in post-Freudian theory, an emphasis that continues even in most non-Freudian circles. To some theorists, predetermination based on the workings of the unconscious mind has been replaced by predetermination based on early family interaction (Clinard and Meier, 1979). Although such psychiatrists as Seymour Halleck (1967) and Bernard Diamond (1968) suggest the need for a broad cultural perspective, the importance of environmental factors is recognized by most psychoanalysts only in the most severe cases.

Sociologists tend to react adversely to the individual determinism stressed in the psychiatric approach. If crime is totally a matter of individual characteristics, then the incidence of criminality would be randomly distributed throughout society. However, crime appears to be concentrated in some parts of the society and relatively absent from others. Sociologists therefore attempt to look at the characteristics of the high-crime areas.

Many of the early American sociologists—partly because they came from rural areas and were theologically oriented—were concerned with the negative impact of large industrialized urban centers on the waves of new immigrants. These sociologists were morally and ethically disturbed by the poverty and vice of the slums and felt committed to working toward the ame-

Early
Sociological
Explanations

lioration of the social conditions giving rise to them. It was this background, combined with the intellectual influences of the time, that produced what is referred to as the "social pathology" approach to all social problems, including crime (see Mills, 1943).

Criminological theories of this period were closely linked with the early development of sociology. The social pathology outlook, which focused on general social problems, was dominant in criminology from the turn of the century to about World War I. It was a perspective strongly influenced by the French tradition of the Enlightenment, where human nature was idealized and social ills were perceived as repressing or inhibiting the goodness of the human being.

The orientation of the early "pathologists" leaned heavily upon the earlier work of Auguste Comte (b.1798–1857), a founder of the scientific approach to the study of human behavior and the man who in fact coined the word "sociology." Using the analogy of a biological organism, he saw society as a relatively harmonious, interdependent system subject to the same laws of growth, change, and decay that govern other biological entities. Comte stressed that society is more than the sum of its individual members and must be understood as a complex whole. The ills of society, in this view, are diseases that attack the organic social system. Social ills are manifestations of pathology, and the social scientist is obligated to ameliorate these conditions.

American sociologists at the turn of the century tended to emphasize the individual in society, both as a basis for understanding crime and as a source of change. Amelioration would involve the correction of the maladjusted person, restoration of mental health, improvement of social relationships, and ultimately the development of a healthy society. The faith and inspiration of the social pathologists were set back by World War I, but its critics also helped doom the movement as a theoretical perspective. They argued that the definition of a social problem was too often based upon the moral standards of the sociologists themselves, not on any objective criteria. Explanations for pathological conditions were hazy, often ad hoc, and suffered from a lack of clear definitions. The writings of social pathologists were moralistic and encumbered with borrowed scientific jargon and analogies. While claiming to be scientific, the so-called pathologists produced very little of an empirical nature.

During the early decades of the twentieth century, the center of academic sociology in the United States was the University of Chicago. There a primary concept, social disorganization, was generated; it was defined as "a decrease of the influence of existing social rules of behavior upon individual members of the groups" (Thomas and Znaniecki, 1927). Crime came to be seen as an indicator of social disorganization, social disorganization as a cause of crime. Social disorganization was also viewed as a concomitant of urbanization, immigration, mobility, and population growth, and consequently these factors became associated with crime causation. The theorists of the Chicago school pioneered in efforts to discover the dynamics of disorganization, examine delinquent neighborhoods (Breckinridge and Abbott, 1970), and study the spatial distribution of social phenomena within the city (Park, 1925). Sections of Chicago were labeled delinquency areas by the marking off of homes of "official" delinquents on maps of the city. Clifford Shaw (1929) concluded from this mapping of delinquency areas that crime rates *systematically* declined as one moved outward from the center city through a series of concentric zones. Delinquency was therefore seen to be highest in areas of physical decay, poverty, bad housing, adult crime, suicide, and other characteristics of social disorganization.

The patterns found in Chicago were also observed, with some variations, in Birmingham, Cleveland, Denver, Philadelphia, Richmond, and Seattle. Studying these cities, Shaw and his colleague Henry McKay (1931, 1942) obtained reinforcement for their concept that certain urban environmental conditions are significant factors in producing delinquency. Central to their analysis is the proposition that the pattern of delinquent responses is transmitted from one generation to the next. The cause of crime, then, is the "cultural transmission" of norms, roles, and responses indigenous to the delinquent areas. Irrespective of the group living in these areas, crime remains high. In Chicago, as immigrant ethnic groups changed, the crime rate in these areas remained relatively stable, indicating that the cause of crime rests more with environmental conditions than with the individualized factors proposed by psychiatric theorists.

This approach was tested in studies of Minneapolis by Calvin Schmid (1937), which supported the spatial-location and concentration-of-delinquency hypothesis, and of Detroit by Stuart Lottier (1938). Continuing this work, Roland Chilton (1964) attempted to clarify the relationship between crime areas and delinquency by elaborating upon economic variables. However, Bernard Lander (1954) in his study of Baltimore failed to support the ecological determinism of earlier studies.

The orientation of the Chicago school was a dramatic break with the determinism of the psychiatrists, with its emphasis on individual and family factors. The association of degenerative and disorganized social conditions with crime had intuitive appeal and considerable lay support, as it does today.

The Chicago study of urban behavior and social disorganization resulted in about two dozen published books over a twenty-year period. The first was *The Hobo* by Nels Anderson (1923); it concerned homeless migratory men, and continues to be read today. It was followed by such works as *The Gold Coast and the Slum* by Harvey Zorbaugh (1929), an investigation of a Chicago slum area adjacent to a wealthy strip; *The Taxi-Dance Hall*, by Paul Cressey (1932); *Vice in Chicago*, by Walter Reckless (1969); and *Twenty Thousand Homeless Men*, a study by Edwin Sutherland and Harvey Locke (1971) including a description of how these men adapted to poverty and became beggars.

The primary emphasis in these works was on the natural forces that seemed to underlie the ecological development of the city. Such development is not planned or necessarily desired but happens to be present in natural, day-to-day urban life. The case studies provided evidence of the disorganization within so-called zones of transition. Using a demographic approach and supporting it with statistical analysis, the investigators developed a broader view of the effects of social disorganization across the entire city. The official records of law enforcement and other governmental agencies were the major sources of data. When the concentric zone maps were combined with data from official records, the city itself was seen to create crime.

The consequence of adding yet another causal factor into the equation explaining crime was serious debate over the nature and expectations of criminological theory. Instead of revealing a single cause of crime, further study showed the phenomenon to be more complex. The positivist school of criminology had attempted to apply natural scientific methodology to the study of crime and focus on discovery of *the* cause of crime. Indeed throughout history, a strong force motivating the investigation of criminality was the hope of being able to postulate that if X occurs then Y must follow. But as social causes became more widely embraced, simple explanations appeared to be less acceptable or even appropriate.

Psychological explanations of crime had a strong appeal, particularly in the United States, because of the strong individualistic tradition and because they appeared to separate the good people from the bad. However, the early ecological arguments of the sociologists also made sense; thus theory was left in a state of confusion. Nathaniel Cantor (1932) argued that the concept of causation in the natural, physical sciences could not be applied in the same way to the social sciences, and that, consequently, criminological theory tended to treat the idea of causation rather loosely and eclectically. A tendency was developing to try to explain crime in terms of all of the conditions that appear to be associated with it—low IQ, personality deficiency, broken family, poverty, and a long list of other factors. This is often called the multicausal or multiple-factor theory of crime.

Multiple-Factor Theory

Historically, multiple-cause theories of crime developed after the early biological and psychological ones, not solely as a result of the influence of sociological explanations, though compounded by them. When Enrico Ferri published his *Criminal Sociology* in 1881, he estimated that the multiple-factor approach had many hundreds of adherents (see discussion by Schafer, 1969). Awareness of the complexity of the criminal's nature and situation and of the diversity of the surrounding biological, psychological, and social conditions produced numerous explanations, all of which had some intrinsic appeal as "truth," while none could absolutely claim to state *the* cause. As a result, there developed many theories of crime, of types of crime and criminals.

The divergent and discrepant theories ultimately produced a school of thought geared to compromise and to the position that elements of all theories are applicable. Since each individual is different and each crime relatively unique, no single explanation was considered sufficient. It was postulated that there are many crime-producing factors operating simultaneously, not only on an individual but on each other. What emerged was the multiple-factor orientation, which aims at finding the individual factors surrounding particular cases. Those who study individual cases by this approach are convinced that one crime is caused by one combination of circumstances, another crime by another set.

American criminologists working in the early decades of the twentieth century were clearly oriented toward multiple-factor explanations. During the World War I years William Healy (1969) analyzed over 800 delinquent cases and found no fewer than 138 factors associated with their criminality, while Sheldon and Eleanor Glueck (1950) "unraveled" the causes of crime in terms of a multiplicity of factors. David Abrahamsen, in *The Psychology of Crime* (1960), noted that the etiology of criminal behavior is related to the interplay of multiple causative factors. Though he saw psychiatric problems as primary, in his view socioenvironmental factors also influence the individual, varying in each case in quantity and quality and thus acting in diverse ways.

A modification of the mulitiple-factor approach stresses sociological factors statistically associated with crime. This viewpoint holds that a configuration of background characteristics, environmental conditions, and personality types appears to lead or is significantly related to certain forms of criminal behavior. It may be contended, for example, that the combination of a deficient home, lack of job skills, low social class, low intelligence, and alienation leads to aggressiveness and perpetration of a specific type of crime.

Multicausality seems on its face to be convincing. There is indeed a multitude of circumstances surrounding any single event, and there are many forces impinging on an individual, either encouraging or discouraging a potential action. But such an approach is of limited usefulness. In its efforts to accomplish so much, it fails to offer any systematic framework whereby theoretical understanding can be utilized or enhanced. For example, Marvin Wolfgang has offered an excellent summary of the major factors contributing to crime, but his description does not easily lend itself to further theoretical understanding or social policy recommendations:

> Urban life is commonly characterized by high population density, spatial mobility, ethnic and class heterogeneity, reduced family functions, and . . . greater anonymity. When these traits are found in high degree, and when they are combined with poverty, physical deterioration, low education, residence in industrial and commercial centers. unemployment or unskilled labor, economic dependency, marital instability or breaks, poor or absent male models for young boys, overcrowding, lack of legitimate opportunities to make a better life, the absence of positive, anti-criminal behavior patterns, higher frequency of organic diseases, and a cultural minority status of inferiority, social and psychological mechanisms leading to deviance are more likely to operate. These factors include frustration, lack of motivation to obey external demands, conflicting norms, anomie and so forth. [Wolfgang, 1970: 296–297]

Albert Cohen (1951) criticizes the multiple-factor approach on three major grounds. He contends, first, that there has been confusion between a single-*factor* explanation and a single-*theory* explanation. A single theory does not necessarily explain crime in terms of a single factor, but can be concerned with a set of variables. To make a statement about one fact (single factor) or a series of facts (multiple factor) does not constitute a theoretical explanation. *Theory is an abstract statement of how the known variations in one variable are related to known values of other variables.* Cohen argues that multiple-factor approaches fail to distinguish causal factors from variables:

> A multiple-factor approach is not a theory; it is an abdication of the quest for a theory. It simply asserts that this particular event is "caused" by this particular combination of concrete circumstances and that particular event by another combination of circumstances. [Cohen, 1951]

Cohen's second criticism of the multiple-factor approach is that the factors are used in such a way that theorists are no longer concerned only with single causes; rather, each condition is assumed to have the power to generate crime. In some cases, a factor may require additional crime-producing factors which are cumulative and additive. Often, assessment of the cumulative power of factors is determined by the independent correlations between individual social and economic conditions and crime rates. The logic behind such causal implications is fallacious (Robinson, 1950), since one cannot infer that the individuals who commit crimes necessarily have the characteristics statistically associated with the rates.

In addition, the factors associated with crime become so numerous that they encompass almost all personal, familial, cultural, and social conditions surrounding the life history of an individual; hence the crucial conditions that lead to crime are lost in the medley. As David Matza has argued:

> When factors become too numerous, there is a tendency for them to be not factors at all but rather contingencies. The term *factor*, after all, means something. A factor is a condition that is applicable to a given universe. It has an effect on everyone, not equally, to be sure, but according to degree. It is not something that may or may not matter. Factors may matter to varying extents, but every factor must by definition matter to some extent. Is the way in which a policeman responded to a child on their first meeting a factor? Does it matter or not? Is American foreign policy a factor? Does it matter or not? Is the demeanor of a child's sixth-grade teacher a factor? Does it matter or not? And so on, endlessly. Common sense tells us that these occurrences may matter or not, depending on many other things that may more legitimately be considered factors. Some occurrences may or may not matter. Thus, they are contingencies and not factors. If we insist on considering them factors, we are in the hopeless position of arguing that everything matters. [Matza, 1964: 24]

Moreover, to impute causality to a diverse set of factors is more a reflection of the subjective, intuitive judgment of the investigator than of objective reality, and provides little understanding of the processes operating. These judgments frequently reflect what Cohen has termed the "evil causes evil fallacy" in his third criticism. While this is neither a necessary part of the multiple-factor approach nor peculiar to it, the belief that evil results (crime) must have evil precedents (broken home, poverty, psychopathic personality) fails to consider conditions within the social system or community that in themselves may appear "good" and yet be criminogenic. What may have bad results need not have bad roots. In fact, as sociologists involve themselves more and more in the etiology of crime and deviance, it becomes clearer that deviant and conformist behavior can both be products of the same social processes in numerous cultural or situational variations that are not necessarily or always evil.

While some of the factors associated with crime in the multicausal approach may contribute to criminality, the approach provides neither clarity nor utility and therefore contributes little to our understanding of crime. This perspective, like any other, should be evaluated not on the basis of being right or wrong but on its relative utility (Sagarin, 1975). This is why multiple-factor approaches are generally discarded: they are less useful than other approaches.

Contemporary Sociological Perspectives

One of the above-mentioned criticisms of the multiple-factor approach is of its assumption that "evil causes evil." It has never been formally stated that current sociological thinking is a direct reaction to that assumption; nonetheless, the underlying theme of the numerous theories that have emerged during the current century has been that normal, natural social processes that may not be evil in themselves can create conditions that increase the probability of any one individual engaging in crime. The emphasis thus has changed from the absolute determinism of the past to the need to understand the social interaction and social *processes* of becoming criminal.

This perspective, linking crime to social interaction, has its historical roots in Europe and in the Chicago school. However, as an orientation and as a basis for theory construction, it has received its strongest support and propagation in the past quarter century. Sociological criminology owes a clear debt to Gabriel Tarde (b. 1843–d. 1904) and his work *Penal Philosophy* (1968), in which he argued that crime patterns are learned and adopted as are fashions and fads in clothing; this learning is through either conscious imitation or unconscious suggestion. But Tarde's theory had little impact in the United States until it was developed by Edwin Sutherland and his followers (although Sutherland specifically denied that his theory of cultural learning was a perspective based on a theory of imitation). In Chicago, Clifford Shaw (1931a, 1931b, 1938) suggested that crime is a product of the social relationships of offenders with others: criminal acts are prescribed by peers and result from the social and cultural setting, in which different opportunities are available to various segments of the population. Even earlier, Ernest Burgess (1923) proposed that the individual delinquent can be studied as a product of social interaction with others. In fact, wrote Burgess, not only crime

> but all social problems, indeed the entire area of group behavior and social life, is subjected to sociological description and analysis. The person is concerned in his interrelations with the social organization, with the family, the neighborhood, the community, and society. Explanations of his behavior are found in terms of human wishes and social contacts and social interaction, conflict, accommodation and assimilation. [Burgess, 1923: 679]

Contemporary sociological thinking on the causes of crime makes the assumption that criminality is a function of the individual's interaction with other individuals and elements of the society. Etiology, therefore, focuses on social structure and social processes.

Much of the confusion over the state of criminological thinking is rooted in the number and diversity of theories that have been proposed. Though numerous theories have been offered, none can be considered a complete or unrefuted explanation. This is not to say none is correct, but that for the most part any one theory focuses on only a single element or aspect of the process. Theories need to be understood in terms of what they hope to explain and the level of analysis they employ and generalizations they offer.

Little is gained if modern theories are presented solely in chronological order. Instead, it is more important to understand theories in terms of the procedural elements with which they deal. To help clarify the issue, we suggest that there are three levels of analysis:

1. The *structural level*, consisting of theories explaining crime as a product of forces external to the individual and beyond his or her control, such as urbanization, industrialization, social class, and political economy.
2. The *systems level*, comprised of theories explaining crime as a function of institutions, such as the family, peers, and voluntary associations; each of the system forces is directly related to structural conditions, but the individual has some interaction with a unit of each system and some impact on that unit in turn.
3. The *individual level*, consisting of theories focusing on the conditions surrounding the act itself.

The British criminologists Ian Taylor, Paul Walton, and Jock Young (1974: 270–271) refer to the first two levels as the wider and the immediate origins of the criminal act, respectively, and to the third level as the circumstances surrounding the act itself.

The commission of a criminal act has been seen as the product of the interaction of forces on all levels. Viewing the process somewhat as a funnel (see Figure 4–1), we can see the act as both unique and determined by these forces. Once committed and detected, the act precipitates a reaction on the other levels and the process may repeat itself.

To date, no one has integrated all levels of analysis by means of a single systematic theory; yet the possibility for development of such a theory is increased if current explanations are placed in perspective. To do so, the next two chapters will deal with these theories by the level of analysis they employ.

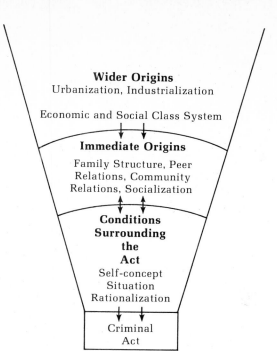

Wider Origins
Urbanization, Industrialization

Economic and Social Class System

Immediate Origins

Family Structure, Peer
Relations, Community
Relations, Socialization

**Conditions
Surrounding
the
Act**
Self-concept
Situation
Rationalization

Criminal
Act

FIGURE 4-1
**The Funnel Effect of
Forces Contributing to
the Commission of the
Criminal Act**

Wider-Origin Theories

The structural level of analysis suggests that crime and criminals result from beyond the control of the individual, although the individual may still be the controlling force over the behavior. These causative forces lie in the rapidly changing economic, political, and social characteristics of society, and ultimately determine the probable rate of different types of acts in various sectors of the population. These variables are structural in the sense that they are part of the fabric of society; they determine the nature of the society, defining its character and the quality of relationships within it. Structural variables include urbanization and industrialization, the economic system, and the educational and religious institutions. They are examined in terms of their effect on individuals, particularly through the distribution of power and wealth.

Urbanism and Crime

Structural-level explanations of crime developed out of the observations and studies of the early Chicago sociologists, who noted that crimes were more prevalent in urban than rural areas (an observation as true today as it was in the 1930s, though the difference between urban and rural crime rates has diminished in the intervening decades). In studies in the United States and abroad, Marshall Clinard (1942, 1953, 1960) found that the greater the degree of urbanism the higher the rate of property offenses. Paul Spector (1975) took note of a significant positive relationship between city size and violence. The pattern is worldwide: it is seen in the United States (Clinard and Meier, 1979; Uniform Crime Reports, 1980), in industrialized Europe

(Christiansen, 1960; Szabo, 1960), the Far East (UN, 1958), Latin America (Hauser, 1960), and Africa (Clinard and Abbott, 1973). The statistical association between crime and urbanization seems relatively established.

The explanation for this relationship seems to lie in the nature of the urban environment itself. The urban population, particularly in the twentieth century, has tended to be more and more heterogeneous, with greater concentrations of unlike peoples in one area, resulting in conflicts between people of diverse cultural backgrounds. Crime and delinquency are products of a breakdown in social-control mechanisms fostered by decline in the unity of the primary group as a result of rapid increases in population size, density, and heterogeneity.

The condition in which social control over individual behavior breaks down was initially called "social disorganization." However, the concept of disorganization has been discarded by many sociologists and criminologists on the grounds that it is subjective and vague (Clinard and Meier, 1979) and is frequently used as both cause and effect. Further, what seems like disorganization may actually be the effect of conflict between quite organized social groups composing society (Ibrahim, 1968: 47–48).

For an understanding of crime and its higher rate in urban than in rural areas, insight may be obtained by contrasting the ways of life of urban and rural people. Rural areas, it has been contended, are held together by similarities among group members. The social cohesion and integration of such areas have been called "Gemeinschaft" (Tönnies, 1957), "mechanical solidarity" (Durkheim, 1964), and "sacred society" (Becker, 1956). Social interaction in the rural society is based on a strong collective identification. The homogeneity of culture and custom lends uniformity to belief and behavior. There is comparatively little role differentiation and mobility.

Urban society, on the other hand, tends to be organized on the basis of differences between group members, termed "Gesellschaft," "organic solidarity," or "secular society" by Tönnies, Durkheim, and Becker respectively. Urban living thus creates mutual dependence and exposes people to more potential conflict resulting from the close contact of heterogeneous groups. Relationships between persons tend to be restricted to specific needs. There is no universally accepted culture or custom, and thus no uniformity in belief and behavior. People living in urban areas vary in age, race, ethnicity, norms, and values. Each group brings with it its own expectations of behavior. No group completely dominates. Urbanism—and especially the quality of urban living—is sociologically distinct from simple population growth, density, or what would be called urbanization (Wirth, 1938). Urbanism is often characterized by conflicts in cultural norms and values, increased mobility, impersonality and anonymity, rapid social change, and an emphasis on material goods and individualism.

Urbanism may transcend metropolitan boundaries and is not unique to city living, particularly today when media and technology have made all areas more "urbanistic." It is not that urban living directly results in criminality, but rather that to a preponderant degree urban conditions are conducive to it.

Industrialization and Crime

There is an interdependence between urbanism and industrialization. The latter requires human resources in large numbers, and when large groups of individuals converge they bring with them a diversity of interests and backgrounds. The greater the concentration of population, the greater the anonymity; thus, there is an increased emphasis on formal, as opposed to informal, social control in the cities. Youths may be simply reprimanded for certain behavior in one instance and subjected to police and family-court agencies for the same behavior in another. Rural deviance and urban deviance belong to the same kind of sociocultural phenomenon (Hartung, 1965), yet they tend to produce different social responses. In rural areas, for example, the parents of young people are known to other adults and are more likely to be contacted if delinquency is observed. In urban areas, such acquaintanceship is rare. The use of formal controls, it has been found, may severely affect an individual's self-conception and subsequent role-playing. The formally sanctioned youth is more likely to be labeled delinquent or bad, and subsequent offenses will more often be handled by police than by friends or neighbors. Rural malfeasants more frequently are conceived of— and conceive of themselves—as merely "wild" and "reckless," whereas the urban delinquents carry a conception of themselves as "hard," "tough," or "no good" (Hartung, 1965: 119). Edwin Lemert (1951) believes that a negative self-concept leads to role-playing appropriate to the conception, so that this change from an informal to a formal way of handling deviants might account for much of the delinquency in urban areas.

Industrialization also changes the technology for modern living by providing an array of luxury goods and services which become part of the social identity of individuals. Urban living is especially materialistic, and is usually surrounded by affluence; this affects participation in crime. The more anonymous the social setting, the more individuals rely on outward appearances and definitions of success. Many luxury items become important as "status symbols" (Goffman, 1959), and people increasingly judge others by how well they display their wealth and how much they seem to have to display. Of course, not all urban inhabitants have equal access to these goods; this is particularly true of youth. Advertisers appeal to a potential consumer group, presenting their products as symbols of, let us say, the "jet set," the "in crowd," or the "good life." As mass media and rapid transportation bring the same messages to rural areas, rural youth will be increasingly exposed to these new values and patterns of behavior, although not to the same anonymity that surrounds city youth.

Urbanism is also characterized by rapid cultural change and population mobility, which tend to facilitate changes in norms and ideology. Traditional norms and beliefs are often debunked, leaving few sacred "truths" to define acceptable conduct and a general lack of specific prescriptions and proscriptions for behavior. Mobility, both horizontal and vertical, increases the individual's contact with different groups and customs and hence exposure to and potential conflict with divergent norms. The conditions of urbanism decrease the saliency and consistency of norms and thus tend to break down the traditional informal controls exercised by the primary group. This process has been summarized by Clarence Schrag (1971).

One of the major theoretical orientations to develop out of studies of urbanism and crime focuses on the importance of culture conflict in precipitating violations of the law. Under the impact of rapid or sudden change, or under conditions of urbanism, gaps develop between traditional and new norms and values, between indigenous and imported expectations.

In the 1920s and 1930s a number of sociologists, criminologists, and anthropologists shifted their attention to the problem of the conflict of norms. Clifford Shaw and Henry McKay (1931) indicated that urban areas with certain characteristics tend to give rise to attitudes and behavior which are in conflict with legal norms. Frederic Thrasher (1927) and later Lewis Yablonsky (1962) stressed the critical importance of cultural definitions of behavior by gang members for an understanding of the dynamics of gang behavior.

Louis Wirth (1931) maintained that all conduct has reference to cultural codes. In fact, each community, each gang, each family has a culture of its own which is in competition with other cultures for an individual's allegiance. Adherence to the norms of one group may involve violation of the norms of another, creating internal conflict over the appropriate conduct code to follow.

Thorsten Sellin, in *Culture Conflict and Crime* (1938), became one of the most prominent advocates of the theme that crime is an expression of conflict between different cultures, peoples of different cultures, and codes of conduct embodied in such cultures. He agreed with Wirth that any individual is identified with a number of social groups, each with conduct norms for a different set of situations. The extent to which the individual receives divergent rules of conduct from these groups (and the more complex the culture, the greater the probability that this will occur), the greater the possibility of crime. The conduct norms to which an individual may conform may be neither the socially dominant ones nor those embodied in law. Thus, law violation may occur without internal conflict, simply in the process of offenders adhering to the dominant codes of their reference groups.

To Sellin, cultural conflict can develop in several different ways, and each form of conflict is potentially related to crime. Of primary importance here is conflict developing from contact with divergent cultural codes; this Sellin termed a conflict of *conduct* norms. What is customary behavior within a minority culture group may be regarded as illegal by the dominant group, which is in a position to legally define criminality. This concept of minority-group definition has been observed to be especially applicable to such behavior as traffic-law violation, black-market activity, alcohol and drug violation, white-collar crime, organized crime, sex crime, and other types of activity, especially those devoted to economic gain (Vold, 1979).

Sellin also pointed out that the law, the basis for defining criminality, is itself a product of conduct norms. According to Sellin, the criminal law is a mechanism whereby one group may coerce adherence to its cultural norms:

> Among the various instrumentalities which social groups have evolved to secure conformity in the conduct of their members, the criminal law occupies an important place, for its norms are binding upon all who live within the political boundaries of a state and are enforced through the coercive power of the state. The

criminal law may be regarded as in part a body of rules, which prohibit specific forms of conduct and indicate punishments for violations. The character of these rules, the kind or type of conduct they prohibit, the nature of the sanction attached to their violation, etc. depend upon the character and interests of those groups in the population which influence legislation. In some states these groups may comprise the majority, in others a minority, but the social values which receive the protection of the criminal law are ultimately those which are treasured by dominant interest groups. [Sellin, 1938: 21]

The relationship of law, crime, and culture conflict was also described in an early article by Edwin Sutherland (1929), who contended that criminal behavior, the law, and punishment are all parts of the same process that "begins in the community before the law is enacted, and continues in the community and in the behavior of particular offenders after punishment is inflicted." When a politically influential group, Sutherland maintained, feels that one of its important values—life, property, beauty of landscape, theological doctrine—is seriously endangered by the behavior of others, it secures the enactment of appropriate laws and thus wins the cooperation of the state in an effort at self-protection.

This same theme serves as a basis for more recent political analyses of crime. Before discussing the current extensions of the concept of culture conflict reflected in the law, let us consider another view of culture conflict, which sees its roots in the values of the society as a whole.

Looking at American society, Donald Taft (1966) has suggested that forces in the general culture may be criminogenic. Taft recognizes culture conflict between different groups but insists that for crime to flourish there must be nonetheless some core emphasis that, by its nature, encourages criminal activity. American society is seen here as dynamic, complex, materialistic, and competitive, with an emphasis on individualism and status. Concurrently, there is a tolerance of political corruption, a disrespect for some specific laws, and acceptance of quasi-criminal exploitation.

The mechanism by which culture is related to criminal behavior has been expressed by Taft, in collaboration with Ralph England:

Given a culture dynamic, complex, materialistic, and admiring the successful in a competitive struggle but with many falling short of success, relative failures will collect in its slums and there develop patterns of behavior hostile to the interests of the general community but in harmony with the community's basic values. Assume such a society nominally approving democracy but in practice often rating its members not on the basis of individual virtues but on their accidental membership in such social groups as races, classes, nationalities, or cliques. Weaken in such a culture primary-group controls which prevent serious departure from approved traditional patterns. Develop in such a culture, through processes of social change, a confusion of tongues in definitions of morality and hypocritical rationalizations as to contrasts between the criminal and the noncriminal. . . . Permit white-collar criminals to receive but mild punishment and no status loss. Permit also gigantic social swindles . . . and injuries to the body politic to go unpunished, while no more serious injuries, classed and treated as crime, result in severe punishment. . . . Assume in this culture a holdover of frontier traditions, involving approval of the use of force and mob action by "respectable" groups against those who oppose their interests or arouse their hostile prejudices. Grant the prevalence in that society of Puritanical traditions preventing the legal or "moral" expression of basic sex and other drives—traditions to which lip service continues to be given long after large minorities, at least, cease to follow them. [Taft and England, 1964: 277–278]

These criminogenic forces serve as the background for crime; they set the stage, so to speak, in such a way that the probability of criminality is increased. Many of these values serve as the basis for "success" in the legitimate world, and are fostered—in fact rewarded—by our social institutions, such as the schools. Schools and mass media emphasize competitive and individualistic rather than collective or socializing activities. And, as Taft and England have indicated, the law forbids many satisfactions that are in wide demand.

Among those who have looked at the major historical and social currents as sources of crime was Mabel Elliott (1952). She contended that the "rugged individualism" in the American heritage has led to a great deal of unwillingness on the part of citizens to accept the restraints of law. Like Taft, she stressed the influence of pervasive attitudes and beliefs of the society on individual commitments to accept or reject social norms. Edwin Schur (1969) took this theme much further, suggesting that American society is in and of itself criminogenic because of the manner in which these beliefs are applied in daily practice. Specifically, Schur wrote, America is a criminal society because (1) it is an unequal society, (2) its foreign policy relies particularly on the use of violence, (3) its cultural emphasis on money, individualism, competition, and personal success creates pressures and frustrations, (4) it has passed idealistic and unenforceable moral and social laws, and (5) it has adopted an unworkable orientation to crime problems that stresses repression rather than eradication of the basic causes (1969: 16–21).

In sum, these are expressions of a view that the dominant culture is the basis for molding and shaping behavior, not only of the law-abiding citizens but also of criminals. Those who internalize the values of success, status, and power and make them preoccupations (as do most adult and adolescent Americans) are potential sources for a criminal population when legitimate means to obtain these ends are blocked and when they are surrounded by a culture that glorifies the achievements of violence.

This perspective, as cogent as it may sound, is not without its critics. It does not explain the differential involvement in crime and delinquency of various segments of the American population. As a concept, culture is an ensemble of ideas that embody meanings attached to customs, and is thus too broad as a basis for theory and research (López-Rey, 1970). As a dominant criminogenic force, cultural values are difficult to substantiate.

While the culture-conflict perspective may be criticized for its inability to explain individual criminality, it does provide a framework for analysis of the creation of criminal law, its application, and the response of individuals to being defined as deviant.

The Social Reality of Crime: Theory and Perspective

Both the law and crime have been viewed as cultural products (Kadish, 1967; Wolfgang, 1966). An act codified as criminal by law reflects cultural patterns believed to be unacceptable within the normative social structure. The law reflects the values of those in a position to define acts as criminal. The objects stolen or damaged in these acts and even the victims attacked usually represent culturally important choices.

Much of the recent attention focused on crime has dealt less with the individual criminal than with the development of criminal law and normative judgments of behavior. The political turmoil in the United States during the 1960s led many to reevaluate the role and function of law (Reasons, 1973: 471). Consequently, there developed a reanalysis of the definition of crime, an urging of demystification of the law, and, in response to "overcriminalization," a movement for decriminalization of certain acts deemed in the realm of personal morality rather than antisocial behavior (Schur, 1965; Geis, 1979; Morris and Hawkins, 1970; Hart, 1963). The emphasis shifted essentially from the criminal to the "other side" of criminology (Hoefnagel, 1973)—the political, cultural, and social aspects of law. In describing the reality of crime, criminologists turned their attention to the way in which certain behavior comes to be defined as criminal (Turk, 1964).

Richard Quinney (1970) has strongly contended that criminologists previously avoided studying the criminal law for a number of reasons, including fear of being legalistic, lack of knowledge about the law, general acceptance of law and society as they exist, and belief that the study of criminal law is unrelated to an explanation of crime. All of this, he contends, indicates a need for reorientation in criminology.

Criminal law provides a definition of acceptable and unacceptable behavior in the society; yet the norms defined and the values they reflect are not universal truths and do not represent consensus, in the view of many conflict-oriented criminologists. Rather, they are a product of the conflict of power groups. Law is affected by the dynamics that mold the society's social, economic, and political structures (Quinney, 1975). In any society, the laws enacted primarily reflect the interests of those who control the economic or political institutions of the society (Chambliss and Seidman, 1971). In America, this means that the wealthy, the top management of large corporations, and the professionally powerful groups will have more success in getting laws beneficial to them passed than will poorer citizens. Those laws that appear not to reflect the interests of the wealthy, such as antitrust and environmental protection statutes, rarely involve severe penalties against individual violators and are seldom enforced as vigorously as laws that do reflect those interests (Kolko, 1963).

From this perspective the laws, which define illegality, are viewed as the product of value conflict and political activity. The definition of certain acts as criminal depends on the interests of those with sufficient political power and influence to make their views prevail. It is also assumed by adherents of this view that the same political forces are reflected in the implementation of law as in its enactment.

The conflict criminologists note the changes over time in the definition of certain behaviors as legal or illegal. They deny that there is any "natural law," citing the fact that even acts on the criminality of which there is now general agreement were not always so defined. In the early history of English criminal law, theft was not a criminal act but a civil wrong (J. Hall, 1952) —that is, a thief could not be punished by the government for his wrongdoing but could be sued by the victim for the recovery of what he had appropriated. Theft only became criminal with the rise of commerce and increased demands by merchants for protection of their goods. In fact, some claim that every detailed study of the emergence of legal codes shows the importance of activities of special interest groups—not the public interest—in the formulation of legislation (Chambliss and Seidman, 1971: 73).

Quinney has proposed a theory of the social reality of crime that reflects the assumptions of the culture-conflict perspective. His theory is stated in six propositions, listed with our commentary below.

I. THE OFFICIAL DEFINITION OF CRIME: Crime is a definition of human conduct that is created by authorized agents in a politically organized society. [Quinney, 1970: 15]

The starting point here is a definition of crime that itself is based on the legalistic approach. Crime, as officially determined, is a definition of behavior conferred by those in power. Agents of the law (legislators, police, prosecutors, judges) are responsible for formulating and administering criminal law. Upon the formulation and application of these definitions of crime, persons and behaviors become criminal.

Crime, according to this first proposition, is not inherent in behavior but is a judgment made by some about the actions and characteristics of others. This proposition allows us to focus on the formulation and administration of criminal law as it applies to the behaviors defined as criminal. Crime is here seen as a result of the class-dynamic processes that culminate in defining persons and behaviors as criminal. The greater the number of activities defined as crime, the greater the amount of conduct perceived as and reacted to as crime.

II. FORMULATING DEFINITIONS OF CRIME: Criminal definitions describe behaviors that conflict with the interests of the segments of society that have the power to shape public policy. [Quinney, 1970: 16]

Definitions of crime are formulated according to the interests of those who have the power to translate those interests into public policy. These definitions are ultimately incorporated into the criminal law. Furthermore, definitions of crime change as the interests of the dominant class change.

The powerful interests are reflected not only in the definitions of crime and the penal sanctions attached to them, but in the legal policies on handling those defined as criminals. Procedural rules are created for enforcing and administering the criminal law. Policies are also established for treating and punishing the criminally defined, and for programs to control and prevent crime. From the initial definitions of crime to the preventive and penal programs, those who have power regulate the behavior of those without it.

III. APPLYING DEFINITIONS OF CRIME: Criminal definitions are applied by the segments of society that have the power to shape the enforcement and administration of criminal law. [Quinney, 1970: 18]

The dominant interests intervene in all the stages at which definitions of crime are created. Class interests cannot be effectively protected merely by formulating criminal law; the law must be enforced and administered. The interests of the powerful, therefore, also operate when definitions of crime reach the application stage. As Vold (1979) argues, crime is political behavior, and the criminal becomes in fact a member of a "minority group" without sufficient public support to dominate the control of the police power of the state. People whose interests conflict with those represented in the law must either change their behavior or run the risk that it will be defined and treated as criminal.

The probability that definitions of crime will be applied to behavior varies according to how much the behaviors of the powerless conflict with the interests of those in power. Law-enforcement and judicial activity is likely to increase when the interests of the dominant class are threatened. Fluctuations and variations in applying definitions of crime reflect shifts in class relations. The likelihood of application of criminal sanctions depends further on discretionary actions of the legal agents having the authority to enforce and administer the law. The definition of crime that is applied is based on their evaluation. Austin Turk has argued that during the process of "criminalization," a criminal label may be affixed to people because of real or fancied attributes rather than actual behavior: "Indeed, a person is evaluated, either favorably or unfavorably, not because he does something, or even because he is something, but because others react to their perceptions of him as offensive or inoffensive" (1966: 34). The evaluations by the definers are affected by the way in which the suspect handles the situation, but ultimately the decisions of the legal agents are the crucial factors in determining the criminality of human acts. As legal agents evaluate more and more persons and instances of a behavior as worthy of being defined as criminals and crimes, the probability that a definition of crime will be applied increases.

IV. HOW BEHAVIOR PATTERNS DEVELOP IN RELATION TO DEFINITIONS OF CRIME: Behavior patterns are structured in segmentally organized society in relation to criminal definitions, and within this context persons engage in actions that have relative probabilities of being defined as criminal. [Quinney, 1970: 20]

Although behavior varies, all forms of behavior have in common that they are patterns found within subgroups of the society. All persons—whether they create definitions of crime or are solely the objects of such definitions —act in reference to normative systems learned in their own social and subcultural settings. Because it is not the quality of the behavior but the action taken against it that gives it the character of a crime, that which is defined as criminal is relative to the behavior patterns of the class formulating and applying the definitions. Consequently, people whose normative systems and behavior patterns are not represented when definitions of crime are formulated and applied are more likely to act in ways defined as criminal than are those making the definitions.

People construct their own patterns of action in participating with others. It follows, then, that the probability that persons will develop action patterns with a high potential of being defined as criminal depends on (1) structured opportunities, (2) learning experiences, (3) interpersonal associations and identifications, and (4) self-conceptions. Throughout these experiences, individuals create conceptions of themselves as human beings. Thus prepared, they behave according to the anticipated consequences of their actions.

Those who have been defined as criminal (because of their mischief or delinquency, official suspicion, or some other reason) may begin to conceive of themselves as criminal. As they adjust to the definitions imposed upon them, they learn to play the criminal role (Lemert, 1967). As a result of the reactions of others, therefore, they may develop patterns of action that increase the likelihood of their being defined as criminal in the future. That is, increased experience with definitions of crime increases the probability of their developing self-conceptions and actions that may cause them to be defined as criminal.

V. CONSTRUCTING CONCEPTIONS OF CRIME: Conceptions of crime are constructed and diffused in the segments of society by various means of communication. [Quinney, 1970: 22]

This conception is created in the ideas people are exposed to, the manner in which people select information to fit their image of the world they are shaping, and their way of interpreting this information. People behave in reference to the social meanings they attach to their experiences.

Conceptions that develop in a society relating to what people regard as crime must of course be accompanied by ideas about the nature of crime. Images develop about the relevance of crime, characteristics of offenders, the appropriate reaction to crime, and the relation of crime to the social order. This constitutes an ideology that is diffused throughout the society.

VI. CONSTRUCTING THE SOCIAL REALITY OF CRIME: The social reality of crime is constructed by the formulation and application of criminal definitions, the development of behavior patterns related to criminal definitions, and the construction of criminal conceptions. [Quinney, 1970: 23]

Crime, in this view, is a social-class phenomenon; crimes are defined by the class in power and are generally perceived as being committed by the lower classes—those without political power and influence. Historically, most crime has been assumed to be conventional lower-class activity, and theorists have attempted to explain it in just those terms. Much theory therefore uses social class as a structural variable in the development of the etiology of crime.

Some would argue that many crimes are not class-related, and that modern societies, it is contended, cannot exist without social control over homicide, theft, forcible rape, and other types of universally forbidden conduct. It is contended that, although the powerful when apprehended are usually treated with deference, as in corporate swindles involving millions of dollars, this fact demonstrates the social-class nature of criminal justice but not of the formulation and application of definitions of crime.

Social-Class Theories of Crime

On the basis of official statistics—which, as we have seen in Chapter 2, present problems of reliability—youth crime has commonly been described in the literature as a phenomenon of the lower classes. Studies have tended to demonstrate that the largest proportion of the criminal population comes from the lower classes and the crime rates of those classes exceed those of others. The Gluecks (1950) found that a lower percentage of the parents of delinquents had businesses of their own, and that the fathers of delinquents tended to fall into the unskilled category. In "Yankee City" (Newburyport, Mass.)—subject of a study by W. Lloyd Warner—the lower class constituted 25 percent of the population but accounted for 65 percent of all arrests over a seven-year period (Warner, 1963). In "Elmtown," August Hollingshead (1949) found that not one person in the two upper social classes had been sentenced for any crime, but 46 percent had been sentenced in the lowest class.

On an international scale, the pattern has also been supported by statistical evidence. In England, for example, Arnold Rose (1954) indicated that 40 percent of the fathers of the deviants in his studies came from the unskilled classes. A study by Lynn McDonald (1969) added support to this finding, particularly with regard to property damage and violent offenses. Hermann Mannheim and Leslie Wilkins (1955) found a similar trend in a study of boys sent to Borstal, a so-called training school for juvenile delinquents in England. Swedish data have indicated the same relationship between social-class position and involvement in crime; using official statistics for 1962, Karl-Erik Forsström (1965: 49) found that 82.7 percent of those charged for offenses were from the lower class while only 5.9 percent could be considered upper class. According to Carl-Gunnar Janson (1968), however, the increase in deviance since World War II has been most evident in the lower middle class, a conclusion based on a study of over 4,500 males born in 1925 and 1940, of known social-class position, and officially registered with the police. In a nationwide representative sample in Denmark, Preben Wolf (1962) showed that this relationship between class and violation of the penal code was statistically significant.

Not all researchers have been willing to accept the association between class and crime. Studies of social-class relationships are questionable on the ground that they are based on court records, police files, and other official statistics. F. Ivan Nye and his colleagues (1958) have contended that while these statistics may be an adequate basis for an examination of official deviance, they are unreliable as an index of actual deviance within the general population. Others have tended to challenge the implicit assumptions behind the apparent correlations, rather than the correlations themselves.

Along this line, it is the position of Albert Reiss and A. Lewis Rhodes (1961) that no simple relationship between class and criminality exists. Statistically, they find greater deviance in the lower classes, but state that this might be due to differential life chances and to traditions of marginal activity in lower-class neighborhoods. Carrying this argument further, LaMar Empey and Steven Lubeck (1971) conclude that the effects of social class are mediated by intervening influences of family and ethnic status, the prevailing ethos of the community, and the existence of particular kinds of peer subcultures.

Given the fact that official statistics demonstrate the difference in criminal behavior between classes, the question arises whether and to what extent such difference is due to contrasting attitudes taken by police and other officials toward lower- and middle-class deviants. In many instances, the deviant acts of middle-class children are never reported, but handled informally. An expectation that crime is to be found among the poorest people may lead police to more concentrated activity in the areas where they live. When they occur in a middle-class community, many deviant acts do not go beyond the stage of being reported. Parents know how to make use of other community resources, such as child-guidance clinics, and the police are often hesitant to proceed with a case if the family is attempting to deal with it. Among those who have found juvenile middle-class theft not uncommon, and perhaps as widespread as lower-class juvenile thievery, are Edmund Vaz (1967, 1969) and Howard and Barbara Myerhoff (1964).

Walter Reckless, another critic of the assertion that crime rates are higher among the lower classes, has suggested (1973) that the class distribution of crime is a U-shaped curve, with both the lower and upper classes having high rates and the middle class low rates. He bases this contention on the opportunity of the upper classes to commit white-collar crime and the fact that the middle-class subculture tends to insulate itself against activities usually considered crimes.

Other arguments, particularly within the conflict perspective, perceive crime as ubiquitous but the system of justice to be highly selective and discriminatory against the lower classes. It is charged that the public and the media pay little attention to white-collar crimes, which are economically more costly than ordinary property crimes, and that the government is biased in enforcement and administration of justice. "The public system concentrates on crimes committed by the poor," writes David Gordon (1974: 68), "while crimes by the more affluent are left to private auspices." When the poor get into trouble, Gordon contends, they go to prison, whereas the more affluent go to private psychiatric and counseling services that supplant prosecution.

In the conflict perspective power is the central concept, particularly its potential for abuse. The more powerful a group, the greater the probability of its defining other groups' behavior as criminal; the less powerful a group, the more likely that its members will be defined as criminal. Thus, the differential in the power to make a legal definition of crime explains the overrepresentation of the lower classes in the criminal justice system. William Chambliss argues, for example:

The lower-class person is (1) more likely to be scrutinized and therefore to be observed in any violation of the law, (2) more likely to be arrested if discovered under suspicious circumstances, (3) more likely to spend the time between arrest and trial in jail, (4) more likely to come to trial, (5) more likely to be found guilty, and (6) if found guilty, more likely to receive harsh punishment than his middle- or upper-class counterpart. Even after sentence is passed, the built-in biases continue—among those sentenced to death for murder, lower-class persons are more likely to be executed than are the others. [1969: 86]

Ultimately, the determination of the relationship between class and crime lies in the accumulation of empirical evidence. To date, such evidence is far from conclusive, with the contention that the lower classes have higher rates of illegal behavior than the middle and upper classes challenged by several studies (Short, 1957; Nye, 1958; Dentler and Monroe, 1961). In general, these studies reveal no significant class differences in the incidence of certain illegal behaviors. Robert Dentler and Lawrence Monroe (1961) conclude that middle- and upper-class arrest rates are inaccurate and unreliable. In order to avoid reliance on official statistics, Nye, Short, and Olson (1958) sampled high school students in six Western and Midwestern areas. Using the father's occupation as the basis of defining social status, they identified four groups: unskilled and semi-skilled labor, skilled labor and craftsmen, white collar and small business, and professional and large business. Their findings suggest that there are no significant differences in these occupational and socioeconomic strata in the incidence of self-reported delinquency. John Clark and Eugene Wenninger (1963) have criticized these findings in that they felt the study was based on too limited a sample, consisting only of persons from rural communities and small cities but not urban centers. In addition, they criticized the study because of the absence of sufficient subjects at the extreme ends of the upper and lower classes, such as would be present in larger metropolitan areas. Finally, they find that there is more than one kind of lower class, and in rural areas they were simply more likely to have low rates of delinquency.

Using the self-reporting approach, Clark and Wenninger (1963) themselves sampled public high school students in Northern Illinois communities selected on the basis of their class structure. These communities included rural farm, lower urban, industrial, and upper urban settings. The results were mixed: no significant differences in illegal behavior between the classes in either rural or small urban areas were found, a conclusion similar to that of Short and Nye (1958) and Dentler and Monroe (1961). However, significant differences were found between communities that could be characterized as having one predominant socioeconomic class. In these cases the lower-class areas had a higher rate of illegal behavior than the upper-class areas, especially in the more serious kinds of offenses. (Differences between the classes within each of these "status areas" were insignificant.) The authors concluded that a community must reach a certain population size (about 40,000) before social class becomes a significant factor in delinquencies. Crime rates in these larger communities are affected not only by social class but by ethnic composition, prestige of the dominant class, and proportion of social-class representation. In contrast, in the smaller communities juveniles are affected by community-wide norms rather than by their own social-class origins. Generally, the social class that dominates the community to a large extent affects the types of delinquency that will occur. The implication here is that the lower-class delinquent subculture is primarily a product of the larger metropolitan areas.

Clearly, the relationship between class and delinquency is complex. Albert Reiss and A. Lewis Rhodes (1961) found, for example, that both the status structure and the extent of delinquency as a cultural tradition in an area significantly affect delinquency regardless of social class. While, in general, the probability of becoming delinquent is greater for lower-status youths than higher-status ones, a low-status youth in a predominantly high-status area with a low rate of delinquency is unlikely to become a delinquent. The chances of becoming a delinquent are greatest in the lower-status and the high delinquency areas, regardless of the individual's social-class origins.

In a recent assessment of thirty-five studies examining the relationship of social class to crime and juvenile delinquency, Charles Tittle and his colleagues (1978) found only a slight negative relationship between class and criminality, with self-report studies demonstrating lower associations than official data. An important aspect of this study is that there was an apparent decline in the magnitude of the relationship during the 1970s.

While official and unofficial data regarding social class and criminality are inconclusive and class per se cannot be considered an explanation, a number of theorists, accepting the validity of overrepresentation of lower-class youth in the crime statistics, have attempted to explain it. One of the problems in all of these studies is that significant differences can arise as one shifts focus from juvenile delinquency to adult criminality.

ANOMIE THEORY

One of the most widely discussed approaches to criminality is Robert Merton's theory of anomie (1968), in which he explains certain types of crime in terms of social structure. Merton stresses the role of structural conditions that limit access to the culturally emphasized economic and power goals of the society. In this view, criminality is a function of the social structure that produces a strain toward relative normlessness or social alienation. This strain is seen as a result of a disequilibrium between established goals in a society and institutionalized means to achieve those goals. Merton states that anomie is "conceived as a breakdown in the cultural structure, occurring particularly when there is an acute disjunction between cultural norms and goals and the social-structural capacities of members of the group to act in accord with them" (1968: 162). Inspired by the classic work of Durkheim (1951) on suicide and anomie, Merton sees the relative normlessness in society as deriving from the nature of modern social structures.

According to Travis Hirschi (1969), criminality results from an emphasis in society on goals, particularly materialistic ones, that are unattainable for certain segments or classes of the population through legitimate or accepted means. In anomie theory, Hirschi points out, it is assumed that rates of criminality within a given society vary according to social class, ethnic or racial status, and other characteristics that can limit access to legitimate means. In the United States, the major goal stressed is wealth, but Merton contends that this is done without equivalent emphasis on the legitimate, normative means to acquire that wealth. It is this clash between the goals with which members of the society are inculcated and the inaccessibility of their attainment through acceptable means that produces strain. People can adapt to a strain toward anomie in a number of ways. Merton offers a schematic paradigm of possible individual responses in terms of acceptance or rejection of the socially approved goals and the means for their attainment (Table 5–1).

Conformity consists of acceptance of both the goals and the normative methods of reaching them—although one may be defeated in the effort or forced to compromise short of success. Innovation—which would account for most property crime—is a success-oriented response in which persons use deviant or criminal (here called innovative) means to attain socially approved goals. Ritualism is the reverse of innovation: the ends, if they are not rejected, just do not count; all that is important is the means. Retreatism is a rejection of both means and goals; some would account for alcoholism and narcotics addiction in these terms, and others likewise for mental illness, though dispute surrounds such statements (see Clinard, 1964, for a series of original papers on the validity of anomie theory). Finally, rebellion is not so much the acceptance or rejection of ends and means as their replacement with new proposals.

Merton qualifies his anomie approach by stating, "The theory only holds that those located in places in the social structure which are particularly exposed to such stresses are more likely than others to exhibit deviant behavior" (1968: 183)—that is, social-class membership automatically exposes some individuals (those in the lower echelons of a society) to greater stress, and hence they are more likely candidates for deviance. For it is "only when [this] system of cultural values extols, virtually above all else, certain common success-goals for the population at large while the social structure rigorously restricts or completely closes access to approved modes of reaching these goals for a considerable part of the same population that deviant behavior ensues on a large scale" (Merton, 1968: 146).

Essentially, anomie theory proposes that three factors operate to produce criminality: cultural goals, institutionalized means for achieving these goals, and social-class differentials in access to the means. The dichotomy between goals and means in Merton's theory is a general conception, so that "*any* cultural goals which receive extreme and only negligibly qualified emphasis in the culture of a group will serve to attenuate the emphasis on institutionalized practices and make for anomie" (1968: 181). Some criminologists, such as Marshall Clinard (1964: 55), object that within a given modern, complex society it may be difficult to ascertain the presence of any universal cultural goal.

Research on anomie has been abundant, perhaps inconclusive, largely because of the inability of the theory to generate testable hypotheses. To test the hypothesis that criminality results from a discrepancy between goals and means requires the measurement of two independent variables simulta-

	Ends	Means	
Conformity	+	+	**TABLE 5-1**
Innovation	+	−	**Modes of Adaptation**
Ritualism	−	+	**to Goal Attainment**
Retreatism	−	−	
Rebellion	±	±	

neously, but researchers have not been able to reach consensus on how to measure these variables.

The inability to test the model directly has led to indirect tests. Thus, Bernard Lander (1954) attempted to measure anomie by way of factor and correlation analysis of cases in Baltimore. He contended that there are two essential sets of factors operating in the juvenile delinquency rate of a given area. The socioeconomic cluster consists of the more conventional factors of substandard housing, overcrowding, and low median figure for years of education completed. The anomic cluster consists of the delinquency rate, percentage of nonwhite population, and percentage of owner-occupied homes. Lander concluded that the rate of anomie is essentially determined by the instability and transitory nature of the area, more so than by the economic structure or personal alienation.

Shortly after the work of Lander, David Bordua (1958) replicated the Baltimore study in Detroit and arrived at similar conclusions, although he implied that the use of the term "anomie" largely serves to obscure the analysis. Both the Lander and the Bordua studies show that structural variables within neighborhoods are correlated. The term "anomie" has been applied to these variables collectively, but no evidence has been presented to suggest that this factor is an indicator of structural strain or related to individual deviations from the norm.

Other attempts have been made to test the anomie proposition by measuring feelings of strain in individuals. Leo Srole (1956) devised a scale to measure an individual's perception of his environment and his place in it. Subsequent research using this scale has shown that anomia—the term employed to distinguish the psychological from the structural concept of anomie—was more prevalent in the lower than the upper classes.[1]

Research, however, has not demonstrated the alleged disjunction between goals and normative means in society, but has merely indicated that deviance is officially higher in certain sections of urban areas, a fact that offers little empirical proof or disproof of Merton's theoretical propositions. Furthermore, as Dorothy Meier and Wendell Bell (1959) have pointed out, the indicator of anomie on Srole's scale appears to measure little else than despair, hopelessness, and a sense of discouragement.

Some researchers have cited the paucity of empirical data in the United States that might support the theoretical propositions stated by Merton.

1. For studies that demonstrate the inverse relationship between social class and anomia, see Meier and Bell (1959), Mizruchi (1960), Roberts and Rokeach (1956), McDill (1961), and Tumin and Collins (1959), as well as Simpson and Miller (1963), who support the contention of the inverse relationship but venture beyond differences between classes to find variations of greater importance within classes.

Clinard (1964) has contended that this is essentially due to basic problems with the theory itself. For example, anomie fails to consider the importance of the interaction process, group expectations of subcultural influences, and aspects of personal interaction.

**DIFFERENTIAL
OPPORTUNITY**

While anomie theory itself appears untestable, modifications of it have been proposed that appear to overcome this shortcoming. This is especially true of the concept that came to be known as differential opportunity, first introduced by Richard Cloward (1959) and later expanded by Cloward and Lloyd Ohlin (1960).

The Cloward and Ohlin reformulation focuses on the problem of goal-means discrepancies but stresses the role of the opportunity structure—i.e., the chances one has to achieve a goal either legitimately or illegitimately. The central hypothesis is described thus:

> The disparity between what lower-class youth are led to want and what is actually available to them is the source of a major problem of adjustment. Adolescents who form delinquent subcultures . . . have internalized an emphasis upon conventional goals. Faced with limitations on legitimate avenues of access to these goals, and unable to revise their aspirations downward, they experience intense frustrations; the exploration of nonconformist alternatives may be the result. [Cloward and Ohlin, 1960: 86]

Delinquency is thus seen as both adaptive—i.e., instrumental in the achievement of "the same kinds of things" everyone wants—and reactive—i.e., generated by a sense of injustice at having been deprived (Nettler, 1978: 227). Both goals and means are culturally determined by the structure of the society.

Not everyone who experiences barriers to the use of legitimate means is in a position to deviate. Cloward and Ohlin proposed that the emphasis of the Chicago school on cultural transmission and differential association essentially referred to access to illegitimate means, and that the availability of *illegitimate* alternatives must also be considered as a variable in crime and delinquency. In this way, they attempted to combine the class-oriented theory of Merton and the theory of Sutherland and Cressey (1978), which did not have a social-class base.

Differential opportunity, when analyzed closely, incorporates the basic propositions of the theory of anomie, although the former is more easily made operational. At the same time, the differential-opportunity formulation attempts to account for subcultural variations in the adaptations made by individuals and groups faced with opportunity barriers.

For Cloward and Ohlin, both legitimate and illegitimate opportunity are regulated by neighborhood structure and the corresponding subculture. In the "criminal subculture," participants are devoted to theft and other illegal means of securing income. Youths learn to use adult criminals as role models. In the "conflict subculture," violence dominates as a way of winning status. There are no strong adult role models, and thus status is achieved through peer recognition. The "retreatist subculture" stresses the use of drugs, the participants being unable to achieve goals either legitimately or illegitimately (Cloward and Ohlin, 1960: 178–186).

Later empirical findings have not been conclusive regarding differential opportunity. Studies have failed to distinguish clearly the specific types or activities of gangs in the typologies of Cloward and Ohlin (see Schrag, 1971; Spergel, 1964; Short, Rivera, and Tennyson, 1965; Downes, 1966). In addition, the association between opportunity and criminality has not been clear, particularly if viewed in terms of economic opportunity.

Some criminologists have concluded that it is not, for example, the absolute rate of unemployment but "relative deprivation," or unemployment in a prosperous economy, that creates the greatest frustration and dissatisfaction (Taft and England, 1964). However, the relationship of unemployment to crime rate appears to be different for juveniles and adults: Daniel Glaser and Kent Rice (1959) found that the frequency of crimes committed by juveniles varies inversely with unemployment rates, and that in contrast the frequency of property crime committed by adults varies directly with such rates.

From this, it would appear that, in studying youth deviation, one should consider the degree of commitment to the occupational goal and the importance attached to that goal. It is believed by many researchers that the economic and employment goals of the general adult population may not after all be the goals of youth (Short, 1964; Short and Strodtbeck, 1965; Bordua, 1961; Friday, 1972, 1974; Hirschi, 1969; Quicker, 1974) and that the achievement of these goals in the immediate future is not important to youth. Those holding this view seriously doubt the assumption both of Merton and of Cloward and Ohlin that blockage of legitimate channels for goal achievement is an important determinant of illegal behavior for youth, although it may be a plausible explanation of such behavior in adults.

A modification of the differential-opportunity thesis might flow from this. The blockage may in fact be a function of discrepancy between the achievement aims of a youth and that individual's confidence in being able to reach the goals. This view discards the idea that all or most lower-class youth generally seek the same goals. What is involved here can be termed perceived (or self-perceived) discrepancy. James Short (1964) has found high discrepancy scores among black youths, for both those involved with gangs and others. If racial discrimination is assumed to be a factor of blocked opportunity perceived by the youths, this would tend to support the Cloward-Ohlin hypothesis. Paul Friday (1972), however, has found occupational goal discrepancy in Sweden to be unrelated to involvement in crime. Both Travis Hirschi (1969) and John Quicker (1974) have indicated that postulated long-range goal discrepancy is untenable as a cause of delinquency, although immediate goal discrepancy is strongly related. Deviation committed by young people may be incidental to the existence of blocked long-term occupational opportunity. Instead, youth appear more concerned with less concrete goals, such as the utilization of leisure or the development and maintenance of status within the peer group (Short and Strodtbeck, 1965). Employment opportunity as a variable may be more significant for older youth.

Whether opportunities are blocked may not be so important a factor in delinquency as whether they are perceived as blocked. Friday (1970) has found the perception of blockage—in contrast to actual blockage—to be significantly related to involvement in crime in Sweden, while Short, Rivera, and Tennyson (1965) found that gang members perceived legitimate opportunities as blocked more often than other boys did. It is not clear, however, whether this blockage perception precedes gang membership or is a function of it. In fact, official adjudication and labeling as criminal may precede opportunity perception.

Research to date attempting to relate degree of opportunity and deviance has not controlled for appearance before official sanctioning bodies. Short, among others, did not control for such contact. Studies using Srole's anomia scale have systematically made correlations between anomia or deviation and social class without controlling for interaction with such formal agencies as police and the courts (Bell, 1957; Mizruchi, 1960; Simpson and Miller, 1963). Virginia Lambert (1969: 167) made a study of adjudicated juveniles in Milwaukee and concluded that the data showed anomie "to be more pronounced following adjudication." Although she indicated that one cannot draw conclusions regarding the actual genesis of deviance in relation to anomie, the factor of adjudication does appear to play a major role in changing an individual's self-concept. These and many other studies parallel the orientation in the study of victimless crimes and noncriminal deviance put forth for many years by the "societal reaction" or "labeling" school (Becker, 1973; Kitsuse, 1962; Lemert, 1951), which emphasized the effect of a negative label on subsequent behavior of the person so tagged.[2]

Thus, most studies have left unanswered the question of whether perception of blocked opportunities leads to deviance, or official sanction for a deviant act leads to such perception. Differential opportunity may indeed play a significant role in recidivism and continuation of deviation, but as an explanation of a first offense it may not be very relevant.

SUBCULTURAL SOCIAL-CLASS THEORIES

Albert K. Cohen (1955) found Merton's anomie theory plausible as an explanation of adult professional crime and property delinquency by older juveniles, but suggested that it is not applicable to the delinquent subculture as he understood it. For Cohen, lower-class juvenile delinquency is nonutilitarian, malicious, and negativistic (the three key words that distinguish, in his orientation, youthful from adult criminality). This delinquency results from adjustment to the frustration of lower-class status. Lower-class youths, in Cohen's view, internalize middle-class goals and values, find the opportunities to reach them blocked, and then experience a reaction formation or internal rebellion against the norms that they have found they cannot use in their own success strivings. In this reaction they form delinquent subcultures that are outlets for aggression and they ostensibly, on an outward and conscious level, reject the middle-class ideologies.

The delinquent response, then, appears to be an explicit and wholesale repudiation of middle-class standards (Cohen, 1955: 129–130), but in reality

2. The labeling perspective is discussed in detail in Chapter 7, particularly on pp. 133–137.

it conceals the internalization of middle-class norms by lower-class delinquents. Socialization within the lower class fails to equip male youth to meet the criteria of the middle-class measuring rod. As David Bordua (1960) has put it, a little internalization is a dangerous thing.

However, research generally fails to support Cohen's thesis. Reiss and Rhodes (1961) reported that the *more* the lower-class youth is in the minority vis-à-vis the larger society, the less likely he is to be delinquent. Lois DeFleur (1969) found no evidence of a reaction formation among delinquents in Argentina. Marshall Clinard (1949) qualifies Cohen in holding that, in addition to permitting protest against middle-class values, lower-class delinquency serves such simple needs as adventure, excitement, protection, and identification. Any protest is seen here as likely to be against older adults who thwart adolescent participation rather than against the middle class as a whole.

Walter Miller (1958) has rejected Cohen's reaction-formation hypothesis and suggested instead that the lower class possesses a relatively distinct and autonomous value system. He has asserted that the delinquent acts of lower-class youth have as their "dominant component of motivation" the directed attempt by the actor to adhere to forms of behavior and achieve standards of value as defined by the community—meaning the lower-class community. He implies that lower-class and gang values emphasize elements ("focal concerns") that differ markedly from middle-class codes. David Downes (1966: 69) has summarized Miller's concept of focal concerns and the perceived alternatives as follows:

Focal Concerns	*Perceived Alternatives*
1. Trouble: law-abiding behavior; i.e. the avoidance of contacts with authorities	Law-violating behavior
2. Toughness: physical prowess, skill; "masculinity," fearlessness, etc.	Weakness, effeminacy, timidity, ineptitude, cowardice, caution
3. Smartness: ability to outsmart, making money by "wits"; shrewdness, adroitness in repartee	Gullibility; making money by hard work, dull-wittedness, verbal maladroitness; slowness
4. Excitement: thrill, danger, risk; change, activity	Boredom; "deadness"; safeness; sameness, passivity
5. Fate: being "lucky," favored by "fortune"	Ill-omened, being "unlucky"
6. Autonomy: independence; freedom from external restraint, especially superordinate authority	Dependency, "being cared for," presence of external constraint and strong authority

Consequently, conformity to certain lower-class values may automatically cause violation of the law. Although Miller assumes that violations may be traced to these conflicts, his theory cannot adequately explain the increase in middle- and upper-class delinquency.

Cohen and Miller offer divergent views of the role played by social-class values. Essentially, the issue is whether a society is based on a common value system or a class-differentiated value system. Hyman Rodman (1963) argues that neither perception is completely accurate. Instead, lower-class persons, without abandoning the general values of the society, develop or "stretch" them into an alternative set. In the "value-stretch" thesis, as Rodman calls it, the values of success, high income, and educational and occupational attainment are not discarded but stretched so that lesser degrees of success become desirable. The result is that many members of the lower class have a wider range of values—some divergent—than do upper-class members, values that help them adjust to their deprived circumstances. In the end, many deviant and criminal acts become easily rationalized.

Solomon Kobrin (1951) has seen the effects of social class somewhat differently. Adult criminality, he has maintained, tends to be systematic and organized, with groups of adults engaging in the promotion and management of consistently profitable illegal enterprises. With these enterprises, leaders "frequently maintain membership in such conventional institutions of their local communities as churches, fraternal and mutual benefit societies, and political parties" (p. 657). Thus two value systems operate simultaneously, with "leaders of illegal enterprise participating in the primary orientation of the conventional elements in the population, and the latter, through their participation in a local power structure sustained in large part by illicit activity, participating perforce in the alternate, criminal value system" (p. 658).

By contrast, in delinquency areas there is an absence of systematic and organized adult activity in violation of law, despite the fact that many adults do commit violations. Thus, Kobrin contends:

> The presence of violators as adult models in the community legitimizes activity in opposition to law from the point of view of delinquent juveniles. In this situation conventional and criminal systems of values are not merely not integrated, but are in extreme and open opposition to one another. As a consequence, the delinquency in areas of this type tends to be unrestrained by controls originating *at any point* in the adult social structure. . . .
>
> Thus, duality of value orientation in the high rate urban areas may be regarded as a fundamental property of a wide variety of specific community situations. While delinquency areas may move toward or away from the integration of these opposing systems of values, the basic character of the social life of these communities appears to be determined in large part by the explicit presence of this duality. [Kobrin, 1951: 658, 659]

Poverty and Crime

The overrepresentation of the lower classes in officially reported, conventional criminality has been a concern for decades. While crime and delinquency are not confined to the poor, and poverty has not been "proved" to be a cause of crime, there is nonetheless considerable lay support for such a thesis. Historically, poverty has been viewed as the most conducive milieu for crime (Schafer, 1969).

Explanations of crime as a function of poverty have taken two general forms: In one instance, poverty is seen as an entrapped way of life, a "culture of poverty" found in urban slums and other economically depressed areas such as Appalachia and the Ozarks; over time, residents of these areas develop a way of life, a subculture, largely as an adjustment to deprivation. The second view sees poverty as a function of the political economy of industrialized capitalist societies and crime as a product of the structured inequalities in the system.

The "culture of poverty" explanation envisions crime and deviance as natural byproducts of a fact of life, much as Miller's theory hypothesized. In describing the poor in San Juan and New York, Oscar Lewis (1966) characterized their activities as a struggle for survival. Living under conditions of unemployment and blocked opportunities, they frequently resort to violence in order to discipline children and settle interpersonal disputes. There is a strong sense of authoritarianism, male superiority, and fatalism. These adjustments to economic conditions are transmitted to the young, and thus the "culture" becomes self-perpetuating.

The second view of poverty does not focus on individual adjustments but on the economic conditions themselves. Such a theoretical orientation has not been particularly popular in the United States. This analysis of economic conditions and crime predates modern criminological thought, and serves as a basis of the Marxist perspective.

While they did not directly address the problem of crime, Karl Marx and Friedrich Engels established the theoretical foundation for the view that the economic structure of capitalist society is responsible for creating crime. Engels (1892) pointed out the six-fold increase in criminality during the depression of 1844, and concluded that crime depends upon the economic position of the workers—i.e., a disadvantaged position conducive to alienation.

Stephen Schafer (1969) reviewed in detail the historical application of the economic determinist view of crime, as based on the works of Marx and Engels. The essence of the argument was made early in the twentieth century by the Dutch criminologist and socialist Willem Bonger (1967), who contended that the structure of capitalist society exerts differential pressures on the various social classes. The capitalist mode of production, based on private property and individual profit, is inimical to the development of collective social instincts. Since Bonger, Marxist and neo-Marxist criminologists have developed numerous different orientations, and have differed among themselves on the nature of European and Asian regimes claiming to follow Marx's teachings and on the extent of crime in the Soviet Union, China, and elsewhere. However, they have agreed on the general proposition that capitalistic economic institutions give rise to criminality. This is where the Marxist analysis starts. As David Gordon writes, such analysis

> presumes, first of all, that the basic structure of social and economic institutions in any society fundamentally shapes the behavior of individuals in that society and, therefore, that one cannot in fact understand the behavior of individuals in a society like the United States without first understanding the structures and biases of the basic "system-defining" institutions in this country. It argues, furthermore, that the "social relations of production" in capitalist societies help define an economic class structure and that one cannot therefore adequately understand the behavior of individuals unless one first examines the structure of

institutionally determined opportunities to which members of the respective economic classes are more or less confined. The analysis depends, at another level, on the radical theory of the State, according to which radicals hypothesize that the activities of the State in capitalist societies serve primarily to benefit members of the capitalist class—either directly, by bestowing disproportionate benefits upon them, or indirectly, by helping preserve and solidify the structure of class inequalities upon which capitalists so thoroughly depend. The radical analysis expects, finally, that various social problems in capitalist societies, although they may not have been created by capitalists, cannot easily be solved within the context of capitalist institutions because their solution would tend to disrupt the functioning of the capitalist machine. If the disruptive potential of solutions to solve problems therefore inclines the state to postpone solution, one can expect to solve those problems only by changing the power relationships in society so that the State is forced to serve other interests than those of the capitalist class. [Gordon, 1974: 73]

There is a wide range of perspectives attempting to explain crime on a structural rather than individual level. Each of the structural forces generating crime—whether urbanization, culture, class, or political economy—operates to sift and sort the population and creates probabilities that some groups will be more likely than others to engage in crime.

Within each group, however, some members do not commit crime. What is needed is an explanation that will help differentiate between the criminal and the law-abiding individual within the most crime-prone segments of the population. Such explanations lie closer to the individual's experience. They deal with the immediate origins of the criminal act, and are discussed in the next chapter.

Immediate-Origin Theories and the Focus on Delinquency

In order for one to reach the point of committing a criminal act, there is usually a developmental process that takes place. Individuals do not one day wake up to find themselves suddenly catapulted into full-fledged criminality. Rather, the act occurs as a result of a long series of events and interactions involving not only the offender but numerous associates, the situation of which the act is part, and the wider political, economic, and historical context in which the offender lives.

In the search for explanations of criminality, it is often difficult if not impossible to grasp all of the complexities of this developmental process. Critical events and problems tend to compound themselves. Once a person has been caught, arrested, prosecuted, and convicted—even for a relatively minor crime—it may become difficult to distinguish between the conditions affecting the initial involvement in the act and the consequences of having been caught, processed, and labeled. For that reason, many of the early theories of crime, which were based on comparisons between prisoners and civilians, were biased, as prison inmates are not necessarily representative of the "criminal element" in the society (as offenders were once called). The inmates were simply those who had been caught and processed through the criminal justice system.

Recognizing the potential bias in drawing theoretical conclusions from the study of those apprehended or incarcerated, criminologists have tended to focus their attention on those relatively unformed by imprisonment and labeling as ex-convict—the juvenile population—and this has especially been true of those researchers developing what can be called immediate-origin theories. The causes of crime are seen as a complex meshing of personal characteristics, social structure, culture, and patterns of relationships, all

113

leading up to initial involvement in a criminal pattern. These first experiences are largely those of young people; in fact, persons under the age of eighteen make up a considerable percentage of those apprehended for conventional crime. Efforts to determine the relative importance of factors leading up to this initial involvement are often made by looking closely at this crime-prone population.

Many of the dominant theories in criminology have grown out of studies of youth. What has emerged is a profuse literature on the etiology of juvenile delinquency—which can be applied to adult crime only indirectly, in the sense that large numbers of adult criminals were once youthful delinquents.

However, with the recent increased emphasis on upperworld crime, the focus of attention may now shift from juveniles to adults. One might assume —subject of course to empirical investigation—that most corporate and other white-collar offenders did not begin their criminal careers as juvenile delinquents, and that many propositions on crime developed through the study of youth may not be applicable to this population. However, theories of adult crime still lean heavily on studies of youth, and this will be particularly apparent as we look into theories dealing with the family, peer groups, and other immediate influences upon the development of each of us.

People are not simply products of structural determinants. Structural forces set the conditions that increase the probability that certain groups of individuals will engage in crime, but not all members of these groups do so. Other forces operate to influence individuals in their adjustments to structural conditions: these involve the immediate origins of the criminal act. Whereas wider-origin theories stress the nature of social institutions (the family, the school, and the peer and work reference groups), immediate-origin theories are concerned with the impact on some individuals of such groups and institutions. These institutions provide the individual with definitions for adjustments, attachments, meanings for actions, and rationalizations for behavior. A major assumption of theorists who emphasize immediate-origin "causes" is that both criminal and conforming behaviors are learned through association with meaningful others and through the socialization process. Family, peer, and other primary groups aid individuals in interpreting their positions in society and the expectations others have for them. In turn, individuals have an impact on these forces—forces which, unlike structural conditions, may be accepted or rejected.

*Crime as
Learned
Behavior:
Differential
Association*

114

Gabriel Tarde (b.1843–d.1904), French jurist and social thinker, was one of the first to view crime as a type of interaction process. His emphasis on social learning and imitation (Tarde, 1968) is considered "a cornerstone of present American criminological theories" (Vine, 1972: 292). For Tarde, crime was intimately tied to the individual's personal identity or self-concept and the customs, interests, and education transmitted through interaction with others and imitation of what is seen in the surrounding culture. Criminality thus represented socially acquired conduct.

Although Edwin Sutherland rejected this idea of imitation, he was the outstanding American adherent of learning theory, closely associated with Tarde. Sutherland proposed a model that he called differential association. The central thesis of his approach is that

> criminal behavior is learned with others in intimate personal groups. The learning includes techniques of committing criminal acts, plus the motives, drives, rationalizations, and attitudes favorable to the commission of crime. [Sutherland and Cressey, 1974: 75]

Thus, people become criminals not by imitating others but by being "taught" by others. Criminality is learned through social interaction, particularly in small, intimate groups. The content of the learning includes techniques of crime, a vocabulary of criminal rationalizations, and criminal conceptions of property, law, and the person. The formation of one's self-concept as a criminal or as a law-abiding citizen, or as both, is a function of observation, association, and identification with those who conceive and interpret the law in a manner favorable to its violation or to its observance, or to both. The concept of differential association hypothesizes that a person will become criminal if interpersonal relations present him or her with an excess of definitions favorable to the violation of law.

The basic principles of differential association have been put forth by Sutherland and Cressey (1974: 75–77) along the following lines:

1. Criminal behavior is learned. Negatively, this means that criminal behavior is not inherited as such; also, the person who is not already trained in crime does not invent criminal behavior, just as a person does not make mechanical inventions unless he has had training in mechanics.

2. Criminal behavior is learned in interaction with other persons in a process of communication. This communication is largely verbal but also includes "the communication of gestures."

3. The principal part of the learning of criminal behavior occurs within intimate personal groups. Negatively, this means that the impersonal agencies of communication, such as films and newspapers, play a relatively unimportant part in the genesis of criminal behavior.

4. When criminal behavior is learned, the learning includes both techniques of committing the crime—which are sometimes very complicated, sometimes very simple—and the specific direction of motives, drives, rationalizations, and attitudes.

5. The specific direction of motives and drives is learned from definitions of the legal codes as favorable or unfavorable. In some subcultures an individual is surrounded by persons who invariably define the legal codes as rules to be observed, while in others he is surrounded by persons whose definitions are favorable to the violation of the legal codes. In American society, these definitions are almost always mixed, with the consequence that there is culture conflict in relation to the legal codes.

6. A person becomes delinquent because of exposure to more definitions that favor violation of the law than definitions unfavorable to such violation. This is the principle of differential association. It refers to both criminal and

law-abiding associations and involves countervailing forces. When persons become criminal, they do so because of both contact with criminal patterns and isolation from anticriminal patterns. Any person inevitably assimilates the surrounding culture unless other patterns are present and in conflict with it. Negatively, the proposition of differential association means that associations that are neutral as far as crime is concerned have little or no effect on the genesis of criminal behavior. Much of a person's experience is neutral in this sense: e.g., learning to brush one's teeth has no negative or positive effect on behavior patterns relevant to law. Neutral behavior is important, however, especially insofar as it occupies the time of youth, so that they are not in contact with criminality while engaged in such neutral conduct.

7. Differential associations vary in frequency, duration, priority, and intensity. This means that associations with criminal and anticriminal behavior vary in these respects. "Frequency" and "duration" as modalities of associations are obvious and need no explanation. "Priority" is assumed to be important in the sense that lawful (or delinquent) behavior developed in early childhood may persist throughout life. This tendency, however, has not been adequately demonstrated, and priority seems to be important principally through its selective influence. "Intensity" is not precisely defined, but has to do with such things as the prestige of the source of a criminal or anticriminal pattern and with emotional reaction related to the associations. In a precise description of the criminal behavior of a person these modalities would be stated in quantitative form. Such a mathematical formula has not yet been developed, however.

8. The process of learning criminal behavior by association with criminal and anticriminal patterns involves all of the mechanisms involved in any other learning. Negatively, this means that the learning of criminal behavior is not restricted to the process of imitation. A person may be persuaded, for instance, to participate in criminal acts by associates; this process would not ordinarily be described as imitation.

9. While criminal behavior is an expression of general needs and values, it is not explained by those general needs and values, since noncriminal behavior is an expression of the same needs and values. Thieves generally steal in order to secure money, but, likewise, honest laborers work in order to secure money. The attempts by many scholars to explain criminal behavior by such general drives and values as the happiness principle, striving for social status, the money motive, or frustration have been and must continue to be futile, since they explain lawful behavior as completely as they explain criminal behavior.[1]

The theory of differential association does not explain why some people choose certain associations or become committed to a given set of definitions. Making the theory operational has centered primarily around the association with individuals, as opposed to the association with definitions. This has been necessary because of the inability to measure exposure to differing definitions adequately. Further, Sutherland's emphasis on the com-

---

1. The above is in part a quotation fom Sutherland and Cressey (1974: 75–77), in part a condensation and paraphrase.

munication and interaction process has led researchers to concentrate on measuring the interaction with deviant individuals.

Differential association as a theoretical perspective stresses the importance of interaction in intimate personal groups. Melvin DeFleur and Richard Quinney have indicated that Sutherland's proposition is internally consistent and capable of producing testable hypotheses. They have suggested that it can be reduced to a number of propositions, summarized as follows:

> Overt criminal behavior has as its necessary and sufficient conditions a set of criminal motivations, attitudes, and techniques, the learning of which takes place when there is exposure to criminal norms in excess of exposure to corresponding anticriminal norms during symbolic interaction in primary groups. [DeFleur and Quinney, 1966: 14]

Criminal behavior, then, is learned, and the learning is seen as a product of exposure to both norms and persons.

Robert Burgess and Ronald Akers (1966) have sought to elaborate the learning process suggested in this theory. They have pointed out that learning occurs as a process of reinforcement or punishment, and have reformulated Sutherland's original propositions to account for differential reinforcement. This learning process adopts the principles of operant conditioning, which means that stimuli following or contingent upon behavior determine the probability of its future occurrence. The amount and frequency of reinforcement for criminal acts and definitions increase the probability of crime.

In the approach of Burgess and Akers, learning is reinforced by those groups that create or control reinforcements. The responses of the most salient reference groups tend to encourage or inhibit behavior. The strength of the deviant behavior is a direct function of the amount, frequency, and probability of its reinforcement.

Reed Adams (1973) criticizes this application of operant principles by stressing the necessity of distinguishing between the acquisition and the maintenance of behavior. Sutherland, as Adams maintained, was concerned with acquisition, whereas differential reinforcement involves only maintenance.

However, the point at which operant learning takes place seems incidental to the theory's ability to explain involvement in crime. The theory has been criticized on the ground that it cannot explain certain types of criminality (Ball, 1957; Clinard, 1942; Hartung, 1965), yet it is one of the most widely tested theories proposed to date. Data supporting this theory have been both direct and indirect. Some research has provided evidence consistent with the theory, though not necessarily demonstrative of it. The implications for differential association have frequently been missed because they are not obvious or immediately apparent (Short, 1960).

In *Studies in Deceit*, for example, Edward Hartshorne and M. A. May (1928) presented a table of correlations of conceptions of right and wrong found among children and their associates. The highest correlations were for children and their parents, whereas progressively lower ones were obtained between the children and their friends, club leaders, and public school and Sunday school teachers (in that order). Since the priority, frequency, intensity, and duration of the children's associations descended in the expected order, the data were consistent with the differential association theory.

James Short initiated investigations into the relationship between differential association and delinquency, drawing his data from both institutionalized and noninstitutionalized groups (1957 and 1960 respectively). He focused his attention on companionship or interaction with friends defined by respondents as delinquent, rather than on officially defined deviants. His conclusions supported differential association as a significant variable in distinguishing deviants from others. Harwin Voss (1964) replicated Short's study in Hawaii, and similarly concluded that differential association with deviant friends can distinguish deviants from conforming people. Working in Sweden, Paul Friday (1972) used the scale developed by Voss and was able to make the same distinction; he was likewise able to distinguish between self-reported deviants and those who admitted few or no deviant acts. In Friday's Swedish study, differential association is the single strongest variable linked with theft.

Albert Reiss and A. Lewis Rhodes (1964) have attempted to test the theory in Tennessee. Basing their conclusions on a sample of 378 boys, ages twelve to sixteen, they found that the probability of committing a deviant act is highest when that act has also been committed by a member of one's peer group. This finding supports earlier studies by Marshall Clinard in both Iowa (1942) and Sweden (1960), where he found a significant relationship between stealing and membership in groups that steal. On the other hand, Reiss and Rhodes (1964) have noted that a distribution of six different lawbreaking acts among youths having various traits associated with delinquency conformed more closely to a random model than to differential association theory.

Further research, however, has supported the notion that an individual's deviant association is highly related to the commission of a deviant act. A national survey by the President's Commission on Law Enforcement and Administration of Justice (1967: 66) concluded, "The typical delinquent operates in the company of his peers, and delinquency thrives on group support. It has been estimated that between 60 and 90 percent of all delinquent acts are committed with companions." Companionship, then, as a component of initial deviation is strongly supported. Thomas Eynon and Walter Reckless (1961) also have documented this, in their study of Ohio youth. John Ball (1957) has found that youth associated with delinquents consistently hold positive attitudes toward stealing, while Daniel Glaser (1960) has contended that the most accurate factors in criminological prediction are consistent with the propositions of differential association.

Empirical criticisms of differential association theory center around the operational definitions given the terms "excess," "favorable," and "unfavorable." The empirical evidence for the theory has been based on implication and perceived association rather than a clearly measurable index. Other criticisms have suggested that the theory cannot account for episodic offenses. Donald Cressey (1953)—student and collaborator of Sutherland and a foremost adherent of the theory—nonetheless has found that embezzlers could not identify specific persons or agencies from whom they had learned behavior patterns favorable to trust violation. Other types of criminality do not fit in well with the theory—for example, "accidental" criminals, occasional situational offenders, and the nonprofessional shoplifter. To Don Gibbons (1971), differential associations may not be operative at all; instead, law-breaking may arise out of a combination of situational pressures and opportunities for criminality.

Reference Group and Subcultural Theories

Modifications have been suggested for the differential association model. Daniel Glaser (1956: 440) believes, for example, that the empirical referent for differential association would be more easily understood in terms of reference groups. He uses the term "differential identification," and suggests: "A person pursues criminal behavior to the extent that he identifies himself with real or imaginary persons from whose perspective his criminal behavior seems acceptable."

Support for the concept of differential association has been offered by Victor Matthews (1968), who has found that those who identify closely with delinquents are themselves more likely to be delinquent, while those who show low delinquency involvement are more likely to identify with nondelinquents. This identification with other delinquents and their norms, values, and beliefs has been referred to as "identification with a delinquent subculture." As Short (1968: 12) has indicated, one facet of delinquency essential to understanding it is the nature of the social relationships within the group: "The influence of particular subcultures on an individual's behavior depends, to a considerable extent, on the nature of his relations with other carriers of these subcultures."

Four major explanations have emerged that attempt to explain the origin and importance of subcultures (Hood and Sparks, 1970). An explanation popular in the late 1930s suggests that the subculture is a product of urban social disorganization. Youth develops an autonomous "society" as a consequence of lack of parental control and low emotional stability in the home.

Walter Miller (1958) offered a second view, that the subculture is generated from stable one-sex peer groups in the lower-class culture. In such groups, high value is placed on toughness, smartness, and excitement (see pp. 109–110).

To a third group of theorists (Cloward and Ohlin, 1960; Cohen, 1955), the subculture develops as a collective solution to shared problems, among which are status frustration and blocked opportunities. In joining together, youths are able to provide definitions, beliefs, and expectations for themselves and establish an achievable criterion for success.

A fourth view of the delinquent subculture is that it emerges out of leisure pursuits that emphasize toughness and masculinity (Matza and Sykes, 1961). Delinquency is seen as incidental, not inherent to the subculture. Youths are not committed to full-time conflict with conventional society;

119

their delinquent acts are episodic, and thus they only "drift" occasionally into them (Matza, 1964). The subculture provides a set of rationalizations necessary for neutralizing negative reactions to the act (Sykes and Matza, 1957) but does not necessarily require criminality.

Irrespective of the origin of the subculture, its role as a reference group for the individual is critically important for an understanding of youth criminality. This factor has been developed by Martin Haskell (1960–1961) as a theory of juvenile delinquency. In short, he contends that the family is the first reference group of the child and serves as a normative reference group —i.e., a group whose norms conform to those of the larger society. Prior to a city youth's participation in a delinquent act, a street group has usually become a personal reference group for him, and such a group, consisting of lower-class youths, is likely to have a delinquent culture.

Social Institutions and Social Control

Differential association and reference group theories suggest the importance for criminal involvement of identification with the peer group and its definitions of appropriate behavior. The importance of the peer group cannot be understood independently of the individual's interaction with others, particularly his family and school associates, and the degree of conventional control exerted by these groups on his behavior.

According to Ronald Akers (1977), effective control occurs when social sanctions successfully reinforce conventional behavior by rewarding it and punishing nonconformity. Conforming behavior develops over time through socialization by the family and other relations. The more that groups other than delinquent peers control rewards, the less is the probability of criminality. Therefore, some theorists have concentrated on the family as a factor in the cause of crime.

FAMILY AND CRIME

The family is considered important because of its early socialization role in shaping values, morality, and consequently behavior. The family has almost exclusive contact with children when they are the most dependent and easily influenced, and has continued intimate contact over a subsequent period of several years. It is the first social institution to affect behavior and provide knowledge of and access to the goals, means, and social expectations of the wider society. However, there may be deficiencies in the integration process between parent and child, so that the child fails to learn appropriate behaviors (Bredemeier and Stephenson, 1962: 126). Socialization may be inadequate for dealing with societal expectations, and youth may not learn clear definitions of appropriate norms (Toby, 1974: 87).

Families from which delinquent children come are frequently characterized by one or more of the following conditions: (1) other members of the family are criminalistic, immoral, or alcoholic; (2) one or both parents are absent by reason of death, divorce, or desertion; (3) there is a lack of parental control because of ignorance, indifference, full-time employment of both parents or illness; (4) home uncongeniality exists, as evidenced by domination of one member, favoritism, over-solicitude, over-severity, neglect, jealousy, or interfering relatives; (5) religious or other cultural differences, or differences in conventions and standards, are present; (6) there are economic difficulties, such as unemployment, poverty, crowded housing conditions, or poor arrangement of financial affairs (Davies and Day, 1974).

The family may affect crime directly by imparting delinquent behavior. Henry McKay and James McDonald in *Brothers in Crime* (1966) have indicated that older siblings may teach younger ones to steal. The Gluecks (1950) found that 70 percent of their delinquents had at least one parent with a criminal record. According to the Gluecks, drunkenness, crime, or immorality at home was found in 90 percent of delinquents but in only 54 percent of the control group. Joan and William McCord (1958) found the sons of offenders to have higher rates of criminality than the sons of others.

Above all, the family sets a value system which may be indirectly favorable to crime. Just as family values may predispose youth to choose certain types of recreational or sport activity or career, so too do they transmit basic values regarding response to threats, challenges, or frustrations. Adelaide Johnson and S. A. Szurek (1954) have concluded that parents' unwitting sanction or indirect encouragement is a major stimulus for truancy and other kinds of delinquency. Likewise, the subculture-of-violence thesis of Marvin Wolfgang and Franco Ferracuti (1967) is predicated on the assumption that families transmit basic values that in certain circumstances call for and expect violent responses. For example, a father who stresses physical prowess as a requirement for masculinity may easily transmit this definition to his son and directly or indirectly define violent behavior as acceptable—which may lead to assaultive criminality. Lawrence Severy (1973) studied delinquent and law-abiding high school students over a four-year period. Among these youths, when there had been low exposure in early years to the deviance of family members, greater exposure during adolescence led to increasing deviance. On the other hand, when family exposure had originally been high, increasing exposure led to rejection of delinquency.

Other perspectives dealing with the family and crime have stressed the role of the "broken home." In a controversial study, the Gluecks (1950) concluded that such a family pattern is a major cause of delinquency. Several studies since have tended to confirm this conclusion, but others have suggested that the broken home is but one of a number of variables that act together to generate illegal conduct. Studies demonstrating a relationship between broken homes and delinquency may be biased since most have sampled only lower-class delinquents. Jackson Toby (1957) found the broken home to be more significant if the family controls are traditionally strong; if family controls are weak, the broken home has little direct effect.

As early as 1929, Cyril Burt found no difference between delinquent and nondelinquent groups as a result of the father's death, but was of the opinion that divorce, separation, and desertion have a marked influence on delinquency.[2] Subsequent research conducted during the 1950s and 1960s

2. Much of Burt's work was later discredited. Today it is not clear how much of it was fraudulent, how much genuine.

revealed that while the broken home plays a major role in delinquency, the effect differs considerably among youths. The effect was greater in the working class than in other social classes.

In Norway, Nils Christie (1960) studied statistics for all males born in 1933, and found that 5 percent had become registered offenders by 1958. Comparing home structure for offenders and nonoffenders, he found that the home was broken 17 and 13 percent of the time respectively, a statistically insignificant difference. From this one would conclude that broken homes are not necessarily linked with delinquency for adolescent males. A study in Sweden showed a positive relationship between broken homes and delinquency among working class male youths only where other criminogenic factors were also present (Olofsson, 1971). The differential effect on females was investigated by Thomas Monahan (1957), who found that in the United States broken homes appear to have a greater effect in generating delinquency for females and blacks than for white males.

It is quite understandable that a parent's absence for whatever reason can be experienced as personal rejection, and that this in turn can weaken the sense of identity. Likewise, it is easy to appreciate that parents can be physically present but psychologically and socially absent. It is not necessary for divorce to occur to have a broken home (Glueck and Glueck, 1950). A low frequency of interaction between parents and between parents and children has consequences analogous to those of a broken home, in that it involves the giving of little sentiment or affection (Homans, 1950). The President's Task Force on Delinquency and Youth Crime emphasized the family interaction pattern as more significant in the etiology of delinquency than the physical structure of the familial unit (see Rodman and Grams, 1967).

The family may contribute to delinquency by tacitly condoning minor delinquent acts or failing to discipline appropriately or consistently (McCord and McCord, 1959). Parents may reinforce deviance by offhandedly bragging about their own adventurous acts when they were young, or may neutralize punishment by openly disagreeing over the appropriate response, thus reducing its effectiveness. One of the most important elements in the parent-child relationship seems to be consistency (Mays, 1972).

Finally, the family may predispose a child to delinquency through neglect and general deprivation. This may be not simply physical but may be personal neglect, as, for example, with the "poor rich kids" whose parents spend more money than time on them. Parental rejection and neglect create a condition wherein the child does not internalize parental norms. In such a situation, there is a predisposition to defy parents and others (Parsons, 1951). Neglect also reduces the efficacy of reward controls, and the youth may feel less guilty in identifying with his peers and using them as his dominant reference group.

Increasingly, researchers have come to the conclusion that the structure of the family is less important than the nature of the interaction within it. For example, F. Ivan Nye (1958) and Charles Browning (1960) have concluded that the legally and psychologically broken home is not as sure an indicator of delinquency as are other factors of family disorganization. The

McCords (1959) found that the quarrelsome home where the children are neglected leads to more delinquency than the broken home. Marital adjustment of the parents and overall family solidarity are significant, but Donald Peterson and Wesley Becker (1965) contend that the quality of parent-child relations is even more important. Above all, discipline, fairness, and consistency play a major role in inhibiting delinquency. Toby (1957) has suggested that American families exercise such weak control over adolescent males that there is in effect little difference in supervision between a well integrated family and a disorganized one. Thus, one would not expect the parent-child relationship to be as strong for adolescent boys as for girls. The well integrated family does give firm supervision to girls and preadolescents, whereas the disorganized family cannot. Therefore, girls and preadolescents from disorganized homes—in which discipline, fairness, and consistency are lacking—are more likely to be exposed to other criminogenic forces than are girls and preadolescents from well-organized homes.

In terms of discipline, parents of delinquent children more frequently resort to physical punishment than to reasoning, according to the Gluecks (1950), but Nye (1958) found that love-withdrawal is more significant than physical punishment in delinquency causation. In any case, the degree of parental affection appears to play an important role in the occurrence of delinquency.

In general, the family can have a positive impact in insulating individuals from criminal patterns, provided that it retains its ability to control rewards and effectively maintain positive attachments within the family unit. Commitments to family—what Hirschi (1969) has called attenuated attachments—reduce the probability of involvement in acts of deviance. Research by Michael Hindelang (1973) reaffirms the importance of family interaction and attachment. Delinquency is highest when family interaction and controls are weak (Rodman and Grams, 1967). Some parents do not supervise the recreational activities of their children, enforce bedtimes, perform activities as a group with them, or even eat meals together with them (Nye, 1958). For the delinquent this is a life free of restraint but without guidance. Studies have shown that these weak controls and low-frequency interaction patterns are more common in low income and ethnic minority families (Lewis, 1966). Edmund Vaz and John Casparis (1971) have reached a similar conclusion in their comparison of Canadian and Swiss youth. They indicate that the Canadian sample tended to be more peer-oriented and more deviant, while the Swiss favored their parents and engaged in fewer criminal acts. Further, the Swiss boys interacted more frequently with adults than with their peers.

Milos Kobal (1965), studying delinquency in Yugoslavia and England, has concluded that there tends to be more openness, communication, and general contact between youth and adults in Slovenia than in London. Marshall Clinard and Daniel Abbott (1973) found crime rates to be higher in Africa in those areas less likely to have stable family relationships. A report on living conditions of delinquents, prepared by the criminological institute at Ljubljana, Yugoslavia, states that one of the characteristics of families producing juvenile delinquents is the lack of an emotional bond between parents.

Przemyslaw Mackowiak and Stanislaw Ziembinski have reported a study in Poland that stresses the importance of socially positive role models (1971), and Albert Bandura and Richard Walters (1963) in the United States have reported that behavior copying is more frequent when a positive relationship exists. Paul Friday and Jerald Hage (1976) stress that isolation from the family is likely to increase a child's peer or deviant associations.

The family is thus seen as important as an immediate point of origin of crime, not because it causes crime per se, but because relationships within the family effectively influence the exposure to and importance of other norm-defining reference groups.

SCHOOLS AND CRIME

In our highly technical, industrial culture, education and schools play a key role in determining the eventual placement of an individual in society. In terms of length and intensity of exposure, education is considered, next to the family, the major force shaping the lives of American youth. The most general societal function of schools is to transmit knowledge, norms, and values, along with their orientational and motivational underpinnings (Clausen, 1968: 153). In essence, Emile Durkheim maintained, the school functions as the primary regulator of moral education for a nation and is "the sole moral environment where the child can learn methodically to know and to love" (1963: 67).

While the school functions as a major social integrator, it can also be viewed as a major contributor to delinquency. John Feldhusen and his colleagues (1973) have concluded after an eleven-year longitudinal study that only the family and the peer group are more pervasive influences in causing delinquency. Kenneth Polk and David Halferty (1966) found that delinquency is highly related to poor adjustment in school, being uniformly low among boys of all social classes doing well in school, while uniformly high among those doing poorly. Another follow-up study by Delbert Elliott and Harwin Voss (1974) found school to be the most critical institution in affecting patterns of delinquent behavior. The school ranks as more important than family or peers as an influence on exposure to and attitudes toward conforming and deviant behavior patterns.

Failure at school is often interpreted as failure of the pupil to respond rather than failure of the school to stimulate interest and develop a commitment to conformity. School success is vital in achieving favorable occupational and economic status; in Robert Merton's (1968) terms, it is a legitimate means to achieve social goals. School performance is dependent upon both the home and the neighborhood from which the children come and upon the way they are treated once in school, as well as upon individual, innate talents, abilities, and temperament. Recent teacher-writers clearly argue that lower-class "culturally disadvantaged" children are eager to learn and excited by the initial experience of school, but the schooling process, reliance on IQ tests that are social-class biased, "tracking," the physical condition of the school, and the attitudes of teachers soon deplete this initial motivation.

Social relationships within the school are important in understanding why those who do well have lower delinquency and crime rates than those who fail. Sutherland and Cressey suggest a sequential pattern that helps identify this process:

1. Some students, especially working-class students, lack the role-playing abilities necessary to meet the demands of the teachers and, especially, of the other students in school.

2. These students enter school at a competitive disadvantage because their life experiences have not provided the social skills, verbal skills, attitudes toward students, teachers, and scholarship, and familiarity with pencils and reading materials that are common among other students. To take a simple example, some first-graders have never seen an adult reading a newspaper, magazine, or book.

3. These disadvantages are enlarged rather than diminished when teachers and other students assume that the students experiencing them are bad, undesirable, stupid, or even sick, and then devote their time, attention, and affection to students assumed not to have these characteristics. In high schools, this "locking out" process has been shown to occur even among students who have verbal abilities such that they are capable of excellent work.

4. The eventual outcome is alienation from school, truancy, drop out, or the passive compliance necessary to graduate from high school, but without the social skills necessary for getting along with employers, fellow workers, and unfamiliar settings generally.

5. Some such youngsters do not become delinquent; they are so well integrated into families or peer groups placing a high value on conformity and educational success that they do not even become truant. But others are not thus "held into" the legitimate system for achieving success, and they drift into association with delinquent subcultures. [Sutherland and Cressey, 1978: 248–249]

Walter Schafer and Kenneth Polk (1967: 223), in a report for the Presidential Task Force on Delinquency and Youth Crime, state that "available evidence strongly suggests that delinquent commitments result in part from adverse or negative school experiences of some youth, and, further, that there are fundamental defects within the educational system, especially as it touches lower income youth." Students who fail become progressively excluded by individual teachers and other achieving students. Failure and rejection in turn make the school experience increasingly unsatisfying and frustrating.

There is an interaction between home and school that affects the school's ability to be a rewarding experience and to facilitate and reinforce commitments to conforming norms. Cultural background and socialization processes, based as they are on social-class distinctions, to a great extent determine children's behavioral patterns and personality structures before they enter school. Once in school, their behavioral patterns are observed and evaluated by the teacher—usually on the basis of middle-class role expectations, which may either reinforce the student's identity or tend to alienate that youth from the socialization and norm-transmission role of the school (Marshall, 1973). The alternative faced by youth is either to accept the social-role definitions given by the dominant interactive partners in the school, or to reject those definitions, thereby reducing the impact of school relationships in fulfilling their integrative functions.

The youth who is not performing adequately in school—socially or academically—often compensates by attempting to achieve prestige among peers who themselves are not achievers (Coleman, 1961). LaMar Empey and Steven Lubeck (1971: 50) found that decreased achievement results in strain, and increased strain enhances identification with delinquent peers. Peer group identification in turn can further increase strain and consequently lead to a search for delinquent solutions.

The effect on delinquency of competition and strain in school is shown in a study by Delbert Elliott (1966). He has hypothesized that if school adjustment and experience are causally related to delinquency, then delinquency will be lower among out-of-school youth than those in school. His findings indicate the highest delinquency rate to be among lower-SES dropouts *prior* to their leaving school. He also found the same boys to have the *lowest* rate of all *after* dropping out of school. Their out-of-school rate was less than one-third of their in-school rate. He thus concluded that the school experience contributes to and sustains delinquency.

This finding is supported by Elliott and Voss (1974), who for four years followed 2,600 students who entered junior high school in 1963. They found the delinquency rate to be significantly higher for those continuing in high school than for those who actually had dropped out. Furthermore, the evidence indicated that the dropouts had delinquency problems that began while in school but declined upon departure from school.

The school becomes an important factor in delinquency causation since it is at once both a socializing, integrating element and, ultimately, the source of economic reward. A person's anticipation of success in either deviant or conforming activities is in part a function of the degree of prior success (Glaser, 1972). Rewards for conforming behavior in school compete with rewards for deviant activities, and often a child can realistically anticipate deriving feelings of competence, self-esteem, and support more from delinquent peers than conforming adults. If rewards are greater out of school, truancy will increase. The interaction process and reward structure in school are therefore critical in understanding delinquency, and help to explain why truancy is one of the best statistical predictors of later delinquency (Glaser, 1962).

School, family, and peers should not be considered independent factors in the causation of crime. Each contributes to a process that affects the probability that a given individual will engage in crime. This process involves the development of commitments to either deviant or normative patterns and to the groups that transmit those patterns. Hirschi (1969) has argued that attachment to parents generates a wider concern for the approval of other authority figures and ultimately a belief that societal norms bind one's conduct. Michael Hindelang (1973) has empirically demonstrated an inverse relationship between attachments to parents, teachers, and school and school-related activities, on the one hand, and delinquency on the other. Predominant attachment to peers, in contrast, is related directly to involvement in crime. This, in essence, is what Sutherland's differential association theory implies: criminality increases with isolation from conventional norms; when isolation, rejection, and alienation decrease, there is a general reduction in criminality. Larry Karacki and Jackson Toby (1962) have indicated that lack of commitment to the adult way of life is at the root of delinquency. When they examined the shift of many delinquent gang members to law-abiding behavior, it appeared that these erstwhile delinquents tend to have moved from participation in the youth culture to adult roles, successfully returning to school or engaging in work. Ronald Akers (1977) contends that a lack of attachment to conventionality means that the youth is isolated from or unable to obtain sufficient reward for conformity in the family, school, or conforming peer groups. The lack of ties with a major socializing institution precedes deviance (Empey and Lubeck, 1971, ch. 13; Matza, 1964; Schur, 1973: 157–165; Short and Strodtbeck, 1965, ch. 10, 12).

Theory and
the Nature of
the Criminal Act
and Actor

Theories dealing with the wider and the immediate origins of crime both tend to isolate and evaluate forces that are primarily external to the individual. These forces serve systematically to determine the probability that some groups in the society will commit a criminal act, but in themselves they cannot explain that involvement. The "funnel effect"—the term used to describe the interaction of these forces—shows that urbanization, industrialization, and the impact of various social interactions tend to increase the risk that a person will feel that a deviant action offers a solution to immediate and chronic problems. Yet not everyone who shares these circumstances—whether blocked opportunity, poor integration at home or school, or high frequency and intensity of association with those following criminal patterns—will actually commit illegal acts.

Few attempts have been made to apply sociological principles to individual cases, but the critical point at which the criminal act takes place requires some analysis of this type. Two interacting elements seem to operate at this point: first is the self-image held by the individual and the role that he or she perceives can or should be played; second is the situation itself and the definition the individual applies to it. Once the criminal act occurs, a third element—the reaction of others—affects future situational definition and self-image.

The Self
and Crime
128

In all social conduct, an understanding of the sense of self and the playing of social roles is important in the interpretation of behavior. This is no less true for criminal than normative behavior. The self is developed through social experiences whereby the person obtains a sense of identity in the course of interaction with others. This self-image is largely a reflection of the view that others take of the individual as "good" or "bad," depending upon their consistency—except, of course, that some individuals may misperceive others' views or deliberately and consciously ignore or reject them. In most instances, however, a pattern of behavior develops that is consistent with the collective expectations of those surrounding the individual. George Herbert Mead (b.1863–d.1931)—a social psychologist and philospher who has had a notable influence on American social thought—refers to the wide gamut of people whose collective attitudes and responses impinge upon the person as "the generalized other." The individual, incorporating and often internalizing the attitudes of the generalized other, becomes subject to its control. Supplementing this generalized other are the values and attitudes of those surrounding people—family and peers and members of various reference groups—who have been termed "the significant others" (Mead, 1944).

A primary factor affecting whether one will commit a criminal act is self-concept, influenced by the perception of whether an act appears to be consistent with the expectations of significant others and will meet with their approval. The self-concept may act to precipitate crime or it may be an insulator against criminal values. Walter Reckless and his colleagues (1957) studied the "good" boy in the "bad" neighborhood in an attempt to determine why some boys follow acceptable patterns even in high-delinquency areas. They concluded that "good" boys are those capable of maintaining images of themselves as good. This favorable concept of self acts as an inner buffer, a containment against deviance (Reckless and Dinitz, 1967).

The positive self-concept represents an internalization of normative attitudes and meanings and reflects favorable socialization (Dinitz et al., 1962). The source of the self-concept and consequent behavioral expectations has been traced to primary group relations. Generally, boys conforming to behavioral patterns demanded by society think of themselves as "good" and are also thought of as "good" by parents and teachers. Michael Hindelang (1973) supports this view in his finding that attachments to parents and teachers are inversely related to attachments to peers and delinquency. Thus, when attachments to the primary socializing agents are high and internalization of their norms is strong, an inner containment against deviance tends to result.

Reckless (1961, 1973) proposes what has come to be known as the "containment theory." In this view, there are two dimensions of the individual's situation that determine his proneness to crime. In one, an effective family life and other *external* factors act as structural buffers to the individual's immediate social world and are able to hold him or her within bounds. In the other, *internal* containment involves self-control, good self-concept, high resistance to diversions, and the ability to handle conflict, direct oneself away from exciting risks, and stay out of trouble.

When a person conforms, it is because the external and internal containments are strong. In opposition to the containment forces are "*pull*" factors —such as "bad" companions, delinquent and criminal subcultures, and deviant groups—which draw the individual away from accepted norms. "*Push*" factors also operate against the containment forces. They include inner tensions, aggressiveness, and feelings of inadequacy and inferiority

(Reckless, 1973: 55–57). In a mobile, urban society internal containment takes on added significance; given a highly delinquent situation, the strength of an individual's positive self-concept may be the critical determinant of whether a criminal act will be performed.

Containment theory provides an explanation of a critical point in the process of becoming or not becoming criminal, and does so in terms of factors (such as self-concept) that can be abstracted, tested, and quantified. The paradigm provides an identification of immediate forces acting within and on the individual at any given moment and offers insight into the form that behavior is apt to take. Its disadvantage lies in the complex problem of balancing the various pushes and pulls in a manner allowing predictive statements to be made. Walter Reckless and Simon Dinitz have conducted studies over the years that support the relationship between self-concept and delinquency. Other researchers, however, have suggested that modifications are needed. Richard Quinney (1970) believes that "good" and "bad" concepts of self have been assumed rather than empirically verified, a criticism likewise made by Sandra Tangri and Michael Schwartz (1967: 187), who add, "A delinquent self-concept is not necessarily a negative concept." Along this line, Gary Jensen (1972: 94) found that many adolescents who think of themselves as delinquent still maintain positive self-esteem scores. Others have concluded that the relationship between self-concept and delinquency varies from context to context, depending upon social class, nature of peer group orientation, and other factors (Short and Strodtbeck, 1965: 140–184; Hall, 1966). None of the research, however, refutes the basic importance of the concept of self in either permitting or containing deviant acts.

Self-concept and behavior patterns are interdependent, notes Quinney (1970: 238). An individual develops a self-concept through interaction with others, and plays the role deemed appropriate to that self-image. In his developmental theory of delinquency, James Hackler has set forth the sequence through which the self and delinquent acts are linked:

> This developmental sequence could be made still more explicit and systematic by linking specific variables in a causal chain as follows: (a) having low esteem leads to (b) the anticipation on the part of others that ego will act badly or at least not be able to act properly; this leads to (c) ego's perception that others anticipate improper behavior if (i) opportunities to play conforming roles are perceived as blocked by those in dominant positions, such as teachers, and if (ii) ego views these self-relevant responses from primary and non-primary significant others as valid; this would lead to (d) the development of a delinquent self-concept; which leads to (e) the search for roles compatible with a delinquent self-concept; this leads to (f) delinquent behavior; and finally leads to (g) the selective endorsement of delinquent norms through dissonance-reducing mechanisms. [Hackler. 1971: 64]

The Situation

Delinquent and criminal acts constitute a small percentage of all acts committed by an individual. Few persons are career criminals in the sense that the systematic and regular pursuit of criminality is their main activity. Most

Chap. 7
*Theory and the
Nature of the Criminal
Act and Actor*

criminal acts are typically episodic, goal-oriented, and committed in response to certain stimuli. The nature of the situation becomes important, therefore, for purposes of interpretation and understanding. How an individual defines an immediate situation and the role he or she feels obligated to perform is critical. The meaning attached to given behavior and the way in which the situation is defined are cumulative results of wider-origin and immediate forces and self-concept.

Situational factors can confront individuals with conflicts, opportunities, pressures, status threats, and temptations. The pressures of the moment can affect, to varying extents, the values and behaviors of those involved. Scott Briar and Irving Piliavin (1965: 36–37) declare that delinquent acts of males "are prompted by short-term situationally induced desires experienced by all boys to obtain valued goods, to portray courage in the presence of or be loyal to peers, to strike out at someone who is disliked, or simply to 'get kicks.' "

The actual circumstances in which a person finds himself, and the meanings attached thereto, should not be minimized as etiological forces. As Kurt Lewin put it:

It is a simple fact, but still not sufficiently recognized in psychology and sociology, that the behavior of a person depends above all upon his momentary position. Often, the world looks very different before and after an event which changes the region in which a person is located. [Lewin, 1951: 137]

The situation acts as an inducement to reaffirm self-concept and identity, whether positive or negative. To many delinquent gang boys, attributes that they prize highly can be claimed only in social situations where something of consequence is risked. It is impossible to prove that one is "cool," "courageous," or "smart" without a situation in which there is something to be cool, courageous, or smart about (Wertman, 1967). A fight, for example, is defined by gang youths as a situation in which reputation or rank can be won or lost. Lewis Yablonsky has offered the following statement by a gang boy to illustrate this point:

I was walkin' uptown with a couple of friends, and we run into Magician and them there. They asked us if we wanted to go to a fight, and we said "Yes." When they asked me if I wanted to go to a fight I couldn't say, "No." I mean I could say, "No," but for old-time's sake, I said, "Yes." [Yablonsky, 1962: 13]

An intensive study of Chicago gangs by James Short and Fred Strodtbeck (1965) reinforces the importance of the situation as a precipitator of criminal activity. They have interpreted much aggression and other misbehavior as a response to individual status within the gang. The delinquent boy's self-concept in the context of the group is important. Some delinquent acts, therefore, are seen to have status-maintaining functions; much misconduct is designed to preserve the boys' reputations as courageous fighters. Thus, gang behavior may be seen as a rational balancing of the risk of immediate loss of status within the group against the risk of societal punishment.

According to Short and Strodtbeck, the delinquents they studied generally enforced middle-class values and standards, yet were more tolerant of "bad" behavior than were boys not associated with gangs. On the other hand, the gang boys showed limited social skills, poor intelligence scores, and anxiety over sexual adequacy and identity. The researchers have interpreted much of their behavior as responsive to the fragile sense of status of the youths studied.

Status is an important element in social relations. All persons, conforming or deviant, seek to define themselves as having some worth or value. Herbert Bloch and Arthur Niederhoffer (1958) have argued that adolescence, a period in which a great amount of criminality can occur, is by definition a time when clear-cut status is lacking. The individual is neither child nor adult, and our society places inconsistent and at times conflicting demands on those in that age group. There are few socially approved rites formally indicating that the adolescent has been transformed into an adult.

There are many conditions that may serve as a basis for the development of commitments to conformity. Among these, Briar and Piliavin (1965: 41) name belief in God, occupational aspirations, desire to perform well in school, and fear of material deprivation and punishment if arrested. However, even persons with strong commitments to conformity are sometimes tempted to engage in criminal acts, when their commitments do not appear threatened or when the motives to deviate are exceptionally strong.

For those caught between conflicting expectations or attachments, the choice between a normative and a criminal response may hinge upon the ability to rationalize or "neutralize" the deviant act. Studies of criminality indicate that most offenders recognize both the legitimacy of the social order and their own delinquency. What then, in a particular situation, accounts for the decision to violate known rules of conduct? Donald Cressey (1953) introduced the concept of rationalization to characterize the last phase of the embezzlement process; rationalization permits the embezzler to look upon his trust violation as noncriminal, justified, or part of a general line of action and chain of events for which he is not responsible and hence not accountable.

Gresham Sykes and David Matza (1957) have expanded the concept to apply to juvenile delinquent acts. A youth involved in a criminal act may define the circumstances and redefine the social rules so as to maintain an acceptable self-concept. A number of rationalizations or "techniques of neutralization" are employed. These allow the delinquent to engage in criminality without extreme psychological maladjustment (Downes, 1966: 75). Through neutralization, apologies are made but violations are deemed "acceptable" though not necessarily "correct." Previously inculcated norms, morals, and values are neutralized *before* or *while* the person engages in the conduct. The nature of the neutralization is contingent upon the self-concept and the situation itself.

Sykes and Matza (1957) identify five major techniques used in the process, which we paraphrase as follows:

1. *Denial of responsibility.* In this instance the delinquent deflects blame from himself by rationalizing that he was really not responsible for his acts.

CHAP. 7
*Theory and the
Nature of the Criminal
Act and Actor*

2. *Denial of injury.* Through rationalization the delinquent denies that he hurt anybody, cost anyone his property, or engaged in any major delinquent or ciminal activity.
3. *Denial of the victim.* In this instance, the delinquent accepts the fact that his act may have caused harm or injury but argues that the victim deserved such injury for previous acts committed against others.
4. *Condemnation of the condemners.* Focusing upon the motives and shortcomings of those who sit in judgment, he shifts blame from himself to his accusers. In exposing their shortcomings he silences his own sense of guilt or qualms concerning his deviance.
5. *Appeal to higher loyalties.* Ties and commitments to companions, family, or primary groups supercede other loyalties and take precedence over conformity to laws and social norms.

These techniques deflect disapproval by society and self and permit the maintenance of a positive self-image. They are, ironically, extensions of general "defenses to crime" contained in the conforming culture and incorporated into the criminal law (Akers, 1977).

The situation precipitating criminality cannot be viewed independently of the wider and immediate origins of the criminal act. This is brought out by Don Gibbons.

> The major implication of this work for the study of crime causation should be clear: perhaps more attention ought to be given to the possibility that a number of kinds of criminality are the work of individuals who are not characterized by any sort of clear-cut motivation toward law-breaking, that their behavior is not the outcome of some kind of differential learning. Instead, there may be a number of forms of criminality in which situational elements loom much larger than acknowledged heretofore. [Gibbons, 1971: 270]

A situation by itself is not sufficient to produce criminality, but it is critical; an act can be understood only in the light of the overall social processes operating on the individual at the time that the situation becomes real and a choice can be made. For some youths, no conscious choice may be involved at all; instead, their past experience, class position, and self-concept will dictate either a delinquent or normative solution.

Reactions to the Act: Labeling

Once an act has been committed, another and final stage in the process begins. Others react to it and sanction the actor in accordance with the meaning imputed to the particular act. The meaning of the act changes according to the surrounding situation, the nature of the offender and the victim, the visibility of the action, and the response of the enforcer. Some people apparently consider many criminal acts "all right"—e.g., burglaries by the FBI and CIA in the name of national security, or acts of retaliation and revenge by victims and their families. This means that the universality of law-breaking is attended by extensive particularism in the definition of an act as criminal (Phillipson, 1974: 115).

The differential response to acts and the relativity of the label "criminal" for some actors has received major attention from the so-called "labeling school" of theorists, which focuses less on the act itself and more on the application of the label "deviant" or "criminal" to the act. Howard Becker has argued (1973), "Deviance is *not* a quality of the act the person commits, but rather a consequence of the application by others of rules and sanctions to an 'offender.' The deviant is one to whom that label has successfully been applied."

Edwin Lemert (1951) was among the first to discuss the implications of reactions to deviant acts. He proposed that simple violation of societal rules may be situationally determined and considered as "primary" deviance. The intensity and severity of the reaction to this then affect the actor's attitudes and self-concepts, leading in some cases to subsequent changes in behavior and self-image. These changes create a new, "secondary" form of deviance which is far more harmful than the original act for which the individual was labeled deviant.

Literature analyzing the effects of labeling was quite popular during the 1970s, finding adherents in sociology and psychiatry. Some social scientists have combined labeling theory with conflict theory, conceiving of the criminal justice system as an expression of the differential power of political agents of society in formulating and administering criminal law (Quinney, 1970: 15–20). Quinney argues that the application of the criminal label reflects the vested interests of those who possess this power.

This perspective assumes the validity of the process of moving from primary to secondary deviance and emphasizes perceptions of acts by control agents rather than the meaning for the actors themselves. The societal reaction of norm enforcers is interpreted in terms of the class position and interests of the agents of social control and the class position of the deviant. Once they encounter deviant behavior, the agents of social control react in a manner that depends on their own social-class position, their perception of the dominant norms, the social class of the actors, and the discrepancy between the social-class position of the control agents and their perception of the expected role of the actor. Irving Piliavin and Scott Briar (1964) have observed that a youth becomes a "juvenile delinquent" because someone in authority has defined him as one, more often on the basis of color, attitude, or demeanor than the offense committed.

While the act itself may be a commonly assumed form of criminality, such as larceny or burglary, the conflict-labeling theorists argue that the creators of social policies, those who provide guidelines for societal reaction, are not neutral or impartial in their interpretations of what the norms or laws should be. At least in regard to criminal policy, Quinney points out what he feels are the biases. He asks:

> What, then, is the economic and political nature of criminal policy-making in America? My argument is that the ruling class formulates criminal policy for the preservation of domestic order, an order that assures the social and economic hegemony of the capitalist system. [Quinney, 1974: 59]

CHAP. 7
*Theory and the
Nature of the Criminal
Act and Actor*

The ruling class, the argument states, is able, directly and indirectly, through its economic, political, and social powers to determine, influence, and condition the construction of the normative structure that defines social order. It uses its powers to perpetuate the capitalist social and normative order by prescribing which social acts and actors will effectively be labeled deviant. Herbert Schiller, in discussing the normative manipulation of society, contends:

> The means of manipulation are many, but clearly, control of the informational and ideational apparatus at all levels is essential. This is secured by the operation of a simple rule of the market economy. Ownership and control of the mass media, like all other forms of property, is available to those with capital. Inevitably, radio- and television-station ownership, newspaper and magazine proprietorship, movie-making and book publishing are largely in the hands of corporate chains and media conglomerates. The apparatus is thus ready to assume an active and dominant role in the manipulative process. [Schiller, 1973: 4]

The act of labeling is not evil per se; it is the differential application and consequent implications of the label that are of primary importance in this perspective. Public stigma can carry devastating and permanent effects: the ex-con cannot get employment, the juvenile delinquent is shunned by other youths, the individual who once committed a sex crime is held in suspicion. Labeling theorists cite the possibility that societal responses may change a casual rule-breaker into a career criminal because of the disapproving, degrading, and isolating reactions to the behavior (Lemert, 1967; Becker, 1973).

There are no uniformly accepted propositions of labeling theory, though there are a number of underlying assumptions and themes central to the perspective. Clarence Schrag (1971: 89–91) and Edward Sagarin (1975: 128–129) have outlined a number of them. They include the following:

1. Actions derive their characteristics of "badness," not from their intrinsic content, but from the way in which they are defined by others, particularly by the rule-makers and rule-abiders in a society. In essence, no act is intrinsically criminal, nor for that matter evil.

2. It is not especially useful to look at the nature of the act or the characteristics of the individual in order to understand the phenomenon; rather, one must examine the nature of the condemning society and the process by which some people gain the power to place the label of deviant or criminal on others—i.e., a person does not become a criminal by violating the law but only by being designated a criminal by authorities.

3. The act of getting caught begins the labeling process. (This proposition—defended most vigorously by Kitsuse (1962)—appears to ignore the powerful effect that self-labeling has on the secret and unapprehended criminal or deviant; it has lost much of its support among the labeling adherents.)

4. The process of placing the label of deviant on an individual and reacting to him as a transgressor differs not only with the nature of the act but

with who he is. Official and unofficial reaction to deviance is not predictable from the act itself, but varies according to social class and power relationships, which would include factors of age, occupation, education, race, and others.

5. A label of deviant—or more frequently a label embodying the negative character of deviance without being the word itself—is placed on an individual, and this results, usually although not invariably, in new, secondary deviance that is more severe and hurtful to society than was originally the case. The placing of this label and the public identification of the individual as deviant, in this perspective, act to reinforce or "fix" the individual in that status.

6. There are careers in deviance, as in other roles and in occupations. These careers are facilitated by the official reaction to persons as deviant, particularly by their exclusion from the society of normals and incarceration with others cast out by society. Labeling is a process that eventually produces identification with the deviant image and subculture.

Considerable controversy has centered around the labeling perspective. Charles Wellford (1975) has evaluated empirical data for a number of these assumptions and found support for them to be weak. He concludes that there *are* intrinsically criminal acts, and seriously questions the assumption of extreme relativism. He presents conflicting evidence regarding the differential effect of personal characteristics in relation to societal reaction to an act, and cites William Hohenstein (1969), Donald Black and Albert Reiss (1970), and Jay Williams and Martin Gold (1972) among others who find the *act* the most important factor in assigning a label. On the other hand, Irving Piliavin and Scott Briar (1964), Aaron Cicourel (1968), Nathan Goldman (1963), Terence Thornberry (1973), and David Petersen and Paul Friday (1975) all reach the opposite conclusion. The data neither negate nor support the assumptions, perhaps because of research and methodological difficulties. In a collection edited by Walter Gove (1980), the social scientists generally agree that the labeling approach has not been empirically validated. In this work Travis Hirschi and Charles Tittle in particular take a strong position against the labeling perspective when applied to juvenile delinquency and crime. The entire controversy, with numerous citations, is nicely summarized by Fred Montanino (1977).

Joseph Rogers and M. D. Buffalo (1974) emphasize the interaction that occurs when a label is applied: there is negotiation between actor and labeler, and in the end this is what defines the label and affects its permanence—and thus the subsequent identity and activity of the alleged deviant. This is summarized by Edwin Schur (1971: 56) thus: "As imputation of deviant character inevitably incorporates some exercise of power . . . it is not surprising that various forms of negotiation and bargaining have been found to be a crucial element in labeling."

In this thinking, the secondary deviance does not come about in one fell swoop; simply to become caught and sanctioned does not necessarily and automatically produce acceptance of the deviant role. Instead, the impact of the societal reaction depends upon the nature of the interaction, the significance of the reactors, and shifting definitions of situations (Schur, 1971: 71).

In the face of deviant labeling, a number of alternatives may be pursued by the labeled individual. These are summarized by Rogers and Buffalo (1974) roughly as follows:

1. *Acquiescence.* He or she acknowledges the face validity of the deviant label.
2. *Repudiation.* The person rejects the label. There may be forthright denials: "I didn't do it!" "I've been framed!"
3. *Flight.* He or she attempts to flee from the label by running away, committing suicide, feigning insanity, or actually becoming mentally ill. Flight may be literal or figurative, physical or emotional.
4. *Channeling.* The label is assented to and utilized as a fulfilling means of self-expression and identity. A negative label is translated into a positive one—e.g., by joining Alcoholics Anonymous or another self-help group.
5. *Evasion.* The individual verbally excuses or neutralizes the label by offering explanations: broken home, parental rejection, bad companions, and the like.
6. *Modification.* He or she attempts to exchange the negative label for a better one. This is accomplished by changing the name, adjective, or image —as in "sick" for criminal, or "heavy drinker" for "alcoholic."
7. *Reinterpretation.* The deviant label and responsibility are accepted but verbally interpreted so as to put the actor in a favorable light. The terrorist for one side is the freedom fighter for the other.
8. *Alteration.* This is the rehabilitation goal, in which there is a change in behavior and with it a change in the label and accompanying identity.

These do not exhaust the possibilities. A ninth mode is mentioned by Rogers and Buffalo, which they term "redefinition." It consists of a change by society in its norms so that formerly deviant behavior becomes tolerated or accepted, if not encouraged (nonmarital sex, possession of marijuana). This does not represent a mode of individual adaptation, however, as do the others.

Some negatively labeled persons cope with the societal reaction by publicly embracing a highly valued status. Religion has served this purpose for some of those convicted in the Watergate scandal, for pornographers, and for violent criminals, including murderers.

Many criminologists are dismayed that labeling ignores the problem of etiology. However, it does provide some basis for interpreting reinvolvement in crime and redefining situations for which some people find a deviant solution. The label in effect may alter an individual's patterns of association and attachments, thus having an impact on the immediate origins of an act. But it may also affect the wider origins by blocking opportunity for jobs and effective integration into the conventional economic and social life of the community.

The conditions surrounding the criminal act must not be seen independently of the other forces in the society. Criminality emerges out of a continuous process of social interaction, not as a simple choice; it is dynamic, not simplistic, and can be viewed only in the context of the interaction between the actor and his immediate and wider social conditions.

On Theory: Summing Up

The century that has passed since Lombroso has thus seen a large number of efforts to arrive at a plausible explanation of crime. Some of these explanations have been reflections in the area of criminology of major intellectual movements that put forth new images of the human being; noteworthy examples along this line are theories influenced by Darwin, Marx, and Freud.

Although many theories have gained ascendancy at various times, only to be replaced by others at a later date, the earlier explanations were seldom entirely discarded. Rather, they were seen as having somewhat weaker explanatory power than their adherents first claimed, but they survived, perhaps in some weaker form, or they reappeared in a new form. Despite Sutherland's disclaimer, there is a clear line of development from the earliest imitation theories of Tarde to differential association, the latter in turn continuing to have its influence in the form of learning and reference group theories, to differential identification and other thrusts that have their vocal supporters. Biological theory has been reborn under the more careful name of biosocial, a clear effort not to fall into the pessimistic and socially dangerous orientations of Hooton and others who saw criminal tendencies in body build and physical stigmata and who thought in terms of criminal destinies and bad seeds. The new biosocial is more sophisticated, it will not be led into the trap of calling for wholesale elimination of unredeemable people, but it is again a nice example that theory is not so much discarded as it is renewed in an ever more acceptable form. And conflict theory, which had its strong supporters among the Marxists from late nineteenth century through the first decades of the twentieth century, was to make its reappearance in many forms: studies of conflict between groups in a heterogeneous society, as set forth by Wirth and later Sellin; the work of Merton on anomie which goes to the heart of conflicts that are built into the social structure; the emphasis in recent years on pluralism, neo-Marxism, and other forms of conflict by Vold, Quinney, Turk, and many younger and some older criminologists. Even the labeling perspective had it antecedents: as long ago as the turn of the century when W. E. B. DuBois saw many of the defeats and degradations of the black people as a result of the way they were defined in a hostile society; by Merton, who in an exquisite essay made a household term of the phrase "the self-fulfilling prophecy"; and all leading up to Tannenbaum, Lemert, and Becker, who saw people being tagged or labeled as deviant, delinquent, even criminal, and as a result of this label turning into what they had originally been defined (often wrongly, prematurely, or exaggeratedly) as being.

Theories have their own life histories. But although they have their lineage from previous theories that now appear archaic and good only for discard, this does not mean that all of the approaches formerly or presently being put forth can be reconciled. Nevertheless, just such reconciliation is a major focus, to which some people have turned their attention.

Those who develop theory cannot ignore that societies are undergoing rapid change. The influence of the mass media is no doubt greater than at any previous stage in history; whether this is a factor to account for the increased crime is something still too early to grasp. But it is worth serious investigation.

To sum up the numerous theories presented in these chapter, we would emphasize two issues:

First, there is a growing recognition that crime can only be understood in interdisciplinary terms. The three major disciplines that are coming together appear to be sociology, psychology, and biology. Some would reduce biology to the negligible; some would elaborate on the sociology by stressing political economy; and others would want to be certain that psychiatry is included somewhere, whether it comes under the rubric of psychology or biology or some new heading of its own. But without an interweaving of specialists who look at the phenomenon of crime from their various vantage points, theory is unlikely to advance.

Second, what has been, and is, remiss in theoretical criminology, in the opinion of many, is the spurious attempt to explicate all crime on the basis of one unitary, universal theory. Any theory that attempts to explain all crime, it is charged, cannot escape being a general theory of all human behavior, because criminal behavior encompasses a wide and divergent body of conduct. A general theory of crime would have to explain too much and therefore would explain too little. The essential questions are: What kinds of criminals, and what kinds of circumstances, result in the commission of what kinds of crime? In short, the development of criminal typologies, in this view, offers the most plausible approach to the etiology of crime.

ABRAHAMSEN, DAVID. *The Psychology of Crime.* New York: Columbia University Press, 1960.

ADAMS, REED. "Differential Association and Learning Principles Revisited." *Social Problems,* 1973, 20: 458–470.

AKERS, RONALD. *Deviant Behavior: A Social Learning Approach.* 2d ed. Belmont, Calif.: Wadsworth, 1977.

ANDERSON, NELS. *The Hobo: The Sociology of the Homeless Man.* Chicago: University of Chicago Press, 1923.

BALL, JOHN. "Delinquent and Non-Delinquent Attitudes Toward the Prevalence of Stealing." *Journal of Criminal Law, Criminology and Police Science,* 1957, 48: 259–274.

BANDURA, ALBERT, and RICHARD H. WALTERS. *Social Learning and Personality Development.* New York: Holt, Rinehart & Winston, 1963.

BECCARIA, CESARE. *Dei delitti delle pene.* 1764. Translated by E. Ingraham: *Essay on Crimes and Punishments.* Stanford, Calif.: Academic Reprints, 1953.

BECKER, HOWARD. "A Sacred-Secular Evaluation Continuum of Social Change." In *Transactions of Third World Congress of Sociology,* vol. 6. London: International Sociological Association, 1956.

BECKER, HOWARD S. *Outsiders: Studies in the Sociology of Deviance.* 2d ed. New York: Free Press, 1973.

BELL, WENDELL. "Anomie, Social Isolation, and the Class Structure." *Sociometry,* 1957, 20: 105–116.

**References
for Part**

BENTHAM, JEREMY. *An Introduction of the Principles of Morals and Legislation.* New York: Hafner, 1973. (First published in 1825.)

BLACK, DONALD, and ALBERT J. REISS, JR. "Police Control of Juveniles." *American Sociological Review,* 1970, 35: 63–77.

BLOCH, HERBERT A., and ARTHUR NIEDERHOFFER. *The Gang: A Study of Adolescent Behavior.* New York: Philosophical Library, 1958.

BONGER, WILLEM A. *Criminality and Economic Conditions.* New York: Agathon Press, 1967. (First published in English in 1916.)

BORDUA, DAVID. "Juvenile Delinquency and Anomie: An Attempt at Replication." *Social Problems,* 1958, 6: 230–238.

_____. *Sociological Theories and Their Implications for Juvenile Delinquency.* Washington, D.C.: U.S. Children's Bureau, 1960.

_____. "Delinquent Subcultures: Sociological Interpretations of Gang Delinquency." *Annals of American Academy of Political and Social Science,* 1961, 338: 120–136.

BRECKINRIDGE, SOPHONISBA P., and EDITH ABBOTT. *The Delinquent Child and the Home.* New York: Arno Press, 1970. (First published in 1912.)

BREDEMEIER, HARRY C., and RICHARD M. STEPHENSON. *The Analysis of Social Systems.* New York: Holt, Rinehart & Winston, 1962.

BRIAR, SCOTT, and IRVING PILIAVIN. "Delinquency, Situational Inducements, and Commitment to Conformity." *Social Problems,* 1965, 13: 35–45.

BROWNING, CHARLES. "Differential Impact of Family Disorganization on Male Adolescents." *Social Problems,* 1960, 8: 37–44.

BURGESS, ERNEST W. "The Study of the Delinquent as a Person." *American Journal of Sociology,* 1923, 28: 657–680.

BURGESS, ROBERT L., and RONALD L. AKERS. "A Differential Association-Reinforcement Theory of Criminal Behavior." *Social Problems,* 1966, 14: 128–147.

BURT, CYRIL. *The Young Delinquent.* London: University of London Press, 1929.

CANTOR, NATHANIEL. "The Search for Causes of Crime." *Journal of Criminal Law and Criminology,* 1932, 22: 854–863.

CHAMBLISS, WILLIAM J. *Crime and the Legal Process.* New York: McGraw-Hill, 1969.

CHAMBLISS, WILLIAM J., and ROBERT B. SEIDMAN. *Law, Order and Power.* Reading, Mass.: Addison-Wesley, 1971.

CHILTON, ROLAND J. "Continuity in Delinquency Area Research: A Comparison of Studies for Baltimore, Detroit, and Indianapolis." *American Sociological Review,* 1964, 29: 71–83.

CHRISTIANSEN, KARL O. "Industrialization and Urbanization in Relation to Crime and Juvenile Delinquency." *International Review of Criminal Policy,* 1960, 16: 3–8.

CHRISTIE, NILS. *Unge Norske lovovertraedere.* Oslo: Universitetsforlaget, 1960.

CICOUREL, AARON. *The Social Organization of Juvenile Justice.* New York: Wiley, 1968.

CLARK, JOHN P., and EUGENE P. WENNINGER. "Goal Orientation and Illegal Behavior among Juveniles." *Social Forces,* 1963, 42: 49–59.

CLAUSEN, JOHN, ed. *Socialization and Society.* Boston: Little, Brown, 1968.

CLINARD, MARSHALL B. "The Process of Urbanization and Criminal Behavior." *American Journal of Sociology,* 1942, 48: 202–213.

_____. "Secondary Community Influences and Juvenile Delinquency." *Annals of American Academy of Political and Social Science,* 1949, 261: 42–54.

_____ "Urbanization and Crime." In Clyde B. Vedder, ed., *Criminology: A Book of Readings,* pp. 238–246. New York: Dryden, 1953.

_____. "A Cross-Cultural Replication of the Relation of Urbanism to Criminal Behavior." *American Sociological Review,* 1960, 25: 253–257.

CLINARD, MARSHALL B., ed. *Anomie and Deviant Behavior.* New York: Free Press, 1964.

CLINARD, MARSHALL B., and DANIEL J. ABBOTT. *Crime in Developing Countries.* New York: Wiley, 1973.

CLINARD, MARSHALL B., and ROBERT F. MEIER. *Sociology of Deviant Behavior.* 5th ed. New York: Holt, Rinehart, & Winston, 1979.

CLOWARD, RICHARD A. "Illegitimate Means, Anomie, and Deviant Behavior." *American Sociological Review*, 1959, 24: 164–176.

CLOWARD, RICHARD A., and LLOYD E. OHLIN. *Delinquency and Opportunity: A Theory of Delinquent Gangs.* New York: Free Press, 1960.

COHEN, ALBERT K. "Juvenile Delinquency and the Social Structure." Ph.D. dissertation, Harvard University, 1951. Excerpted, "Multiple Factor Approaches," in Marvin E. Wolfgang, Leonard Savitz, and Norman Johnston, eds., *The Sociology of Crime and Delinquency*, pp. 77–80. New York: Wiley, 1962.

———. *Delinquent Boys: The Culture of the Gang.* New York: Free Press, 1955.

COLEMAN, JAMES S. *The Adolescent Society.* New York: Free Press, 1961.

CORTÉS, JUAN B. (with Florence M. Gatti). *Delinquency and Crime: A Biopsychosocial Approach.* New York: Seminar Press, 1972.

CRESSEY, DONALD R. *Other People's Money: The Social Psychology of Embezzlement.* New York: Free Press, 1953.

CRESSEY, PAUL G. *The Taxi-Dance Hall: A Sociological Study in Commercialized Recreation and City Life.* Chicago: University of Chicago Press, 1932.

DAVIES, LYNN, and E. C. DAY. "The Criminal and Social Aspects of Families with a Multiplicity of Problems." *Australian and New Zealand Journal of Criminology*, 1974, 7: 197–213.

DEFLEUR, LOIS B. "Alternative Strategies for the Development of Delinquency Theories Applicable to Other Cultures." *Social Problems*, 1969, 17: 30–39.

DEFLEUR, MELVIN, and RICHARD QUINNEY. "A Reformulation of Sutherland's Differential Association Theory and a Strategy for Empirical Verification." *Journal of Research in Crime and Delinquency*, 1966, 3: 1–22.

DENTLER, ROBERT, and LAWRENCE J. MONROE. "Social Correlates of Early Adolescent Theft." *American Sociological Review*, 1961, 26: 733–743.

DIAMOND, BERNARD L. "The Psychiatric View." In Seymour Halleck and Walter Bromberg, eds., *Psychiatric Aspects of Criminology*, pp. 40-52. Springfield, Ill.: Thomas, 1968.

DINITZ, SIMON, FRANK R. SCARPITTI, and WALTER C. RECKLESS. "Delinquency Vulnerability: A Cross Group and Longitudinal Analysis." *American Sociological Review*, 1962, 27: 515–517.

DOWNES, DAVID. *The Delinquent Solution.* New York: Free Press, 1966.

DRIVER, EDWIN D. "Charles Buckman Goring." In Mannheim, 1972: 429–442.

DURKHEIM, EMILE. *Suicide: A Study in Sociology.* New York: Free Press, 1951. (First published, in French, in 1897.)

———. *The Division of Labor in Society.* New York: Free Press, 1964. (First published, in French, in 1893; in English in 1933.)

———. *Education and Sociology.* New York: Free Press, 1963.

ELLIOTT, DELBERT S. "Delinquency, School Attendance and Dropout." *Social Problems*, 1966, 13: 307–314.

ELLIOTT, DELBERT S., and HARWIN L. VOSS. *Delinquency and Dropout.* Lexington, Mass.: Lexington Books, 1974.

ELLIOTT, MABEL A. *Crime in Modern Society.* New York: Harper & Row, 1952.

EMPEY, LAMAR T., and STEVEN G. LUBECK. *Explaining Delinquency.* Lexington, Mass.: Lexington Books, 1971.

ENGELS, FRIEDRICH. *Die Lage der Arbeitenden Klasse in England.* Stuttgart, 1892. Translated by W. O. Henderson and W. H. Chaloner: *The Condition of the Working Class in England.* Stanford, Calif.: Stanford University Press, 1968.

EYNON, THOMAS G., and WALTER C. RECKLESS. "Companionship at Delinquency Onset." *British Journal of Criminology,* 1961, 2: 162–170.

FEDERAL BUREAU OF INVESTIGATION. See Uniform Crime Reports. 1980.

FELDHUSEN, JOHN F., JOHN R. THURSTON, and JAMES J. BENNING. "A Longitudinal Study of Delinquency and Other Aspects of Children's Behavior." *International Journal of Criminology and Penology,* 1973, 1: 341–351.

FORSSTRÖM, KARL-ERIK. *Brottslighet i siffor.* Stockholm; Aldus/Bonniers, 1965.

FOX, RICHARD G. "The XYY Offender: A Modern Myth?" *Journal of Criminal Law, Criminology and Police Science,* 1971, 62: 59–73.

FRIDAY, PAUL C. "Differential Opportunity and Differential Association in Sweden." Ph.D. dissertation, University of Wisconsin, 1970.

_____. "La verifica delle teorie della struttura differenziale della opportunità delle associazioni nella societa Svedese." *Quaderni di Criminologia Clinica,* 1972, 14: 279–304.

_____. "Research on Youth Crime in Sweden: Some Problems in Methodology." *Scandinavian Studies,* 1974, 46: 20–30.

FRIDAY, PAUL C., and JERALD HAGE. "Youth Crime in Postindustrial Societies: An Integrated Perspective." *Criminology,* 1976, 14: 347–368.

FRIEDLANDER, KATE. *The Psychoanalytic Approach to Juvenile Delinquency.* New York: International Universities Press, 1947.

GEIS, GILBERT. *Not the Law's Business.* 2d ed. New York: Schocken Books, 1979. (First published in 1972.)

GIBBONS, DON C. "Observations on the Study of Crime Causation." *American Journal of Sociology,* 1971, 77: 262–278.

GLASER, DANIEL. "Criminality Theories and Behavioral Images." *American Journal of Sociology,* 1956, 61: 433–444.

_____. "Differential Association and Criminological Prediction." *Social Problems,* 1960, 8: 6–14.

_____. "The Differential Association Theory of Crime," In Arnold M. Rose, ed., *Human Behavior and Social Processes,* pp. 425–442. Boston: Houghton Mifflin, 1962.

_____. *Adult Crime and Social Policy.* Englewood Cliffs, N.J.: Prentice-Hall, 1972.

GLASER, DANIEL, and KENT RICE. "Crime, Age, and Employment." *American Sociological Review,* 1959, 24: 679–686.

GLUECK, SHELDON, and ELEANOR GLUECK. *Unraveling Juvenile Delinquency.* Cambridge, Mass.: Harvard University Press (for the Commonwealth Fund), 1950.

_____. *Physique and Delinquency.* New York: Harper & Row, 1956, Reprinted, New York: Kraus Reprint Co., 1970.

GOFFMAN, ERVING. *The Presentation of Self in Everyday Life.* Garden City, N.Y.: Doubleday, 1959.

GOLDMAN, NATHAN. *The Differential Selection of Juvenile Offenders for Court Appearance.* New York: National Council on Crime and Delinquency, 1963.

GORDON, DAVID M. "Capitalism, Class and Crime in America." In Charles E. Reasons, ed., *The Criminologist: Crime and the Criminal,* pp. 66–88. Pacific Palisades, Calif.: Goodyear Publishing, 1974.

GORING, CHARLES. *The English Convict: A Statistical Study.* Montclair, N.J.: Patterson Smith, 1972. (First published in England in 1913.)

GOVE, WALTER R., ed. *The Labelling of Deviance: Evaluating a Perspective.* 2d ed. Beverly Hills, Calif.: Sage, 1980.

HACKLER, JAMES C. "A Developmental Theory of Delinquency." *Canadian Review of Sociology and Anthropology*, May 1971, 8: 61–75.

HAKEEM, MICHAEL. "A Critique of the Psychiatric Approach to the Prevention of Juvenile Delinquency." *Social Problems*, 1958, 5: 194–206.

HALL, JEROME. *Theft, Law and Society*. Indianapolis: Bobbs-Merrill, 1952.

HALL, PETER M. "Identification with the Delinquent Subculture and Level of Self-Evaluation." *Sociometry*, 1966, 29: 146–158.

HALLECK, SEYMOUR L. *Psychiatry and the Dilemmas of Crime: A Study of Causes, Punishment, and Treatment*. New York: Harper & Row, 1967.

HART, H.L.A. *Law, Liberty, and Morality*. Stanford, Calif.: Stanford University Press, 1963.

HARTSHORNE, EDWARD YARNELL, JR., and M. A. MAY. *Studies in Deceit*. New York: Macmillan, 1928.

HARTUNG, FRANK. *Crime, Law, and Society*. Detroit: Wayne State University Press, 1965.

HASKELL, MARTIN R. "Toward a Reference Group Theory of Juvenile Delinquency." *Social Problems*, 1960–1961, 8: 220–230.

HAUSER, PHILIP, ed. *Urbanization in Latin America*. New York: Columbia University Press, International Documents Service, 1960.

HEALY, WILLIAM. *The Individual Delinquent: A Text-Book of Diagnosis and Prognosis for All Concerned in Understanding Offenders*. Montclair, N.J.: Patterson Smith, 1969. (First published, Boston: Little, Brown, 1915.)

HINDELANG, MICHAEL J. "Causes of Delinquency: A Partial Replication and Extension." *Social Problems*, 1973, 20: 471–487.

HIRSCHI, TRAVIS. *Causes of Delinquency*. Berkeley: University of California Press, 1969.

HOEFNAGEL, G. PETER. *The Other Side of Criminology*. Deventer, Holland: Kluwer, 1973.

HOHENSTEIN, WILLIAM. "Factors Influencing the Police Disposition of Juvenile Offenders." In Thorsten Sellin and Marvin Wolfgang, eds., *Delinquency: Selected Studies*, pp. 138–149. New York: Wiley, 1969.

HOLLINGSHEAD, AUGUST. *Elmtown's Youth*. New York: Wiley, 1949.

HOMANS, GEORGE. *The Human Group*. New York: Harcourt Brace Jovanovich, 1950.

HOOD, ROGER, and RICHARD SPARKS. *Key Issues in Criminology*. London: World University Library, 1970.

HOOK, SIDNEY, ed. *Psychoanalysis: Scientific Method and Philosophy*. New York: New York University Press, 1959.

HOOTON, EARNEST A. *Crime and the Man*. Cambridge, Mass.: Harvard University Press, 1939.

IBRAHIM, AZMY ISHAK. "Disorganization in Society, But Not Social Disorganization." *American Sociologist*, 1968, 3: 47–48.

JANSON, CARL-GUNNAR. *Det differentierade samhället*. Stockholm: Prisma, 1968.

JENSEN, GARY F. "Delinquency and Adolescent Self-Conceptions: A Study of Personal Relevance of Infraction" *Social Problems*, 1972, 20: 84–103.

JOHNSON, ADELAIDE M., and S. A. SZUREK. "Etiology of Antisocial Behavior in Delinquents and Psychopaths." *Journal of American Medical Association*, 1954, 32: 814–817.

KADISH, SANFORD H. "The Crisis of Overcriminalization." *Annals of American Academy of Political and Social Science*, 1967, 374: 157–170.

KARACKI, LARRY, and JACKSON TOBY. "The Uncommitted Adolescent: Candidate for Gang Socialization." *Sociological Inquiry*, 1962, 32: 203–215.

KITSUSE, JOHN I. "Societal Reaction to Deviant Behavior: Problems of Theory and Method." *Social Problems*, 1962, 9: 247–256.

KOBAL, MILOS. *Delinquent Juveniles from Two Different Cultures*. Ljubljana: Revija za Kriminalistiko in Kriminologijo, 1965.

KOBRIN, SOLOMON. "The Conflict of Values in Delinquency Areas." *American Sociological Review*, 1951, 16: 653–661.

KOLKO, GABRIEL. *The Triumph of Conservatism*. New York: Free Press, 1963.

KRETSCHMER, ERNEST. *Physique and Character*. New York: Harcourt, Brace, 1926.

LAMBERT, VIRGINIA. "An Investigation of the Relationship of Self-Conception to Adjudication for Delinquency." Ph.D. dissertation, University of Wisconsin, 1969.

LANDER, BERNARD. *Toward an Understanding of Juvenile Delinquency*. New York: Columbia University Press, 1954.

LEMERT, EDWIN M. *Social Pathology: A Systematic Approach to the Theory of Sociopathic Behavior*. New York: McGraw-Hill, 1951.

_____. *Human Deviance, Social Problems, and Social Control*. Englewood Cliffs, N.J.: Prentice-Hall, 1967.

LEWIN, KURT. *Field Theory in Social Science*. New York: Harper & Row, 1951.

LEWIS, HYLAN. "Child Rearing among Low-Income Families." In Louis A. Ferman, Joyce L. Kornbluh and Alan Haber, eds., *Poverty in America: A Book of Readings*, pp. 342–353. Ann Arbor: University of Michigan Press, 1965.

LEWIS, OSCAR. *La Vida: A Puerto Rican Family in the Culture of Poverty—San Juan and New York*. New York: Random House, 1966.

LINDESMITH, ALFRED A., and YALE LEVIN. "The Lombrosian Myth in Criminology." *American Journal of Sociology*, 1937, 42: 653–671.

LOMBROSO, CESARE. *Crime: Its Causes and Remedies*. Montclair, N.J.: Patterson Smith, 1968. (First published in English in 1911.)

LOMBROSO-FERRERO, GINA. *Criminal Man, According to the Classification of Cesare Lombroso*. Montclair, N.J.: Patterson Smith, 1972. (First published in 1911.)

LÓPEZ-REY, MANUEL. *Crime: An Analytical Appraisal*. New York: Praeger, 1970.

LOTTIER, STUART. "Distribution of Criminal Offenses in Metropolitan Regions." *Journal of Criminal Law and Criminology*, 1938, 29: 37–50.

MACKOWIAK, PRZEMYSLAW, and STANISLAW ZIEMBINSKI. "Social Aspects of Sources of Criminality and Its Prevention and Control." *International Review of Criminal Policy*, 1971, 29: 25–31.

MACNAMARA, DONAL E. J., and EDWARD SAGARIN. *Sex, Crime, and the Law*. New York: Free Press, 1977.

MANNHEIM, HERMANN, ed. *Pioneers in Criminology*. 2d ed. Montclair, N.J.: Patterson Smith, 1972.

MANNHEIM, HERMANN, and LESLIE WILKINS. *Prediction Methods in Relation to Borstal Training*. London: H. M. Stationery Office, 1955.

MARSHALL, T. F. "An Investigation of the Delinquency Self-Concept Theory of Reckless and Dinitz." *British Journal of Criminology*, 1973, 13: 227–236.

MATTHEWS, VICTOR M. "Differential Identification: An Empirical Note." *Social Problems*, 1968, 14: 376–383.

MATZA, DAVID. *Delinquency and Drift*. New York: Wiley, 1964.

MATZA, DAVID, and GRESHAM SYKES. "Juvenile Delinquency and Subterranean Values." *American Sociological Review*, 1961, 26: 712–719.

MAYS, JOHN BARRON. *Juvenile Delinquency, the Family, and the Social Group*. London: Longmans, 1972.

MCCORD, JOAN, and WILLIAM MCCORD. "The Effects of Parental Role Model on Criminality." *Journal of Social Issues*, 1958, 14(3): 66–75.

MCCORD, WILLIAM, and JOAN MCCORD. *The Origins of Crime*. New York: Columbia University Press, 1959.

MCDILL, EDWARD L. "Anomie, Authoritarianism, Prejudice, and Socio-Economic Status: An Attempt at Clarification." *Social Forces*, 1961, 39: 239–245.

McDonald, Lynn. *Social Class and Delinquency*. Hamden, Conn.: Archon Books, 1969.

McKay, Henry D., and James F. McDonald. *Brothers in Crime*. Chicago: University of Chicago Press, 1966.

Mead, George Herbert. *Mind, Self and Society*. Chicago: University of Chicago Press, 1944.

Mednick, Sarnoff, and Karl O. Christiansen eds. *Biosocial Bases of Criminal Behavior*. New York: Gardner Press, 1977.

Meier, Dorothy L., and Wendell Bell. "Anomia and Differential Access to the Achievement of Life Goals." *American Sociological Review*, 1959, 24: 189–208.

Merton, Robert K. *Social Theory and Social Structure*. New York: Free Press, 1968.

Miller, Walter B. "Lower Class Culture as a Generating Milieu of Gang Delinquency." *Journal of Social Issues*, 1958, 14(3): 5–19.

Mills, C. Wright. "The Professional Ideology of Social Pathologists." *American Journal of Sociology*, 1943, 49: 165–180.

Mizruchi, Ephraim H. "Social Structure and Anomia in a Small City." *American Sociological Review*, 1960, 25: 645–654.

Monachesi, Elio. "Cesare Beccaria." In Mannheim, 1972: 36–50.

Monahan, Thomas P. "Family Status and the Delinquent Child: A Reappraisal and Some New Findings." *Social Forces*, 1957, 35: 250–258.

Montanino, Fred. "Directions in the Study of Deviance: A Bibliographic Essay, 1960–1977," In Edward Sagarin, ed., *Deviance and Social Change*, pp. 277–304. Beverly Hills, Calif.: Sage Publications, 1977.

Morris, Norval, and Gordon Hawkins. *The Honest Politican's Guide to Crime Control*. Chicago: University of Chicago Press, 1970.

Myerhoff, Howard L., and Barbara G. Myerhoff. "Field Observations of Middle-Class 'Gangs.' " *Social Forces*, 1964, 42: 328–336.

Nettler, Gwynn. *Explaining Crime*. New York: McGraw-Hill, 1978.

Newman, Donald J. "Sociologists and the Administration of Criminal Justice." In Arthur B. Shostak, ed., *Sociology in Action*, pp. 177–187. Homewood, Ill.: Dorsey Press, 1966.

Nye, F. Ivan. *Family Relationships and Delinquent Behavior*. New York: Wiley, 1958.

Nye, F. Ivan, James F. Short, Jr., and Virgil J. Olson. "Socioeconomic Status and Delinquent Behavior." *American Journal of Sociology*, 1958, 63: 381–389.

Olofsson, Birgitta. *Vad var det vi sa!* Stockholm: Utbildningsforlaget, 1971.

Park, Robert E., ed. *The City*. Chicago: University of Chicago Press, 1925.

Parsons, Talcott. *The Social System*. New York: Free Press, 1951.

Petersen, David M., and Paul C. Friday. "Early Release from Incarceration: Race as a Factor in the Use of 'Shock Probation.' " *Journal of Criminal Law and Criminology*, 1975, 66: 79–87.

Peterson, Donald R., and Wesley C. Becker. "Family Interaction and Delinquency." In Herbert C. Quay, ed., *Juvenile Delinquency: Research and Theory*, pp. 36–99. Princeton, N.J.: Van Nostrand, 1965.

Phillipson, Michael. *Understanding Crime and Delinquency*. Chicago: Aldine, 1974.

Piliavin, Irving, and Scott Briar. "Police Encounters with Juveniles." *American Journal of Sociology*, 1964, 70: 206–214.

Polk, Kenneth, and David S. Halferty. "Adolescence, Commitment, and Delinquency." *Journal of Research in Crime and Delinquency*, 1966, 4: 82–96.

President's Commission on Law Enforcement and Administration of Justice. *The Challenge of Crime in a Free Society*. Washington, D.C.: Government Printing Office, 1967.

Quicker, John C. "The Effect of Goal Discrepancy on Delinquency." *Social Problems*, 1974, 22: 76–86.

QUINNEY, RICHARD. *The Social Reality of Crime*. Boston: Little, Brown, 1970.

———. *The Problem of Crime*. New York: Dodd, Mead, 1975.

———. *Critique of Legal Order: Crime Control in Capitalist Society*. Boston: Little, Brown, 1974.

RACHMAN, STANLEY, ed. *Critical Essays on Psychoanalysis*. New York: Pergamon Press, 1963.

REASONS, CHARLES E. "The Politicizing of Crime, the Criminal, and the Criminologist." *Journal of Criminal Law and Criminology*, 1973, 64: 471–477.

RECKLESS, WALTER C. *Vice in Chicago*. Montclair, N.J.: Patterson Smith, 1969. (First published, Chicago: University of Chicago Press, 1933.)

———. "A New Theory of Delinquency and Crime." *Federal Probation*, December 1961, 25: 42–46.

———. *The Crime Problem*. 5th ed., New York: Appleton-Century-Crofts, 1973.

RECKLESS, WALTER C., and SIMON DINITZ. "Pioneering with Self-Concept as a Vulnerability Factor in Delinquency." *Journal of Criminal Law, Criminology and Police Science*, 1967, 58: 515–523.

RECKLESS, WALTER C., SIMON DINITZ, and BARBARA KAY. "The Self Component in Potential Delinquency and Potential Non-Delinquency." *American Sociological Review*, 1957, 22: 566–570.

REISS, ALBERT J., JR., and A. LEWIS RHODES. "The Distribution of Juvenile Delinquency in the Social Class Structure." *American Sociological Review*, 1961, 24: 720–732.

———. "An Empirical Test of Differential Association Theory." *Journal of Research in Crime and Delinquency*, 1964, 1: 5–18.

ROBERTS, ALAN H., and MILTON ROKEACH. "Anomie, Authoritarianism, and Prejudice: A Replication." *American Journal of Sociology*, 1956, 61: 355–358.

ROBINSON, WILLIAM S. "Ecological Correlations and the Behavior of Individuals." *American Sociological Review*, 1950, 15: 351–357.

RODMAN, HYMAN. "The Lower-Class Value Stretch." *Social Forces*, 1963, 42: 205–215.

RODMAN, HYMAN, and PAUL GRAMS. "Juvenile Delinquency and the Family: A Review and Discussion," In President's Commission on Law Enforcement and Administration of Justice, *Task Force Report: Juvenile Delinquency and Youth Crime*, pp. 188–221. Washington, D.C.: Government Printing Office, 1967.

ROGERS, JOSEPH W., and M. D. BUFFALO. "Fighting Back: Nine Modes of Adaptation to a Deviant Label." *Social Problems*, 1974, 22: 101–118.

ROSE, ARNOLD. *Five Hundred Borstal Boys*. Oxford: Blackwell, 1954.

SAGARIN, EDWARD. *Deviants and Deviance: An Introduction to the Study of Disvalued People and Behavior*. New York: Praeger, 1975.

SALTER, ANDREW. *The Case Against Psychoanalysis*. New York: Citadel Press, 1963.

SCHAFER, STEPHEN. *Theories in Criminology*. New York: Random House, 1969.

SCHAFER, WALTER E., and KENNETH POLK. "Delinquency and the Schools." In President's Commission on Law Enforcement and Administration of Justice, *Task Force Report: Juvenile Delinquency and Youth Crime*, pp. 222–277. Washington, D.C.: Government Printing Office, 1967.

SCHILLER, HERBERT. *The Mind Managers*. Boston: Beacon Press, 1973.

SCHMID, CALVIN F. *Social Saga of Two Cities: An Ecological and Statistical Study of the Social Trends in Minneapolis and St. Paul*. Minneapolis: Minneapolis Council of Social Agencies, 1937.

SCHRAG, CLARENCE. *Crime and Justice: American Style*. Washington, D.C.: Government Printing Office, 1971.

SCHUESSLER, KARL F., and DONALD R. CRESSEY. "Personality Characteristics of Criminals." *American Journal of Sociology*, 1950, 55: 476–484.

SCHUR, EDWIN M. *Crimes without Victims*. Englewood Cliffs, N.J.: Prentice-Hall, 1965.

———. *Our Criminal Society*. Englewood Cliffs, N.J.: Prentice-Hall, 1969.

———. *Labeling Deviant Behavior: Its Sociological Implications*. New York: Harper & Row, 1971.

———. *Radical Non-Intervention: Rethinking the Delinquency Problem*. Englewood Cliffs, N.J.: Prentice-Hall, 1973.

SELLIN, THORSTEN. *Culture Conflict and Crime*. New York: Social Science Research Council, Bulletin 41, New York, 1938.

SEVERY, LAWRENCE J. "Exposure to Deviance Committed by Valued Peer Groups and Family Members." *Journal of Research in Crime and Delinquency*, 1973, 10: 35–46.

SHAH, SALEEM A., and LOREN H. ROTH. "Biological and Psychophysiological Factors in Criminality." In Daniel Glaser, ed., *Handbook of Criminology*, pp. 101– 173. Chicago: Rand McNally, 1974.

SHAW, CLIFFORD R. *Delinquency Areas: A Study of the Geographic Distribution of School Truants, Juvenile Delinquents, and Adult Offenders in Chicago*. Chicago: University of Chicago Press, 1929.

———. *The Jack-Roller: A Delinquent Boy's Own Story*. Chicago: University of Chicago Press, 1931a.

———. *The Natural History of a Delinquent Career*. Chicago: University of Chicago Press, 1931b.

———. *Brothers in Crime*. Chicago: University of Chicago Press, 1938.

SHAW, CLIFFORD R., and HENRY D. McKAY. *Social Factors in Juvenile Delinquency*. National Commission of Law Observance and Enforcement: Report on the Cause of Crime, vol. 2, no. 13. Washington, D.C.: Government Printing Office, 1931.

———. *Juvenile Delinquency and Urban Areas: A Study of Rates of Delinquents in Relation to Differential Characteristics of Local Communities in American Cities*. Chicago: University of Chicago Press, 1942.

SHELDON, WILLIAM H. (with Emil M. Hartl and Eugene McDermott). *Varieties of Delinquent Youth*. Darien, Conn.: Hafner, 1970. (First published, New York: Harper & Row, 1949.)

SHORT, JAMES F., JR. "Differential Association and Delinquency." *Social Problems*, 1957, 6: 233–239.

———. "Differential Association as a Hypothesis: Problems of Empirical Testing." *Social Problems*, 1960, 8: 14–25.

———. "Gang Delinquency and Anomie." In Marshall B. Clinard, ed., *Anomie and Deviant Behavior*, pp. 98–127. New York: Free Press, 1964.

———. "On Gang Delinquency and the Nature of Subcultures." In James F. Short, Jr., ed., *Gang Delinquency and Delinquent Subcultures*. New York: Harper & Row, 1968.

SHORT, JAMES F., JR., and F. IVAN NYE. "Extent of Unrecorded Juvenile Delinquency: Tentative Conclusions." *Journal of Criminal Law, Criminology and Police Science*, 1958, 49: 296–302.

SHORT, JAMES F., JR., and FRED L. STRODTBECK. *Group Processes and Gang Delinquency*. Chicago: University of Chicago Press, 1965.

SHORT, JAMES F., JR., RAMON RIVERA, and RAY A. TENNYSON. "Perceived Opportunities, Gang Membership and Delinquency." *American Sociological Review*, 1965, 30: 56–67.

SHORT, JAMES F., JR., RAY A. TENNYSON, and KENNETH I. HOWARD. "Behavior Dimensions of Gang Delinquency." *American Sociological Review*, 1965, 28: 411–428.

SIMPSON, RICHARD L., and H. MAX MILLER. "Social Status and Anomia." *Social Problems*, 1963, 10: 256–264.

SPECTOR, PAUL E. "Population Density and Unemployment: The Effects on the Incidence of Violent Crime in the American City." *Criminology*, 1975, 12: 399–401.

SPERGEL, IRVING. *Racketville, Slumtown, Haulburg: An Exploratory Study of Delinquent Subcultures*. Chicago: University of Chicago Press, 1964.

SROLE, LEO. "Social Integration and Certain Corollaries: An Exploratory Study." *American Sociological Review*, 1956, 21: 709–716.

SUTHERLAND, EDWIN H. "Crime and the Conflict Process." *Journal of Juvenile Research*, 1929, 13: 38–48.

SUTHERLAND, EDWIN H., and DONALD R. CRESSEY. *Criminology*. Philadelphia: Lippincott. 9th ed., 1974; 10th ed., 1978.

SUTHERLAND, EDWIN H., and HARVEY J. LOCKE. *Twenty Thousand Homeless Men: A Study of Unemployed Men in the Chicago Shelters*. New York: Arno Press, 1971. (First published, Philadelphia: Lippincott, 1936.)

SYKES, GRESHAM M., and DAVID MATZA. "Techniques of Neutralization: A Theory of Delinquency." *American Sociological Review*, 1957, 22: 664–670.

SZABO, DENIS. *Crimes et villes: Etude statistique de la criminalité rurale en France et en Belgique*. Paris: Editions Cujas, 1960.

TAFT, DONALD R. "Influence of the General Culture on Crime." *Federal Probation*, September 1966, 30: 16–23.

TAFT, DONALD R., and RALPH W. ENGLAND, JR. *Criminology*. 4th ed. New York: Macmillan, 1964.

TANGRI, SANDRA S., and MICHAEL SCHWARTZ. "Delinquency Research and the Self-Concept Variable." *Journal of Criminal Law, Criminology and Police Science*, 1967, 58: 182–190.

TARDE, GABRIEL. *Penal Philosophy*. Montclair, N.J.: Patterson Smith, 1968. (First published, Boston: Little, Brown, 1912.)

TAYLOR, IAN, PAUL WALTON, and JOCK YOUNG. *The New Criminology: For a Social Theory of Deviance*. New York: Harper & Row, 1974.

THOMAS, W. I., and FLORIAN ZNANIECKI. *The Polish Peasant in Europe and America*. New York: Knopf, 1927.

THORNBERRY, TERENCE P. "Race, Socioeconomic Status and Sentencing in the Juvenile Justice System." *Journal of Criminal Law and Criminology*, 1973, 64: 90–98.

THRASHER, FREDERIC M. *The Gang: A Study of 1,313 Gangs in Chicago*. Chicago: University of Chicago Press, 1927. Abridged ed., 1963.

TITTLE, CHARLES R., WAYNE J. VILLEMEZ, and DOUGLAS A. SMITH. "The Myth of Social Class and Criminality." *American Sociological Review*, 1978, 43: 643–656.

TOBY, JACKSON. "The Differential Impact of Family Disorganization." *American Sociological Review*, 1957, 22: 505–512.

_____. "The Socialization and Control of Deviant Motivation." In Daniel Glaser, ed., *Handbook of Criminology*, pp. 85–100. Chicago: Rand McNally, 1974.

TÖNNIES, FERDINAND. *Community and Society*. Trans. by Charles P. Loomis. New York: Harper & Row, 1957.

TUMIN, MELVIN, and RAY C. COLLINS. "Status Mobility and Anomie: A Study in Readiness for Desegregation." *British Journal of Sociology*, 1959, 10: 253–267.

TURK, AUSTIN T. "Prospects for Theories of Criminal Behavior." *Journal of Criminal Law, Criminology and Police Science*, 1964, 55: 454–461.

_____. "Conflict and Criminality." *American Sociological Review*, 1966, 31: 338–352.

UNIFORM CRIME REPORTS. *Crime in the United States, 1979*. Washington, D.C.: Federal Bureau of Investigation, 1980. (Published annually.)

UNITED NATIONS. *Urbanization in Asia and the Far East*. Proceedings of the Joint U.N./UNESCO Seminar, Bangkok, August 8-18, 1958. SS.57.V7A. New York: United Nations.

VAN DEN BERGHE, PIERRE L. *Man in Society: A Biosocial View.* 2d ed. New York: Elsevier, 1978.

VAZ, EDMUND W. "Delinquency and the Youth Culture: Upper and Middle-Class Boys." *Journal of Criminal Law, Criminology and Police Science,* 1969, 60: 33–46.

———. *Middle Class Juvenile Delinquency.* New York: Harper & Row, 1967.

VAZ, EDMUND W., and JOHN CASPARIS. "A Comparative Study of Youth Culture and Delinquency: Upper Class Canadian and Swiss Boys." *International Journal of Comparative Sociology,* March 1971, 12: 1–23.

VINE, MARGARET S. WILSON, "Gabriel Tarde." In Mannheim, 1972: 292–304.

VOLD, GEORGE B. *Theoretical Criminology.* 2d ed., revised by Thomas J. Bernard. New York: Oxford University Press, 1979. (First published in 1958.)

VOSS, HARWIN L. "Differential Association and Reported Delinquent Behavior." *Social Problems,* 1964, 12: 78–85.

WARNER, W. LLOYD. Yankee City. New Haven, Conn.: Yale University Press, 1963.

WASHBURN, S.L. "Review of *Varieties of Delinquent Youth,* by W. H. Sheldon." *American Sociological Review,* 1951, 16: 10–14.

WELLFORD, CHARLES. "Labeling Theory and Criminology: An Assessment." *Social Problems,* 1975, 22: 332–345.

WERTMAN, CARL. "The Functions of Social Definitions in the Development of Delinquent Careers." In President's Commission on Law Enforcement and Administration of Justice, *Task Force Report: Juvenile Delinquency and Youth Crime,* pp. 155–170. Washington, D.C.: Government Printing Office, 1967.

WILLIAMS, JAY, and MARTIN GOLD. "From Delinquent Behavior to Official Delinquency." *Social Problems,* 1972, 20: 209–229.

WILSON, EDWARD O. *Sociobiology: The New Synthesis.* Cambridge: Belknap Press of Harvard University Press, 1975.

WIRTH, LOUIS. "Culture Conflict and Misconduct." *Social Forces,* 1931, 9: 484–492.

———. "Urbanism as a Way of Life." *American Journal of Sociology,* 1938, 44: 1–24.

WOLF, PREBEN. "Crime and Social Class in Denmark." *British Journal of Criminology,* July 1962, 13: 5–17.

WOLFGANG, MARVIN E. "A Preface to Violence." *Annals of American Academy of Political and Social Science,* 1966, 364: 1–17.

———. "Urban Crime." In James Q. Wilson, *The Metropolitan Enigma,* pp. 270–311. New York: Doubleday, 1970.

———. "Cesare Lombroso." In Mannheim, 1972: 232–291.

WOLFGANG, MARVIN E., and FRANCO FERRACUTI. *The Subculture of Violence: Towards an Integrated Theory in Criminology.* London: Tavistock, 1967.

YABLONSKY, LEWIS. *The Violent Gang.* New York: Macmillan, 1962.

ZORBAUGH, HARVEY W. *The Gold Coast and the Slum: A Sociological Study of Chicago's Near North Side.* Chicago: University of Chicago Press, 1929.

PART III

Criminal Behavior: Systems, Offenders, Victims

Violent
Personal Crime

For purposes of orderly description, study, analysis, and derivation of theory, it is desirable to have a method of grouping into subsystems or categories the various phenomena, events, people, and ideas that relate to the object of attention. In criminology, there have been a number of such systems. In this chapter and the four following, we shall deal with the nature of offenses, leaning heavily on the typology of the criminal behavior systems constructed by Marshall B. Clinard and Richard Quinney (1973). They view criminal behavior systems as constructions of types by which "concrete occurrences can be described and compared within a system of theoretical dimensions that underlie the types." They conceptualize nine types among the criminal behavior patterns extracted from the research literature, and describe each along five theoretical dimensions:

1. Legal aspects of selected offenses
2. Criminal career of the offender
3. Group support of criminal behavior
4. Correspondence between criminal and legitimate behavior
5. Societal reaction and legal processing

In using the Clinard-Quinney system, we introduce some modifications of our own. We have singled out for study and analysis eight overlapping areas among criminal behavior patterns:

1. Violent personal crime
2. Professional and career crime
3. Conventional crime against property
4. Organized crime

5. White-collar and upperworld crime
6. Political crime
7. Public-order offenses
8. Sexual crime

We believe that almost all offenses can be subsumed under one of these categories. One can make entirely different categories, in which there might be a special group, for example, consisting of narcotic offenses. However, in this example, the most serious violations are probably part of organized crime, and the least serious part of public-order offenses (particularly if one includes the marijuana trade). Most narcotic addicts who become caught up in the criminal justice system do so because of their involvement with other crimes, and it is these other crimes—such as burglary, robbery, or interpersonal violence—that are described here, rather than whether the offender is addicted to drugs.

More difficult is the problem of overlapping areas. Organized crime contains a great deal of violence against the person, and white-collar crime violations of property; political crime can be extremely violent, as can a sexual offense. However, a remedy that would divide crime merely into violent and nonviolent acts would cover too broad a spectrum for analysis and would not isolate the special character of some offenses as, for example, political, sexual, or others as part of organized crime. Nevertheless, the descriptions here are not meant to preclude other methods of classification that can be more useful for different purposes.

Our discussion of the eight categories follows, with one exception, an order of what appears to be decreasing public concern, indignation, and fright. This order does not represent a normative judgment. We are not contending that white-collar or political crimes are inherently less threatening than organized crime, the latter less so than professional and career crime —but only that public concern appears to follow such an order. The public is, of course, heterogeneous and fickle, and shows different degrees of concern for various individual acts and types of acts found within any of our groupings. Even violent crimes arouse more or less indignation depending upon the motive, offender, victim, circumstances, and the other elements surrounding the act.

The exception is sexual crime, which we place last, outside our continuum from most to least anxiety-provoking. As a category, it includes forcible rape—certainly one of the most important violent acts—and prostitution, generally regarded as a nuisance and at worst a public-order offense.

We start, then, with violent personal crime.

A violent personal crime is an illegal act that inflicts or attempts to inflict physical injury upon another person. Criminal homicide and aggravated assault represent clear-cut, well-researched patterns of violent personal criminal behavior. So does forcible rape, but it will be discussed later, in the section on illegal sexual conduct (Chapter 12), as it constitutes an offense— the most serious—in that category. Sometimes child molestation is included as a violent crime against the person, but it too is better studied as a sexual crime; it is probably accompanied quite frequently not so much by violence or even the threat or fear of it as by intimidation of the young victim. Kidnapping certainly can involve violence, but it has a low incidence and has not been widely researched.

We have excluded robbery from this category because it is primarily a property crime associated with a career of theft, although it has a potential for violence. Similarly, arson is a crime against property, although it can result in many deaths and injuries (such deaths are not generally studied as part of the statistics on murder). Many individual acts of violence, such as assault, murder, rape, arson, and vandalism, are committed during wars, riots, and demonstrations but are different in origin, nature, and motivation from such acts of individual violence as homicide and assault. Violence occurring in labor or race riots, lynching mobs, juvenile delinquent gang fights, or violence utilized by syndicate criminals is collective in nature and does not lend itself to analysis as acts of individual violence. Finally, there is political terrorism—best understood, we believe, as an aspect of political crime.

LEGAL ASPECTS OF SELECTED OFFENSES

Criminal homicide means murder (usually differentiated by degree, depending on premeditation and other factors), described in the Uniform Crime Reports as "the willful (nonnegligent) killing of one human being by another." Excluded from the official count are "deaths caused by negligence, suicide, or accident; justifiable homicides, which are the killings of felons by law enforcement officers in the line of duty or by private citizens; and attempts to murder or assaults to murder, which are scored as aggravated assaults." The unintended killing of someone during the commission of a crime is termed "felony-murder," although the slaying itself may not have been premeditated, and is officially counted as murder and handled as such by the criminal justice system.

According to Uniform Crime Reports, there were 21,456 murders in the United States in 1979. The murder rate—expressed as the number of people reported killed per 100,000 population—ranged from a low of 8 in the Northeast to 13 in the South; for the country as a whole it was 9.7. It is generally agreed that the majority of all murders are committed by a relative or other person having a close interpersonal relationship with the victim.[1] For 1979, the FBI reported that 52 percent of the murder victims were acquainted with the assailant, and 16.8 percent related to the offender. A great deal of interest has centered around the type of weapon used; as shown in Figure 8-1, handguns account for half of all murders.

Aggravated assault is an illegal attack upon a person for the purpose of inflicting severe bodily injury, usually attempted or accomplished by the use of a weapon or other means likely to produce serious bodily harm or death.

1. This is often referred to as murder by "relatives or friends," an expression we abjure as it seems to take liberties with the concept of friendship.

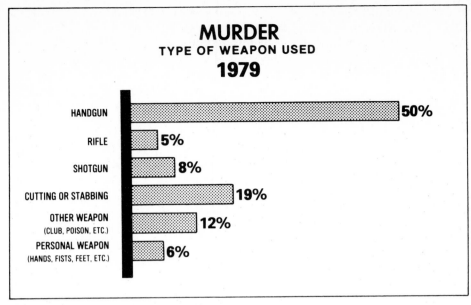

MURDER
TYPE OF WEAPON USED
1979

HANDGUN	**50%**
RIFLE	**5%**
SHOTGUN	**8%**
CUTTING OR STABBING	**19%**
OTHER WEAPON (CLUB, POISON, ETC.)	**12%**
PERSONAL WEAPON (HANDS, FISTS, FEET, ETC.)	**6%**

FIGURE 8-1

SOURCE: Uniform Crime Reports, 1980, p. 12.

However, if death results, the offense is escalated to murder and is not categorized as aggravated assault. In 1979 there were some 614,000 aggravated assaults committed in the United States and reported to police. The rate per 100,000 inhabitants was 279.1, a sharp rise from the early and middle 1960s and a rise of 69 percent during the decade.

In the nature of the victim-offender relationship and the attack (the use of physical force to settle an argument or disagreement) this offense is similar to murder. As contrasted with the 63 percent of murders committed with firearms (handguns, rifles, and shotguns), 23 percent of serious assaults were committed with such weapons in 1979.

The element—usually one of chance—that prevents aggravated assault from becoming criminal homicide by death of the victim is related in part to the use or non-use of a firearm. However, better medical technology and more rapid movement of the victim to medical facilities are believed to have simultaneously slowed down the increase in the murder rate and accelerated that of aggravated assaults. Despite the similarity in the behavior and sometimes in the intent, the legal definitions of aggravated assault and murder are quite distinct. As might be expected, reports of aggravated assault to the police are not as accurate as those of criminal homicide. On the basis of victimization studies, many scholars believe that aggravated assaults are grossly underreported. Both the offenders and the victims of murder and aggravated assault are most frequently males between the ages of eighteen and thirty. The proportion of female victims is rather low because assaults upon them are often categorized as rape or attempted rape, but even if rape and aggravated assault were combined, male victims would far outnumber female.

Except for paid killers and enforcers utilized by crime syndicates, murderers and assaulters do not generally have criminal careers centered on systematic violence. Some offenders identify with criminal subcultures, others do not—but very few see themselves as professional criminals utilizing a violent modus operandi. However, research reports on arrests for these two offenses conflict: some find the offenders relatively free from previous arrest for crimes of violence, some claim that they have for the most part no previous arrest record at all, while others find a high incidence of arrest for property crime and violent personal crime as well (Clinard and Quinney, 1973: 27–34). It seems likely that these divergent studies have tapped different types of arrested offenders. These types can include first offenders who under pressure reacted once in a violent fashion; conventional property offenders, habitual and recidivistic (convicted of three or more violent offenses), who resort to violence when apprehended or impeded during the commission of a property crime; and finally, a truly violent group of offenders whose life-style involves physical violence as a built-in reactive mechanism to problematic contingencies. In a study of all persons arrested for murder in Philadelphia during a two-year period, Marvin Wolfgang (1958) found that 66 percent had a previous arrest record. Of these, more had been previously arrested for aggravated assault than for all types of property offense combined.

F. H. McClintock (1963) examined the criminal records and social backgrounds of offenders convicted of crimes of violence in London during the years 1950, 1957, and 1960. The acts included homicide, attempted murder, felonious assault, rape and other violent sex crime, and possession of firearms and other offensive weapons. The report found that 80 percent of these violent offenders had no previous convictions for violent crime. However, 20 percent of them had previously engaged in indictable violent acts for which they were not convicted (fighting while drunk, intimidating and attacking citizens, disturbances in public places, and gang fights). Violent offenders for the most part were single, unskilled, and living away from home in high-crime areas.

In the McClintock study, a hard-core group of violent recidivists, comprising 4 percent of all persons convicted for crimes of violence in 1950 and 1957, emerged as a significant class of offenders. In contrast with others convicted of violent crime, the hard-core recidivists had in their records more serious property offenses, malicious damage, sex violations, fights and attacks in public houses, attacks on police as well as strangers and neighbors, aggressive behavior in everyday life, and unreported violence. They had usually been incarcerated as juveniles and had served time repeatedly in various jails and prisons. In a five-year follow-up study of the hard-core recidivists convicted in 1950, McClintock found that 60 percent had again been convicted (half of them for violent offenses).

In an examination of the arrest histories of 400 inmates of the District of Columbia Reformatory, Julian Roebuck (1967) found two mixed patterns of violence: the first a triple pattern consisting of assault, drunkenness, and larceny; the second a double pattern of assault and drunkenness. The former offenses were more episodic and were conventional crimes against property. Those in the double-pattern group consisted of hard-core violent types in terms of life-style. Few of them had ever been arrested for property crime, but they were more psychopathic, were unlike offenders in other categories who resorted to criminal violence, and displayed an early and continuing pattern of violence in their criminal and social histories.

Marvin Wolfgang (1974: 248–249) studied a birth cohort consisting of almost 10,000 boys born in 1945, most of them in Philadelphia. Of these boys, 627 were defined as chronic offenders. Although representing only 6.3 percent of the entire cohort, they accounted for more than half of all the delinquent acts committed by the group and were heavily represented among those who had perpetrated violent offenses. The chronic offenders accounted for 53 percent of the serious personal attacks, 62 percent of property offenses, and 71 percent of robberies (not included in the two previous figures). Of all violent acts committed by white males in the cohort, 45 percent could be accounted for by the hard-core group; for nonwhites, the figure rose to 70 percent. Wolfgang concluded that the chronic offenders represented hard-core delinquents.

GROUP SUPPORT OF CRIMINAL BEHAVIOR

It has often been stated that acceptance of the use of violence varies by country, region, state, neighborhood, social class, occupation, race and ethnicity, sex, and age (see Beattie and Kenney, 1966; Clinard and Quinney, 1973: 30–39; Wolfgang and Ferracuti, 1967; Gastil, 1971; Miller, 1958). Sociologists have attempted to explain these differentials in terms of general cultural or subcultural patterns of violence. Some have claimed—with others offering counterarguments and strong denials—that there is a high incidence of violent crime and personal violence in the United States that derives from the unique American experience (see discussion of this in Skolnick, 1969). The country was settled, they assert, in large part by European adventurers, renegades, transported criminals, and malcontents, who seized land and subdued with force the native Americans, and then built a part of their wealth by exploiting kidnapped slaves. They achieved nationhood by violent revolution and moved westward in a continuous struggle with a hostile physical and social environment. The frontier saw the violence of sheriff and posse, and after the Civil War the South witnessed the destructive violence of the march through Georgia and the resubjugation of the freedmen by night terror, hooded riders, and lynch law.

The American character, it is said, has embodied two conflicting elements, puritanism and sensuality. The passage of unenforceable laws in the area of personal morality has led to the organized dispensation of illegal goods and services (syndicated crime), based upon corruption and violence. Politics in the United States is fraught with violence, assassinations, and political riots (Nieburg, 1969).

Nonetheless, this thesis does not easily withstand cross-cultural examination. There are many nations with more violent politics, more murders, assassinations, palace coups, and acts of political terrorism, and far smaller rates of interpersonal violence. Australia was founded, even more so than the United States, by transported convicts, had a great struggle to subjugate the native population, and engaged in a long effort to come to grips with a hostile environment, but did not emerge with interpersonal violence on the scale known in America.[2]

Some have seen American group and institutional support for violence in the media, on the one hand, and in the "politics of overkill," on the other. The literature is preoccupied with violence and the language replete with it, particularly in its colloquialisms. Our national sports represent the epitome of acceptable violence. All of these factors reflect and generate personal violence, according to this thesis (see Hartogs and Artz, 1970).

Critics of this thesis, such as Harold Nieburg (1969: 22–25), argue that all governments are based upon a legal monopoly of force and violence, and that violence has played an important role in the creation and development of new nations.

The contention that television is at least in part responsible for the high level of American personal and political violence has been set forth most vigorously by Marshall McLuhan (1964). He maintains that the very dynamics of the electronic media compel individuals and groups to seek exposure and attention by doing something different or new, inventing tactics that will maximize shock value. Again, Nieburg refutes this contention. He notes the pluralistic nature of media coverage, in which various approaches and messages serve as countervailing forces against one another. Further, he claims that the television viewer edits the content of the message in accordance with his own structures, images, predispositions, and needs. Thus, to Nieburg television does not generate violence unless the content is interpreted by a predisposed individual as an adaptive and useful method to cope with the problems of everyday life.

Probably the most forceful concept of group support for violent criminal behavior arises from subculture-of-violence theories. For Marvin Wolfgang and Franco Ferracuti (1967), such a subculture embraces the normative system of a group or groups within the larger society that differs from the dominant culture. Some populations within the society inherit and continue a set of shared values in which physically aggressive responses by members are approved, expected, and even adulated. Violence is not synonymous with illegal conduct, and its users suffer no guilt about their aggressions. Rather, it is a part of a life-style, is a method for solving problems, and is used primarily among persons who themselves rely upon the same supportive value system.

Not all members of a subculture share its values. For those who do, the greater the degree of the individual's integration into the subculture of violence (in terms of expected responses to certain types of stimulus and to the meaning of human life and limb), the more likely it is that he will resort to violence in a problem situation. In a subculture of violence the proof of mascu-

2. The Australian case differs from the American in many respects and is cited here only to indicate that certain similarities—the large numbers of transported felons that founded the countries and the violent struggle with native populations and a hostile environment—are not sufficient to account for the difference in the level of violence. Australia did not suffer a civil war, did not have a heritage of slavery, maintained a rather homogeneous population after the subjugation of the natives, and even in its urban centers does not have the population density of the United States.

linity is "toughness," and it frequently requires the display of physical prowess, the exploitation of women, quick aggressive response to perceived affront, personal redress of wrongs, and a constant show of bravado (Clinard and Quinney, 1973: 29–39; Miller, 1958).

Wolfgang (1974: 246–248) sees the subculture of violence in the United States as arising out of certain characteristics of urban life: population density, social and geographic mobility, ethnic and class heterogeneity, reduced family functions, and anonymity. Some, but not all, of these features are universal. When they are found in combination with poverty, physical deterioration, and a social-psychological ambience that promotes violence, the subculture not only develops but also gives support to values of force, toughness, prowess, and aggression as favored problem-solving devices.

PERSONALITY DIMENSIONS

Various writers have sought to explain violence on the basis of psychological or biological factors and processes. Although the approaches overlap, we shall here discuss them separately.

Psychogenic formulations maintain that violent offenders are responding to stress, pressure, and personality difficulties such as chronic frustration, anger, hatred, paranoia, prejudice, neurosis, and animalization, all of which can drive them to violence (Ball-Rokeach, 1973). The psychogenic position has been put forth in the frustration-aggression theory (Dollard et al., 1939), which maintains that aggressive behavior presupposes the existence of frustration, with violence against the person actually defined as an extreme form of such aggression. Some frustration-aggression theorists place all situations and individuals along a continuum. Other writers point to a specific personality syndrome, termed "sociopathy" or "psychopathy," that predisposes to violence. The psychopath is guiltless, loveless, asocial, impulsive, aggressive, and unconditionable (McCord and McCord, 1964). Lewis Yablonsky (1962) has described such persons in *The Violent Gang*, Julian Roebuck (1967) in his double-pattern concept of drunkenness-assault, and Don Gibbons (1968) in his "psychopathic assaultist." In addition to the assaultive psychopath, there are also, in the view of some researchers, "conniving" psychopaths.

Studies of criminality in twins, adopted children, and others (see Mednick and Christiansen, 1977) are at the basis of some biogenic views of violence. Among the anatomical and physiological features studied are abnormality in the hypothalamus, chromosomal and endocrine structures, and brain waves; also neurological disorder, epilepsy, episodic dyscontrol syndrome, schizophrenia, innate aggressive drive, and neurological unconditionability. In this list, some items can be thought of as causes, others as symptoms or even consequences.

Several scientists (Mark and Erwin, 1970; Wasman and Flynn, 1962) have proposed that violent behavior is inseparably linked to the structure and functioning of the brain—i.e., that the brain is the storehouse of all human experience and the generator of all human behavior, both peaceful and violent. Although aware that behavior is influenced by social and economic conditions as well as all other aspects of a person's environment, they emphasize that such influences and events impinge on the brain and are stored in and translated into patterns of action by it. Thus we return to the primary importance of the brain in understanding conduct.

Extensive research along these lines has been conducted to determine the specific neurological structures that elicit and control different types of violent behavior. Most of this research has been done with animals, and its applicability to humans is debatable. It has, however, disclosed strikingly diverse forms of attack behavior. For example, stimulation of the lateral hypothalamus elicits intense but selective attack on a selected object, unaccompanied however by high levels of emotion. Stimulation of the medial hypothalamus, on the other hand, elicits equally intense but emotional attack directed indiscriminately toward any handy object, including stuffed animals and experimenters. Stimulation of the amygdala in cats produces a fear-aggression response, as it was called by Alfred Freedman and Harold Kaplan (1972). Animals under such stimulation frequently endeavor to escape the experimental locale. If escape proves impossible, however, an attack is directed against the most available object even when a suitable one is not present.

Relating these and other findings to humans, Vernon Mark and Frank Erwin (1970) hold that many violent crimes, especially the more brutal, "senseless" murders and assaults, result from neurological malfunctions caused by some kind of structural damage, often traceable to birth complications, disease, accidental head injury, or brain tumors. The case of Charles Whitman, who committed mass murder at the University of Texas in Austin in 1966, is an example (Johnson, 1972). Previous to the murder spree, Whitman had complained to a psychiatrist about periodic uncontrollable violent impulses. On the eve of the murders, he wrote a letter expressing bewilderment and concern about his impulses and at the same time announcing that he was going to kill his wife and mother, both of whom he claimed to love. Later that night, he did kill them, and the next morning he barricaded himself on the observation deck at the top of the university tower. With a high-powered rifle, he gunned down thirty-eight people in 90 minutes, killing fourteen. A post-mortem examination revealed a brain tumor the size of a walnut in the area of the amygdala.[3] Other less extreme examples are given by Mark and Erwin, who estimate that ten million Americans have serious and observable brain damage, and another five million minor, less observable brain disorder.

Interest in genetic explanations of violence was regenerated by the discovery in the 1960s of an apparently disproportionately high percentage of XYY karyotype males in prisons and maximum-security hospitals. P. Jacobs and his colleagues (1965) conducted the first study that indicated a relationship between an extra Y chromosome and aggressive behavior. But later findings have cast doubt on this, and many researchers are not at all certain

---

3. There is, however, considerable dispute over this interpretation of the Whitman case. Some deny that such a brain tumor could have been related to his murder spree. It may be that biology has been less an explanation than an excuse for the criminal behavior of this "all-American boy."

that there is greater incidence of uncontrolled violence among XYY males than among other males (for a discussion of this issue, see Shah and Roth, 1974).

Ethologists such as Konrad Lorenz (1966, 1974) have proposed that humans as well as other animals possess innate aggressive drives that seek expression. Lorenz contends that such drives are more dangerous to humans than to other animals, which have evolved inhibitory responses to prevent intraspecies killing. Man did not develop an inhibition against killing other humans—except possibly for a repugnance for cannibalism (Arens, 1979)—and as a result often "fights to the death." Ethologists readily agree that there are environmental conditions that can enhance the aggressive drives. For example, Lorenz (1974) points out the unusual irritability and aggression experienced by animals crowded together in a laboratory, and suggests that the crowding effect of large cities may bring forth similar responses in people.

No other form of criminal activity lends itself to studies of biological predisposition so much as violent personal behavior, particularly among recidivists. However, such behavior, even if it has biological roots, can thrive only in a favorable cultural and subcultural environment, is capable of being rechanneled into socially acceptable directions, and is seldom if ever manifested as a case of anatomy being destiny.

CORRESPONDENCE BETWEEN CRIMINAL AND LEGITIMATE BEHAVIOR

Both the criminal law and the dominant cultural-religious systems in the United States are ambiguous regarding violence. Some forms of aggression are negatively sanctioned, some socially approved. Examples of approval are found in the killing of enemy soldiers during wartime (including undeclared war), the legalized assault involved in many sports, violence in situations of real or perceived self-defense, corporal punishment against children by parents and teachers, human carnage on the highways due in part to the negligence of automobile makers, and ill health and death caused by corporate polluters. Somewhat less legitimated, although not without cultural support, are killing of civilians during wartime, physical attacks upon members of minority groups, physical force and the use of firearms against protesters and dissenters (less so after the 1960s), acceptance of gangland killings with the complacent attitude that they are good riddance, undue and at times illegal force by the police, corrections officers, and other prison officials in attempting to maintain order, violent redress of personal wrongs involving harm to members of one's family, and violence as the symbolic expression of manhood in situations involving honor and esteem.

The degree to which the legitimate behavior implants, fosters, and encourages the illegitimate is a matter of deep concern to all those interested in the reduction of criminal violence.

SOCIETAL REACTION AND LEGAL PROCESSING

Criminal law does not allow for the differential subcultural norms among many lower-class groups that regard the use of violence to settle some disputes as legitimate. Murder and assault are heavily sanctioned by law, not only because they comprise a threat to the political and economic order but also because of the injury inflicted upon the individual. A severe punitive reaction is invoked, whether as retribution, deterrent, or for purposes of incapacitation. Despite the close relationship between aggravated assault and murder, the former results in relatively shorter sentences. Thus, the law takes account of the fact that these offenses differ in their consequences, although they may not in motivation. Frequently only fortuitous circumstances separate the victim of violence from the perpetrator (a fact that should not be generalized to cover other types of crime).

For homicides, the 18–29 age group is most heavily represented among both perpetrators and victims. In 1979, of all homicides reported to the police, 73 percent were cleared by arrest. However, many of those arrested are not then brought to trial, because of insufficient evidence or for other reasons. Some are tried and found not guilty; the police consider the investigation closed. As in other types of crime, there may be plea bargaining.

Probably many aggravated assaults are not reported to the police, especially when they involve members of the same family (such as assault by a husband on his wife). In the 1979 figures, 59 percent of assaults reported to police resulted in arrest. Of the index crimes other than murder and aggravated assault, only forcible rape has a sizable percentage of the cases reported to police resulting in arrest—48 percent, with the next highest figure in the index being 25 percent, for robbery.

The arrest rates for reported crime, high for violent personal crime as compared with other index offenses, may reflect either a strong societal reaction to violence or the greater ease of escaping arrest for those offenses in which most criminals have had no previous acquaintance with the victim.

Crime against Property

Most crimes are committed against property. The motivation is financial gain. According to the crime clock of the Uniform Crime Reports, an average of one property crime is committed every three seconds in the United States, a figure that goes much higher if one includes property crimes not found in the index—not to speak of the dark figure of unreported crime.

For analytic purposes, we divide this larger category into (1) professional and career crime and (2) ordinary crime against property. We exclude organized crime and treat it as a separate category (Chapter 10).

Professional and Career Crime against Property

By professional criminal behavior, we refer to conduct engaged in by thieves who have highly developed criminal careers which they pursue habitually and as a livelihood, but who are not part of syndicated organized crime. Professional crime is characterized by dimensions similar to those found within legal occupational patterns—e.g., recruitment and training measures, skill, search for status among peers, shared world-views, widely accepted rules and codes of behavior, organization, and occupational vicissitudes. Like a business, this type of career crime is concerned with targets of operation, supply and demand, protection, new methods of operation, and the accumulation of profits. Professional crime is engaged in by skilled individual offenders operating within small informal groups (usually called "mobs") organized for specific purposes. This is in contrast to the large-scale organization of syndicated crime ("the mob").

The way in which a crime is executed, the type of perpetrator, and the organizational structure involved in the criminal activity distinguish professional crime from most other criminal behavior. The professional is a skilled person who carries out his acts with a finesse that has led to and made possible an at least moderately successful career. The illegal acts committed fall into several categories: shoplifting, pickpocketing, sneak-thievery, confidence swindling, robbery, burglary, forgery and counterfeiting, gambling, fencing, and extortion are among the most common. Forms of professional crime shift with changing social conditions—that is, with changes in the economic structure, the credit structure, the illegal market and illegal opportunity structure, criminal laws, police technology, the administration of criminal justice, and general technology. A pattern of hustling ("scoring" for whatever comes up) is found among many professional criminals that may include a series of diversified offenses (such as auto theft, fraud, involvement in illegal abortions, stealing of credit cards, arson, murder, hijacking, narcotics violations, and pornography).

Professional criminals spend their working time on illegal enterprises directed toward economic gain, on which they are financially dependent. The offenders view themselves as professional thieves, define criminal activities as a "calling," look down upon amateur thieves, show contempt for both victims and personnel in the administration of justice, rationalize away their crimes as business activities, and see all men as dishonest, all social arrangements and institutions as corrupt. Operating in small, informally organized, versatile working groups consisting of two to five persons (usually all males), they improvise by cashing in on criminal opportunities as they arise, and they plan others. The more successful the professional, the more likely he is to specialize in one type of crime. Both specialists and generalists move in and out of criminal mobs organized to handle one specific job at a time.

CRIMINAL CAREER OF THE OFFENDER

Relationships among professional criminals are structured primarily around the criminal job at hand and the composition of the mob (Walker, 1974). Most have developed skills necessary for the commission of several types of property crime. Status among peers in the professional underworld depends on skill, money, reputation as a "right guy," life-style (usually luxurious living geared toward material comforts, ostentatious living quarters, high-priced cars, beautiful women, and conspicuous consumption), and the ability to avoid frequent arrests and incarcerations. With these criteria, there is a wide variation in success among professional criminals.

Recruits come from all class levels. Some shift from legitimate occupations to career crime; some graduate from petty crime; still others without criminal experience are hired by mobs, usually to carry out some of the more dangerous missions. Most recruits come to this type of crime with a great deal of knowledge about "the life," gained from prior contacts with underworld people in such hangouts as poolrooms, bars and restaurants, "girlie" joints, gambling joints and casinos, fencing operations and pawnshops, cheap hotels, even dance halls and amusement centers. Many of these are located in the "tenderloin" or "vice" areas of big cities (Inciardi, 1975: 51). Intimate association with established members of the criminal fraternity precedes a career in crime. During the apprenticeship, the skills, techniques, argot, codes, and knowledge about the underworld are handed down from the experienced to the novice.

Professional criminals rely heavily on "the fix"—a loose phrase that describes payoffs, bribery, and other methods of dealing with law enforcement officials to prevent harassment and arrest and, if arrested, avoid prosecution and incarceration. To the fix, they add their strong relationships with criminal lawyers. However, when they do fall (that is, go to jail or prison), they accept the "bit" philosophically as an occupational hazard, much in the same fashion that the professional soldier accepts the contingency of capture, injury, or even death. While incarcerated, they do their time as quietly, unobtrusively, and comfortably as possible, without getting caught up in or dedicated to the inmate prison subculture. Their reference group is outside prison walls, though they may have to temporize with the inmate code. Although they may pretend to cooperate with the correctionally oriented prison officials, they actually resist any rehabilitation efforts and return to their illegal pursuits upon release. Many look forward to the one big score that will permit retirement. Little is known about the highly successful thief's exit from the world of crime. A few graduate to syndicate crime, and still others enter legitimate enterprises (usually connected with the bar, hotel, or entertainment industry in marginal areas of cities).

We do have some material on those who exit the profession as losers (Inciardi, 1975: 72–74). Some die young as a consequence of alcohol or drug abuse or disregard for health care. Some are murdered. Others are expelled from the underworld because of a serious violation of the code. Unable to locate confederates, shunned, they find it difficult to pursue the life of crime. Some cease their law-breaking activities because of loss of protection. Others are shocked out of crime by long prison sentences after which they no longer have the youth, vitality, strength, morale, or connections to continue. The poor, disabled, demolished, and inept losers retire to skid-row cultures. Inciardi (1975: 74) quotes a professional burglar as saying: "The Bowery has always been a hiding place, a retiring place and a burial ground."

Ascribed and Achieved Characteristics.   There are small working groups of moderately successful thieves. The membership is constantly in flux, yet group cohesion is strong, with one or two leaders generally emerging to form an enduring core.

Julian Roebuck and Wolfgang Frese (1976) have studied twenty professional thieves, whom they observed over a period of two years at play and work in an after-hours club and some of whom Roebuck later interviewed in their homes.[1] In addition, they studied twenty female professional thieves. In this overwhelmingly male-dominated area of crime, Roebuck and Frese

1. Much of the material in this section of the chapter is based on the work of Roebuck and Frese (1976).

found, the females more often are loners, with the males operating in small groups. More females than males had worked at legitimate employment at one time or another, and more frequently the women were involved in legitimate moonlighting on their main job (the criminal one) when it did not pay enough.

Among males, three or four criminals with certain specialties may band together for the execution of one crime. Subsequently they may remain together or disband—possibly later reassembling for the same or another kind of criminal job. Loyalty to a mob is based on business and the particular criminal task at hand; it is somewhat independent of personal bonds among members. Thieves systematically engage in a wide variety of specialized crimes, all of which are directed toward economic gain: unorganized gambling (owners, managers, and dealers working one or two table dice or card games), auto theft, forgery, check passing, confidence games, fencing,[2] pimping, burglary, shoplifting, robbery (usually as planners rather than executors), pickpocketing, credit-card theft, short-changing, and street drug retailing.

Thieves have a tendency toward specialization, and most of them have a preferred criminal activity. However, considerable criminal versatility occurs, varying with the opportunities for law-breaking behavior. Generally, the more successful the thief in terms of skill, scores, reputation, and the ability to avoid arrest, the greater the specialization.

These habitual thieves, usually products of the lower and lower-middle classes, are not well educated and for the most part lack legitimate work skills (forgers are an exception). There is little regular legitimate employment for extended periods of time among the professionals, although many moonlight at one time or another at unskilled jobs. They make no pretense in this respect and boast that the sole source of their income is derived from criminal pursuits (perhaps a self-aggrandizing exaggeration). Roebuck and Frese found that the thieves varied widely in age (twenty-five to fifty-five) and marital status. Most were single or divorced, assumed no family responsibilities, and lived with a series of women on a one-after-another schedule. Residence was usually in hotels or apartments situated in lower-middle-class areas near commercial zones, but the interiors of their rooms or apartments were better appointed than those of neighbors.

Most of the thieves studied had been adjudicated juvenile delinquents and had spent time in juvenile correctional institutions. As youths, their violations were in the main for property-related gang offenses. All had adult arrest records—on the average four to five arrests each—and had served time, about one-third of it for felonies. Despite the arrest histories and criminal processing, only small staggered bits of their lives had been spent behind bars. All were social drinkers, and while in part this may be explained by the hangout where they were met by the researchers and studied (an after-hours club), it is likely that social drinking is widespread among these marginal people. However, few appeared to have problems of alcoholism: it is

2. Fences studied by Roebuck and Frese were much more specialized and secretive in their operations than was Vincent, the professional fence described and analyzed in impressive detail by Carl Klockars (1974).

likely that alcoholism would make the pursuit of their criminal activities difficult if not impossible. Many had experimented with various drugs, including marijuana, hashish, and cocaine, but none was addicted to heroin. Their recreational pursuits revolved around women and gambling. Most gambled heavily at various games—including cards and dice—and on numbers and horse races.

Identities and Perspectives.   Professional thieves speak in the criminal argot and define themselves as solid (honest, stand-up guys), cool (nervy and composed), and skillful (having finesse and being masters of criminal techniques). They identify generally with crime and with the lower echelons of the underworld. Working at different criminal trades, they form a subculture, belong to the same criminal world, and are isolated from conventional society. They share acquaintances, friends, and criminal connections and negotiate with those who seek, steal, sell, and buy contraband. Residing usually in the same neighborhoods, they patronize the same restaurants and bars, run with the same class of women (frequently the same women), and know and deal with the same police, fences, "juice men" (loan sharks), criminal lawyers, bondsmen, and district attorneys. Most retain criminal lawyers, and all say they have paid off policemen at one time or another for immunity from arrest or permission to operate illegally, but this is difficult to verify. Thieves exchange goods and information and can provide one another with social and emotional support, physical protection, financial aid, loans, and work skills. Self-styled successful criminals, they are proud of their prestige, success, and underworld reputation (however limited), their monetary rewards, and their life-style. As one thief commented to the researchers while standing at the bar:

> Any way you want to look at it, I'm a success. Every all-right thief in town knows I'm a stand-up guy. We're all in this together. It don't make no difference if you steal it or sell it. I got a lot of friends in this business. I've been fencing for fifteen years and been busted only three times. You don't have to pay off all the cops, just those in your precinct. Look at my pad. You've seen my Cadillac. I live good. My women are the finest, nothing but table stuff. I lead a good life.

Thieves proclaim that most men, particularly "straights," are dishonest hypocrites. Good thieves, as they profess to be, are "right" and "solid," honest, loyal, and responsible people who pay their debts, meet their obligations, keep appointments, and show up when needed by colleagues. Espousing a code of honor based on the cardinal principle "don't squeal," thieves agree that the only way a poor, honest man can achieve a decent life-style in an unfair society is to steal. Reluctantly they admit that their code, like all others, is broken now and then by some thieves who "don't hold up."

Professional thieves express negative views about all the basic institutions of society, especially all facets of the administration of criminal justice, with which most of their contacts have been of a negative nature: arrest, bond, trial, fines, probation, parole, incarceration, payoffs. They are especially vituperative in their display of contempt and hostility for the police.

Professional criminals share a subculture of values and norms antithetical to those of conventional society. Lasting friendships among them are few, because of the mobility factor. Life- and work-styles and security needs preclude intimate association with members of conventional society. Self-concept and social isolation concur. James Inciardi (1975: 69) records the normative code that ideally guides the professional criminal:

GROUP SUPPORT OF CRIMINAL BEHAVIOR

1. Do not hold out money or property from fellow criminals.
2. Pay debts to other criminals as rapidly as possible.
3. Deal honestly with other members of your mob.
4. Do not cut in on the operations of other mob members.
5. Always endeavor to fix cases involving other mob members.
6. Never inform the police about crimes of fellow thieves.

This normative code, however, is not inviolate. Adherence or violation depends upon pragmatic considerations, including interpretations of the social situation. Thieves are not supposed to be loyal to or protective of fellow members who have "finked" on them, double-crossed other thieves, or otherwise flagrantly violated the code. Informing is at times expected and, less frequently, tolerated if a thief faces a long prison sentence unless he talks; under these severe conditions, however, the violator is expected to give out the least damaging information possible. Lip service and a degree of obedience to the code are ensured by the individual thief's desire to remain viable in the underworld. Violations of the code may bring ostracism, loss of the fix, damage to professional reputation, physical violence, and sometimes death.

Professional criminal behavior is similar to legitimate behavior patterns in several respects: it is engaged in systematically as a full-time pursuit for economic gain; its personnel are self-employed or, more frequently, work for a mob, with a system of organizational and operational rules; they possess a degree of skill above that of the amateur; some skills and operations parallel those utilized in conventional activities—e.g., the fence is in some respects like the legitimate retailer, and in fact may have a legitimate retail business as a cover for the fencing operation (Klockars, 1974).

CORRESPONDENCE BETWEEN CRIMINAL AND LEGITIMATE BEHAVIOR

Professional criminals see themselves as having a career that separates them from the sporadic law-breakers. They enjoy a certain status among peers, and many of their activities depend upon the cooperation of law-abiding accomplices. They must have flexibility in their operations, bending with changes in the social and economic climate. They respond to a market of supply and demand and to technological developments—e.g., credit-card theft and usage has developed as a new form of professional crime, while safe-cracking has been on the decline.

For several reasons, professional criminals tend to be favored over conventional offenders by public officials. Skilled and rational people, they are willing, able, and financially equipped to negotiate with the police and court officials and with their victims before and after apprehension. Unlike run-of-

SOCIAL REACTION AND LEGAL PROCESSING

the-mill offenders, they understand how the administration of justice can be made to work to their advantage. Some escape arrest through regular ("up-front") payoffs. Protection money permits them to operate with impunity in certain areas, and assures them quick release on various grounds when arrested. Some carry "fall money" (one or two thousand dollars) on their persons at all times, and if arrested while performing a criminal act, attempt to make a payoff on the spot. In many cases, they hire professional fixers after arrest; these are lawyers, businessmen, politicians, private citizens with influence, who have access to whatever level of the judicial system it may be necessary to reach for the next level of negotiation.

Professional criminals usually retain criminal lawyers on a permanent basis. They like to boast that they can "get to" arresting officers, investigative detectives, prosecutors, bondsmen, judges, jurors, victims, others. Jury fixing is apparently difficult; a single juror can result in a hung jury, but not without bringing down some element of suspicion upon himself. Restitution, bribe money, or just threat may convince the complainant not to press charges, and if the district attorney will not then drop the charges completely, he is usually amenable to plea bargaining, which can include the reduction of the charge from a felony to a misdemeanor. (See discussion of plea bargaining in Chapter 18.)

Perhaps the greatest barrier to any form of social control of the professional criminal is his low visibility. The public knows little of arrests and convictions of such persons. In addition to the large amount of unreported crime—particularly shoplifting and pocket-picking, among other types—the crimes committed by professionals that are reported and make their way into the Uniform Crime Reports and other records are presented in such a way that it is not possible to distinguish the sporadic and amateur offender from the professional. It is probably the case that while more burglaries, larcenies, and robberies are committed by amateurs, the total value of money and goods stolen by professionals far exceeds the take of their amateur competitors.

Conventional Crime against Property

From the perspective of the amount of money that changes hands illegally, white-collar, organized, and professional crime constitute the dominant forces in American and no doubt other modern industrialized societies. Nonetheless, ordinary or conventional small-time crime by people who do not have particular criminal skills, are not specialists, and do not pursue crime as an occupation, career, or profession is extremely significant in the lives of most citizens. This is the type of crime that is felt most directly, is visible and threatening, is directed against the average individual in the pursuit of his mundane daily activities, frequently victimizes the poor, and has the greatest impact on spreading a climate of fear and affecting adversely the quality of life.

LEGAL ASPECTS OF SELECTED OFFENSES

To refer to any property crime—or any crime at all—as conventional may be a contradiction, for that it is a crime is itself a statement that it contravenes the conventions of society. But this type of property crime is conventional, or can be conceived of as such, in the sense that it is not extraordinary in its scope and network, its required skills, its ramifications and traditions, its targets and frequency of occurrence.

The most common such events include burglary, larceny (grand and petty), theft of (or from) motor vehicles, and probably robbery, although the latter is also conceptualized as a violent crime against the person because it is committed in the presence of the victim (by definition) and hence has a strong potential for resulting in injury, including murder. We exclude from this category, for purposes of description and of analysis, such crimes as embezzlement, forgery, counterfeiting, smuggling, extortion, fraud, and trafficking in stolen property. Most of these activities are practically the exclusive domain of white-collar, professional, or organized crime—although they might be conducted in a small way by amateur, inept persons attempting to hustle in on something they know little about and for which their skills are inadequate. Arson also is outside this category; although directed against property, it appears to be most frequently either a white-collar act or an act of revenge, and sometimes its aim is injury to the person.

Yet, the classifications do overlap. There seems to be good reason to believe that a considerable amount of automobile theft is professionally committed by networks of skilled persons who steal cars to order (with the make, year, even the color as desired) and deliver them, with altered plates and papers, to a prearranged destination. Others remove automobiles from streets and garages to points from which they are exported. Finally, some groups of car thieves work with garage owners; they quickly strip a car of its valuable parts and then crush whatever remains so that it becomes scrap metal, beyond recognition or identification. Sometimes motor vehicles are stolen for the purpose of committing other, more serious crimes, including violent ones; at the other end of the spectrum vehicles are taken for a joyride and returned or abandoned shortly thereafter. Nonetheless, when all of these and still other motives and descriptions of skilled car thieves are listed, what remains is a considerable residue of automobile thefts committed by people who are not so highly skilled and do not have such broad network connections as to be part of professional or organized crime groupings. For them, the theft is conventional or ordinary crime.

Motor-vehicle theft is a specific instance of the general crime of larceny, often divided in state penal codes into grand and petty larceny. This distinction depends on the amount of money or value of the goods stolen. It sometimes proves useful in plea bargaining, when a plea of guilty to petty larceny may be entered and accepted although the accused had been charged with taking amounts far exceeding the maximum for that offense.

Larceny—or, more technically, larceny-theft, as the crime is called in the Uniform Crime Reports—is defined as "the unlawful taking, carrying, leading, or riding away of property" from the possession of another, without the use of force, violence, or fraud. "It includes crimes such as shoplifting, pocket-picking, purse-snatching, thefts from motor vehicles, thefts of motor vehicle parts and accessories, bicycle thefts, etc."[3] The UCR definition does not include embezzlement, confidence games, forgery, and writing or pass-

3. This is more a description than a legal definition. The crimes are legally defined in the various state penal codes, and wording differs from one jurisdiction to another.

ing worthless checks; it also excludes automobile theft, for crime-reporting purposes only, because this is a separate index offense. Some might think that pickpocketing could qualify as robbery rather than property theft, because it involves taking something from a person in his presence, and that purse-snatching is even more closely related to robbery, but both have been categorized as larceny for purposes of crime reporting. Figure 9–1 shows an approximate analysis of 1979 larceny offenses known to the police. The extremely high percentage of these offenses represented by thefts from motor vehicles or of motor vehicle accessories may be traceable to the fact that losses from such larcenous acts are often covered by insurance and hence are generally reported to the police. Also, automobiles are vulnerable because they are left on streets and in unattended garages, parts are easily removable, passersby are unlikely to be able to distinguish thief from owner, and extreme inflation in the cost of parts has made such crimes more tempting than ever.

Not all shoplifting is easily classified as conventional or ordinary crime. Some of it, as Mary Cameron (1964) has convincingly shown in her study of this widespread type of activity, is committed by career and professional criminals, who have regular fences and other outlets for their stolen goods and have developed highly skillful techniques to carry out their crimes without being detected. But that a good part of shoplifting is amateur and that a not inconsiderable amount of ordinary and conventional crime consists of shoplifting are both pretty well established.

Other than larceny-theft, a good deal of conventional property crime takes place in the form of illegal breaking and entering (burglary) and robbery, with or without weapons.

CRIMINAL CAREER OF THE OFFENDER

The conventional or ordinary criminal is almost by definition devoid of a criminal career. Although part of his life is spent in crime, he does not make a career out of these activities, even during a given period when he is committing them. The criminal act is carried out with little skill and training, sporadically, usually in an unplanned manner. Some of these acts occur when an opportunity presents itself and the prospect of getting something for nothing beckons.

Except for shoplifting, most of the conventional acts against property are performed by the young, strong, and agile. Some of these persons commit the acts to support a drug habit. While a great deal of adolescent and teenage depredation may be considered by the perpetrators as nothing more than mischief (sometimes reported or recorded as malicious mischief or vandalism), for others the acts may be the prelude to a drift into career or professional crime, but probably not organized crime. Whether this drift into career crime would be accelerated by a stint at a juvenile detention home—where the new inmate can learn greater skills and make contact with those having a greater commitment to a life of crime—is a matter widely debated in circles interested in juvenile corrections.

The conventional property criminal is usually a petty criminal; the take is small, and if it has to be disposed of through fences it becomes even smaller.

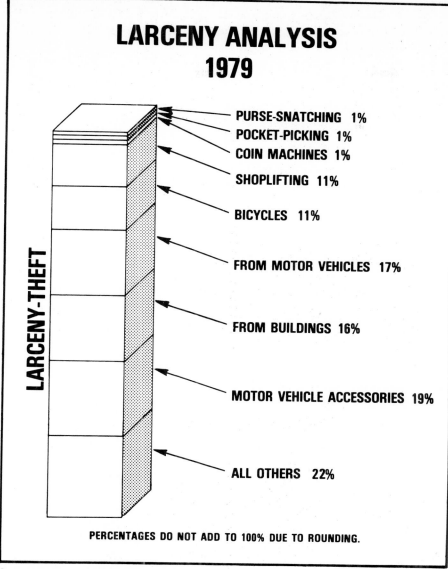

LARCENY ANALYSIS 1979

LARCENY-THEFT

PURSE-SNATCHING 1%
POCKET-PICKING 1%
COIN MACHINES 1%

SHOPLIFTING 11%

BICYCLES 11%

FROM MOTOR VEHICLES 17%

FROM BUILDINGS 16%

MOTOR VEHICLE ACCESSORIES 19%

ALL OTHERS 22%

PERCENTAGES DO NOT ADD TO 100% DUE TO ROUNDING.

FIGURE 9-1

SOURCE: Uniform Crime Reports, 1980, p. 29.

Despite stories of mothers who send their children through college with the fruits of shoplifting and other ill-gotten gains,[4] only the drifter can live off this type of occasional crime. Most of these offenders are people with jobs but few skills, students still in high school or even junior high school, drop-outs, hangers-on, or recently discharged veterans. Often their property crime is against their employer.

4. Where no doubt the sons and daughters receive high grades in their courses in ethics, not to speak of criminology.

173

GROUP SUPPORT OF CRIMINAL BEHAVIOR

Generally, one can divide conventional property offenders into two types: the loner and the individual working with a peer group. Even the loner is not devoid of support in all instances. Although the act is carried out without accomplices or possibly with only one other, by its nature it has group support, in the sense that Sutherland indicated in his theory of differential association—that is, the offender is mingling and exchanging values with others in a similar position who take a favorable attitude toward his activity. He learns in a company, for example, that employees steal—or at least he believes they do—and that only a fool does not do so. Thus he uses many rationalizations to justify the act. Sometimes the stealing is in concert with other employees (particularly those working in a stockroom); but even when it is not, this is only because of his general mistrust toward sharing his secret, not because he believes others do not indulge in such activities.

Strong peer-group support for other types of ordinary crimes, particularly by the young, may come about through either a selective search for peers who offer support or strong associations with those already committed to the activity. For young males, some of the acts have symbolic value as forms of bravado, machismo, courage, heart: they constitute proof that the youth is a right-on guy, that he is not a square or a straight, not afraid of "the man." The successful fulfillment of the crime is achievement: he can boast to peers of a watch obtained illegally, and it glitters the more because of the story behind its passage from its former to its present possessor.

PERSONALITY DIMENSIONS

It is probably hazardous to try to develop a psychological profile on haphazard and sporadic property offenders. They are not violent, although they may have the potential to become so (as have many others who do not go through the earlier stage of property offense). They are seldom psychopaths; often they will outgrow their occasional criminal forays and become no more law-breaking in their patterns than most citizens, and no less. If they graduate into other types of career and professional crime, they may develop personality traits (if they did not already possess them) associated with the group into which they are entering.

Nevertheless, a few generalizations seem to be in order. For the most part, we may be dealing here with the most normal cross-section of the crime-producing sectors of the populace. It is doubtful whether the policeman who takes a bribe or the fireman who steals from a building he has been authorized to enter has personality differences or defects that separate him from the many policemen and firemen who would not commit such acts. While it is undoubtedly an exaggeration to state, as the old cliché would have it, that there is a little larceny in the heart of everyone, very large numbers of people with no special personality problems can indeed be tempted.

There is no evidence that property crimes are carried out by people with low IQ. In fact, the mentally subnormal are often incapable of effecting these events, and do not attempt them. These crimes are not the work of compulsive people, although compulsivity may be a convenient excuse when one is caught red-handed. The desire in youthful groups to display ability and courage in beating the system hardly appears to be an unusual personality trait.

A relatively recent phenomenon, and one little studied, is the involvement of elderly people in petty thievery, especially shoplifting. This is of course a far less serious matter than the victimization of the elderly, by both violent offenders and swindlers operating in such fields as, for example, realty sales and tourism.

CORRESPONDENCE BETWEEN CRIMINAL AND LEGITIMATE BEHAVIOR

On the surface, it might appear that people who take property or money from others by illegal means have no models or precedents in the legitimate society. Nevertheless, we are surrounded by acts of a predatory nature, in which some people enrich themselves at the expense of others, by means that if not illegal are on the fringe of legality, are unethical, and are what is referred to in the common language of everyday life as rip-offs. Storekeepers in poor neighborhoods charge more, offer lower-quality merchandise, and do not stand by guarantees (Caplovitz, 1963). A large motor company, earning hundreds of millions of dollars, substitutes an inferior motor in a higher-priced car. Frauds abound; the emergence of television and consumerism means that the rip-offs have become highly publicized.

The motive is profit, and with some modifications the reality is "caveat emptor." A vision of society in which the respectable, the well-to-do, and the pretentiously proper are engaged in enriching themselves through any means, at the expense of anyone, may be an exaggeration, but it is one easily believed by those who want to rationalize their stealing.

SOCIETAL REACTION AND LEGAL PROCESSING

The societal reaction against small-time predators is mixed. Small shoplifters, petty white-collar criminals, and employees who steal small amounts from their employers through padded expense accounts or by taking small tools and inexpensive equipment rather than salable merchandise are hardly considered threats. They are warned but seldom discharged and very rarely prosecuted. Shoplifting and inventory shrinkage are regarded as more serious when larger sums are involved, although such activity does not directly appear to threaten anyone but the storekeeper or the company and then only on the bottom line—something which hardly elicits great public indignation. That the consumer pays in higher prices, because of shrinkage and the cost of additional security in warehouses, stores, and other establishments, seems to be widely recognized and accepted as part of the burden of living in an inflationary economy.

On the other hand, property crime directed against people in their homes —or, more literally, against their homes—pocket-picking and purse-snatching constitute, together with robbery, the type of "street crime" or "ordinary crime" against property that elicits the greatest public concern. The reaction is sharp, and the public calls for protection and even retaliation. Even those who demand slum clearance, job creation, better education, and a resurgence of moral commitment to a set of values other than accumulation of profit usually insist that these ordinary criminals must be prosecuted and incarcerated so that their depredations will cease.

Public outrage over automobile theft does not seem to be as strident as that over burglary and street crime. This may be due in part to the nature of

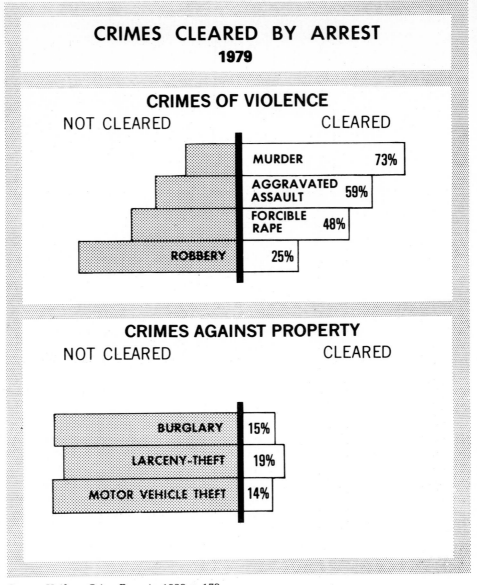

CRIMES CLEARED BY ARREST
1979

CRIMES OF VIOLENCE

NOT CLEARED   CLEARED

MURDER   73%

AGGRAVATED ASSAULT   59%

FORCIBLE RAPE   48%

ROBBERY   25%

CRIMES AGAINST PROPERTY

NOT CLEARED   CLEARED

BURGLARY   15%

LARCENY-THEFT   19%

MOTOR VEHICLE THEFT   14%

FIGURE 9-2

SOURCE: Uniform Crime Reports, 1980, p. 178.

the act—in burglary one's home is entered, and robbery is by its nature a threat to the person—but also because the stolen car is almost universally covered by insurance. The insurance companies are not concerned, as their rates are based upon tables of past and anticipated payments. The owners of stolen cars usually sustain a loss (in addition to the cost of their insurance payments), but not sufficient to bring forth the same outcry as when a house is burglarized.

If we assume that most burglary, larceny-theft, and motor-vehicle theft constitute conventional or ordinary crime against property, we find that the percentage of such crimes cleared by arrest is dismayingly small, as shown by the statistics for 1979 (Figure 9–2). Moreover, since only a small portion of these crimes is ever reported to the police (with the exception of theft of motor vehicles), then "cleared by arrest" must make up an even smaller section of the total number of such acts committed.[5]

Twice as many males as females were arrested for larceny-theft in 1979, and twice as many whites as blacks. Those under twenty-one accounted for 59 percent of those arrested, those under eighteen for 42 percent. But these figures have to be analyzed with the realization in mind that 80 percent of the cases known to the police were not cleared by arrest; there is thus some doubt whether those apprehended were representative of the total population of offenders.

Recent research on professional criminals indicates that they are decreasing in number. The highly skilled specialist is giving way to the generalist, a hustler who seeks scores whenever he can find them; criminal mob status has given way to individual criminal status; and the criminal code of the professional has been weakened. In short, it is argued that the theoretical frame established by Edwin Sutherland, based on status, consensus, organization, differential association, and the learning of technical skills, is no longer tenable (Walker, 1974). Nonetheless, Sutherland's theoretical frame retains some validity as a research tool, and his description of behavior systems is not entirely outdated. It is true that the highly skilled specialist is not as much in evidence as in years gone by. Mob organization and status seem to have been replaced by organization for a particular criminal job, and status as a career criminal is no longer conferred by a permanent mob but rather by the "in-the-life" community (Prus and Irini, 1980). Furthermore, consensus that emphasizes cooperation and harmony has been weakened among career criminals (Miller, 1978).

In a study of deviant and criminal types in an urban hotel community (a subculture), Prus and Irini (1980) demonstrate the existence of a behavior system process model comprising rounders (professional criminals), hookers, strippers, and bar and hotel employees and patrons. The model includes career contingencies (individual career identity, activity careers, career relationships), initial involvements (closure, seekership, recruitment), drift, multiple routings, continuity (conversion, continuance commitments, activity entanglements, embeddedness in the social life of the deviant community, self-other identities), disinvolvement, and deviance as joint activity. In this process model, several common achieved and ascribed characteristics of professional criminals are noted, along with world views, work and recreation routines, and modus operandi.

---

5. In UCR, a crime is cleared "when a law enforcement agency has identified the offender, has sufficient evidence to charge him, and actually takes him into custody. In exceptional instances, crimes may be cleared when some element beyond police control precludes taking the offender into custody" (Uniform Crime Reports, 1980: 177).

Organized Crime

Organized crime consists of networks of persons engaged in the systematic dispensation of illegal goods and services, usually within specific geographic areas. Generally, the enterprises operate with a bureaucratic type of organizational structure affording a division of labor, specialization with delineated relationships, a hierarchical chain of command, and a mutually agreed-upon set of obligations and privileges based on work role, secrecy, loyalty, and a code of conduct. These enterprises are complex organizations as well as secret societies, with members employing an argot of their own and with rules, personnel, and a sort of "government." Like legitimate organizations operating in a capitalist society, these enterprises seek monopolistic control of markets and tend to expand their operations. This leads them to the infiltration of legitimate businesses. Furthermore, these enterprises seek protection from the law via political connections and payoffs to public officials. Organized crime in a sense is the white-collar crime of the underworld.

There are two divergent views among those studying syndicated crime in the United States. One viewpoint holds that it comprises a confederation of "families," mainly if not entirely under the control of a few Italian-Americans. Although the number is fluid, there are as of the early 1980s perhaps twenty-four in all, operating as criminal cartels in large cities throughout the nation. This confederation, sometimes called the Cosa Nostra or the Mafia, controls most large-stakes illegal gambling, loan-sharking, and narcotics traffic and is involved in prostitution, labor racketeering, and many legitimate businesses as well (including in all likelihood legalized gambling). A crime "commission" composed of the leaders of the most powerful families serves in a loose sense as a combination legislature, supreme court, and board of directors.

The second viewpoint contends that syndicated crime consists of several independent "local" collectivities organized in the major metropolitan areas without regional or national linkages.

The first view is supported by many law-enforcement agencies, as well as some criminologists and other authorities, such as Donald Cressey (1969) and Ralph Salerno and John Thompkins (1969). The second view is advocated by Daniel Bell (1967), Ramsey Clark (1970), Norval Morris and Gordon Hawkins (1970), Dwight Smith (1975), Joseph Albini (1971), and Francis Ianni (1972, 1974), among others.

The primary goal of organized crime, as of big business itself, is financial gain. Through illegal means, organized crime provides its clients with goods and services that are otherwise unavailable; this is of course a simplification, because it provides many unwanted "services" as well, such as protection. A gambler, instead of going to the racetrack, uses the illegal services of a bookmaker; a drug addict finds a dependable supplier because organized crime sees to it that the dealers are well stocked; and a businessman who has exhausted all legal resources for borrowing goes to a loan shark when he needs money. Thus, in many instances, clients seek out the services of organized crime. But, as with legitimate business, the reverse is also true: business must be drummed up, converts sought for the product—thus there are drug pushers. And in some cases the supplier imposes the service on the reluctant client.

LEGAL ASPECTS OF SELECTED OFFENSES

Traditionally, organized crime has been found operating in the areas of illegal gambling, narcotics, and prostitution. Current data suggest that syndicate operations are extensively involved in illicit gambling, the burgeoning world of casinos, loan-sharking, narcotics importation and distribution, labor racketeering, extortion, takeover of legitimate businesses through economic and physical pressure, dealing in illegal and stolen securities and bonds, illegal transportation and sale of highly taxed products such as cigarettes, control of many bars and restaurants, and distribution of pornography. Legitimate enterprises are used as fronts for criminal activities, offer a major source of income, provide a legal façade for tax and other purposes, and are utilized to "launder" money obtained illegally.

The continued licit and illicit operations of organized crime may be associated with the failure of the legal system to check its growth and curtail its influence. But some of the activities of organized crime receive considerable indirect support from large numbers of people, who constitute a willing market for products and services. In the United States, many laws have been passed to control and even thwart the operations of organized crime in gambling, prostitution, trafficking in drugs, racketeering, legitimate business. These have been largely futile. As Marshall Clinard and Richard Quinney (1973: 20) put it, "Since organized crime is closely tied to the general business economy, these laws tend to invade the privacy of all citizens rather than to control organized crime."

Legal methods have failed because syndicated crime has gained virtual immunity from the interference of law-enforcement agencies. This is demonstrated by the fact that none of the criminal syndicates has been successfully broken up by government action. (Sometimes, however, internecine warfare has accomplished this.) Few of the ringleaders have ever been convicted or imprisoned.

Upper-echelon members of criminal organizations are buffered from the street-level operations they control. When low-ranking members are arrested, their leaders may obtain their release through competent legal assistance or a fix. In this way, the possibility of prosecution is minimized. The lack of effective legislation and the weakness of law enforcement reflect the public's toleration of organized crime in America. The FBI and local law enforcement agencies have been more concerned with street crime and the capture of traditional criminals than with the apprehension of the syndicate people. Ordinary men and women feel more threatened by the robber accosting them on the street or the burglar breaking into their homes than by something apparently far removed from their everyday lives, as is organized crime. In short, conventional criminals are both easier targets for law enforcement and of greater concern to citizens.

The lack of a centralized federal mechanism for crime control impedes the fight against organized crime. As described by Stuart Hills (1969: 27), America has a "splintered system of decentralized and overlapping law enforcement agencies having separate jurisdictions. . . . Political investigation and court action are vested in separate agencies—the sheriff, district attorney, and judge. . . . All can operate independently of one another—and are further divided into federal, state and local levels."

Organized crime thrives by accommodating to the changing times and consumer habits and tastes. It gains and maintains its strength and influence through the nullification and corruption of the political structure and law enforcement machinery.

CRIMINAL CAREER OF THE OFFENDER

The structure of organized crime groups provides roughly three echelons of position for members: a top leadership level for those who determine policy, a management segment that oversees operations and implements policy (serving also as buffers), and a lower stratum of operators who engage in direct criminal activity, deal with the public, and involve nonmembers in specialized tasks. Recruitment and progression from one level to the other depend upon the interplay of many variables, such as loyalty, dependability, ability to fit in with personnel and operations, length of service, nepotism, and ethnicity. Individual mobility within the organization depends as well on qualifications as money managers, enforcers, corrupters, or some other capacity.

Specifics about recruitment and career dimensions are hard to come by because organized crime constitutes a secret society. It appears that some members with specialized training are directly recruited from law and accounting, while some well-connected younger men are provided with college training contingent upon an agreed-on career in the syndicate. Still others—generally recruits at the lowest level—have already established conventional criminal careers, having "progressed" from juvenile delinquent and criminal youth gangs to some form of activity in association with organized criminals. Most people of this group grow up in slum areas that offer an opportunity structure in criminal careers. These recruits are selected by organized criminals on the basis of being loyal, willing, and trustworthy, rather than for technical skill. Organized crime seeks younger men with "brains," "heart," "connection," and "trust" (Spergel, 1964: 159–163).

Organized crime provides persons having certain attributes with the opportunity for a lifetime career in crime. The choice of a syndicate career rather than an ordinary criminal one appears to be largely dependent upon the opportunity structure available in the area in which the aspirant lives. As the offender becomes increasingly involved in organized crime he becomes more committed to the underworld and more detached from many aspects of conventional society. He develops a self-concept and world view that enable him to rationalize his offenses as necessary services. Society to him is corrupt and full of injustice, and justice is a commodity one pays for as with everything else. The intelligent and elite rule and prosper in the social jungle. Some leaders of organized crime may choose to live segmented lives that permit them to enjoy power and luxury in both the criminal and the legitimate worlds.

Organized Crime Figures: A Portrait.   In organized crime, the term "businessman" refers to owners of "books" for illegal off-track betting and other sports gambling; owners, managers, and employees of illegal gambling houses; numbers writers and backers; wholesale pilferers dealing with large-scale, warehoused, transported, and resold stolen goods; loan sharks; and racketeers engaged in such activities as control and protection in the trucking of perishable goods and vegetables. A study of fifteen such persons indicates that they engage in crime as a livelihood and have an organizational structure, a code of conduct, prescribed methods of operations, and a security system.[1]

The fifteen are affluent, middle-aged (forty to sixty) products of stable lower- or middle-class backgrounds. Their highest educational levels are graduation from grammar school or high school. They have apparently good or at least stable marriages, and are "family men" in the ordinary sense of that word. They engage in lucrative legitimate businesses such as: real estate, trucking, legal money lending, importing and exporting, laundry and cleaning services; operation of poolrooms, night clubs, restaurants, bars, movie houses, liquor stores, and hotels and motels; and sale and distribution of vending machines. These profitable enterprises function as tax shelters and provide a channel for the investment and movement of illegal money.

These men can be said to be successful in a combination of underworld and upperworld endeavors. They reside in upper-middle- to upper-class neighborhoods and live surrounded by material possessions and comfort. They have legitimate work skills that would equip them for occupational adjustment in legitimate society. Most have an arrest and conviction record as adults—usually for gambling or property offenses—and most had a previous

1. This entire section is based on Roebuck and Frese (1976: 167–174), where these crime figures are described as conforming to the "patron" type.

juvenile delinquency record; the adult records are brief and mainly misdemeanors. Represented by excellent lawyers on a retainer basis and reported to have connections within the administration of criminal justice, these businessmen usually receive light dispositions: dismissal of case for lack of evidence, a fine, probation, or short jail term. In fact, most have served at least one such term, but felony time was rare. Incarcerations were brief and staggered; none had been "prisonized" (that is, socialized into the world of prisoners). All are social drinkers, none is alcoholic, and none admits to the use of nonalcoholic drugs.[2] They dress conservatively, speak in the vernacular of the street (with frequent use of criminal argot), and appear to be deficient in the vocabulary of middle-class and white-collar people.

Streetwise, shrewd, aloof, and arrogant, these men are superficially sophisticated in specific areas. They are knowledgeable about criminal and civil law, food and drink, sports, gambling, clothes, jewelry, night life, and sex but are limited in general knowledge of middle-class life-styles, values, and standards. Parochial, sensual, and materialistic—the emphasis is on comfort, money, food, and sex—they view the world as a jungle where the strong and clever not only survive but prosper and rule behind the scenes. They visualize themselves as a criminal elite who have attained success in certain financial, commercial, social, and religious circles. Moreover, they rationalize their criminal pursuits as connected with the dispensation of goods and services that the public demands and "is going to get one way or the other anyhow." The following comment overheard at a bar is typical:

> Who's kidding who? I'm just like any other businessman trying to make a buck. I offer here what is legal in Las Vegas. My odds beat theirs or the odds given by any legal gambler. I didn't start at the top, you know. It's taken me years to get where I am. But some people think of men like me as ordinary criminals. I know less about street criminals than you do. I don't associate with heistmen, burglars and con men. They are not my kind of people. The public and the cops have to be concerned with muggers, freaks and sex criminals—not with decent people like me.

These organized crime figures are proud of their purported success, which they account for in terms of individual initiative, brains, and courage. They express little bitterness toward the administration of criminal justice (including law enforcement personnel, the courts, and the correctional system), though they deprecate its effectiveness. This statement was made to an observer sitting at the bar:

> Why should I feel bitter toward jail? I don't go there. District attorneys and police —who's worried about them? Those that got any brains can be had [bought] one way or another. Everybody goes for something—money, booze, broads, gambling. Don't you go for something? Just find out what a man goes for. That's all you need to know. Then it's just a question of how much of whatever he likes it takes.

2. As with the professional criminals discussed in Chapter 9, that they are social drinkers may be due in part to the fact that the sample was encountered in an after-hours nightclub. There is however reason to believe that in the world of organized crime there are many social drinkers and few alcoholics.

In brief, this type forms a group of class-conscious, monetarily successful, highly committed career criminals, whose role identities receive self-support as well as group support. They share an investment in crime as a way of life which has thus far paid off for them.

GROUP SUPPORT OF CRIMINAL BEHAVIOR

Structural Arrangements. Before World War II criminal organizations existed that were composed almost exclusively of Italians, particularly Sicilians, in Chicago, Kansas City, New Orleans, and New York. But even then, as after World War II, the composition of most syndicates was ethnically and in some cases racially mixed. "Lucky" Luciano's group, the Lansky-Siegel people, and the Irish gangs from Hell's Kitchen in New York often worked closely together in bootlegging, gambling, prostitution, hijacking, and narcotics smuggling and trading.

To what extent these groups were modeled along the lines of or reflected the influence of the Sicilian Mafia is widely debated. In many respects, they appeared to resemble American organizations in structure and function. They were indeed "organizations" or "families," and sometimes the word "families" has here a double meaning, for some of the people in a group might be related by blood or marriage. They exhibited such structural features as a hierarchy and a strict code of conduct to maintain social order, instill camaraderie and loyalty, and ensure discipline. They enforced their orders and their code of silence ("*omertà*") with the threat of retaliation—often carried out; these are widely shared norms governing behavior in the criminal underworld, and are not unique to any single ethnic group.

Within the American organized crime groups that have come to public attention, there appears to have been a prolonged involvement of Italian-Americans in the higher echelons, traceable perhaps to the relatively late massive immigration of Italians into the United States; some of the socio-political traditions which they brought from the Old World; their slow assimilation into the mainstream of American culture, from which they were separated by both religion and language; and economic conditions that simultaneously yielded enormous profits from illicit activity and offered little opportunity for mobility in the world of legitimate jobs and careers. Once a strong, lucrative position in the leadership of organized crime had been attained, it was not likely to be easily abdicated.

According to Francis Ianni (1972), crime families are not really structured along corporate lines, although there is some rational division of labor based on skill and background. Kinship plays an extremely important role in selection of personnel for positions at all levels of a crime group. However, as organized crime in recent years has become more heterogeneous both racially and ethnically, kinship and nepotism have declined as important means of attaining entry and mobility within this world.

Organized crime groups seek to establish monopolistic control over various enterprises, such as gambling, but this is usually only within a given territory. The concept of a national confederation of such groupings is probably largely mythical, although there may be enough contact, knowledge, mutual respect and fear, and tacit and explicit understanding so that the idea of something approaching a national supreme body is not entirely far-fetched.

The Enforcer: Violence and Corruption.   A unique and essential feature of syndicate organization is the configuration of three positions, described by Donald Cressey (1967: 6) as enforcer, corrupter, and corruptee. The importance of these positions inheres in their integration within a broader division of labor, but it should not be thought that in the criminal underworld there is a division of labor, clear-cut positions, and specific responsibilities and titles such as might be found in the legal bureaucracies of a corporation, governmental agency, or religious group.

Any man who is a member of a "family" or syndicate can be ordered to take a "contract"—which simply means an order to perform a task—from a boss or higher functionary within the organization. If a "button man"—that is, a member who is implicitly trusted and given duties and rights not accorded others affiliated with the group—thinks an assigned job too difficult or has misgivings about his ability to carry it out successfully, he can ask others, usually subordinates and colleagues, to help him or even do it for him. Whichever option is chosen, the man given the contract remains responsible for its success or failure.

Some syndicate members develop reputations as "hit" men and enforcers because of their willingness or skill in murder, mayhem, and violence; others develop a reputation because of a single widely publicized event. Nevertheless, this does not mean that the underworld activities of such persons are limited to one activity and one role. The violent enforcement of agreements is only one of many aspects of syndicate involvement, and it is not the exclusive domain of specialists. In short, syndicate members inhabit roles that are not very explicit as to obligations and expectations, although the activities in carrying out a given contract will no doubt be very specific.

Some writers claim that organized criminals have been using violence less in recent years than formerly. This contention is questionable in the light of gangland killings in the late 1960s and early 1970s in New York City and Gary, Indiana (Homer, 1974). Violence is used to maintain internal security and discipline and to deal with persons outside the organization who constitute a threat to it. By striking fear in the hearts of would-be "squealers," the purveyors of violence minimize betrayal and thereby nullify legal authority.

The world of organized crime perpetuates four types of violence: client-centered, interorganizational, interethnic, and intraorganizational (Homer, 1974). Client-centered violence takes place between organized criminals and their clients. For example, a person unable to pay interest on money borrowed from a loan shark may be threatened or beaten up. Racketeering also involves violence. The *New York Times* of October 6, 1971, reported a typical case: A sales company tried to force the local A&P stores to buy a detergent that was rejected because it did not meet company standards. Two A&P managers were murdered and sixteen supermarkets were set afire by arsonous efforts believed traceable to this event.

Interorganizational group violence is generated by rivalry between criminal organizations or families, each striving for monopoly over territory or over business interests. Sometimes these rivalries are also interethnic, with various syndicates—each dominated by a single ethnic stamp of identity—vying for a piece of the action, often a sizeable one.

Violent conflict between two factions of a criminal family flares up as intraorganizational struggle, often reflecting intergenerational conflicts between the "old guard" and the "young Turks" who want to bring radical changes to the structure and operation of the organization. The Gallo-Profaci and the Bonanno wars are cases in point (Homer, 1974: 43).

Although the threat of violence is felt in all operations of organized crime, it is used on a continuous basis only by enforcers performing special functions—e.g., in loan-sharking and bodyguard activities. Sometimes the enforcers hire others to do "minor" jobs for them. Organized crime does not have legal recourse; therefore, the use of violence has always inhered in the formation and maintenance of syndicate crime.

The corrupter also occupies an important position in the crime family hierarchy. He bribes, buys, intimidates, threatens, negotiates, and sweet-talks himself into a relationship with police, public officials, and anyone else who might help family members maintain immunity from arrest, prosecution, and punishment. These corrupting functions are not centralized in a single position, but are shared by several corrupters. For instance, one corrupter may take care of the police or city hall while another may be assigned some other department. Corruption takes place whenever a public official violates duty in exchange for some private gain or becomes otherwise obligated to criminals. Patronage, on the other hand, is the act of granting governmental favors in exchange for political support. Official corruption is generally exercised in three ways: nonfeasance, or failing to perform a required duty (e.g., ignoring statutory duties on gambling and overlooking other illegal activities); malfeasance, or the commission of an unlawful act by a public official under the color, cloak, and protection of the office (e.g., extorting money under the guise of soliciting a "political contribution"); misfeasance, or illegal, morally wrong, and improper conduct by a public official (e.g., demanding a kickback or taking bribes for city bids on contracts). (See President's Commission, 1967b: 64–74.) The corrupt official may rationalize his activities by viewing the ill-gotten gains as fringe benefits of the job.

Corruption takes place at various levels of government in a variety of agencies. The rewards for actions of public officials beneficial to organized crime vary from the delivery of votes to cash payments. Corrupt officials may be required by the corrupter to take positive action or merely exercise "ignorance" and neglect. For example, a customs official may not inspect the bag of a traveler, a judge may let someone go free, or a mayor may tell his police force to go easy on gambling.

Evidence shows that organized crime may try to buy legislators by helping them win elections, sometimes by making campaign contributions. For example, the Kefauver Committee estimated that 15 percent of all political contributions come from criminal sources. In the 1972 presidential campaign, Nixon was supported by the Teamsters Union, often said to have close associations with organized crime. Subsequently, the Nixon White House granted two favors to the union: cancellation of an investigation of an alleged Teamster mobster, and commutation of the prison sentence of former union head James Hoffa (Hammer, 1974: 215).

Organized crime may nullify the legal process by bribing, threatening, or even murdering witnesses. Former Attorney General Nicholas Katzenbach noted that in cases involving organized crime, key witnesses frequently suffer "accidents" and are found in a river wearing "concrete boots." He claimed to have lost more than twenty-five informants in this way during a period of four years. He also mentioned his inability to bring hundreds of other cases to trial because fearful key witnesses would not testify.

Many instances of police corruption involving organized crime have come to light. In 1960, nationwide publicity was given to the actions of some New York City policemen, who issued illegal licenses to syndicate members to operate illegal lotteries (Cressey, 1969: 261). Ralph Salerno and John Thompkins (1969) have illustrated how the police collected commissions from numbers operators. Each policeman collected two dollars a day from each spot in his area. Two men in the squad car patrolling the area collected thirty-five dollars weekly. Detectives, sergeants, lieutenants, other officials of precincts, divisions, borough commands, vice squads, gambling squads, and officials from police headquarters sent their own special pickup men to collect fees totalling about two thousand dollars a month.

Organized crime may even arrange for the comfort of its incarcerated members by seeking to bribe prison authorities. Joseph Valachi's testimony revealed that his former criminal boss arranged for a reassignment of cells so they could room together. Sam Giancana, an organized crime figure serving a sentence in an Illinois county jail, made arrangements for his daily quota of steaks and cigars in addition to being lodged in the most comfortable quarters (Salerno and Thompkins, 1969: 16). Inmates associated with the Mafia are said to help run a Northeastern maximum security institution while enjoying many luxuries unheard of for other inmates, including immunity from many prison rules (Carroll, 1974: 67–71).

Ethnic Support. Two opposing views are expressed in the literature and popular press regarding the ethnic composition of organized crime. Homer (1974) calls these views "the garlic and guns position" and "the melted pot position." The former holds that ethnicity explains everything in organized crime and that Italian-Americans are the very embodiment of this endeavor, with other ethnic groups playing subordinate roles. The latter position holds that other variables, such as class or age, rather than ethnicity alone or even primarily, may explain the nature of organized crime. Daniel Bell (1967), for example, claims that organized crime is not a Sicilian-American invention but a part of the American way of life and a "queer ladder of social mobility" used by all newly arriving immigrant groups.

Joseph Albini (1971) has developed a more complex perspective. He cites the evolutional-centralization approach, which assumes that syndicates in the United States represent the evolution of an organization that has its roots in Sicily and Naples. Once established in the United States, it developed into a national association with a centralized structure. On the other hand, there is also the developmental-association approach, a perspective—supported by considerable empirical research—that views the origin and development of syndicate crime as emerging from social conditions and factors within American society itself. This point of view looks upon the structure of syndicate crime as including not one national, centrally organized group, but many organizations which may or may not cooperate with one another.

Certainly, no one particular ethnic group or set of variables can wholly explain the complex social phenomenon of organized crime. There is a great deal of interchangeability of roles in this enterprise. No longer is "money moving" the monopoly of Jews, nor is enforcement a purely Italian thing (Homer, 1974: 76). A flexible pattern appears to be emerging, embracing various ethnic groups that play roles respective to their circumstances. Salerno and Thompkins (1969: 370) have observed that black and Puerto Rican gangs have begun making criminal alliances similar to those made by Italians and Jews in the past. Many other Latin Americans appear to be involved in high-echelon organized crime. It would appear that the Colombians and Cuban exile and refugee groups are highly represented in drug smuggling, that Puerto Ricans are assuming the one-time Jewish role of money manager and businessman for the ghetto alliances, while blacks are providing a good deal of the muscle that was once the more or less exclusive Italian domain. It is said that as the Italians as a group become better educated, those who once might have joined the syndicate instead move increasingly into the professions and legitimate business, thus making way for blacks and Puerto Ricans in organized crime.

Despite these trends, many law enforcement personnel and some scholars believe that organized crime is still primarily Italian at the top, and that this will remain the case for a long time to come. Established institutions and those in positions of power and privilege have a way of maintaining and perpetuating themselves in substance, though outward forms may change.

Code of Conduct. Organized crime has a well-defined, though unwritten, code of conduct to which members must adhere, a code not dissimilar to that among other professional, career criminals or among prisoners, except perhaps that it is more strictly enforced. The rules demand loyalty to the family and the boss, honesty in relations with family members, secrecy regarding structure and operations, and "honorable" behavior toward outsiders (Cressey, 1969: 171). The President's Commission (1967b: 40–50) has noted the following chief tenets of the code:

1. Be loyal to members of the organization. Do not interfere with each other's interests. Do not be an informer.

2. Be rational. Be a member of the team. Don't engage in battle if it can be avoided.
3. Be a man of honor. Respect womanhood and your elders. Don't rock the boat.
4. Be a stand-up guy. Keep your eyes and ears open and your mouth shut. Don't sell out.
5. Have class. Be independent. Know your way around the world.

Through the code of conduct the top members of the hierarchy maintain their power positions. The code stipulates that underlings should not interfere with leaders' interests and should not go to the police for protection. When arrested, members must be willing to go to jail if the fix fails. Though the code enables the boss to exploit underlings (who must honor and respect him) and to maximize profits at the expense of subordinates, many rewards are available to those who follow it. Granted, the rewards are not equally distributed in such a feudalistic society, but neither are they for most citizens in the present capitalist system. The conformist is offered a lifetime criminal career with great protection from arrest and a prison sentence. Should he go to jail his family is cared for financially while expert lawyers ("springers") work for his early release. Depending on ability, industry, style, and opportunity, underlings have the chance to rise in the hierarchy. Those who do not still have steady jobs. The code operates for the safety and well-being of all members of organized crime.

The code's rules are inculcated in family members through ritualistic initiation and family customs, and are enforced through material reward, cameraderie, and violence. Internal informants keep the boss alerted to instances of disloyalty, betrayal, or misconduct. Despite the ultimate sanction of death, the code is based on mutual aid and cooperation, and serves to instill and maintain a "we feeling" among the membership.

CORRESPONDENCE BETWEEN CRIMINAL AND LEGITIMATE BEHAVIOR

In a purely economic sense, organized crime is an integral part of American culture. The economic motives of those involved are similar to those of people engaged in free enterprise. Like legitimate business, organized crime attempts to achieve maximum profit through efficient organization and management with a minimum of expenditure and risk. George Vold (1979) claims that the evolution of organized crime in America recapitulates the origin and development of Western and, more specifically, American capitalism. Initially capitalism, like organized crime, was ruthlessly violent. Parallels between the financial and criminal syndicate are striking—e.g., bureaucratic design, the economic ends, ruthless means, a monopolistic trend, violence, a struggle for respectability, political designs. Vold regards organized crime as a natural developmental adjunct to our system of a private-profit economy. He concludes that though business, industry, and finance are legal competitive enterprises, there is also an area of genuine economic demand for certain illegal goods and services. Organized crime is a business system that functions in this area, and, facing competition, must organize for self-protection and control of the market.

Alfred Lindesmith (1941: 120) has recorded several cultural factors in the United States that foster organized crime: an individualistic predatory philosophy of success, indifference to public affairs, general disregard for law, the profit motive, decentralized government, laissez-faire economics, and some corrupt political practices. Moreover, he has claimed that organized crime is culturally perpetuated because respectable people demand illicit goods and services. The activities of gambling, drug use, and moneylending have become common features of modern life, and such activities have supported organized crime as an important part of American culture.

In many instances it is difficult to distinguish between the activities of organized criminals and those of so-called respectable businessmen because the two are frequently intertwined. Thus, on a theoretical plane, it may be argued that illicit businesses are only morally—not economically—distinguishable from licit businesses (Merton, 1968: 134). Both licit and illicit businesses sell goods that people want to buy, and both the business world and the underworld possess many basic similarities of organization, demands, and operation. The criminal activities of organized crime arising from its infiltration into legal businesses and industries operate within the same legal framework to amass huge profits. These activities are technically legal until proved otherwise; thus organized crime flourishes, since the line of demarcation between legal and illegal activities is not always clear. In short, from a functional point of view, organized crime at present "fulfills some functions for these diverse subgroups which are not adequately fulfilled by culturally approved or more conventional structures" (Merton, 1968: 134). In a democracy such as ours it is unlikely that large segments of the population would accept the legal and police controls necessary for the effective elimination of the goods and services provided by the underworld.

There is considerable public toleration, apathy, and ambivalence toward organized crime. Gamblers, for example, are willing clients who do not want their bookmakers shut down. A covert tolerance of vice, combined with a refusal to approve of it openly, appears to be ingrained in the American ethos. Many desire to enjoy the illicit services provided by organized crime while officially prohibiting other people from partaking of these pleasures. Robert Woetzel (1963: 8) succinctly notes the American hypocrisy with regard to vice. Many Americans affirm values that are not in keeping with their wishes. Consequently, law and a high degree of lawlessness exist side by side, and the moralists and gangsters complement each other. Furthermore, the public that purchases the illicit goods and services of organized crime does not know—or care to know—about the many illegal activities, including violence, that are tied in with these products. Many syndicate offenses are not visible to the public, their harm not apparent.

Beyond the absence of a strong public reaction against organized crime, there are other aspects of the American social structure that foster weak reactions to this type of activity. From a purely legalistic perspective, organized crime was for a long time "a social category, rather than a legal category" (Cressey, 1969: 229). Neither the founding of such organizations nor

**SOCIETAL
REACTION AND
LEGAL
PROCESSING**

active membership in them constituted a criminal offense. Only participation in specific crimes, such as drug trafficking, loan-sharking, or murder, subjected a person to arrest and prosecution. Therefore, law enforcement authorities did not have the legal mandate (nor did they have the technical knowledge) to delve into the organizational structure of syndicate crime. The law enforcement process was by and large designed to control individuals, not organizations (Hills, 1969); it was no more applicable to criminal organizations than to corporate entities.

However, in 1970 this appeared to change, when Congress passed and President Nixon signed the Organized Crime Control Act, of which Title IX is known as RICO (Racketeer Influenced and Corrupt Organizations). This is one of twelve substantive titles in the act, the purpose of which is to eliminate organized crime. It intends to accomplish this "by establishing new penal prohibitions and by providing enhanced sanctions and new remedies to deal with the unlawful activities of those engaged in organized crime." Among the many problems posed by RICO is its establishing that organized crime is a very definite group, having members whose unlawful activities are to be controlled in some special manner not applicable to unlawful activities of other people.

The penalties for violations under RICO are more severe than those that would ordinarily prevail should the same crimes be committed and prosecuted under other statutes. A crime that comes under the category of "racketeering activity" is defined as "any act or threat involving murder, gambling, arson, kidnapping, robbery, bribery, extortion, or dealing in dangerous or narcotic drugs which is chargeable by state law and punishable by imprisonment of more than one year."

According to a study conducted by the National Association of Attorneys General (1975), several states have enacted statutes modeled after RICO. These include Connecticut, Florida, Hawaii, Pennsylvania, and Rhode Island, but only Florida has brought actions under it and that state's statute has been declared unconstitutional because of vague draftsmanship.

Although RICO has been in effect since 1970, few cases were brought under the act until 1975. Jeff Atkinson points out (1978) that there were no cases brought in 1970 and 1971, and in the six years that followed, from 1972 to 1977 inclusive, there were one, two, three, seven, ten, and fourteen respectively.

The Organized Crime Control Act of 1970 does not actually define organized crime. Perhaps the definition is too difficult to summarize in such a manner that it would stand up under the scrutiny of defense attorneys and appellate courts. But as a result, in the opinion of many, RICO is vague and may draw into its net only minor figures, while major ones remain unapprehended or at least not prosecuted or convicted. A problem that has not been dealt with is whether following an acquittal under state law, federal prosecution for the offense under RICO would constitute double jeopardy.

According to Atkinson (1978), criminal penalties under RICO are far more severe than with similar state laws. In Illinois, for example, delivery of thirty grams of marijuana could draw a maximum of three years imprisonment, while the RICO prosecution would mean either a fine of $25,000, imprisonment for a maximum of twenty years, or both.

Because of certain defects in the legal and political system, most prosecutions against organized crime figures either are dropped or end in light sentences. Among other problems, there are difficulties in obtaining proof, a lack of specialized knowledge and resources, a lack of agency coordination, failure to use available sanctions, lack of public and political commitment, and the ubiquitous fix—bribes, patronage, and payoffs. At the local level, one is faced with the possibility of police corruption. The FBI for many years did little to investigate organized crime, perhaps guided by the statement of J. Edgar Hoover, "Crime is essentially a local matter." For thirty-seven years Hoover avoided any assignment that would involve the FBI directly with problems that could not be resolved in a manner reflecting favorably on the agency.

What happens when organized crime figures are brought to court? In many instances, lenient treatment is accorded them, by agreement among judges, prosecutors, and defense attorneys. Convictions are often for minor offenses. Some judges give defense attorneys adjournments stretching over months and even years to accommodate the defense's schedule, a practice that consistently undermines a case and reduces the possibility of obtaining witnesses willing to testify.

The organized underworld is neither a person nor a corporation and in this sense has no legal existence. Yet, as a secret organization, it has a "government" equipped with money, manpower, and muscle. Through and by legal and illegal contacts, the fix, the placing of henchmen in important business and local political offices, the relationships with politicians, and the use of secret business transactions, organized crime escapes for the most part from local and federal business regulatory legislation and authority (Tyler, 1981: 287–290).

Nicholas Gage (1973) conducted a study to determine some of the factors accounting for the wide discrepancy in the treatment of racketeers and ordinary defendants in the courts. In the 193 instances in which organized crime figures were actually convicted, his study showed that judges gave suspended sentences or fines in 46 percent of the cases. Most judges were especially lenient for "victimless crimes" such as gambling, judges in state courts giving short jail terms in a small number of cases and fines in all the others. Furthermore, he found state judges to be much easier to pay off than federal judges. They were also "hung up" on conventional street crime. Finally, political influence is often used in such cases. Gage further notes that our judges come up through political organizations and build up obligations along the way. Racketeers cultivate these political figures, attempting to gain the political influence of those they have befriended. Justice and politics on the American scene are thus intertwined.

Crimes at the Citadels of Power

11

Crimes of the powerful and against the powerful have attracted increasing attention, particularly in America, during the middle and later decades of the twentieth century. Roughly they can be divided into white-collar and political crimes, although many crimes by industrial executives are outrightly political in their nature and aims.

White-Collar Crime

White-collar crime encompasses a wide range of illegal behavior by both individuals and corporate bodies. Until recently, there has been a marked tendency to concentrate on white-collar offenses as discrete, individual instances of conduct violating certain laws rather than to relate such offenses to the larger social, historical, ideological, political, and economic contexts of which they are a part (Edelhertz, 1970; Geis, 1974; Jaspan, 1960). That is, the emphasis has been on the offender, whether an individual or a corporation, and the problems presented by such offenses, not on the structure of society from which the offender emerges and within which he (or it) operates. However, the thrust of studies of white-collar crime does indicate that criminality characterizes our organizational structures, occupational groups, and corporate entities; that the criminality is not anomalous but on the contrary is part of the ethos of a profit-making economy.

In short, much white-collar crime is organizational crime, in that the persons or groups within corporations who commit such crimes often are doing so in pursuit of organizational goals—though they may simultaneously be enhancing their personal fortunes or organizational careers through these violations. The offense patterns are engendered and supported by the internal operating norms of the organization; peer groups within the organization accept and implement violations based upon these norms. Frequently there is collusion between so-called "regulatory" governmental agents (e.g., Federal Trade Commission, Interstate Commerce Commission), and corporate agents, which is clearly illegal and serves to prevent or attenuate the government's control of big business.

Edwin H. Sutherland (1949) produced the classic work in the field of white-collar crime, documenting evidence of widespread illegality and criminality on the part of leading corporations in the United States. Almost single-handedly, he focused the attention of sociologists, criminologists, the lay public, and the body politic on illegal activity that hitherto had been virtually ignored. Because Sutherland conceptualized as crime the corporate violations of rules made by government regulatory agencies, and conceptualized as criminal many people who had not been legally indicted and found guilty, his work was attacked by some, most notably Paul Tappan (1947), but nevertheless has had considerable influence in the social sciences. Following soon after Sutherland were several significant studies of business and corporate illegality: an investigation of offenses in the wholesale meat industry of Detroit by Frank Hartung (1950), violations of financial trust by Donald Cressey (1953), black markets during World War II by Marshall Clinard (1952), and public attitudes toward white-collar offenses by Donald Newman (1957, 1958). By the 1960s, the concept of white-collar crime had gained wide acceptance, and compilations by Gilbert Geis (1968) and by the same criminologist with Robert Meier (1977) mark the ablest efforts to present the best available material on this subject. Geis (1974) started to use the term "upperworld crime," which broadened the concept to include many types of political activity, a perspective reflected in his collaboration with Meier and in the work of others, such as that of Jack Douglas and John Johnson (1977).

LEGAL ASPECTS OF SELECTED OFFENSES

A white-collar criminal is generally defined as a person of high socioeconomic status who violates laws designed to regulate his or her occupational or business activities when a criminal penalty can be imposed for such violation. When the concept is broadened to upperworld crime, it would include all persons of respectability and high status who commit illegal acts. However, upperworld homicide would generally not be thought of as part of white-collar crime. Rather, the concept includes violations of legal codes controlling certain occupations and professions, as well as such patterns as restraint of trade, monopolistic practices, income tax evasion by super-rich individuals and large corporations, fraudulent advertising and sales, manufacture and sale of unsafe and improperly tested foods and drugs, corporate pollution, national and international bribery by corporate executives, suppression of damaging reports and evidence on the part of corporate bodies, illegal lobbying and campaigning, pension fraud by corporations against employees, and a myriad of other criminal activities.

However, despite frequent attempts to clarify the concept, there is no clear and brief accepted definition of white-collar crime that includes all the types of acts considered as falling within this category. This is not only be-

193

cause of the many diverse laws involving such offenses, but because the laws are formulated, enforced, and administered primarily according to the wishes, needs, and goals of that segment of society that has the power to impose its will and ideology upon the whole legal process: namely, the upper corporate class. This is not to deny that there are countervailing forces: consumer groups, environmental groups, and conflicts of interest within the upper class, all of which make even more difficult a clear formulation of what constitutes white-collar offenses.

Herbert Bloch and Gilbert Geis (1962: 307–308) point out that one of the difficulties in the study of white-collar crime "has been the failure of researchers to delineate clearly homogeneous types of offenses in terms of such things as modus operandi, legal categories, characteristics of the perpetrators, impact on particular victims, or the social context in which the offenses arose." They distinguish among offenses committed

1. by individuals as individuals (lawyers, doctors),
2. by employees against the corporation or business (embezzlers),
3. by policy-making officials for the corporation (antitrust cases),
4. by agents of the corporation against the general public (advertising fraud), and
5. by merchants against customers (consumer frauds).

One could add to this list acts by policy-making officials of the corporation against employees (union-busting, spying, pension fraud), and collusion between corporate officials and members of government regulatory agencies to "deregulate" rather than regulate business.

In most of the literature on white-collar offenses, the law has been taken as a given and infrequently scrutinized, which ignores the fact that rules are created and codified into law to protect the interests of the economically powerful (except when strong counterforces compel action restraining their depredations). In capitalist countries, laws generally serve the interests of the economically powerful upper class, and in socialist societies the interests of the highest political bureaucrats.[1] The white-collar offender and the "ordinary" or "common" criminal face charges for violations of different laws and are treated differently by the agencies that enforce and administer the criminal justice system.

The American government has historically tried to avoid control of business through criminal law, and has sought to ensure this by establishing supposedly independent regulatory commissions. Corporate acts that violate the law or are clearly not in the public interest have been placed outside the realm of criminal law in America and many other societies, being processed for the most part by administrative agencies. As social-conflict theorists have pointed out, powerful groups manage to get their norms and values embodied in both criminal and administrative law. Just as personal acts and some individuals are labeled criminal in the interests of the powerful who have the ability to so define them, so are such acts and people protected from that label when they emanate from a class at the highest level of socie-

---

1. For a discussion of crime by bureaucrats in socialist societies, see Alexander Solzhenitsyn, *The Gulag Archipelago* (New York: Harper & Row, 1974).

ty. Herbert Marcuse (1969: 67) stated, "There is no enforceable law other than that which serves the status quo, and . . . those who refuse such service are 'eo ipso' outside the realm of law before they come into actual conflict with the law."

Some claim that a legal system that holds the individual ultimately to blame, because he has *mens rea*, does not necessarily negate the role the social system plays in creating crime. As Albert Reiss (1966: 8) has pointed out, there is no individual criminal act that does not involve social interaction and organization. Much of what is termed individual crime is intricately linked to organized systems and organizations which are also susceptible to a criminal definition. The legal process in America appears to consider irrelevant the fact that the social system creates crime, so to speak, through its daily operation (see Schur, 1969, on the criminogenic nature of society). American economic organizations are rooted in property relations which the law serves to protect. By and large, criminal law is designed to control the activities of those who are dispossessed and marginal to the needs of a social system. The legal superstructure is designed to work not on a due process model but on a crime control model (Packer, 1968). When the public outcry becomes too loud, laws are passed to restrict business in the area of most notorious danger, such as consumer safety, harmful foods and drugs, and air and water pollution. Yet the influence of corporate elites over the administrative agencies seriously impedes the enforcement of even such weak laws. Elected officials are most reluctant to invoke criminal sanctions against corporate managers who violate air and water pollution laws or safety laws governing the mining industry (affecting employees) and the automobile industry (affecting consumers and, in fact, the public at large). Moreover, all recent federal administrations, under the guise of energy crises—however real these may be—have put pressure on Congress either to repeal or restrict the application of existing regulatory laws. Thus have legal sanctions been eroded.

Historically, the American legal system was engendered by, has been penetrated by, and has responded to the interests of the upper classes. In a rather general way, C. Wright Mills (1957: 131) has recorded that in the second half of the nineteenth century, beginning with the expansion of banks and other financial institutions and the growth of railroads, the large corporations became dominant in the business world. They grew until they were the core of the national economy, and eventually gained enormous influence over those governmental regulatory agencies that developed in order, supposedly, to control them. Muckraking social movements and later attempts by local and state governments to regulate big business gave way to the façade of control by the federal government. Regulatory agencies and their measures have largely served the interests of big business. Gabriel Kolko (1963) has shown with massive documentary evidence that during the Progressive Era, the establishment of the Federal Trade Commission, the Federal Reserve Board, and the Food and Drug Administration was not opposed by business, for large corporations had little to fear from such agencies. At a time when clamor against many corporate activities was increasing, these regulatory commissions served industry's purposes by having improper activities deflected from the control of criminal law, helping to set up markets on a rational basis, and limiting competition from smaller businesses.

The first regulatory agency, the Interstate Commerce Commission, established in 1887, served as a prototype. In the twenty years following the Civil War, small businessmen and farmers joined forces to demand government action to outlaw abuses practiced by the railroads (Bernstein, 1955). Their organization, the Grange, opposed the setting of transportation rates by the railroads, as such rates tended to favor big business and drive others to economic ruin. When state legislation proved inadequate, the Grange turned to the federal government, demanding absolute laws, including but not limited to the supervision of railroad activities, rather than mere reviews of violations and violators.

What the Grange obtained, after some twenty years and 150 bills, was an independent tribunal that adjudicated disputes between private parties. There would be no criminal sanctions against violators. The first chairman of the ICC (one Judge Cooley) was himself a former spokesman for the right of private property against any governmental interference. Thus, at the outset, those who were supposed to regulate business were selected on the basis of their favorable attitudes toward the continued monopolistic and possibly illegal activities of such enterprises. The appointments themselves were justified on the ground of the experience of the personnel selected, experience that reflected the intimate association of the appointees with the businesses they were appointed to oversee.

Another illustration of the economic interests of a big corporation being served by political means is the case of El Paso Natural Gas (Harris, 1973). In the late 1950s, El Paso secured control over its only interstate competition in California, the Pacific Northwest Pipeline Company. With this acquisition El Paso became the largest single gas pipeline company in America. In 1964, after numerous civil court (not criminal court) battles, the issue of the legality of this acquisition reached the U.S. Supreme Court, which ruled that it was in violation of the federal Sherman Antitrust Law. The Court ordered El Paso to divest itself of the illegal purchase. Undaunted by the Supreme Court decision, El Paso kept the case in the courts, presenting various plans to reorganize itself. In 1967 and again in 1969, the Supreme Court overruled these plans. Faced with these setbacks, El Paso then turned to Congress, seeking retroactive legislation to make its activities legal. With almost unlimited funds, the corporation mounted a lobbying campaign in support of its position. "If, because of its wealth," writes Fred Harris (1973: 33), "a company can hire the best lawyers, the best public relations firm, and the best economists, and can invest thousands of dollars in explaining its case to the public, I think we can fairly say that it has bought political power through lobbying."

In summary, laws that appear to control big business in America are usually weak, involve criminal sanctions only on the rarest of occasions, permit socially injurious action with impunity or with mild fines or cease-and-desist orders, and frequently reflect nothing more than the inner conflicts within the economic upper class.

Studies of white-collar criminals show that they are respectable members of the community. They are of middle- or upper-class origin and status, married, middle-aged, well educated (often at elite schools), economically successful, and, so far as is known, without more pathological problems than the average criminal. Subscribing to the American business ideology, they think of themselves as highly respected and respectable people, and are in turn so defined by others. Despite systematic law-breaking activity, they are able to rationalize their violations as good business practice even if illegal, as not harmful to the public, and certainly as not criminal.

The interactional setting of white-collar offenses is one in which the offenders ostensibly perform conventional occupational tasks while secretly engaging in illegal acts. In their efforts to keep their activities secret from those outside an inner circle, they often develop their own argot, not unlike that used for the same purpose in the criminal underworld. In the great electrical equipment price-fixing conspiracy, brought to court in 1961, the opportunity for collusion was provided by meetings of the National Electrical Manufacturers Association (Smith, 1961). Private hotel discussions followed the formal meetings. Executives were informally introduced to the practices of price-rigging by their superiors. "We gradually grew into it," an executive reported. "We understood this was what the company wanted us to do." From time to time the conspiracy was halted because of fear of federal investigation. This was known as "going behind the curtain." General Electric executives taking part in the conspiracy were instructed not to reveal their actions to company lawyers and to avoid mentioning the places they visited in their expense account reports. The attendance list was known as the "Christmas card list" and meetings as "choir practice."

Many writers have maintained that white-collar offenders use various rationalizations and techniques of neutralization to protect their self-images, in the manner described for ordinary criminals by Gresham Sykes and David Matza (1957). For example, they might deny personal responsibility. An executive in the 1961 electric company antitrust case claimed that his job required his illegal action. The rationale of the executives involved was that they were all "gentlemen," no more inclined to gouge the consumer than crowd a competitor. "Sure, collusion was illegal," one executive explained, "but it wasn't unethical" (*Fortune*, 1960: 135). In that sense it was no more criminal, in the minds of the offenders, than such harmless illegal acts as double parking.

It is not clear whether such a line of thinking is a rationalization to protect self-image or a depiction of the reality of the situation in which executives must operate. Raymond Baumhart (1961: 19), in his study of the ethics of businessmen, notes that many profess high levels of personal ethical aspiration but deny that other businessmen hold equally high standards. He argues that the judgments they make of the activities of other businessmen are probably closer to the actual conduct of affairs than are their self-serving claims about themselves. Baumhart's businessmen reported the widespread incidence of unethical and illegal activities in the business community: the use of call girls, giving and receiving lavish gifts that actually are bribes, pricing violations, and dishonest advertising. If this is the case, then business for some people may offer a continuing career in unethical, marginal, and often illegal activities.

Serious white-collar offenders usually work within a corporate structure that enjoys high status despite any systematic criminality: e.g., the nation's leading corporations repeatedly commit illegal acts against the environment as part of standard operating procedures. Indictments have been brought against several of the largest corporations for dumping toxic wastes into lakes and rivers, thus poisoning fish and birds and eventually causing health hazards to humans as well. A copout is frequently invoked: namely, that this is not the responsibility of any one individual in the corporation. Yet, when one states that the corporation is the criminal, there is still a denial of responsibility. Violating corporations respond to criminal allegations in much the same way as do violating individuals: they feign surprise, indignation, and ignorance of their criminal activities.

GROUP SUPPORT OF CRIMINAL BEHAVIOR

White-collar criminals and the corporate structure in which many of them operate receive a great deal of peer support. Edwin Sutherland and Donald Cressey (1966) have noted the importance of peer group associations in the support of white-collar offenses. They maintain that criminal behavior in general is learned from others who define such behavior favorably, and this would be true of upperworld offenses. Robert Lane (1953) supports this thesis. He studied patterns of labor relations in the New England shoe industry, and found rates of violation to vary from town to town. He concluded that one of the reasons for these differentials is the attitude of businessmen toward the law, the government, and the morality of illegal behavior; that is, those manufacturers who associate with people whose attitudes favor violations are more likely to break the law than manufacturers isolated from people harboring such values. In small communities, Lane found, the violations of some firms received support from local newspapers.

Richard Quinney (1963) found support for the importance of peer group association in his study of prescription violation among retail pharmacists. The occupation of retail pharmacist, Quinney points out, consists of two different role expectations—the businessman and the professional. The tendency of a pharmacist to violate prescription laws is dependent upon which role orientation he favors. Those with a professional occupational view of self are bound by a system of normative controls and guidelines that precludes any violation in the compounding and dispensing of prescriptions. Pharmacists who are not professionally oriented have no such inner controls. The business-oriented are interested primarily in monetary gain. They also subscribe to the popular idea that self-employment carries with it independence and freedom from control.

As Marshall Clinard and Richard Quinney (1973: 213–215) report, crime by corporations or corporate officials receives support from similar—even from competing—individuals and businesses. Some corporations have in fact developed a normative pattern of law-breaking that is shared with other corporations. Officials and employees are provided with a work situation that enables them to learn the necessary values, motives, and techniques favorable to this type of criminal activity. Since businessmen and corporate officials have a consciousness of kind and associate with one another at work and play, they are isolated in part from the wider society's strictly legal definitions of proper business conduct. Moreover, the laws and rules of government agencies purportedly regulating business conduct are frequently ambiguous and negotiable. Perhaps this must be the case in a capitalist democracy. In any event it is far from clear in many cases just how far a corporation or business may go in its drive for profits; therefore corporate lawyers and regulatory agency officials have much to negotiate. For example, cases of antitrust violations are not always clear-cut but fraught with legal complexities and interpretations. This situation invokes violation attempts. In the case of a business monopoly (e.g., ITT) or a multinational corporation where regulatory efforts under our present system are weak and problematic, built-in supports for systematic illegal practices are thus available.

CORRESPONDENCE BETWEEN CRIMINAL AND LEGITIMATE BEHAVIOR

White-collar crime is consistent with modern technology, its sophisticated bookkeeping and accountancy practices, widespread computerization, telephone transactions involving huge sums, bugging and other surveillance equipment, and numerous other advances of the modern era. It is consistent with the Protestant ethic, which calls for hard work, individual achievement, getting ahead, winning the game while retaining a semblance of respectability. And, finally, it is consistent with the profit motive, as it is designed to increase profits by controlling production and encouraging unnecessary consumption. It employs ruthless methods in the expansion of local and international markets, the exploitation and pollution of the natural environment, and false and compelling advertising. It cynically scoffs at regulatory rules and systems, whose weaknesses are notorious. In a heterogeneous society where progress is defined in terms of materialistic acquisition and consumption and financial success is proclaimed for all but available to few, one would expect to find white-collar crime in abundance, paralleling and imitating legitimate business activities.

SOCIETAL REACTION AND LEGAL PROCESSING

The United States Congress has institutionalized a special set of rules to govern the socially injurious activities of the upper class—that is, the wealthy, the politically and militarily powerful, the owners and top managers of big business—through the establishment of regulatory commissions and agencies. These commissions provide administrative and civil hearings and sanctions for corporate offenders, rather than criminal trials and criminal sanctions. Implementation of the rules of the regulation commissions is weak. Even when the criminal law is invoked against corporations or their top executives, the corporate structures themselves are rarely brought to trial, because the legal system is based upon the theory that only the individual is ultimately to blame, for he alone can have *mens rea* (criminal intent). Therefore, corporate crime enjoys low visibility and corporate executives

199

usually escape a criminal label, in contrast to the ordinary citizen tried in criminal court as a "natural person" when accused of breaking the law.

Neither strong criminal sanctions nor effective regulatory measures are utilized in cases against individual and corporate white-collar offenders. The punitive measures are usually mild. They consist of fines, cease and desist orders, or restitution; only on rare occasions are there prison sentences.

Historically, public reaction to corporate crime has been weak, because consumer consciousness has been weak and the public rarely perceives the corporate criminal act as causing severe victimization. When discovered, the offenders are seen as law-breakers at worst, not as criminals. The violators are often viewed as instruments of a corporation who have been coerced to act on its behalf. It is the profit-making system that has generated the attitudes and values of the offender, who has done nothing more, in the perception of large parts of the public, than carry out such values with loyalty and ardor.

Victims of white-collar crime are scattered throughout the social structure. When an entire class of consumers is victimized—and they may number in the millions—the individual usually suffers so slightly that indignation is difficult to arouse. C. Wright Mills (1957: 95) states, "It is easier to take one dime from each of ten million people at the point of a corporation than $100,000 from each of ten banks at the point of a gun. It is also safer."[2]

Nevertheless, some individuals suffer very severe harm from white-collar crime. There are the tragic stories of the thalidomide children, the disasters at Love Canal from chemical wastes, and numerous other instances that have resulted in deformity, disease, or death.

Regulatory agencies have failed in the past to keep the public posted about consumer fraud. The task has been left to muckraking journalists and such consumer advocates as Ralph Nader and his coworkers. Edwin Sutherland (1949) recorded the existence of corporate propaganda campaigns designed to develop favorable public sentiment for upper-class interests.

Neither the criminal law nor regulatory agencies are effective in controlling corporate violators. When, on rare occasions, the white-collar offender is brought before a criminal court, there is a class congruence between the defendant and the judge who tries him. Glynn Mapes (1970) notes an interesting example. In 1969, in federal court in New York City, a partner in a stock brokerage firm pleaded guilty to $20 million of illegal trading with Swiss banks. His high-priced attorney pleaded the stockbroker's case by comparing it to a parking ticket. Judge Irving Cooper gave the defendant a tongue-lashing, a $30,000 fine, and a suspended sentence. A few days later, the same judge heard the case of an unemployed shipping clerk who pleaded guilty to stealing a television set from an interstate shipment in a bus terminal. He was sentenced to one year in jail.

It is clear that under the American legal system white-collar offenders are better equipped than others to defend themselves, since their attorneys'

2. Along this line, James Turner (1970: 63) notes that when the warehouse of Caltec Citrus Company was staked out by the Food and Drug Administration, adulterant substances not allowed in pure orange juice were found. Estimates indicated that the adulteration cost consumers $1 million in lost value. This represented a loss for the average customer of a nickel per can of misrepresented orange juice.

fees are often paid by their corporations. In the extremely unlikely event that the white-collar offender is convicted, he usually receives a short sentence and is confined in a minimum-security, comfortable penal institution.

Political Crime

Political crime is a broad and ill-defined category. Many nations vehemently deny that they have any political prisoners, maintaining that the men and women in question have been convicted or simply detained because of violations of (or dangerous intentions to violate) laws that protect persons and property. The crime, whether homicide, assault, curfew violation, or disorderly conduct, such nations contend, does not become political crime because of the motives of the offender. Criminologists generally recognize that there is a special category of crime that is more readily understood if seen in the context of the act's relationship to the distribution of power in a society.

In a sense, all crimes are political, as pointed out by William Chambliss (1974), Richard Quinney (1970), and others. They are political because a body politic has created the criminal law, has legislated that certain acts should be handled as crimes, and has given certain individuals and bodies unique powers to arrest, prosecute, and imprison people for violation of these rules. Chambliss (1964) has argued persuasively that vagrancy became a crime only when the criminalization of such behavior suited the needs of the English industrial system, and Jerome Hall (1939) has traced the history of the criminalization of theft, demonstrating that it was a political elite that brought such conduct under the rubric of criminal law when it became advantageous and necessary to do so to protect the political-economic structure.

Nevertheless, to state that all crimes are political is to miss the special character of some acts. Such acts, we would suggest, are political either because they are directed toward influencing (continuing, changing, toppling) power relationships in a society and thus violate the law, or because they are committed by people in political power in the course of their occupational activities (whether for reasons of retaining power or attaining financial gain, or for other motivations—but the latter are subsumed under organizational goals). In short, political crime is a form of organizational crime.

Some political criminals, in contrast to almost all others, announce their intentions publicly, challenge the very legitimacy of laws or their application in specific situations, aim to change norms, do not have personal gain as their goal, and appeal to a higher morality by pointing out the gap between the professed beliefs and actual practices of those in power (Merton and Nisbet, 1971: 829–832). These offenders have a moral commitment to a "higher social order" different from the one that currently exists (Cavan, 1964; Clinard and Quinney, 1973).

However, this idealistic assessment is limited to some offenders against the state: traitors motivated by ideology rather than greed, antiwar demonstrators, civil disobedience activists, draft resisters. It is hardly applicable to what might be called "state lawlessness" (e.g., any illegal acts committed by agents of the FBI and CIA or by persons on the staffs of the White House and federal regulatory agencies, in the course of their assigned activities). Government offenders, in contrast to their adversaries, generally wrap their true intentions in a cloak of secrecy, uphold their legitimacy as agents of the government, publicly support the very norms they privately violate, may or may not seek personal gain, and extol their own moral virtues while deceptively broadening the gap between their professed beliefs and their actual practices.

There is still another group, likewise wrapped in secrecy and believing in the righteousness of their way, but seeking not to alter but to preserve privilege and oppression in a society. They are represented in the United States by such groups as the Ku Klux Klan. In contrast to the Klan, there are those who commit "ordinary crimes," particularly crimes of violence but sometimes against property as well, for the purpose of furthering a political cause. This is represented by acts of personal and collective terrorism in many parts of the world, including the United States; and by kidnappings to obtain ransom money or funds, bank robberies, extortions, and other crimes done in order to support a revolutionary movement (as when Stalin, along with some comrades, participated in a bank holdup in Tiflis in order to support the underground and emigré Bolshevik movement).

The evidence thus underscores the need to distinguish between the action patterns of government or its agents, upholders, and supporters, and those of citizens acting against a government. Acts against a government are defined as political crime when the state perceives the actors as a threat to the distribution of power and privilege. By contrast, state officeholders may commit political crime when they violate the civil liberties and rights of citizens and other residents, engage in illegal acts while enforcing the law, or under the pretext of enforcing one law break another. On rare occasions, and usually under the pressure of civil libertarian gatekeepers, such persons are prosecuted.

Several postulates are useful to form a foundation for study of political crime:

1. The American social structure is characterized by extreme differences in the distribution of personal income and wealth (Kolko, 1962) and a consequent unequal distribution of power (Domhoff, 1970).

2. There is an elite, a privileged group, sometimes referred to as a ruling class. It is made up of the owners and managers of large banks and corporations, who share many economic and political interests with one another and have in common many conflicts with ordinary working people. Members of this group are part of interlocking social circles which perceive each other as equals, belong to the same clubs, interact frequently, intermarry, and have access to centers of power and privilege largely closed to others.

3. Political power stems for the most part from economic power and upholds the structural inequality. It is realized when the upper class uses political means to maintain its economic advantage. Some leading agents of government play an active collusive role in this endeavor. Members of the executive branch, heads of regulatory agencies, senior Congressmen, government lawyers, the courts, and the police occupy positions which allow them to appropriate, distribute, or protect large sums of capital. Some

agents of government are themselves members of the ruling class, and this collusion benefits both groups (which are already partially amalgamated). Corporate campaign contributions help to elect favorable politicians (Green, Fallows, and Zwick, 1972; Sherrill, 1974). Politicians direct favorable appointees to the regulatory bureaucracies. Politicians and bureaucrats consult corporate executives and lawyers in formulating laws, regulations, and public policy. This last favor is accomplished by calling these executives and lawyers to testify before Congress, having them serve as consultants to regulatory agencies and other governmental committees and commissions, and cooperating with them in such policy-planning organizations as the Business Council, the Council on Foreign Relations, the Council on Economic Development, and the Round Table. These various consultations are enhanced by the rapid movement of corporate lawyers and executives in and out of government positions (Kolko, 1962: 17). Moreover, in some cases the political-business bond is strengthened by a social network. Finally, the collusive arrangement comes full circle when politicians solicit reelection funds by threatening to withhold business favors (Sherrill, 1974; Cockburn, 1974).

4. The ruling class therefore controls the political process that determines who gets the greatest share of economic rewards. Conflict ensues between those possessing political power and those seeking access to it. Agents of government want to maintain the existing relations of power so as to remain in their positions of authority. The powerless (the politically and economically dispossessed) seek a "higher order" contingent upon drastic structural change that will allow them as well as others to participate in political decision-making.

5. Political crimes are committed in order either to maintain or change the existing structural relations of power. The former are mainly but not exclusively the acts of governmental agents, the latter of oppositionists.

LEGAL ASPECTS OF SELECTED OFFENSES

As with any other type of crime, political offenses are illegal when participating actors violate established legal codes. However, sometimes political oppositionists are punished not for the behavior that has aroused the indignation of those in power but on some technical, legalistic ground, whether of a minor nature—such as criminal trespass, parading without a permit, or curfew violation—or a more serious one—treason, sedition, espionage. This process—which might be termed vicarious or substitute illegality—occurs because the American legal system does not officially recognize dissent itself as criminal. Finally, actions may be paralegal, meaning that the actor functions with authority derived from a position of power, as with an executive appointed by the President. This authority may appear to have a legal base, but in fact has no legislative determination or definition, as it is beyond Congressional control. This condition exists especially in the secret deliberations of executive committees where there may be no Congressional oversight.[3]

3. These penetration tactics are among those employed by the CIA in their covert operations. For a brief overview of such tactics, see Victor Marchetti and John D. Marks (1974) and Robert Borosage (1975).

For purposes of this discussion, actions that are illegal, vicariously illegal, or paralegal are all considered criminal if they violate the criminal law or a criminal penalty can be attached to them. In point of fact, many regulatory decisions (or non-decisions) never reach a criminal court, but, as Sutherland pointed out the actions they deal with could best be conceptualized as crimes.

From the research literature and media observation, there appear to be four current types of political crime in the United States: intervention, surveillance, confrontation, and evasion. We suggest that terrorism by the Klan against blacks and others, by Puerto Rican nationalists and independence advocates, by various ethnic and political groups against enemies who happen to be in this country, can all be understood and analyzed in terms of these four types. We shall look at each of them in terms of crimes against the government and by agents of government.

INTERVENTION

Intervention refers to all acts designed to effect change in the political structure of a sovereign state. These acts are carried out by those seeking a redistribution of power relations. The agents of change may be acting on behalf of their own government and seeking alterations in a foreign nation, or they may be attempting to make changes within their own country. They seek to effect change through systematic manipulation of events or penetration of members into the institutional life of the nation. Such efforts to bring about change may be not only legal but even institutionalized, as often is the case in the United States, or they may violate the law.

Crimes of Intervention by Government. Both manipulation and penetration have been the norm in government intervention. These types of action became particularly notorious during the Nixon administration, as a result of the Watergate scandal and the efforts of the administration to defeat the movement against the war in Vietnam.

Agencies in the federal bureaucracy that fail to carry out their administrative functions illustrate another form of manipulation, as, for example, in the deliberate nonenforcement of laws. (Activities of this type have been discussed as white-collar or upperworld crime, but they can also be conceptualized as political crime.)

Penetration followed by manipulation has been charged to the CIA, as well as to the corresponding organizations of many other powers. In Ecuador it is widely stated that the CIA funded the labor organizations, the press, and anti-Communist factions that in concert eventually disposed of the Aromsemana regime in 1962 (Morris, 1975: 76–377). The importance of the CIA in overthrowing the Mossadegh regime in Iran and installing the Shah, thus instituting a quarter century of terror and tyranny, has not been denied, and in fact has been widely admitted. The CIA played a major role in the Bay of Pigs invasion of Cuba and is said to have plotted the assassination of Fidel Castro, in cooperation with organized crime. In Chile, the CIA spent $20 million to boost Eduardo Frei into power, and later another $8 million to "destabilize" the Allende government (after it had been democratically elected). It is difficult to assess the role of large American corporations, particularly ITT, in the Chilean events, but they are said to have been paramount, involving such gross criminal acts as plans for sabotaging the economy, fomenting violence, and preparing for a military takeover. Finally Allende was assassinated. The CIA is suspected of involvement in other assassination plots against heads of states in addition to the successful one against Allende and the unsuccessful one against Castro (Marchetti and Marks, 1974; Wise, 1975).

The goals of these interventions were to gain a political victory and maintain the new structural relations of power. The domestic Watergate intervention had but one objective: the reelection of President Nixon. All government interventions of the types described above—both within and without American borders—are clearly illegal. The violations range from burglary and the breaking of federal political campaign laws to such serious crimes as murder in other countries. (There are also violations of the United Nations charter, which protects the political independence of sovereign states, but there is some question whether such violations per se constitute crimes.) Foreign covert operations by the CIA—particularly those related to violence, assassination, and the overthrow of existing political regimes—may be considered paralegal as well as illegal. This is because authority for such CIA operations is derived from secret National Security Council directives, handed down since 1948. These directives appear to have a legal basis in that they are approved by an executive committee of government, but because the secret deliberations are beyond the reach of Congress, the directives do not in fact have any legislative determination or definition (Wise, 1975). Finally, the nature of these interventions may be violent or nonviolent; most are covert, though some may be overt.

Crimes of Intervention against Government. There are many manifestations of intervention against the government. These have taken place at nuclear plants, at recruitment stations for the armed forces, and at draft boards, among other sites. They are led by forces that would often be regarded on the American scene as "radical" and by other forces that would be called "retrogressive" or "reactionary." An example of the latter is the 1962 riot at the University of Mississippi. Following a federal order that demanded the integration of the university and the admission of its first black student, James Meredith, some 300 deputy federal marshalls were stationed in the university administration building to protect Meredith when he registered for classes. Earlier, the governor of Mississippi and other high-ranking state officials had resisted federal court orders to enroll Meredith. One local citizen was charged with insurrection for his role in organizing a group of rioters.

Joseph Mouledous (1967) has argued that the harassment of Meredith and other Southern blacks during the 1960s was an attempt to maintain the existing white supremacist power structure, based on the exclusion of the black people as a legal and political entity. In Meredith's case, such harassment clearly violated federal civil rights laws. The nature of this intervention was both violent and nonviolent and was an open manipulation in full view of the public.

SURVEILLANCE

Surveillance, commonly referred to as intelligence gathering, is the accumulation of information without the knowledge and consent of those from whom or about whom the information is being obtained. Unlike intervention, which attempts to change certain conditions, surveillance is intended only to monitor them. Information is gathered systematically by electronic or classical espionage methods. The development of electronic surveillance methods is relatively recent and involves a full range of technology, including "bugs" and wiretaps, hidden cameras, and other sophisticated and often minute inventions (see Westin, 1967). Classical espionage, on the other hand, employs human rather than electronic means of collection. Human spies serve as monitors, informers, or infiltrators who gain access to certain bodies of information.

Crimes of Surveillance by Government. The government employs both electronic and human agents to gather information about citizens, tourists, alien residents, diplomats, and others, including some of its own elected or appointed officials. Much of government surveillance is legal and authorized, some illegal. From 1969 to 1971, President Nixon had wiretaps placed on thirteen people who were either ranking members of his own administration or journalists. Later, in 1972, the White House bugged the Democratic National committee. Electronic surveillance has also been used by the CIA, which bugged and placed wiretaps on thirty-two of its own employees during the 1960s—all this of doubtful legality (*Newsweek*, 1975).

Over a twenty-year period, the CIA opened and photographed the contents of over 215,000 letters, including some addressed to prominent and powerful Americans, which had been sent to or from the Soviet Union. In addition, two CIA spy projects, Operation CHAOS and Project 2, were carried out by sending agents into radical groups to produce dossiers on thirteen thousand Americans believed to be dissidents (*Newsweek*, 1975). It has been charged that agents of the Internal Revenue Service dug up details on the sex lives and drinking habits of thirty political figures in Florida, again without authorization and probably illegally. And the FBI harassed and attempted to discredit Martin Luther King, Jr. for a period of six years before his murder, at a time when he was the acknowledged leader of the civil rights struggle and one of the most eloquent voices against the war in Vietnam. Among other things, the bureau tapped his telephone, bugged various rooms in which he was present, sent him anonymous threatening letters, and sent his wife a tape recording purportedly of King in a sexually compromising situation.

The objectives behind surveillance by government are clear: to secure a political victory, to maintain internal security, or to quell dissent. This type of surveillance is basically illegal, although in some instances it can be legal when authorized by a court. In the case of the CIA, domestic activities, whether by electronic or human agents, violate the National Security Act, which states that the agency "shall have no police, subpoena, law enforcement, or internal security functions." Unwarranted wiretapping of any kind in most instances violates the Fourth Amendment, even when directed toward "subversives" allegedly threatening the national security (*Vanderbilt Law Review*, 1971). Covert data collection on American citizens violates sections of the Right to Privacy Act, passed by Congress in 1974.[4] The nature of government surveillance is nonviolent and by definition covert.

Crimes of Surveillance against Government. Agents collecting information against the American and other governments have made use of the same tactics as those the governments have used against private citizens. Bugging was used by the Soviet KGB against the American Embassy in Moscow (Marchetti and Marks, 1974), and there is reason to believe that similar actions of governments against one another are widespread. From time to time, spies have been arrested by the United States and charged with espionage and other crimes. The goal of such spies has been to obtain classified information and pass this on to foreign powers, particularly the Soviet Union.

The Ellsberg-Russo case was unusual in that the defendants had revealed the information they obtained not to a foreign government but rather to an American newspaper. Daniel Ellsberg turned over the documents that came to be known as the Pentagon Papers to the press, as a personal protest against American involvement in Vietnam in "a hopeless war" and in order to assist the antiwar movement by revealing the information.

Thus, surveillance against government can be undertaken either to aid a foreign government or to protest a specific issue such as the war in Vietnam. Espionage is itself illegal, in America and in all other countries; in the United States it is a violation of 18 U.S. Code 793–798. However, as a charge it can also fall into the category of substitutive illegality. Thus, in the Ellsberg-Russo case the espionage statutes were apparently used as legalistic substitutes invoked for the purpose of embarrassing, punishing, discrediting, and crushing an opponent of the administration. In fact, the specific sections of the espionage act on which the government based its case had never before been implemented. The government was actually asking the courts to establish a precedent that would criminalize the actions of the defendants ex post facto (*Columbia Law Review*, 1973: 935).

CONFRONTATION

Confrontation refers to overt contact between groups, individuals, or an individual and a group when this contact is between adversaries, the individuals and groups have continued conflict with one another, and one of the adversaries is representative of the power center in the society. Patterned confrontation may take on several forms. One is face-to-face contact with

---

4. There have been many legal challenges to government surveillance, and in some instances lawsuits have resulted in monetary compensatory damages.

others within the context of controversy over a specific issue or closely related issues. A second form is symbolic contact, in which the conflicting parties need not meet face-to-face. Finally, there is covert conflict, from which some persons are able to accumulate unauthorized reward or gain. While in America there are many legal forms that such conflict can take, there are also criminal forms; as with other types of political crime, these can be manifested in crimes by the government and crimes against it.

Crimes of Confrontation by Government. Two groups of government agents—the police and the National Guard—have on occasion been accused of confrontation offenses of the face-to-face variety. During the 1960s, such confrontations were well-known and highly publicized, and sometimes resulted in death. There were student demonstrations in which the National Guard and other armed government agents were accused of having used illegal force: at Kent State University in Ohio (where four students protesting the war in Vietnam were killed), at Jackson State in Mississippi (again, students were killed), at the Democratic National Convention in Chicago in 1968, and in battles between police and protestors at Columbia University and San Francisco State College, among other campuses. Some of these actions have been referred to by students and their partisans as "police riots," a phrase that was also applied to the confrontation at People's Park in Berkeley in 1969, struggles between police and blacks in many major cities of the United States, and clashes between students and police in France and Germany, particularly in 1968. The fact that these can be conceptualized as illegal government activity against students, black urban residents, and others does not preclude the possibility that latter groups may have themselves been engaging in illegal activity (as discussed below), nor does it imply that they were. Confrontation is often a two-way mutually escalating series of steps.

However, these incidents are not to be seen merely as clashes between groups of individuals. The police are guardians of the government in power, of its social institutions and class and property relationships. They do not determine policy, except to a limited extent on a local scale. Policemen who confront political dissidents of whatever nature must keep them in line, whether in the United States, the Soviet Union, or elsewhere. Demonstrators must not disrupt the established economic and political order. As stated by Austin Turk (1975), the police are involved in political policing; in times of stress, political policing makes political prisoners.

Situational confrontation may be illustrated by police corruption, which is political crime only in the sense that it is committed by people representing the political structure of the society; it does not usually have the redistribution, change, or continuity of power as its aim. The police may demand payoffs in return for protecting gamblers, prostitutes, and burglars from arrest. Other types of rewarding and corrupt practices by police include opportunistic theft, shakedowns, fixing criminal cases, participation in direct criminal activities (such as robbery and burglary), and internal payoffs involving sale of assignments, evidence, and other in-house commodities. To the extent that these actions represent patterns of behavior endemic to some police organizations in the United States rather than isolated incidents, they are police crime that has political implications. An investigation of police corruption has concluded that most new officers are "faced with the situation where it is easier for them to become corrupt than to remain honest" (Roebuck and Barker, 1974).

Confrontation crimes by the government are propelled by the desire for personal gain (police corruption), for political power (Watergate), and for quashing dissent (police violence). Offenses are in violation of many criminal laws, ranging from robbery and burglary to bribery and extortion. As crimes by the government, some are more accurately described as crimes by persons in government positions who are able to commit these illegal acts only because of the positions they hold.

Crimes of Confrontation against Government. Acts of confrontation against the government can be personal, face-to-face, symbolic, or have a combination of these characteristics. These represent many of the most important and best-known of the acts most frequently associated with political crime.

Large-scale protests can be included in this category. They range from the previously described demonstrations against the integration of the University of Mississippi to the many demonstrations against the war in Vietnam on college campuses and in Washington during the 1960s. Although such demonstrations, like the police efforts to contain them, are for the most part peaceful, many have been punctuated by violence. In addition to demonstrations, individual violent acts, often for the purpose of making a symbolic dramatic expression of a view antithetic to the political power structure, have frequently taken place. In the early part of the 1970s, during a fifteen-month period 1,425 terrorist bombings could be counted in the United States (Karber, 1971: 523). Bombings in America later declined in number, but continued to take place from time to time, attributed to or with credit claimed by Puerto Rican nationalist-independence groups, Croatian nationalists, and others. Kidnapping for purposes of political terrorism rather than financial gain, as was traditionally the case, emerged mainly in Europe and South America, and it sometimes resulted in the murder of the kidnapped person, as in the case of Aldo Moro, former premier of Italy. In the United States, this type of symbolic expression has been rare, probably limited to the abductions of newspaper heiress Patricia Hearst and Reginald Murphy, editor of the Atlanta Constitution.

The goals of these confrontations included the desire for symbolic communication (as in the case of terrrorism), protest on specific issues, and search for change in the structure of society and distribution of power. Symbolic communication is often a factor in terrorist acts, although they may be counterproductive; specific issues are protested in antiwar actions; and the quest for change in power distribution is dramatically brought forth during

209

political trials such as that in Chicago of eight defendants (later reduced to seven) who had been arrested and charged with conspiracy in the violent demonstrations that accompanied the Democratic National Convention of 1968.

Confrontation against government becomes criminal action when it is planned as or results in destruction of property or injuring or killing of persons. In such instances it is clearly illegal. However, in most cases it is quasi-illegal or substitutively illegal. Although quelling dissent is the object, protestors are usually arrested not for dissent as such but for legalistic substitutes. For example, 208 protestors were arrested in 1967 for failing to honor the expiration deadline of their parade permit in the march on the Pentagon. Conspiracy laws may also be considered substitutes. These laws (18 U.S.C. 2101–2102) stipulate that it need not be proven that the conspirators planned any activity but only that they said something about such activity to one another.

Confrontation actions against the government can be violent or nonviolent. All are overt, although the people responsible for them may decide to keep secret their identities. Conspiracy laws to the contrary, the evidence suggests that such "conspirators" act in an open and announced manner, at least prior to trial (Sternberg, 1974: 197). Terrorists of course plot secretly, but for their actions to be effective in communicating a message they must identify their ideology and social movement with the terrorism.

EVASION

Unlike other types of political crime, evasion involves a disavowal or retreat from a condition that the participating actors define as undesirable. Patterns of evasion include denial and flight. In the former, the actors disclaim knowledge of or responsibility for an action that may be attributed to them. In the latter, the actors seek physical displacement or escape in order to avoid acting in a manner prescribed by law.

Crimes of Evasion by Government.   High government officials, especially heads of state, routinely deny complicity in questionable decisions that they had previously approved. In some instances this is a traditional part of international diplomacy: that is, the denial is, although the complicity itself could not stand up to international approval if all the facts became known.

It is more likely that historians will describe illegal and unauthorized flights over the Soviet Union in time of peace (as in the U-2 incident) as a type of espionage activity that all countries capable of so doing actually perform than that they will call them crime, whether political, international, or any other sort. The Bay of Pigs invasion was only one of thousands of such events committed by numerous powers in this century; it is only from the viewpoint of the Cuban government that the invaders were criminals. (The Cuban government did react in this manner toward them, imprisoning them and refusing to give them prisoner-of-war status, as the country was not at war.) However, the involvement of President Nixon in the Watergate scandal—the full extent of which is not at all certain—and his subsequent activities, which might have been adjudicated as obstruction of justice, conspiracy to commit burglary, and other crimes had he been obliged to stand trial, cannot possibly be thought of as routine government diplomacy.

In all of these instances the rationale offered was that executive authority and national security were being protected. In the U-2 and Bay of Pigs event this is at least debatable, but in the Watergate case it is apparent that this rationale was employed only as further excuse for continued illegality. One of Nixon's tape recordings summarizes the purpose of the cover-up: "We're going to protect our people [the White House staff] if we can" (U.S. House of Representatives, 1975: 147).

In Watergate, the evasion by agents of government was clearly illegal, and in fact eight of President Nixon's aides were convicted of various crimes for their roles in the cover-up. Spy flights over other countries in peacetime (the outstanding example was the U-2 flight over Russia) and assistance given to military intervention in another country (as with the Bay of Pigs in Cuba) were paralegal. The National Security Council directives allowing for foreign intervention by the CIA were so secretive that presidents, who in fact gave final approval for all CIA clandestine operations in foreign countries, could plausibly deny any complicity with the CIA should it fail in its task or otherwise embarrass the United States. Therefore, with authority vested in an executive body unaccountable to Congress and legislative control, presidents are not committing crimes, whatever one's judgment of their morality may be, when they lie to the public and cover up illegal activities of the CIA. In fact, some would say that it was the duty of the president to lie; in fact, when President Eisenhower made the admission with regard to the U-2, stating publicly what everyone assumed to be true, he was not acclaimed but rather scoffed at for this act of honesty. Finally, the nature of an evasion is nonviolent and generally covert, though it may be overt.

Crimes of Evasion against Government.   Persons evading specific laws and government regulations are most likely to flee to a jurisdiction outside the United States, go underground, or in some instances try to conceal their criminal act entirely. Some 10,000 draft evaders, for example, emigrated to Canada each year from 1965 to 1970. Underground evaders may have accounted for most of the 15,310 Americans listed as "delinquent" by the Selective Service in 1968. The latter men were primarily draft registrants who fled to ghettoes, communes, or other areas where no questions were asked or they could find friendly refuge. In addition, there were noncooperators, who refused to register or claim conscientious objection, the latter on the ground that even such a claim was cooperation with a political act of which they strongly disapproved. Finally, there were those who refused to flee, and chose rather to go to prison for their opposition to the war.

Emigrant draft evaders had lost faith in the American government because of their feelings regarding its conduct of the war in Vietnam. Neither emigrants nor undergrounders attempted to change the system, except to the extent that any resistance or even noncooperation contributes toward change; instead, they followed their own independent judgment and abandoned the system altogether. Evaders used illegal, nonviolent means to escape prosecution and, beyond a handful of helpful intimates, covert means to avoid selective service.

CRIMINAL CAREER OF THE OFFENDER

Political offenders against the state do not conceive of themselves as having criminal careers (with the exception of professional assassins and spies willing to be double agents). However, when sanctioned by the state as criminals or outlaws, they proclaim themselves political prisoners and demand that that classification be used. (This demand is itself part of the political propaganda to further a cause.)

Some offenders attempt to legitimate a conventional criminal career by claiming to be political prisoners. However, if all prisoners, or just all those who came out of oppressive social conditions, are categorized as political prisoners (although most will have perpetrated robberies, burglaries, and other acts for personal rather than political gain), the separate idea of political crime would lose its meaning.

The political offender is committed to social or political goals that may or may not require law-breaking in order to be attained but for which he or she opts to use law-breaking methods. In contrast, political offenders in government who use their office to attain private illegal gain may be more akin to upperworld white-collar criminals than to political criminals in the general sense in which this term is used.

Political criminals vary in ethnicity, goals, age, sex, and social class, among other factors. Many are well educated; many are of radical political leanings. Women have been prominently represented in the leadership of such groups, but have probably been outnumbered by men. In the 1960s in the United States, young people were overrepresented, because of the draft and the movements taking hold among students.

It is likely that most antigovernment offenders are much more cognizant of the social, economic, and political inequalities in America and elsewhere in the world, and the causes of such inequality, than their conservative counterparts. Various groups of political offenders share value systems that comprise countercultures.

Government personnel who are political offenders are generally similar to white-collar criminals in that they are educated, upperworld, and respected persons, and they commit offenses against the public in the course of their everyday occupations and professions. Often—as with the police, the FBI, and the CIA—they operate within a framework of secrecy. They claim that any law-breaking in which they indulge (other than corruption) is necessary in order to enforce the law.

Thus, crimes by government agents have two separate but often interlocking goals: maintenance of the existing system, and attainment of private but ill-gotten gain. Some have claimed that Nixon and his aides were not political offenders but simply unscrupulous individuals who broke the law to maintain personal political power. Their strongest financial backers and political supporters before and during their "travail of tears" were economically and politically powerful elites. Nixon and Agnew not only rewarded these people with financial and political gains but also obtained in return improper favors from them. It was big business that supported Nixon, and it was Nixon who supported big business.

Many government policy-makers, military men, and diplomats routinely commit illegal acts in other countries. They do this in the interest of their concept of desirable American foreign policy, and defend this as simply being a matter of doing their job, and as illustrating their higher loyalty, all this being necessary because other powerful nations do the same and American failure to do so would jeopardize this country.

Many antigovernment political criminals belong to well-organized groups or informal radical subcultures from which they derive considerable support. Some of these organizations are formed along ethnic, racial, political, or economic dimensions. As ideological offenders, they mingle with those whose views they share.

GROUP SUPPORT OF CRIMINAL BEHAVIOR

The government offender receives support from several sources: his operating peer groups, officials above and below him, socioeconomic elites outside the government on whose behalf he is acting, and large sections of the conservative masses. When their violations are an integral part of the governing or regulating process, offenders have built-in support for their illegal activities. When their offenses constitute a departure from overtly accepted procedures, as in the Watergate scandal and police corruption, the offenders may be denounced, often by people whose own conduct differs little from what they publicly declare to be so reprehensible.

Crimes against government often arise out of situations consistent with democratic values of American society, as supported particularly by the First Amendment to the Constitution. Many of the offenses are violations of state laws and city ordinances that themselves nullify the rights of petition, association, dissent, and freedom of speech, laws ostensibly promulgated in the name of public order and safety but actually designed to discourage, defeat, and give an excuse for the arrest of protestors.

CORRESPONDENCE BETWEEN CRIMINAL AND LEGITIMATE BEHAVIOR

Constituted authority often contrives to prevent public protests that call for structural changes in society. In any society, there is continual tension between activist dissenters who clamor for observance of civil liberties that would enable them to present programs for structural change and government agents interested in maintenance of the status quo. There is conflict over the definition of political freedom and over the limits of behavior consistent with such freedom.

However, when such dissent takes on the form of sabotage, spying, espionage, assassination, looting, rioting, the destruction of property (as in arson), or attacks against persons, there is no analogous legitimate and legal behavior to support it.

213

SOCIETAL REACTION AND LEGAL PROCESSING

Political crime, more than any other type of criminal conduct, can be understood in the context of the sociopolitical setting in which it is cultivated. Because it is ideological or convictional crime, it is the least likely to be diminished by the usual punitive measures. It demands analysis in terms of the prevailing political climate and social structure, change in which can sometimes bring about diminution of the offenses or even a redefinition of the offenders as righteous and their opponents as criminal. Martin Luther King, Jr., for example, was jailed some sixty times for violations of the law. After a few years, however, the violations for which he was prosecuted were no longer crimes under any criminal codes.

Crimes against Public Order and against Sexual Mores

There is a strange overlapping of crimes against public order with certain sex crimes, and then again there is wide divergence. Whereas some sex crimes are against the person and are violent as well, others are disturbances only to a community whose moral values are outraged.

Crimes against Public Order

The various offenses that are grouped as crimes against public order are for the most part marginal acts committed by marginal or deviant people. They are relatively unthreatening and are perceived as such; they comprise disturbances rather than manifestations of criminality. In some instances, statutes covering public order offenses are utilized as legal substitutes in arresting political protestors or others behaving in a manner that arouses the ire of officials or police. Frequently these laws provide the basis for police harassment and lend themselves to the corruption of police officers, who have discretionary powers in deciding how vigorously to enforce.

LEGAL ASPECTS OF SELECTED OFFENSES

Drunkenness—which becomes a police issue only rarely when in the privacy of home, office, or restaurant—accounted for more than one and a third million arrests in 1970, a figure that had dropped to 864,000 by 1975, only to rise to almost 1.2 million by 1979. The fluctuations reflect changes not in the amount of public drunkenness but in facilities and interest in handling inebriates through the police, courts, and jails.

In addition, the offense of driving under the influence of alcohol—to which large numbers of highway deaths are attributed—accounted for another 365,000 arrests in 1970, more than half a million in 1975, and more than 1.3 million in 1979.

These figures do not indicate the number of different individuals counted; if they did, the arrested population in the first group would be much smaller than indicated above, as many of the offenders, about 90 percent of them male, go in and out of local lockups to be "dried out" and then released in what has been called "revolving door" justice.

In an instance of drunken driving, there may be considerable dispute as to whether the individual is intoxicated. There are various tests that are given, which bring up complex questions of constitutional rights, particularly the right to avoid taking the tests on the ground of self-incrimination. For street drunkenness, this is usually not perceived as a problem, as the charge is slight, the penalty not severe, and the arrested person often homeless, with the arrest constituting a way of obtaining a warm place to sleep, a meal, and a place to rest until a state of sobriety is reached.

Arrests are made in these cases simply because society provides no other services for these people, no paramedical or social service workers to pick them up from the street, protect them from accidental or deliberate injury, and take them somewhere to be held and assisted, if only temporarily. Elimination of the statutes from the criminal law would be useful provided some service were offered to the inebriates. In that case, it would serve the purpose of freeing the police for more important tasks in the struggle against crime and for the preservation of order in a community (that is, if new services were offered by some agency other than police), and it would also create the illusion of a reduction in crime because of lower arrest statistics. In urban centers, there is some tolerance of the chronic inebriate if he drifts to the "skid row" area. However, in other neighborhoods he is not accepted, and even in skid row there are businesses and families nearby that often create pressure to remove the intoxicated people.

Driving under the influence of alcohol is of course a much more serious offense than simple drunkenness, and it seldom involves the same people. Those arrested for drunkenness in public are lower class, if not in origin then in present status; they are drifters, unemployed, and in most cases unlikely to become rehabilitated. In contrast, the drunken driver may be working class, middle class, professional, or upper class. The offense is liable to severe penalty, which is, however, seldom invoked because such persons are generally seen as social drinkers who made an error.

In a study conducted in England, T. C. Willett (1964) concluded that those found guilty of reckless driving under the influence of alcohol are often not only recidivists but offenders with other kinds of criminal convictions. Those who drive recklessly live what he called a "reckless life-style." Julian Roebuck and James Landrum (1981), dealing with a subsample of drivers under the influence (mostly lower-class, underemployed, problem-drinking petty offenders), showed that more than two-thirds of persons arrested had several arrests for other criminal offenses. This supports Willett's conclusion that people tend to drive as they live.

Among the most important crimes against public order are the offenses that are directly or indirectly linked to drugs. These are generally part of what is conceptualized as victimless crime, a category that includes adult consensual sexual activity not socially approved, gambling, and other types of activity in which no one is hurt except possibly the willing participants.

Many drugs are either totally banned or restricted as regards their manufacture, sale, purchase, and use in the United States as well as in most other countries of the world. These include marijuana, heroin, cocaine, LSD and other hallucinogens (i.e., mind-altering substances that produce temporary hallucinations), and such prescription items as tranquilizers, amphetamines, and barbiturates. Laws pertaining to these materials cover importation (or smuggling) into the United States, and unauthorized manufacture, transportation, and possession. It is widely believed that trading in heroin is under the effective control of organized crime, but it is the user on the street who constitutes a public order problem in major American cities.

Many crimes against public order are covered by statutes that are written broadly. People often come into court under some catch-all category such as disorderly conduct, vagrancy, loitering and curfew violations (the latter almost entirely for children and adolescents), or some such vague category as those encompassed in the Uniform Crime Reports under "all other offenses except traffic."

CRIMINAL CAREER OF THE OFFENDER

The public drunkenness offender is a chronic offender. He is arrested because of alcoholism and life-style rather than injury to person or property. It might be said that his way of life is offensive when it becomes visible, and if invisible would not be subject to punishment. That is why the laws are written in such a way as to criminalize *public* drunkenness rather than drunkenness itself, although in the Uniform Crime Reports the world "public" is omitted.

If being drunk in public can be considered criminal, then one might say of these people that they not only have a criminal career but have no other career.

Some people arrested as public nuisances or for disorderly conduct are involved in chronic life-styles that likewise tend to preempt any other career: Examples would be skid row alcoholics, vagrants, and some public transvestites.

GROUP SUPPORT OF CRIMINAL BEHAVIOR

There is a modicum of group support for the chronic inebriate, in the sense that some very tenuous community-type relations are formed in what can be described as a pathetic lumpenproletarian subgroup of society. A suggestion of just such a community was found by Harvey Siegal (1978) in his study of a single-room-only hotel (or "welfare" hotel, as it is commonly called) in New York City. Indeed, skid row alcoholics have been known to form "bottle clubs."

From time to time, soup kitchens, Salvation Army hostels, religious groups, and others provide skid row alcoholics with physical sustenance. Religious conversion is often also attempted with these derelicts.

217

Some vagrants and beggars are loners, but for the most part they huddle with others like themselves. The support for transvestites comes not only from those of similar bent, but from many gay people who oppose police harassment, although they distinguish themselves from flagrant effeminate activity.

Few crimes receive so much group support as drug use. The user is seldom able to survive as a loner, for he needs a network if for no other reason than to obtain the goods. His peers, schoolmates, and friends may have induced him to use heroin, and then may offer him considerable social and psychological support in continuing its use should he at any time waver and be on the verge of renunciation of his dependency.

CORRESPONDENCE BETWEEN CRIMINAL AND LEGITIMATE BEHAVIOR

There is a close relationship between legal and criminal behavior in almost all public order offenses. Not only is social drinking approved in our society, but intoxication is widespread and affects persons in all social classes, including some of the highest public officials. Although most such people are carefully guarded from displaying their intoxication in public, even when they do make a display, it is usually readily excused, and reacted to with more sympathy than anger—depending upon where they are, with whom they are drinking, and the nature of their political support or opposition (if indeed they are political figures).

Other public order crimes show an equally great correspondence between law-abiding and law-breaking behavior. Whether noisy, congregating adolescents or older people are ignored, politely told to break up their group or remain more subdued, or are hauled into court will depend primarily upon social class and the specific setting as well as degree of deference shown to police officers.

The line between legal and illegal behavior, always difficult to define in penal codes, is left to the discretion of police officers and judges in cases of disorderly conduct and other offenses against the public order, more so than in most other types of conduct that lead to arrest.

SOCIETAL REACTION AND LEGAL PROCESSING

Most people in public avoid situations in which there is a disturbance. If there are complaints, they are sometimes anonymous, and are made only when boisterousness seems to be escalating into interpersonal violence. If hard-core pornography, streetwalking transvestites, and peep shows beckon the passerby to partake of some forbidden delights, those who find these activities reprehensible tend to avoid the areas—which is not easy to do if they live or work there. Still, many people support crusades for decency. Those who abjure them often do so stating that the work of police would be better focused on more serious and threatening problems.

Nevertheless, politicians and journalists occasionally find useful issues in crusading against "vice," "sin," and public expressions of behavior widely held to be distasteful. Thus, periodic campaigns take place, sometimes without high regard for the rights of those swept up in the nets of arresting and raiding officers.

riage no longer exists. But because it is largely viewed as a private matter between the persons directly involved, efforts to control or handle it in the context of criminal law fail. Because it is not enforceable, legal processing of adultery cases opens the door for prosecution of a selective nature—e.g., for political or other undesirable reasons.

By contrast, there is consensus about some other sex crimes and the necessity for their prosecution, as for example forcible rape.

Two offenses will be discussed in detail here because they constitute criminal behavior of deep concern to the public: forcible rape and adult-child sexuality. In addition, several other offenses will be mentioned because of the relatively large portion of the population involved and the debates over legal and public policies pertaining to them: statutory rape, adult consensual homosexuality, and prostitution. These are, however, overlapping areas. For example, prostitution can be heterosexual or homosexual, although it is usually the former. Sexual assault can be against a female or against a male, although it is not classified legally as rape if the victim is male. A child can be the victim of force and violence, even without a legal definition that force is inherent in the condition in which an adult is confronting a child.

LEGAL ASPECTS OF SELECTED OFFENSES

Forcible rape is defined in Uniform Crime Reports as "the carnal knowledge of a female forcibly and against her will." In the early period of the gathering of UCR statistics, statutory rape (sexual acts between an adult male and a minor female—not a child—without the use of force) was included in the figure for rape, but there has since been a separation of these two quite distinct forms of behavior, and statutory rape is no longer an index crime. State definitions and case law are sometimes more specific than the UCR definition of rape, often requiring that the act be penile-vaginal (otherwise it is classified as sexual assault or sodomy, or placed in some other category), and some jurisdictions have in the past required ejaculation to have occurred for the conduct to be classified as rape. UCR handles this problem by using the phrase "carnal knowledge," which includes sodomy or any other type of enforced sexual relation, coital or noncoital. UCR also includes "assaults to commit forcible rape" in the same category as completed acts. This is controversial as a classification method for the purpose of amassing crime statistics, because it introduces a greater possibility that there will be inconsistency between one state and another in reporting, and it involves the element of motivation or intention, which may or may not be clear-cut.

For 1979, UCR reported 75,089 forcible rapes (including attempts, limited to heterosexual) in the United States, for a rate of 34.5 per 100,000 inhabitants. However, this rate rises to about 70 when only female inhabitants are considered as potential victims, and again doubles when only the most vulnerable age group is considered, reaching its highest rates for young black females.

Menachem Amir (1971), in his studies of all rapes committed and reported to the police for two calendar years in the 1960s in the city of Philadelphia, focused on several concepts. These included group rape, in which two or more males are accomplices in subduing the female and all participate in the assault; felony rape, in which the sexual act was apparently unplanned but occurred when a male in the course of committing another crime, usually a burglary, was confronted with a female; and victim-precipitated rape, in which the victim plays a role leading up to the act and does not employ ordinary care and prudence in seeking to prevent it.[1]

Adult-child sexuality—usually called child molestation—is found in the penal law as carnal abuse of a child, carnal knowledge of a child, or under other headings. Sometimes the act is accompanied by violence, even murder. The act itself can be heterosexual or homosexual. Some offenders have been known to be oriented toward children as such, rather than to girls or boys exclusively. The acts can range from making a pass or a suggestion to fondling, exhibitionistic exposure, oral-genital relations, and in rare instances actual intromission. Some of the acts are incestuous; many college-age students, male and female, have memory of sexual solicitation and activity with adults, relatives and others, when they were children (Finkelhor, 1979). The highest incest rate appears between stepfather and stepdaughter, but there is a high rate between blood relatives also. The offender in child molestation cases may be a friend of the family or a neighbor. Legal definitions generally revolve around the question of the age of the child, which is defined differently in various jurisdictions; in fact, the distinction between sex with a minor and with a child is a matter of the child's age; generally if she (or he) is over the age of thirteen, the act is treated as statutory rape. The American Law Institute (1962), in its Model Penal Code, has made the further suggestions that for the act to be child molestation the male should be at least four years older than the female, and that the male should not be permitted a defense of not knowing the child's age if she (or he) was under ten.

There are no reliable figures on the amount of child molestation reported to the police, arrests, or prevalence of the behavior. Probably large numbers of children have experienced sporadic and occasional advances, but perhaps of so ambiguous a nature that the child either was unaware of what was occurring or rejected the molester, forgetting about the incident soon thereafter. How many such acts take on a form that objectively or subjectively (that is, in the view of the child) could be considered serious and overtly sexual is a matter of speculation. The UCR does not have a separate category of child molestation or carnal abuse of a child. These acts, when not reduced to disorderly conduct, vagrancy, or some other legal category, are found in UCR in the catch-all group "all other sex offenses," meaning those not classified as forcible rape, sexual assault, prostitution, and commercialized vice. Only a research study could indicate how many such arrests (UCR data cover arrests rather than cases known to the police) would fall under a category of adult-child sexuality. In 1979, there were 67,400 arrests for all sex offenses other than forcible rape and prostitution; it is likely that most were for homosexual conduct in public or semi-public places. However, many child molestation arrests may find their way into official records as

---

1. There has been widespread objection to the term "victim precipitation" when applied to rape. Amir (1971) is here using a concept obtained from Wolfgang (1958), whose analysis of victim precipitation in homicide cases was far less controversial. For a discussion of this issue, see MacNamara and Sagarin (1977).

disorderly conduct or offenses against family and children, or under some other heading.

An indication of the frequency of arrests for child molestation or related charges can be gleaned from the work of Charles McCaghy (1966, 1967), who studied the records of persons convicted of violation of any law or section of the penal code if the offense actually covered sex with a child. The study, made in selected counties in Wisconsin, turned up 181 persons, 121 of whom were incarcerated at the time, the remainder on probation. It is difficult to extrapolate these figures for the entire nation; it is uncertain whether the area is typical in the population that is attracted to it and stays there, in attitudes of the public toward making a complaint and pursuing a criminal prosecution, and in other respects. One can safely assume that the McCaghy figures indicate several thousand such prosecutions in the United States each year. However, this offers no indication at all of the amount of such activities themselves, as there is little reason to believe that a close correlation exists between arrests and incidence of the conduct.

Statutory rape is defined as consensual sexual relations between an adult male and a female under the age of consent but not so young as to be classified as a child. It is called rape because the youth of the female is considered to deprive her of the right to decide for herself that she could enter into such a relationship. Hence, by logic, she has been "forced" into the act, not by violence or the threat of it but the superior age of the male. When the act is between an adult male and a boy (again, too old to be a child), there is often more vigorous prosecution and extremely severe sentencing, but enforcement and punishment have been erratic in this respect, with many cases handled through psychiatric referral while others have resulted in prison sentences of thirty years or more.

Homosexual assault, or sexual assault of one male upon another with the use of violence or the threat of it, is probably almost completely confined to jails, prisons, juvenile detention homes, and other institutional settings, in some of which such activity is said to be not at all rare. There is seldom prosecution in these cases, although many reports have made their way into the public domain and judicial notice has been taken of prison rape. In one instance, a young convict was freed on the ground that prison authorities had failed to give him adequate protection against assaulters.

There are many other legal offenses among sex activities. Throughout the United States, except some counties in Nevada, prostitution is illegal. Notwithstanding, prostitution (both heterosexual and homosexual) is thriving, and functions quite openly in big cities. Arrests are sporadic, and are more an occasional harassment and occupational hazard than a deterrent force.

Adult consensual homosexual activity is usually not classified as such in the penal codes, but is put under such headings as sodomy, crime against nature, or others. The criminal laws of the various states describe a wide spectrum of sexual acts and positions here—oral-genital, penile-anal, and others, whether between persons of the same or different sexes. Some of these laws have been repealed, but the U.S. Supreme Court has held that they are not unconstitutional. This is considered a classic example of victimless crime. There are few arrests for such activities, and the laws are unenforce-able, but arrests for consensual homosexual acts in public or semi-public places could not be called rare.

CRIMINAL CAREER OF THE OFFENDER

It appears that many rapists have previous arrest records, some for sex crimes but most for other crimes. With a few exceptions, one does not en-counter career rapists. It is likely that most of these people are violence-prone individuals who on occasion add rape to their repertory of illegal be-havior. Some offenders are found who have had no previous difficulty with the law and who contend that they interpreted the woman's refusal as a coy invitation that she wanted to be "taken." However, this claim is seldom be-lieved by law enforcement officers, correctional personnel, or researchers. For the most part, convicted rapists do not appear to be free of serious per-sonality problems.

How many of the persons involved in sexual activity with children have made a "career" of this, how many have persistent orientation toward chil-dren (a Lolita complex) with little or no interest in adults, is difficult to say. Of the sample of incarcerated offenders studied by Paul Gebhard and his colleagues (1965) from the Institute for Sex Research, it was found that rela-tively few of the offenders against children were pedophiles. Many of them were drifters, psychotics, mental defectives, or men with sexual interest in both children and adults; few had criminal records of sexual or other crimes, and only a handful had records of sex crimes against children. Mc-Caghy found that many of the men accused of molesting little girls claimed that they were drunk at the time; those accused of offenses against little boys did not make the intoxication defense. In Gebhard's study, of the victim-ized minors (pubescent and post-pubescent youths under the age of consent), the girls more frequently denied that the sex had been voluntarily entered into, although the offender may have claimed that no force or threat of force was used; the boys more readily admitted the voluntary nature of the act and seldom claimed that they were frightened, threatened, or overpowered.

By definition, prostitution is a career or at least an occupation, although sometimes short-lived. However, the occupational nature of prostitution more accurately describes the female prostitute than the male. The latter is more likely to be a part-timer, a student or worker or more probably a drifter who once in a while comes out on the street or enters a bar to "hus-tle," and who is not systematically pursuing the sale of sex as a means of earning a living. The female prostitute—who may be a loner or work in groups—very often has a pimp, a role that has been played exclusively by males until very recently. There are ancillary crimes associated with both female and male prostitution: some robbery, assault, theft of the prostitute's services—as might be anticipated in a marginal occupation that does not have the support, either for prostitutes or clients, of police or of a normative value system in the society.

Such victimless illegal behavior as is defined as criminal, under head-ings of crimes against nature or other, whether heterosexual or homosexual, would almost always be a more or less continuing although not a rigidly fixed and inescapable pattern. The illegal act is not sporadic, but is part of a pattern that may continue over months, years, or the entire adult life of the person. However, there is no reason to believe that persons involved in such behavior are more frequently engaged in other criminal patterns than is the general population.

Forcible rape and child molestation receive almost no group support, in the United States or elsewhere. Both come so close to modern universal condemnation as to suggest that "natural law" requires that they be defined as crime; however, examination begins to reveal exceptions and complexities.

GROUP SUPPORT OF CRIMINAL BEHAVIOR

Violent rape has a long history, and upon careful study one finds that condemnation has usually been limited to the violence committed against women of one's own group in society. The ravishing of "enemy" women in wartime has received at worst complete approval and at best only mild disapproval throughout history. Only in recent years has it been discouraged and prosecuted, as a result of wide publicity given to such conduct and the changed role of occupied and invaded peoples in the last half-century.

In addition, violence was used in some primitive and occasionally more advanced societies to effect bride capture. A woman might be stolen from neighboring territories or kidnapped by marauding invaders and then taken by the man who subdued and ravished her as his wife or one of his wives. Inasmuch as a woman was valuable property for families, particularly fathers, it appears that this was in part a mechanism by which the abductor could avoid the payment of the bride price. In societies in which a woman did not expect to be able to choose a mate for herself, the entire experience may not have been as devoid of group support as the modern-day viewer might expect. Robert LeVine (1959) has described a particularly aggressive type of sex play, bordering on institutionalized rape, among the Gusii, a tribe in Kenya; it appears, however, that the women are not unwilling but have been brought up to want to be captured. As far as is known, only Sicily for a period gave some group support to forcible rape, but under the special condition that the male remedy the ravishing he has inflicted by marrying the female. He chooses for rape a virgin (or a woman having the reputation of one), takes her by force, kidnaps her, rapes her, and then—since once despoiled she is impure and hence not good for marriage to another—she would accept the man who raped her as her husband. This system has been challenged with some success and appears to be on the decline, but even in its heyday it could hardly qualify as group support for forcible rape in the sense in which the term is known today. The Sicilian chose a woman because he wanted her as his wife and mother of his children; bride capture and forcible sex were his way of expressing his indisputable domination in making the decision that they would marry.

As for sex of any type between an adult and a child, there is little evidence of group support. Among many primitive tribes, such an interest in an adult was considered peculiar, and the man was an object of ridicule rather than punishment in the more formal sense (Ford and Beach, 1951). In prison in modern America, the child molester is greeted with contempt, often expressed in physical violence, when his crime becomes known to other inmates.

Probably in no area of social life is there such wide divergence between the ideal and the real culture as in matters pertaining to sexuality. Only a few years ago spokesmen for society—particularly its political, educational, and religious leaders—were still pretending that this is a world of married and single people, in which the latter live celibate lives and the former confine their sexual activities to relationships with their legally wedded mates. A double standard permitted premarital sexual activity by males, but only with "bad girls"—whether prostitutes or not—and these "fallen women" were not marriageable.

Although the law traditionally reflected this theme—sometimes illegalizing unmarried sexuality between even a consenting man and woman—disobedience was widespread, if seldom articulated. Prostitution, although illegal, was openly practiced (often with the support of local political and police officials), thriving side by side with kept women and other activities bordering on legitimacy and respectability.

While child molestation appears never to have had any legal and legitimate analogue, the same cannot be said of adult-minor relationships or statutory rape. The man who could capture the heart, love, and body of a younger woman, so long as she was not a child, was envied rather than assailed. The line was tenuous between the older man with a beauty in her late teens and one whose companion had not quite reached the chronological age of consent, even though she may have been mature and worldly. In statutory rape the offender could show the strong resemblance of his act to those of others not arrested; for child molestation such corresponding activity can hardly be cited.

With forcible rape there is a more complex relationship between legal and illegal behavior. People have generally been socialized to believe that the male should be the aggressor in seeking heterosexual relationships and that the female does not accede without some male insistence, cajoling, and persuasion. A man is often little trained to distinguish between a woman who rejects his proposal because the idea is repugnant to her and one who does so in order not to appear to be eager and is really awaiting further persuasion. If, because she is afraid of being brutalized or is for some other reason frightened, she does not resist, he may interpret this passivity as acquiescence (failing to do so at the time, he may nonetheless make such an interpretation ex post facto).

In a case where a woman shows physical injury, was not acquainted with the man before, and makes a report to the police immediately after the event, the correspondence between the criminal and legitimate behavior lessens. The offender may still hold on to it—a slender reed to assist in his defense should he be brought to trial and which allows him to think of himself as having captured a woman by personality, persuasion, and physical attractiveness, not by brutality, superior strength, or weaponry.

Societal reaction differs considerably for the various sex crimes. For sexual relations between adult and child there has been traditional hostility in Western society. Legal processing is often hindered, however, by the reluctance of some people to prosecute on the ground that the courtroom appearance may be more traumatizing to the child than the sexual act itself (a highly controversial contention). And, short of a confession, it is sometimes difficult to establish that touching or fondling constituted sexual acts.

Statutory rape, particularly when the female is not far below the age of consent or has a record or reputation as a prostitute or a "promiscuous" girl, is no longer prosecuted with the vigor that once was the case. The societal reaction is often more hostile to the girl than to the man.

Despite generally more lenient social and (in many jurisdictions) legal attitudes toward consensual homosexuality, when the younger of the partners is under the age of consent such activity meets with extremely strong sanctions. It is not unusual to find vigorous prosecution when sex has been with boys fourteen or fifteen years old; sentences of from twenty to fifty years in prison have been meted out as recently as the latter 1970s. But there is wide discrepancy here, that derives from social class and power relationships; when the older man is rich or influential, he is often sent to a psychiatrist and offered an outpouring of sympathy instead of prison.

Until the feminist movement was reborn in America in the 1960s, developing greater vigor in the decade that followed, forcible rape met with ambiguous social and legal reaction. Only blacks accused of raping whites were certain to be prosecuted; if not lynched out of court, they were not infrequently executed or sentenced to life imprisonment. The black female victim, whether of a black or white man, was given little sympathy, and the white woman accusing a white man was often similarly looked upon with skepticism, sneeringly asked if she enjoyed the act and subjected to considerable interrogation in court about matters embarrassing to her. Further, the rape victim has traditionally all over the world been a pariah: this is the classic case of blaming the victim, to use the phrase made widely known by William Ryan (1971).

This societal reaction against the victim has undoubtedly abated. Prosecution continues to be difficult when there is no witness—as often is the case, except with a fellow offender in multiple or group rape. Further difficulties in prosecution are encountered when there has been no physical injury, and where the case hinges either on differing versions of the encounter —her claim that it was involuntary, his that it was voluntary—or on identification of the accused by a victim. Cases of misidentification, in good faith, of so-called "look-alikes" continue to occur. However, the placing of the onus upon the victim is no longer prevalent, because of feminist pressure and legal reform. The changes that continue to be demanded by feminists—which must not place the burden to prove his innocence upon the defendant, for the burden of proof in a criminal case is always on the prosecution—constitute a difficult but necessary task facing the criminal justice system.

Classification of Offenders

Who are the offenders? What early life experiences, personality traits, social and demographic variables do they have in common? Can similar biological and physiological characteristics be found among them?

Historically, a major interest of criminologists has been the classification of offenders.[1] It used to be assumed that there are differences in background between those who commit crimes and those who do not. The post-Darwinian school of criminology—particularly in Italy where the outstanding figure was Cesare Lombroso (see Chapter 4)—sought to discover factors that distinguish the criminal from the law-abiding population. Psychoanalytic and psychological schools continued these studies, emphasizing distinctions among people in early stages of life—infancy and early childhood—although the Freudians never excluded the possibility that some people have inborn or "constitutional" characteristics that produce predilections toward crime. Some of the early American criminologists had strong leanings toward what would now be considered racism, noting the disproportionate numbers of juvenile delinquents and adult criminals among certain immigrant, ethnic, and racial groups (see particularly Healy, 1969). In Europe, twentieth-century Marxist criminologists, especially the Dutch socialist Willem Bonger (1967), emphasized differences in social class and economic background between criminals and the rest of the population. Sheldon

1. "Classification of offenders" is also used to refer to a process that takes place upon intake into prison, in which skills, previous vocational training, age, the nature of the offense, and other characteristics are taken into account by administrators of the institution in order to make a decision regarding work assignments and other tasks during confinement. However, as used in this chapter, "classification" has a different meaning: it refers to placing offenders into one or more categories for analytic, research, or social policy purposes (see Glaser, 1974, on the purposes of classification systems).

and Eleanor Glueck (1970) were much more eclectic in their search for background distinctions between delinquents and nondelinquents, studying no fewer than sixty-three factors, physiological and environmental.

Some criminologists have now turned away from all attempts to establish physical and personality distinctions and have declared that there are no differences between law-abiding and law-breaking sectors of the populace except that the former have the power, make the rules, and hence are able to conceal their own criminality. In his work on the stereotyping of criminals, the English author Dennis Chapman (1978) strongly advocates this position. The work of Edwin Sutherland (1949) on white-collar crime has given great impetus to this perspective. (Many have questioned why no one has studied the IQ, ethnic background, and unresolved Oedipus complexes of perpetrators of corporate fraud, bribery, price-fixing, illegal lobbying, and other such crimes.) A new group of criminologists contends that study of the characteristics of offenders is a wrong focus: one should rather ask why certain acts are criminal and others are not, or why certain crimes (and those who perpetrate them) are prosecuted while others of an equally heinous nature are not (Quinney, 1975).

Nevertheless, offenders have been studied and classified for various purposes, among them to highlight a number of characteristics. Under Anglo-American law, it is important to know whether an accused person was sane at the time of the crime and is mentally competent to stand trial and assist in his own defense. Thus, the law itself requires a distinction according to the mental state of offenders, even if research goals do not. Offenders are divided into those who are and who are not psychopathic, with borderline psychopathological cases identified as well; it would appear that the psychopath-offender is by no means a myth (McCord and McCord, 1964). To establish whether an apprehended person is psychopathic is difficult, and it is only rarely possible to know whether the crime of someone never caught was the work of a psychopath. When such a characterization is made, it mainly derives from the nature of the event rather than information about its perpetrator.

This relates to a major problem in the study of offenders—that so little is known about those who never get caught. The exception is probably forcible rape, where victims' descriptions of the men and events can offer some information. Thus, an assumption almost of necessity has to be made that the apprehended are not different from the unapprehended, and that those adjudged guilty are typical of a wider population. But when we derive our image of the criminal from studies of the incarcerated, we are removed still further from the original scene.

Most arrests for index crimes in the United States are of people between the ages of seventeen and twenty-nine, although that group makes up only 20 percent of the total population. But it is estimated that only one out of every ten index crimes results in an arrest. Are the young less likely to escape detection or more vulnerable to suspicion and arrest than those ten or twenty years older? Or can we assume—as has sometimes been validated with unofficial statistics from sociological research—that the under-thirty age group *does* account for as much of total crime as the UCR figures indicate?

When race and ethnicity are taken into account, the gap between actual offenders and those known through arrest is probably even greater. Blacks, Hispanics, and American Indians make up a disproportionate percentage of the inmates of America's prisons and jails. But there is great difficulty in determining whether and to what extent the figures misrepresent the true situation, because of the greater suspicion falling upon these groups and because of discretionary arrests, prosecutions, and imprisonment. This is not to say that the data are useless, but that they have to be interpreted with great caution.

Both age and race are characteristics that can conceal another variable—namely, social class, income, and wealth. The young are generally poorer and have lower earning power than the middle-aged, and the proportion of families below the poverty level is extremely high in the three ethnic groups mentioned above. William Wilson (1978) contends that race is of declining significance in American life: it is class that determines life chances. If income or social class were to be held constant, the disproportionate figures on the crime rates among some ethnic groups would be far less striking. Again, this is a matter that does not impugn the validity of the statistics but acts as a warning as to how they should be interpreted and what theoretical and policy conclusions can be drawn from them.

Below, the three variables of age, sex, and race-ethnicity are discussed in more detail separately. These are the variables on which official and unofficial information is most readily available, and for which comparisons can be made between their distribution in the total population and their distribution among those arrested, convicted, or in prison at any given time.

Age of Offenders

The study of offenses by youths has come to be a separate sub-area of criminology, known as juvenile delinquency. Some of the acts for which people under the age of sixteen are incarcerated would not be crimes if committed by an older person, such as sexual promiscuity, running away from home, buying beer or whiskey, "playing hookey," or being "incorrigible." Since the turn of the century, youthful offenders have been taken before family courts or special juvenile courts, where they have not been given the opportunity to defend themselves against the charges (for a history of the juvenile court movement, see Platt, 1969). The myth was created that they were not being charged as criminals but being treated as persons, juveniles, or children "in need of supervision" (generally known as PINS, JINS, and CHINS, respectively). Hence, their guilt or innocence on any specific charge was irrelevant. This argument was finally challenged in the Gault decision (In re Gault, 1967), when the U.S. Supreme Court declared that a juvenile has the right to a trial with most of the constitutional protection and privileges of an adult.

Leaving aside the issue of whether an illegal act committed by a juvenile under a given and specified age ought to be classifiable as a crime, it appears that a lower age group has recently entered into certain criminal activities. While there is a long history of the arrest of youths as young as nine or ten on charges of robbery and burglary, purse-snatching, street mugging, school assault, serious vandalism, racially violent acts, and trafficking in narcotics or assisting in such acts, both the seriousness and the quantity of such events attributed to extremely young people have increased. Burglaries that require considerable skill, robberies in which guns are used, and sexual assaults have reportedly been committed by delinquents in their early teens or even preteen years.

This is in contrast to the generally accepted image of juvenile delinquency in the earlier decades of this century. The pattern of that period was believed to take on the form of gang wars. When there was violence it was directed at rival gangs, in the fight over girls or "turf" (see Thrasher, 1927). The thesis of Albert Cohen (1955), that juvenile delinquency differs from adult crime not only in that it is committed by younger people but in that its major thrust is malicious, mischievous, negativistic, and lacking in rational goal orientation, has been an important contribution to the understanding of youth in the 1950s and 1960s, but it might have to be seriously revised, if not entirely withdrawn, as a description of youthful crime of the 1970s and later.

Of the almost two and a third million index crimes cleared by arrest in 1979, approximately 39 percent of the accused offenders were under the age of eighteen. When the figures are analyzed further, it is found that about 20 percent of arrests for violent crimes and 43.5 percent for index property crimes were in the under-eighteen age group. Almost all such persons were at least ten years old, so these figures should be studied while bearing in mind that the age group involved—youths between ten and seventeen—constitute 13.8 percent of the American population.

In Figure 13–1, the arrest distribution by age in 1979 is contrasted with the percentage of persons in the population for each age group. Even if the under-twelve and the sixty-five and over groups are omitted, one finds a dis-

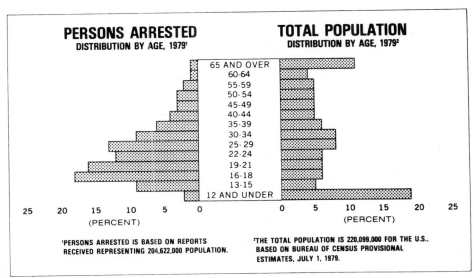

FIGURE 13-1

Source: Uniform Crime Reports, 1980, p. 187.

[11,758 agencies; 1979 estimated population 204,622,000]

Offense charged	Total all ages	Ages under 15	Ages under 18	Ages 18 and over	Age									
					10 and under	11–12	13–14	15	16	17	18	19	20	21
TOTAL	9,506,347	662,043	2,143,369	7,362,978	74,652	136,754	450,637	407,152	515,979	558,195	595,798	550,079	504,901	466,326
Percent distribution[1]	100.0	7.0	22.5	77.5	.8	1.4	4.7	4.3	5.4	5.9	6.3	5.8	5.3	4.9
Murder and nonnegligent manslaughter	18,264	206	1,707	16,557	14	25	167	283	559	659	884	902	934	931
Forcible rape	29,164	1,081	4,651	24,513	66	183	832	900	1,213	1,457	1,801	1,701	1,755	1,682
Robbery	130,753	10,622	41,157	89,596	392	1,837	8,393	8,327	10,480	11,728	11,559	9,955	8,627	7,721
Aggravated assault	256,597	10,688	39,860	216,737	898	2,173	7,617	7,248	9,866	12,058	13,325	13,145	13,090	12,970
Burglary	468,085	81,703	227,680	240,405	9,366	17,215	55,122	46,620	50,508	48,849	41,524	32,041	24,263	20,011
Larceny-theft	1,098,398	182,220	444,053	654,345	23,037	44,947	114,236	81,749	90,788	89,296	78,170	62,013	50,718	43,192
Motor vehicle theft	143,654	18,199	70,676	72,978	466	2,164	15,569	17,213	18,842	16,422	12,241	9,228	7,061	6,012
Arson	18,387	5,233	9,012	9,375	1,669	1,289	2,275	1,440	1,276	1,063	959	754	702	566
Violent crime[2]	434,778	22,597	87,375	347,403	1,370	4,218	17,009	16,758	22,118	25,902	27,569	25,703	24,406	23,304
Percent distribution[1]	100.0	5.2	20.1	79.9	.3	1.0	3.9	3.9	5.1	6.0	6.3	5.9	5.6	5.4
Property crime[3]	1,728,524	287,355	751,421	977,103	34,538	65,615	187,202	147,022	161,414	155,630	132,894	104,036	82,744	69,781
Percent distribution[1]	100.0	16.6	43.5	56.5	2.0	3.8	10.8	8.5	9.3	9.0	7.7	6.0	4.8	4.0
Crime Index total[4]	2,163,302	309,952	838,796	1,324,506	35,908	69,833	204,211	163,780	183,532	181,532	160,463	129,739	107,150	93,085
Percent distribution[1]	100.0	14.3	38.8	61.2	1.7	3.2	9.4	7.6	8.5	8.4	7.4	6.0	5.0	4.3
Other assaults	451,475	28,108	84,258	367,217	2,953	6,308	18,847	15,621	18,959	21,570	22,487	22,942	22,817	22,968
Forgery and counterfeiting	70,977	1,707	9,933	61,044	71	279	1,357	1,718	2,663	3,845	4,331	4,362	4,257	4,122
Fraud	243,461	1,570	8,372	235,089	105	241	1,224	1,417	1,985	3,400	6,551	9,090	11,214	12,104
Embezzlement	7,882	185	996	6,886	6	30	149	124	268	419	405	467	397	358
Stolen property; buying, receiving, possessing	107,621	10,178	35,630	71,991	583	1,851	7,744	7,333	8,802	9,317	9,082	7,695	6,398	5,426
Vandalism	239,246	61,960	129,603	109,643	13,230	16,018	32,712	21,990	23,173	22,480	16,628	12,870	10,086	8,673
Weapons; carrying, possessing, etc.	152,731	5,847	24,991	127,740	366	1,031	4,450	4,623	6,537	7,984	9,546	8,811	8,330	8,151
Prostitution and commercialized vice	83,088	373	3,319	79,769	24	46	303	487	781	1,678	4,742	7,468	7,619	8,091
Sex offenses (except forcible rape and prostitution)	62,633	4,217	11,368	51,265	382	839	2,996	2,250	2,290	2,611	2,719	2,762	2,745	2,818
Drug abuse violations	519,377	16,832	114,356	405,021	502	1,585	14,745	21,157	33,690	42,677	48,880	46,253	41,724	37,491
Gambling	50,974	266	2,107	48,867	15	31	220	357	618	866	1,106	1,293	1,300	1,442
Offenses against family and children	53,321	1,137	2,571	50,750	599	158	380	412	487	535	2,111	2,102	2,179	2,369
Driving under the influence	1,231,665	548	29,830	1,201,835	162	38	348	1,077	7,793	20,412	46,310	54,399	60,308	61,715
Liquor laws	386,957	10,361	139,286	247,671	195	715	9,451	20,009	44,101	64,815	65,282	48,265	33,675	13,367
Drunkenness	1,090,233	4,689	45,700	1,044,533	524	383	3,782	6,721	12,810	21,480	42,440	43,673	43,325	48,553
Disorderly conduct	711,730	32,180	125,536	586,194	3,318	6,839	22,023	22,180	30,508	40,668	51,514	48,425	46,149	44,488
Vagrancy	34,662	1,245	4,956	29,706	178	203	864	942	1,264	1,505	2,230	2,155	2,045	2,255
All other offenses (except traffic)	1,595,864	87,133	295,838	1,300,026	10,728	16,992	59,413	53,909	77,577	77,219	97,427	96,016	92,090	87,849
Suspicion	18,135	1,454	4,910	13,225	170	260	1,024	952	1,137	1,367	1,544	1,292	1,093	1,001
Curfew and loitering law violations	78,147	19,676	78,147	....	909	3,183	15,584	17,710	23,146	17,615	....	....	....	....
Runaways	152,866	62,425	152,866	....	3,724	9,891	48,810	42,383	33,858	14,200	....	....	....	....

SOURCE: Uniform Crime Reports, 1980, pp. 196–197.

TABLE 13-1
Total Arrests, Distribution by Age, 1979

proportionate representation of people between the ages of fifteen and twenty-nine, continuing for males in their thirties, and thereafter diminishing to a small number of persons and a small part of the populace.

Probably the most accurate data on arrests for individual crimes in 1979, showing breakdown by age, can be found in Table 13-1. Persons under the age of thirty accounted for over 70 percent of arrests in 1979 (except for traffic·violations, excluded from the figures). By contrast, cohorts between ages ten and twenty-nine (inclusive) constitute about 35 percent of the

Offense charged	Age												
	22	23	24	25–29	30–34	35–39	40–44	45–49	50–54	55–59	60–64	65 and over	Not known
TOTAL	425,099	382,882	353,421	1,279,025	827,300	564,716	418,477	329,217	271,102	186,336	104,507	94,264	9,528
Percent distribution[1]	4.5	4.0	3.7	13.5	8.7	5.9	4.4	3.5	2.9	2.0	1.1	1.0	.1
Murder and nonnegligent manslaughter	955	913	847	3,326	2,241	1,401	996	731	578	379	225	304	10
Forcible rape	1,671	1,535	1,474	5,276	3,241	1,852	1,039	596	405	214	125	130	16
Robbery	6,807	6,020	5,402	17,411	8,247	3,660	1,844	1,068	563	359	137	157	59
Aggravated assault	12,850	11,764	11,026	43,241	28,887	18,862	12,818	9,076	6,501	4,231	2,307	2,389	255
Burglary	16,835	14,199	12,143	38,981	18,584	9,250	4,887	3,204	1,955	1,124	509	460	435
Larceny-theft	38,166	33,799	30,078	111,083	65,610	39,816	26,993	21,056	18,302	13,179	8,915	12,223	1,032
Motor vehicle theft	5,202	4,242	3,661	11,624	6,093	3,146	1,756	1,150	699	407	176	147	133
Arson	571	470	425	1,664	1,049	767	491	344	272	147	89	85	20
Violent crime[2]	22,283	20,232	18,749	69,254	42,616	25,775	16,697	11,471	8,047	5,183	2,794	2,980	340
Percent distribution[1]	5.1	4.7	4.3	15.9	9.8	5.9	3.8	2.6	1.9	1.2	.6	.7	.1
Property crime[3]	60,774	52,710	46,307	163,352	91,336	52,979	34,127	25,754	21,228	14,857	9,689	12,915	1,620
Percent distribution[1]	3.5	3.0	2.7	9.5	5.3	3.1	2.0	1.5	1.2	.9	.6	.7	.1
Crime Index total[4]	83,057	72,942	65,056	232,606	133,952	78,754	50,824	37,225	29,275	20,040	12,483	15,895	1,960
Percent distribution[1]	3.8	3.4	3.0	10.8	6.2	3.6	2.3	1.7	1.4	.9	.6	.7	.1
Other assaults	22,229	20,587	19,755	75,006	48,853	31,534	21,261	14,540	9,919	5,936	3,068	2,880	435
Forgery and counterfeiting	4,097	3,739	3,692	14,337	8,064	4,209	2,547	1,492	985	462	173	110	65
Fraud	13,006	13,445	13,289	55,530	39,563	25,133	15,439	9,121	5,760	3,134	1,393	1,207	110
Embezzlement	392	362	333	1,335	996	670	463	316	215	95	42	24	16
Stolen property; buying, receiving, possessing	4,766	4,160	3,710	12,860	7,076	4,080	2,507	1,605	1,168	701	343	324	90
Vandalism	7,239	5,903	5,342	17,723	9,761	5,640	3,439	2,258	1,637	930	474	547	493
Weapons; carrying, possessing, etc.	7,715	6,921	6,544	24,752	15,629	10,314	6,940	5,031	3,748	2,463	1,332	1,374	139
Prostitution and commercialized vice	7,977	6,646	5,743	16,027	6,601	3,130	1,927	1,344	1,044	700	355	336	19
Sex offenses (except forcible rape and prostitution)	2,592	2,451	2,406	9,456	7,117	5,011	3,413	2,553	2,015	1,412	842	908	45
Drug abuse violations	32,917	27,978	24,354	78,051	34,851	15,046	7,315	4,295	2,643	1,589	673	574	387
Gambling	1,412	1,369	1,408	6,401	6,025	5,436	4,913	4,865	4,072	3,269	2,132	2,418	6
Offenses against family and children	2,554	2,595	2,705	11,539	8,788	5,942	3,623	2,032	1,168	548	264	190	41
Driving under the influence	57,460	55,454	52,270	210,986	154,675	117,993	94,678	78,666	65,519	46,018	25,400	19,130	854
Liquor laws	10,152	7,752	6,300	19,111	10,900	7,878	6,557	5,483	4,727	3,378	1,991	1,914	939
Drunkenness	44,088	40,274	37,538	149,041	117,286	100,700	89,660	83,856	81,183	59,773	34,546	28,400	197
Disorderly conduct	38,539	32,944	30,323	101,735	60,618	38,908	28,059	21,741	17,381	11,697	6,555	6,421	697
Vagrancy	2,008	1,738	1,509	5,394	3,115	2,002	1,476	1,182	1,041	770	392	365	29
All other offenses (except traffic)	81,996	74,801	70,382	234,681	152,074	101,665	72,988	51,307	37,381	23,278	11,981	11,148	2,962
Suspicion	903	821	762	2,454	1,356	671	448	305	221	143	68	99	44
Curfew and loitering law violations	......	......	......	......	......	......	......	......	......	......	......	......	......
Runaways	......	......	......	......	......	......	......	......	......	......	......	......	......

[1]Because of rounding, the percentages may not add to total.
[2]Violent crimes are offenses of murder, forcible rape, robbery, and aggravated assault.
[3]Property crimes are offenses of burglary, larceny-theft, motor vehicle theft, and arson.
[4]Includes arson, a newly established Index offense in 1979.

population, and those between fifteen and twenty-nine (inclusive) some 27 percent.

Analysts of this information generally agree that it gives a partially, but not entirely, distorted view. The younger age groups do account for violent and other index crime to a greater extent than would be anticipated from their numbers in the population, but they are probably less capable of escaping arrest than older offenders. And if one is going to exclude infants and young children in determining the proportion in the total population that a crime-prone age group constitutes, one might exclude the elderly as well, or at least those seventy-five and older (about 4 percent of all Americans), thus slightly reducing the discrepancy between the proportion of crimes committed by the young and the percentage of youths in the total American population.

There are only rare instances in which information on the age of criminals other than that from arrests can be obtained. In a study of forcible rape, Menachem Amir (1971) found that information on age and other characteristics of alleged offenders, as given by victims, correlates closely with the same characteristics of those arrested. However, there is a built-in bias toward finding correlation here, because a suspect is much more likely to be arrested if the description given by the victim is accurate.

If some of the information in Table 13–1 is deleted, the relationship of youth to crime becomes clarified. Arrests for curfew and loitering violations and for being a runaway are for the most part "status offenses"—that is, offenses only because they are committed by young people; if these are eliminated, the under-fifteen percentage of all arrests drops from 7.0 to 6.2; the under-eighteen from 22.5 to about 20.6. What begins to emerge is that youths between the ages of ten and fourteen are represented in arrests for other than status offenses in approximately the same proportion as their numbers in the total population of the United States; with the ten-to-eighteen age group, 13.7 percent of the population accounts for more than 20 percent of the arrests. Youths aged fifteen, sixteen, and seventeen make up about 15 percent of all those arrested, except for status offenses. This is almost three times their proportion in the population. While this figure is high, it would have to be modified, for children under the age of ten should apparently be eliminated from consideration, as they are not part of the population likely to be arrested for criminal activity. With infants and very young children removed from the population under study, the youths of fifteen, sixteen, and seventeen are disproportionately represented to the extent of about two and a half rather than three times their number in the population.

Some criminologists emphasize that arrest figures conceal the true incidence of serious crime, because white-collar and organized crime, drug smuggling, and other major illegal activities involve relatively few arrests and the perpetrators are no doubt older. Youth participation in serious crime is high and has been growing, but it is index crime, street and conventional, violent and nonviolent. It does not generally involve sums of money as large as those that change hands illegally through corporate, white-collar, political, and organized crime, but it does involve death, bodily harm, fright, and threat to individuals and the quality of their lives.

It is sometimes suggested that the baby boom following World War II is largely responsible for the rise in crime in the 1960s and 1970s. On the basis of this argument, as the proportion of the population under age thirty (currently responsible for about 70 percent of all arrests) diminishes, as it will do in the 1980s, some criminologists predict a drop in crime derived from this changing demographic distribution.[2] However, a major difficulty with

2. The statistics tell the story. People between the ages of fifteen and twenty-nine (inclusive) constituted 27 percent of the U.S. population in 1980, and will go down to 22 and 20 percent in 1990 and 2000, respectively, according to projections by the Bureau of the Census. However,

predictions for crime based on demography is that they do not take into account the continued high birth rates among those social classes and ethnic groups in which street and other ordinary crime are most frequently found.

Many factors can affect this situation and alter the otherwise optimistic prediction: the state of the economy and unemployment; the attitudes and values of youth in the years ahead; the dynamism of crime and its tendency to continue on its own momentum, be imitated, and become epidemic; the entry of new groups (particularly women) into criminality; and the shifts of "high risk" populations to urban areas.

Against such factors one can look to innovations in education, the course of civil rights achievements and their effect on crime, improvement in job opportunity, and any movement toward unifying community or national values. Demographic trends alone, in our view, are unlikely to lead to the long-sought dramatic reduction in serious crime.

Sex of Offenders

After age, it is sex that is most easily studied. Again one must rely almost entirely on arrest records, although reports by victims or onlookers are occasionally available.

Crime has traditionally been considered a male pursuit. Although there have been famous female criminals in history and fiction (such as Daniel Defoe's Moll Flanders), the activities of a woman criminal usually have been confined to acting as lookout while her lover or husband commits the crime. Crime in this view is a man's job, and requires such putatively manly qualities as strength, brutality, proneness to violence, speed, and toughness, characteristics not found in the "delicate sex."

There are two crimes in which women have appeared to be highly represented. One is prostitution, although women probably never have had as complete a monopoly in this field as has generally been believed, and it is today indisputable that there are many male prostitutes. Pimping has traditionally been seen as a job for a man—although it is believed that some women have now entered this field—whereas the allied occupation of running a house of prostitution has usually been in the hands of a woman (sometimes a former prostitute herself). And shoplifting is thought to be carried out to a considerable extent by women (see Cameron, 1964).

Freda Adler (1975) and Rita Simon (1975), among others, have found a notable increase in female criminality, including violent crime, during the 1960s and early 1970s. The increase has extended, they contend, to crimes in which women were formerly little represented. The rise appears to be real, but the total number of women involved—that is, the absolute figures—may in some instances be so low that the percentage jumps are misleading. The proportion of female arrests to total arrests continues to be small for al-

---

during the same period, youths from fifteen to nineteen (inclusive), who in 1980 were 9 percent of the population, will decline to 6.9 by 1990, only to go up to 7.5 at the beginning of the new century. This indicates that the decline of the most crime-prone age group as a percentage of the total population will be ending in the 1990s, and the trend will then be reversed.

most all crimes except prostitution. However, this proportion appears to be increasing as women enter the work force and encounter the same opportunities for law-breaking behavior as have confronted men for many years.

One of the problems in dealing with the extent of female participation in crime has developed over what is sometimes called the role of chivalry. It has often been asserted that the participation of women in crime would show up as a higher proportion of total crime were it not for the desire of male criminals to protect women and exclude them entirely from dangerous pursuits, the reluctance of police to arrest, of bystanders and victims to report, and of judges to sentence female offenders. Feminists have recently been challenging the accuracy of this widely held belief, concluding that on the contrary women have often been more harshly treated at the hands of police and in the halls of justice than have men, the latter being shown solidarity by their same-sex comrades in power.

While the evidence is being amassed and debate rages, it appears to us that both sides are partially correct. Females have received far harsher treatment than men for victimless crimes such as prostitution: the "Johns" are usually completely vindicated, seldom arrested, often ignored, and not at all stigmatized, and in many jurisdictions their activities are not illegal although those of females from whom they buy sex are. Women have been more harshly treated than men in cases of adultery—although this might not show up in crime statistics—for the woman often suffers (or did until recently) court-ordered loss of custody of a child, while the husband's adulterous relationships are considered hardly relevant.

However, if sex crime is excluded—and for the area of female arrests it is a major exclusion—there appears to be a preponderance of evidence of greater leniency for women than men in otherwise similar cases. The indications are that this is more true of sentencing than of parole, however. Even sentencing becomes complex, for the female is often relegated to the role of accessory, a category that might have been treated with leniency regardless of sex.

The problem has been further obscured by ideological controversy involving feminism. Some of those who find a great increase in female criminality over the 1960s and 1970s, a rise out of proportion to the general increase, note that this is concomitant with female militancy and the general feminist movement. Women imbued with the idea that they can do anything a man can will go out, it is argued, and become policewomen and firefighters, painters, construction workers, surgeons, "customer's men"—and robbers, pickpockets, pimps, and street muggers. Now, women did all of these things before the recent period, or at least aspired to do so, but as they move into almost every sector of the labor market and seek to attain all types of positions, this will motivate the criminally inclined in the same way as with other women.

This appears to be the thesis—much oversimplified, here—of Freda Adler's influential book, *Sisters in Crime* (1975). But while some people simply deny such a cause-and-effect relationship, others denounce this viewpoint as an insult to the feminist movement stemming from male chauvinist ideology. Rita Simon comments on this question in a manner that would probably meet wide approval from feminists:

> If one of the consequences of sexual equality should turn out to be higher crime rates among women, the women's movement would not feel that it has all been in vain. The contemporary leadership might then do what the leaderships of earlier women's movements have done after their immediate goals were realized: turn their efforts and energies to treating other important social ills that affect both men and women. [Simon, 1975: 106]

Simon further points out that criminologists have denied that women are more endowed with morality and decency than are men. Refuting this view, she holds that the roles women perform in society assume "goodness, charity, and morality, and it is those roles that serve as useful masks for hiding criminal activities" (Simon, 1975: 9). With changing sex roles, not only would women have more opportunity to commit crime but the assumptions about their delicacy and noncriminality would be dropped and their criminal activities become as visible as those of men.

Figures on female crime must be examined with the same reservations as for other aspects of illegal conduct. For the most part, the statistics report arrests, not offenders. Three sets of figures are here examined, dealing with arrests by sex for 1970 and 1979, 1975 and 1979, and for 1979 alone, as shown in Tables 13–2, 13–3, and 13–4, respectively. (Note that these tables differ considerably with regard to the number of persons arrested in 1979, because the figures have been adjusted so as to be comparable to the population studied in the earlier years.)

In Table 13–4, where 1979 figures are used alone, total arrests for the year amount to nine and a half million people. Of these, 15.7 percent are female, but this figure rises to 19.5 for index crimes. We will set aside forcible rape, overwhelmingly a male crime (the 219 female arrests here are evidently for being an accessory to rape, not for a lesbian assault or sexual assault on a man by a woman, as neither of these falls within the purview of rape as defined by UCR). Thus, omitting rape, we note that the female rate of arrest is far lower than the male rate for robbery, burglary, motor vehicle theft, homicide, aggravated assault, and arson. However, it rises to as high as 30.3 percent for larceny-theft, probably owing to arrests for shoplifting. Females account for approximately 10 percent of violent index crimes and almost 22 percent of property index crimes (the former after the exclusion of rape from the statistics), these figures being based on arrests, not on police reports or victimization surveys.

When one looks at arrests for a diversity of offenses, women appear to be overrepresented in some of the white-collar crimes and underrepresented in drunkenness. The latter constitutes so large a part of all arrests in a given year that the unusually small number of women involved distorts the total arrest figures, much more than do the disproportionate arrests for prostitution and of teenage females for curfew and loitering-law violations and for being runaways. When some of the doubtful entries are removed,

[3,943 agencies; 1979 estimated population 114,952,000]

Offense charged	Males						Females					
	Total			Under 18			Total			Under 18		
	1970	1979	Percent change	1970	1979	Percent change	1970	1979	Percent change	1970	1979	Percent change
TOTAL	4,440,899	4,590,254	+3.4	1,026,652	1,069,362	+4.2	743,226	923,363	+24.2	287,250	288,306	+.4
Murder and nonnegligent manslaughter	8,247	9,530	+15.6	1,027	919	−10.5	1,524	1,497	−1.8	73	120	+64.4
Forcible rape	11,754	17,904	+52.3	2,472	2,811	+13.7	3	136	+4,433.3	1	38	+3,700.0
Robbery	56,651	77,032	+36.0	18,035	23,765	+31.8	3,580	6,241	+74.3	1,237	1,806	+46.0
Aggravated assault	82,221	129,499	+57.5	13,211	20,785	+57.3	11,906	18,934	+59.0	2,083	3,646	+75.0
Burglary	212,245	267,226	+25.9	112,435	133,539	+18.8	10,737	18,430	+71.6	5,424	9,338	+72.2
Larceny-theft	350,992	493,752	+40.7	183,111	214,333	+17.1	138,826	224,769	+61.9	64,476	81,427	+26.3
Motor vehicle theft	95,284	80,169	−15.9	53,991	40,832	−24.4	5,329	8,207	+54.0	3,113	4,730	+51.9
Arson	6,454	9,491	+47.1	3,986	5,158	+29.4	611	1,232	+101.6	287	539	+87.8
Violent crime[1]	158,873	233,965	+47.3	34,745	48,280	+39.0	17,013	26,808	+57.6	3,394	5,610	+65.3
Property crime[2]	664,975	850,638	+27.9	353,523	393,862	+11.4	155,503	252,638	+62.5	73,300	96,034	+31.0
Crime Index total[3]	823,848	1,084,603	+31.7	388,268	442,142	+13.9	172,516	279,446	+62.0	76,694	101,644	+32.5
Other assaults	196,384	240,377	+22.4	33,221	46,231	+39.2	29,220	39,410	+34.9	8,160	12,312	+50.9
Forgery and counterfeiting	25,077	28,959	+15.5	2,715	4,481	+65.0	8,366	13,590	+62.4	975	1,913	+96.2
Fraud	44,423	73,076	+64.5	1,914	3,077	+60.8	16,673	51,041	+206.1	598	1,351	+125.9
Embezzlement	4,610	3,065	−33.5	137	511	+273.0	1,704	1,059	−37.9	58	129	+122.4
Stolen property; buying, receiving, possessing	34,794	56,775	+63.2	12,108	21,175	+74.9	3,600	6,865	+90.7	949	2,040	+115.0
Vandalism	79,543	134,131	+68.6	58,896	75,181	+27.7	6,759	12,616	+86.7	4,340	6,473	+49.1
Weapons; carrying, possessing, etc.	73,520	90,206	+22.7	12,943	16,025	+23.8	5,321	7,504	+41.0	517	1,070	+107.0
Prostitution and commercialized vice	7,662	19,288	+151.7	210	647	+208.1	26,771	36,847	+37.6	547	1,655	+202.6
Sex offenses (except forcible rape and prostitution)	34,707	38,494	+10.9	6,438	6,962	+8.1	5,427	3,645	−32.8	1,908	615	−67.8
Drug abuse violations	211,824	273,117	+28.9	48,300	60,009	+24.2	42,329	44,786	+5.8	14,630	12,129	−17.1
Gambling	56,992	32,875	−42.3	1,340	1,410	+5.2	4,981	3,497	−29.8	44	59	+34.1
Offenses against family and children	39,108	21,385	−45.3	455	982	+115.8	4,095	3,108	−24.1	217	612	+182.0
Driving under the influence	337,786	540,905	+60.1	4,062	13,402	+229.9	24,558	55,219	+124.9	227	1,583	+597.4
Liquor laws	151,899	187,616	+23.5	49,867	63,329	+27.0	22,408	33,324	+48.7	10,586	17,909	+69.2
Drunkenness	1,195,079	641,367	−46.3	30,273	23,966	−20.8	91,143	51,745	−43.2	4,634	3,982	−14.1
Disorderly conduct	428,046	401,003	−6.3	85,551	70,866	−17.2	73,481	78,386	+6.7	18,010	14,947	−17.0
Vagrancy	46,452	15,737	−66.1	7,242	2,459	−66.0	6,847	2,487	−63.7	1,740	524	−69.9
All other offenses (except traffic)	508,542	622,746	+22.5	142,109	131,978	−7.1	103,245	127,961	+23.9	48,634	36,532	−24.9
Suspicion (not included in totals)	49,617	9,190	−81.5	13,830	2,714	−80.4	7,995	1,632	−79.6	2,774	537	−80.6
Curfew and loitering law violations	70,169	43,649	−37.8	70,169	43,649	−37.8	18,286	11,585	−36.6	18,286	11,585	−36.6
Runaways	70,434	40,880	−42.0	70,434	40,880	−42.0	75,496	59,242	−21.5	75,496	59,242	−21.5

[1]Violent crimes are offenses of murder, forcible rape, robbery, and aggravated assault.
[2]Property crimes are offenses of burglary, larceny–theft, motor vehicle theft, and arson.
[3]Includes arson, a newly established Index offense in 1979.

SOURCE: Uniform Crime Reports, 1980, p. 191.

TABLE 13-2
Total Arrest Trends, Sex, 1970–1979

one still has a picture of women as constituting about one-fifth of the population of adult arrestees but far less a proportion of prisoners.

Now, let us look at what the trends have been over shorter and longer periods of time. In 1979, all arrests had risen slightly over the previous year, a rise that would have been greater had there not been a decline in the large drunkenness arrest figure. For index crimes, female arrests had decreased slightly while the male figure went up, but for violent index crime female arrests rose, although not quite so much as male.

One-year changes are not particularly meaningful; one must look to five- and ten-year periods and longer to see whether female arrests have been

[8,688 agencies; 1979 estimated population 179,932,000]

Offense charged	Males						Females					
	Total			Under 18			Total			Under 18		
	1975	1979	Percent change	1975	1979	Percent change	1975	1979	Percent change	1975	1979	Percent change
TOTAL	6,744,051	6,854,777	+1.6	1,647,021	1,482,686	—10.0	1,266,788	1,274,168	+.6	438,289	381,755	—12.9
Murder and nonnegligent manslaughter	14,500	13,335	—8.0	1,490	1,289	—13.5	2,657	2,150	—19.1	165	162	—1.8
Forcible rape	22,389	25,564	+14.2	3,992	4,185	+4.8	226	203	—10.2	59	55	—6.8
Robbery	124,367	106,642	—14.3	42,668	34,118	—20.0	9,408	8,595	—8.6	3,395	2,577	—24.1
Aggravated assault	182,427	200,560	+9.9	30,565	31,062	+1.6	27,528	28,702	+4.3	5,754	5,416	—5.9
Burglary	433,298	382,934	—11.6	226,209	187,376	—17.2	24,930	26,076	+4.6	12,531	13,115	+4.7
Larceny–theft	657,914	664,293	+1.0	309,840	285,590	—7.8	301,529	297,807	—1.2	123,705	107,708	—12.9
Motor vehicle theft	114,732	114,861	+.1	61,399	56,319	—8.3	8,576	11,212	+30.7	4,964	6,392	+28.8
Arson	13,100	14,146	+8.0	6,978	7,179	+2.9	1,662	1,809	+8.8	723	760	+5.1
Violent crime[1]	343,683	346,101	+.7	78,715	70,654	—10.2	39,819	39,650	—.4	9,373	8,210	—12.4
Property crime[2]	1,219,044	1,176,234	—3.5	604,426	536,464	—11.2	336,697	336,904	+.1	141,923	127,975	—9.8
Crime Index total[3]	1,562,727	1,522,335	—2.6	683,141	607,118	—11.1	376,516	376,554	(*)	151,296	136,185	—10.0
Other assaults	306,598	327,311	+6.8	54,819	57,380	+4.7	49,151	52,407	+6.6	14,774	14,914	+.9
Forgery and counterfeiting ...	41,804	42,572	+1.8	5,314	6,276	+18.1	16,811	18,952	+12.7	2,129	2,585	+21.4
Fraud	99,375	116,847	+17.6	3,418	5,232	+53.1	51,872	77,200	+48.8	1,273	1,932	+51.8
Embezzlement	6,705	4,771	—28.8	526	671	+27.6	3,121	1,683	—46.1	134	201	+50.0
Stolen property; buying, receiving, possessing	91,864	84,497	—8.0	30,060	28,774	—4.3	11,053	10,216	—7.6	2,821	2,796	—.9
Vandalism	162,689	189,455	+16.5	106,476	104,980	—1.4	14,309	17,397	+21.6	8,625	8,958	+3.9
Weapons; carrying, possessing, etc.	122,767	118,793	—3.2	20,209	20,228	+.1	10,648	9,352	—12.2	1,330	1,271	—4.4
Prostitution and commercialized vice	13,176	23,917	+81.5	593	1,060	+78.8	37,886	45,513	+20.1	1,801	1,877	+4.2
Sex offenses (except forcible rape and prostitution)	47,466	51,134	+7.7	9,643	9,410	—2.4	3,862	4,497	+16.4	1,099	733	—33.3
Drug abuse violations	452,777	405,601	—10.4	105,987	82,936	—21.7	72,425	60,749	—16.1	20,726	16,601	—19.9
Gambling	47,179	36,729	—22.1	1,757	1,337	—23.9	4,395	3,720	—15.4	103	60	—41.7
Offenses against family and children	49,672	37,000	—25.5	3,528	1,422	—59.7	6,044	4,482	—25.8	2,010	868	—56.8
Driving under the influence	864,561	977,267	+13.0	16,202	23,170	+43.0	75,099	94,433	+25.7	1,355	2,597	+91.7
Liquor laws	229,060	295,426	+29.0	83,538	97,559	+16.8	37,807	51,075	+35.1	21,293	27,173	+27.6
Drunkenness	1,111,675	877,768	—21.0	36,864	33,730	—8.5	85,181	69,456	—18.5	5,550	5,385	—3.0
Disorderly conduct	453,447	445,141	—1.8	96,943	82,876	—14.5	115,324	74,780	—35.2	19,976	17,940	—10.2
Vagrancy	28,440	24,475	—13.9	4,453	3,661	—17.8	6,226	7,589	+21.9	809	888	+9.8
All others (except traffic)	879,460	1,166,892	+32.7	210,941	208,020	—1.4	162,531	205,797	+26.6	54,658	50,475	—7.7
Suspicion (not included in totals)	26,976	13,187	—51.1	7,448	3,467	—53.5	4,311	2,232	—48.2	1,309	670	—48.8
Curfew and loitering law violations ...	93,283	54,693	—41.4	93,283	54,693	—41.4	22,545	14,965	—33.6	22,545	14,965	—33.6
Runaways	79,326	52,153	—34.3	79,326	52,153	—34.3	103,982	73,351	—29.5	103,982	73,351	—29.5

[1]Violent crimes are offenses of murder, forcible rape, robbery, and aggravated assault.
[2]Property crimes are offenses of burglary, larceny–theft, motor vehicle theft, and arson.
[3]Includes arson, a newly established Index offense in 1979.
[*]Less than one-tenth of 1 percent.

SOURCE: Uniform Crime Reports, 1980, p. 193.

disproportionately rising or merely keeping pace with total arrest figures for the country as a whole. Arrests of males over a ten-year period (1970–1979) were up 3.4 percent, and those for under-eighteen males rose 4.2 percent; the corresponding figures for females were 24.2 and 0.4 percent. Examining the ten-year period, two questions are of interest: (1) What crimes account in the main for the increase in women arrested (from 743,000 to over 900,000)? (2) For what crimes were the increases disproportionately high as compared to arrests for men?

More than 47 percent of the increase in the total number of women arrested is accounted for by larceny-theft, and the next largest portion by

TABLE 13-3
Total Arrest Trends, Sex, 1975–1979

239

Offense charged	Number of persons arrested			Percent male	Percent female	Percent distribution[1]		
	Total	Male	Female			Total	Male	Female
TOTAL	9,506,347	8,011,417	1,494,930	84.3	15.7	100.0	100.0	100.0
Murder and nonnegligent manslaughter	18,264	15,761	2,503	86.3	13.7	.2	.2	.2
Forcible rape	29,164	28,945	219	99.2	.8	.3	.4	(2)
Robbery	130,753	121,107	9,646	92.6	7.4	1.4	1.5	.6
Aggravated assault	256,597	224,753	31,844	87.6	12.4	2.7	2.8	2.1
Burglary	468,085	438,411	29,674	93.7	6.3	4.9	5.5	2.0
Larceny-theft	1,098,398	765,862	332,536	69.7	30.3	11.6	9.6	22.2
Motor vehicle theft	143,654	130,840	12,814	91.1	8.9	1.5	1.6	.9
Arson	18,387	16,303	2,084	88.7	11.3	.2	.2	.1
Violent crime[3]	434,778	390,566	44,212	89.8	10.2	4.6	4.9	3.0
Property crime[4]	1,728,524	1,351,416	377,108	78.2	21.8	18.2	16.9	25.2
Crime Index total[5]	2,163,302	1,741,982	421,320	80.5	19.5	22.8	21.7	28.2
Other assaults	451,475	390,055	61,420	86.4	13.6	4.7	4.9	4.1
Forgery and counterfeiting	70,977	49,016	21,961	69.1	30.9	.7	.6	1.5
Fraud	243,461	145,185	98,276	59.6	40.4	2.6	2.0	6.6
Embezzlement	7,882	5,884	1,998	74.7	25.3	.1	.1	.1
Stolen property; buying, receiving, possessing	107,621	96,107	11,514	89.3	10.7	1.1	1.2	.8
Vandalism	239,246	219,118	20,128	91.6	8.4	2.5	2.7	1.3
Weapons; carrying, possessing, etc.	152,731	141,496	11,235	92.6	7.4	1.6	1.8	.8
Prostitution and commercialized vice	83,088	26,992	56,096	32.5	67.5	.9	.3	3.8
Sex offenses (except forcible rape and prostitution) ..	62,633	57,764	4,869	92.2	7.8	.7	.7	.3
Drug abuse violations	519,377	449,137	70,240	86.5	13.5	5.5	5.6	4.7
Gambling	50,974	46,151	4,823	90.5	9.5	.5	.6	.3
Offenses against family and children	53,321	48,031	5,290	90.1	9.9	.6	.6	.4
Driving under the influence	1,231,665	1,124,798	106,867	91.3	8.7	13.0	14.0	7.1
Liquor laws	386,957	330,180	56,777	85.3	14.7	4.1	4.1	3.8
Drunkenness	1,090,233	1,010,569	79,664	92.7	7.3	11.5	12.6	5.3
Disorderly conduct	711,730	602,336	109,394	84.6	15.4	7.5	7.5	7.3
Vagrancy	34,662	26,851	7,811	77.5	22.5	.4	.3	.5
All other offenses (except traffic)	1,595,864	1,359,734	236,130	85.2	14.8	16.8	17.0	15.8
Suspicion	18,135	15,502	2,633	85.5	14.5	.2	.2	.2
Curfew and loitering law violations	78,147	60,923	17,224	78.0	22.0	.8	.8	1.2
Runaways	152,866	63,606	89,260	41.6	58.4	1.6	.8	6.0

[1]Because of rounding, the percentages may not add to total.
[2]Less than one-tenth of 1 percent.
[3]Violent crimes are offenses of murder, forcible rape, robbery, and aggravated assault.
[4]Property crimes are offenses of burglary, larceny-theft, motor vehicle theft, and arson.
[5]Includes arson, a newly established Index offense in 1979.

SOURCE: Uniform Crime Reports, 1980, p. 199.

TABLE 13-4
Total Arrests, Distribution by Sex, 1979

fraud and driving under the influence of alcohol. The rest are small increases except for the catch-all category of all other offenses except traffic. Females accounted for almost half of the arrests on larceny-theft charges in 1979, as contrasted with about two-fifths a decade earlier, a change that one might attribute to a greater willingness to arrest women for shoplifting, rather than a larger proportion of women engaging in this type of activity.

In traditionally male crimes, greater increases in arrests were noted for females, but the crimes continued to be male-dominated nonetheless. Note that over a ten-year period, increases in arrests of males and females, respectively, for robbery were 36.0 and 74.3 percent; for aggravated assault, 57.5 and 59.0; arson, 47.1 and 101.6; and burglary, 25.9 and 71.6. Arrests for motor vehicle theft declined 15.9 percent among men and increased 54.0 percent among women. Similar increases are found for arrests of women as compared to men on charges of receiving stolen property, forgery and counterfeiting, fraud, vandalism, stolen weapons, driving under the influence of alcohol, and many other crimes.

A major problem here—one that has been widely discussed—is that we are dealing with small figures that look big when offered as percentages. Robbery, for example, remains overwhelmingly a male crime. In 1979, after the ten-year rise, women accounted for only about 8 percent of all arrests on this charge; this casts a different light on the previously cited figures showing increases in male arrests during this period of a little more than 36 percent, as contrasted with the female rise of 74.3 percent. It might be objected that women in reality account for a greater percentage of the total robberies than arrest figures indicate (only about 15 percent of those reported resulted in arrest), but this is conjecture and most unlikely. When one shifts from percentages to real numbers, the role of women in robbery, as in other crimes, appears to be even less startling. From 1970 to 1979, arrests nationwide of women on charges of robbery rose from 3,580 to 6,241; of men, from 56,651 to 77,032. The spectacular percentages of increase begin to take on a different aspect when the actual numbers of arrested people are examined.

When the number of women arrested is compared with the larger group of offenders unapprehended or unknown, does the total image of the place of women in crime change? The answer can only be speculative. There appear to be more women in crime than before, but they continue to make up a very small percentage of the total offender population. While the proportion may increase over the years, it is unlikely that women will catch up with men or surpass them. Whether this is solely because of the cultural ambience in which all people are raised and the culturally appropriate behavior that more easily permits males to enter the criminal world; or because of lack of opportunity available to women for certain types of crime; or because women still spend large amounts of time as homemakers and mothers, leaving them less time for crime; or because of innate male tendencies toward higher energy levels, greater aggression, and greater predilection for violence; or because of a complex combination of these various factors, probably cannot be answered in a definitive manner at the present time.

Recent statistics show that whereas about 3 percent of all adult prisoners in America are female, about 22 percent of those in juvenile detention homes are female. This is probably due to the greater amount of confinement of girls to such centers on charges of curfew violations, being runaways, and sexual promiscuity, but it may also indicate that the increased female participation in ordinary crime may be manifesting itself more in the lower age groups than in older ones.

Race and Ethnicity of Offenders

The third important variable studied by those who look at offenders, arrested persons, and convicts is race and ethnicity. This is a sensitive area, filled with misunderstanding.

Most criminologists agree that the official figures on racial distribution of crime are seriously distorted. The statistics conceal—not necessarily deliberately—those crimes in which whites are most likely to be highly represented, particularly corporate and white-collar crime, fraud and large embezzlements. Some criminologists argue that blacks, Hispanics, American Indians, and a few other ethnic groups are under greater suspicion when a crime is committed, more likely to be arrested, more likely to be mistreated at the hands of police, less able to find competent lawyers and sympathetic juries (except in cases that have attained national and, particularly, international publicity), more often found guilty, and when convicted more likely to be sent to prison and given long sentences. At any one time, figures for the prison population may present a greater distortion because whites are more readily and quickly paroled than others.

There is a great deal of evidence to support these contentions, but let it be noted that there are some countervailing forces, particularly that most crime appears to be intra- rather than interracial and that black community leaders have charged that the police are far less interested in making an arrest when the victim of a robbery, burglary, assault, or forcible rape is black. It is doubtful that these two forces cancel each other out: the stigmatized and oppressed minorities probably find their way into crime statistics as offenders and convicts in greater proportion to their actual numbers and percentages in the population than would be the case if one had access to complete data on all criminal offenders.

Historically, the blacks were the victims of crime, as were the American Indians and many other ethnic groups. Slave-running continued long after it was outlawed. Brutality, including murder, against slaves was a moral crime against humanity for which white offenders often went unpunished. Many of those glorified as founders of the United States and among its leaders for the first eight decades after the founding of the Republic were themselves slaveholders and espoused slavery as an American institution. Thousands of the lynchings that took place, primarily but not exclusively in the South, from the Reconstruction period until the 1930s were directed against black victims. If one had been able to count the offenders in the method used by the FBI to count homicides, the total number of such participants would be extraordinarily high. Blacks have been otherwise victimized by whites, in frauds, assaults, and numerous other crimes.

Using official arrest records, the thrust of which is verified when possible with descriptions by victims that did not lead to arrest, one finds an overrepresentation of certain minority groups in various types of crime. Whether this would be seriously reduced if there were no discriminatory police and judicial procedures is a disputed question. However, if one accepts the aforementioned thesis put forward by William Wilson (1978), in which he contends that race (and apparently ethnicity) is of declining significance in the United States and that social class can explain and predict behavior with little regard to race, the crime picture appears in a different light. Blacks, Hispanics, and American Indians are overrepresented among the poor, and the poor are overrepresented among offenders for ordinary street crime and most violent crimes. If social class, economic conditions, and education are held constant, some crimes emerge largely as lower-class phenomena rather than as activities in which racial and ethnic minorities play a disproportionate role. In other words, blacks, Chicanos, Puerto Ricans, and a few other minorities are highly represented among the poor, and when the crime figures are recomputed and placed in the context of the social class of the offender, the overrepresentation of these ethnic minorities is reduced, but not to the point of being evenly balanced with their proportions in the populace. White-collar and corporate crimes are seldom reported, and in these there is little doubt that blacks and other minorities are underrepresented. Crime emerges as a phenomenon committed primarily by those who have the opportunities and who represent those social groups—rather than ethnic and racial groups—in which crime-producing factors are found in abundance.

Still another problem is that few reliable census reports are available that show how large a portion of the American population is made up of each of the minorities. Blacks, for example, have been variously estimated as at between 10 and 20 percent of the population. If the latter figure is correct, then the disproportion of blacks among total arrested persons is far less striking than if the lower figure is accepted. Similarly, blacks and other minorities are highly concentrated in urban areas, where there is generally a larger amount of crime and a higher crime rate than in small cities or rural areas. The cause-and-effect situation here can be complex: it is easy to say that the blacks bring crime to the cities, but it may be just as true—or more so—that the city (with its anonymity, crowding, and greater opportunities for law-breaking) brings crime to the city residents.

Some official statistics on race and crime are shown in Table 13-5. The statistics offer no breakdown for Hispanics, which makes the analysis somewhat less useful. In 1979, blacks accounted for almost 25 percent of all arrests in the United States, which is more than the highest estimate of their proportion in the population but not higher than their proportion in the lower social classes, in which most arrests occur. However, blacks accounted for about 44.1 percent of arrests for index violent crime and 29.4 percent for index property crime. The high figure for murder and nonnegligent manslaughter, in which the black proportion of arrests amounts to 47.7 percent, may be due in part to the discretionary judgment of police and prosecutors, who more often charge whites with negligent manslaughter for crimes that with others would result in the more serious charge. When a comparison is made of only rural districts, the black proportion for arrests for violent and property crime is much smaller (but the black portion of the population is smaller as well).

The question of ethnicity and race in crime remains a delicate one, easily leading to distortions and misunderstandings. So long as various ethnic and racial groups have differential opportunities, different roles in the society, and in some instances suffer from stigma, crime will not be evenly distributed among them. The evidence that this is socially and not biologically caused seems beyond dispute among most scientists, but widely held views to the contrary among large sections of the population can have serious repercussions on race relations and on the struggle against crime.

243

TABLE 13-5
Total Arrests,
Distribution by Race,
1979

[11,689 agencies; 1979 estimated population 204,363,000]

Offense charged	Total arrests							Percent distribution[1]						
	Total	White	Negro	Indian	Chinese	Japanese	All others	Total	White	Negro	Indian	Chinese	Japanese	All others
TOTAL	9,467,502	6,849,179	2,342,664	102,392	6,089	7,668	159,510	100.0	72.3	24.7	1.1	0.1	0.1	1.7
Murder and nonnegligent manslaughter	18,238	9,010	8,693	155	16	8	356	100.0	49.4	47.7	.8	.1	(*)	2.0
Forcible rape	29,068	14,578	13,870	235	15	12	358	100.0	50.2	47.7	.8	.1		1.2
Robbery	130,585	53,527	74,275	743	124	76	1,840	100.0	41.0	56.9	.6	.1	.1	1.4
Aggravated assault	255,987	155,821	94,624	2,684	280	105	2,473	100.0	60.9	37.0	1.0	.1		1.0
Burglary	464,099	322,489	133,011	3,097	280	347	4,875	100.0	69.5	28.7	.7	.1	.1	1.1
Larceny-theft	1,093,998	735,651	330,325	8,971	1,381	1,169	16,501	100.0	67.2	30.2	.8	.1	.1	1.5
Motor vehicle theft	143,197	100,193	38,905	1,482	121	98	2,398	100.0	70.0	27.2	1.0	.1	.1	1.7
Arson	18,304	14,450	3,513	112	5	15	209	100.0	78.9	19.2	.6		.1	1.1
Violent crime[3]	433,878	232,936	191,462	3,817	435	201	5,027	100.0	53.7	44.1	.9	.1		1.2
Property crime[4]	1,719,598	1,172,783	505,754	13,662	1,787	1,629	23,983	100.0	68.2	29.4	.8	.1	.1	1.4
Crime Index total[5]	2,153,476	1,405,719	697,216	17,479	2,222	1,830	29,010	100.0	65.3	32.4	.8	.1	.1	1.3
Other assaults	448,893	293,805	144,324	3,719	314	265	6,466	100.0	65.5	32.2	.8	.1	.1	1.4
Forgery and counterfeiting	70,486	47,038	22,630	399	47	29	343	100.0	66.7	32.1	.6	.1		.5
Fraud	241,731	164,185	75,037	1,460	95	51	903	100.0	67.9	31.0	.6			.4
Embezzlement	7,873	5,899	1,862	36	9	8	59	100.0	74.9	23.7	.5	.1	.1	.7
Stolen property; buying, receiving, possessing	106,727	70,909	34,253	582	95	94	794	100.0	66.4	32.1	.5	.1	.1	.7
Vandalism	237,595	195,976	36,805	1,634	131	147	2,902	100.0	82.5	15.5	.7	.1	.1	1.2
Weapons; carrying, possessing, etc.	152,096	92,861	54,964	849	138	123	3,161	100.0	61.1	36.1	.6	.1	.1	2.1
Prostitution and commercialized vice	83,035	37,845	43,706	282	134	66	1,002	100.0	45.6	52.6	.3	.2	.1	1.2
Sex offenses (except forcible rape and prostitution)	62,371	48,265	12,607	593	102	37	767	100.0	77.4	20.2	1.0	.2	.1	1.2
Drug abuse violations	516,142	396,065	112,748	1,984	223	374	4,748	100.0	76.7	21.8	.4		.1	.9
Gambling	50,840	14,057	34,540	40	240	291	1,672	100.0	27.6	67.9	.1	.5	.6	3.3
Offenses against family and children	53,042	33,439	18,739	523	10	9	322	100.0	63.0	35.3	1.0			.6
Driving under the influence	1,224,126	1,048,154	151,168	14,050	596	1,320	8,838	100.0	85.6	12.3	1.1		.1	.7
Liquor laws	385,709	347,357	25,338	6,786	151	86	5,991	100.0	90.1	6.6	1.8			1.6
Drunkenness	1,089,965	876,132	181,483	26,577	422	161	5,190	100.0	80.4	16.7	2.4			.5
Disorderly conduct	709,888	466,712	210,678	9,552	193	238	22,515	100.0	65.7	29.7	1.3			3.2
Vagrancy	34,613	21,434	12,291	622	34	22	210	100.0	61.9	35.5	1.8	.1	.1	.6
All other offenses (except traffic)	1,590,936	1,083,037	430,490	12,823	843	2,410	61,333	100.0	68.1	27.1	.8	.1	.2	3.9
Suspicion	17,903	12,132	5,557	48	4	12	150	100.0	67.8	31.0	.3		.1	.8
Curfew and loitering law violations	78,067	59,795	16,907	825	25	26	489	100.0	76.6	21.7	1.0	.1		.6
Runaways	151,988	128,363	19,321	1,529	61	69	2,645	100.0	84.5	12.7	1.0	.1		1.7

SOURCE: Uniform Crime Reports, 1980, pp. 200–202.

Offense charged	Arrests under 18							Percent distribution[1]						
	Total	White	Negro	Indian	Chinese	Japanese	All others	Total	White	Negro	Indian	Chinese	Japanese	All others
TOTAL	2,133,626	1,628,819	456,638	15,813	1,450	1,411	29,495	100.0	76.3	21.4	.7	.1	.1	1.4
Murder and nonnegligent manslaughter	1,704	877	751	16		1	59	100.0	51.5	44.1	.9			3.5
Forcible rape	4,641	2,003	2,531	36	2	2	67	100.0	43.2	54.5	.8	(²)		1.4
Robbery	41,122	14,393	25,697	170	55	17	790	100.0	35.0	62.5	.4	.1		1.9
Aggravated assault	39,765	25,221	13,777	309	65	13	380	100.0	63.4	34.6	.8	.2		1.0
Burglary	225,478	162,560	58,401	1,383	132	192	2,810	100.0	72.1	25.9	.6	.1	.1	1.2
Larceny–theft	442,253	309,373	121,451	3,282	494	516	7,137	100.0	70.0	27.5	.7	.1	.1	1.6
Motor vehicle theft	70,444	52,815	15,292	735	74	54	1,474	100.0	75.0	21.7	1.0	.1	.1	2.1
Arson	8,973	7,522	1,283	42	2	5	119	100.0	83.8	14.3	.5		.1	1.3
Violent crime[3]	87,232	42,494	42,756	531	122	33	1,296	100.0	48.7	49.0	.6	.1		1.5
Property crime[4]	747,148	532,270	196,427	5,442	702	767	11,540	100.0	71.2	26.3	.7	.1	.1	1.5
Crime Index total[5]	834,380	574,764	239,183	5,973	824	800	12,836	100.0	68.9	28.7	.7	.1	.1	1.5
Other assaults	83,806	55,377	25,946	572	66	69	1,776	100.0	66.1	31.0	.7	.1	.1	2.1
Forgery and counterfeiting	9,815	7,785	1,913	51	4	7	55	100.0	79.3	19.5	.5		.1	.6
Fraud	8,347	5,890	2,329	40	9	3	76	100.0	70.6	27.9	.5	.1		.9
Embezzlement	996	808	170	6	2	1	9	100.0	81.1	17.1	.6	.2	.1	.9
Stolen property: buying, receiving, possessing	35,333	25,031	9,684	196	36	29	357	100.0	70.8	27.4	.6	.1	.1	1.0
Vandalism	128,827	110,614	16,007	611	61	66	1,468	100.0	85.9	12.4	.5		.1	1.1
Weapons; carrying, possessing, etc.	24,902	17,611	6,501	131	33	24	602	100.0	70.7	26.1	.5	.1	.1	2.4
Prostitution and commercialized vice	3,311	1,593	1,654	16	7		41	100.0	48.1	50.0	.5	.2		1.2
Sex offenses (except forcible rape and prostitution)	11,318	8,177	2,897	53	41	5	145	100.0	72.2	25.6	.5	.4		1.3
Drug abuse violations	113,603	97,718	14,147	456	35	69	1,178	100.0	86.0	12.5	.4		.1	1.0
Gambling	2,103	403	1,558	1		5	136	100.0	19.2	74.1			.2	6.5
Offenses against family and children	2,529	1,846	655	14	1		13	100.0	73.0	25.9	.6			.5
Driving under the influence	29,734	28,361	940	295	4	11	123	100.0	95.4	3.2	1.0			.4
Liquor laws	138,965	133,218	3,175	1,688	45	35	804	100.0	95.9	2.3	1.2			.6
Drunkenness	45,714	42,263	2,418	815	11	7	200	100.0	92.5	5.3	1.8			.4
Disorderly conduct	125,235	93,335	27,737	809	27	25	3,302	100.0	74.5	22.1	.6			2.6
Vagrancy	4,929	3,893	961	20	6	6	43	100.0	79.0	19.5	.4	.1	.1	.9
All other offenses (except traffic)	294,788	228,276	61,323	1,708	148	153	3,180	100.0	77.4	20.8	.6	.1	.1	1.1
Suspicion	4,936	3,698	1,212	4	4	1	17	100.0	74.9	24.6	.1	.1		.3
Curfew and loitering law violations	78,067	59,795	16,907	825	25	26	489	100.0	76.6	21.7	1.1		.1	.6
Runaways	151,988	128,363	19,321	1,529	61	69	2,645	100.0	84.5	12.7	1.0		.1	1.7

TABLE 13-5
(continued)

Offense charged	Arrests 18 and over							Percent distribution[1]						
	Total	White	Negro	Indian	Chinese	Japanese	All others	Total	White	Negro	Indian	Chinese	Japanese	All others
TOTAL	7,333,876	5,220,360	1,886,026	86,579	4,639	6,257	130,015	100.0	71.2	25.7	1.2	0.1	0.1	1.8
Murder and nonnegligent manslaughter	16,534	8,133	7,942	139	16	7	297	100.0	49.2	48.0	.8	(*)	...	1.8
Forcible rape	24,427	12,575	11,339	199	13	10	291	100.0	51.5	46.4	.8	.1	...	1.2
Robbery	89,463	39,134	48,578	573	69	59	1,050	100.0	43.7	54.3	.6	.1	.1	1.2
Aggravated assault	216,222	130,600	80,847	2,375	215	92	2,093	100.0	60.4	37.4	1.1	.1	...	1.0
Burglary	238,621	159,929	74,610	1,714	148	155	2,065	100.0	67.0	31.3	.7	.1	.1	.9
Larceny-theft	651,745	426,278	208,874	5,689	887	653	9,364	100.0	65.4	32.0	.9	.1	.1	1.4
Motor vehicle theft	72,753	47,378	23,613	747	47	44	924	100.0	65.1	32.5	1.0	.1	.1	1.3
Arson	9,331	6,928	2,230	70	3	10	90	100.0	74.2	23.9	.8	...	.1	1.0
Violent crime[2]	346,646	190,442	148,706	3,286	313	168	3,731	100.0	54.9	42.9	.9	.1	...	1.1
Property crime[3]	972,450	640,513	309,327	8,220	1,085	862	12,443	100.0	65.9	31.8	.8	.1	.1	1.3
Crime Index total[4]	1,319,096	830,955	458,033	11,506	1,398	1,030	16,174	100.0	63.0	34.7	.9	.1	.1	1.2
Other assaults	365,087	238,428	118,378	3,147	248	196	4,690	100.0	65.3	32.4	.9	.1	.1	1.3
Forgery and counterfeiting	60,671	39,253	20,717	348	43	22	288	100.0	64.7	34.1	.6	.1	...	.5
Fraud	233,384	158,295	72,708	1,420	86	48	827	100.0	67.8	31.2	.6	...	...	.4
Embezzlement	6,877	5,091	1,692	30	7	7	50	100.0	74.0	24.6	.4	.1	.1	.7
Stolen property; buying, receiving, possessing	71,394	45,878	24,569	386	59	65	437	100.0	64.3	34.4	.5	.1	.1	.6
Vandalism	108,768	85,362	20,798	1,023	70	81	1,434	100.0	78.5	19.1	.9	.1	.1	1.3
Weapons; carrying, possessing, etc.	127,194	75,250	48,463	718	105	99	2,559	100.0	59.2	38.1	.6	.1	.1	2.0
Prostitution and commercialized vice	79,724	36,252	42,052	266	127	66	961	100.0	45.5	52.7	.3	.2	.1	1.2
Sex offenses (except forcible rape and prostitution)	51,053	40,088	9,710	540	61	32	622	100.0	78.5	19.0	1.1	.1	.1	1.2
Drug abuse violations	402,539	298,347	98,601	1,528	188	305	3,570	100.0	74.1	24.5	.4	...	.1	.9
Gambling	48,737	13,654	32,982	39	240	286	1,536	100.0	28.0	67.7	.1	.5	.6	3.2
Offenses against family and children	50,513	31,593	18,084	509	9	9	309	100.0	62.5	35.8	1.0	...	...	.6
Driving under the influence	1,194,392	1,019,793	150,228	13,755	592	1,309	8,715	100.0	85.4	12.6	1.2	.1	.1	.7
Liquor laws	246,744	214,139	22,163	5,098	106	51	5,187	100.0	86.8	9.0	2.1	...	...	2.1
Drunkenness	1,044,251	833,869	179,065	25,762	411	154	4,990	100.0	79.9	17.1	2.5	...	...	.5
Disorderly conduct	584,653	373,377	182,941	8,743	166	213	19,213	100.0	63.9	31.3	1.5	...	...	3.3
Vagrancy	29,684	17,541	11,330	602	28	16	167	100.0	59.1	38.2	2.0	.1	.1	.6
All other offenses (except traffic)	1,296,148	854,761	369,167	11,115	695	2,257	58,153	100.0	65.9	28.5	.9	.1	.2	4.5
Suspicion	12,967	8,434	4,345	44	...	11	133	100.0	65.0	33.5	.3	...	.1	1.0
Curfew and loitering law violations														
Runaways														

[1] Because of rounding, the percentages may not add to total.
*Less than one-tenth of 1 percent.
[2] Violent crimes are offenses of murder, forcible rape, robbery, and aggravated assault.
[3] Property crimes are offenses of burglary, larceny-theft, motor vehicle theft, and arson.
[4] Includes arson, a newly established Index offense in 1979.

Victims
and Victimology

14

There are many types of victims: sufferers from birth defect and disease, natural disaster, accident, prejudice, and crime, to name but a few. Thus, a complete study of victims—who they are, how they arise, under what circumstances—would be broader than is encompassed by criminology. There are some interesting and important analogies to be drawn between victims of crime and victims of other forces, events, and people. In the context of criminology, however, the study of victims—victimology—focuses on those who have suffered death, injury, or loss because of the criminal activities of others or, in some circumstances, of themselves as well.

Victimology as a field of study has developed primarily since the 1930s. It embraces a variety of interests and raises a number of problems, many of them quite controversial. These interests and problems include the amassing of information on and study of characteristics of victims, relationships between offenders and victims, alleged proneness of some persons to being victimized, contributions that some victims make toward the crime by precipitation or provocation, the use of victimization surveys to correct crime statistics, role of the victim in prosecution of the offender, protection of the victim during prosecution and thereafter from further victimization and retaliation, mass victimization of large sectors of the public in the case of political and other upperworld crimes, victimization of disvalued persons (such as homosexuals and inebriates) with seeming impunity, victimization of entire peoples in officially sponsored genocide, victimization of offenders in the correctional system, efforts to make the victim whole through compensatory programs paid for by government or the offender, and informal but severe sanctions often imposed by family, friends or vigilantes in society on some victims (as in cases of rape). This list is not exhaustive, but it contains some of the many facets of this aspect of criminology that have attracted considerable attention.[1]

The Historical Rights of Victims

In most societies up until a few centuries ago, the victim or family had not only the right to retaliate but an obligation to do so in order to protect the honor of family, clan, or group. Such retaliatory measures frequently resulted in so-called blood feuds that continued over long periods of time.

In the development of modern law, the right to retaliate was taken away from the victim and placed in the hands of a governmental apparatus. This meant that someone accused of a crime could not be punished by the superior strength or numbers of victims and their allies, but was given a trial to determine innocence or guilt, crude as such a trial might seem from the vantage point of modern standards of criminal justice.

In certain respects this new situation sometimes proved unsatisfactory. Victims who were certain of the identity of the offender were not always able to prove their case in court or could not always convince authorities even to prosecute, thus leaving them with a sense of frustration. But perhaps more important, in property crimes the victims frequently did not recover the value of their losses, and even if they had the satisfaction of seeing the offender apprehended and punished (until the mid-nineteenth century, capital punishment was not at all rare for many property crimes), they were nonetheless left bereft of their treasures or other belongings. This has led to two modern debates: over victim compensation or restitution, and over retaliatory actions by some victims.

Crimes, Victims, and Demographic Variables

Who are the victims? This is an important question for many reasons, particularly as it may offer a potential for greater public protection as reliable information on this subject is amassed.

In a few instances, victims are defined by the crime or circumstances surrounding it. Only children can be victims—by definition—of child abuse or child molestation, impairing the morals of a child, or similar types of criminal activity. Only close relatives can be victims of incest. If forcible rape is defined to exclude assaults upon boys and other males, then only females can be victims of that crime. However, these tautologies leave unanswered such questions as age, race, and social class when crimes of these types are considered.

The victim differs according to the nature of the crime committed, the characteristics of the offender, and other factors. One of the founders of victimology, Hans von Hentig (1979) has made a tentative typology of victims in which he has emphasized a series of characteristics, some demographic and some psychological, often both. His categories of victims include children,

1. Some have suggested that a word is needed, the analogue of criminality, to cover this phenomenon. They have suggested the word "victimity," a neologism that has not, however, gained a foothold.

females, lonely people, the mentally ill, and the emotionally disturbed, among others. The groupings of von Hentig are not particularly useful as a classification system, but his work does highlight the special vulnerability of some kinds of people to victimization at the hands of others. In recent years, particularly in the United States, attention has focused on blacks and other minorities illegally discriminated against and, until the 1950s, not infrequently subjected to lynchings, courtroom frameups, and brutality at the hands of police and sheriffs; on women as victims of rape and young men in prison as victims of sexual assault; on the elderly as an exceptionally helpless group; and on battered spouses, especially wives. MacNamara and Sagarin (1977) suggest that the deviant, particularly the sex deviant, is often victimized, not merely in the sense of being an object of social hostility, but as a target of such crimes as blackmail, extortion, murder, assault, and robbery. Along similar lines, the "rolling" (robbing) of alcoholics has a long and seamy history. A number of occupational roles have been identified as especially vulnerable to victimization: taxi driver, filling-station operator, liquor store clerk.

Nonetheless, although many of these variables suggesting enhanced vulnerability can be substantiated, they do not account for a large proportion of criminal victimizations. For instance, males are the objects of violent crime more frequently than females, youth more than the elderly.

According to studies made by the President's Commission on Law Enforcement and Administration of Justice (1967a:38), "the highest rates of victimization occur in the lower income groups when all index offenses except homicide are considered together." This is shown in Table 14–1. The information here is based on incomes in the early to mid-1960s, but the general relationship of the ratios to one another as one goes up the income scale would probably hold true at this writing, although the income figures in absolute numbers and the ratios themselves would be higher. Forcible rape, robbery, and burglary indicate a definite trend toward greater victimization

**TABLE 14-1
Victimization by
Income**

(Rates per 100,000 population)

Offenses	Income			
	$0 to $2,999	*$3,000 to $5,999*	*$6,000 to $9,999*	*Above $10,000*
Total	2,369	2,331	1,820	2,237
Forcible rape	76	49	10	17
Robbery	172	121	48	34
Aggravated assault	229	316	144	252
Burglary	1,319	1,020	867	790
Larceny ($50 and over)	420	619	549	925
Motor vehicle theft	153	206	202	219
Number of respondents	(5,232)	(8,238)	(10,382)	(5,946)

SOURCE: Philip H. Ennis, "Criminal Victimization in the United States: A Report of a National Survey," Field Survey II, President's Commission on Law Enforcement and Administration of Justice. Washington, D.C.: Government Printing Office, 1967.

as one goes down the income scale; aggravated assault shows a checkered line suggesting that this crime does not discriminate economically among victims. (This finding is difficult to reconcile with theories of subcultures of violence among lower-income groups.) Larceny of more than fifty dollars goes up with higher income families, possibly because of their greater possessions, and motor vehicle theft likewise goes up, as would be expected, because of the greater number of vehicles owned by families in middle and upper income brackets.

Patterns of victimization by race indicate that nonwhite people (a category made up overwhelmingly of blacks) are victimized at rates much higher than whites for all index crimes except homicide (excluded from this study) and grand larceny, as shown in Table 14-2. The high victimization rate among nonwhites for motor vehicle theft is difficult to reconcile with the low figure for poor families shown above in Table 14-1, but all the other information follows a predictable course. In short, the poor and the black are heavily victimized, and insofar as these two categories overlap, one would expect to find somewhat similar results in both sets of data.

As shown in Table 14-3, males are victimized far more frequently than females—almost three times as often—although there is some indication that the trends for the years since this study may have brought the sexes closer to equality in this respect. The victimization of males according to these data is greater than that of females for all index crimes except rape (excluded for definitional reasons) and homicide (also excluded), but other statistics show that men are much more frequently the victims of murder than women.

There is an interesting aspect to presentation of material regarding the gender of the victim in burglary. Most burglaries are committed against businesses or residential premises, and, while single people may be especially vulnerable, it is unlikely that they can account for a large percentage of all burglarized homes, because they account for a low percentage of all homes owned or rented. Nevertheless, the table shows that the rate of male victimization is about five times as high as that of females. However, this is mainly because of a peculiarity in reporting in which the male was most fre-

**TABLE 14-2
Victimization by
Race**

(Rates per 100,000 population)

Offense	White	Nonwhite
Total	1,860	2,592
Forcible rape	22	82
Robbery	58	204
Aggravated assault	186	347
Burglary	822	1,306
Larceny ($50 and over)	608	367
Motor vehicle theft	164	286
Number of respondents	(27,484)	(4,902)

SOURCE: President's Commission on Law Enforcement and Administration of Justice, 1967a. Adapted from a study conducted by National Opinion Research Council.

TABLE 14-3
Victimization by
Age and Sex

(Rates per 100,000 population)

| Offense | Male | | | | | | |
	10–19	20–29	30–39	40–49	50–59	60 plus	All ages
Total	951	5,924	6,231	5,150	4,231	3,465	3,091
Robbery	61	257	112	210	181	98	112
Aggravated assault	399	824	337	263	181	146	287
Burglary	123	2,782	3,649	2,365	2,297	2,343	1,583
Larceny ($50 and over)	337	1,546	1,628	1,839	967	683	841
Motor vehicle theft	31	515	505	473	605	195	268
	Female						
	10–19	20–29	30–39	40–49	50–59	60 plus	All ages
Total	334	2,424	1,514	1,908	1,132	1,052	1,059
Forcible rape	91	238	104	48	0	0	83
Robbery	0	238	157	96	60	81	77
Aggravated assault	91	333	52	286	119	40	118
Burglary	30	665	574	524	298	445	314
Larceny ($50 and over)	122	570	470	620	536	405	337
Motor vehicle theft	0	380	157	334	119	81	130

SOURCE: President's Commission on Law Enforcement and Administration of Justice, 1967a.
Adapted from a study conducted by National Opinion Research Council.

quently identified as "head of household." Certainly, when a family consisting of husband, wife, and children has had its home burglarized, the fact that the man is the chief breadwinner or for some other reason is identified as the head of household does not make the woman or children in the home any the less victimized.

Correcting, then, for the burglary figure, one still finds that males are victimized for four other index crimes (robbery, aggravated assault, grand larceny, and motor vehicle theft) more frequently than females. To these a fifth can be added—homicide. (As with burglary, the victim of automobile theft is most often listed as male, although the car may be owned and used by the entire family, because of the greater number of family-owned vehicles that are registered in the name of the husband-father.) Depending on whether one includes rape and corrects for the burglary and automobile theft data, male victimizations are from two to three times as frequent as female victimizations.

When examining Table 14–3 for age, one finds young people, both male and female, especially between the ages of twenty and thirty-nine, to be the most frequently victimized. The rate for the males in this age group is in the neighborhood of 6,000 per 100,000; it declines for each decade of life thereafter. However, for many individual crimes, victimization does not follow such a predictable pattern. Robbery declines as one gets older, with an inexplicably low rate in the male thirty to thirty-nine cohort, and aggravated assault likewise shows a steady decline, in fact a precipitate one, from the twenties to the thirties for males. Burglary is somewhat more steady, although there are some peaks that do not readily lend themselves to easy explanation.

For other types of crime—those not included in the index—victimization according to race, age, sex, and income is more difficult to unravel. It would appear that the poor and sometimes the very wealthy, including corporations and banks, are victims of white-collar crimes, ranging from consumer fraud to embezzlement. Crimes against the state (such as treason) can best be conceptualized as not victimizing any one individual or group more than another. And some types of illegal action have become widely identified as victimless.

A great deal of public indignation is expressed when violent crimes victimize the elderly and others who are relatively weak and helpless. It has not been established that the elderly are victims of assaults, robberies, and rape out of proportion to their numbers in the population, but any of these crimes committed against them carry an aura of moral decay that makes them abhorrent even to many criminals and often brings down the wrath of juries and judges.

The relationship of the nature of the victim to the disposition of a case, especially to sentencing of a convicted defendant, is an interesting field of study. It has long been noted that blacks and other minorities have received particularly harsh treatment when convicted of crimes (a finding that has been challenged by a few criminologists, although many if not most appear to uphold it); similarly, the question whether women offenders have been treated with "chauvinistic" severity by male judges or with chivalrous leniency is still being debated. Statistics on capital punishment amassed by Haywood Burns (1970), Frank Hartung (1952), and others indicate that, of blacks and whites convicted of murder, rape, and other capital crimes, a disproportionate number of blacks were executed. However, more recent studies tend to show that it is the race of the victim rather than the offender that seems to be the important factor. When the victim is white, there is greater likelihood of a severe sentence and, where it is still in effect, of capital punishment. If one takes this a step further, it suggests that interracial crime of blacks against whites is more severely punished than white crime against blacks, or any form of intraracial offense.

Demographic variables on victims have been studied in considerable detail by Marvin Wolfgang (1958) with regard to homicide, and Menachem Amir (1971) with regard to rape. Both studies were conducted in Philadelphia. While they show a great deal of victimization of blacks, young people, and persons from lower income families and lower class origins, both studies focused primarily on the previous relationship, interaction, and contribution (if any) of the victim to the crime.

The Criminal-Victim Relationship

No part of the burgeoning field of criminology is so fraught with misunderstanding, misrepresentation, and real and potential prospects for damage or aid to victims as is the effort to focus on the offender-victim relationship in all its phases: long before the crime, immediately before it, while it is taking place, and sometimes immediately thereafter.

While von Hentig was emphasizing psychological and other factors that make some people more likely targets for criminal acts, Benjamin Mendelsohn (1963), likewise a pioneer in victimology, was pursuing the possibility that sometimes the victim provokes, encourages, or precipitates the act. Mendelsohn made a logical typology, starting with those events in which the victim possesses pristine innocence, moving to others in which he or she is free of any wrongdoing but fails to use ordinary care and prudence to prevent the crime from occurring, and continuing on the gradation until reaching crimes in which there is an ongoing relationship resulting in assaultive behavior between parties and eventually severe injury or perhaps death for one party, with the injured or deceased no less guilty of the escalation of the altercation than his or her adversary.

For some crimes, however, victim precipitation hardly seems relevant. Except for a small number of self-punishing and self-destructive persons— who probably constitute a minuscule proportion of the victims of property crime—people are not robbed, burglarized, or mugged because they invited, provoked, or incited the event, although they may well have been less than completely prudent. For homicide, in contrast, contribution by the victim to the victimization does not appear to be rare, nor for aggravated assault as well. Whether it is useful to develop the concept of victim precipitation for rape is a controversial question.

Mendelsohn seems to have been strongly influenced by a novel by the then popular writer Franz Werfel—*The Murdered One Is Guilty* (*Der Ermordete Ist Schuld*). It was a curious influence, for in Werfel's novel a son murders his father after many years of suffering from misguided paternal discipline, but in no sense did the father instigate, precipitate, or provoke the act. If Werfel's novel is taken as the model for victimology, then almost all crime can be placed in the framework of victim precipitation—and in fact this position has been taken by some criminologists, as we shall presently see.

As one of the major founders of victimology, Mendelsohn conceived of crime as an interactive event. Although he very specifically exempted certain experiences from having influence on an interaction's becoming criminal—there are many instances after all when the attacker is a complete stranger—he emphasized that in numerous cases the victim makes a distinct contribution to being victimized. To some extent, the rise of such a theme in Europe in the 1930s may have been an expression of the strong influence of Freud; both Mendelsohn and von Hentig were quite explicit in stating that the alleged contribution of the victim to the injury sustained may in some instances be derived from unconscious motivation.

Later, Stephen Schafer (1968), a prominent European criminologist and legal scholar who emigrated to the United States, where he became a champion of victim compensation programs, even more strongly emphasized the victim's contribution to the criminal event. Schafer appeared to allow very few if any exemptions. Whereas the major work of von Hentig is called *The Criminal & His Victim*, Schafer turned this upside down, placing the emphasis and by implication a greater degree of responsibility on the victim, when he called his brief book on the subject *The Victim and His Criminal*. Several passages from this will indicate the extent to which he, and a few other scholars, carried the notion of victim precipitation:

> In a way, the victim is always the cause of a crime, even if the crime is motivated for abstract reasons such as intellectual integrity, freedom of religion, public health, the safety of a nation. All crimes necessarily have victims, and, necessarily, the existence of the victim or something material or immaterial that belongs to him makes for crime and may actually produce a criminal effect. However, as so often happens, the victim not only creates the possibility of a crime but precipitates it. In other words, the victim may develop the direction of the offender's criminal conduct toward himself. Even if he is an innocent bystander, in certain cases his silent "bystanding" may make him not only a psychological accomplice but at the same time the one who establishes the criminal motive and encourages the criminal action. He may motivate the criminal unconsciously. Or he may motivate him consciously, disregarding the risk he is taking. Or he may feel that his provocation is justified. Or he may want to be victimized. [Schafer, 1968: 79–80)

Even when the victim resists, thus ostensibly demonstrating a strong unwillingness to allow the event to proceed, Schafer sees an element of participation:

> Resistance may be a kind of provocation, it may increase the criminal effort; this may be especially true in sex crimes. [p. 81]

All members of society, Schafer points out in another passage, are potential victims. Then he goes on to qualify his own statement:

> But, and this is what the study of criminal-victim relationships is aiming at, not all victims are wholly passive sufferers of the attacking criminal, and the terms "offender" and "victim" fundamentally designate a legal position. Many offenders are offended by the victim, or, better, many victims victimize the offender; thus, the doer-sufferer distinction does not mean the exclusive doing of one party and the suffering of the other. [p. 102]

Many object to the formulations of Schafer. At their most extreme it is as if one were to say that a woman is the cause of her being raped because she is a woman, alive and beautiful, or is in a particular place at a given time, a place where she had every right and need to be. Rather than say that in a way the victim is "always the cause of a crime" it would be more logical to think of a gradation based on the extent, if any, of the victim's contribution. At one extreme, the victim initiates and provokes; at another point in the spectrum are victims who do not take ordinary care and prudence and hence are "guilty" of what might be considered contributory negligence. Finally, there are victims who are completely innocent of any responsibility for what has befallen them. Only the first would qualify for the concept of victim precipitation, bringing with it shared responsibility. Others may be said to be prone to victimization.

**VICTIM
PRECIPITATION** The concept of victim precipitation, derived from the early European works on victimology and studied in more detailed fashion by Marvin Wolfgang

(1958), refers to the degree to which the victim makes a contribution to a crime by acts that challenge, entice, or in other ways assist in bringing about an interaction culminating in the crime itself. Homicide, the crime studied by Wolfgang, lends itself particularly well to this analysis, for many victims and offenders are involved in an ongoing relationship. In some instances, the person who was ultimately murdered evidently initiated or escalated the altercation, or failed to terminate it.

When Amir (1971) attempted to apply the same concept to forcible rape, the idea of precipitation appeared to many to be too strong. He was actually referring—although he did not make the distinction—to vulnerability and imprudence.

Other than homicide and assault, few crimes are precipitated by victims. In swindles and confidence games of various sorts, the tables are sometimes turned: what can be involved here, not infrequently, is the effort of two swindlers to outdo each other, with the victorious one being called the criminal and the vanquished the victim. However, to speak of the greedy and acquisitive who fall prey to the swindler as precipitators is, in our opinion, a distortion. When a con artist is outconned, that is victim precipitation; when someone naive wants to get rich and places his money in the hands of a swindler, he is the victim of his own naivete and the other's criminality, but he, the victim, has not precipitated the crime.

The problem of resistance and its relationship to contribution by victims to their own victimization is an important one. In our view, a storekeeper being held up or a woman being raped is in no sense precipitating his or her own murder by fighting back. Even granting that the chances may be slim that murder will occur if no resistance is offered, it is the original crime, not the struggle against it, that is the cause of the homicide. Resistance may or may not be ill-advised (when we can make ex post facto judgments we usually applaud it as well-advised and heroic if successful) but it is in no sense a precipitating factor in the escalation of a crime from armed robbery or rape to homicide.

Victim precipitation occurs when there is illegal, criminal, assaultive, violent, or some other type of antisocial interpersonal behavior emanating from the one who eventually becomes the victim. This behavior need not be initiated by the victim, although sometimes this is the case. If the act was initiated by the victim, he is the victim of his own criminal activity, not that of another. However, one cannot usefully speak of precipitation when the victim has acted in self-defense. In precipitation, there is shared responsibility; normally, this means that the victim must assume his share but that a part falls upon the other as well. This would not be true in self-defense.

RISK OF VICTIMIZATION

Risk of victimization, or vulnerability, involves the differential probability that certain innocent persons will be victimized in criminal encounters. These risks may derive from variables of demography, neighborhood, type of work engaged in, physical prowess or lack thereof, and a host of other traits and characteristics.

Risk of victimization is a purely statistical category. It places no shared blame or responsibility on an individual for being female, elderly, crippled, or a salesman who must carry cash. For an elderly couple to continue to live in a dangerous neighborhood, stubbornly refusing their children's offers to move them elsewhere, does not make them partners in responsibility when they are victimized.

As with other crime statistics, the usefulness of data on risk of victimization is not always apparent, and in some instances presentation of the figures can be misleading, for it may seem that the victim is being blamed rather than studied. Still, knowledge as to who is being victimized and in what types of crime may lead to greater understanding of the criminal events themselves and enhanced protection for the most vulnerable sections of the populace. That it might also lead to public withdrawal, hysteria, and epidemic fear is a price that may have to be paid in a high-crime society in which warnings to potential victims are necessary aids to self-protection.

The serial murderer—a special type of mass murderer who kills an entire group of victims not within a few minutes as part of a single event but over a period of time—creates considerable hysteria within the locale where he is striking. A pattern is usually discovered; certain types of persons are known to be the victims. Such was the case with Jack the Ripper (whose victims were prostitutes), the Boston Strangler, the Hillside Strangler in Los Angeles, and the .44-caliber killer in New York (also known as "Son of Sam"). Some victims of serial murders simply disappear and are not heard from, their bodies undiscovered for months or even years, and no one links the disappearances to one another. This was the situation recently in two separate events, in Illinois and in Texas, in which boys were killed in serial fashion in homosexual sadistic activities. A study of the victims in serial murders may lead not only to solving the case but to increased vigilance by others who may share with the dead some major characteristic, be it a demographic trait or life-style.

**PRONENESS TO
VICTIMIZATION**

There are situations in which the victim neither precipitates nor provokes victimization but pursues a type of behavior for which the likelihood of becoming a victim is enhanced. This involves lack of care, prudence, and vigilance, and often a life-style that lends itself to victimization. It does not mean that the victim is necessarily doing anything improper, illegal, or unethical (although some might define a promiscuous search for sex partners and a willingness to go with strangers for this purpose as being improper, or at least marginal).

It was this category that informed the major work of von Hentig, when he focused on the feeble, the alcoholic, the very young and the elderly, and the lonely and forlorn. All of them are easy marks for robbers, rapists, swindlers, and murderers. Hitchhikers constitute another victim-prone group (particularly the female or lone hitchhiker), as do the men and women who pick them up in their cars. The woman who accompanies a stranger to his apartment can hardly be said to be precipitating or provoking a rape, but she is acting with careless disregard of the dangers, whether motivated by alcoholic intoxication, loneliness, a trusting faith in people, or a momentary sexual attraction that she then decided she did not wish to carry to fruition.

Precipitation, risk, and proneness are overlapping but separable entities, and the pursuit of their study is highly desirable.

The Problem of Retaliation

As crime has increased in the United States and large numbers of people have begun to lose faith in the ability, willingness, or power of the police and courts to apprehend criminals and impose punishment upon them, some victims and their friends and families have turned to extralegal retaliation.

Neighborhood vigilante groups formed to combat crime may be purely defensive or may serve only to intimidate the would-be offender. Such groups have often turned to making unofficial "arrests" and punishing alleged offenders without benefit of trial. When, as punishment, beatings or even murders have taken place upon apprehension of a criminal during the commission of an illegal act, they might be thought of as constituting an unnecessarily violent, yet understandable, form of self-defense. However, when they are directed against someone spotted a day, a week, or more after the crime, the possibility of misidentification is extremely high; history indicates that there is good reason to suspect interethnic and interracial bigotry in many cases, including blind revenge against an entire group for the alleged misdeed of one or two of its members.

Murder of a spouse has not been uncommon in America and most other countries. According to Uniform Crime Reports for 1979, 9 percent of all murder victims that year were slain by their husbands or wives, and if one were to include cohabiting but unmarried men and women, this proportion would no doubt be higher. Many surviving spouses have claimed to have been battered, although the crime itself (i.e., the murder) may not have been committed in a context of self-defense. Where constant battery upon a wife is established, juries have been reluctant to convict, even for a lesser charge, usually accepting the idea that the murderer had been so thoroughly and relentlessly victimized and the murdered person so provocative that the act was an extended form of self-defense. Nonetheless, society, through its legal codes, does not approve such conduct—offering divorce, legal separation, and complaint to authorities as legal alternative remedies—and some spouses have been found guilty of murder and given long sentences despite their defense of having been battered.

The retaliation of a victim or victim's family, except in the course of the crime itself (such as when Joan Little killed her jailer in North Carolina during what she claimed was an attempted rape, and so convinced a jury), while seldom vigorously prosecuted, is still unacceptable in modern systems of jurisprudence. In addition to circumventing the law and often initiating a cycle of feuding it deprives the accused of a fair trial or any trial at all. It offers the possibility for deliberate expression of revenge against a traditional enemy innocent of any wrongdoing, enhances the danger that an innocent bystander will be caught up and treated as if part of the criminal action, and increases the likelihood of persons being beaten, assaulted, or even killed because they are members of a racial or ethnic group that has incurred the ire of another group in the area. Retaliation offers dangers that someone will be mistakenly identified and gives enticements for the commission of serious crime, especially murder, with a handy but false defense argument.

While this book was in preparation, one of the authors had two students who were victims in different incidents of false identification and accusation, each time no doubt in good faith. Both students are white males, and both were accused of mugging white victims. (Race is mentioned here because had accusers and those accused been of different racial groups, the possibility of mistaken identification would have been greatly increased.) In the first case, the student had a police record of minor transgressions and was identified from his picture in a "rogues' gallery." However, the crime took place while the student was with the author in his office, many miles from the scene; and the youth could convincingly trace his steps before he came to that office and after. Nevertheless, it took a lot of persuasion to convince the assistant district attorney to drop the case, the strength of the alibi notwithstanding. In the second instance, the student was grabbed by the collar from behind by a woman who screamed that he had mugged her the week before. A policeman soon came to the scene, and the woman summoned a friend who had been with her during the robbery. Her friend arrived only to say, "That's not him, what's the matter with you?" Had on-the-spot justice been administered in these incidents, they would have ended far more tragically. This is, as we see it, the chief danger in victim retaliation, but sentiment for such retaliation will continue to be strong unless the public receives assurances of better crime control with more frequent apprehension and punishment of offenders, or unless it experiences revulsion over such retaliation resulting in some scandal due to the brutalization of persons later exonerated of any wrongdoing.

False Cries of Victimization

Reports by some persons that they have been victims of crimes that actually never took place have rarely been studied. While the giving of such false reports to police, district attorneys, and other officials is a criminal act, it is seldom prosecuted, and there has been little research to indicate the extent, motivations, and patterns of such activities.

A false report of having been victimized seems to take place under several types of circumstances, among which are the following:

1. A person falsely claims to have been a victim of a burglary or a robbery for the purpose of making an insurance claim. Insurance fraud is probably rather widespread, usually involving exaggeration of loss rather than complete fabrication. Some automobile owners have deliberately abandoned their cars in places where they are unlikely to be found, including the bottom of a river, so they could make an insurance claim on a stolen car (the claim amounting to more, evidently, than could have been obtained from a sale). Persons who have spent, gambled, or squandered money for which they were accountable have been known to report that they had been robbed and to claim insurance.

2. Accomplices to a crime, particularly robbery and hijacking, may pretend to be overcome or assaulted, and actually show some signs of physical injury. Messengers carrying valuable negotiable securities, bank tellers and

clerks, truck drivers, and many others have been apprehended as accomplices to crimes in which they had reported being victimized, even assaulted. Although the alleged assault is a possible false cry of victimization, the accomplice would not have been able to claim being a victim of robbery even had he not been a cooperative conspirator, for it was not his own money, securities, or property that were taken.

3. People who have won money in gambling activities that had to be shared with others, or who were carrying money in numbers games or for drug running, may seek to escape having to turn over such funds to partners, confederates, and superiors by claiming to have been robbed. Similar claims are made by people seeking to establish a tax loss.

4. Many people have reported victimization falsely for purposes of political gain, personal revenge, extortion, income tax evasion, providing an alibi, or a variety of other reasons. Prostitutes have been hired to entrap prominent people, particularly politicians. A small percentage of all charges of forcible rape are believed to be entirely false. In a study of all cases of rape reported to the police in Denver in a two-year period, the authorities concluded that 9.6 percent of the cases were false accusations; 3 percent of the complainants later confessed that they had falsely accused the men of rape (Sheppard, Giacini, and Tjaden, 1976). At one time, false accusation of rape was not rare in the United States, as witness the Scottsboro case in Alabama that became a cause célèbre throughout the world in the 1930s, when it was related to racial oppression, but it is doubtful if such a situation remains current (Carter, 1971).

5. There have been rumors and for the most part unsubstantiated claims by persons accused of kidnapping that the seized individual was a willing "victim" interested in publicity or a co-conspirator trying to extort money from his or her own family. Most of these claims have been rejected by juries, although in some instances juries have brought in verdicts that could be described as ambiguous.

The problem of fake victimization is quantitatively small but qualitatively significant. Only a small proportion of crime consists of falsified reports of victimization, as compared to the total number of forcible rapes, kidnappings, street muggings, hijackings, and burglaries. Only insurance fraud and income tax evasion appear to be common motivations for false victimization reports, but this seems to involve more exaggeration of amounts of loss than total fabrication of the event itself. When a false report results in an indictment, trial, or guilty verdict of the accused, as in the Scottsboro rape case or in slander against an innocent person, as in some of the kidnapping cases, the consequences are serious, although the number of such instances has been small.

An effort to gain a more accurate picture of the extent, nature, and scope of crime in the United States has been undertaken through victimization surveys. These consist of studies of specific locales to determine how many and what types of crimes have been committed against persons in households over a specific period of time.

Victimization Surveys

Victimization surveys have by and large been regarded as correcting rather than distorting the official crime statistics. Nonetheless, they do violate the warning once made by Manuel López-Rey (1970), that the victim is not a highly reliable source of information about the crime. James Levine (1976) has emphasized that there are tendencies among victims to exaggerate, and that victimization surveys may be giving an image of serious crime greater than that warranted by events themselves.

The use of the victims to obtain a fuller appreciation of the scope of crime may be one of the most interesting developments in victimology, as this subdiscipline of criminology unfolds.

Victim Compensation and Restitution

The problem of the victim of a brutal crime who, besides being deprived of money and belongings, is left with the ongoing problems of serious injuries, large medical bills, and diminished earnings is not uncommon. Whereas the criminal who is apprehended and convicted is given nourishing food, free medical and dental care, and even some psychiatric assistance (inadequate as it may be) at the expense of the government, the impoverished victim is often left to a sad fate—to public welfare and clinics and his or her own wits in coping with staggering debts.

Few seriously question the desirability of offering the convicted individual food, medical and dental care, and even such rehabilitative counseling as may be appropriate. The penal system is much more frequently criticized for giving too little to the inmates than for giving too much. Actually, contrasting the fate of the criminal and the victim is not entirely relevant, for the need to give the criminal both punishment and proper and humane care is seldom disputed. The contrast is usually drawn in order to highlight the burdens of the victims and the failure of government to come to their aid.

There has been a major drive in some parts of the United States and several other areas of the English-speaking world (such as Australia and New Zealand) to correct this situation and offer some form of victim compensation or restitution. Donal MacNamara and John Sullivan (1974) cite the fact that there is an often overlooked distinction between compensation and restitution. The former refers to efforts to assist someone in need because of loss of property or physical injury; the latter to efforts to restore the victim to the situation that prevailed before the crime. There is an underlying assumption here of liability, if not responsibility, on the part of the state, and not merely of the perpetrator. The state is liable in this view because it has assumed the responsibility for protection against crime, and because all of us, including the victims, pay for that protection.

Just how far compensation should go has been much debated. Some would offer it only in cases of financial need. Others would tie it in to the amount of pain and suffering, not merely loss of money or cost of medical care. And there is a problem in determining the relationship of compensation programs to insurance.

As to restitution, there is a limit on its possibilities. Property losses can be quantified in dollars. Injuries have long resulted in financial awards to victims through civil law, although this has frequently hinged on the question of blame (more accurately, negligence). A financial award, no matter the size, does not restore a victim to the condition that prevailed before the criminal assault, particularly if it left permanent injuries. Monetary awards cannot be any more restitutive in cases of forcible rape. That the same can be said of murder is too obvious to belabor. Psychological fear and memories continue after compensation, and their lingering effects can be most damaging. In crime, *status quo ante delictum* is impossible to achieve; in fact, in all interpersonal and social situations there is just no status quo ante anything.

Summary

The issues discussed above are a few of the major aspects of victimology, perhaps the newest and most interesting focus of recent criminological thought. Victimology is concerned with the questions, Who is the victim? Of what crime was he or she victimized and why? (Rather than, Why did the offender commit the act?) Those who have doubts about victimology demand to know how a knowledge of such victimization can be utilized to protect others from a similar fate.

The study of the victim should make clear-cut distinctions among victims who precipitate crimes and contribute as much to the criminal act (sometimes even more, frequently less) as does the victimizer; those who are vulnerable to crime or in a high-risk category, but have not provoked the act; and those who are prone to crime because of psychological difficulties, behavioral patterns, or lack of caution. Special studies of the self-destructive, accident-prone, and suicidal, on the one hand, and of the overly scrupulous and self-judgmental, on the other, would be useful to determine what correlations there are between such persons and their victimization, if any.

Care is needed that victims, their friends and family do not take the law into their own hands, because this is not only inimical to the legal process and deprives an accused of a day in court, but can lead to gross injustice. To balance this, however, greater care on the part of government personnel is needed to prevent the victim from being turned into an "accused" in court and to see that cross-examination never becomes harassment or a fishing expedition into private and potentially embarrassing matters irrelevant to the case at issue.

References for Part III

ADLER, FREDA. *Sisters in Crime: The Rise of the New Female Criminal.* New York: McGraw-Hill, 1975.

ALBINI, JOSEPH L. *The American Mafia: Genesis of a Legend.* New York: Appleton-Century-Crofts, 1971.

AMERICAN LAW INSTITUTE. *Model Penal Code.* Philadelphia: American Law Institute, 1962.

AMIR, MENACHEM. *Patterns in Forcible Rape.* Chicago: University of Chicago Press, 1971.

ARENS, W. *The Man-Eating Myth: Anthropology & Anthropophagy.* New York: Oxford University Press, 1979.

ATKINSON, JEFF. " 'Racketeer Influenced and Corrupt Organizations,' 18 U.S.C.: §§1961–68: Broadest of the Federal Criminal Statutes." *Journal of Criminal Law and Criminology*, 1978, 69: 1–18.

BALL-ROKEACH, SANDRA. "Values and Violence." *American Sociological Review*, 1973, 38: 736–749.

BAUMHART, RAYMOND C. "How Ethical Are Businessmen?" *Harvard Business Review*, July-August 1961, 39: 6–19, 156–176.

BEATTIE, RONALD H., and JOHN P. KENNEY. "Aggressive Crimes." *Annals of American Academy of Political and Social Science*, 1966, 365: 73–85.

BELL, DANIEL. *The End of Ideology: On the Exhaustion of Political Ideas in the Fifties.* New York: Free Press, 1967.

BERNSTEIN, MARVER H. *Regulating Business by Independent Commission.* Princeton, N.J.: Princeton University Press, 1955.

BLOCH, HERBERT A., and GILBERT GEIS. *Man, Crime, and Society.* 2d ed. New York: Random House, 1962.

BONGER, WILLEM A. *Criminality and Economic Conditions.* New York: Agathon Press, 1967. (First published in English in 1916.)

BOROSAGE, ROBERT. "Secrecy vs. the Constitution." *Society*, March-April, 1975, 12: 71–75.

BURNS, HAYWOOD. "Can a Black Man Get a Fair Trial in This Country?" *New York Times Magazine*, July 12, 1970, pp. 5 ff.

CAMERON, MARY OWEN. *The Booster and the Snitch: Department Store Shoplifting.* New York: Free Press, 1964.

CAPLOVITZ, DAVID. *The Poor Pay More: Consumer Practices of Low-Income Families.* New York: Free Press, 1963.

CARROLL, LEO. *Hacks, Blacks, and Cons.* Lexington, Mass.: Lexington Books, 1974.

CARTER, DAN T. *Scottsboro: A Tragedy of the American South.* New York: Oxford University Press, 1971.

CAVAN, RUTH SHONLE. "Underworld, Conventional and Ideological Crime." *Journal of Criminal Law, Criminology and Police Science*, 1964, 55: 235–240.

CHAMBLISS, WILLIAM J. "A Sociological Analysis of the Law of Vagrancy." *Social Problems*, 1964, 12: 67–77.

———. "The State, the Law, and the Definition of Behavior as Criminal or Delinquent." In Daniel Glaser, ed., *Handbook of Criminology*, pp. 7–43. Chicago: Rand McNally, 1974.

CHAPMAN, DENNIS. *Sociology and the Stereotype of the Criminal.* London: Tavistock, 1978.

CLARK, RAMSEY. *Crime in America.* New York: Simon & Schuster, 1970.

CLINARD, MARSHALL B. *The Black Market: A Study of White-Collar Crime.* New York: Rinehart, 1952.

CLINARD, MARSHALL B., and RICHARD QUINNEY. *Criminal Behavior Systems: A Typology.* 2d ed. New York: Holt, Rinehart and Winston, 1973.

COCKBURN, ALEXANDER. "Sweet Mysteries of Watergate." *New York Review of Books*, November 28, 1974, 21: 8–16.

COHEN, ALBERT K. *Delinquent Boys: The Culture of the Gang.* New York: Free Press, 1955.

COLUMBIA LAW REVIEW. "The Espionage Statutes and Publications of Defense Information." *CLR*, 1973, 73: 929–1087.

CRESSEY, DONALD R. *Other People's Money: The Social Psychology of Embezzlement.* New York: Free Press, 1953.

———. "Organized Crime as a Social System." *Law Enforcement: Science and Technology*. Vol. 1. Washington, D.C.: Thompson Book Co., 1967.

_____. *Theft of the Nation: The Structure and Operations of Organized Crime in America.* New York: Harper & Row, 1969.

DOLLARD, JOHN, NEAL E. MILLER, LEONARD W. DOOB, O.H. MOWRER, and ROBERT E. SEARS. *Frustrations and Aggression.* New Haven, Conn.: Yale University Press for the Institute of Human Relations, 1939.

DOMHOFF, G. WILLIAM. *The Higher Circles.* New York: Random House, 1970.

DOUGLAS, JACK D., and JOHN M. JOHNSON, eds. *Official Deviance: Readings in Malfeasance, Misfeasance, and Other Forms of Corruption.* Philadelphia: Lippincott, 1977.

EDELHERTZ, HERBERT. *The Nature, Impact and Prosecution of White Collar Crime.* Washington, D.C.: Government Printing Office, 1970.

FEDERAL BUREAU OF INVESTIGATION. See Uniform Crime Reports.

FINKELHOR, DAVID. *Sexually Victimized Children.* New York: Free Press, 1979.

FORD, CLELLAN S., and FRANK A. BEACH. *Patterns of Sexual Behavior.* New York: Harper & Row, 1951.

Fortune. Editorial, September 1960, p. 135.

FREEDMAN, ALFRED M., and HAROLD I. KAPLAN. *Human Behavior.* New York: Atheneum, 1972.

GAGE, NICHOLAS. "Study Shows Courts Lenient with Mafiosi." *New York Times,* September 25, 1973.

GASTIL, R.D. "Homicide and a Regional Culture of Violence." *American Sociological Review,* 1971, 36: 412–437.

GAULT. See In re Gault.

GEBHARD, PAUL H., JOHN H. GAGNON, WARDELL B. POMEROY, and CORNELIA V. CHRISTENSON. *Sex Offenders: An Analysis of Types.* New York: Harper & Row, 1965.

GEIS, GILBERT. "Upperworld Crime." In Abraham S. Blumberg, ed., *Current Perspectives on Criminal Behavior,* pp. 114–137. New York: Knopf, 1974.

_____. *Not the Law's Business.* 2d ed. New York: Schocken, 1979.

_____, ed. *White-Collar Criminal: The Offender in Business and the Professions.* Chicago: Aldine, 1968.

GEIS, GILBERT, and ROBERT F. MEIER, eds. *White-Collar Crime: Offenses in Business, Politics, and the Professions.* New York: Free Press, 1977.

GIBBONS, DON C. *Society, Crime, and Criminal Careers.* Englewood Cliffs, N.J.: Prentice-Hall, 1968.

GLASER, DANIEL. "The Classification of Offenses and Offenders." In Glaser, ed., *Handbook of Criminology,* pp. 45–83. Chicago: Rand McNally, 1974.

GLUECK, SHELDON, and ELEANOR GLUECK. *Physique and Delinquency.* New York: Kraus Reprint Co., 1970. (First published in 1956.)

GREEN, MARK H., JAMES M. FALLOWS, and DAVID R. ZWICK. *Who Runs Congress?* New York: Bantam Books, 1972.

HALL, JEROME. *Theft, Law and Society.* Indianapolis: Bobbs-Merrill, 1939.

HAMMER, RICHARD. "Playboy's History of Organized Crime." *Playboy,* June 1974.

HARRIS, FRED R. "The Politics of Corporate Power." In Ralph Nader and Mark J. Green, eds., *Corporate Power in America,* pp. 25–41. New York: Grossman, 1973.

HARTOGS, RENATUS, and ERIC ARTZ. *Violence: Causes and Solutions.* New York: Dell, 1970.

HARTUNG, FRANK E. "White Collar Offenses in the Wholesale Meat Industry in Detroit." *American Journal of Sociology,* 1950, 56: 25–34.

_____. "Trends in the Use of Capital Punishment." *Annals of American Academy of Political and Social Science,* 1952, 284: 8–19.

HEALY, WILLIAM. *The Individual Delinquent: A Text-Book of Diagnosis and Prognosis for All Concerned in Understanding Offenders.* Montclair, N.J.: Patterson Smith, 1969. (First published in 1915.)

HILLS, STUART L. "Combating Organized Crime in America." *Federal Probation*, March 1969, 33: 23–28.

HOMER, FREDERIC D. *Guns and Garlic: Myths and Realities of Organized Crime*. West Lafayette, Ind.: Purdue University Press, 1974.

IANNI, FRANCIS A. J. *Black Mafia: Ethnic Succession in Organized Crime*. New York: Simon & Schuster, 1974.

IANNI, FRANCIS A. J. (with Elizabeth Reuss-Ianni). *A Family Business: Kinship and Social Control in Organized Crime*. New York: Russell Sage Foundation, 1972.

INCIARDI, JAMES A. *Careers in Crime*. Chicago: Rand McNally, 1975.

In re Gault, 387 U.S. 1, 1967.

JACOBS, P., M. BRUNTON, M. MELVILLE, R. BRITTAIN, and W. MCCLERMONT. "Aggressive Behavior, Mental Subnormality, and the XYY Male." *Nature*, 1965, 208: 1351–1352.

JASPAN, NORMAN (with HILLEL BLACK). *The Thief in the White Collar*. Philadelphia: Lippincott, 1960.

JOHNSON, ROGER N. *Aggression in Man and Animals*. Philadelphia: Saunders, 1972.

KARBER, PHILLIP A. "Urban Terrorism: Baseline Data and a Conceptual Framework." *Social Science Quarterly*, 1971, 52: 521–533.

KLOCKARS, CARL B. *The Professional Fence*. New York: Free Press, 1974.

KOLKO, GABRIEL. *Wealth and Power in America*. New York: Praeger, 1962.

————. *The Triumph of Conservatism*. New York: Free Press, 1963.

LANE, ROBERT E. "Why Businessmen Violate the Law." *Journal of Criminal Law, Criminology and Police Science*, 1953, 44: 151–165.

LEVINE, JAMES P. "The Potential for Crime Overreporting in Criminal Victimization Surveys." *Criminology*, 1976, 14: 307–331.

LEVINE, ROBERT A. "Gusii Sex Offenses: A Study in Social Control." *American Anthropologist*, 1959, 61: 965–990.

LINDESMITH, ALFRED R. "Organized Crime." *Annals of American Academy of Political and Social Science*, 1941, 217: 119–127.

LÓPEZ-REY, MANUEL. *Crime: An Analytical Appraisal*. New York: Praeger, 1970.

LORENZ, KONRAD. "Lorenz Warns: Man Must Know That the Horse He Is Riding May Be Wild and Should Be Bridled." *Psychology Today*, November 1974, 8: 83–93.

————. *On Aggression*. New York: Harcourt Brace Jovanovich, 1966.

MACNAMARA, DONAL E. J., and EDWARD SAGARIN. *Sex, Crime, and the Law*. New York: Free Press, 1977.

MACNAMARA, DONAL E. J., and JOHN J. SULLIVAN. "Making the Crime Victim Whole: Composition, Restitution, Compensation." In Terence P. Thornberry and Edward Sagarin, eds., *Images of Crime: Offenders and Victims*, pp. 79–90. New York: Praeger, 1974.

MAPES, GLYNN. "A Growing Disparity in Criminal Sentences Troubles Legal Experts." *Wall Street Journal*, September 9, 1970.

MARCHETTI, VICTOR, and JOHN D. MARKS. *The CIA and the Cult of Intelligence*. New York: Dell, 1974.

MARCUSE, HERBERT. *Essay on Liberation*. Boston: Beacon Press, 1969.

MARK, VERNON H., and FRANK R. ERWIN. *Violence and the Brain*. New York: Harper & Row, 1970.

MCCAGHY, CHARLES H. *Child Molesters: A Study of Their Careers as Deviants*. Ph.D. dissertation, University of Wisconsin, 1966. Excerpted in Marshall B. Clinard and Richard Quinney, eds., *Criminal Behavior Systems: A Typology*, pp. 75–88. New York: Holt, Rinehart and Winston, 1967.

MCCLINTOCK, F. H. *Crimes of Violence*. New York: St. Martin's Press, 1963.

MCCORD, WILLIAM, and JOAN MCCORD. *Psychopathy and Delinquency*. New York: Grune & Stratton, 1964.

McLUHAN, MARSHALL. *Understanding Media: The Extensions of Man.* New York: New American Library, 1964.

MEDNICK, SARNOFF, and KARL O. CHRISTIANSEN, eds. *Biosocial Bases of Criminal Behavior.* New York: Gardner Press, 1977.

MENDELSOHN, BENJAMIN. "The Origin of the Doctrine of Victimology." *Excerpta Criminologica*, May–June 1963, 3: 239–244.

MERTON, ROBERT K. *Social Theory and Social Structure.* New York: Free Press, 1968.

MERTON, ROBERT K., and ROBERT NISBET. *Contemporary Social Problems.* New York: Harcourt Brace Jovanovich, 1971.

MILLER, GALE. *Odd Jobs: The World of Deviant Works.* Englewood Cliffs, N.J.: Prentice-Hall, 1978.

MILLER, WALTER B. "Lower-Class Culture as a Generating Milieu of Gang Delinquency." *Journal of Social Issues*, 1958, 14(3): 5–19.

MILLS, C. WRIGHT. *The Power Elite.* New York: Oxford University Press, 1957.

MORRIS, NORVAL, and GORDON HAWKINS. *The Honest Politician's Guide to Crime Control.* Chicago: University of Chicago Press, 1970.

MORRIS, ROGER. "The Aftermath of CIA Intervention." *Society*, March/April 1975, 12: 76–80.

MOULEDOUS, JOSEPH C. "Political Crime and the Negro Revolution." In Marshall B. Clinard and Richard Quinney, eds., *Criminal Behavior Systems: A Typology*, pp. 217–231. New York: Holt, Rinehart and Winston, 1967.

NATIONAL ASSOCIATION OF ATTORNEYS GENERAL. Committee on the Office of Attorney General. *Organized Crime Control Units: Special Report.* Raleigh, N.C.: The Committee, 1975.

NEWMAN, DONALD J. "Public Attitudes toward a Form of White Collar Crime." *Social Problems*, 1957, 4: 228–232.

_____. "White Collar Crime." *Law and Contemporary Problems*, 1958, 23: 735–753.

Newsweek. "The Cloak Comes Off." June 23, 1975, pp. 16–22.

NIEBURG, HAROLD L. *Political Violence: The Behavioral Process.* New York: St. Martin's Press, 1969.

PACKER, HERBERT L. *The Limits of the Criminal Sanction.* Stanford, Calif.: Stanford University Press, 1968.

PLATT, ANTHONY M. *The Child Savers: The Invention of Delinquency.* Chicago: University of Chicago Press, 1969.

PRESIDENT'S COMMISSION ON LAW ENFORCEMENT AND ADMINISTRATION OF JUSTICE. *The Challenge of Crime in a Free Society.* Washington, D.C.: Government Printing Office, 1967a.

_____. *Task Force Report: Organized Crime.* Washington, D.C.: Government Printing Office, 1967b.

PRUS, ROBERT, and STYLLIANOS IRINI. *Hookers, Rounders, and Desk Clerks: The Social Organization of the Hotel Community.* Toronto: Gage Publishing, 1980.

QUINNEY, RICHARD. "Occupational Structure and Criminal Behavior." *Social Problems*, 1963, 11: 179–193.

_____. *The Social Reality of Crime.* Boston: Little, Brown, 1970.

_____. *The Problem of Crime.* New York: Dodd, Mead, 1975.

REISS, ALBERT J., JR. "The Study of Deviant Behavior: Where the Action Is." *Ohio Valley Sociologist*, Autumn 1966, 32: 1–12.

Robinson v. California, 370 U.S. 660, 1962.

ROEBUCK, JULIAN B. *Criminal Typology: The Legalistic, Physical-Constitutional-Hereditary, Psychological-Psychiatric, and Sociological Approaches.* Springfield, Ill.: Thomas, 1967.

ROEBUCK, JULIAN B., and THOMAS BARKER. "A Typology of Police Corruption." *Social Problems*, 1974, 24: 427–434.

ROEBUCK, JULIAN B., and WOLFGANG FRESE. *The Rendezvous: A Case Study of an After*

Hours Club. New York: Free Press, 1976.

ROEBUCK, JULIAN B., and JAMES LANDRUM. Report on DUI Follow-Ups Project (1977–81), conducted by Mississippi State University Social Science Research Center for National Highway Traffic Safety Administration. 1981.

RYAN, WILLIAM. *Blaming the Victim.* New York: Pantheon, 1971.

SALERNO, RALPH F., and JOHN S. THOMPKINS. *The Crime Confederation.* New York: Popular Library, 1969.

SCHAFER, STEPHEN. *The Victim and His Criminal: A Study in Functional Responsibility.* New York: Random House, 1968.

SCHUR, EDWIN M. *Crimes without Victims.* Englewood Cliffs, N.J.: Prentice-Hall, 1965.

_____. *Our Criminal Society: The Social and Legal Sources of Crime in America.* Englewood Cliffs, N.J.: Prentice-Hall, 1969.

_____. *The Politics of Deviance: Stigma Contests and the Uses of Power.* Englewood Cliffs, N.J.: Prentice-Hall, 1980.

SHAH, SALEEM A., and LOREN H. ROTH. "Biological and Psychophysiological Factors in Criminality." In Daniel Glaser, ed., *Handbook of Criminology,* pp. 101–173. Chicago: Rand McNally, 1974.

SHEPPARD, DAVID I., THOMAS GIACINI, and CLAUS TJADEN. "Rape Reduction: A Citywide Program." In Marcia J. Walker and Stanley L. Brodsky, eds., *Sexual Assault: The Victim and the Rapist,* pp. 169–175. Lexington, Mass.: Lexington Books, 1976.

SHERRILL, ROBERT. *Why They Call It Politics.* New York: Harcourt Brace Jovanovich, 1974.

SIEGAL, HARVEY A. *Outposts of the Forgotten: Socially Terminal People in Slum Hotels and Single Room Occupancy Tenements.* New Brunswick, N.J.: Transaction Books, 1978.

SIMON, RITA JAMES. *Women and Crime.* Lexington, Mass.: D. C. Heath, 1975.

SKOLNICK, JEROME H. *The Politics of Protest.* New York: Ballantine, 1969.

SMITH, ALEXANDER B., and HARRIET POLLACK. *Some Sins Are Not Crimes.* New York: Franklin Watts, 1975.

SMITH, DWIGHT C., JR. *The Mafia Mystique.* New York: Basic Books, 1975.

SMITH, RICHARD A. "The Incredible Electrical Conspiracy." *Fortune,* April 1961, 63: 132–137, and May 1961, 63: 161–164.

SOLZHENITSYN, ALEXANDER I. *The Gulag Archipelago.* New York: Harper & Row, 1974.

SPERGEL, IRVING. *Racketville, Slumtown, Haulburg: An Exploratory Study of Delinquent Subcultures.* Chicago: University of Chicago Press, 1964.

STERNBERG, DAVID. "The New Radical-Criminal Trials: A Step Toward a Class-for-Itself in the American Proletariat." In Charles Reasons, ed., *The Criminologist: Crime and the Criminal,* pp. 189–209. Pacific Palisades, Calif.: Goodyear, 1974.

SUTHERLAND, EDWIN H. *White Collar Crime.* New York: Dryden, 1949.

SUTHERLAND, EDWIN H., and DONALD R. CRESSEY. *Principles of Criminology.* 7th ed. Philadelphia: Lippincott, 1966.

SYKES, GRESHAM, and DAVID MATZA. "Techniques of Neutralization: A Theory of Delinquency." *American Sociological Review,* 1957, 21: 664–670.

TAPPAN, PAUL. "Who Is the Criminal?" *American Sociological Review,* 1947, 12: 96–102.

THRASHER, FREDERIC M. *The Gang: A Study of 1,313 Gangs in Chicago.* Chicago: University of Chicago Press, 1927.

TURK, AUSTIN. *Political Criminality and Political Policing.* New York: MSS Modular Publishers, 1975.

TURNER, JAMES S. *The Chemical Feast.* New York: Grossman, 1970.

TYLER, GUS. "The Crime Corporation." In Abraham Blumberg, ed., *Current Perspectives on Criminal Behavior,* pp. 273–290. 2d ed. New York: Knopf, 1981.

UNIFORM CRIME REPORTS. *Crime in the United States, 1979.* Washington, D. C.: Federal Bureau of Investigation, 1980. (Published annually.)

UNITED STATES HOUSE OF REPRESENTATIVES. *Impeachment of Richard M. Nixon, President of the United States: The Final Report of the Committee on the Judiciary.* New York: Bantam Books, 1975.

VANDERBILT LAW REVIEW. "Warrantless Wiretapping of Suspected Domestic Dissident Group's Conversation Violates Fourth Amendment." *VLR,* 1971, 24: 1259–1295.

VOLD, GEORGE B. *Theoretical Criminology.* 2d ed., revised by Thomas Bernard. New York: Oxford University Press, 1979.

VON HENTIG, HANS. *The Criminal & His Victim.* New York: Schocken, 1979. (First published in 1948).

WALKER, ANDREW. "Sociology and Professional Crime." In Abraham S. Blumberg, ed., *Current Perspectives on Criminal Behavior,* pp. 87–113. New York: Knopf, 1974.

WASMAN, N., and J. P. FLYNN. "Direct Attack Elicited from the Hypothalamus." *Archives of Neurology,* 1962, 6: 60–67.

WESTIN, ALAN F. *Privacy and Freedom.* New York: Atheneum, 1967.

WILLETT, T. C. *Criminal on the Road.* London: Tavistock, 1964.

WILSON, WILLIAM JULIUS. *The Declining Significance of Race: Blacks and Changing American Institutions.* Chicago: University of Chicago Press, 1978.

WINICK, CHARLES, "Maturing out of Narcotic Addiction." *Bulletin on Narcotics,* January–March 1962, 14: 1–7.

WISE, DAVID. "Cloak and Dagger Operations: An Overview." *Society,* March/April, 1975, 12: 26–32.

WOETZEL, ROBERT K. "An Overview of Organized Crime: Mores vs. Morality." *Annals of American Academy of Political and Social Science,* 1963, 347: 1–11.

WOLFGANG, MARVIN E. *Patterns in Criminal Homicide.* Philadelphia: University of Pennsylvania Press, 1958.

———. "Violent Behavior." In Abraham S. Blumberg, ed., *Current Perspectives on Criminal Behavior,* pp. 240–261. New York: Knopf, 1974.

WOLFGANG, MARVIN E., and FRANCO FERRACUTI. *The Subculture of Violence: Towards an Integrated Theory in Criminology.* London: Tavistock, 1967.

YABLONSKY, LEWIS. *The Violent Gang.* New York: Macmillan, 1962.

PART IV

Criminal Justice: Prevention and Control of Crime

Concepts of Crime Prevention

Terms such as "prevention," "control," and "deterrence" are frequently encountered in the literature of crime. However, their meaning often varies from one text to another. In this respect, criminology is like most social sciences—that is, there are few rigorous and universally accepted definitions. Rather, certain terms and concepts take on a general meaning, with more agreement on usage than on definition.

"Crime prevention" is a term that is often used very broadly. It has served to justify many diverse programs. Thus, proposals to censor children's television, raise the minimum wage, or require school prayer all have proponents who argue that these measures will contribute to a reduction in crime and delinquency.

While most of the basic constraints on criminal behavior are established by such institutions as the family, schools, media, and other forces that inculcate general cultural values, there are other institutions involved, more directly connected to the prevention of crime. The most apparent of these is the criminal justice system, with its concepts of deterrence and its mechanisms for apprehension of offenders, adjudication of their guilt or innocence, and the punishment and hopefully the rehabilitation of those found guilty of violating the law.

Crime prevention and control are usually differentiated, in that prevention is thought of as the effort to forestall or deter the commission of a crime while control refers to measures of dealing with the crime and the criminal after the act has been committed. Thus, police patrol, job-training, and

Prevention and Control

youth counseling can all be seen as preventive measures. In contrast, arrest, trial, and incarceration are aspects of control. Some would argue, however, that police patrol is also an aspect of crime control, since an effective patrol instills a fear of arrest and punishment in the potential offender and thus discourages crime. In a similar vein, treatment programs aimed at convicted offenders can be considered control measures because they occur after a crime has taken place.

An official agency distinguishes between crime control and crime prevention in an interesting manner:

> "Control" refers to those activities (detection, apprehension, prosecution, adjudication, and post-adjudicatory efforts) in which society primarily engages in response to criminal acts once they have occurred. . . . "Prevention of crime" denotes a range of societal activities which are designed to inhibit the occurrence of criminal behavior by interrupting the social, psychological, and situational processes believed to encourage it, and by supporting those processes which are believed to encourage law-abiding behavior. [New York State Division of Criminal Justice Services, 1975: III-C-42]

In practice most people do not make such theoretical distinctions, and in common parlance any measures taken to deter the commission of an offense are usually considered crime prevention. The prevention/control, before/after dichotomy is useful, however, in focusing attention on philosophical approaches to the crime problem. An emphasis on prevention aims at significantly reducing, even eradicating, crime. Control, on the other hand, concedes that a certain amount of crime will always occur and emphasizes measures to keep it within bounds. The practical effect of this distinction will be apparent when we discuss anticrime policies.

Models of Prevention and Control

All systems of prevention and control are implicitly or explicitly based on theories of causation. Adherents of the classical school of criminology subscribe to the belief that offenders knowingly choose to engage in wrongful acts and that therefore the best means of preventing crime is to make punishments for criminal behavior greater than anticipated rewards. While few contemporary policy-makers totally accept such tenets, classical philosophy still underlies our criminal law in what might be termed the *punitive* or *rational-legal* model of prevention and control. This and two other models—the *correctional* and *mechanistic*—are shown in Table 15–1 and discussed in detail below.

**TABLE 15-1
Models of Crime
Prevention and
Control**

Punitive	*Correctional*	*Mechanistic*
Deterrence:	Treatment:	Reduction of opportunity
General	Social causation	Increase of risk to offender
Specific	Individual	

The functions of arrest, prosecution, and punishment can of course be carried out by the criminal justice system only after the commission of a crime has occurred, when general and specific (or special) deterrence are called into play.

THE PUNITIVE MODEL

The imposition of criminal penalties on convicted offenders is the essence of the punitive model. The basic rationale is that punishment of convicted offenders "teaches them a lesson" while it serves as a deterrent to others (Morris, 1966). The former is known as specific deterrence, the latter as general deterrence.

At one time it was widely accepted that punishment must be severe in order to have the desired effect of deterrence. Therefore, in some societies, such as eighteenth-century England, hanging was common for even the pettiest offenses. An alternative notion is that severity of punishment is less important than its certainty. One problem arises from the differential impact of sanctions on individuals. To some people the mere fact of an arrest, even without prosecution or further punishment, would constitute such a severe disgrace in their own minds or public reputations that they would never chance its happening. To others a jail term may mean little unless it is of considerable duration. Differences of opinion are rife in criminological and political circles over the effect of punishment on inhibition of criminal behavior, reaching the point of sharpest debate over the death penalty.

A view that has received considerable attention is a modified version of the punitive model. Adherents argue that apprehended criminals must be incarcerated in order to "incapacitate" them—a technical term that covers all methods of making a person incapable of committing another criminal act, methods that may include execution, exile, detention, physical mutilation, and incarceration. For example, one study suggests that the rate of serious crime would be reduced by two-thirds if every person convicted of such an offense was incarcerated for three years (Shinnar and Shinnar, 1974). However, other research studies have disputed this finding (Van Dine et al., 1979).

THE CORRECTIONAL MODEL

Explanations of crime causation other than the classical one suggest alternative rationales for prevention and control. The tenets of positivism have given rise to what might be termed the sociopsychological or correctional concept of crime prevention. This holds that criminal offenders are motivated by either individual personality defects or societal imperfections or by both. The means used for the prevention of crime will largely depend on which aspect of causation is embraced. For example, the notion that criminal behavior is primarily a result of individual maladjustment suggests that attempts be made to identify potential offenders through their personality patterns, and that they be offered treatment before engaging in crime or after conviction to discourage further illegal activity. Counseling, behavior modification, transactional analysis, drug treatment, psychotherapy, and other methods have been tried for effecting change in prospective or actual offenders. In this approach, correctional concepts can serve as both preventive and control measures because they can be administered before or after the commission of a crime.

If the etiology of crime is believed to be rooted in the social organization, or lack of it, the correctional model proposes that the remedy is to "treat" society itself. This may involve programs to eliminate poverty and racial discrimination or create a sense of community. It might also mean basic structural changes in the economic and political system. Some schools of thought, for example, contend that only a socialist state can adequately meet the problem of crime.

THE MECHANISTIC MODEL

A third approach to crime prevention involves measures to reduce the opportunity for crime to occur. For example, placing strong locks on apartment doors may discourage all but the most skilled burglar; use of exact-fare systems in public transportation often seems to reduce the robbery rate. Opportunity reduction has been called mechanical or mechanistic prevention because it seeks to redesign the environment (not because it necessarily involves any mechanical device).

The mechanistic model differs from other types of prevention because it emphasizes the victim or object of crime rather than the offender, and does not primarily involve punishment or rehabilitation. Certain aspects of the mechanistic approach do, however, depend on altering offender perceptions. These are measures designed to increase the risks in committing crime. For example, the rationale for the installation of bright street lighting is that it will make street crime more visible and therefore more likely to be interrupted, either directly by police or by citizens who may summon them. Thus the preventive aspects of the mechanistic model interact with the control aspects of the punitive model, since it would not be worthwhile to increase the risks of apprehension if there were no possibility of punishment.

Policy Implications: The Models Weighed and Considered

Over the past few decades, the essence of crime prevention and indeed of the overall system of criminal justice in America has been a combination of punitive and correctional concepts. The dominant theme of the system is that criminals must be caught and processed, but those who are convicted should be rehabilitated rather than punished. Therefore, when a criminal is sent to prison, the proponents both of punishment and of rehabilitation can feel some satisfaction, the former because the offender is getting his due and the latter because the maladjusted individual is receiving treatment.

In the real world, both ordinary citizens and policy-makers are constantly accepting or rejecting various strands of criminological theory, even though they may not be aware of it. Political candidates who promise mandatory prison sentences for drug dealers are espousing the tenets of classical criminology, urging a punitive model of crime prevention. That is, they are arguing that the behavior of drug dealers is essentially rational and can therefore be prevented by making the penalty sufficiently severe. Newspaper columnists who urge that prisons be closed and inmates transferred to community treatment centers are affirming their faith in the correctional model, as developed in theories of positivism. A community group that petitions the city to install street lights is in effect supporting the mechanical model of crime prevention, since its members evidently believe that the lights will reduce the opportunity for crime and therefore the likelihood of its occurring. Then there are those who contend that priorities must be reordered—that, for example, the most serious public danger is posed by white-collar and corporate offenders who commit crimes with far-reaching effects but are rarely caught, tried, or punished, and if punished generally receive lenient treatment.

These examples are common enough that we can easily recognize them, yet it is often difficult to decide which course of action policy-makers should choose. Some argue for the simultaneous adoption of all of these approaches in the hope that at least one will work. This position requires that most criminals be sent to prison (punitive model) and that at the same time they be sent to community treatment centers (correctional individual treatment) and also unconditionally released (on the ground that the criminal act is sociogenic and not the fault of the individual). Obviously all three cannot be done for any individual offender at one time, or for most offenders, although all can be invoked as alternatives for different individuals or various types of offender or for the same person at different times. Those pointing to the virtual immunity of white-collar and corporate offenders call for basic changes in the definition and administration of civil and criminal law that would facilitate the apprehension, conviction, and punishment of many who now escape the hand of justice. Some scholars claim, along these lines, that structural changes in the advanced capitalist state would eliminate most of these offenses.

It is of course possible to undertake a number of conceptually distinct crime prevention programs simultaneously. For example, an administration can install street lights, increase police patrols, and provide more community-treatment centers. However, resources are rarely abundant enough to permit such lavish expenditures, and in many instances the programs may not be compatible. For instance, it could be argued that increasing police patrols would be dysfunctional to the goal of reducing juvenile delinquency, since it could increase friction between police and youth.

One problem in determining crime prevention policies is the fact that in speaking of crime people are using a single term to describe what we have seen is a considerably complex array of heterogeneous human behavior. Even index crime covers a wide range of activities, and conventional street crime covers such disparate acts as juvenile automobile theft for joyriding purposes to burglary, which does not literally occur on the street. As a result, there has emerged among criminologists a movement to deal with the various types of crime in a narrower and more specific context. These crime-specific analysts seek to study a particular offense, such as burglary or robbery (or, even more precisely, street mugging), in all its dimensions, including the offender, victim, environmental factors, and legal processing, in the hope of arriving at more realistic policy recommendations. In a similar vein, one can study a specific geographical area and the forms, nature, and impact of crime as it occurs in that locality. Such studies are based on the concept that references to crime and criminals are too broad and discussion should focus on particular types of crime and offender, geographic areas, and other relatively narrow aspects of the general crime scene. All of these factors come into play in weighing the three major models.

The various models and the concepts that underlie them contain many contradictions and shortcomings as well as advantages. Arguments can be offered for or against any of them.

THE PUNITIVE MODEL

Over the centuries the punitive model has been the dominant approach to crime prevention and control in many countries. It has the advantage of being the cheapest to implement, since it requires only a rudimentary criminal justice system which does not come into operation until a crime has been committed and someone has been arrested. Even then it focuses on only an individual case and one or several offenders. A familiar, extreme example of this system was prevalent in the American West. There was no established and formal police patrol; rather, when a crime took place the sheriff would form a posse and pursue the suspects. If they were caught, they were often dealt with in summary fashion. There was here an assumption that the apprehended persons were the guilty ones; in innumerable instances, however, this was not true.

The rationale of the punitive model is that it inhibits offenders through fear of punishment. Its effectiveness is based on two assumptions. First, that most offenders behave rationally, in that they calculate, at least in rough fashion, the anticipated costs and benefits of a particular offense. Second, given that rational calculations are made, the possibility of apprehension and punishment is such that most potential offenders are deterred. That is, if would-be criminals reason that there are effective measures of apprehension and punishment related to the type of crime they are considering, they will be less likely to proceed with the act, at least at that time and place.

With regard to the first proposition, analysis of conventional offenders tends to call it into question. Index crime offenders who are apprehended tend to be young and to represent disproportionately the lower levels of educational and economic achievements—segments of the population in whom rational decision-making is generally not a highly developed skill. Motivations also tend to vary greatly within the index categories. Murder, rape, and assault frequently result from uncontrolled passion, whereas robbery, burglary, and larceny are often more calculated offenses (although not necessarily planned more than a few moments before the event). But even with property crime, there are some offenders (drug addicts, for example) whose needs may be so compelling that cost factors are outweighed by immediate benefits. A study of property offenders (robbers, burglars, and thieves) in the nation's capital has indicated that they are not highly rational or fearful of consequences, or, if fearful, are able at the time of committing the crime to block out the fear (Goodman, Miller, and DeForrest, 1966). A study of robbery offenders in Boston found that one-third did not fear capture, one-third blocked out the fear, and one-third thought chances of capture were minimal (Conklin, 1972: 134). Most white-collar and corporate criminal offenders who are engaged primarily in organizational crime, rather than such individual offenses as embezzling, have little if any fear of apprehension or punishment (Roebuck and Weeber, 1978). Patently, these offenders are among the most rational of all criminals, and thus it is among them that the punitive model should be tested.

Thus, even if offenders do calculate risks, there is evidence that they often rationally determine that chances of capture are minimal. As regards these chances, Table 15-2 presents the findings of a Rand Corporation study of New York City Police Department apprehension activities for index crimes. If the New York figures are typical, it would appear that police arrest offenders for about 50 percent of index crimes against persons and about 5 percent of index crimes against property. These figures would be even lower if data on unreported crime were included, since obviously these result in no arrests whatsoever. When the Rand data are adjusted for estimated total index crime, including unreported offenses, the arrest figures may be closer to 25 percent for offenses against persons and 2.5 percent for those against property. Of those arrested, only a minority are convicted and an even smaller proportion incarcerated. A Presidential crime commission has calculated that fewer than 10 percent of all those arrested for index crime actually serve time in prison (President's Commission on Law Enforcement and Administration of Justice, 1967a: 262–263).

Various studies have determined, however, that most routine property offenders frequently repeat their crimes and are eventually caught (Wolfgang, 1973; Reppetto, 1974). Thus the great majority of offenders do come into contact with the criminal justice system. The Washington study mentioned above examined the "losers" of the system—that is, persons who have been frequently apprehended, convicted, and incarcerated, and have spent considerable time in jails and prisons (Goodman, Miller, and DeForrest, 1966). Not surprisingly, most thought that if they continued to commit crimes they would actually be caught and severely punished; yet they intended to return to criminal behavior upon release.

The correctional model is based on the proposition that the formation of criminal desire should be prevented before offenses are perpetrated, or, if this is not successful, that such desire should be eradicated from convicted offenders. The implementation of correctional efforts on a broad scale can be most costly. The varied approaches may be directed toward individuals or whole societies. However, correctional approaches differ widely from

**THE
CORRECTIONAL
MODEL**

Crime	Cases	Arrest Index[a]
Homicide	338	.7130
Rape	906	.4834
Robbery	15,847	.1327
Assault	13,392	.4599
Burglary	67,028	.0434
Grand larceny	40,822	.0420
Motor vehicle theft	20,792	.0810

**TABLE 15-2
Arrests in New York
City for Index Crimes**

[a]The percentage of cases in which one or more persons were charged with the crime.

SOURCE: Greenwood, 1970, p. 24.

one another in their policy implications. Those who believe that crime is a function of individual maladjustment do not differ from those who support punitive concepts in their approval of the arrest of offenders. Indeed, some support the use of legal authority to compel individuals to be "treated." This is not the case with those who view crime as a failure of society. If criminals are victims of society, it follows (for some people) that they should not be punished and cannot be treated, since it is society that is the culprit. The proponents of societal guilt occasionally contend that the logical extension of this viewpoint is to arrest virtually no conventional index crime offenders, although most shrink from the full implications of this position. Rather, they combine the responsibility of society for its inequities with the necessity of social defense against their consequences: that is, one must work toward radical change in society, while at the same time protecting its members from being victimized by its victims (i.e., potential or actual offenders). Radical criminologists, neo-Marxists, and others take the latter view, admitting that even socialist societies have a lumpenproletarian class that is criminally dangerous and some of whose members must be controlled and punished.

In the 1970s considerable doubt was cast on the notion that the correctional system can rehabilitate offenders. Indeed, the system was characterized as providing only human warehouses where no rehabilitation can take place. Proposals for reform range from abandonment of the idea of rehabilitation in favor of a return to punitive functions (with mandatory prison sentences) to closing of penal facilities in favor of an alternative system of treatment. It is generally agreed, however, that some form of incarceration must continue in all societies, if for no other reason than that incapacitation, at least temporarily, protects society from dangerous offenders.

THE MECHANISTIC MODEL

The mechanistic or mechanical model concentrates on the victims of crime, the persons and objects injured or threatened, and the material property vulnerable to theft or actually stolen. It seeks to foreclose criminal opportunities. It overlaps with the punitive in that both seek to increase the risks and hazards of crime and thus discourage the criminal. The mechanical approach, however, poses a problem in that it fails to come to terms with the dedicated offender. Since not all opportunities can be foreclosed at all times, the criminal may simply move from one target to another. As one study has warned, "The traditional 'valve' theory of crime shifts asserts that the volume of crime is not reduced by 'hardening targets.' If one type of crime, such as robbing buses, is 'shut off,' crime will shift to other targets, such as robbing taxicabs or stores" (National Commission on Causes and Prevention of Violence, 1969: 717). Thus the mechanical model appears weak in the light of crime displacement, a phenomenon that has major policy implications for crime prevention efforts but has been little studied.

Crime Displacement

When crime is displaced, the risk of victimization is transferred from one target to another. The displacement potential inherent in a particular anticrime model or strategy is an important consideration. On its face, displacement appears to be less likely with correctional or rehabilitative strategies, since offenders whose propensity for crime is eliminated or diminished presumably would cease or curtail their illegal activities. However, in one attempted application of these principles, efforts to curb violence among New York street gangs seem to have produced a retreatist posture wherein many gang members turned to drugs (Cloward and Ohlin, 1960: 25–27).

Pure mechanical prevention, because of displacement, offers no promise of crime reduction. The house securely locked, the street well patrolled, lessen an offender's criminal propensities not in an absolute sense but only with regard to those potential targets. Whether he will find other targets depends upon several factors, including his commitment to illegality.

At least five forms of displacement might occur after the initiation of a crime prevention program: temporal, tactical, target, territorial, and functional. Perhaps the simplest displacement for the offender is temporal—to continue the same type of crime in the same places, against the same targets, using the same tactics, but at a different time. For example, intensive police patrolling of the Bronx in New York City during evening hours reportedly produced a reduction in certain types of crime, but at the expense of an increase in crime occurring in the late afternoon (Maltz, 1972: 21).

Alternatively, offenders may continue to commit the same crime at the same time and place and against the same target, but using different tactics. Installation of alarms in commercial establishments may cause burglars to switch from breaking and entering a store to smashing and grabbing (i.e., breaking a window, seizing something, and running away).

When one target appears relatively impervious to any criminal tactics, offenders may switch to another target. After an increase in police patrols in New York City subways, there was an apparent increase in bus robberies. Later, a system was introduced requiring that all bus passengers have the exact fare, to be dropped into a box accessible to neither the driver nor the would-be offender; as a result, bus robberies dropped and subway robberies rose. A displacement occurred because of perceived or actual changes in the relative attractiveness of buses and subways as targets (Chaiken, Lawless, and Stevenson, 1974).

Offenders may move not only from target to target but also from place to place. A substantial increase in police manpower in one Manhattan precinct apparently produced a reduction in street robberies but may also have been responsible for a simultaneous increase in the same crime in adjoining precincts (Press, 1971).

Finally, offenders may simply switch functionally from one crime to another: robbers become burglars and vice versa.

Displacement is a major constraint in various crime prevention strategies, particularly those of a punitive or mechanistic type. However, adherents of the displacement concept, who argue that mechanistic measures do not reduce crime, make two assumptions: First, they claim that the offender's behavior is totally determined and therefore inelastic. In this view, an offender must commit X number of crimes per day, week, or month. Thus, nothing will be accomplished toward lessening the frequency of criminal activity by foreclosing opportunities or increasing risks. Second, they assume that offenders possess total mobility in terms of crime, time, target, tactics, and area. In this view, the young burglar who by day climbs through the windows into apartments in the inner-city housing project where he lives is entirely capable of moving his operations to the suburbs, cracking safes, working late at night, or becoming a holdup man.

Against the first of these contentions, several studies have noted that some offenders, particularly the very young, do not necessarily set out to commit a crime but rather act on impulse when opportunity presents itself. A California study reported that many robbers (albeit a minority) had not started a day's activities with the intent to rob but became involved in somewhat ambiguous and spontaneously created situations. The adults in this study were more likely to have planned their robberies than the juvenile offenders, although with both adults and youths the intention had been present in a majority of instances (Weir, 1973: 164).

It appears, then, that even if the primacy of individual motivation in determining criminal behavior is conceded, it must be acknowledged that motivation is not a constant for all offenders, with the exception of those who engage in corporate crime that ties in with the goals of a formal organization dedicated to profit at any price (Ermann and Lundman, 1978). The motivation of these offenders is clear: in pursuing the goals of the corporation in a systematic fashion, they may resort to illegitimate means and as a result receive personal financial rewards.

As for the assumption of infinite mobility, a number of relatively inelastic factors seem to limit such mobility. Various studies have determined that individuals choose to become robbers or burglars because of their basic personalities which limit their adaptability; for example, many burglars prefer stealth to confrontation. Some offenders, particularly young ones, are often limited to operating in their own neighborhoods. Indeed, the most striking fact about many conventional offenders is their extremely limited geographic range. A study of robbers in Philadelphia found that the mean distance between the scene of the offense and the offender's residence was 1.57 miles. A study of juvenile delinquents in the same city found that the mean distance from residence to place of offense was 0.4 miles and that three-quarters of all offenses occurred within one mile of the offender's home (Turner, 1969).

Given the various factors that limit crime displacement, it is possible to design anticrime efforts to minimize the displacement effects, but the potential success of such measures should not be overemphasized. Because offenders are of different types and activated by different motivations, perhaps we should utilize differential prevention and control models in a typological fashion; i.e., it takes different strokes for different folks. This approach calls for treatment typologies that exist in the literature (Gibbons, 1968).

The Police

The most visible agency of crime prevention is the police force, the responsibilities of which extend to a whole range of tasks related to general social control. Virtually every modern society has developed some form of police system (Reith, 1952), ranging from part-time volunteers to highly organized bureaucracies. From one perspective, the police can be seen as a semimilitary force the chief goal of which is to repress crime and disorder. To facilitate this purpose, it seeks to deter, detect, and apprehend offenders. Such a view emphasizes the classical theories of criminology and punitive or mechanistic methods of crime control. In contrast, the police can also be seen as a type of social service organization that deals with maintaining social order and with those behavioral problems manifested in crime and disorder. This perspective deemphasizes the punitive, repressive aspects of policing and emphasizes the correctional functions of counseling, treatment, and prevention.

Most studies of the police, particularly in the United States, find both viewpoints reflected in day-to-day operations. For example, each year the police arrest and charge a substantial number of persons with serious criminal offenses. Units such as detective divisions and tactical patrol forces are devoted almost exclusively to apprehending criminal offenders. Yet most policemen are assigned to uniformed patrol, and most patrolmen interact with citizens mainly in resolving order-maintenance situations involving family and neighborhood quarrels, barroom fights, noisy youngsters, and disorderly or intoxicated persons—that is, cases that society does not see as necessarily requiring invocation of the criminal process. Indeed, in most instances, the police resolve such matters on the spot through counseling or warnings, friendly or otherwise. Certain police units, such as juvenile bureaus, are often based on the philosophy of counseling and referral to treatment rather than punitive action. Traffic control is another police function that, while carried out within the framework of law enforcement, is largely noncriminal in nature.

The police also perform tasks beyond maintenance of order and prevention and control of crime. They enforce various administrative and licensing regulations governing the conduct of businesses, and provide a wide variety of miscellaneous services, such as responding to emergency cases, diverting traffic during a fire, and rescuing pets that have wandered into a dangerous spot from which they cannot extricate themselves. Finally, the police are a public relations arm of the government. They are quite visible, and if they present a good image it reflects favorably on their political superiors.

Thus, a police department encompasses many roles and has many tasks, ranging from directing traffic and writing parking tickets to investigating homicide. Adding to this complexity is the fact that in the course of a single day an individual policeman's focus of activity can cover this entire range.

Early Police Systems

Although the police function evolved early in Western societies, police departments of the modern variety first developed in the eighteenth and particularly the nineteenth centuries, largely as a result of the rise of urban, industrial societies. In earlier times, when the nations of Europe were predominantly agricultural countries, the prevention of crime and the maintenance of order were the responsibility of every citizen, or at least of every adult male. In a rural village or small town all residents were acquainted, and any strangers who appeared were kept under observation. Anyone who discovered a crime would raise what was called a hue and cry, and neighbors would respond to help capture the perpetrator. Normally, citizens undertaking law enforcement tasks would be subject to the supervision of an appointed officeholder, such as a justice of the peace or sheriff. However, in the few cities of any size and on the King's highways, there was need for more permanent policing arrangements. On occasion the military would be employed to hunt down bandits or suppress disorder. From the late Middle Ages on, British cities utilized night watchmen, who at first were ordinary citizens serving an allotted term in the manner of modern jurors. Since the task was an onerous one, by the eighteenth century it had devolved on paid regulars. Some were moonlighting workmen, and others members of the community who because of age, infirmity, or disposition could find no better-paying position.

London in the late eighteenth and early nineteenth century provides a good example of policing in the preindustrial era. In that city, each neighborhood—or parish, as these areas were called—maintained a force of watchmen to patrol the streets. Normally they did not wear a uniform or bear arms save for a stout stick, and often their duties included many of the service tasks necessary to city life, such as lighting lamps, noting accumulations of sewage, and placing lanterns over holes in the street to warn passersby. Standards of order and safety were low, and the city was racked with crime, disorder, and periodic rioting as greater numbers of the rural dispossessed arrived. In such circumstances the well-to-do generally found it necessary to arm themselves and their attendants before venturing out, particularly at night.

As a supplement to the watch system, there were forces of special constables attached to the magistrates or justices of the peace. The best of these constabulary groups was the Bow Street Runners, who operated out of the court at that location, presided over by Henry Fielding, author of *Tom Jones*. For a fee the Runners would undertake to investigate a crime in the manner of modern detectives. Often the line between law enforcement and law-breaking was blurred, as in the case of the notorious Jonathan Wild, a master fence who also doubled as a thief catcher (Babington, 1969: 127–128).

New Model of Police

In the nineteenth century, as the industrial age flowered and cities grew rapidly, the old haphazard systems of urban policing proved to be inadequate. Nevertheless, in England there was resistance to any move to strengthen the police, because of the fear of tyranny or military rule. Finally, in 1829 Parliament approved a plan submitted by the Home Secretary, Sir Robert Peel, for the creation of a London Metropolitan Police Department. The new model provided a single police department having military structure and discipline. Its members were uniformed but unarmed except for clubs, and each constable had only the powers of an ordinary citizen and was responsible to civilian law. Thus the police combined some of the advantages of a military force without posing a threat to liberty.

At first the new police were resented, but within a generation London had become a much safer city, and the image of the friendly but firm "Bobby" (after Sir Robert Peel) had become a symbol of democratic law and order, of government with the consent and support of the citizenry. In 1842, a detective branch was created at police headquarters (Scotland Yard) to assume the investigative function previously exercised by the magistrate and constable system. Other British cities and counties created similar police forces, and in the 1840s and 1850s American cities followed, beginning with New York, Boston, and Philadelphia.

While many American cities adopted the forms of the London police—a hierarchical military structure, uniforms, and integration of detective and patrol forces into a single organization—there was a significant difference. Unlike the British police, who were placed under the direct or indirect control of the national government, American police were made subordinate to local city governments. Despite some experiments that had taken place with state control of local police, the states exercised little responsibility for municipal policing and the national government none. The police service was thus shaped by the prevailing ethos of corruption and spoils which was at its height in municipal American politics of the nineteenth and early twentieth centuries.

By the latter part of the nineteenth century, American police departments had assumed the organizational forms that they manifest to this day.

Police service was fragmented among thousands of local municipalities without any central direction or coordination. It was common practice for the commanding officer of a neighborhood police station to pay closer heed to local politicians than to the chief at headquarters. The ward boss and the police district captain often ruled their domains in a manner reminiscent of the feudal barons.

By the turn of the century detective forces, which had originally been small adjuncts to the patrol force, had grown to become major units; assignment to the detective bureau, whether located at headquarters or at the local stationhouse, became much sought after. The rise of popular newspapers catering to a mass readership brought public emphasis on sensational crime stories of the type normally handled by detectives, and the new, key position of detectives vis-à-vis the media greatly enhanced their primacy within police departments.

Throughout its history, much of the concern of American police administration has been directed toward the enforcement of so-called "vice" or morals laws. Drinking, gambling, prostitution, and other indulgences were often the subject of bitter debates between native-born Americans, particularly white Anglo-Saxon Protestants, and immigrant newcomers. For example, so seemingly simple a question as the nature of Sunday was the cause of police raids, riots, and legislative debates. Most native-born Americans of Anglo-Saxon background viewed Sunday as a day for prayer and meditation. However, many immigrant groups were accustomed to the continental Sunday of sport, drinking, and music. This question of whether Sunday was to be the occasion for turning inward or outward was usually settled by the political strength of the native-born, who passed Sunday "blue laws" forbidding many activities. The personal values of some were thus mandated as the rule for all. As Raymond Fosdick noted, in the early part of this century:

> It suits the judgment of some and the temper of others to convert into crimes practices which they deem mischievous or unethical. . . . Meanwhile our police are caught in an embarrassing dilemma and there is little hope for a sound and healthy basis of police work until our law-making bodies face the fact that men cannot be made good by force. . . . Permanent advance in human society will not be brought about by nightsticks and patrol wagons. [Fosdick, 1969: 56]

The practical result of the "embarrassing dilemma" was for the police to temporize. William Whyte, writing just prior to World War II of efforts to regulate gambling in a minority-group neighborhood of Boston, described what this meant in practice:

> [The police] must play an elaborate role of make believe . . . serve as a buffer between divergent social organizations with their conflicting standards of conduct. . . . On one side are the "good people" . . . who have written their own moral preferences into law. . . . On the other . . . people who have different standards. [Whyte, 1955: 138]

The perceived excesses of immigrant self-government in the cities at the turn of the century produced a powerful movement for municipal reform, one element of which was aimed at police improvement. An early victory of the reformers was the appointment in 1895 of Theodore Roosevelt as president of the New York City Board of Police Commissioners. Roosevelt's appointment—in the wake of revelations of massive scandal in the police department controlled by Tammany Hall—led to a general streamlining of management, improved personnel practices, and less apparent corruption. However, Roosevelt soon departed, and every decade or so thereafter New York City has experienced a major police scandal, followed by certain predictable events, in sequence:

1. breakdown in the internal control procedures of corrupt police departments
2. mobilization by outside organizations (e.g., the press) against scandal in the corrupt police department as well as against dominant coalitions that are themselves deviant or are tolerant of deviant activities within the force
3. reorganization of the police by external and inside influences
4. return of internal control, but without removal of the external environmental influences encouraging corruption (e.g., continuing to permit corrupt politicians with ties to the gambling world to exert operational control over the department) or provision of controls through a separate unit of "spies" to monitor ongoing police activities and procedures, particularly those having to do with vice (prostitution, drugs, liquor, gambling)
5. further scandal, and a repetition of the process (Sherman et al., 1978).

A similar pattern has prevailed in many other American cities.

As we enter the last two decades of the twentieth century, police service is still set in the mold of one hundred years ago. Of some 500,000 police and law enforcement officers at present in the United States, approximately 80 percent are employed by local governments scattered into some thirty-nine thousand separate departments, ranging in size from one officer to thirty thousand. However, the latter figure is unusual; only about sixteen units of local government employ two thousand or more police officers, mostly males (Municipal Year Book, 1979).

Municipal police departments are very similarly structured, regardless of locale. Virtually all are organized in hierarchical pyramids. At the base is the patrolman level, consisting of 75 to 80 percent of the force. The apex is occupied by a single head, variously called chief, director, commissioner, or superintendent (see Figure 16–1). He in turn usually reports directly to the local chief executive, such as the mayor or city manager.

The most striking fact about American police organization is the wide variation in numerical strength among cities of comparable population size and apparent demographic and physical similarity. Thus, police strength in cities of twenty-five to fifty thousand in population ranges from a low of 0.7 policemen per thousand to a high of 6.3 (Municipal Year Book, 1979: 447). The reasons for these differences are not readily apparent, although the most plausible explanation is generally found in local traditions and perspectives. Cities that view the police as municipal watchmen, available to carry out a wide range of duties, including various clerical and housekeep-

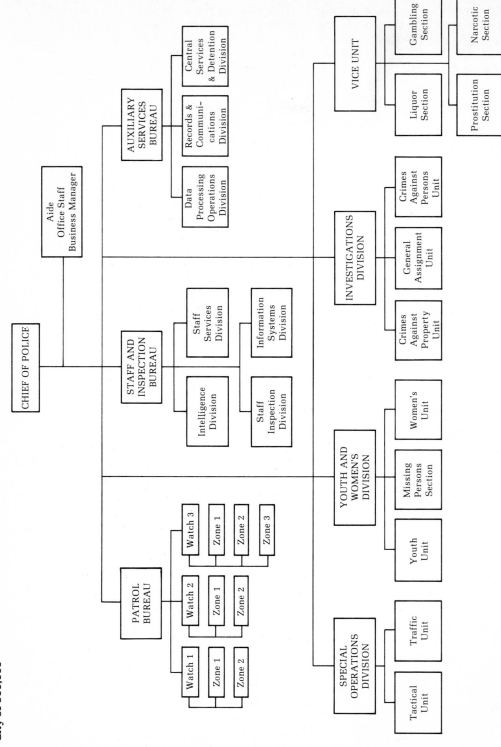

FIGURE 16-1
Structural Organization Chart for Police Department Serving City of 500,000

CHIEF OF POLICE

Aide
Office Staff
Business Manager

AUXILIARY SERVICES BUREAU
- Data Processing Operations Division
- Records & Communications Division
- Central Services & Detention Division

STAFF AND INSPECTION BUREAU
- Intelligence Division
- Staff Services Division
- Staff Inspection Division
- Information Systems Division

PATROL BUREAU
- Watch 1
  - Zone 1
  - Zone 2
- Watch 2
  - Zone 1
  - Zone 2
- Watch 3
  - Zone 1
  - Zone 2
  - Zone 3

SPECIAL OPERATIONS DIVISION
- Tactical Unit
- Traffic Unit

YOUTH AND WOMEN'S DIVISION
- Youth Unit
- Missing Persons Section
- Women's Unit

INVESTIGATIONS DIVISION
- Crimes Against Property Unit
- General Assignment Unit
- Crimes Against Persons Unit

VICE UNIT
- Liquor Section
- Gambling Section
- Prostitution Section
- Narcotic Section

SOURCE: George and Esther Eastman, eds., *Municipal Police Administration*, 7th ed. (Washington, D.C.: Inter City Management Association, 1971), p. 34.

ing functions, require larger outlays of personnel than do communities that assign their policemen tasks more directly related to law enforcement and the maintenance of order.

Styles of Policing

Despite similarities in organizational form, there are differences in operational style among police departments. At least three styles have been distinguished—*traditional* (watchmen), *professional* (legalistic), and *service* (Wilson, 1968).

The traditional force is one governed by particular policies that vary according to individual attributes and the nature of the situation. For instance, whether a traffic violator is arrested, given a ticket, warned, or ignored depends on who he is, what section of town the incident occurs in, and which officer handles the affair. Police personnel are recruited from among local residents of limited educational attainment. Their training usually stresses department lore and local mores. Such a force is usually loosely controlled, and in many instances its informal authority relationships are more important than the formal structure. At the operating level, the patrolman is required to keep a beat orderly but is not expected to be overzealous in enforcement of the law, since this only stirs up antagonism. However, the public relations image of a traditional force is usually a poor one. Buildings and equipment are often old and in poor repair, individual officers are sometimes unkempt, routine business is conducted in a haphazard fashion, and scandals are frequent. Finally, traditional style forces are usually unable or unwilling to eliminate organized crime and vice activities.

In contrast to the traditional style, there has developed, particularly in California, what is termed a professional or legalistic style of policing. The professional style force is one that adheres to general, impersonal rules whose relevance is considered independent of time, place, and personality. Personnel are recruited on the basis of open competition, without regard to residency, and their training is based on texts written by experts in the field. Many recruits possess college training, and the department makes it clear that higher education will play a significant role in individual career progress. Such a force is usually highly centralized, both to prevent corruption and ensure that uniform policies apply throughout. Authority accrues to formal position and discipline is strict. Such departments posit crime control as their prime mission, and quantitative measures are used to gauge the productivity of officers in bringing about arrests and curbing crime. Routine business is efficiently conducted according to detailed procedures, scandal is rare, and anti-vice activity minimal, provided that: (1) the dominant coalition of police officers who run the department is honest (i.e., does not foster police corruption as an organizational goal); (2) the department enjoys relative autonomy and insulation from political officeholders and their backers; (3) a vigilant premonitory focus, in the form of a separate, secret corruption control unit, is present; and (4) the community environment is not saturated with illegal organizational vice supported by powerful politicians who are themselves corrupt (Sherman et al., 1978: 30–56).

Most policemen and all police unions are opposed to a premonitory focus, which entails use of covert internal regulatory techniques (police spies, informers, wiretaps, etc.), on the grounds that it results in low police morale and is an infringement on due process and other rights of police officers. On the other hand, those favoring it claim that such spying activities are necessary for the deterrence of police corruption. Only the guilty, it is argued, would have anything to fear.

Some contend that maintenance of liberty depends so greatly on the conduct of law enforcement agents that it may be necessary for them to relinquish some of their own personal liberty so that it can be ensured that they do not violate the rights of the public. In reference to the factor of morale, it is argued that it may be in the best public interest to have a "demoralized" police department as long as police performance does not deteriorate, rather than a police department with corruption and high inner morale (Sherman et al., 1978: 256–261). In any event, special premonitory units would probably prove too expensive for small police departments (those with fewer than 100 patrol officers, for example). However, size would not preclude a few specially selected officers from engaging in limited premonitory activities from time to time, under the tight control of the chief executive police officer (1978: 242–263). These arguments can be summarized by pointing out that a truly professional department usually enjoys a favorable public relations image and hence is a better force both for its own personnel and for the public.

The third style of police operation is a blending of the two previous ones. This is the so-called service style, in which discipline, technical efficiency, and good public relations are stressed, with less emphasis on law enforcement and more on satisfying local citizens through courteous service. The service style is generally found in suburban areas with homogeneous middle-class populations, where a consensus exists as to what constitutes appropriate behavior.

Until the mid-1960s, the thrust of police reform had been directed toward urging the adoption of the professional style of policing. However, cities with professionalized police were not spared destructive riots in this period any more than were cities with traditional forces descended from the old-line watchman type. Indeed, in some instances community-police relations were at their worst in urban centers with professional style departments. Thus concerted efforts began to be made to blend what were perceived as the best features of the various styles of policing.

Another significant tendency has been the increase in police services provided by governments other than municipalities. Because of the movement of population to the suburbs and the widespread use of automobiles, some state and county governments have had to provide substantial police departments organized along the lines of municipal forces and performing many of the same tasks. However, most state police officers still spend the greatest portion of their time on highway traffic duty. Despite the growth of a few large county police departments such as those that service the suburbs of Los Angeles and New York, the more common trend has been to expand municipal police departments in suburbia.

In the same vein, the increasing federal regulation of domestic affairs since the First World War has provided impetus for a twenty-fold increase in organizations such as the FBI and drug enforcement agencies. Federal law enforcement agencies, though still relatively insignificant in the volume of crimes they deal with, handle many of the most important and sensitive types of cases, including those relating to internal security, racketeering, interstate corporate and other white-collar crimes, kidnapping, bank robbery, smuggling, and skyjacking. The philosophy, nature, and operations of these agencies vary significantly from those of municipal police. Indeed, there is no authorization in law for the federal government to maintain a general police force, and each agency must relate its functions to the specific authority contained in the relevant federal statutes. Thus, for example, federal officers operating in the District of Columbia, in national parks, or at border stations do not wear uniforms or engage in patrol activities. Rather, they conduct criminal investigations somewhat in the manner of local detectives.

The fragmentation of police authority among a number of jurisdictions and levels of government strikes many observers as wasteful and inefficient. Yet there are few who seek the creation of a national police force. To many Americans the preservation of local control over the potentially awesome power of the police is considered worth any cost in efficiency. However, it imposes a tremendous financial burden upon the cities, which lack the necessary revenue-raising powers. Some would argue that we already have two organizations, the FBI and the CIA, that function as national police forces in their policing activities, but many of their past activities (involving so-called political prisoners) have been illegal; the CIA is expressly forbidden to participate in domestic policing, as is now generally conceded it has done in the past (see Turk, 1975).

Police Problems

A number of problems beset contemporary police activity. In some communities they are of such moment that they shape anti-crime efforts, transcend them, or make them difficult to carry out. Chief among them are community relations, administrative discretion in enforcing the law, enforcement of vice laws, and the maintenance of police integrity.

COMMUNITY RELATIONS

In essence, "community-police relations" refers to the interaction between bureaucratic professional police departments and the citizenry and other residents they serve. In the past, when the tasks of policing were carried out by the citizenry at large, the potential for friction between residents and police was small if not absent. Today, a police force that does not have the support and confidence of the residents in its area cannot function effectively. There is reason to believe that most American police departments have impressive public support (see Table 16–1). However, the findings in Table 16–1 mask considerable dissatisfaction with police on the part of certain segments of the community, particularly disadvantaged blacks and Hispanics. As Figure 16–2 indicates, there is a far smaller percentage of white than black citizens with unfavorable opinions of the police, although in all cities

**TABLE 16-1
Rating of Way Police
Treat People in
Neighborhood, by City**

Response	Albuquerque	Atlanta	Baltimore	Boston	Denver	Kansas City, Kansas	Kansas City, Missouri	Milwaukee	Nashville	San Diego
Very good	47%	37%	30%	29%	44%	44%	50%	52%	40%	51%
Good enough	34	38	48	44	29	42	35	32	41	34
Not so good	6	7	16	12	8	7	3	5	6	4
Not good at all	2	5	5	6	4	2	3	4	2	3
Not ascertained	11	13	1	9	15	5	9	7	11	8
Total	100%	100%	100%	100%	100%	100%	100%	100%	100%	100%
(N)	(471)	(469)	(500)	(507)	(357)	(193)	(383)	(443)	(426)	(517)

SOURCE: Fowler, 1974, p. 167.

shown the majority of blacks see police in a favorable light. Nonetheless, in some cities "community relations" is a polite euphemism for problems in public relations with black or Hispanic residents, particularly those under the age of thirty. This is not a new problem. To a great extent the police have been most visible in their enforcement role among the disadvantaged segments of the population regardless of ethnic origin, especially among low-income males. The natural habitat of such individuals is often the streets and other public places of the urban environment—which may constitute virtually their only free recreational areas—and a prime objective of the police is to control the public streets. Indeed, safe passage through the public ways is a hallmark of a civilized society; its absence is beyond the level of tolerance of any society.

Beyond the public duty to control the streets, the police have strong intrinsic feelings of personal worth and power which explain and buttress their public goals. After all, the streets also comprise the natural occupational habitat of policemen. This territory of theirs is a milieu that from their standpoint is filled with an ever-shifting population of criminal, deviant, and marginal types, and must be occupied and controlled at all costs by themselves (see Rubinstein, 1973). Policemen see and interact every day with a number of people more powerful economically and politically than they are, and encounter many professional and organized criminals who appear to operate with impunity. This is particularly true of rank-and-file policemen who are not engaged in detective work or the control of vice.

Many politicians, organized crime figures, and even petty criminals disdain the police, some overtly, others condescendingly. Often, small-time habitual criminals and some members of minority groups display open hostility. As a result, many policemen feel besieged, put upon, and compelled to defend their turf (the streets) with the power inherent in their official position. This is the resource available to them in everyday life, a resource that gives them some edge over other street inhabitants.

In recent years the police, local government, and citizens' groups have promoted extensive community relations efforts. In some instances these are little more than public relations or image-making; in others they are genuine

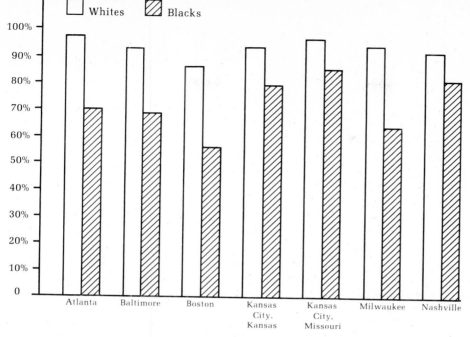

Whites   Blacks

SOURCE: Fowler, 1974, p. 168.

**FIGURE 16-2
Percent Who Say
Police Treat People
"Very Good" or "Good
Enough," by Race**

attempts to open lines of communication. However, the problem of police-community relations transcends simple lack of communication. Police are the cutting edge of real conflicts over values and prerogatives in everyday affairs. While all parties may be sensitized to the nature of existing conflicts, in any given situation it may be difficult for police to act in a way satisfactory to all concerned. Some community relations programs however, appear to have met with success, e.g., a program in San Jose, California.

Related to the problem of community relations is the role of the police as interpreters of the law. Ideally, a statute would be drafted to be clear in almost all situations. In the instance of felony crimes, this is generally the case. If individual A holds up individual B at gunpoint, A has committed robbery and police officers who happen on the scene are obliged to try to arrest him. A police officer who fails to make this attempt is aware of his own legal culpability. Thus, while disputes may occur over procedures used to effect arrest—search, seizure, interrogation, and identification—there is no question of the officer's duty to apprehend robbers.

In contrast, if individuals A and B were engaged in a street fight, the police officer's duty is less certain. He may arrest A on the word of B or vice versa, may charge both or neither. While the law clearly prohibits assault and battery and public brawling, it is often difficult to determine who assaulted whom. Furthermore, public attitudes about brawling vary according to such factors as status of the combatants, geographic location, and extent

**ADMINISTRATIVE
DISCRETION**

of injuries. If the incident has taken place in a part of town where such matters are normal occurrences between two well-matched combatants who are willing to shake hands and resume their former friendship, the officer may overlook enforcement of the law. If the incident had occurred between the same people in the downtown business district, he might have arrested both parties. Unlike laws forbidding felonies such as murder, robbery, or burglary, those forbidding offenses such as assault, public intoxication, disorderly conduct, and loitering afford wide room for interpretation. And it is this last category of offense that is most likely to be encountered by the police.

In the judgment of many observers, at least three positions can be discerned regarding police discretion in enforcing the law. One is to deny its legitimacy, arguing essentially that laws can be written to define clearly what conduct is criminal, and administrative procedures can be promulgated to require police adherence to these laws (Goldstein, 1964). A second view argues that police discretion is inevitable and even desirable lest the courts be needlessly overburdened and justice be denied through the subjecting of citizens to unnecessary arrest. Proponents of this view would leave statutory definitions somewhat broad, supplementing them with widely publicized administrative policy guidelines. Thus, discretion would not be randomly exercised according to each individual officer's whim but rather through department policies arrived at publicly. In general, this viewpoint has received the endorsement of the various official bodies that have examined the question (President's Commission, 1967c; National Advisory Commission, 1973: 21–22). The third outlook holds that the statutes dealt with by patrolmen are such that no truly suitable general guidelines can prescribe the "correct" action to be taken for every incident (Wilson, 1968: 293–294). In any event, a negotiating process between policemen and the people with whom they interact will continue, regardless of any model agreed upon in this area.

ENFORCEMENT OF VICE LAWS

A great deal of the resources of policing have gone into the enforcement (or nonenforcement) of laws governing gambling, sexual behavior between consenting adults, and use of alcohol and drugs. The rationale for enforcement of such laws has varied with time and place, ranging from the moral outrage of one group at the behavior of another, to concern about the dangers that such conduct can create for other citizens. Whatever the rationale or its legitimacy, the police force is faced with the practical problem of enforcing these laws. The historic posture of the police has been to enforce vice laws to an extent sufficient to satisfy one segment of the population without antagonizing others. Not surprisingly, this posture has often led to widespread corruption.

The de facto organizational goals of several large police departments in the United States have from time to time fostered the protection and regulation of big-city vice activities (gambling, illegal drug sales, prostitution, liquor violations, abortion rings, pornography rings, homosexual establishments, and after-hours clubs). That is to say, the dominant coalition or ruling group in several police departments, along with other personnel (in particular members of the vice squad), has protected and regulated vice activities in collusion with entrepreneurs and underworld figures involved in the world of vice. The police rationalize their role here by noting that the vice exists because the public demands it and is willing to pay for it; therefore someone is going to provide it. Moreover, the rationalizations continue, the public is not really interested in eliminating vice but rather in having it continue in a regulated but surreptitious manner. Policemen see themselves as performing a function in assisting in this regulation, so that everyone benefits—the public, the entrepreneurs, and the police (Barker and Roebuck, 1973).

In recent years, several new trends seem to have emerged. One is the diminishing public pressure to enact laws simply out of moral disapproval. Current debates on the legalization of marijuana, for example, do not explicitly revolve around the alleged immorality of its use but rather whether it has a deleterious or dangerous effect on the user or on others. A similar situation is noted in respect to prostitution and gambling (Schur, 1965; Geis, 1979). As the range of law narrows to cover only those areas where consensus exists, enforcement problems will be lessened but by no means eliminated. The sale of liquor, for example, is legal in most areas of the United States, but it is still a regulated activity, and questions of license eligibility, operating hours, and age of clientele pose problems of police enforcement.

Another trend is to favor a medical or treatment approach to the use of alcohol or drugs, as opposed to the criminalization approach (Skolnick and Dombrink, 1979). In many locales police now deliver intoxicated persons to a medical facility rather than the city jail. This ameliorates part of the problem, but police still continue to be involved.

A third approach is for the police department itself to announce that it will no longer enforce certain vice laws since they are virtually unenforceable and lead to corruption. An example of this is the policy of many departments in large cities not to arrest street-level gamblers. Concurrent with this policy is the fact that some city and state governments have themselves gone into the gambling business in the form of lotteries, off-track betting, and numbers games (no longer referred to as the "numbers racket" since the entry of local governments into this business).

Two major complaints have frequently been made against the police. One concerns corruption and bribery and is largely a result of police discretion and vice-law enforcement. The second is police brutality, particularly toward disadvantaged individuals.

In the past brutality usually referred to physical violence by officers against civilians. In the earlier years of this century, it was routinely accepted by police and public that police manhandled so-called "hoodlums" or members of the "criminal classes." By the second half of the twentieth century, most Americans, despite apprehension over the rise of crime, were probably of the opinion that the police should not use unlawful force against any person. The term "brutality" itself has been expanded in meaning, so

MAINTENANCE OF INTEGRITY

293

that in common parlance it now refers to a variety of conduct including harassment, verbal abuse and psychological pressure to obtain a confession or for some other purpose.

There is no accurate means of determining whether the extent of corruption and excessive force is as great today as in the past. The best verdict seems to be that there is probably less of both but that public expectations are higher, so that any deviation from acceptable standards tends to generate greater criticism.

In regard to the problem of integrity, one viewpoint is the so-called "rotten apple" theory, which holds that misconduct by police officers is largely confined to a few individuals, who give the force a bad name.[1] An alternative notion is that police misconduct is principally organizational in nature and therefore widespread. Proponents of the latter view argue that corruption and brutality arise from the nature of the police function and the ambiguities of society—that is, the police must cope with crime, violence, and vice without clear rules to guide them, since large segments of the public often disagree on what is right.

The "rotten apple" theory generally receives little support among professional analysts of the criminal justice system. Instead, they accept the notion that the roots of police misconduct lie in the nature of policing and the society itself. This does not imply that all or most policemen routinely engage in misconduct, but rather that inherent pressures to do so are great and cause many officers to succumb, at least occasionally (see Skolnick, 1966). The debate on police misconduct thus shifts from its extent to the means of controlling it.

One concomitant of the "rotten apple" theory has been an all-or-nothing response to accusations of misconduct: the accused officer has either been "hung" or "whitewashed." An alternative approach, more in accord with the systemic view of corruption, is to establish and exercise strong controls to prevent corruption, such as training, socialization, and supervision. Along this line, many police departments conduct special anticorruption programs and maintain relatively large internal affairs units that not only investigate complaints but ferret out wrongdoings and, perhaps more important, what are termed "wrong situations"—i.e., those procedures most likely to give rise to misconduct.

An unresolved issue is whether the control of misconduct should be handled almost exclusively by police themselves or whether there should be a significant civilian input. Some communities have created, or been urged to create, civilian review boards to investigate complaints. Others have given the task of overseeing the police to government officials, such as special prosecutors or ombudsmen. There are many who argue that the only real monitor of a policeman's conduct is the police force itself. Others doubt that any bureaucratic organization, particularly one so noted for secrecy, can monitor, supervise, and control itself and its own members.

1. This is a curious use of the expression "rotten apple," which ordinarily refers to "badness" that spreads, whether in a barrel of fruit or among people. When used about police (most generally by police officers and their most ardent defenders), it implies that the few bad officers are not typical of the rest of the force, not that the good officers will be corrupted by the spread of "rottenness."

Regarding the first and probably most important complaint against the police, corruption, it would be helpful to have a definition that is both analytic and pragmatic. Police corruption has been operationally defined as any type of proscribed behavior engaged in by a law enforcement officer who receives or expects to receive for it, by virtue of his official position, an unauthorized material reward or gain. Behavior defined as police corruption transgresses several normative systems: (1) formal (written) departmental administrative rules, laws, regulations, policies; (2) informal rules (standard operating procedures); and (3) criminal laws.

Transgressions of norms prescribed by a law enforcement officer's sworn oath of office or of other formal departmental norms are not always violations of criminal laws, but all violations of criminal laws are violations of an officer's sworn oath of office and other formal norms. Informal rules (governing informal practices) may or may not be in accord with formal or legal norms; i.e., they may be in contradiction with either or both. Violations may vary, then, from transgression of prescribed ethical conduct to engaging in criminal activity. Obviously, it is more serious to violate the criminal law, as in accepting bribes, than such formal rules as may forbid acceptance of free lunches, tickets to a sports event, and other gratuities. However, both comprise corrupt police behavior. In the latter case, the officer's authority is corrupted when he receives officially unauthorized, unearned material gain by virtue of his position as a police officer, though he does not strictly violate the law. One type of corrupt act, such as receiving gifts, may lead to other, more serious violations. As the saying goes, "Once you've been had, you've been had!"

The definition offered here covers both corrupt activities of individual police officers and organizational deviance of the department. Police corruption in a large Southern city, with a population of just over three-quarters of a million, was found to occur within a number of specific patterns, each of which was analyzed along the following dimensions: goal of the individual corrupt officer, corrupt acts and the people involved, norm violations and situational social meanings, support from the peer group (fellow officers), degree of organizational deviant practices, and reaction of the police department as such (Barker and Roebuck, 1973: 18–20).

Other definitions of police corruption are simpler but much less comprehensive in scope. For example, Lawrence Sherman (1978: 30) defines it as "an illegal use of organizational power for personal gain." In this definition, as in that of Thomas Barker and Julian Roebuck, police corruption is distinguished from brutality, perjury, illegal search, and other violations of the law committed in support of such legitimate organizational goals as the control of crime. Individual criminal acts, such as murder, rape, assault, or burglary, committed by policemen but not associated with their policing role or the organizational goals of the department, are excluded from these definitions of corruption.

For Sherman, as long as the illegal use of police power for personal gain is not fostered by the dominant coalition of a police department, police corruption is only a form of individual deviance in an organization, though one that is harmful to legitimate organizational goals.

It is likely that all large police departments have individual policemen who at one time or another engage in individualized corrupt behavior, but no department, in the view of Sherman (1978: 31), is corrupt if the dominant coalition does not foster corruption as an organizational goal. His analysis—based on empirical studies of four police departments, including that of New York City—appears to foster an either/or vision: there is either a corrupt department or a department free of corruption. In contrast, in the previous definition degrees of corruption can be ascertained within a department.

Corrupt police behavior appears to be a dynamic, progressive form of deviant behavior. It exists as a process, generally traveling along the path from (1) corruption of authority to (2) kickbacks to (3) opportunistic theft from arrestees and victims and of unprotected property at the scene of crime to (4) shakedowns to (5) protection of illegal activities to (6) the fix to (7) direct criminal activity to (8) internal payoffs.

PROSPECTS AND OUTLOOK

While "police reform" is raised as a slogan with greater or lesser intensity in each generation, its accomplishment is no simple matter. Americans have generally tried to effect a balance between efficient and responsive government. No doubt American police would be more technically proficient if they were a constabulary force living in barracks or if the chief executive officers were appointed by the national government (both situations are common arrangements in many countries). However, the relationship with local residents might be little better than that of an army of occupation. On the other hand, if the police were organized on the basis of neighborhood control, as is often suggested today, it is likely that efficiency and integrity would not be much different than they were with the London watchmen of the eighteenth century or American municipal police at the height of the machine-politics era.

The police constitute a large, highly visible branch of government. Local police officers for the most part interact with many civilians daily. The very nature of police work often requires an authoritarian and coercive role. Some citizens look upon the police as a "necessary evil"—i.e., required when they are in distress but unwanted when they themselves deviate. In short, policemen perform necessary but "dirty" work and as a result are frequently subjected to vigorous denunciation.

Often the attacks made on the police are self-serving, although sometimes they are justified by an event, such as the unwarranted killing of an innocent youth. However, utilizing the concept of the latent function (Merton, 1965), denunciations can also serve the interests of those who control the police, for the latter can be likened to a lightning rod, deflecting extreme heat and energy to a safe target. Thus, attacks on corruption have historically led to the dismissal of a few officers, the installation of a reform chief, and perhaps the elevation of a crusading district attorney to the governor's chair, but with the basic social conditions that produced the corruption left unchanged.

Some of these social conditions have been researched and spelled out:

1. A police department may be captured by surrounding political and business enterprises. That is, corrupt political control may be effected by in-

formal administrative systems that permit politicians and others to influence personnel and operating decisions. Political leaders protecting vice operations for pay on behalf of criminals sometimes determine who will occupy key positions of power within a police department. Thus, the political leaders are able to impose their own corrupt goals on the department, including the protection of vice for personal, financial, and perhaps party benefit. Strong community tolerance or even support for illegal vice activities facilitates police corruption and the capture of a police department. The business community in many cities fosters police corruption by a whole series of illicit exchange mechanisms; e.g., businessmen may give policemen secret bonuses for extra and special police protection of their property.

2. There may be an absence of external or internal premonitory control of corruption.

3. The dominant coalition in a police department may be committed to personal gain through the protection of vice enterprises, independent of local politicians or any third party. Here the police deal directly and exclusively with criminals and marginal people.

4. There may be weak internal and external administrative control in the department, sometimes inherited from previous administrations and perpetuated because of lack of adequate leadership.

5. Large segments of the population may perceive policemen as regulators rather than opponents of vice activities. At the same time, these civilians expect policemen to control street crime, especially violent and property crime.

6. There may be a dearth of police activity in the area of organizational white-collar or corporate crime. However, the responsibility for this rests outside the municipal and state levels of government and outside the scope of police departments. Very few policemen are adequately trained for such work, and few are assigned to it; when they are, it is doubtful if their activity can be successful unless conducted in coordination with and under the supervision of federal authorities.

7. Finally, though recognizing the need for some autonomy, the police department, as a necessary paramilitary branch of government, in a democratic society falls under the observation and control of a higher governmental authority. Some would implement this by having a local civilian review board (elected or appointed) empowered to review certain police operations (e.g., conduct of police officers in contact with residents, especially during a stop and search incident or during arrest). Those who advocate this position stress that the police, like the army or other branches of military and national defense operations, should not be in a position to implement an independent policy without outside scrutiny and restraint.

The Police, Crime, and Crime Prevention

Historically, the American public has viewed the principal function of the police as being the control of crime, and has viewed the police as the principal means of combatting crime. Police administrators and citizens alike have tended to emphasize law enforcement responsibilities to the exclusion of other tasks. Consequently, when a community has perceived an increase in its crime rate, a typical response has been to demand more police protection. Of late, however, there has been a greater appreciation of the fact that the police have wider concerns than crime, and that they may not even be the principal means of controlling criminal behavior. While this realization is a healthy one for police and citizens alike, it is sometimes carried to extremes, as in the arguments that the police can do nothing about crime and that their work primarily involves noncriminal tasks. The evidence in support of these propositions seems deficient.

The Role of the Police in Combatting Crime

Proponents of the view that police work is primarily noncriminal in nature often point to various police workload studies indicating that only a small proportion of all police calls involves law enforcement. However, this excludes the many that involve taking crime reports and that concern problems related to the maintenance of order. While the activities for which the police are called in such instances are not serious or index crimes, they are illegal acts; any view that they are "minor" or "noncriminal" affairs is somewhat elitist. Middle- and upper-class people who live in the suburbs or exclusive city neighborhoods are relatively untroubled by street beatings, harassment, and disorder as compared with the residents of inner-city slums, who often find it difficult to walk the streets or even sleep peacefully because of disorderly conduct and other maintenance-of-order offenses.

In addition to answering calls, a significant portion (more than half) of a typical uniformed officer's time is devoted to patrol, an activity designed to deter crime (Reiss, 1971: 95). Whether this is justified on a cost-benefit basis is a question that must be seriously considered. It may be correct to assert that most day-to-day police work does not involve felony crimes, but it is also accurate to note that policing is primarily concerned with crime and the maintenance of public order. Furthermore, an analysis of the workload based on the number of calls, or on the amount of time expended on a given activity, does not reflect the role of police as primarily involved in deterring crime and apprehending offenders.

The police occupy a key position in the society's formal arrangements to prevent and control crime. The criminal justice system is an amalgam of federal, state, and local police, with prosecutorial, judicial, probation, parole, and custodial agencies, occasionally augmented by private security forces. Normally, each component maintains its own records and devises its own goals and work methods; this partially explains why the criminal justice system is sometimes referred to as a "nonsystem." Probably the most important single agency within the system is the police. By mandate of law, they are charged with the prevention of crime, investigation of all reported and suspected offenses, and legal processing of offenders and victims up to the point when the courts and correctional agencies take over these tasks. The judicial and correctional agencies in large measure must wait for police initiative.

It is sometimes said, not that the police do little about crime, but that they *can* do little. If this is so, one might reasonably ask: What, then, is the sense of maintaining a police force? A possible answer is that the police constitute something close to a social service and public relations agency dealing with a variety of urban ills, of which crime is one. Indeed, the role of policeman has been described as that of philosopher, guide, and friend—i.e., community service officer (Cumming, Cumming, and Edell, 1965). However, most police officers possess little training in the behavioral sciences. Other professionals, such as social workers, teachers, or clergymen, appear to be better equipped to perform the community service role.

While the social-psychological dimensions of policing are important, it is doubtful that police departments can be justified solely or even principally on the basis of their community service functions. The chief justification for the maintenance of the police force lies in its ability to prevent and control crime and maintain order. For this purpose society confers considerable authority, especially for making arrests. It is this authority that distinguishes the police from other agencies.[1]

1. In the United States, any resident, whether citizen or alien, can technically make an arrest. In practice, the right is seldom carried out; usually it could not be brought about without coercion except in the presence of a policeman. A person making a "citizen arrest" is liable for false arrest damages should the charge not be upheld, whereas a policeman is very rarely held responsible for false arrest. An individual holding another by force as a citizen arrest may even be charged with kidnapping or some other major crime. Thus the statement that the power to make arrests is vested in the police is modified only to very small degree by the existence of citizen arrests.

If in fact the ability to set the criminal justice process in motion by making an arrest is the distinguishing feature of the police, then some consideration must be given to the utility of the arrest sanction. There are many who doubt that arrests constitute an effective tool for crime control. Some police officers, for example, feel that because of alleged court leniency, arrests are futile. Others argue that individuals cannot be coerced into proper behavior. Yet it is true that almost no one will commit a crime knowing that a police officer is present, and that virtually all offenders seek to avoid arrest.[2]

The contradictions between the enforcement and the social service aspects of policing have led to tensions within and outside of police organizations. Old-style police chiefs normally stressed the enforcement function, and the professional school of police administration attempted to convert order-maintenance situations into enforcement ones by specifying that minor assaults and disorders would be either handled by arrests or ignored (Wilson, 1968: 172). In this way it was hoped to avoid corruption and the criticisms that arise when discretion is exercised. Clearly this exclusive emphasis on enforcement is unrealistic. It is equally unrealistic, however, to stress the primacy of social service, because there are many occasions when enforcement is the only possible police action. A citizen who believes the police are social workers would be understandably confused if this "treatment worker" suddenly exercised coercion by invoking the criminal process, the first step of which is usually a trip to jail.

In sum, policing has many dimensions, but its distinguishing feature and most important concern is its role in relation to crime.

Police Organization and Methods

According to the Uniform Crime Reports, most index crimes, and apparently most other serious crimes, occur in the cities, and it is there that police resources are concentrated. Thus, it is the municipal police that bears the primary burden for dealing with crime. To carry out the task of combatting crime, municipal police departments contain two basic organizational elements, each of which involves a process or technique of crime control. These are the patrol and the investigative divisions.

PATROL

The patrol division comprises the bulk of police personnel, normally two-thirds or three-quarters of the sworn complement. The patrol force is the element with which most citizens come in contact, since it is the most visible and frequently called upon. For example, in a city of a half-million population, it is normal for the police to be dispatched to 350,000 or more calls annually (President's Commission, 1967d: 11). The public's view of the police is largely shaped by the patrol force, and secondarily by information in the news media on crime-solving successes and failures, although news reports are mainly restricted to a small number of highly publicized crimes.

2. Sometimes, as in a political act such as the burning of draft cards or other conduct conceptualized more as civil disobedience than as traditional crime, the offender does not seek to avoid arrest. But in general the perceived presence of the police acts as a deterrent to crime.

In the larger cities, the administration of the patrol function is decentralized on a territorial basis. A local precinct may constitute a mini-department, so that residents with complaints about crime or other problems find it more convenient to deal with the neighborhood station than with headquarters. Even the establishment of a central telephone emergency number in large cities has not diminished the relationship with local stations, as complaints received centrally are regularly routed through neighborhood precinct quarters.

In order to combat crime, the patrol force utilizes three basic techniques —omnipresence, aggressive patrol, and rapid response.

Omnipresence. Omnipresence involves efforts to convey to potential offenders the high probability of police presence at any given point in time and space, thus heightening the would-be offenders' perception of risk. The basic means of creating a sense of omnipresence has traditionally been through visible patrol by uniformed officers. Whereas in the past patrol activities were largely carried out by officers on foot, automobile patrol has become the most common method in large cities of the United States.

Omnipresence is probably the most important technique in fighting crime, since it is the central concept around which police departments are organized. In the 1970s, however, there was major rethinking concerning this arrangement.

Aggressive Patrol. Aggressive patrol has traditionally been conceived of as the effort by the police to prevent crime by locating and challenging suspicious persons through methods sometimes referred to as stop-and-frisk or field interrogation. Such activities have been characterized as offensive by many people, particularly minority groups. The problem of combatting crime in minority neighborhoods has created a dilemma for police administrators. The residents of these areas are the ones most often victimized, and they naturally demand a high level of protection. These are the same neighborhoods where complaints of mistreatment and police-citizen confrontations have been most common.

In short, while it is desirable for police to take strong action against crime in ghettoes and other such neighborhoods, great care must be exercised over the manner in which this is done. The proposal has been offered that this can best be carried out by police of the same racial and ethnic identification as that of the people in the neighborhood. This is a highly controversial question, and social science has not offered convincing evidence that such an arrangement would or would not be beneficial in protecting people from victimization by neighborhood offenders or by police, and from humiliation and improper treatment at the hands of police.

Rapid Response. The technique of rapid response to calls is based on the belief that the more quickly the police arrive at the scene of a crime, the more likely they are to effect an arrest. In general, various studies support this proposition (President's Commission, 1967d: 100). However, certain qualifications are apparent. Workload studies usually find that the largest portion of the typical uniformed officer's case assignments involves order maintenance. The deployment of police resources to maximize arrests by rapid response may not be compatible with the need for crime prevention by methods other than arrest.

To facilitate crime prevention, it may be necessary to have a large number of officers on roving motor patrol, while maintenance of order may be better served by having foot officers talking to people on their beat. A patrolman must often choose whether to spend more time on an order maintenance call than on motor patrol, thus promoting better police-citizen relations but diminishing his availability for radio dispatch, or vice versa.

INVESTIGATION   The second major element of the police department in fighting crime, the investigative force, contains an important minority of the sworn complement. Members of the investigative units, mainly detectives, are almost totally concerned with crime. The basic technique they utilize is the follow-up investigation, in which they employ deductive methods to apprehend perpetrators after a crime has been committed. The detective forces, unlike patrol, cultivate low visibility. Most ordinary citizens seldom encounter working detectives, and public understanding of their investigative operations is often distorted, in part as a result of dramatizations and media reports.

The vast majority of arrests for homicide, rape, and assault are made by detectives; for burglary, robbery, and motor vehicle theft, by the patrol force. Some cases are solved through informants or negotiation with the suspect rather than classic deductive methods. Often someone will "squeal" on a suspect, usually in the hope of gain (e.g., immunity for his own misdeeds) or to attain revenge or because of jealousy. The offender who confesses to one or more crimes often implicates others in order to obtain a more lenient disposition of his case or even complete immunity (Skolnick, 1966).

While conventional wisdom holds that the patrol division should conduct the preliminary investigation and detectives the follow-up, in practice it is difficult to delineate the boundaries between the two. In some cities detectives are organized into special groups, such as homicide or robbery squads, and given citywide scope; in others they are attached to a local precinct station and work on a wide variety of cases. This can be characterized as the headquarters specialist pattern versus the precinct generalist. Precinct level detectives are expected to draw on their local knowledge and contacts to clear crimes. For common offenses such as street robbery and residential burglary, which frequently involve local offenders (or offenders known to local people), this arrangement has great utility. In effect, the precinct detective is an arm of the patrol division.

At the citywide or major case level, the situation is quite different. In order to solve crimes committed by skilled and mobile offenders, such as master burglars and armed robbery gangs, it is necessary to possess specialized, expert knowledge. Major case detectives are required to be acquainted with the offenders, tipsters, and fences who constitute the burglary or robbery network. At this level, functional specialization is more vital than area or territorial knowledge.

One noteworthy feature of detective work in the United States is that the federal government employs nearly as many criminal investigators as do local governments. As a result, the federal presence constitutes a significant influence on detective activities. This is in sharp contrast to the situation of the uniformed patrol forces, which comprise the bulk of local police services but are a negligible factor at the federal level. Because of the existence of organizations such as the FBI, certain law enforcement problems—for example, organized crime—can be brought within the federal purview by relatively simple legislative or administrative action. This cannot be done for other problems, notably street crime, because there is no federal law enforcement machinery to deal with them.

Problems of Crime Control through Police

The ultimate potential for effective use of the police to combat crime is not certain. As frequently noted, most crimes do not result in an arrest. On the other hand, most habitual criminals are caught rather frequently, and those who continue their career over a period of time are likely to be incarcerated.[3] Viewed in this light, the impact of the police is much greater than arrest figures for individual crimes suggest. It is also true that no one knows what the crime rate would be if the police did not exist or if they altered their basic operating strategies.

One constraint on police effectiveness is the relatively small force available for the struggle against crime. In a typical city, only 13 percent of the total force is likely to be engaged in patrol duty at any given time (National Advisory Commission on Civil Disorders, 1968: 327). In a city of a half million, this might amount to a little more than 100 officers, and at peak periods a large percentage of these (50 percent or more) is likely to be tied up answering calls. One solution often advocated is to increase the size of the police department. This is a measure traditionally favored by many politicians, police administrators, and ordinary citizens. It is not clear, however, that an increase in police personnel is the correct answer to the problem.

For practical purposes, a common crime of stealth such as burglary (typically, breaking into and entering a structure whose occupants are away) is relatively invisible to patrolling police. In contrast, street robbery can be highly visible, although rarely conducted with this optimum visibility. The relationship among manpower resources, number of potential crime targets, and frequency of criminal attack is illustrated by a calculation that in Los Angeles a patrolling policeman's chance of encountering a robbery in progress is once in fourteen years (President's Commission, 1967d: 12). Similarly, a close study of patrol activity in three major cities found that the police role in crime control was largely "reactive" rather than "proactive." That is, 87 percent of all criminal arrests were initiated by citizen calls rather than ob-

3. The exceptions are probably white-collar and organized crime figures.

servations by cruising officers. The study concluded, therefore, that patrol activity as then constituted was ineffective in controlling crime (Reiss, 1971: 94–96).

A more detailed study in Kansas City divided a section of the city into three areas. In one area, police patrol was substantially increased. In a second, it was substantially decreased. (Indeed, it can be said that for practical purposes police patrol was withdrawn from the second area, and officers entered there only when called.) In the third area, police patrol was kept at normal levels. After one year, no significant differences were noted in the rates of crime or in citizen attitudes among the three areas (Kansas City Preventive Patrol Experiment, 1974). A similar experiment in Nashville, Tennessee, however, found a significant decrease in the rate of home burglaries following an increase in the patrol force, indicating that preventive patrol does have significant impact (*Criminal Justice Newsletter*, 1977: 3).

Two studies conducted in New York City appear to confirm the Nashville rather than Kansas City results. In New York a significant increase in visible police patrol led to major reductions in visible crime such as street robbery (Press, 1971). When the number of police on duty in the subway system was nearly tripled, for example, crime decreased—but, somewhat unexpectedly, it decreased also in the hours when the additional officers were off duty. This so-called "phantom effect" lasted for eight months, whereupon crime returned to its normal level and then began to rise (Chaiken et al., 1974).

Another study which compared police performance in two apparently similar cities suggested that the style of policing might have a major impact on performance in fighting crime. Professional style police departments appeared to produce more arrests and clearance and to effect lower crime rates than did traditional type forces (Reppetto, 1975).

Innovations and Proposals

Police departments have sought a diversity of methods to improve their effectiveness in crime control. One basic theme has been to move police from a reactive to a proactive posture—that is, from cruising around waiting for a crime to occur, to doing something to prevent it.

**CRIME
PREVENTION**

A development of interest has been the creation of crime prevention units in police departments. Traditionally, the crime prevention section of municipal police departments was primarily engaged in social service work with male juveniles (and to a lesser extent female). There too, however, the general posture was usually reactive: wait until the youngster was arrested and then conduct an investigation followed by a court referral or, in lesser crimes, stationhouse counseling. The more progressive juvenile units, by contrast, devoted a considerable portion of their time to case finding and community referral. This meant that, instead of waiting for a crime to occur, they sought out youngsters who were exhibiting signs of delinquency but had not committed any acts serious enough to warrant apprehension. The officers would then undertake a social (rather than a criminal) investigation of the case and seek to refer the youngster to a community social organization for counseling and perhaps treatment.

While this activity still continues in many police departments, the term "crime prevention" is now more likely to refer to mechanical prevention or opportunity reduction programs. In a typical crime prevention section, a specially trained officer will conduct security inspections of a home, place of business, or residential neighborhood on request, in order to pinpoint such security deficiencies as poor lighting and inadequate locks. The officer will then recommend means of correcting these deficiencies and in some instances assist in drawing up a security plan for an organization such as a block association or business enterprise.

The crime prevention section, whether correctionally or mechanically oriented, is usually a small adjunct to most police departments. In contrast, three other models require larger changes in the traditional patterns of operation. These are the crime attack, community service, and regional squad approaches.

The crime attack model, in essence, is based on classic police strategies that assume that crime is deterred by patrol and that the arrest of offenders, whether during the event or by a follow-up investigation, is useful both to incapacitate them and to deter others. Thus, the goal of crime attack is to assign police so as to prevent crime. This means that most manpower is deployed at the times and places of high probability for the occurrence of serious crime. To further this effort, some police departments utilize sophisticated information systems that in effect "predict" when or where offenses are likely to occur. Of late, there has been a shift in patrol tactics associated with this strategy: formerly, the patrols were largely conducted in uniform; then the preference shifted to plainclothes patrols, utilizing stakeouts and decoys.

One of the most effective programs has been carried on by the New York City Police Department. This consists of deploying about one thousand officers dressed in civilian clothes to operate in high-crime areas. Although the unit has never comprised more than 5 percent of the field personnel, it accounted in 1973 for over 18 percent of the felony arrests, including more than half the arrests for robbery and about 40 percent of those for burglary and auto theft. Furthermore, three-fourths of arrests by this unit resulted in conviction (by trial or guilty plea); this was far higher than the citywide rate (Wilson, 1975: 92–93).

CRIME ATTACK

The community service model is sometimes referred to as the "neighborhood police team" (Sherman, Milton, and Kelly, 1973). Three factors characterize this concept: geographic stability, community integration, and administrative decentralization.

Geographic stability means that officers are regularly assigned to the same small area, such as a local neighborhood, rather than shifted through-

COMMUNITY SERVICE

out the city. There is an effort to dispatch all calls in a particular area to the local officers, even though they may not be as readily available as outside units, on the ground that speed of response is less important than close familiarity with local residents.

Community integration is much more than traditional public relations or community relations, largely ineffective in the past. Instead, it means a systematic effort to know the community residents, determine their needs, and involve them in efforts to combat crime.

Administrative decentralization means that major decisions, such as personnel deployment and operational tactics, are established at the local level rather than at central headquarters. In this way, police can respond to neighborhood needs quickly and flexibly. In the past, uniform citywide policies have tended to clash with or be irrelevant to the needs of specific neighborhoods.

Some neighborhood police operations have also adopted the full service component and participatory management. Full service means that local officers do not turn cases such as robberies or rapes over to specialists from headquarters but follow through themselves. Participatory management provides lower-level officers, such as patrolmen, a chance to have an influence in the formation of policy.

The basic rationale of community service policing is that a sense of territorial identity and mutual understanding among police and citizens will produce more efficient service and reduce levels of crime. The most noteworthy experiment in this respect has been conducted in Cincinnati, Ohio. There, a normally highly centralized police department has conducted an experiment in one district, utilizing all features of the community service model including full service and participatory management. Preliminary results indicate that the burglary rate has declined, but that citizen attitudes toward police (generally favorable) are the same as before and that citizens do not feel any safer.

REGIONAL SQUAD

At higher levels of police organization, there has been a movement toward establishing regional investigative squads or strike forces combining local, state, and even federal officers. Such units usually concentrate on major crimes and organized racketeering; their area of operation transcends municipal boundaries. The regional concept seeks to provide both a wider authority and a level of expertise beyond that of traditional municipal departments. It is at this level that trained personnel are needed to investigate, arrest, and prosecute organizational corporate offenders.

Crime Control: Innovation or Fad?

Many experiments in policing have been proclaimed as "new," "innovative," or "successful," but close examination often has failed to support these assertions. Special units consisting of carefully selected officers have a long history. In the 1920s and 1930s, roving squads of detectives were utilized to deal with organized gangs and street crime. Later, in the 1950s and

1960s, uniformed tactical patrol forces played a similar role. While it is clear that elite squads can produce a disproportionate number of arrests, it is not clear what effect this has on the crime rate. Elite units tend to use aggressive tactics and produce complaints, particularly when citizens are accosted in the streets by armed persons in civilian dress who only later reveal themselves as policemen.

The community service or neighborhood team model of policing represents the idealized "police precinct and cop on the beat" of yesteryear. Once again, despite these romantic visions of the past, it is not clear that this arrangement reduces crime or even improves police-citizen relations. Historically, precinct stations were often centers of corruption and inefficiency; the reforming trends in police administration from the turn of the century to the mid-1960s sought to reduce this local autonomy.

To be effective, regional squads or multilevel strike forces must transcend various political rivalries between city and suburb, on the one hand, and state and federal administrations, on the other. Often the power to investigate such sensational matters as organized crime, official corruption, or subversion is a sought-after political prize, since it greatly enhances some individual careers, destroys others, and brings a spotlight of publicity on a few key people. Sometimes it is claimed that special investigative units, particularly those created outside normal governmental channels or official scrutiny, have employed questionable methods and become a greater menace than the evil they were formed to combat. This argument may be created to protect corruption, or may derive from a deep concern over civil liberties.

Nonetheless, for all of the important functions of the police with regard to crime, one should not automatically conclude that the police are the only or even the best means of deterring unlawful behavior, or that arrests are the most effective technique they can use in most situations. A society that places prime reliance for its internal security on police activity is a society in grave difficulty, and is veering dangerously close to what is rightly characterized as a "police state." A police force is one means of preventing and controlling crime, and no modern society can dispense with such an agency. However, in a democratic society, most persons are believed to be restrained from criminal activity by their shared values and other institutional supports. It is left to the police, then, to deal with those whose propensities for crime lead them to commit criminal acts, and to inhibit those who would in all likelihood do so were it not for the police presence.

Urban Development and Crime

The modern crime problem is to a large extent a product of the growth of urban areas. In 1790 only 5 percent of the American population lived in urban settings; by 1900 this figure had risen to 40 percent, and by 1960 to 70 percent (Hauser, 1965: 61).

Crime in its various forms has been known since time immemorial, but the development of cities has created whole districts where crime, vice, and disorder flourish and where youthful and adult criminals operate in gangs with virtual impunity. This was true even in the relatively small preindustrial cities of London and Paris. With the coming of the giant cities of the industrial age, the situation became even more serious. A writer describing New York in 1887 noted:

In all the eastern part of New York City . . . there is an overcrowding of human beings in a degree far beyond anything that has ever been known in any civilized country. . . . The most densely populated districts of London do not approach anywhere near. . . . Some 500,000 persons live in the tenement houses of this city. . . .

What refining or restraining influence of family life is possible under such surroundings? . . . The younger criminals seem to come almost exclusively from the worst tenement house districts; that is, when traced back to the very places where they first had homes. Those very domiciles are nurseries of crime, and of the vices and disorderly courses which lead to crime. . . .

Whatever may be the cause or causes, whether intemperance, overcrowded tenements, ignorance, or inherited depravity, the unwelcome fact remains that crime is steadily on the increase, and outstrips in proportion the growth of populations. [Costello, 1972: 525–526]

The prevalence of high crime rates in the central parts of cities continues to be a feature of American life. Year after year, official statistics indicate that American crime rates are much higher in the cities than in suburban and rural areas. This fact has also been reflected in the vast crime control systems that have been established as part of the urban scene.

COMMUNITY SOCIAL ORGANIZATION

One of the most striking features of urban crime is its grossly differentiated spatial distribution. Thus, certain city neighborhoods have exceedingly high crime rates while nearby urban areas might experience comparatively little crime. While this fact has been noted for generations—particularly since criminal statistics began to be kept in the nineteenth century—one of the most influential findings was presented by University of Chicago sociologists in the 1920s. They noted that the highest rates of juvenile delinquency were found in areas adjacent to the city's central business district, and that these rates tended to vary inversely with the distance from the center of the city (Shaw and McKay, 1968). The same findings have been made regarding crime and juvenile delinquency in other cities (President's Commission, 1967b: 61, 143–149).

There are of course certain qualifications to the general findings. Not all cities have developed outward in a concentric pattern as did Chicago. In other cities, natural barriers (rivers) and those constructed by the city builders (railroads and major highways) were among the factors that caused growth to move in radial, star-shaped, and other patterns. And particular types of crime vary in their pattern of concentration. In a typical city, robbery tends to be much more highly concentrated by area than burglary. Nevertheless, the heaviest concentrations of crime—and the residences of most offenders—are found in the central areas of the city.

Given the findings that crime and criminals are disproportionately located in the central city sections, it is not surprising that these areas are the ones populated by the disadvantaged elements of society. Whether one believes that crime is rooted in failures of social organization, in social injustice, or in individual personality defects, all of these causal factors can be encompassed in the notion of urban slums as one source and locale of street crime and lower-class criminals. Of course, not all slums are the same. One study of urban crime found sharp differences in the nature of crime between certain low-income central city areas. One neighborhood produced a large number of conventional property-crime offenders, while another produced recruits for organized racketeering. In a third area, the prevalent mode of criminal behavior for the young was participation in combative gangs, and for males in their post-teen years, drug use and drug-related crime. These findings suggest that crime is associated with the opportunities provided by the local social organization (Spergel, 1964). Crime patterns are area-specific, but only to a limited extent: that is, they are also related to the character of the local community.

One school of thought has sought to explain crime in terms of human ecology:

> Human or social ecology is concerned with the relationships which exist between people who share a common habitat or local territory and which are directly related to the territory itself; it is a study of social structure in relation to the local environment. [Morris, 1958: 1]

Along this line, a major thrust of criminology has been to seek the roots of crime through the study of urban areas and to develop means of crime prevention through the strengthening of such areas—in effect, to prevent crime through action within the community. This approach has characterized several crime prevention programs.

One such program was the Chicago Area Project. In the 1930s, as an outgrowth of the findings of the University of Chicago sociologists, certain neighborhoods were chosen as sites for programs designed to strengthen their capabilities for the control of crime. Since the nineteenth century, settlement houses had been located in high-crime slum areas to provide constructive resources for delinquent youth and others who might otherwise be easily drawn into a criminal life. However, the settlement houses often displayed an elitist approach, stressing the values of upper-class citizens who looked down on the immigrant masses. The Chicago Area Project, in contrast, sought to build indigenous leadership, arguing that youngsters must be led by those whom they respect and with whom they can and wish to identify.

Such a "grass roots" or community approach to crime prevention is a common one, and has often been a reaction to the presumed failure of the so-called "establishment" or its representatives. However, with this approach, it has often been found difficult to sustain the interest of ordinary citizens over long periods of time. Grass-roots groups also tend to be parochial, and may adopt policies that clash with the values of the larger society. One well-known program, an offshoot of the Chicago school of sociology, eventually became a "keep-'em-out" group whose principal interest was to maintain a particular pattern of ethnic exclusion in the area.

A generation later, another major effort was undertaken in New York City. In this instance it was argued that it is not enough simply to provide more leadership; instead, opportunities must be made available to permit slum youth to have the same life chances as middle-class youngsters. The New York project, called Mobilization for Youth, utilized paid professional staff, enormous resources, and a variety of activities. In fact, it was a prototype of the national "war on poverty" of the 1960s. While the final verdict on these programs has not yet been rendered, many people were disappointed that these large expenditures did not produce more tangible results (Moynihan, 1969).

COMMUNITY SELF-POLICING

After the creation of professional police departments, citizens were for the most part not directly involved in patrol or apprehension activities, but instead played only an indirect role by notifying police of crimes in progress or those that had already occurred, providing information leading to arrests, and appearing as prosecution witnesses. Later, some citizen groups went beyond this role. In many communities they formed their own security forces. Sometimes this was in response to official requests from police and other municipal authorities. In these instances, civilians provide additional eyes as police surrogates in block-watch and citizen-alert programs. In certain instances, residents may patrol their neighborhoods equipped with walkie-talkies or other devices for summoning police. Other neighborhoods use citizen-band radios to alert police, who monitor the channel.

In many localities citizen patrols have been organized, with or without official sanction. Among the voluntarily instituted citizen patrols, not serving as direct adjuncts to the police, there is a shared belief in the failure of the police to provide adequate protection and justice. However, the citizen patrols usually do not show any consensus on the assessment of blame and on their own objectives. Some such groups see police as well-meaning but "handcuffed" and overextended; hence they seek to supplement the regular police. Other citizen groups see police as uncaring or even hostile, and their patrols may seek to monitor or even replace the regular security forces. In any event, citizen patrols are often perceived as a threat to professional police and a danger to the community. One writer, discussing citizen patrols, has observed:

> Experience has shown that it is not alone the sober defenders of hearth and home who clamor for an opportunity to serve. Truculent, disorderly, intolerant, and downright vicious elements also flock to police standards . . . from motives of their own and with objectives foreign to the maintenance of civil peace. [Smith, 1960: 314]

There are some reports of citizen forces being effective in reducing crime, although they are often difficult to confirm. More important, however, is the fact that in many instances such forces provide a spur to community morale (Marx and Archer, 1973), and some police agencies now seek to cooperate with them.

Another approach to community crime prevention arises out of concepts of both social organization and mechanical prevention (i.e. opportunity reduction). A number of analysts have sought to develop a positive correlation between crime and such factors of urban design as land use and population density. While density per se does not seem to be a crime predictor, overcrowding—particularly number of persons per room—may well be (Harries, 1974: 83). One study found population density and ratio of police to citizens to have the high positive correlation of .75 (McDowell, 1975: 85). Another study found a high correlation between incidence of burglary and such factors as the percentage of overcrowded housing units, percentage of lower-cost rental units and percentage of lower-cost housing units (Scarr, 1973: 104–110).

One of the most influential theories relating crime to urban design factors has been promulgated most notably by Jane Jacobs, who has argued that informal street surveillance is the key to crime prevention:

> The first thing to understand is that the public peace—the sidewalk and street peace—of cities is not kept primarily by the police, as necessary as police are. It is kept primarily by an intricate, almost conscious network of voluntary controls and standards among the people themselves, and enforced by the people themselves. [Jacobs, 1961: 31–32]

Jacobs opposes the tendency of urban planners to divide the city into specialized districts along functional lines (commercial, residential, industrial, recreational, and other). Instead, she argues for diversifying land use so as to create more street activity, thereby stimulating informal social controls and creating more natural surveillance possibilities. For Jacobs, the essentials in crime prevention are the sense of community cohesion and feelings of territoriality and responsibility for an area or "turf." Jacobs has been criticized on the one hand for projecting a romanticized return to the industrial cities of the nineteenth century, and on the other for promoting a security-phobic view of modern urban life.

A neighborhood frequently cited by Jacobs and others as having a low rate of street crime and being highly cohesive is the North End section of Boston. Although a low-income neighborhood of older, multi-unit dwellings in the core city, it registers little conventional crime. The population is predominantly Italian-American, and a vigorous street life is carried on through the day and most of the evening. However, while such ethnic blue-collar enclaves were once common in American cities, they are for the most part dying out, and attempts to recreate them artificially have often been disappointing. The trend of postwar urban development has been for large segments of the middle-class population to move to homogeneous suburbs, and for upwardly mobile young professionals—often with two incomes in the family—to move to the former ethnic blue-collar enclaves. Thus, despite the view of Jacobs and others, most people have opted against diversity. As James Q. Wilson has remarked:

> A small fraction of the population (in my judgment, a very small fraction) may want diversity. . . . And even the few probably exaggerate just how much diversi-

ty they wish. . . . The desired diversity is a "safe" diversity—a harmless variety of specialty stores, esoteric book shops, "ethnic" restaurants and high-brow cultural enterprises. . . . This tolerance, however, does not extend to "unsafe" diversity—street crime, for example. [Wilson, 1975: 28]

Other writers have argued that it is difficult to apply Jacob's ideas in reality, since the typical city does not contain a sufficient number of evening establishments to provide stimulus for widespread street activity after dark. One study (Angel, 1968) hypothesized that public areas become unsafe not when there are few or many potential victims present, but when there are just enough people to attract the attention of potential offenders but not enough for surveillance of the area to occur—a condition found in "critical intensity" zones. On the basis of this hypothesis it has been recommended that the physical configurations of the city be altered to concentrate pedestrian circulation and thereby eliminate such zones. This would involve developing commercial strips along main arteries, some of which would be open in the evening and some closed. Main pedestrian routes from high-density developments would be located close to that part of the artery that remains open, and the concentration of the few all-night establishments in those routes would create opportunities for mutual surveillance. These evening town "squares," equipped with every possible design offering assurance of maximum safety, would cater to citywide or regional populations. Smaller gathering places would serve high-density neighborhoods and would be part of a citywide network serviced by public transportation.

Somewhat later, Oscar Newman (1972) and C. Ray Jeffery (1977) developed the concepts of defensible space in environmental design. These were meant to refer to the manipulation of spatial arrangements and other surroundings to alter social behavior in the interest of increased security. For example, the impersonality created by high-rise apartment buildings and large undifferentiated open spaces is seen as contributing to the crime problem. In public housing in postwar America, older inner-city neighborhoods have been torn down and replaced by double-load high-rise projects utilizing the super-block concept. ("Double-load" projects are those in which apartments are placed on each side of a corridor; in single-load projects, they are all on the same side. In the "super-block" concept, city streets are closed off and the space within used for a common recreational area.) This means that there are no streets between certain buildings for the police to drive through, and that residents must often walk a considerable distance through the interior area to reach home, thus leaving themselves vulnerable to attack.

The large open-space recreational area, not part of any particular dwelling and therefore not the specific turf of any one family or group, often becomes a no-man's-land and falls under the control of the strongest element, usually adolescent males. This phenomenon frequently occurs in public parks, where ordinary citizens are afraid to venture because the area has been taken over by teenage gangs.

High-rise buildings also utilize a common entrance for a large number of apartments, thus making it difficult to determine who is a stranger on the premises. A study examining two adjacent projects with similar populations, one high-rise and the other low-rise, found the crime rate of the latter to be significantly lower. This was attributed to the fact that they had fewer units per entrance, which meant that people could more easily recognize their neighbors (Newman, 1972).

Public housing policy has often tended to put families with many problems into multi-unit high-rise environments. Such families frequently have many children and may have one parent. The number of teenagers tends to be disproportionately high, and their values become dominant in the project. Such housing areas have been known to exist under a teenage "reign of terror" so great that even the police are fearful of entering them. As one writer described the situation in Philadelphia:

> Public-housing projects are the most disliked and feared places where a patrolman is obliged to work. Even before he has to do the work for which he has been summoned, he must pass beneath high roofs which frequently are used as platforms for launching attacks. He does not bother to look up since he knows it will do him no good. If he is on an emergency call, he may run; but otherwise he cannot give the impression of haste or appearing frightened, lest he betray to watchful eyes, including his own, evidence that will make it more difficult to do an almost impossible job. He must enter a densely packed building and ascend in a slow elevator, which takes him away from the radio and the street. He enters a place filled with terror, and regardless of his feelings for the people who must live there, he considers it an act of courage to even walk in the main door. But that is only the beginning. There are other places where the patrolman is exposed to danger, streets where he does not linger to do his paperwork, bars he does not walk into casually or alone. But these are places which can be discreetly avoided; the projects cannot, and they combine the characteristics the policeman most fears—an uncontrollable space, arduous and restricted passage to the street, and hostile people. [Rubinstein, 1973: 298]

A so-called model public housing development in St. Louis became so crime-ridden that even the poorest residents of the city refused to move there from their slum homes. Finally, a large part of the project was demolished by the authorities.

While environmental-protection and defensible-space concepts can be designed into new or modified construction, much of this work is prohibitively expensive, not to mention the redesigning of structures already in existence. For the latter, several means of achieving security have been suggested, including (1) creation of a fortified area with limited and controlled access; (2) subdivision of large residential complexes into smaller components so that each can be controlled "naturally" by a number of residents; and (3) relocation of a vulnerable group such as the elderly into a safe area, wholly occupied by that group alone. This last proposal has met opposition. Some people, including many of the elderly, have claimed that it involves the creation of age ghettoes, representing a step toward accepting a view of the elderly as "useless" and discardable persons.

Clearly, there are many crime prevention possibilities available to a community, including such major programs as revising police operations; providing for special strike forces at larger regional levels; developing community so-

**COMPREHENSIVE
CRIME
PREVENTION**

cial organization; creating citizen patrols; and utilizing urban design techniques. In fact, there are so many possible measures that it is difficult to choose among them and decide where to place priorities or allocate funds and other limited resources.

Some cities have attempted to combine various features of these approaches in comprehensive models of crime prevention. For example, in Hartford, Connecticut a program has been undertaken to organize local citizens and involve them in various block-watch and other surveillance techniques. While this is taking place, the urban design features of the neighborhood can be altered to reduce crime opportunity and heighten the sense of community. And the local police may be restructured to facilitate greater police-citizen cooperation and territorial dedication by local officers.

Despite these and other possible crime prevention programs, many residents of American cities, perceiving themselves as engulfed by crime, have opted to move to the suburbs. There, the nature and intensity of crime is expected to be less acute. However, this is a choice that most inner-city residents do not have or at least cannot put into effect without great difficulty, and that many others find unappealing as a way of life. If such movement—caused not only by fear of crime but by many other factors, such as quality of public school facilities and availability and price of housing—eventually results in our great cities becoming residential areas of only the very rich and the very poor, tremendous damage to urban America will have been done.

Arrest,
Charge,
and Plea

18

The process of crime control essentially involves two types of operation; prevention and apprehension. No matter how great preventive measures may be, some crime will take place, and a society requires authorized personnel and a set of rules to govern the apprehension of suspects, the determination of guilt, and, if guilt is found, the imposition of prescribed punishment. It is necessary to have such a set of rules for two different but interrelated reasons: first, without the rules, no citizen or resident would be free from persecution by unrestrained government personnel; second, without personnel authorized to apprehend and process suspects, crime would go unpunished or be subjected to punishment only at the hands of a mob.

Apprehension of the suspect is the domain of the police; processing of the suspect, determination of innocence or guilt, and imposition of sentence on the guilty are all the domain of the judiciary; and post-sentence processing of the offender is the domain of correctional personnel.

Just as with the definition of crime and to some extent the nature of the police force, so in the administration of justice pertaining to processing the suspect from arrest through trial, there are vast differences from one jurisdiction to another within the United States. Although such differences have diminished during the twentieth century—especially since 1930—they still are to be found. Geographic mobility, industrialization, urbanization, and technological developments that have made the entire country and even the world aware of what happens in one court all have brought pressure for uniformity in courtroom procedures. The civil rights movement of the 1960s and 1970s focused attention on miscarriages of justice, problems with all-white juries, lack of adequate counsel, and other difficulties experienced by minorities, especially but not exclusively in the Southern states. Increasing pressure has been placed upon local courts to abide by procedures already in effect in some states, procedures that offer greater protection to the rights of the accused and greater assurance of a fair trial. Several organizations, including the American Law Institute, have campaigned for some degree of uniformity in courtroom procedures, and the American Civil Liberties Union has initiated and supported legal action that would establish uniform national procedures for police in making arrests and interrogating suspects. Starting in the 1930s and continuing through the 1960s various clauses of the Bill of Rights that concern diverse procedures in criminal cases were made applicable to state cases, not merely federal ones.

The description of arrest, charge, detention, bail, plea, and trial procedures given in this and the following chapter is presented in general terms. In the majority of instances the information applies to federal and most state jurisdictions, but unusual definitions, rules of procedure, and exceptional conditions may prevail in a given state.

Arrest

It is difficult to make an exact definition that would cover all circumstances in which there is an arrest and pinpoint the time that the event took place. In a comprehensive work devoted to the subject, Wayne LaFave (1965: 3) uses the word "arrest" to refer to "the decision to take a suspect into custody," but such a decision could be determined only by overt action, and not by the state of mind of the decision-making officer. The arrest may be said to occur when police put into effect a decision to detain an individual against his will and bring him to police headquarters or elsewhere for further questioning. LaFave sees arrest as "a distinct operational step in the criminal justice process, involving all police decisions to interfere with the freedom of a person who is suspected of criminal conduct to the extent of taking him to the police station for some purpose" (1965: 4).[1]

LaFave's concept would exclude from the category of arrest an act of stopping, interrogating, and frisking a person, although this may be done against his will, and he may be angry or upset and may submit only because he fears the consequences of resistance. Some, however, question whether a distinction between street frisking and detention for the purpose of taking a suspect to a police station is meaningful. LaFave contends that, in asking a person whether he has ever been arrested, it would be expected that a person "who has only been questioned on the street, frisked or searched, would most likely answer no" (1965: 5).[2] In response to this critics contend that any detention by the police, for no matter how short a period, in which there is coercion or the threat of it in order to effect detention, constitutes an arrest. The fact that a person is being held involuntarily, they maintain, is far more significant than the duration of detention or the place where it occurs.

An arrest can take place with or without a warrant; most arrests by patrolmen occur without one. The warrant itself is a document issued by an au-

---

1. In many countries there are house arrests, in which a person is confined to his home or a small immediate surrounding area. This practice does not occur in the United States and is omitted from the present discussion.

2. Many object to the question itself: "Have you ever been arrested?" Or, worse: "Have you ever been arrested or detained by the police?" They contend that such questioning should be confined to instances where a person has been found guilty, for otherwise an arrest followed by dismissal of the charges or a not guilty verdict would become part of a permanent record, stigmatizing the innocent and possibly resulting in a great deal of discrimination.

thorized court that grants permission to the police to take certain steps that they would not otherwise be allowed to take, including the search of private premises or the seizure of someone who is not, at the time that he is taken, committing a crime. Without a warrant, the police may make arrests during the commission of the crime, immediately thereafter when in pursuit of the suspect, or if they have reason to believe that a crime is going to be committed or has already taken place and that the offender will escape if an arrest is not made. Nonetheless, as late as 1980, warrantless searches, in order to make a routine felony arrest, had been authorized by New York State law, and were upheld by the U.S. Supreme Court (see Payton v. Riddick, 1980).

Yet, not everyone taken to the stationhouse and detained there can be said to have been arrested. People may be taken as material witnesses (deemed essential for a prosecution, but not charged with a crime), held over for handling by a juvenile home, or given to a hospital and treated as mentally ill. In addition, some suspects are taken in for questioning at the stationhouse and then released without having been charged or booked (a process known as custodial interrogation). The exact time of an arrest is significant for legal purposes, in determining not only whether a person has an arrest-free record but also whether his rights have been observed in the period of custodial detention by the police.

Following an arrest, a defendant is booked and charged. Booking is the process of taking down in writing the name, address, and other vital information about the suspect, obtaining fingerprints and sometimes snapshots (front and side views), and entering the fact of arrest in police records. Charging is the process of writing down the nature of the offense that the suspect allegedly has committed, and making the charge known to the suspect. That is, the suspect has a right to an answer to the question, "Why am I being held?" The charge is that answer.

In some jurisdictions, and especially for minor cases, the police are authorized to make a decision as to disposition of the suspect during the preliminary period awaiting the first appearance (or arraignment) in court. If the court is open at the time of arrest, the suspect is supposed to be brought there without delay, except for a reasonable amount of time for interrogation. If the court is not open, police may have discretionary powers to have a suspect released on his own recognizance (known as ROR) for court appearance, to hold him until a court opens (usually the following morning, in which case the holding is in a locked cell), or in a routine case to set bail and make arrangements for granting of bail through a bondsman or someone named by the suspect.

While in the hands of the police—whether on the street, in a police car, or at the stationhouse—the detainee may be interrogated. The police are required by law to tell the suspect before interrogation that he may remain silent if he so chooses, that if he answers questions he does so voluntarily and that anything he says may be held against him in court, and that if he wishes to have a lawyer present he may do so, although the police do not provide stationhouse lawyers. These requirements followed many cases of repudiated confessions and charges of police brutality, trickery, and other illegal means to obtain statements. While such interrogation in some instances may have led to the solution of crimes, in others they resulted in grave miscarriages of justice. In one of many such cases, that of George Whitmore, a confession to two long unsolved murders that had baffled and in fact embarrassed the New York police was repudiated the moment the defendant, in handcuffs, left the area where he had been questioned, and it was later established beyond any doubt that it had been a false confession. Rulings on the rights of suspects following arrest and at the stationhouse were laid down by the Supreme Court in a series of decisions, including particularly Miranda v. Arizona (1966).

Preliminary Hearing

Soon after arrest, a preliminary hearing or an arraignment is held before a judge, generally a magistrate. This is supposed to take place very shortly following arrest, most often within a day or two, but there may be slight delays. In many misdemeanor cases, particularly those that might be considered of a minor nature, the magistrate actually hears the case and disposes of it then and there. Arrests for prostitution, drunkenness, and vagrancy are often handled in this manner, and frequently follow the routine of a guilty plea and a fine or short sentence (sometimes suspended), all within a few minutes.

In more serious cases, particularly felonies, the arraignment is not a trial. It is a courtroom procedure in which the accused, present and often represented by an attorney, is taken before a magistrate who determines whether to hold him at all, whether to send the case to a grand jury or directly to a court having jurisdiction over it, and, if held, what to do with the defendant in the interim.

At this preliminary hearing, the prosecution tries to present sufficient evidence for the judge to be able to make a determination of the next step. This may mean calling one or several witnesses, but does not involve presenting the entire case against the defendant. The witnesses can be cross-examined, but the attorneys are primarily involved in demonstrating the probable degree of gravity of the case if it does come to trial. In addition to hearing these witnesses and brief statements from both sides, the judge has before him what is colloquially called the "rap sheet," the record of the defendant's previous arrests and the disposition of the cases, including arrests that resulted in dropping or dismissal of charges and in not-guilty verdicts. While this practice has been deemed outrageous by some critics, it is one of the ironies of the system that it may be to the advantage of a defendant to have had a series of arrests if he has established a "track record" of reporting to court as required, for he becomes a good risk for low bail or even ROR, as contrasted with a first offender who it is thought may never show up at the trial.

Bail and Pretrial Detention

Bail is anything of value (bond, property, cash) placed in the hands of the court to guarantee that the defendant will make an appearance on the trial date, to be forfeited should he fail to appear. The Eighth Amendment to the Constitution guarantees that excessive bail shall not be imposed, but this has historically been applied only to federal jurisdictions, not to state ones. There is of course no precise definition of "excessive" and nothing in the amendment that declares that bail shall be granted at all (only that, if granted, it shall not be extraordinarily high). Even small amounts may prove beyond the means of the poor. If a bail bondsman is obtained, the fee can be extremely onerous for a poor defendant and his family. And if an employed defendant awaiting trial cannot raise bail, failure to allow him provisional freedom on his own recognizance may force the family to seek public assistance, thus in the end costing the government far more than a bail bondsman's fee, which a welfare program does not provide.

Studies made by the Vera Institute of Justice (1977) and Legal Aid Society in New York found that when defendants of the same background charged with the same crime were divided into two groups, one freed on their own recognizance and the other held pending trial for inability to make bail, those on ROR were more likely to be found not guilty, even though the jury did not know of their pretrial status. This may be due to the better impression made by the demeanor of a person who has not been incarcerated before trial, or to the ability of a free person to participate fully and actively in an investigation of the background of the crime and preparation for trial. Thus, those held in jail for inability to make bail are doubly punished, first by confinement, second by the greater likelihood of being found guilty.

One might argue that a free person can utilize his time to fabricate alibis, intimidate witnesses planning to testify against him, and coach other witnesses to give false testimony. But this is entirely conjectural, and if it is a path followed by some RORs to obtain eventual exoneration, it is an alternative open to those defendants able to make bail with ease. White-collar defendants are almost invariably given ROR, and organized crime figures usually manage to post very high bail, so these categories of offenders benefit from a system that penalizes the poor.

The Vera Institute study likewise demonstrated that for large numbers of defendants bail is unnecessary to assure appearance at trial. In the Vera project, "no shows" were few, no greater than when bail was set by the usual means in the usual amounts. Employment, family relationships, and community ties often prove to be the best predictors of a defendant's return to court at the appointed time. But some even object to these criteria, on the ground that they favor the employed against the poorest and most distressed unemployed inner-city residents.

A magistrate may hold a defendant without bail, but this practice is rare except in homicide cases. Sometimes extraordinarily high bail is set in the knowledge that in effect it means holding the defendant without bail, although technically not doing so. During the course of a few days of appeal to another court to lower the bail, the magistrate has succeeded in effect in imposing a short jail term, albeit in a manner that circumvents the judicial rules.

To hold pending trial, without bail, is known as pretrial detention. In many parts of the world suspects are held, not for crimes they have committed, but because the authorities charge that if free they would be likely to commit illegal acts, usually of a political nature. This practice is known as preventive detention. What makes pretrial detention in America a difficult problem is that in many jurisdictions there is an extremely long period of time between arraignment and trial. In New York City this may be four or five months, and it is not that rare for it to be closer to a year. This situation is due to crowded court calendars, inefficient use of judicial personnel and space, and requests for postponements from both sides. It is little consolation to a defendant who is eventually exonerated that the judge dismisses him with a word of regret (if even that) for the many long months spent in jail, or to one who has been found guilty that the judge often sentences him to time already served, which may be more than the sentence he would probably have received had he been out on bail (although, of course, not longer than the maximum sentence that the judge is permitted to impose).

The historical purpose of bail is to offer some guarantee that the defendant appear in court as scheduled; should he fail to do so, he becomes subject not only to rearrest but to forfeiture of the bond. Bail was meant not to provide a means of incapacitating a suspect, but the very reverse—to permit him to function while awaiting adjudication of guilt or innocence. Incapacitation is a function of the prison system, to be invoked only after a person has been found guilty.

Yet some argue that bail should have a preventive detention function, that it should not be granted if the defendant is a poor risk to remain lawabiding until the trial. Cases are frequently cited of a defendant out on bail committing robberies and burglaries to pay for the bail bondsman and the lawyer; he is then rearrested and this time freed on higher bail, and thus the cycle continues. Pretrial detention would preclude such a state of affairs, but it is based on a presumption of guilt rather than innocence. Nevertheless, as a practical issue, judges are undoubtedly influenced in making a bail decision by the apparent strength of the case against the suspect.

Another problem with holding a person in jail pending trial—whether bail was denied or could not be made—is that this places pressure upon the defendant to accept an offer to plead guilty to a lesser charge, an offer that he might otherwise find unacceptable. This is particularly tragic in those instances—undoubtedly few in number but nonetheless very important—in which the defendant is innocent but is pressured to buy his way to the freedom due him by offering a guilty plea in exchange for a sentence of time already served (plea bargaining is discussed below, pp. 323–327).

There is still another factor in the bail issue, and that is the condition of the jails in which defendants are held while awaiting trial. These jails or local lockups are overcrowded and generally inferior as confining facilities to state and federal prisons (see Goldfarb, 1975).

Informations and Indictments: Grand Jury

The suspect has thus far been arrested, booked, charged, and arraigned at a magistrate's hearing. At that hearing, the case may have been dismissed, tried, or referred to a trial court or grand jury. If there was neither dismissal nor final disposition at the hearing a decision is made as to what to do with the accused until a trial is held. At this point, he may be released on his own recognizance, released on bail, held without bail, or held because he is unable—or in rare cases unwilling—to meet bail.

The case then proceeds either directly to a trial court or to a grand jury; if directly to a trial court, the prosecution draws up what is called "an information"—a specific statement describing details of the crime of which the defendant is accused. This is made available to the defense. Note that an indictment by a grand jury can also occur before an arrest. The prosecution presents to the grand jury evidence that a crime has occurred, that the identity of the criminal is known, but that he has not been apprehended. The indictment would generally be followed by a warrant for arrest.

In some states a felony case must be presented to a grand jury. The grand jury does not hear the case itself, only limited aspects of it. It has the power to indict (i.e., hand up an indictment). An indictment is an accusation that a person has committed an act in violation of the penal code and must therefore stand trial. The indictment is not meant as a conclusion regarding the suspect's guilt but only as an indication that there is enough evidence against him to make for a triable case; or, to put it in another manner, if what the grand jury has heard were presented in a trial court and should the defendant offer no evidence refuting or counterbalancing it then there would be reason to believe that a crime had been committed and that the defendant had been guilty of committing it.

The grand jury is a body of men and women, usually ranging in number, depending upon the jurisdiction, from sixteen to twenty-six members (twenty-three is a common number). It is a continuing body, convened not for one case but either for a period of time (perhaps six months) or for specific investigation of one issue, situation, or episode. The grand jury meets *in camera* (that is, behind closed doors, with press and public denied access), and its minutes are kept secret. It may deliver an indictment, decline to do so at all, or reduce the charges to a misdemeanor. In some instances, the grand jury initiates its own proceedings, investigations, and indictments, although no prosecutor may have called for such action (this is known as a runaway grand jury).

In some jurisdictions, a suspect may testify before a grand jury and his attorney can be present while he is being examined, but neither the defendant nor his lawyer is otherwise permitted to attend the proceedings of the grand jury or hear its deliberations. The grand jury can indict or fail to indict by a majority vote.

Grand juries have been subject to investigation, criticism, and attack. They have traditionally not included representatives of minority groups and the working class, even less so than have trial juries (also known as petty or petit juries). Grand juries have been accused of reflecting the viewpoints and biases of white, middle- and upper-class males, middle-aged and older, particularly small businessmen. Some changes in this system have been made, but grand juries are still hardly ever a microcosm of a city or community.

Whether an indictment or information, two conditions of specificity must generally be met. First, the document usually names the exact law or laws that the defendant is accused of violating; second, it usually gives details of the violation that allegedly occurred.

1. The defendant must be accused of violating a specific law—e.g., Section 248.2 of the Kansas Penal Code—rather than simply be charged with

having committed fraud, rape, or burglary. For a prosecution of a case, this specificity is important because in many cases the question of whether the act, even if it did occur, violated a particular law as written and as interpreted by higher courts in the jurisdiction becomes the point of contention. In a burglary case, there may be a definition in the law that permits the defense to argue that the act was not burglary because the door had been left open or because the entered building was a barn and the law refers only to a home, business, or structure occupied by humans. The statute may have been the subject of higher court rulings and interpretations on such points; these rulings accumulate and become "case law," which is binding upon all lower courts in the same jurisdiction unless the rulings are overruled by the same or higher courts.

2. Details of the event are given. A charge of burglary, for example, couched as a general accusation without specific details of time and place and other pertinent data would not permit a defense to be mounted. The suspect could not gather witnesses, establish that he was elsewhere at the time of the crime (technically called the alibi), or present other evidence to show that he is not the culpable person. For that reason an indictment or information gives precise details, of which time, place, and name of victim are among the most important. An indictment, for instance, might charge that a given individual (either specifically named or, if the name is not known, called John Doe or Richard Roe) illegally broke into the apartment of, let us say, Jane Jones, occupying the entire third (top) floor of the building at 419 West Sunset Street, Wichita, Kansas, and that he did illegally remove from that apartment money, jewelry, and other valuables having an estimated value of more than one thousand dollars. The document would state that the break-in occurred on January 24, 1981, sometime between the hours of 7 P.M. and 11 P.M., and finally that the act is in violation of a section or sections of the Kansas Penal Code, with specific citations.

The Problem of Over-indictment

In performing a single criminal act, an offender may violate many different statutes—burglary, robbery, assault, carrying an illegal weapon, possession of illegal drugs, driving an automobile with an expired license, speeding, possession of stolen goods, resisting arrest. By obtaining an indictment on all of these counts, the prosecution is in an excellent position to bargain with the defendant, who is now threatened by the specter of being found guilty on a number of charges and subjected to an extremely long prison term. (In actual fact, prison terms on multiple charges are usually served concurrently rather than consecutively.) A defendant is often willing to accept a guilty plea on one count in exchange for the prosecution's offer to drop all the other charges.

Overindictment involves not merely multiple charges but indicting for a more serious degree of an offense. That is, by indicting a suspect for robbery-1 (robbery in the first degree)—which in a given jurisdiction might be defined in the penal code as occurring when a deadly weapon is used or threatened to be used and might carry a penalty of ten to twenty years—the prosecution may be able to obtain a plea of guilty to robbery-3, in which there is no weapon or threat to harm anyone, and which might carry a sentence of one to five years. There may actually not have been a strong case of robbery-1, but it is to the prosecution's advantage to have an indictment for the maximum charge, carrying the maximum penalty, so that it can begin the bargaining from a position of strength. The prosecution does not fear acquittal because of overindictment, because the jury can still bring in a verdict of guilt on a charge less than the most serious one in the indictment.

The Plea and the Bargaining

Following the indictment, the defendant is brought to court, where he enters a plea. There are essentially two major pleas (major in the sense of being frequently invoked) and some minor or infrequently used pleas. The major ones are not guilty and guilty. A defendant may also plead no contest (*nolo contendere*), which is neither a confession nor a request to the court to be treated as if guilty but a statement that he chooses not to contest the charges and accepts the disposition that the court may order, which can be (but usually is not) the same as the punishment available to the court had the accused pleaded guilty. This plea has been used in cases of political and white-collar crime, where influential and powerful defendants avoid the stigma of being officially adjudicated guilty. There is a special plea of not guilty by reason of insanity, in which the defendant does not deny that he committed the act as charged but does deny legal responsibility. Finally, the prosecution can enter a plea of *nolle prosequi*, which means that it chooses not to proceed with the case and asks that the charges be dropped (the prosecution is said to "nol-pros" the case). This plea is an indication of the discretion in the office of the prosecutor, a controversial matter that has had its defenders and detractors (see Newman, 1975).

The question of the plea is extremely important and goes to the heart of the criminal justice system, particularly as practiced in the United States. A plea is not a statement to the court that the defendant admits or denies guilt, although it is often interpreted that way. It is rather a pleading (a request or a prayer, so to speak) by the accused that the court treat him as guilty or not guilty. A defendant can plead separately to each charge, but in practice he usually pleads either guilty or not guilty to all of the charges together, rather than guilty to some and not guilty to others. If he makes a selective guilty plea to one charge, it is almost invariably as part of a pact made with the prosecution whereby all other charges (or counts) are dropped.

After a trial has begun, a defendant who pleaded not guilty may decide to withdraw that plea and change it to guilty. This is not at all a rare experience, as the defense may see that a case is not going in the desired direction. A change of plea suggests that the accused is throwing himself "on the mercy of the court," for which he is more likely to receive lenient treatment than with a guilty verdict after a full trial.[3] A change from guilty to not guilty, on

3. Note that a defendant has not committed perjury or any other offense by having previously entered a plea of not guilty. This is because the plea is not a statement of denial, but a prayer to the court, as explained above.

the contrary, is usually resisted by prosecutors and courts, for once a defendant has been "disposed of" by the guilty plea and the sentencing, the court is reluctant to have guilt once more thrown in doubt, one more case added to a calendar, and the possibility on its hands that an apprehended and sentenced offender may "beat the rap." In one of the best known instances of a defendant's seeking to change his plea from guilty to not guilty, the courts have resisted it and to date have not permitted the change: namely, the case of James Earl Ray, sentenced to ninety-nine years for the murder of Martin Luther King, Jr. The unwillingness of the court to permit the change of plea has thrown a cloud of suspicion over the case, giving rise to rumors that Ray was actually part of a conspiracy that powerful forces do not want aired in open court. However, in most instances where the defendant is denied the right to make a change of plea, the reasons are practical and do not have such broad political implications.

The preponderance of cases in which there is arrest and indictment on one or more felony counts results in a plea of guilty, after a period of negotiation.[4] What takes place is actually a bargaining session between the defendant's attorney and the prosecutor. The prosecution does not really want the case to come to trial, for disposition without trial is fast, inexpensive, excludes the possibility of an acquittal and hence a lost case, and leaves its own staff and the courts free from the burden of a crowded calendar and a heavy caseload. The prosecution must have something to offer, and that is not only its assurance to the defendant that it has an airtight case against him and that a guilty verdict is inevitable, but the gentleman's agreement, tantamount to a promise, that if the defendant accepts a plea and avoids a trial, he will get off with a lighter sentence than he is bound to receive should he go to trial and be found guilty. Here the leverage, already mentioned, of multiple counts and overindictment comes into play.

When attorneys representing both sides arrive at a decision on the fate of the accused, that decision must be presented to two others for approval. The first is the defendant himself, the second is the judge. At this point the defendant frequently begins to see his own counsel as an adversary rather than a defender, for his attorney is in the position of showing him why he should not fight the case, attempt to exonerate himself, and go free, but rather should accept the offer from the other side. Family and friends are often marshaled by the defense counsel to assist in convincing the defendant not to be adamant, to admit guilt and take the lesser punishment rather than fight the case through to what might well be the bitter and disappointing end. In instances where the prosecution offers suspended sentence or probation, or a sentence amounting to time already served awaiting trial, a guilty plea becomes particularly appealing, and little attention is given to the consequences of a record that shows guilt for a felony.

The judge must also be convinced that the bargain is acceptable, but resistance from this source is rather rare. However, if the case is one that has

---

4. As we complete work on this book, one state, Alaska, has abolished plea bargaining. The results of that effort will be watched with great interest; first reports appear to be promising. However, there may be problems in utilizing the Alaskan results in high-crime and densely populated areas.

attracted publicity as an outrageous crime and the newspapers are likely to report the sentence, the judge may be sensitive to the repercussions and their effect on his own reputation, for he will carry the brunt of the responsibility for the sentence even though it is actually arranged by prosecution and defense. Almost invariably the judge goes along. The alternative, that the two sides go to trial, is unappealing. While the judge may be confident of a conviction, he cannot embark on a policy of crowding court calendars to a point at which the system would break down.

After the agreement has been accepted by the accused and the judge, the defendant appears in court and pleads guilty, as prearranged, to the charge. The prosecutor states that he agrees to accept the guilty plea and drop all other charges. The judge asks the defendant if anyone has made any promises to him regarding leniency of sentence or anything else in exchange for his guilty plea, and the defendant dutifully lies as he is expected to do (should he tell the truth in court, the entire edifice would disintegrate). The judge thereupon imposes the prearranged sentence, or remands the defendant to jail, or permits a continuation of bail pending a date set for sentencing. If awaiting sentence, the judge requests a pre-sentence report and presumably will study it, although in fact the sentence has already been agreed upon.

Sometimes the question is asked: What if the judge takes seriously his role as sole determinant of the sentence (within limits set by the legislature) and as a result ignores the bargain and presents himself as a savior, a knight on a white horse forging ahead under the banner of integrity? This does not happen, and it cannot. The entire system of plea bargain justice, to which American criminal justice is committed, would collapse if prosecution and defense could not be absolutely certain that the judge will go along with their agreement, particularly after he has stated privately that he will.

Abraham Blumberg (1967), who has studied plea bargaining at length, particularly as it works in New York, calls it the bureaucratic model of justice. Its purpose is neither to control crime nor to offer a fair trial but is rather to keep the system going, support the criminal justice bureaucracy, move the maximum number of defendants through the courts in the minimum amount of time, keep the local jails from becoming even more overcrowded than they are, and allow the district attorneys to accumulate a good "track record," a good "score card" that shows an impressive volume of cases handled and a large percentage resulting in adjudications of guilt.

The public is often more critical, complaining of criminals who come out of court with short or suspended sentences for very cruel and heinous crimes. Justified as public criticism may be, there is some naiveté as to the *reasons* for this apparent leniency, which the public blames on "soft-headed" or corrupt judges, tricky lawyers, or Supreme Court decisions that favor defendants.

As Blumberg points out, defendants who are guilty of serious crimes are indeed the victors in this system. They know that the district attorney wants to avoid trials, except in highly publicized cases, particularly homicides. In New York City, one trial started in 1978 and lasted well into 1979, some fifteen months, and cost the state over a million dollars; while few trials consume this amount of time, the overwhelming burden of increasing the number of trials five- or tenfold, should the plea bargaining system be dropped, is something that guilty defendants are aware of, and they and their lawyers use this knowledge to advantage.

The big loser is justice in the abstract sense, not only in terms of a public that does not receive the protection it deserves, but in terms of a few innocents who are pressured into accepting a guilty verdict. The number of such cases may be small, but it is an important factor that a system designed to protect the guiltless cannot ignore.

Finally, under the plea bargaining system, if the defendant, whether innocent or guilty, chooses to stand on his constitutional rights and demand a trial, he is risking the possibility of being punished for making that decision. If found guilty, he will surely be given a sentence far more severe than that offered to him by the prosecutor (a procedure upheld by the U.S. Supreme Court). In the view of many, he is being sentenced not only for the crime he originally committed, but also for the "offense" of obtaining the trial guaranteed him by the Constitution.

The winners in this plea bargaining system are the judges, prosecutors, and administrators who clear calendars; the prosecutors who can show a high but spurious rate of convictions; the defense attorneys who handle cases with little investigation and courtroom time; and offenders who have perpetrated serious crimes only to be treated much more leniently than would have occurred had they gone to trial.

It is illusory to expect plea bargaining to be abolished in the United States, writes Milton Heumann (1978), but he does suggest a few minimum remedial steps. He urges that the plea bargaining process be opened up, that all of it be put on the record, thus assuring that the prosecutor will live up to the bargain, that the ceremony of pretending that there has been no bargain be eliminated, and that the defendant be given the opportunity of withdrawing his guilty plea, should the judge renege. But all of these are small changes, to be invoked in the relatively rare circumstances where the bargain is ignored after the guilty plea has been made. Heumann lists several other possible reforms:

> (1) requiring prosecutors to present a prima facie case establishing the defendant's guilt and demonstrating why possible legal challenges would not succeed; (2) requiring defense attorneys to state for the record why they negotiated the settlement; (3) requiring defendant participation in the actual plea negotiations; (4) requiring judges to explain the reasons for a sentence in a particular case; (5) allowing defendants to appeal their sentences. [Heumann, 1978: 167]

We are more sanguine about the first and third of these suggestions than the others. The second might violate confidentiality of lawyer-client relations and require a defense attorney to make damaging statements against his own client; the fourth might be impossible, because the reason for the sentence is only that it was the decision reached in a bargaining session; and the appeal would make the system precarious.

One reform that might be practicable and in the interests of justice would require a not guilty plea and a trial in all cases in which there has been an indictment for specified serious crimes, such as homicide, forcible rape, kidnapping, felonious assault with intent to kill, and any theft (burglary, robbery, or larceny) involving more than one hundred thousand dollars. The criminal justice system, it appears to us, would not collapse under the burden of these additional trials, and justice would be served.

The Trial: Determination of Guilt or Innocence

Historically, two major systems of conducting a trial have evolved in the Western world. One is the Anglo-American adversary system, which prevails in the United States, England, and many countries formerly under English rule. The other is the continental inquisitorial or inquiry system, derived from criminal law as practiced on the European continent and in many parts of the world formerly under the colonial rule of Spain, Portugal, Belgium, France, Germany, the Netherlands, and other continental powers.

The adversary type of trial conceives of the court as a battleground or arena in which the judge is supposed to act as impartial referee handing down rulings to keep either side from gaining an advantage in violation of the rules of the game. Justice, it is believed, will triumph when these opposing teams clash, for the victor will be not the better players and coaches, but the side armed with the weighty weapon of truth.

The inquisitorial type conceives of the court as a house of inquiry. The trial is an investigation process in which all must cooperate in order to arrive at truth and justice, although this may not be to the advantage of one side or the other.

In an adversary system, the court itself (represented by the judge) does not initiate inquiries and investigations, does not call its own witnesses (although on very rare occasions there may be a court-appointed expert witness), and very seldom intervenes in an examination or a cross-examination.[1] Each side is left to fend for itself and find the best method of approach, and work toward winning the case, even if that is not in the best interests of

---

1. In 1979 in New York City a guilty verdict was overturned by an appellate court because of the large extent of examination of witnesses by the trial judge, which constituted an undue interference, in the opinion of the appellant judges, with trial procedures in the adversary system.

justice. While the prosecution is expected to drop a case if it becomes convinced that the accused is innocent, and is obligated to make known to the defense information it possesses that would aid the defendant, in practice these steps are seldom taken and the prosecutor is usually determined to win the game and get the case over with. The defense, of course, has the same aim.

The adversary and inquisitorial methods of courtroom procedure are most sharply divergent regarding the role and duties of the defense attorney and on the issue of self-incrimination on the part of the accused.

A defense attorney is not expected, in the adversary system, to assist prosecution or court if he is convinced that his client is guilty. Officially, he is restrained by certain laws and administrative rules, so that he may not aid and abet perjury by his client or on his client's behalf. Professor of law Lloyd Weinreb recounts a meeting at which Monroe H. Freedman, a prominent member of the bar and later chairman of the Legal Ethics Committee of the District of Columbia bar, discussed three questions with the lawyers present:

1. Is it proper to cross-examine for the purpose of discrediting the reliability or credibility of an adverse witness whom you know to be telling the truth?
2. Is it proper to put a witness on the stand when you know he will commit perjury?
3. Is it proper to give your client legal advice when you have reason to believe that the knowledge you give him will tempt him to commit perjury? [Weinreb, 1977: 107]

With some uncertainty Freedman concluded "that the nature of the adversary system often required affirmative answers to all three questions." Attorneys under the adversary system often protect themselves from the possibility of disbarment procedures or even criminal charges of subornation of perjury (i.e., procuring or assisting someone in committing perjury) by not allowing or encouraging the client to disclose all the facts, despite the old adage that everything should be told to one's lawyer. This method, however, is abjured by many criminal lawyers, who do not want to find themselves unprepared in court and surprised by testimony about which they had not been forewarned.

In an inquiry type of court, cooperation by the defense attorney is expected, even if it leads to a guilty verdict, since the purpose of all members of the court is to arrive at the truth, not to fight in the manner of warring gladiators to see who will emerge victorious.

On the issue of self-incrimination, the Fifth Amendment to the United States Constitution states that no person can be required to incriminate himself in a criminal proceeding. Actually, any testimony by the defendant in a criminal trial was not allowed for a long time in Anglo-American law. Up to the mid–nineteenth century, not only was it forbidden for a defendant to be called by the prosecution, but he could not be called by his own side to testify in his own behalf. The rationale of this now seemingly curious rule was that an accused would obviously lie to save himself, and since his testimony would therefore not carry credibility it ought not to be permitted at all. In later years this was changed and the defendant was allowed to testify, but only if he would submit himself to cross-examination; and many defendants, not wishing to be cross-examined (on their past criminal record, for example, which otherwise is usually not made known to the jury), have preferred to stay off the stand.

In an inquiry trial the defendant has no choice but to testify. He can be examined by judge and counsel for both sides. His examination is meant to throw light not only on his own culpability, if any, but also on that of his confederates, the manner in which the crime was carried out, and all other information that a court might find relevant. A refusal to answer questions would not only make him liable to a charge of contempt but would place upon him a legal presumption of guilt and make his exoneration well-nigh impossible.

Rules of evidence are far more stringent in the adversary than in the inquiry system. The inquiry court is less concerned, for example, as to whether a piece of testimony is rumor, for it will hear it just the same and weigh its validity. The adversary court in this instance will hear lengthy arguments as to the admissibility of a rumor and in the end will almost always exclude it.

Some have stated that a court of inquiry is primarily concerned with solving a crime, and that in such an effort the defendant has no rights except the right to cooperate so that, if he is innocent, the search will uncover that crucial fact. An adversary court, by contrast, is more interested in the inherent rights of the defendant and protection of all persons against governmental power, as vested in the prosecution in a criminal court. If some guilty persons are thus found innocent, this is a price worth paying in order that governmental power be restrained. Although only the adversary system has official recognition in the United States, a few legal authorities, particularly Weinreb (1977), have called for its revision, if not its abandonment, as inconsistent with the goals of justice.

Essentials of Criminality and Guilt

In American law, and for the most part in English law, for a person to be found guilty of a crime, several features must all hold true. Some of these go back to the definition of a crime—that it is an act in violation of a criminal code, for example, and an intentional act committed by an adult not suffering from insanity. Others are important technical questions, such as the amount of time that has elapsed since the crime took place, or whether the suspect has been tried and acquitted once before for the same crime. Finally, there are procedural questions, involving an open court, having counsel, and proof beyond a reasonable doubt.

It would be difficult to catalogue all of the essential features without which the defendant is not supposed to be found guilty. They sometimes differ for various jurisdictions; certainly their interpretations differ. There is in addition a myriad of relatively minor rules, more important to the legal profession than to the student of the criminal justice system. We have isolated several that we consider most significant. They are enumerated below, followed by a brief statement of some of the rationales and ramifications for each:

1. For a crime to have occurred there must have been an overt act, which may be one of commission or omission.
2. The act must have been in violation of a written law.
3. The law must have been enacted before the crime occurred.
4. The offender must have had criminal intent.
5. The offender must have reached a specified age at the time the act was carried out.
6. The offender must have acted voluntarily in committing the offense.
7. The offender must have been sane (of mental competence) according to the criteria of the jurisdiction at the time the offense was perpetrated.
8. The offense must not have been committed at the instigation of a police officer or someone acting in behalf of police for the purpose of making an arrest.
9. The defendant, unless a fugitive or accused of certain specified crimes, must have been apprehended within a set period of time, stated in a statute, after the offense was committed.
10. In being brought to trial, the defendant must not be placed in jeopardy a second time for the same offense.
11. The defendant must be presented with an information, an indictment or some equivalent document giving details of the offense with which he is charged.
12. The defendant is entitled to be represented by counsel.
13. The defendant must be mentally competent to assist in his own defense.
14. The defense is entitled to a trial by jury, but may waive this right in favor of trial by one or more judges.
15. The defendant is entitled to a speedy trial.
16. The defendant must be able to face his own accusers, whose testimony shall be given only in his presence.
17. The defendant may testify in his own defense but is not required to do so.
18. The prosecution must notify the defense of any information it possesses that might be helpful to the defendant.
19. The prosecution is required to give defense advance notice of its plans, including the calling of witnesses, so that there will be no surprise that might cause delays because they find the defense unprepared. The corresponding obligations of the defense are usually more limited, as in New York where advance notice must be given only for an insanity defense or a planned alibi.
20. With rare exceptions, the trial of an adult is open to public and press.
21. The court must exclude testimony of a "privileged" nature, no matter how pertinent it may be.
22. The defendant comes into court presumed to be innocent; therefore:
23. The burden of proof is on the prosecution to prove the guilt of a defendant, never the reverse.
24. Guilt must be established beyond a reasonable doubt.

All these are complex and controversial issues, explained and elaborated on in the sections that follow.

AN OVERT ACT
The criminal offense is an act, not a thought, plan, idea, or hope. Although criminal intent is necessary for an act to be a crime, it is not sufficient, for intent alone does not constitute a crime. However, the act can be one of commission or omission. Failure to report a contagious disease, if this is in violation of the criminal code, is a crime of omission, as is failure to file an income tax return if a person's earnings are sufficient to make filing obligatory, and failure in the armed services to return to post after a leave (going AWOL).

The issue of an act being overt becomes somewhat more complex when a crime is planned in concert with others but is never carried out. Certainly it is the task of the police, upon learning that a crime is being hatched, to prevent it from occurring and make appropriate arrests. Such plans for a criminal act are called criminal conspiracies. There are many problems in deciding, particularly with political acts, whether talk and exchange of ideas constitute a plan to carry out a crime or remain in the realm of free discussion.

VIOLATION OF A CRIMINAL CODE
Among modern societies only Communist China functioned for a long period of time without a written criminal code, and toward the end of the 1970s steps were taken there to change this. No matter how seriously an act may offend public morality, it is not a crime and is not legally punishable if it is not in contravention of a written law. (The recent movement toward decriminalization of certain activities, such as adult consensual incest, is intended not to give social approval to these acts but simply to remove the criminal sanctions.)

In the United States the criminal law that is violated may be state, federal, or both, or may be a military law (see Bryant, 1979, for a thorough review of violations of military law). A law is not constitutional if, in the view of the higher courts, it is written in such broad and general terms that a potential offender cannot be expected to know that what he is doing is in violation of it, or a court cannot determine whether a given act falls within the area of conduct proscribed by that law.

THE LAW PRECEDES THE ACT
A person cannot be arrested, tried, and punished for behavior if the law making the behavior criminal was enacted after the deed itself took place. In the same way, punishments more severe than those in effect at the time the crime was committed—that is, more severe punishments enacted at a later date—cannot be imposed upon an offender. In the reverse situation—where a punishment has been made more lenient—a defendant would probably not be subjected to the more severe penalty of the old law. In the history of the United States, changes have been made with regard to the abolition and reinstitution of capital punishment, to the criminalization of slavery, to the manufacture and sale of alcohol and other drugs, to diverse types of sexual

behavior, to performance of abortion, and to other conduct; in these instances only the law in effect at the time of the activity could prevail.

The arrest and prosecution of a person for an act made illegal only after it occurred is technically termed an *ex post facto* prosecution, prohibited under the law of most modern nations.

CRIMINAL INTENT

For a crime to have occurred there must have been an intention on the part of the offender to commit a crime: this intention is known as the "guilty mind" ("*mens rea*"). While *mens rea* includes mental capacity (adulthood, sanity, and other features), it also covers deliberate intent. The criminal act cannot have been an accident, although the accident itself may be the result of a crime. If an automobile skids and injures or kills someone, it is an accident, not a crime. If the driver of the car is intoxicated, then the unintended injury or death of the victim is the result of a crime intentionally entered into: namely, driving while under the influence of alcohol. If the accident is instead the result of negligence or carelessness without criminal intent, then the victim (or his or her family) can recover damages in a civil suit, with the one responsible for the accident held civilly but not criminally accountable.

Criminal intent does not have to involve a plan to commit the crime for which the individual is charged. If a man holding up a store grabs a customer and knocks her down so that her head hits the floor and she is killed, he can be charged with homicide even if there is no evidence that he came into the premises with the intention of killing anyone. As a general rule, a crime that occurs in the course of commission of a felony is the responsibility of the felon. His criminal intent was to be felonious, and that is sufficient to place upon him the burden of all illegal acts that took place while he was pursuing his unlawful behavior.

The situation can become very complex, as when police, called by an alarm during a bank robbery, have a shootout with the robbers and as a result a bystander is killed. As a matter of law, most jurists would agree that the robbers can be charged with homicide. However, as a practical issue the charge would often be only bank robbery or armed robbery; the fact that the act resulted in the death of a bystander would lead to more severe punishment, within the limits set by legislation.[2]

AGE OF THE CRIMINAL

By and large, a child is not considered capable of committing a crime, although the act itself may be in violation of the penal code. (Some offenses with which children are charged are not in themselves crimes but become delinquent acts only because the offender is below some specified age, such as truancy and drinking beer on the street. These are known as status offenses, because they are illegal only because of the age-status of the person committing the act.)

2. The number of innocents killed by police in these situations is unknown but probably small. The police tend to be cautious when there are bystanders or passersby who might be hit by stray bullets. Nonetheless, in New York City in 1978 a policeman shot and killed an innocent girl on a subway platform while in pursuit of an assailant. Such instances often result in civil suits against the municipality.

Officially, a child who has done something that would be criminal if performed by an adult is regarded as a "person in need of supervision" and assistance ("PINS").[3] As a result, he is not given a "trial" and is not adjudicated guilty or innocent; rather, a hearing is held to determine whether he is in need of treatment or aid and for how long (sometimes for an indeterminate period which cannot continue after he has reached the age of maturity). However, many scholars have looked upon this treatment orientation as a cruel and deceptive fiction that has resulted in victimizing children under the pretense of a big-brotherly attitude, depriving them of the right to a trial to determine innocence or guilt, and sending them off to some jail or prison that is masquerading under another name. Incarceration is a hardship, no matter what the institution is called, and involuntary confinement, even if treatment is given, does not differ greatly from prison except that all the inmates are juveniles.

A serious challenge to what many have regarded as a denial of constitutional rights was mounted in the Gault case (In re Gault, 1967). In this most important decision, the U.S. Supreme Court ordered the release from confinement at a treatment-oriented facility of a youth who, prosecution had claimed, had made obscene telephone calls to an elderly woman but had not been given the opportunity to defend himself at a trial.[4] It is still too early to determine the extent to which changes in the trial of youths on criminal charges will be effected by the Gault decision.

The age at which a person attains full responsibility for doing something unlawful varies from one jurisdiction to another and from one act to another. The range is broad, from as low as eleven years of age to as high as eighteen. (Age is counted as of the time the illegal act took place, not the time of apprehension or trial.) Not infrequently a group of youths arrested for acting together in the commission of a crime will vary in age and will include some under and some over the specified age dividing the juvenile from the young adult offender. In this case, the older youths may be tried as adults and the others handled as juveniles, even though they may be separated in age by as little as a few weeks. The older ones may receive long prison terms, far greater than those given to the younger, who can be sentenced to a juvenile center for a limited period only, until a given age is reached, at which time they are automatically released. However, the very opposite often occurs: the adults are tried and found not guilty or given an opportunity to plea bargain and walk out with probation or suspended sentences, whereas the young offenders are sent to juvenile centers without benefit of trial.

Under the impetus of widespread fear of serious youthful crime, many jurisdictions have recently lowered the age at which a suspect can be tried as an adult, so that a youth accused of murder or rape, for example, cannot

3. Acronyms are also used for "juveniles in need of supervision" and "children in need of supervision"—JINS and CHINS, respectively.

4. The extent to which the judiciary can be a bureaucratic maze is illustrated by one aspect of Gault. For a considerable period, the youth was not allowed to file an appeal; there was nothing to appeal, since he had not been tried! If not tried, why was he confined? But he was not confined—at least not in a prison—he was being cared for. Cared for, but against his will? Of course, since he was a child and could not know whether the care was in his own best interests!

count on automatic release when he reaches eighteen. Some of these same jurisdictions, however, have not created facilities for detention of youths apart from those for adults—which are usually full of older, hardened, and often extremely exploitative men—a problem that will have to be faced by the American correctional system if youthful crime and the trend toward handling at least some young offenders as adults persist.

VOLUNTARISM OF THE ACT

Most acts are carried out voluntarily; this is true of the law-abiding as well as law-breaking ones. It would be an effective defense against a charge of committing a crime if the suspect could demonstrate that he had literally been compelled to carry out the illegal act. Such a defense in a court of law is rather rare. It is sometimes claimed that a defendant was forced at the point of a gun to commit the crime, was hypnotized at the time and acting under the hypnotic spell, or was "brainwashed"—that is, that some individuals had used systematic psychological efforts to impose their will on him so that he no longer had the capacity to control his own mind. When the newspaper heiress Patricia Hearst was kidnapped by a radical group, only to join her abductors later in a bank robbery, the defense claimed both that she had participated with a gun pointed at her and that she had been subjected to brainwashing by her kidnappers some months earlier. These two defenses are not incompatible: both could have occurred, and either would be sufficient to exonerate her. The jury in the Hearst case rejected both, however.

The requirement of voluntarism in a crime—as with the age of the offender and the degree of sanity at the time the event took place (discussed below)—is derived from this principle: for a crime to have been committed, the perpetrator not only must have had criminal intent but must have been capable, in terms of state of mind and development of the mind at a certain age, of having had that intent. This is the concept of *mens rea*. There cannot be *mens rea* without the mental capacity for its existence in the offender.

SANITY

A fundamental requisite for a crime to be committed and for the offender to have *mens rea* is sanity. Although the plea to process a defendant as sick rather than as criminal goes back many centuries in English law, it was not until 1843 that the first clear-cut statement was made of the conditions under which an offender might be declared not guilty by reason of insanity. In that year, Daniel McNaughtan (one of several spellings of his name) shot and killed the secretary to the prime minister of England, evidently mistaking his victim for Sir Robert Peel, the prime minister himself. After hearing testimony about McNaughtan's behavior from companions and family and expert statements about him from the medical profession, the judge stopped the trial and ordered the jury to find the defendant not guilty on the ground of insanity. McNaughtan was not freed as a result but spent the rest of his life, upward of twenty years, in two institutions for the insane. His having been saved from the gallows resulted in a thorough examination of the insanity defense. Debate and hearings took place on the subject of criminal responsibility, and out of these came the McNaughtan Rules, the first guidelines for determining when a person is to be held insane for the purpose of criminal prosecution. In the best known of these rules, a defendant is freed from criminal responsibility if he cannot distinguish right from wrong and does not know that what he is doing is wrong. Later, there were more debates, and many exceptions and new features were established, including the concept of compulsivity: that the defendant could not refrain from doing what he did, even though he knew it was wrong.

The insanity defense has been much abused, by both government and defense. It has been used to exculpate the rich and the powerful. In one instance a jury reached a "not guilty by reason of insanity" verdict on the basis of medical testimony that the defendant suffered from a mental disease which had never before been known, mentioned, or diagnosed! The insanity charge has also been used to discredit political dissidents, putting a label of lunacy rather than political criminality on those who struggle against the powers-that-be, thus diverting attention from their cause. In fact, Richard Moran (1981) suggests that this is the key to an understanding of the McNaughtan case itself.

Few believe that the insane should be treated as criminals. A woman puts her infant in a lighted oven to exorcise the demon she believes inhabits his body; a man with tools in hand attacks Michelangelo's sculpture of the Pietà, shouting words of rage against his own mother. We are dealing here with the demented and the mentally ill. But these are clear-cut instances in which there would be general agreement that the offender is not of sound mind. A greater problem arises in borderline cases, where the crime may appear bizarre, repulsive, and blatantly irrational, yet the accused shows no other signs of insanity.

The distinguished British jurist H.L.A. Hart (1965) has suggested that adjudication of guilt or innocence should be made without an insanity defense—that is, the state of mind of the accused should be irrelevant. For practical purposes, *mens rea* would then disappear as a concept in criminal law. Following a guilty verdict, Hart has proposed a post-trial hearing or second trial solely to determine the competence of the criminal and what disposition should be made in sentencing him. Others have also urged that the state of mind be abolished as a mitigation of guilt (Szasz, 1965, 1981).

INSTIGATION BY POLICE ENTRAPMENT

In the United States, though in few other places of the world, a person is exculpated for an illegal act if it took place at the instigation of a police officer or someone acting as an agent of the police for purposes of making an arrest, and if the court is convinced that the crime would not have occurred without such instigation. This is the concept of entrapment.

Entrapment takes place not when police officers with advance knowledge of a planned crime (perhaps through a covert agent) pounce upon the offenders during the course of their criminal activities; it occurs only when the police have done more than aid and abet in the planning, more than go along with the activities under surveillance. The key to the entrapment defense is that, were it not for the intent of police to arrest someone, the crime would never have occurred. For example, the police can properly participate in, even start, a fencing operation in order to obtain information on stolen goods—who is stealing them, how they are disposed of. But it cannot convince neighborhood people to go out and steal so that an arrest can be made.

Inasmuch as the crime does eventually take place, many might wonder whether a defendant who has violated the law at the instigation of the police should go free when a defendant who has broken the law at the instigation of peers, family, or business associates does not. The Supreme Court, in formulating the entrapment concept, stated that it is not the function of law enforcement to manufacture crime (Sherman v. United States, 1958).

STATUTE OF LIMITATIONS

In all American and many other jurisdictions the law specifies for most but not all crimes a length of time after commission of the act during which the arrest must take place or a warrant obtained for the arrest of the suspect. If this period of time should elapse without arrest or warrant, the offender becomes protected by what is known as the statute of limitations. He is from then on no longer subject to arrest or trial for the act, even if he acknowledges his guilt.

The statute of limitations is based on the rationale that a criminal act should not pursue the perpetrator throughout his entire lifetime; that if he has "turned his life around" and become a law-abiding citizen without committing further offenses, his mind should be freed of the burdensome fear that one day the past will be unearthed and he will be seized. Presumably, the years that have elapsed after the event must have been law-abiding ones; this is regarded as evidence of rehabilitation.

Some crimes are exempt from "forgiveness" through the statute of limitations. In the United States this is generally true of treason, murder, and kidnapping. In addition, there is no time limitation for a fugitive from justice: that is, an escaped convict or a person for whom there is an active arrest warrant. For this reason, it is not infrequent for one to read in the newspapers of an escapee, now an upright citizen, being discovered some fifteen or twenty years after a jailbreak and held for extradition to the state from which he escaped. The public sentiment favorable to the detainee that frequently occurs is at the foundation of the rules governing limitations.

DOUBLE JEOPARDY

Early in the history of the administration of criminal justice, it was determined that a suspect, once acquitted, should not be subject to retrial for the same crime, even though new evidence might have been unearthed that would make a conviction more likely. The rationale for the rule against double jeopardy is that it serves as a protection, perhaps the most important one, against continual governmental persecution. If a jury has found a person not guilty, it has been argued, the government should not have the right to present the same case to a second jury, and then even to a third, fourth, or fifth, until a guilty verdict is attained (see Sigler, 1969).

A second trial is, of course, possible, and frequently occurs when a defendant who has been found guilty successfully appeals for a new trial. It is legal and legitimate also when a jury is unable to reach a verdict (a "hung jury") and is dismissed; for the legal record, the case is retried as if there had been no previous trial. And it is permissible to have a new or second trial if something improper occurs during the first trial and the judge, usually upon request of the defense, declares a mistrial (i.e., because of an error, the trial is discontinued and for all practical purposes treated as if it had never been held).

However the public may respect the idea of protection against double jeopardy, with its real possibility of persecutorial prosecution, it would probably express some dismay and frustration, if not outrage, were a defendant to be found not guilty without taking the stand in a murder or forcible rape case and then walk out of the court and admit to reporters that he was indeed guilty. A situation not far removed from that took place in a New York case in which a woman was accused of murdering her husband. She was found not guilty when the defense called to the stand her niece, who insisted that she herself had committed the murder when the husband had seduced her. Then, when the niece was brought to trial for murder, she denied the story and insisted that she had not done the killing at all. While there could have been a charge of perjury against both women, the fact is that the murder charge could never be reinstated against the wife.

Double jeopardy, like almost all other concepts in the administration of criminal justice, is replete with ambiguity. It is not at all certain at what point a defendant is being placed in jeopardy. In one case the judge declared a mistrial when there was a death in the family of one of the attorneys and postponement to the next week would have inconvenienced many of the jurors, not to mention the judge himself, who was about to embark on a vacation. Both the prosecution and defense argued against the mistrial ruling and warned that a second trial might be considered double jeopardy. The judge, ignoring the warnings, declared a mistrial. The defendant was later tried again and found guilty, and eventually the verdict was overturned on appeal. In another case a man was accused of raiding a gambling game and executing several people there. He was arrested and tried specifically for the murder of one of the victims, for which he was found not guilty. Thereupon he was rearrested and tried for killing another victim at the same time and place; this trial resulted in a guilty verdict. However, on appeal, the U.S. Supreme Court declared that he, too, had been deprived of his rights under the double jeopardy rule.

One looks upon such cases with dismay, on the one hand, that the rather small number of arrests and convictions for major crimes should be eroded further by such devices, and, on the other, with a feeling of satisfaction that rules exist to protect all defendants against improper prosecution at the hands of an awesomely powerful government. In the multiple-murder event, for example, suppose one were to shift the scene to that of a swindle in which an executive allegedly perpetrated a computer scheme involving 100 different companies. Should he be subject to a possible 100 trials, one after another, until a jury is found that would convict him? If the same evidence is to be used in each trial, then obviously not. In the mistrial case suppose that the judge had been hostile to the accused and had noticed that the prosecution was bungling its case and the jury was sympathetic to the defendant.

Should he have been permitted to declare a mistrial on any flimsy excuse, including his own plans for vacation, so as to have the case retried under circumstances which he believed might be less favorable to the defendant? Again, the answer is obviously in the negative.

A major exception to the double jeopardy law takes place when in a single act a defendant violates both state and federal law. He may be found innocent in a state trial and then guilty in a federal one. This has occurred most frequently with regard to gross violations of civil rights, including murders of blacks and other minorities. The legalistic defense of this two-trial system is that in each trial a different law and a different jurisdiction are involved. Some contend that this has been a method—perhaps a necessary and socially desirable one—for the federal government to thwart the Southern courts at a time when they were systematically excluding blacks from juries, juries which would not bring in a verdict of guilty even in a clear-cut case, when the victim was black or a civil rights advocate.

In a well-publicized case involving charges of vehicular homicide and driving under the influence of intoxicating liquor—a case in which the accused was the son of a prominent jurist—a trial was arranged with unseemly haste and the defendant was exonerated. After a public clamor there was another trial, at which he was found guilty, a verdict that was subsequently overturned by a higher court on the ground of double jeopardy. It might appear that such abuses could be remedied by ruling that a trial arranged only for the record and the purpose of avoiding a trial is not a trial at all, and that the accused had thus never been placed in jeopardy. However, such a ruling would lend itself to considerable abuse. In the case of the hasty trial, the remedy may rest with prosecution of the responsible judges for obstruction of justice, not the abrogation of the rule against double jeopardy.

DETAILS OF THE CRIME

The defense is entitled to details of the crime or crimes that the accused is charged with having perpetrated, and the specific law that it is claimed he violated. These details are necessary for an investigation of the event, for legal determination of whether the incident did indeed violate the law as written, and for mounting a proper defense in court. If the time and place of the crime are not given, and are not known to the accused in advance of the trial, it would be difficult if not impossible for him to establish a credible alibi (that is, that he was in a different place at the time that this event occurred).

The details of the event are usually contained in the indictment handed down by the grand jury, an information (usually brought forth by the prosecutor), or some similar document. Donald Newman (1975: 481) writes, "The evidentiary standard for the information, like that of the indictment, is probable cause that the defendant committed a crime and should be 'bound over' for trial."

RIGHT TO COUNSEL

Courtroom procedures are extremely intricate, and without specially trained personnel at his disposal a defendant is usually unable to put up an effective struggle to exonerate himself. Although the right to counsel is written into the Bill of Rights, it was not until the 1930s, in the Scottsboro case, that it was established that this constitutional provision can apply to trials in state courts (Powell v. Alabama, 1932). Later, in Gideon v. Wainwright (1963), the U.S. Supreme Court ruled that the right extends to all felony cases (Scottsboro was a capital case), even if the defendant does not request counsel at the time of the trial. Finally, the right to counsel was extended to cover misdemeanants in the case of Argersinger v. Hamlin (1972).

That the rich defendant is at an advantage over the poor one is hardly deniable, at least in terms of marshaling resources for the investigation, preparation, and presentation of a case. If the defendant is indigent, he may call on public defenders, legal aid societies, or court-appointed attorneys for assistance; there is considerable dispute as to their effectiveness. Many difficulties have arisen when an accused person has sought to function as his own attorney, acting alone or in conjunction with hired or appointed lawyers. The judge may exercise discretion and refuse to permit a defendant to represent himself; however, increasingly in the United States higher courts are ruling that the defendant has this inherent right. It gives the defendant the advantage of having a voice without actually having to take the stand and be subject to cross-examination. Although relatively infrequent, it is a highly publicized occurrence; in some instances, particularly where the crime has political implications, publicity is exactly what the defendant is seeking.

Problems may arise for indigent defendants because of the cost of appeal. This can be extraordinarily high in long and complex cases; the transcript alone can cost thousands of dollars. In cases involving capital punishment, appeal is automatic and mandatory in many states, and here the state often assumes the cost of paying for the transcript. But one stops to wonder at the possible cost in other types of trial of the transcript and other work on the appeal, especially for a trial that lasted, let us say, fifteen months.

This issue notwithstanding, the right to counsel is well established in American courts. That it will be counsel faithful to the interests of the client can probably be assured, but that it will be effective and competent is more difficult to control. Yet without that competence a defendant is scarcely better off than if he came into court unaccompanied by a member of the bar.

MENTAL COMPETENCE

A person cannot stand trial unless he is capable of understanding the proceedings and thus assist in his own defense. Sometimes there is a judgment before trial that the accused is incompetent, or this judgment may be rendered by a jury. The accused is thereupon confined, without trial, for an indeterminate period in a mental institution. This is sometimes accomplished with the connivance of the defendant in order to avoid a trial, but more often it is without his consent.

Pretrial detention in a mental institution without an opportunity to defend against the charges may be inflicted on an innocent person. Confinement itself, because it is indeterminate, can take place for periods far longer than the defendant would have served had he been found guilty and given a maximum sentence (Szasz, 1965). The constitutionality of such pretrial confinement has been challenged.

A trial by jury (technically known as a trial jury or a petty jury, sometimes a petit jury, to distinguish it from a grand jury) is guaranteed by the Constitution. A defendant has the right to a jury trial, but it can be waived voluntarily, and in fact most American cases that are not settled by guilty plea do not go to jury trial at all, but are tried before a judge or a panel of judges, the latter known as a bench trial (Kalven and Zeisel, 1966). **TRIAL BY JURY**

It is frequently stated that a person is entitled to a trial by a "jury of his peers." This expression has come down to us from English law, where the practice was meant to protect the aristocracy from a vengeful trial at the hands of commoners and, on the face of it at least, the reverse. In America it lost this meaning, as there has been no official and titled aristocracy. Occasionally it has been suggested that the poor should be jurors of the poor, the blacks of blacks, but these suggestions are seldom thought through carefully. This would mean that the white man accused of killing a black would be tried by an all-white jury (this is what usually takes place, but is under increasing attack), and that the rich would be entitled to a jury of the rich.

A jury is selected from a larger group, called "the venire," made up of voter lists, citizen lists, and volunteers who have asked that their names be used for prospective jury duty. Members of the venire are questioned by both prosecution and defense counsel (a process called "voir dire"), and each side can ask for the disqualification of an unlimited number of prospective jurors *for cause*; e.g., admission of prejudice, having personal knowledge of the defendant or victim, or having formed an opinion about the guilt or innocence of the defendant that is unlikely to be modified. In addition, each side is given a limited number of challenges without having to state any reason; these are known as peremptory challenges and are often used for the systematic exclusion of blacks, poor, the young, or others from juries.

A study of verdicts rendered by juries shows that, in about 80 percent of the cases, the trial judge would have handed down the same verdict. However, of the remaining cases—those in which the judge disagreed with the decision of the jury—the jury voted not guilty about four out of five times (Kalven and Zeisel, 1966).

When a jury cannot reach unanimity after long deliberation and several votes have been taken, the case can be dropped or retried. The prosecution will often drop a case when unofficial polling discloses that the jury is overwhelmingly in favor of acquittal, but instances are known in which the prosecution will insist on a new trial although the first had resulted in a vote of eleven to one for acquittal.

There has been some movement in the United States to modify the long tradition that a jury must reach a unanimous verdict. Some efforts have been made to give juries the right to find a defendant guilty by a vote of eleven to one or of ten to two. However, others contend that a verdict of guilt by a less than unanimous vote runs counter to the concept that guilt must be established beyond a reasonable doubt.

The efficacy and justice of trial by jury continue to be debated.

The defendant is entitled to a speedy trial. However, a speedy trial is not defined in terms of the calendar and is not meant to permit prosecutors to rush **SPEEDY TRIAL** a defendant to hasty injustice. That many trials up to about a century ago were too speedy should be borne in mind. In 1812, John Bellingham assassinated the prime minister of England. "Within seven days of the crime," write Ida Macalpine and Richard Hunter (1969), "from the Monday when it was committed to the Monday following, he was tried, convicted, sentenced and executed." In the previously mentioned Scottsboro case, the nine black youths were arrested in Alabama on March 25, 1931. During the one week of April 6, they were all tried (this included several different trials), and eight were found guilty and sentenced to death, with a mistrial declared in the case of the ninth youth, then thirteen years old, because the jury could not agree on whether he should receive life imprisonment or the death penalty (Carter, 1971).

The purpose of a speedy trial is to avoid a long period of pretrial detention for the defendant and to avoid an even longer period in limbo in which the suspect, released on bail or on his own recognizance, has been accused of a crime and has not yet been given an opportunity to exonerate himself. He is awaiting his fate, unable to plan his own future because of the uncertainty about adjudication of the charges.

The very volume of arrests, backlog of cases, crowded court calendars, and time consumed in many cases have all resulted in long delays between arrest and trial. Such delay in bringing the accused to trial is often the responsibility of the defense as much as the prosecution, but it is mainly built into the system. If held without bail, or because he is unable to make bail, a defendant eventually found guilty does have the solace of being given credit for the pretrial and presentence detention, but it is really little solace in many cases, because he is often sentenced to time already served, and probably would have received a smaller sentence or none at all if he had not been held in jail.

In contrast with the United States, defendants in Europe generally come to trial within a few days of arrest in minor cases and within a few weeks in major ones.

THE RIGHT TO FACE ACCUSERS

It is extremely important that the defendant have the right to face accusers. This involves essentially two processes: (1) the defendant should be in court during all trial procedures, and (2) there shall be no second-hand (hearsay) testimony, in which a witness states what another person, not the defendant, told him about the culpability of the accused. A rare exception to the hearsay rule is made for deathbed statements, but these almost always have to be verified by several persons present at the time, who should be disinterested parties, and in some instances there must be convincing evidence that the statement was given by a person who knew that he was dying.

In cases in which government spies have infiltrated foreign or domestic networks, it is sometimes difficult to mount a believable case without presenting witnesses, and this would "blow their cover." Some major cases are said to have been dropped because the government felt it more important to protect informants than to proceed with prosecution, or because national security would have been endangered by testimony in open court.

In organized crime and certain other cases, the right of defendants to face their accusers has meant that witnesses have been intimidated and even killed before or after testifying, while others have received assistance and protection from the government during and after the trial. This protection has taken the form of the Witness Relocation Program, in which witnesses are sent to new localities, given a "new identity," and offered financial and other aid.

The defendant has the choice of taking the stand as a witness or remaining silent. If he chooses to remain silent, he cannot be called by the prosecution; the prosecution is not allowed to suggest to the jury that any inferences about guilt should be drawn on the basis of the defendant's failure to testify. Lloyd Weinreb (1977) expresses what may be a widespread belief among attorneys, that the public and jurors, notwithstanding any warnings from a judge, suspect that a defendant who does not testify has something to conceal—namely, his guilt.

TESTIFYING IN ONE'S OWN DEFENSE

Actually, there are many reasons why a defendant chooses not to testify other than complicity that might be uncovered by cross-examination. He might wish to protect a friend or family member; he might be frightened of what will happen to him if he is examined on criminal activities of which he has knowledge but for which he is not on trial; and, perhaps most important, his attorney might feel that the defendant is one who will make an unfavorable impression upon a jury and become easily confused on cross-examination. Finally, should a defendant not take the stand, it is usually difficult for the prosecution to make known to the jury his previous arrest and conviction record.[5]

As noted earlier, at one time the defendant was barred from testifying in his own behalf or in behalf of a co-defendant, a rule that has since been discarded throughout the world.

The prosecution, with its resources and facilities, may uncover information that would be helpful to the defense in establishing innocence, but it may nonetheless not be convinced that the defendant is innocent and should be dismissed without a trial. In the interest of a fair trial, such information may not be concealed. But in actual practice it appears to be concealed quite frequently. When it is uncovered after a defendant has been found guilty, the prosecution will usually argue, on appeal, that it did not have the information, did not believe it relevant, or that the information, even if it had been presented, would not have made sufficient difference in the strong case against the defendant to have changed the verdict. Higher courts on appeal are generally unsympathetic to all of these arguments, especially the last. It appears that, when a higher court does not grant a new trial on the ground

DISCLOSURE OF INFORMATION TO DEFENSE

5. There are, however, other ways in which this can be revealed. If the defense calls character witnesses, for example, they can be asked if they knew that the defendant had had previous arrests and convictions.

of discovery of information concealed by the prosecution, it is because a hard-to-convict person with a notorious reputation has finally been imprisoned; tortuous reasoning prevails in the higher court's effort to sustain the original trial verdict. The same is true of politically sensitive cases.

The defense, in contrast, is not required to disclose information that might hurt the defendant. It is permitted to ignore fact, but not to falsify deliberately. That such falsifications are not infrequent has been stated publicly by well-known legal scholars, who often defend them as part of the adversary system (see Weinreb, 1977, for an interesting discussion of this).

**ADVANCE NOTICE
AND THE
QUESTION OF
SURPRISE**

In order to prepare a case, each side must have some knowledge of the witnesses, evidence, documentation, and line of attack of the other. Otherwise, it could be taken by surprise in mid-trial and find itself in a position where new witnesses would have to be located, alibis investigated, and other work undertaken. Inasmuch as it is not practical or even possible for all details of a case to be laid out beforehand, lawyers will frequently claim surprise during the course of a trial.

Generally, the prosecution has greater obligation than the defense to give advance notice. The latter may be limited in its obligations to disclosure of a proposed alibi (meaning that the defendant was not and could not have been at the scene of the crime at the time that it occurred, because he was at another specifically named place, for which there is proof) or of an expectation that it will offer a defense of not guilty by reason of insanity.

A witness called by the prosecution may make statements entirely unexpected by both sides, but this would usually not constitute surprise because the prosecution could not possibly disclose in advance what it had no knowledge of before it occurred.

OPEN TRIAL

A trial closed to the public (called a "star chamber" proceeding, and said to be held *in camera*) has many dangers. If the public remains uninformed, it becomes possible for the government to persecute minorities, political dissidents, and others in disfavor, without the spotlight of public attention focusing on the proceedings. Improper and unworthy conduct by prosecutors, judges, and others in the court seldom come to light if the public and press are barred.

Traditionally, almost all trials except those in family court were held in public. During the 1970s, the U.S. Supreme Court increasingly leaned toward seeing abuses and dangers in the unrestrained open court and paid particular attention to the problem of publicity before and during the trial. In England there are many restrictions on what the press can report about a case, especially from the time of arrest until the verdict, but American thought has generally seen more danger than protection in such restrictive measures. On rare occasions, pretrial publicity has been made the basis for a successful appeal, but somewhat more frequently it has merely resulted in a change of venue (meaning that the trial is held in a different locality). When a change of venue is demanded, it almost invariably comes from the defense. On some occasions the court that grants the change may specify a new place where the atmosphere is equally hostile to the defense.

Information obtained in certain types of role relationships cannot be divulged in court without the consent of the original informant, usually the defendant. The most common types of privileged information are those derived from relationships between wife and husband, physician and patient, clergyman and penitent, and lawyer and client. Note, however, that parents and children do not have such a protected relationship.

PRIVILEGED INFORMATION

The rationale behind the rule of privilege is that some institutionalized relationships are so vital to the society, and would be so completely hurt and possibly destroyed if confidentiality were not upheld, that their preservation becomes more important than the prosecution of an accused, even for a major crime.

The privileges are complex and contain many exceptions. For example, a spouse who has been victimized can testify against the victimizer; a husband or wife can usually be compelled to testify about a crime committed by the other before they were married; a lawyer or doctor might be compelled to testify about information received from a client or patient in other than a professional–client relationship (that is, as a friend or eyewitness). The limits and extent of privilege are the subject of debates agitating American jurisprudential circles; questions are being raised, for example, as to whether the privilege should be extended to certified psychologists, marriage counselors, social workers, social researchers, criminologists, and journalists.

It is often repeated that the defendant walks into court presumed to be innocent. Yet everyone knows that most defendants are eventually found or plead guilty. The public hence has some difficulty accepting the concept of the presumption of innocence. It is generally felt to be unlikely that a person would be arrested and held if he were totally innocent. In some instances the defendant has been caught red-handed; in what sense can it be expected that he walk into court presumed to be innocent?

PRESUMPTION OF INNOCENCE

The presumption of innocence is a legal, specifically an evidentiary, presumption. It means that, for purposes of a trial and determination of guilt or innocence, one starts the trial with no prejudgment against the defendant. Each point against the accused must be proved. Even a person caught on the scene in the course of the crime, or fleeing from it, may have some explanation that would exonerate him, be it entrapment or hypnosis or any other. A defendant photographed during a bank holdup might claim that the photograph is a look-alike. A fugitive caught fleeing the scene of a robbery might claim innocence in that robbery, charging that it had been staged by the police in order to frame him when they learned his whereabouts.

Drawing a sharp contrast between the in-court presumption of innocence and out-of-court attitudes, Herbert L. Packer (1968) contends that in American society there is actually a presumption of guilt. This appears to be inevitable, although its impact on juries might be diminished if reports in the press gave less information about trials, as the presumption of guilt is likely to be most damaging in influencing the jury. It may also be part of the continued stigma that follows a defendant after exoneration.

BURDEN OF PROOF

As befits a system in which there is a presumption of innocence, the burden of proof is always upon the prosecution to prove guilt, never the reverse. When the defense does offer proof of innocence, this is not because the burden of proof has shifted, but because it wishes to neutralize the evidence brought forth by the other side and bolster the case in its own favor.

Inasmuch as the defendant does not have to prove his innocence, he may stand mute and insist that no case against him has been presented that can withstand the test of proof. Or he may counter the testimony of prosecution witnesses and present proof of innocence (alibi, character witnesses, documents).

"Prove you did not do it" makes no sense in a court of law. Sometimes, from a practical point of view, an innocent person can have no such proof. Only when confronted with witnesses against him can he question them (through his attorney) to find some evidence that the witnesses are themselves less than believable or may be deliberately lying. Only when he sees a signature reputed to be his can he offer proof to the contrary or show that although he did indeed sign the paper, words were altered after he had written his name.

Since the prosecution must prove guilt, it presents its case first. When it has finished (technically, the prosecution "rests"), the defense routinely makes a motion for dismissal of charges on the ground that a *prima facie* case has not been established. The defense here is stating that, even if it presents nothing further to counter what has already been heard in court, the defendant would have to be found not guilty because the prosecution has failed in its task of carrying the burden of proof. On infrequent occasions, the judge grants this defense motion and the case ends.

PROVED BEYOND A REASONABLE DOUBT

In a criminal case the prosecution must prove its case "beyond a reasonable doubt" in order to justify a verdict of guilt. This is in contrast to a civil case, where the two sides—in contention in an adversary relationship—battle it out and the winner is the side that establishes its case "by a fair preponderance of the credible evidence."

Proof beyond a reasonable doubt does not and cannot mean beyond any scintilla of a doubt whatsoever. A flicker of doubt is almost inevitable. A confession, even if offered by a defendant in court, might be made to protect another person; documentary evidence, fingerprints, signatures can be in error or forged; and eyewitness identification, even when given in good faith, has a long history of error (Buckhout, 1974).

In Scotland there is a verdict that permits a man to go free but does not exonerate him—"not proved" (known, appropriately enough, as "the Scotch verdict"). In the United States and all other jurisdictions, an accused is never legally found *innocent* of the crime of which he is charged; rather, he is found *not guilty*. In terms of freedom from punishment and rearrest on the same charge, "not guilty" and "innocent" are synonymous, but in their social and sometimes even legal repercussions, there can be vast differences.

Criminal Justice and the Bill of Rights

Many of the points made above and others (on search and seizure and on cruel and unusual punishment, for example) involve rights guaranteed to the public in the first ten amendments to the Constitution. However, in the case of Barron v. Baltimore (1833), the Supreme Court, in a decision written by Chief Justice John Marshall, held that the provisions of the Bill of Rights apply only to federal issues, not to state ones, and hence not to most criminal cases. In fact, the only exception to this for almost a hundred years was in the Dred Scott case, an exception made in order to deprive a black man of his freedom.

After the Civil War, the Fourteenth Amendment to the Constitution was ratified; it contains the famous clause that forbids "any state to deprive any person of life, liberty, or property, without due process of law." For more than sixty years following ratification of this amendment in 1868, this phrase was invoked primarily to protect corporations, defined as persons for purposes of coming within its purview. Starting in the early 1930s, massive challenges were launched to deprivations by states of the rights to counsel and to freedom from unreasonable search and seizure, as well as other rights ostensibly guaranteed under the Constitution. This struggle, known as the movement for the nationalization of the Bill of Rights, reached a turning point in 1932 with the Scottsboro case (Carter, 1971), when it was argued successfully before the U.S. Supreme Court that the due process clause of the Fourteenth Amendment gives protection against trial without counsel in a state case.

However, it was not until the last days of the Warren Court that most of the provisions of the Bill of Rights became nationalized. Justice Hugo Black had argued that the entire Bill of Rights should apply to state issues, but this approach was resisted; instead a gradual process occurred in which individual amendments, or parts of them, were studied to determine whether, without their protection, a person would be deprived of due process.

Historically, America thus completed a circle. The due process clause of the Fourteenth Amendment had been meant to protect former slaves and to prevent enslavement of any person. After the clause had been used almost exclusively in the interests of large corporations, there came the nationalization movement, and the due process clause was once again in service to protect the poor and, in fact, in the Scottsboro case, the descendants of former slaves.

The Conviction of the Innocent

Notwithstanding all of the safeguards against convicting an innocent person, some innocents are indeed found guilty (MacNamara, 1969). Among them are those who plead guilty, making a bargain despite knowledge of their own innocence. Probably more frequent are those found guilty in a trial by jury or judge. They are generally treated more harshly than those who have pleaded guilty (a practice that has received the approval of the U.S. Supreme Court) and hence are more likely to find their way into prison.

One of the strongest arguments against capital punishment is its irrevocability. The deceased cannot be resurrected to live again, unlike the guiltless who are imprisoned, to whom the gift of freedom can be given, though long overdue. In fact, it was after just such a case, the Christie affair, that revulsion against capital punishment swept through England and that country passed its first abolition law.

Many cases in the United States and abroad that were causes célèbres continue to leave great doubt as to whether the executed person was guilty. Nicola Sacco and Bartolomeo Vanzetti, two Italian-American radicals, were executed in the 1920s after worldwide agitation for their freedom. Millions of people believed that they were victims of anti-immigrant prejudice and "red scare" propaganda; among those who protested their execution was Harvard law professor Felix Frankfurter, later to become a justice on the U.S. Supreme Court. Fifty years after their execution the Massachusetts legislature passed a resolution "rehabilitating" them, and the keys to the City of New York were offered to the grandson of Sacco, a young man who spurned them because the then mayor favored the death penalty. Three decades after the execution of Sacco and Vanzetti, Julius and Ethel Rosenberg were executed on charges of wartime espionage for the Soviet Union, although the law making wartime espionage a capital crime had been intended as protection against the enemy, not an ally, as the U.S.S.R. had been in the Second World War. The trial of the Rosenbergs took place at the height of the cold war and the heyday of blacklisting and other aspects of the red scare aroused largely by the crusade of Senator Joseph McCarthy. Controversy surrounds the case to this day, with many Americans believing that the executions constituted a miscarriage of justice.

American prisons are not filled with people innocent of the crimes of which they were convicted, nor were most of those who have been executed guiltless. But that the prisons harbor some innocent convicts would be foolhardy to deny. Every year brings cases in which people once found guilty are tried again and found not guilty—not proof of their innocence but an indication that the guilty verdict may have been wrong. There are also complete exonerations, involving incontrovertible evidence that the imprisoned person is innocent, sometimes accompanied by the arrest of a different person for the same crime.

In the case in which George Whitmore, charged with the murder of two women, confessed to the crimes and immediately repudiated his admission of guilt, the police faced the embarrassing fact that somehow they had obtained a confession from a man who turned out to be indubitably innocent. They sought to retrieve their credibility by demonstrating that they had apprehended a dangerous criminal after all, even if he had not committed the acts to which he had somehow confessed. So Whitmore was again charged, this time with forcible rape; he was convicted and again eventually exonerated, but only after he had served time in prison. In another rape case, in the early 1970s in Iowa, one David Feddersen was apprehended on the street as the victim was escaping from her assailant. He was convicted, and served almost two years in prison before a witness came forward who had seen the offender flee in the opposite direction from which Feddersen was walking when seized (State v. Feddersen, 1975; Geis and Geis, 1979).

Generally, the law is not sympathetic to civil remedies for false arrest and imprisonment of the innocent. It is reasoned that, on the one hand, there would be an enormous reluctance to make arrests if the arresting officer or municipality could be held financially liable for having detained the accused, should he not be found guilty; and on the other, that juries and judges would be likely to overconvict, or at least be reluctant to find a defendant not guilty, if such a verdict were to result in many lawsuits against cities and states.

To obtain damages for false arrest, the person usually has to demonstrate deliberate and knowing impropriety on the part of the arresting and prosecuting agents. Sometimes, when there has been extraordinary suffering and an innocent person is finally released because of clear proof that he is the "wrong man" or the victim of a frameup, such restitution is offered. But generally little is done for those exculpated except that the door is opened and they are told to walk out of confinement. One of the Scottsboro defendants served some nineteen years before he was finally freed, and no restitution has ever been offered. In the Whitmore case, the judicial system handed down a decision that he could not sue for false arrest or restitution because the statute of limitations for his arrest had expired! In the Feddersen case, the judge was quoted as saying, in what amounted to little more than an irresponsible shrug of the shoulders, "It shows we're all mortals." And in still another instance, in which a confession exonerated a man who had already been found guilty and sentenced to fifty years, a prosecutor remarked, "Nobody is entitled to a perfect trial, just a fair trial." (See Geis and Geis, 1979, for discussion of these last two cases.) What the prosecutor failed to add is that the public is entitled to know what went wrong and why, and to see that measures are taken to reduce substantially the possibilities of reoccurrence.

The Attainment of Justice

It is foolhardy to believe that perfect justice can be attained, but it can be vigorously pursued. In no society do the poor and powerless receive the same justice as the middle and upper classes, nor are minorities anywhere judged without a vestige of prejudice. The only way to be absolutely certain that no innocent person will be imprisoned is to abolish prisons, and without a substitute that would deter as well or better, there would be no justice for the victims of crime.

George Orwell scoffed, in *Animal Farm*, at a "utopia" where some people were more equal than others. Nonetheless, the inequality gaps can be diminished, the extent of inequality can be narrowed. The vigilance of a critical public, combined with the protections of the Constitution, can work to improve the system, so that there is greater likelihood of apprehending and finding guilty those who are guilty, and greater protection than ever for victims, be they victims of the offenders or of a fallible system of criminal justice.

349

ANGEL, SCHLOMO. *Discouraging Crime through City Planning.* Berkeley: University of California Press, 1968.

Argersinger v. Hamlin, 407 U.S. 25, 1972.

BABINGTON, ANTHONY. *A House in Bow Street.* London: McDonald, 1969.

BARKER, THOMAS, and JULIAN ROEBUCK. *An Empirical Typology of Police Corruption: A Study in Organizational Deviance.* Springfield, Ill.: Thomas, 1973.

Barron v. Baltimore, 32 U.S. (7 Pet.) 243, 8 L.Ed. 672, 1833.

BLUMBERG, ABRAHAM. *Criminal Justice.* Chicago: Quadrangle, 1967.

BRYANT, CLIFTON D. *Khaki-Collar Crime: Deviant Behavior in the Military Context.* New York: Free Press, 1979.

BUCKHOUT, ROBERT. "Eyewitness Testimony." *Scientific American,* 1974, 231: 23–31.

CARTER, DAN T. *Scottsboro: A Tragedy of the American South.* New York: Oxford University Press, 1971.

CHAIKEN, JAN M., N. W. LAWLESS, and K. A. STEVENSON. *The Impact of Police Activity on Crime: Robberies in the New York City Subway System.* New York: Rand Institute, 1974.

CLOWARD, RICHARD A., and LLOYD E. OHLIN. *Delinquency and Opportunity: A Theory of Delinquent Gangs.* New York: Free Press, 1960.

CONKLIN, JOHN. *Robbery and the Criminal Justice System.* Philadelphia: Lippincott, 1972.

COSTELLO, AUGUSTINE E. *Our Police Protectors: A History of the New York Police from the Earliest Period to the Present Times.* Montclair, N.J.: Patterson Smith, 1972. (First published in 1885.)

Criminal Justice Newsletter, No. 3, 1977.

CUMMING, ELAINE, IAN CUMMING, and LAURA EDELL. "Policeman as Philosopher, Guide and Friend." *Social Problems,* 1965, 12: 276–286.

ERMANN, M. DAVID, and RICHARD J. LUNDMAN, eds. *Corporate and Governmental Deviance: Problems of Organizational Behavior in Contemporary Society.* New York: Oxford University Press, 1978.

FEDDERSEN. See State v. Feddersen.

FOSDICK, RAYMOND B. *American Police Systems.* Montclair, N.J.: Patterson Smith, 1969. (First published in 1920.)

FOWLER, FLOYD V., JR. *Citizen Attitudes toward Local Government Services and Taxes.* Cambridge, Mass.: Ballinger, 1974.

GAULT. See In re Gault.

GEIS, GILBERT. *Not the Law's Business.* 2d ed. New York: Schocken Books, 1979.

GEIS, GILBERT, and ROBLEY GEIS. "Rape Reform: An Appreciative-Critical Review." *Bulletin of American Academy of Psychiatry and the Law,* 1979, 6(3): 301–312.

GIBBONS, DON C. *Society, Crime, and Criminal Careers.* Englewood Cliffs, N.J.: Prentice-Hall, 1968.

Gideon v. Wainwright, 372 U.S. 335, 1963.

GOLDFARB, RONALD. *Jails: The Ultimate Ghetto.* New York: Anchor Books, 1975.

GOLDSTEIN, JOSEPH. "Police Discretion Not to Invoke the Criminal Process: Low Visibility Decisions in the Administration of Justice." In George F. Cole, ed., *Criminal Justice: Law and Politics.* Belmont, Calif.: Wadsworth, 1964.

GOODMAN, L.H., G. MILLER, and P. DEFORREST. *A Study of the Deterrent Value of Crime Prevention Measures as Perceived by Criminal Offenders.* Washington, D.C.: Bureau of Social Science Research, 1966.

GREENWOOD, P.W. *An Analysis of the Apprehension Activities of the New York City Police Department.* New York: Rand Institute, 1970.

HARRIES, KEITH D. *The Geography of Crime and Justice.* New York: McGraw-Hill, 1974.

HART, H.L.A. *The Morality of the Criminal Law.* London: Oxford University Press, 1965.

HAUSER, PHILIP M., ed. *Handbook for Social Research in Urban Areas.* Paris: UNESCO, 1965.

HEUMANN, MILTON. *Plea Bargaining: The Experiences of Prosecutors, Judges, and Defense Attorneys.* Chicago: University of Chicago Press, 1978.

In re Gault, 387 U.S. 1, 1967.

JACOBS, JANE. *The Death and Life of Great American Cities.* New York: Vintage Books, 1961.

JEFFERY, C. RAY. *Crime Prevention through Environmental Design.* Beverly Hills, Calif.: Sage Publications, 1977.

KALVEN, HARRY, JR., and HANS ZEISEL. *The American Jury.* Boston: Little, Brown, 1966.

KANSAS CITY PREVENTIVE PATROL EXPERIMENT. *Summary Report.* Washington, D.C.: Police Foundation, 1974.

LAFAVE, WAYNE R. *Arrest: The Decision to Take a Suspect into Custody.* Boston: Little, Brown, 1965.

MACALPINE, IDA, and RICHARD HUNTER. *George III and the Mad-Business.* New York: Pantheon, 1969.

MACNAMARA, DONAL E. J. "Convicting the Innocent." *Crime and Delinquency,* 1969, 15: 57–61.

MALTZ, MICHAEL. *Evaluation of Crime Control Programs.* Washington, D.C.: Government Printing Office, 1972.

MARX, GARY T., and DANE ARCHER. *Urban Vigilante.* Washington, D.C.: National Criminal Justice Reference Service, 1973.

MCDOWELL, CHARLES P. *Police and the Community.* Cincinnati: W.H. Anderson, 1975.

MERTON, ROBERT K. *Social Theory and Social Structure.* New York: Free Press, 1965.

Miranda v. Arizona, 384 U.S. 436, 1966.

MORAN, RICHARD. *Knowing Right from Wrong: The Insanity Defense of Daniel McNaughtan.* New York: Free Press, 1981.

MORRIS, NORVAL. "Impediments to Penal Reform." *University of Chicago Law Review,* 1966, 33: 627–656.

MORRIS, TERENCE. *The Criminal Area: A Study in Social Ecology.* New York: Humanities Press, 1958.

MOYNIHAN, DANIEL P. *Maximum Feasible Misunderstanding: Community Action in the War on Poverty.* New York: Free Press, 1969.

Municipal Year Book, 1979.

NATIONAL ADVISORY COMMISSION ON CIVIL DISORDERS. *Report.* New York: Bantam Books, 1968.

NATIONAL ADVISORY COMMISSION ON CRIMINAL JUSTICE STANDARDS AND GOALS. *Police.* Washington, D.C.: Government Printing Office, 1973.

NATIONAL COMMISSION ON THE CAUSES and PREVENTION OF VIOLENCE. Vol. 12: *Crimes of Violence.* Washington, D.C.: Government Printing Office, 1969.

NEWMAN, DONALD J. *Introduction to Criminal Justice.* Philadelphia: Lippincott, 1975.

NEWMAN, OSCAR. *Defensible Space.* New York: Macmillan, 1972.

NEW YORK STATE DIVISION OF CRIMINAL JUSTICE SERVICES. *1975 Comprehensive Crime Control Plan.* New York: The Division, 1975.

PACKER, HERBERT L. *The Limits of the Criminal Sanction.* Stanford, Calif.: Stanford University Press, 1968.

Payton v. Riddick, *United States Law Week,* April 15, 1980.

Powell v. Alabama, 287 U.S. 45, 1932.

PRESIDENT'S COMMISSION ON LAW ENFORCEMENT AND ADMINISTRATION OF JUSTICE. *The Challenge of Crime in a Free Society.* Washington, D.C.: Government Printing Office, 1967a.

_____. Task Force Report: *Crime and Its Impact: An Assessment.* Washington, D.C.: Government Printing Office, 1967b.

_____. Task Force Report: *The Police.* Washington, D.C.: Government Printing Office, 1967c.

_____. Task Force Report: *Science and Technology.* Washington, D.C.: Government Printing Office, 1967d.

PRESS, S. JAMES. *Some Effects of an Increase in Police Manpower in the 20th Precinct in New York City.* Rand Report R-704-NYC. Santa Monica, Calif.: Rand Corp., 1971.

REISS, ALBERT J., JR. *The Police and the Public.* New Haven: Yale University Press, 1971.

REITH, CHARLES. *The Blind Eye of History.* London: Faber and Faber, 1952.

REPPETTO, THOMAS A. *Residential Crime.* Cambridge, Mass.: Ballinger Press, 1974.

_____. "The Influence of Police Organizational Style on Crime Control Effectiveness." *Journal of Police Science and Administration,* 1975, 3: 274–279.

ROEBUCK, JULIAN B., and STANLEY C. WEEBER. *Political Crime in the United States: Analyzing Crime by and against Government.* New York: Praeger, 1978.

RUBINSTEIN, JONATHAN. *City Police.* New York: Farrar, Straus & Giroux, 1973.

SCARR, HARRY A. (with the assistance of Joan L. Pinsky and Deborah S. Wyatt). *Patterns of Burglary.* 2d ed. Washington, D.C.: National Institute of Law Enforcement and Criminal Justice, 1973.

SCHUR, EDWIN M. *Crimes without Victims.* Englewood Cliffs, N.J.: Prentice-Hall, 1965.

SHAW, CLIFFORD R., and HENRY D. MCKAY. "Social Factors in Juvenile Delinquency." In *Wickersham Commission Reports,* No. 13, *Causes of Crime.* Vol. II. Montclair, N.J.: Patterson Smith, 1968. (First published in 1931.)

SHERMAN, LAWRENCE W., CATHERINE H. MILTON, and THOMAS V. KELLY. *Team Policing.* Washington, D.C.: The Police Foundation, 1973.

SHERMAN, LAWRENCE W., and the NATIONAL ADVISORY COMMISSION ON HIGHER EDUCATION FOR POLICE OFFICERS. *The Quality of Police Education.* San Francisco: Jossey-Bass, 1978.

Sherman v. United States, 356 U.S. 369, 1958.

SHINNAR, SHLOMO, and REUEL SHINNAR. *A Simplified Model of Estimating the Effects of the Criminal Justice System on the Control of Crime.* New York: City College of New York, School of Engineering, 1974.

SIGLER, JAY A. *Double Jeopardy: The Development of a Legal and Social Policy.* Ithaca, N.Y.: Cornell University Press, 1969.

SKOLNICK, JEROME H. *Justice without Trial.* New York: Wiley, 1966.

SKOLNICK, JEROME H., and JOHN DOMBRINK. "The Legalization of Deviance." In Edward Sagarin, ed., *Criminology: New Concerns—Essays in Honor of Hans W. Mattick,* pp. 73–88. Beverly Hills, Calif.: Sage Publications, 1979.

SMITH, BRUCE. *Police Systems in the United States.* 2d ed. New York: Harper & Row, 1960.

SPERGEL, IRVING. *Racketville, Slumtown, Haulburg: An Exploratory Study of Delinquent Subcultures.* Chicago: University of Chicago Press, 1964.

State v. Feddersen, 230 N.W. 2d 510 (Iowa), 1975.

SZASZ, THOMAS S. *Psychiatric Justice.* New York: Macmillan, 1965.

_____. "Crime, Punishment, and Psychiatry." In Abraham S. Blumberg, ed., *Current Perspectives on Criminal Behavior,* pp. 342–363. 2d ed. New York: Knopf, 1981.

TURK, AUSTIN. *Political Criminality and Political Policing.* New York: MSS Modular Publishers, 1975.

TURNER, STANLEY. "Delinquency and Distance." In Thorsten Sellin and Marvin E. Wolfgang, eds., *Delinquency: Selected Studies,* pp. 11–26. New York: Wiley, 1969.

VAN DINE, STEVE, JOHN P. CONRAD, and SIMON DINITZ. "The Incapacitation of the Chronic Thug." *Journal of Criminal Law and Criminology,* 1979, 70: 125–135.

VERA INSTITUTE OF JUSTICE. *Felony Arrests: Their Prosecution and Disposition in New York City's Courts.* New York: The Institute, 1977.

WEINREB, LLOYD L. *Denial of Justice: Criminal Process in the United States.* New York: Free Press, 1977.

WEIR, ADRIENNE. "The Robbery Offender." In S. Feeney and A. Weir, eds., *The Prevention and Control of Robbery*. Davis, Calif.: University of California Press, 1973.

WHYTE, WILLIAM F. *Street Corner Society*. Chicago: University of Chicago Press, 1955.

WILSON, JAMES Q. *Varieties of Police Behavior*. Cambridge, Mass.: Harvard University Press, 1968.

———. *Thinking about Crime*. New York: Basic Books, 1975.

WOLFGANG, MARVIN E. "Crime in a Birth Cohort." In Sheldon L. Messinger, ed., *Aldine Criminal Justice Annual*. Chicago: Aldine, 1973.

PART V

Corrections, Rehabilitation, Resocialization

The Sentencing Process

During the 1970s great controversy arose in American judicial, criminological, and political circles over the nature and type of punishment meted out to offenders following adjudication of guilt. Among the controversial issues debated were determinate versus indeterminate sentences; disparities between different judges and jurisdictions; differential severity depending upon age, social class, employment, and race of offender and victim; discretionary powers given to judges, sometimes to juries, and to parole boards; and whether the concept of corrections—and, with it, rehabilitation—would better be abandoned in favor of the idea of retribution (giving the offender his "just deserts"). These arguments continue and go to the heart of the penological-correctional system and the philosophy behind it.

A defendant who reaches the sentencing stage in the criminal justice process has been found guilty of a crime or has pleaded guilty. In a few instances he has pleaded no contest (*nolo contendere*), a plea which gives the court the right to impose the same sentence as for a guilty plea, although there will be no record of the defendant as a convicted criminal and he may deny guilt in a further proceeding. If there has been a jury trial, the jury may make a recommendation on the sentence, sometimes in a separate deliberation after rendering of the verdict. More often, the input of the jury into the sentencing is limited to the charge or charges on which the jury has agreed to render a guilty verdict; for example, a jury can influence a sentence by finding the defendant guilty only of second degree manslaughter, although in the charge to the jury the judge may have given it a right to bring in a guilty verdict for

The Guilty Defendant before the Court

murder in the first degree. In many criminal cases, including serious felonies, the verdict is in fact rendered by a judge, without jury; thus the same individual who has found the defendant guilty is authorized to impose sentence.

The judge, having presided over the trial as a presumably impartial referee, must now decide what disposition to impose—frequently a difficult and complicated task. Faced perhaps with internal conflict between punitive and rehabilitative objectives (which are often basically contradictory), the judge may impose a compromise disposition that achieves neither. The choice may be influenced by subtle and not so subtle pressures from the police, prosecutor, victims and their families, and the general public, all of whom in the present era are increasingly demanding incarceration of offenders for long periods of time.

Ideally, in sentencing a convicted offender, the judge would be weighing two factors: (1) the possible future of the offender under the available alternatives, balanced against his own perceived responsibility to the local community, and (2) the effect of the sentence upon the society, insofar as it may deter or encourage others in the commission of crimes.

In pondering the first question, a judge would have to be able to predict the behavior of the offender, usually on the basis of little factual information and little knowledge of the effect of the prison environment or return to the community upon the convicted individual. In addition, current legal training seldom prepares a judge to understand the psychological and social components of the offender and his potential for rehabilitation. There is inherent difficulty in fitting abstract legal principles to the circumstances of the offense and the characteristics of the offender.

Whatever decision is reached, it will usually be made with one eye on the scales of justice and the other on a host of factors: the administrative ethos of efficiency in processing a huge number of cases, availability of prison space, the need to preserve favorable working relationships with police and prosecutor, public sentiment, and the forthcoming elections (in which most judges will try to retain a seat on the bench). Public sentiment, particularly in controversial cases, may lead a judge to make a severe—or, on rare occasions, lenient—disposition for fear of a loss of votes. In the sentencing process, most judges rely on a pre-sentence investigation report as well as their own experience, imagination, and intuition.

As for the effect of the sentence on others, it is hardly likely for a judge in a single case—except one that has attracted considerable publicity—to take serious account of this factor. And, from the viewpoint of justice, many would argue that a particular defendant should not be penalized more than others in similar situations in order to present him as an example to peers, friends, impressionable people, and the community.

THE PRE-SENTENCE REPORT

After conviction or a plea of guilty, and before imposition of a sentence, the trial judge usually orders an investigation of the offender's background. This investigation is carried out by a staff of probation officers or social workers. It has been estimated that the courts, in more than 85 percent of the states, prepare some kind of pre-sentence report on felony cases. There is, however, widespread variation in the comprehensiveness of the reports and in the extent to which they influence judges. Only about one-fourth of all states make such a pre-sentence report mandatory for felony offenses. It is generally felt, by both scholars and practitioners, that an adequately prepared and researched pre-sentence report can be a valuable asset in assisting a judge in sentencing a defendant. In the case of plea bargaining, such reports either are not prepared at all or, when mandatory, are ignored, as the nature of the sentence has already been agreed upon.

The pre-sentence investigation report and the information it contains can serve a variety of purposes in addition to aiding the court in arriving at a just and appropriate sentence. It can be used later to assist prison personnel in making decisions concerning the prisoner during incarceration; to aid in the use of those treatment facilities, meager as they may be, that may be available for the prisoner; to plan participation in work release or study release programs; to decide on eligibility for parole; and, finally, to place restrictions on the individual during the period of parole. When an offender is paroled, his parole officer can utilize the information in the pre-sentence report for purposes of assisting his reintegration into the community. If the offender is not incarcerated but placed on probation, the pre-sentence investigation report can also be useful to the probation officer. Finally, these reports contain a wealth of information useful for research into the nature and characteristics of convicted offenders. Nonetheless, in actual practice the reports are seldom put to such wide use, as crowded calendars, bureaucratic inefficiency, and political pressures and considerations are often overriding.

A pre-sentence investigation report may combine information from many sources and cover the following material: the present offense (including the offender's role in and attitudes toward it); his previous criminal history; his family circumstances and marital status, including tensions, discords, cohesion, and other factors affecting his well-being; conditions of the neighborhood and immediate environment; educational and school history (highest grade attained, regularity of attendance, and degrees); employment history, (including skills, work habits, stability as a worker); the types of friends and associates with whom he is known to mingle; such habits as drinking, drug use, sexual promiscuity, and gambling; mental and physical health and recommendations to the sentencing judge (Reckless, 1967). A well-prepared report would also contain subjective data, such as the offender's perspective on life (as sensed by the investigator), how he perceives personal problems and difficulties in which he becomes involved, and his attitudes toward the victim, the victim's family, and members of his own family. In the correctional or rehabilitative outlook on punishment, it has been felt that such data can give the judge meaningful insight into what has shaped the offender's past and into realistic possibilities for his future.

There has been considerable disagreement as to whether the defense attorney should have the right to review and challenge points in the pre-sentence investigation report, in order to correct possible errors and clarify ambiguous or misleading information. It appears that such a right was granted by the U.S. Supreme Court in Gardner v. Florida (1976), the full ramifications of which, however, are still to be worked out. It is not unknown in some states for defense attorneys to employ criminologists, social workers, or others for independent pre-sentence investigations of their clients. From the defendant's point of view, given the discretion in the hands of the judge, it is important that the information in any report to the judge be put in as favorable a light as possible; and if there is unfavorable information the accuracy of which the defendant would dispute, a report kept secret would deny access and be manifestly unjust. If the defendant disputes the facts, some jurisdictions permit him to present his own information; others may at least require that the person responsible for the report substantiate the disputed material. At the time of sentencing, both prosecution and defense can make statements in court with regard to the recommended sentence; the defense can present affidavits or oral arguments in favor of leniency, and sometimes counteract the more condemnatory material in the pre-sentence investigation report. The extent to which such activity is permitted is usually left to the discretion of the trial judge (United States v. Needles, 1973), but American courts have been moving in a direction against secret pre-sentence reports, since they might contain false and inflammatory information that could otherwise be counteracted by the defendant.

PRACTICAL PROBLEMS IN SENTENCING

Local, state, and federal correctional systems are limited in the number of offenders that can be incarcerated at any given time. Some facilities have become extremely overcrowded, housing many more inmates than they were built to accommodate; there are limits beyond which such overcrowding cannot go. Courts in fact may well take the current jail and prison population into account when the time for sentencing arrives; if the incarceration facilities are full, an alternative disposition may be selected in marginal cases, which might otherwise have resulted in imprisonment. This was especially apparent in Florida in 1972, when the state prison director refused to accept any more prisoners; courts then ordered that prisoners be diverted to other correctional facilities, and the state parole board began to release proportionately more prisoners during review periods. Sentencing, therefore, reflects not only the offense, information about the offender in the investigation report, and whatever other information may affect a judge, but also the occupancy rate in available penal institutions and the availability of local resources for handling offenders.

Other factors frequently have a strong impact on sentencing. On the one hand, there is the availability of alternatives and services that offer genuine or pretended rehabilitation without imprisonment. And, on the other, there is community sentiment. Political or journalistic pressures or public hysteria may prod a judge into committing the offender to prison; community sentiment translates into votes in an election year.

Dispositional Alternatives

The number and nature of dispositions available to the sentencing judge vary from state to state. Bound in part by legislative mandate, judges can usually make a choice involving either imprisonment (the term of which can vary) or release to the community under some conditions of supervision.

Among frequently used alternatives are fines (which can be suspended, but usually are not), probation, imposition of a jail or prison term and its suspension, actual sentencing to a determinate or indeterminate term in a local lockup or prison, and, in rare instances, death. There are numerous variations within these categories, such as a jail term to be served only on weekends in order to enable the person to continue on his job, or a term to be served with weekend furloughs, to permit the offender to spend time with his family. Some forms of punishment are obsolete in the United States at least on an official level, and, where practiced at all, the punishers do not have legal authority to inflict them: this is the case with corporal punishment. Other forms of punishment, such as banishment or exile, are limited in application to aliens, and then practiced only in the form of deportation.

PROBATION

Probation refers to a system under which an individual is released, generally without being sentenced to any imprisonment; he is placed in the community under the supervision of authorized personnel for a given period of time. The supervising person—the probation officer—may report to the courts further infractions committed by the offender.

Probation generally follows a trial at which the person has been found guilty, or a plea of guilty in lieu of an actual trial. However, probation may also replace the trial entirely, in which instance it is known as probation without adjudication. Actually, this term embraces two sets of programs. In one, the prosecutor, as part of his legal authority, has on his own deferred or terminated prosecution of the accused (Kaplan, 1973). If the prosecutor decides to grant deferred prosecution privileges, the accused may be asked to sign an agreement accepting moral (but not legal) responsibility for the criminal act, make restitution to the victim, actively participate in certain community programs (such as Alcoholics Anonymous or psychotherapy), periodically report to a designated person, and refrain from any further criminal behavior. If these conditions are successfully met, the prosecutor dismisses the charge; if not, the case may be carried forward to court and trial. Dismissal, in such an instance, would not constitute a trial, and hence it would be legally possible, although unlikely, that the person could be tried at some time in the future without violation of the constitutional protections against double jeopardy.

Probation without adjudication, in its other meaning, refers to a judge's alternative disposition wherever statutes provide a bifurcated process: that is, either determination of guilt through jury trial or guilty plea, or through judicial decree. In Florida, where this system is currently in effect, the statute allows the judge to declare the offender guilty while at the same time refraining from labeling him as a convicted felon. He places him on probation without requiring him to register with local law enforcement agencies as a previously convicted felon; without serving notice to prospective employers of a previous conviction; without preventing the offender from holding public office, voting, and serving on a jury; without impeding the offender from obtaining any license that requires "reputable character"; without making it more difficult for him than others to obtain firearms; in short, without public or even private degradation.

By withholding adjudication of guilt, the court gives the offender an opportunity to prove over a limited period of time his willingness and ability to reform and adjust. During this time, the offender knows it is still possible to be brought before the court for sentencing, possibly to a prison term. Both deferred prosecution and probation without adjudication are considerably less expensive to the state than incarceration, and are consistent with the philosophical assumptions of probation in general, combining treatment in the community with use of available resources.

Probation, following a guilty plea or conviction on a felony count or most misdemeanors, is a frequently used alternative to imprisonment. It permits the offender to remain within the community subject to good behavior, no involvement in further illegal behavior, and such other conditions as may be imposed by the court, such as restitution to victims or attending Alcoholics Anonymous. Still subject to the control of the court, the offender will usually be under the supervision and guidance of a probation officer. Probation not only prevents the further stigma of incarceration and its damaging effects, it also allows the offender to continue to work and support any dependents. However, in actual practice, in the larger American cities caseloads of probation officers are too large to permit careful supervision.

Another variation on the concept of probation has become known as "shock probation" or "shock imprisonment." In a strict sense it is not part of a probation system, as it does involve incarceration. As of the end of the 1970s, it was available as an alternative court disposition in Idaho, Indiana, Kentucky, Maine, North Carolina, Ohio, and Texas. It allows the sentencing judge to impose the legal sentence and order incarceration of the offender, only to recall him after a brief, legislatively defined period of imprisonment (in Ohio, a maximum of 130 days). The system derives its name from the shock effects of short-term incarceration, believed to be sufficient to convince certain individuals who have never before been imprisoned that further criminal behavior is too risky and likely to be met with severe punishment. The offender presumably does not know that his term will be shortened, and part of the shock is that he anticipates a long period in prison until the sudden release (Petersen and Friday, 1975).

Something similar to shock probation is found in the federal courts, and is known as "split sentencing." Here the offender is actually sentenced to a term in prison, but is notified in advance that, after a given brief period of satisfactory behavior, he can serve the remainder of his sentence on probation.

Shock probation and split sentencing are closely related to parole (a system widely practiced in the United States, whereby a prisoner is released after a portion of his term has been served—a minimum, which is often one-third of the full term—and is placed under supervision and surveillance for a period following release). With each there is some imprisonment, although traditionally probation has referred to supervision in lieu of and without incarceration, whereas parole involves a period of supervision following incarceration. However, the brevity of the period actually served in prison—often less than the minimum required and, as in shock probation, less than anticipated by the offender—and the fact that the power to release on probation remains with the sentencing judge and not a review board, combine to make shock probation and split sentencing part of a probationary rather than a parole system.

The impact, beneficial or detrimental, of shock probation and split sentencing continues to be debated. David Petersen and Paul Friday (1973) reviewed the results of split sentencing in Sweden, Denmark, and Poland, but found no conclusive evidence that would favor or oppose this practice. Their initial evaluation of the Ohio experience with shock probation revealed an 85 percent success rate. Other prison success rates with similar programs appear to range from 30 to 60 percent.

FINES

A fine is a penalty imposed upon an offender by the judge, either in place of or in addition to a term in prison, in which a stipulated sum of money must be paid to the court. It has been widely used in minor cases as well as major white-collar offenses. With some white-collar crimes, the fine is combined with a prison term, and the latter may or may not be suspended (see below). Even in the case of a victim deprived of money or property, such as a bank from which an executive has embezzled funds, the fine cannot be turned over as restitution; on the contrary, it belongs to the government.

A sentence is sometimes handed down in the form of a choice between a fine or a period of incarceration; for example, a twenty-five dollar fine or ten days in the local lockup. This system has been challenged on the grounds that it penalizes the poor and turns jailing into a matter of incarcerating debtors rather than offenders. In some instances, as in a union-management dispute, persons adjudicated guilty may refuse to pay the fine as a matter of principle, and compel jailing in order to dramatize a cause and embarrass opponents.

Some European countries, particularly Sweden, have instituted variable fines based on the earnings of the offender. In such a case, a fine may consist of a person's wages (or other earnings or income) for one day, two days, or a week. Although this reduces the discrepancy in treatment between people of different income levels before the court, it still does not eliminate it completely, for the poor suffer more from the loss of the income of one day or week than do the rich.

SUSPENDED SENTENCES

A judge may impose a sentence, whether a fine or imprisonment, and thereupon suspend it. If the offender is found guilty of another offense in the future, the suspension of this sentence can be voided and the individual required to pay the original penalty (of time to be served or a fine, as the case may be). In some instances, the judge may suspend only part of a sentence: this is often done if there is both a fine and a prison term—the latter is suspended, but not the former.

IMPRISONMENT

Imprisonment may take place before and during trial (for lack of bail or when no bail is permitted) and after trial as part of the sentence. In the latter instance, time served awaiting trial, during it, or awaiting sentence is recorded as part of total time served, and counts toward the minimum required in order to be eligible for release.

There are several types of detention facilities, or what have come to be known euphemistically as correctional centers or correctional facilities. These include jails, workhouses, and federal and state prisons.

Jails are places for short-term detention, administered on the local level, usually by a sheriff or other local corrections commissioner. Most of them are small and frequently overcrowded, have few if any facilities for recreation or even exercise, and are not managed by trained personnel. They house together convicted persons awaiting sentence, those sentenced to relatively short terms (usually less than a year) that will not be served in a state penitentiary, and those awaiting trial (Goldfarb, 1975). According to the latest available data there were 3,921 jails in the United States in 1972, at that time housing approximately 140,000 inmates on any given day. About three-quarters of these jails accommodated twenty or fewer inmates. This figure does not include juvenile detention centers, "drunk-tanks," and state-operated local lockups such as are found in Connecticut, Delaware, Rhode Island, and Vermont (United States Department of Justice, 1975).

Workhouses are local facilities, frequently under a municipal jurisdiction, housing convicted misdemeanants serving relatively brief sentences. Although the workhouse was originally a place where "ne'er-do-wells," alcoholics, and marginal persons were supposed to be put to constructive employment, in contemporary America few workhouse residents perform any meaningful work and almost no one is paid. The criticisms frequently leveled at jails are also believed to apply to workhouses, although seldom are accused defendants held in these facilities prior to trial. In contrast to prisons (long-term facilities that hold those found guilty of more serious crimes), relatively little research has been done on American workhouses or their populations.

Prisons are correctional facilities for longer-term incarceration, primarily of felony offenders, administered by either the state or federal government. In January 1977 there were approximately 600 state prisons in the United States, under separate administrations (sometimes a single administration has more than one prison under its jurisdiction). These housed approximately 290,000 inmates, a figure that has since been inching upward. At the same time there were some 31,000 inmates in the federal system, although the official maximum capacity of its facilities had been reported a few years earlier as some five to ten thousand fewer than that figure (U.S. Department of Justice, 1975).

In general, contemporary American prisons are characterized by outdated and overcrowded facilities, inadequate and untrained staff, lack of sufficient fiscal support, and widespread inmate idleness, as well as, in some cases, inmates serving the longest sentences in the Western world (Allen and Simonsen, 1978). Further, particularly in the state systems, prison administrators seldom have any long-range planning programs; their overriding emphasis is on the custodial rather than rehabilitative function of the institution.

There are three types of sentences that are imposed upon defendants who have been found guilty, or have pleaded guilty, and who are to be incarcerated: the definite, the indeterminate, and the indefinite sentence. However, a judge may not have a choice among the three, as he may be circumscribed by legislative mandate. In addition, the maximum sentence that may be imposed is set by the state legislatures, and differs depending on the crime. Finally, the judge has a choice, where there is guilt on multiple counts, between consecutive and concurrent prison terms.

In a definite sentence, the judge imposes the precise sentence as established by law for a specific crime. If the judge has no discretion in the matter, the sentence is said to be a mandatory one. In all likelihood this entire sentence will not be served, as there is time deducted therefrom for "good behavior," usually one-third of the imposed term. This time off is itself mandatory, and can be avoided by prison authorities only if the convict has been found guilty of a serious additional crime during the period of incarceration. Other than the good-behavior reduction, the term can be shortened only by successful appeal, pardon, or executive clemency.

THE DEFINITE SENTENCE

Definite and mandatory sentencing (also known as "flat sentencing") went out of favor in the United States during the first half of the twentieth century, when there was a strong orientation toward rehabilitation. It was widely urged that greater discretion be given to the judge, that aggravating or mitigating circumstances should be taken into account, and that a sentence that is not definite would give motivation to the inmate to work toward earlier release by exemplary behavior and a turn toward reform. When mandatory sentences were long and harsh in relationship to the crime committed, often juries were reluctant to convict and judges preferred no punishment to the harsh alternative.

The indeterminate sentence removes length of sentence from jurisdiction of the court, passing the authority to a parole board of several members, who are ideally supposed to be experienced students of human behavior and of rehabilitation. The assumptions are made that the judge cannot predict the optimal time needed for rehabilitation when he is called upon to pass sentence; that rehabilitation of offenders is possible, perhaps through participation in treatment programs available within institutions; and that parole personnel will be able to detect offender rehabilitation. The pronounced sentence is set by law so that it may not go beyond certain limits; in fact it has been known to be as indeterminate as "one day to life." The parole board has the right to order release at any time. What this amounts to in practice is passing the right to impose sentence from the judge to the parole board.

THE INDETERMINATE SENTENCE

Critics of the indeterminate sentence argue that it is impossible for anyone to make an accurate prediction of a person's readiness for release. But by far the most critical argument concerns the administrative abuses of discretionary power by the parole board or releasing authority. It was found, for example, that when California shifted from a definite to indeterminate sentencing pattern, the average period of incarceration jumped from twenty-four to thirty-six months. When questioned about this finding, the California Adult Authority argued that offenders had become increasingly less mature, increasingly needy of longer-term psychiatric treatment, and more hostile and thus more likely to become aggressive upon release. A legislative research group found upon study, however, that there were no significant differences between the types of inmates committed before and after the sentencing changes occurred (Howard, 1979). When California shifted back to determinate sentencing, there was a sharp rise in prison commitments.

Some critics argue that the assumed treatment programs are nonexistent, that the atmosphere of prisons is not conducive to rehabilitation, that inmates change for the worse in prison, and that custody requirements outweigh treatment programs and their impact. Inmates themselves condemn the system for its capriciousness, lack of coherence, and irrationality and for the psychological problems that it creates for them. It has built into it inherent difficulties for achieving impartiality insofar as race and ethnicity are concerned, and favors those inmates who have been psychologically "broken" by the system, who have become sycophantic and have lost their sense of mastery over their own lives. Finally, convicts tend to develop techniques for dissimulation, and the system favors those who are most adept at such procedures. (For an excellent group of articles on the controversy over the indeterminate sentence, see Special Conference on Determinate Sentencing, 1978.)

THE INDEFINITE SENTENCE

The indefinite sentence can be seen as a compromise between the definite and the indeterminate sentence. Here, the state legislature has established a range of years within which the judge can affix the sentence. If, for example, the legislature has established a three-year minimum and a fifteen-year maximum (known as "three-to-fifteen") for armed robbery, the sentencing judge has discretion to make a definite sentence so long as it falls within the established range, or an indefinite sentence in which the minimum and the maximum fall within the range. That is to say, a definite sentence could be five years, or eight, or even fifteen; an indefinite sentence could be as wide as three-to-fifteen, or relatively narrow, such as three-to-five, five-to-eight, or ten-to-fifteen.

CONSECUTIVE AND CONCURRENT SENTENCES

A further important element in sentencing is the authority of the judge to impose consecutive or concurrent sentences when more than one offense is involved. If an offender is found guilty of two separate acts of breaking and entering, for example, the judge may opt for consecutive sentences, such as three years for each offense, giving a total of six, or for two concurrent sentences of three years each, for a total of three. Under consecutive sentencing the complete sentence for the first offense (except for mandatory time off for good behavior) must be met before the offender begins serving time for the second offense. While the specter of consecutive sentences is used by prosecutors in plea bargaining to hold over the head of the defendant the possibility of extremely long imprisonment, in actual fact most multiple sentences are served concurrently.

Consecutive sentencing is generally considered a punitive act on the part of a judge, invoked perhaps because of an offender's refusal to negotiate a plea. In some instances it is designed to appease the public, as in a case that has attracted attention and caused an outcry from politicians, press, and others to "throw away the keys." Thus one will occasionally read of a judge sentencing a defendant to several consecutive prison terms, amounting to a total of several hundred years, in which he will not be eligible for parole, it is emphasized, for seventy-five or a hundred years or more.

Sentencing Power and Discretion

Who should impose a sentence? Who should make the decision as to its type, severity, and conditions? Where sentences are definite, the legislature has limited the judge's discretionary power, although he can still decide on probation or suspended sentence in place of incarceration. However, some definite sentences also have ranges, as illustrated above, and within the range the judge may have considerable power.

In instances of capital punishment, power is often limited. In eighteenth-century England there were 222 offenses punishable by death; once found guilty, the offender could not escape the death penalty through the discretion of the judge, although the latter could accompany the death sentence with a recommendation of mercy, often resulting in commutation by the king. In the United States the question of mandatory death sentence has often been at issue, in a debate that has reached the Supreme Court on several occasions.

In some cases the jury may act as the sentencing body, although generally the judge is not bound by the jury's recommendations (Williams v. New York, 1949). However, the President's Commission on Law Enforcement and Administration of Justice (1967b) has argued against sentencing by juries, contending that sentencing requires the advice of behavior experts and that juries are ill-fitted for this task. Further, the commission has argued that juries might confuse their sentencing role with their adjudication role, leading for instance to a light sentence for a given crime not because of mitigating circumstances but because of reasonable doubt as to the defendant's guilt, with this doubt being resolved not by a verdict of not guilty, as required by Anglo-American law, but by the compromise of offering a light sentence. That juries also do this through another mechanism, however, is widely suspected: namely, by reaching a verdict of guilt on a lesser charge.

Other critics point out that much of the information that judges use in sentencing, such as the pre-sentence report, could be regarded as hearsay or inadmissible in the jury deliberation process. To bifurcate the jury's guilt-determination phase from its sentencing stage, having it deliberate twice, is cumbersome, but has been tried in some jurisdictions, particularly for major felonies.

Thus the sentencing judge is the most frequent authority for determining the appropriate punishment for a given offense. As the prison system has developed in the United States, administrative forms of sentence-shortening have become common, such as "good time" (or time off for good behavior), pardon, parole, and clemency. Thus, any correlation between a judge's sentence and the time an offender will actually serve has all but disappeared. In practice, while the court may establish the minimum and maximum periods of incarceration in a given case, in accordance with legislative statutes, the actual length of time served is now determined by administrators or parole boards within the correctional system, which means by the executive rather than the judicial or legislative branch of government.

Disparity in Sentencing

How should the judge arrive at a proper sentence for an offender? The present method—sometimes caustically referred to as the "hunch system" (Barnes and Teeters, 1959)—can lead to severe disparities in sentencing even by the same judge for the same offense. Figure 20–1, for example, represents the sentencing pattern for thirteen judges in one municipal court. They were meting out sentences for first-degree misdemeanors, for which the statutes allow a fine, incarceration, or a combination thereof. The disparity in sentencing here cannot be explained by the type of case brought before any particular judge, as the municipal court in which the study was made follows a random case assignment policy for judges. This particular system does not permit a practice widespread in many other courts, in

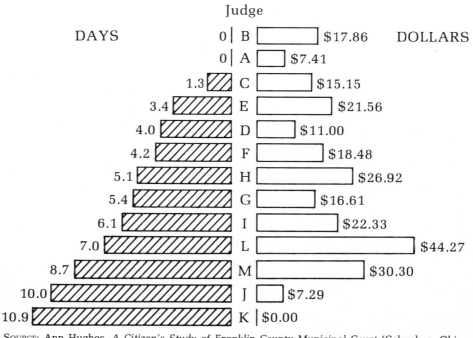

**FIGURE 20–1
Variation in the Use of
Days and Fines by
Judge (average days
and fines combined
for all first degree
misdemeanors)**

SOURCE: Ann Hughes, *A Citizen's Study of Franklin County Municipal Court* (Columbus, Ohio: Academy for Contemporary Problems, 1976), p. 14.

which attorneys—usually for the defense but occasionally for the prosecution—seek postponements until the case comes before a judge deemed friendly or favorable (a practice known as "judge shopping").

The problem of reducing disparity in sentencing has held the attention of judicial authorities and criminologists for many years. To some extent it is related to a defendant's legal representation. The Supreme Court, in a number of decisions has firmly established the right of a defendant to counsel at any critical stage in a criminal proceeding (not merely at the trial itself). Mempa v. Rhay (1967) extended the right of a defendant to counsel in a probation revocation hearing, in this way offering some protection against capricious and arbitrary decisions of the court. Morrisey v. Brewer (1972) did the same for parole revocation hearings.

**REDUCTION OF
DISPARITY**

Appellate courts have the authority to reverse or modify a judge's sentencing decision, but in fact this is seldom done. The appellate court generally takes the position that sentencing is the prerogative of the trial judge, who has observed the offender throughout the trial, heard the evidence in the case, examined the pre-sentence investigation report, and noted the offender's attitude and demeanor (Hagan, 1975). But occasionally the apellate court will find that a trial judge has abused the limits of discretion and will remand the case for a proper sentence (United States v. Wiley, 1960), in which instance it is returned to the original trial judge for a new sentence within new guidelines. This is not to be confused with the much more frequent action of an appellate court in ordering a new trial.

Even denial of a request for probation can be appealed to a federal court when there is an issue of abuse of discretion by the sentencing judge (People v. Andrew, 1968).

At one time, the federal courts were guided by a "hands off" policy toward corrections. The cases cited above are examples that illustrate the erosion, if not the complete abandonment, of this policy. Concern over sentence disparity has now led to the establishment of judicial training conferences, sentencing institutes, and sentencing panels.

**SENTENCING
PANELS AND
INSTITUTES**

In the judicial training conference, newly elected or appointed judges are brought together for a period of pre- or in-service training in sentencing, with special attention given to justice, equality, and individualization. Sample cases are examined in which the judges are asked to indicate their proposed sentences; the reasons for any disparities found are subjected to vigorous analysis and discussion. It is hoped that such conferences will develop a consensus on sentencing policies and practices, and that the judges involved will begin to comprehend the need for similarity and consistency.

Sentencing institutes usually involve a council meeting of judges from a multi-judge court to discuss pending cases and sentencing philosophies and practices. There are also periodic sentencing institutes that bring together judges from diverse court levels and jurisdictions to explore problems in sentencing, look into appellate reviews, and establish policies and guidelines for reducing inequality.

The sentencing panel is usually a group of three judges who discuss the cases for which sentences are to be passed and issue a joint decision as to the appropriate disposition and length of sentence. It is intended that the members of the panel act as influences upon one another. A sentence that one judge might have made extraordinarily lenient, for an arbitrary or capricious reason, may be modified when other judges are present. And judges who can share with one another the public spotlight for resisting political pressure or the urgings of an aroused citizenry, directed toward an extremely harsh sentence, are likely to use the panel for a reduction of disparity.

Recommendations

There have been many recommendations regarding appropriate guidelines for sentencing. The following were put forth by the National Conference on Corrections, Williamsburg, Virginia (1971) and appear to summarize the thinking of many authorities and scholars:

1. It should be mandatory that trial judges have pre-sentence reports in all felony cases. These reports should be prepared by qualified probation or corrections officers.
2. Diagnostic sentencing should be made available to all judges.
3. Indeterminate sentencing should be available to judges in all felony cases.
4. Jury sentencing should be abolished.
5. Sentencing judges should be required to record the reasons for each sentence. These reasons are to be made known to the defendant, with copies to the corrections personnel involved and to the appellate courts in those instances in which the sentences are appealed.
6. The corrections system should provide for appellate review.
7. Sentencing judges should educate their communities on the philosophy of sentencing.
8. Defense counsel and the prosecutor should be consulted by the judge before imposing sentence.
9. Probation officers and judges should receive instructions in sentencing, perhaps attend sentencing institutes.
10. Trial judges should be elected or appointed in as nonpolitical a way as possible.

Some of these recommendations are vague and some utopian, and their likelihood of being put into effect is minuscule (e.g., the second, seventh, and tenth). At least one (the third) has fallen into wide disfavor since 1971. For the most part, however, the Williamsburg conference articulated guidelines that are practical and should work toward justice and equality in sentencing. The same theme pervades the influential Report of the Committee for the Study of Incarceration (von Hirsch, 1976).

Although sentencing the convicted felon remains the task of the judiciary, much of the judge's power to implement sentencing decisions has been eroded by administrative procedures in corrections. The jurist is torn between trying to retain this sentencing power and letting it pass to some form of expert sentencing tribunal. In addition to harboring the understandable desire to protect their domain, judges tend to distrust behavioral scientists with their allegedly "easy solutions to real problems" and see them as a threat to the power and structure of the law. Many committees and commissions of various types have discussed the dilemma of the sentencing process, but the basic burden still remains with the trial judge.

Whatever responsibility lies with the judge, the limits of sentencing have been set by the legislature, the verdict often by a jury, and both verdict and sentence often by the deal between the two sides in the bargaining process. Beyond that, society itself has a vision or philosophy of punishment—perhaps conflicting philosophies—and numerous methods and mechanisms, some age-old and others recent innovations, designed to frighten, incapacitate, deter, cure, or in other ways handle offenders and diminish the likelihood of further offenses.

Responsibility and the Trial Judge

Punishment and Corrections: Meanings, Purpose, Methods

At the heart of all attempts to handle offenders are systematic images of human life and culture, including knowledge, beliefs, and attitudes regarding the human condition and the meanings, purposes, and ethical foundation and rationale of punishment. These ideologies or philosophical approaches provide explanations for the past behavior of the offender, guidelines as to what ought to be done with or to him, and bases for predicting his future after return to the free world.

On Criminal Punishment

"Punishment," writes Herbert Packer (1968: 35), "is a concept; criminal punishment is a legal fact." It is criminal punishment that is meant when the term "punishment" is used in criminology, criminal justice, and criminal law. Packer sets up five criteria, all of which must be fulfilled in order that criminal punishment occur: it must be (1) imposed on an actual or supposed offender, (2) meted out for an offense against legal rules, (3) imposed by an authority constituted by the legal system against which the offense was committed, (4) intentionally administered by human beings other than the offender, and (5) inflict pain or other consequences normally considered unpleasant.

It can easily be seen that, under this definition, severe spanking of a child by parents would not be criminal punishment, nor would action of a vigilante mob, retaliation of a victim, imposition of a high sales tax on cigarettes, enforced isolation of someone with a contagious disease, refusal to allow entry into the country of a member of some foreign Communist Party, or requiring that a driver pay damages to someone he has injured in a traffic accident. On the other hand, the definition is broad enough to include jailing someone during pretrial detention, or compelling him to pay bail money in order to be free pending trial; in both cases he is suffering at the hands of the authorities for being a supposed or suspected offender, although eventually he may be entirely exonerated.

The terms "punishment," "penology," and particularly "punitive" have gone out of fashion, replaced by the word "corrections." The latter embodies the idea that an offender becomes chastised, chastened, rehabilitated, and hence corrected, and that punishment for its own sake, as an imposition of suffering without a correcting function, should be abjured. This turn of terminology away from things punitive has in fact a long history, particularly in the United States, where prisons were established for the express purpose of being houses of penitence and hence were called penitentiaries, and where people have been confined for the purpose of being rehabilitated or reformed and hence have been kept in places called reformatories.

Language of course can conceal meanings, but in so doing it reveals the "up front" part of a society, the supposed and pretended if not actual and dominant cultural themes.

FORMS OF PUNISHMENT

Criminal punishment has taken on many forms down through the ages, some now considered cruel and inhuman—although still practiced in many parts of the world—and others having become outmoded for a variety of reasons. A complete catalogue of mankind's mechanisms of punishment would illustrate the ingenuity and creativity of the human mind in repeatedly proving that Robert Burns was understating the miseries of social reality when he wrote that

Man's inhumanity to man
Makes countless thousands mourn.

Most forms of punishment can be placed into one of the following categories:

1. *Capital punishment* refers to the authorized execution of a convicted felon. Once widely used for hundreds of crimes and conducted in public to serve as an example to the gazing onlookers and those who might hear of the event, capital punishment has fallen into disfavor in the United States and Western Europe, although some public sentiment for its revival appears to have come forward with the recent increase in violence and crime. In America, capital punishment during the twentieth century has been almost completely limited to offenders convicted of murder, forcible rape, and certain wartime activities such as treason. Methods of execution in use in the United States have included the gallows, the electric chair, the firing squad, and the gas chamber (injection of lethal doses of drugs is under study as this book goes to press). In other countries and at different times many other

373

methods have been devised, including burning at the stake, being fed alive to lions and other animals, walking the gangplank (after a trial at sea), and, finally, in the most famous execution in history, nailing to a cross.

2. *Corporal punishment* includes all forms of bodily pain inflicted on an offender by official decree. Hence, psychological and physical torture to obtain confession or injure a suspect or convict for reasons of revenge, persecution, racism, or political enmity—even when conducted by the authorities —would be excluded. Corporal punishment in the past has included the wheel and the rack, often resulting in slow death by exceptionally cruel means. In the United States whipping, sometimes in public and with a stated number of lashes, was an official sentence in some jurisdictions until well into the twentieth century. When it has been used, corporal punishment has sometimes been accompanied by fine or imprisonment, but in the United States this has usually not been the case.

3. *Transportation* refers to a particular form of banishment in which an offender is compelled to move to a colony, a desolate outpost in his own country, or elsewhere. This forced movement was at one time widely practiced by England, with felons being transported to its colonies in Virginia, Georgia, Australia, and elsewhere; by France, which gained notoriety for Devil's Island, its penal colony of transported felons in South America (actually, more a huge concentration camp and prison labor camp than a colony); and by Tsarist Russia, which transported many felons to Siberia (a system of internal exile, one might say). Transportation could be for life or a limited period, and in many instances the family could accompany the felon. Transported convicts played a major role in the development of Australia. With the decline of the colonial system, transportation has recently been little used, although a form of it—internal exile—appears to survive in the Soviet Union.

4. *Excommunication* is the practice of making an individual a complete pariah, so that no one should have any contact with him. In a country where all residents obey the order to avoid relationships, excommunication amounts to a virtual sentence of death. It disappeared as official criminal punishment when theocracies were replaced by secular states. It is still practiced on rare occasions by some orthodox religious orders, but then falls into the category of informal or unofficial rather than criminal punishment.

5. *Exile* or banishment is the act of compelling a person to leave the country in which he resides and of which, usually, he is a citizen. It has fallen into disuse except for political crimes, which generally mean that a new regime has come into power and those associated with the old regime have been sent or permitted to go into exile. Exile is of course dependent upon the offender's finding asylum or haven elsewhere.

6. *Deportation* as a form of punishment, either in lieu of imprisonment or following it, is limited to aliens, who may be returned to their country of origin or of current citizenship.

7. *Slavery*, now almost entirely extinct as an official punishment for crime, was once a widely used form (see Thorsten Sellin, 1976, for a tracing

of its history). The lines of demarcation between slavery and chain gangs, work camps, involuntary labor in prison, and other forms of involuntary work are not always well drawn, and prison work camps in many parts of the world have been called slave camps by political opponents of the regime in which the camps are found.

8. *Permanent physical injury* is a special form of corporal punishment in which a part of the body, often the "offending part," is removed. Thus, the hand of a thief is amputated and a rapist is castrated. In the United States, no such type of injury is legally permitted.

9. *Confinement* or *imprisonment* is now the most widely used punishment inflicted on serious offenders. In past centuries in Europe a small number of prominent offenders were imprisoned in dungeons, towers, and sometimes castles. This amounted to a form of long-range or even permanent internal banishment, employed primarily against political enemies. For larger numbers of convicts, prisons were mainly temporary houses of detention as they awaited execution or transportation. Imprisonment for a definite or indefinite period of time came into its own as the major punishment for a crime in the nineteenth century, with the United States leading the way.

10. *Fines* constitute sums of money to be paid by an offender to the state (specifically not to the victims) and are imposed either in lieu of or in addition to a prison sentence.

11. *Supervision* of an involuntary nature, in lieu of imprisonment (as in probation) or as the result of shortening of a prison sentence (as in parole), has been widely used in the United States. It is part of the concept of community corrections.

12. *Enforced therapy*, usually of a psychiatric nature, is sometimes imposed upon an offender. This can involve confinement in a psychiatric institution, or it can be a substitute for such confinement (see Kittrie, 1971, and Szasz, 1965, for discussion of this controversial subject).

Miscellaneous punishments can be imposed that do not fall under any of these headings. Mothers, for example, have not infrequently lost custody of their children upon conviction of a crime, particularly a sexual offense.

PURPOSES OF PUNISHMENT

It is difficult to imagine a world without a system of criminal punishment. But just what the purpose of punishment may be is sometimes strongly debated. In a long-range, broad sense, punishment, it is hoped, will diminish crime. Beccaria and the English utilitarians such as Bentham thought that this could be brought about by making the anticipated punishment for a criminal act sufficiently severe, and the possibility of being apprehended sufficiently certain, that a person would weigh the probable pain of punishment against the latter. This is based on the image of a rational and calculating human and is called the hedonistic calculus (also known as the felicitic or felicific calculus). Later, the positivists held to a more deterministic view, seeing human beings as having relatively little free will but punishment as necessary insofar as it removes some people from society and in order that the threat of such removal be added to the many environmental forces determining whether people will go in the direction of criminality. Still later, rehabilitation became the ideal, and certain forms of punishment were looked upon as methods of correcting someone who was flawed but not beyond salvage—a soul gone astray.

The purposes of punishment, like the forms and mechanisms, are many, and sometimes more than one is embraced at the same time by a society or a given social thinker. Among them, the following are prominent:

1. *Revenge*, or the idea that society has a right to vent its wrath upon those who have committed heinous acts, is abjured by most modern thinkers as inconsistent with the values of civilized societies, but nonetheless appears to appeal to many people during periods of violent crime.

2. *Retribution* is often confused with revenge, but there are distinct differences. Retribution embodies the concept that an offender should receive what he rightfully deserves (known as "just deserts"), and that society is "made whole" when a criminal has "paid his debt" to it.

3. *Incapacitation* consists of the removal of the offender from society (by execution or confinement), or taking such other measures as to make commission of the crime impossible (amputation, castration, or some other physical injury).

4. *Deterrence* is based on the idea that punishment of an individual offender will deter him from committing the same or other offenses in the future (specific deterrence) and will convince others that "crime does not pay" (general deterrence).

5. *Correction* is a concept that rejects punishment for its own sake and for what it may do in dissuading people from committing crime. It looks upon the task of the government as being to rehabilitate, reform, treat, cure, or correct the law-breaker, changing him into a law-abiding citizen or resident of the country.

There are various philosophical ideologies and underpinnings that are at the basis of the reaction to crime and to the offender. These may not be mutually exclusive, although one or another is usually dominant in an era, in a country, or among groups of criminologists.

The Ideology of Punishment

The punitive ideology accepts the concept of punishment for its own sake: the criminal is a danger to society, he has willfully violated the law, and punishment is both deserved and necessary for the protection of society.

While the ideology of punishment calls for revenge or retribution, it does not neglect deterrence. In order for punishment to serve as a deterrent, professionals who are punitively oriented maintain that it must be visible to potential perpetrators, swift and certain, so closely linked to the crime that it is perceived as punishment for its perpetration, and categorical (i.e., applied so that all persons committing a certain crime receive approximately equal punitive treatment). In addition, the state and its representatives must uphold superior values and behave as ideal examples of good citizenship. If punishment is in the form of a prison term, ideally at its expiration the offender is allowed to resume his previous station in life, free of stigma and further disability.

It can be argued that there are five categories of people, whose probabilities of committing crime are quite diverse. (Figure 21-1 indicates these categories, in order of increasing probability for criminal behavior.)

1. *Gyroscopic nonoffenders* are so tightly enmeshed in the social fabric of group and society, so committed to noncriminal behavior, and so dedicated to the moral order, that almost under no circumstances would they even consider a criminal act, much less perpetrate one. How large this group is in modern, secular, competitive societies is debatable. Some contend that considerable proportions of the population commit at least one serious offense during a lifetime.

2. *Favorable-conditions offenders* are those who, under extreme stress and family or personal need, might consider perpetrating a crime if the situation is favorable (i.e., having a low chance of being discovered or caught and a high probability that the crime would constitute an immediate answer to a one-time need). This is a category of persons generally believed to be easily deterred, although little is known as to who these people are, how to identify them, and what proportion of the total population they represent.

3. *Potential violators* could be characterized as marginal persons who occasionally perpetrate property crimes but draw their main livelihood from basically legitimate enterprises. Their potential for criminal violation theoretically contracts or expands in response to societal economic cycles, perceived presence of police, availability of victims, and perception of risk of detection.

4. *Undetected offenders* can be characterized as persons whose primary source of livelihood is predatory criminal behavior. They appear to be

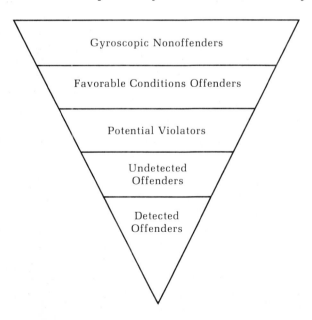

Gyroscopic Nonoffenders

Favorable Conditions Offenders

Potential Violators

Undetected Offenders

Detected Offenders

**FIGURE 21-1
Categories of Criminal Offenders**

little deterred by police presence, patrol practice, length of judicial sentence, or efforts of victims to protect themselves. When police and community activity becomes sufficiently well organized to pose a problem for them, these offenders simply shift to a different neighborhood or district where they can conduct business as usual.

5. *Detected offenders* could be conceived of as inept property violators or persons perpetrating crimes whose violence and enormity make them likely targets for arrest and prosecution.

Only the last two categories are likely to be deterred by the prospect of punishment, but these are not the groups from which the overwhelming majority of criminal offenders are believed to be drawn, although they probably account for a great many of the most serious offenses.

PUNISHMENT AND SOCIAL CONTROL

The early criminologists failed to understand that uniform punishment is not as effective as specialized and selective punishment. This may have been largely responsible for the failure of prisons, based as they were upon the ideology of punishment, to fulfill their missions of deterrence or rehabilitation. In fact, excessive punishment has little deterrent effect. When punishment continues after compliance is achieved, many offenders react negatively. For example, after a prisoner has served his term in prison he must bear the stigma of being an "ex-con" until his death. Finding it almost impossible to get a job because of his criminal record, the ex-offender may decide, "If I'm going to bear the name, I might as well play the game." At that point, neither the prospect of further punishment nor the presence of stigma will deter and the offender is likely to repeat his offenses or, in the language of criminology, to recidivate.

There is some agreement that punishment can be effective if applied in the right amount at the right time. When this ideology is widely practiced in an institutional setting, however, the result is generally negative for both the keeper and the kept. Correctional personnel are usually alert for infractions of minor rules and lack of cooperation by offenders, so they can mete out punishment and tend to overlook the positive behavior of convicts. In prisons the rules—although seldom explicitly stated—are designed to surround the offender with such restrictions as to limit his ability to do anything individual or creative and to ensure that the institution operate smoothly even if it means that rehabilitation is kept to a minimum.

If increasing crime rates are used as indicators, punishment does not appear to be a strong deterrent. Even in those jurisdictions where punishment is relatively swift, certain, and harsh, crimes are on the increase. The overuse of punishment in a social order that purports to be free and open creates a paradoxical situation in which the punished may perceive their punishers as their persecutors—and usually persecutors of the poor, the disadvantaged, and the helpless—thus diverting attention from their own crimes. Minority group members may blame their incarceration on repression by the rich and powerful, on deliberate genocide, on political persecution, or on other forms of injustice toward their group. To compensate for the ineffectiveness of punishment, social control agencies may increase its severity. One consequence of such a reaction may be to stimulate an offender to adopt more sophisticated criminal behavior in the belief that the more skilled are the less likely to be caught. Offenders can become inured to punishment even as administrators increase its severity. Some contend that both sides are degraded in the process.

It appears that no matter how harsh and swift the punitive response, nor even how certain, punishment does not eradicate crime, although it may inhibit and reduce it. Even in highly punitive societies, crime has never been eradicated. No one would deny, however, that in a punishment-oriented society—as all modern societies are and in which the population has been socialized—the abolition of punishment without substitution of a philosophy and outlook based on ethics and shared social values, inculcated into people from the time of early infancy, would result in a tremendous increase in crime. Societies are thus locked into their punishment orientations, although certainly some adjustments are possible.

FROM PUNITIVE IDEOLOGY TO PUNITIVE PROCEDURE

Writing of the function of crime in society, Emile Durkheim (1947) stated that the group must retaliate against offenders in order that all other members of society be reinforced in law-abiding behavior. However, the punishment of offenders turns into the victimization of offenders (a process which the latter have initiated). This victimization is intended to assure social cohesion and conformity to norms.

The behavior of those so punished is frequently unaltered by this treatment, although this fact would not negate the utilization of punishment as a deterrent for others. However, the general public appears to have almost complete faith in punitiveness as the principal vehicle of social control, a faith fed by politicians, the mass media, and the reality of widespread crime. Even if severe punishment is not effective as a deterrent, it appears to gratify the thirst for revenge present in many people, particularly after a highly publicized and very heinous crime.

Elmer Johnson (1964) has argued that punishment is the least effective social control technique to reduce crime: it is hopeless to attempt to construct a sliding scale of appropriate punishments for crimes that range from petty larceny to murder. However, Marvin Wolfgang (1980) has been tapping public attitudes toward crime and finding, among other things, that the public is far more severe in its judgment of white-collar offenders than most criminologists (or other people) had been led to believe. On the other hand, in some instances punishment made particularly severe as a deterrent brings the public to identify with and become sympathetic to the offender.

The imprisoned offender has obviously not been deterred by the specter of punishment. But will punishment serve to restore him eventually to a way of life in which his conflict with society will diminish or disappear? It is through the eyes of the punished offender that the punitive ideology should be viewed. If a felon regards the punishment that he has received as the imposition of the will and power of an unjust establishment, and if this perception is reinforced by his fellow offenders or peer group, punishment will not encourage him to accept a crime-free life. Alternatively, if the offender and his peers perceive the punishment to be both deserved and fair, it may have a positive impact. If an offender not totally committed to a life of crime (what is sometimes called a "prosocial offender") is treated in a manner that he perceives as fair, further criminal behavior may be prevented. If he sees the punishment as excessive or unfair, this may destroy any chance of reform. The perception of the offender may well be incongruent with that of the public, and distorted by personality factors, misinformation, or the belief that he is born to be victimized (the "injustice collector"), but it is a perception that cannot be overlooked. Punished and stigmatized offenders seek and usually find support and comfort from peer groups. They are often in need of hope and faith in self. If embittered by punishment and finding support in a peer group whose perception of abuse is the same as his, the offender is likely to reject the positive values that punishment and imprisonment are intended to reinforce.

The punishment ideology has become fashionable once again, among liberals and conservatives alike. Supporters have found justifications for punishment in theology, economics, and political science. A new ideology of punishment has abandoned the thesis of revenge, and now speaks of retribution: the offender should get his "just deserts," with the question of deterrence being irrelevant to the importance and propriety of meting out justice. A basic argument is put forth that suffering and atonement by the offender serve to cleanse the society as a whole.

In an atmosphere in which a punitive ideology pervades, the routine use of harsh measures in institutions may be as degrading to the offender (who becomes a victim) as to the society whose agents and officers carry out such measures. The punishment ideology is easily transformed into the punishment procedure, which is then routinely applied without regard to the individual nature and needs of offenders. For this reason, prisons develop subcultures in which inmates seek support and values and the agents of law become their enemies. There is a self-segregating procedure among prisoners in which groups are formed according to race, power in the prison, attitudes toward law and the prison administration, need for in-prison protection, and other factors. In many such groups, prisons become "schools of crime," transforming the neophyte and the apprentice into skilled and learned practitioners, and those prisoners with credits and degrees earned in the underworld into respected professors (for a discussion of prison and inmate subcultures, see Sykes, 1958; Clemmer, 1958; Irwin and Cressey, 1962).

Within a large and punishment-oriented institution, there is a tendency to administer punishment in a general and more or less uniform fashion; to the extent that it is limited, it is restrained more by the inmate subculture and its own power structure than by the needs of offenders themselves. Nevertheless, selective punishment, administered in an individual situation to an individual offender, may be an effective and important tool for institutional administrators, although it has great potential for abuse in the form of favoritism and irrelevant criteria used in the selection process.

The abandonment of the word "punishment" in favor of "corrections" was a reflection of a trend favoring an approach to the offender much the same as would be made to the mentally ill, neglected, or underprivileged. It was based on a more humane ideology, a treatment model, in which criminal behavior is seen as a manifestation of pathology that can be handled by some form of therapeutic activity. However, although the criminal may be referred to as sick, a treatment ideology is not analogous to a medical approach. The justification for the comparison with physical and mental illness lies in the assumed need for the offender to recognize the danger and undesirability of his criminal behavior and make a significant effort to renounce it. The treatment model does not "remove" criminal behavior, as surgery might remove a malignancy or chemotherapy extinguish an infection; rather the "patient" or inmate is made to see the rewards of socially acceptable behavior and encouraged to adopt it as a mode of conduct for himself.

Contrary to some popular misconceptions, the treatment ideology does not mean that inmates are "coddled" and permitted to do as they please within an institution. If an institution is not punitive and restrictive—or at least not overly so, for the institution is itself punishment to the extent that it can never be free of restrictions on inmates—this does not necessarily mean that prisoners are being treated with deference and their stay made as pleasant as a vacation, as some journalists and politicians occasionally state. In fact, some form of treatment ideology can permeate the most restrictive and security-oriented institution.

The major difference between the treatment and punishment ideologies is that in the former the inmate is assigned to a correctional program intended to prepare him for readjustment to the community, and in the latter such programs are not available. There is room for punishment in the treatment approach, but little room for treatment in the punitive approach. Treatment methods are intended to be used in conjunction with restriction and authority in a constructive and positive manner. Inmates, it is contended by those favoring treatment, must be allowed to try and to fail. Authoritarian procedures used alone provide little more than ammunition to support the offender's self-image as an "oppressed and impotent pawn of the power structure."

Treatment procedures are almost as varied as the imaginations of the treatment staff that design them. The most common conception of a therapeutic approach is the psychiatric and psychodynamic treatment to assist the offender to adjust. Actually, classic psychiatric treatment techniques are used relatively rarely in the correctional institution. Group therapy has become a more common approach, with groups including staff members as well as offenders. They are attuned to the belief that most criminal behavior is learned from and encouraged by the offender's associates. Group therapy programs are intended to transfer the offender's allegiance from the values and activities of the criminal group to those of the noncriminal group. If the latter's values can be relabeled as desirable, the offender can develop a new behavior model in his future associations, which can represent status and security. Groups conducted in a routine manner, as just another duty that inmates and personnel must perform, have little chance of success. The leader must be a skilled and dedicated therapist, with the ability to stimulate intense exchanges and help both offenders and staff understand what they are learning about themselves.

Other treatment programs within prisons include educational and vocational training, remedial health and medical intervention, religious instruction, and such voluntary group activities as Alcoholics Anonymous. Each of these categories of treatment has an underlying assumption that the offender is in need of assistance to remove a barrier to acceptance of noncriminal behavior as a viable life-style. For example, it is widely believed in contemporary American society that all adults should be able to read and write and ideally should have at least a high school diploma or its equivalent. Many prison systems have schools to teach inmates to read and write and to achieve the General Education Diploma, signifying attainment of high school–completion equivalency.

The main purpose of the treatment approach in corrections is to provide a means by which an individual, possessing some kind of defect or problem that has apparently contributed to his criminal behavior or arisen out of it, can overcome his difficulty. If the offender is placed into confinement, it is to identify and treat this problem, not to be punished for criminal actions regardless of underlying causes.

Treatment in the field of corrections is fraught with problems. The needs of the institution often take precedence over those of the individual, so that treatment programs may be temporarily suspended owing to institutional activity or disciplinary action. For example, an inmate who violates institutional rules may be placed in a disciplinary cell (solitary confinement or isolation) for a period of time, without books or other material to help cope with problems of survival in isolation. (While other deprivations may be far more severe than is lack of books, books are important if the offender is enrolled in an academic program, for he may fall so far behind the rest of the class that it will be necessary to drop out until the next one starts, and it may be six months before he can resume the education program.) Similarly, encounter groups may be broken up, thus losing their effect, when the needs of the institution become paramount.

Despite this handicap, however, group therapy is becoming increasingly popular as a form of institutional treatment, especially for incarcerated juvenile offenders. Group programs that involve correctional personnel can benefit not only the offenders but staff as well. Regular interaction between staff and inmates tends to break down barriers between them and provide insights on problems of both sides.

The administrator who wants to instill a treatment atmosphere in a formerly punishment-oriented institution faces many difficulties. The security staff, generally indoctrinated in the punitive model, will resist such change as a threat to institutional order and their power. Because treatment programs are usually much more expensive than control models, legislatures are slow to allocate the necessary funds. The public, like the staff, exhibits severe fear of crime and presses for more punishment when treatment alternatives are proposed; politicians often bow to the wishes of the voters, even in the face of evidence suggesting that a treatment model is more effective.

Like their social control colleagues in law enforcement, correctional administrators seem to make headlines only during times of crisis or adversity. A criminologist endorsing the treatment ideology would argue that the real hope for its acceptance in corrections is to ensure sufficient security and control so that the successes are not drowned out by failures proclaimed in widely viewed headlines.

Punishment can be part of a treatment program as long as it is a disciplinary procedure and not the overriding emphasis of the program. However, while treatment-oriented correctional personnel might argue that very few inmates are untreatable, it seems that, given the present level of knowledge and interventional technology, there are some offenders (from 5 to 20 percent of the prison population) who cannot be treated and who are too dangerous to release under community supervision. This does not necessarily mean, of course, that their terms of imprisonment should or can be extended beyond the legally permissible sentence for the crimes of which they have been convicted. However, in these cases it is not treatment, but punishment, that may deter future criminality. In sum, diagnosis, classification, and treatment need greater attention, knowledge, and improvement.

The Ideology of Reintegration

The reintegration philosophy is predicated on the assumptions that the offender has failed in an attempt to exist within a sociocultural environment that is either too complex for him or for which his prior education and training are insufficient; that he is a marginal person economically, occupationally, and socially; that given supportive social services gradual absorption into the environment is possible; and that he would prefer to exist within a successful and legitimate life-style. A goal is the development of acceptable living patterns to replace the offender's prior reliance on criminal behavior. This suggests the need for a process of gradual internalization of community standards, some changes in the community, community-based corrections, and continuity of delivery of services between the institution and the community.

The movement toward treatment and corrections in the community has highlighted the need to make treatment programs inside prison walls relate to circumstances in the outside world. Control of crime cannot be achieved by reform of prisoners alone. Continued reformation and reintegration efforts must take place in the community. Toward this end, many of the barriers shutting off the prison from the community have come under severe criticism. The treatment concept has been expanded to encompass efforts of community-oriented professionals and volunteers who have begun to provide offenders with the support and guidance needed to ensure successful reintegration. The main objective of the reintegration model is to return the offender to the community as a responsible and productive citizen, rather than a feared "ex-con" with little hope for legitimate success. Institutions dedicated to this objective have learned to overcome deficits in funding and personnel to some extent by using the ingenuity of prison staff and the resources available in the community.

In many institutions, barriers are coming down for traffic in both directions. Outside activity by inmates and prison personnel ranges from touring lecture programs to work and educational furloughs, which can serve as a method of graduated release back to the community. The rationale for graduated release has been presented as follows:

> There is convincing evidence that the periods immediately before and immediately after release from an institution stand as particularly critical times in an inmate's life. Occasional bravado notwithstanding, most inmates keenly appreciate the fact that they have failed in the past to remain within legal boundaries and that the same or similar conditions that led them to prison in the first place may catapult them back into custody. If nothing else, their incarceration brings into question their adequacy as criminals, that is, the quality of their skill and intelligence, and their ability to evade capture in the future. For those inmates who desire to remain law-abiding, the power of that commitment to withstand social and psychological erosion creates nagging doubts. [NIMH, 1971: 3]

The reintegration model allows the inmate to take on increasing responsibilities before his term expires, until he is ready for acceptance by the community. It is viewed by many as the wave of the future, with treatment programs built around a comprehensive reintegration plan having a much higher possibility of success than the old custody-control methods. The true reintegration model recognizes the need to provide the ex-offender with a reasonable, legitimate means of support—hence the undeniable importance of good vocational training.

The Ideology of Prevention

The problem of crime cannot be distinguished from the problems of the individual offender. Some crime may be prevented by removing the offender from the community, but even the large-scale deportation of hundreds of thousands of felons to the American colonies and Australia did not rid England of crime in the eighteenth and nineteenth centuries. Today, with such mass banishment virtually unknown, the offenders are at least temporarily incapacitated by being sent to prison. Almost all are eventually released, however, and the problem resumes unless the prisoner has been effectively treated while in custody or deterred by the gravity and severity of confinement. Because of the minimal success of present correctional programs (with recidivism rates of from 40 to 70 percent), many communities and governmental agencies are turning to crime prevention as a possible solution.

Much crime prevention activity is designed to steer potential delinquents away from a life of trouble. Such programs generally begin at the school level, where truancy and dropping out are often precursors of criminal activity. These early programs for the most part attempt to identify the first signs of criminal behavior—a complex process, even when carefully controlled. Prevention programs in schools today aim to treat the problem child by providing specialized classes, vocational education, and counseling; they do not aim to get the child out of the picture by expulsion from school. The prevention ideology recognizes that the problem child must have supportive help if he is not to turn to crime as an outlet for his underlying unhappiness and insecurity.

The individual's environment is crucial in the prevention of crime. The prevention ideology emphasizes the need to structure the environment so that criminal opportunity is minimized; this can be accomplished in part by environmental design, but also by working closely with those who constitute the greatest reservoir of potential criminals.

The preventive ideology is usually combined with treatment in the form of community corrections (see Chapter 24). The emphasis is on identification and treatment of the problems that have caused past criminal behavior in order to diminish the likelihood of its recurrence. Eventually, this emphasis may lead to a closer, more interdependent relationship between neighbors and the agencies involved in crime prevention and community services. Diversion and nonjudicial approaches to offenders are seen as potentially valuable alternatives to the more formal punishment-oriented reaction to the problem of crime. Preventive and treatment ideologies constitute the most promising and humane organization of corrections beliefs and practices.

Should "the punishment fit the crime," in the famous phrase of W.S. Gilbert (of Gilbert and Sullivan); or should the punishment fit the criminal? The two orientations cannot easily be reconciled, although with some flexibility a little of each can be used.

*Universality
and
Individuation:
The Enduring
Dilemma*

To make the punishment fit the crime would mean to reduce discretion of judges, racial discrimination and allegations of such discrimination, and disparities between sentences meted out to the powerless (constituting the great majority of convicted felons) and the powerful (a highly publicized and significant minority). It is contended by many that there would thus emerge a more even-handed justice, and that the general belief that such justice exists would diminish both crime and sympathy for the offender and would be a social good in itself.

Individuation does bring about many problems. For example, it is often argued that a defendant who has been found guilty should be released without incarceration because he constitutes no further menace to the society. Under the ideal of rehabilitation, the logic of the argument is apparent. Nevertheless, a consistent program built along this line would elevate injustice to the status of official, institutionalized social policy: a crime has been committed with impunity, simply because the guilty one is a safe bet not to be a repeater. In practice, the better educated, the middle- and upper-class offenders, are almost always the exclusive beneficiaries of such crime without punishment.

Yet, for all of its potential for abuse, individuation—or making the punishment fit the offender—has a strong appeal. It is based upon the idea that different types of criminals require and respond to a variety of treatment programs, as Don Gibbons (1981) has so forcefully demonstrated: individual psychotherapy, group therapy, and community and peer-group assistance. And in some cases, no therapy at all is indicated.

The criminal justice system, in the interest of assisting offenders who can be motivated to change, will sometimes lean to individuation, having found that society is thereby protected from further depredations by those who have been victimizers. But the same criminal justice system will at other times, in the interests of justice, lean to an impartial and even-handed universality of punishment, having found that society is thereby better protected by the wide diffusion of the knowledge that offenders will be handled alike, depending only upon the nature of the offense.

It is an enduring dilemma facing students of criminal punishment.

Misdemeanant Corrections

There is consensus among criminologists that city and county detention centers, correctional farms, workhouses, police lockups, and jails overwhelmingly reflect the punitive and incapacitation aspects of corrections, rather than treatment and prevention ideologies. Local corrections includes misdemeanant probation, city and county jails, and primarily private ancillary service agencies such as halfway houses, drug abuse hostels, and Volunteers of America.

With some exceptions, local tax-supported jails are abysmal in their organization, services, atmosphere, physical plant, management, funding, staffing, staff training, rehabilitative programming, and ideology. Fortunately, most of these jails are short-term detention facilities for misdemeanants. In criminology and penology, overwhelming attention is usually paid to prisons, which house serious criminals, often for a lengthy period of time. Jails and other local lockups deserve attention, however, because almost all suspects must endure a stay lasting at least a few hours, if not overnight or longer, in them; because they are neglected not only by scholars but also by policy-makers; and because they are generally the place where misdemeanant sentences are served.

The offense categories of felony and misdemeanor are important distinctions, made primarily in terms of the punishments that can be imposed. In general, felonies are more serious crimes, for which the offender could be sentenced to death or imprisonment in a state or federal institution for at least a year, whereas misdemeanors are less serious offenses, for which the statutes permit a fine, probation, or short-term incarceration in a local detention facility (usually a county jail, less frequently a workhouse, or, in some jurisdictions, a community correctional center).

Following arrest and in most instances detention at a police station, almost all offenders are processed through jails before disposition of their case. It has been estimated that in one recent year more than seven million persons nationwide were detained in jails long enough for the key to be turned in the lock. This figure includes a wide variety of persons at different stages of the criminal justice process: those arrested and held for investigation, pretrial detainees, offenders adjudicated guilty and serving their entire term in jail or awaiting transfer to federal or state prison, military personnel detained pending transfer to military authorities, persons arrested and awaiting extradition or extradition hearings, material witnesses held by court order, and others. They include a wide range of persons: drug addicts, hardened predatory criminals, some mentally ill people, prosocial offenders, traffic offenders, detained juveniles, and petty property offenders, just to mention a few. Except in larger institutions, little segregation by offense or conviction level is practiced.

In 1972 only 12 percent of the almost four thousand jails in the nation had any sort of in-house medical facility. Only a fraction of the total population of jails that retain adult offenders for forty-eight hours or longer had access to social and rehabilitation programs (U.S. Department of Justice, 1975). There are few recreation programs, and the vast majority of the jail population sits in filthy and overcrowded cells for most of the day with little constructive activity to relieve boredom and "dead time."

In 1970 a comprehensive jail census was made, surveying jails retaining offenders for forty-eight hours or more (U.S. Department of Justice, 1971). This excluded all federal and state correctional institutions (including prisons), juvenile institutions, state-operated jails of three states (Connecticut, Delaware, and Rhode Island), and drunk tanks, lockups, and other facilities that confine offenders for less than forty-eight hours. Generally, it was reported that deplorable conditions were widespread. There were no facilities for recreation or exercise in 86 percent of the institutions surveyed; about 25 percent had no visitation provisions, and some did not even have working flush toilets. The District of Columbia jail was described by the National Advisory Commission on Criminal Justice Standards and Goals in condemnatory terms (since this report little or no improvement was noted):

> The District of Columbia Jail is a filthy example of man's inhumanity to man. It is a case study in cruel and unusual punishment, in the denial of due process, in the failure of justice.
>
> The Jail is a century old and crumbling. It is overcrowded. It offers inferior medical attention to its inmates, when it offers any at all. It chains sick men to beds. It allows—forces—men to live in crowded cells with rodents and roaches, vomit and excreta. It is the scene of arbitrary and capricious punishment and discipline. While there is little evidence of racial discrimination (the Jail "serves" the male population of the District of Columbia and is, therefore, virtually an all-black institution), there are some categories of prisoners who receive better treatment than others.
>
> The eating and living conditions would not be tolerated anywhere else. The staff seems, at best, indifferent to the horror over which it presides. This, they say, is the job society wants them to do. The facilities and amounts of time avail-

able for recreation and exercise are limited, sometimes by a guard's whim. Except for a few privileged prisoners on various details, there is no means by which an inmate may combat idleness—certainly nothing that could be called education, counseling or self-help. [National Advisory Commission, 1973: 275]

When the public's attention is periodically focused on jails—particularly when politicians, the media, or inmates expose appalling conditions on a local level—changes made are generally short-term, and conditions deteriorate to their previous state rather rapidly. Inadequate funds, low priority with local politicians, low-quality staffing, antiquated facilities, overcrowding, and insufficient time to work with offenders have long characterized misdemeanant corrections and hampered efforts to develop relevant programs in jails and other correctional units. However, in some city and county jurisdictions, newer facilities have been constructed to provide better conditions and programs for the misdemeanant, and community programs and facilities have sometimes been marshalled to provide educational and work-release opportunities for short-term offenders. These improved conditions are relatively rare. The availability of Law Enforcement Assistance Administration funds during the 1960s and 1970s generated a number of pilot programs for the improvement of existing jails and for new approaches to short-term and local custody.

*Chronic
Inebriates and
the Revolving
Door*

The common drunk is the major type of client in misdemeanor facilities. Over 50 percent of misdemeanor arrests are for drunkenness or offenses related to drinking, not including driving under the influence of liquor. It is estimated that over two million arrests are made each year for public drunkenness. Of course, this creates problems for the police, not the least of which is the need for vast human resources to handle the inebriates. Another area to feel the impact of this huge volume is the lower court system. With its packed dockets, its personnel are unable to cope with the large numbers, and as a result courts tend to mete out "assembly-line justice." Offenders convicted of public drunkenness represent the largest single sector of the 50 percent of convicted jail inmates who could be treated in facilities other than jail, if they were available.

Most of the offenders arrested for public drunkenness are chronic alcoholics and chronic arrestees. They come to jails for a drying out period, followed by the inevitable return to the streets and the bottle. The situation has been evaluated by Austin MacCormick, former president of the American Correctional Association:

The appallingly poor quality of most of the county jails in the United States is so well known that it is probably not necessary to discuss this point at any great length. The fact that the majority of all convicted alcoholics go to these institutions, however, makes it imperative that the public, and particularly those thoughtful citizens who are interested in the treatment of alcoholics, never be allowed to forget that our county jails are a disgrace to the country . . . and that they have a destructive rather than a beneficial effect not only on alcoholics who are committed to them but also on those others who are convicted of the most petty offenses. [President's Commission on Law Enforcement, 1967a: 234]

The chronic inebriate is neither deterred nor cured by his frequent trips to jail. All that is accomplished is the provision of a brief period of sobriety and removal from public view. The system of misdemeanant corrections is unable to deal with the alcoholic, either medically or from a social standpoint; lockup in jail is usually the only available local response.

The most popular means for diverting alcoholics from the criminal justice system is the detoxification center, a civil (as opposed to criminal) treatment-oriented alternative to the police station as processing point for offenders whose only offense is drunkenness. The offender is retained there until restored to a stable and sober condition. The option of treatment beyond this initial drying-out period is usually left up to the individual; in most detoxification centers the majority elect to stay for more treatment. Detoxification centers are generally staffed with medical and other professional personnel to determine the exact needs of each individual. In the case of serious complications, the patient can be transferred to a public hospital for extensive care.

The Dayton, Ohio, Pilot Cities program (sponsored by the Department of Health, Education and Welfare) is an example of this concept in practice. The structure and goals of the project are outlined in the HEW evaluation report:

> A screening and detoxification center, located in the City Mission, is designated to diagnose medical problems and provide medical treatment to persons suffering from the physical symptoms associated with drinking. Persons coming to the center may be referred from a variety of sources: Police, courts, probation department, hospitals, social agencies, the correctional farm, and volunteer admissions. Disposition of persons from the screening centers can occur in a variety of ways: (1) persons with acute medical problems will be sent to local hospitals; (2) persons progressing in the reduction of medical problems will be sent to a halfway house; (3) persons not having a serious or chronic drinking problem will be returned to society; (4) persons may elect another rehabilitation program such as the one at the City Mission.
>
> The planned procedure to bring persons to the screening center by the police merits special comment. Instead of arresting persons for public drunkenness, police are to bring such persons to the screening center unless the offender refuses or exhibits violent behavior in which case he is arrested. However, there is no legal compulsion imposed on an individual to participate in the program. He may terminate his individual involvement at any time without suffering legal consequences. [Community Research, Inc., 1972]

The removal of over two million chronic alcoholic cases from the workload of the country's law enforcement agencies and jails would allow personnel to concentrate on more serious problems, and in that sense could lead to a significant reduction in major crime in the United States. One model for a comprehensive community-based system for diverting the public drunkenness offender is shown in Figure 22–1.

Referral
Sources

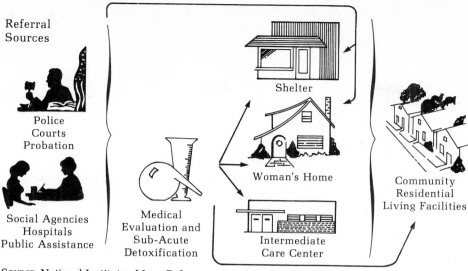

Police
Courts
Probation

Social Agencies
Hospitals
Public Assistance

Medical
Evaluation and
Sub-Acute
Detoxification

Shelter

Woman's Home

Intermediate
Care Center

Community
Residential
Living Facilities

**FIGURE 22–1
Comprehensive Public
Inebriate Diversionary
Program**

SOURCE: National Institute of Law Enforcement and Criminal Justice, *Diversion of the Public Inebriate from the Criminal Justice System* (Washington, D.C.: Department of Justice, 1973), p. 7.

Misdemeanor Probation

The bulk of misdemeanor cases are disposed of through fines, confinement, or misdemeanor probation. While misdemeanor crime occurs in both urban and rural jurisdictions, the majority of adult misdemeanor probation services are available only in urban centers. In a large portion of the United States, there are no probation services whatsoever for the misdemeanant. In some jurisdictions, probation services for felons and misdemeanants have been combined, but this has hardly improved matters, for it has created even heavier caseloads for the already overworked probation officers.

A few states have at least nominal statewide systems for the supervision of adult misdemeanants on probation. In many of these systems supervision is provided only if requested, making the service itself more a check-in formality than a counseling process. Often the offender is seen only once a month for a few minutes, usually in the office of the probation officer. The hopes and promises of the program started early in the nineteenth century in Boston by John Augustus, America's first probation officer, have not been fulfilled in the modern version of misdemeanant probation. One reason is the general overloading of the criminal justice system; another is the short-term nature of misdemeanor sentences.

Other dispositions for misdemeanor offenders include fines, probation without adjudication, and suspended sentences. Fines are often called "price-tag justice." In misdemeanor offenses, the fine is frequently offered as an alternative to a period of confinement, meaning that the offender who cannot pay is in effect confined for being poor rather than for being an offender.

As indicated above, the large number of misdemeanor cases that the lower courts must hear is a major obstacle to any but the most cursory justice. Some lower courts may hear as many as 100 misdemeanor cases in a single morning. In these circumstances it is difficult to conduct any kind of in-depth diagnosis of the offender, the offense, or his ability to pay a fine. The fines for particular crimes have therefore been virtually standardized. For the individual unable to pay, a term in jail is sometimes the only alternative. However, fines can often be paid on the installment plan. This procedure gives the offender a chance to keep a current job or seek work in order to make the payment. This installment system, combined with weekend confinement, has been a major improvement in misdemeanor justice in recent years.

Other alternatives for the misdemeanant are probation without adjudication and the suspended sentence. These are both variations on the same theme: holding formal disposition over the head of the offender for a period of time, often under specified conditions, and then nullifying conviction. In probation without adjudication (deferred prosecution), the offender can avoid prosecution as long as certain established conditions are met, usually for a specific period of time. The judge uses the suspended sentence when the offender does not seem to require supervision to ensure his good behavior. This alternative is generally invoked in the case of first offenders considered to be so impressed with their arrest and possible conviction that further sanctions against them would be of little positive value. The extent to which these two alternatives are employed is not known with any degree of certainty, as little research has been performed in this area; their relative effectiveness is still being examined.

Toward the Future

A serious problem with misdemeanant corrections lies in the hodgepodge of offenders and offenses thrown together in the short-term facilities built primarily for temporary detention. In some misdemeanant facilities, the felons confined for various reasons—with no segregation from misdemeanants—may number as high as 50 percent. Thrown in with the convicted offender (both misdemeanants and felons) is a large group of unconvicted persons who are awaiting trial or other action. The unrestricted mingling of these convicted and unconvicted felons and misdemeanants is now the target for several pilot reform projects across the country.

A number of high-impact treatment programs are specifically designed to be carried out in the brief periods covered by misdemeanant sentences. The development and expansion of these programs, with maximum involvement in the community, should greatly assist the local misdemeanor correctional workers in their efforts.

In Des Moines, Iowa, several innovative programs have been developed that have significantly reduced jail population and costs and diminished such collateral consequences of misdemeanant conviction for offenders as loss of job, family having to go on welfare, repossession of property purchased on the installment plan, and family dissolution. The state saved the average per diem cost of four dollars per person through the literally thousands of misdemeanant cases diverted (some for over 110 days) from jail on ROR. Other persons unable to raise bail bond but not otherwise eligible for

ROR (those who had committed serious crimes against the person), were diverted to the Pretrial Supervision program (probation without adjudication). Still other misdemeanants (and a few felons) were diverted into the Ft. Des Moines Residential Facility for Men. In the latter setting, offenders contract to perform certain tasks (such as getting a job, learning a trade, or participating in personal or marital counseling in order to resolve problems which led them to commit the crime). The offender is told not only that someone cares about him, but that (1) only he can solve his own problems, (2) if he chooses not to do so he is choosing to go to trial, probably be found guilty, and jailed, and (3) if he tries to solve his problems through the available opportunities he will be a free man.

All three of these programs have had remarkably low failure rates; only 1.8 percent of the ROR and pretrial supervision cases have failed to appear for trial, compared to 2.2 percent for the bail-bond procedure. The rearrest rate of the Residential Facility offenders was a mere 36 percent, compared with 50 to 70 percent for release from penal institutions (National Institute of Law Enforcement and Criminal Justice, 1974).

These favorable results did not require large technical, vocational, professional, or academic expenditures; only those resources available in the community were used. Due to the effective use of these local resources and programs as well as the remarkable outcomes, the National Institute of Law Enforcement and Criminal Justice has declared the Des Moines experiment to be an "exemplary project," suitable for replication in other jurisdictions.

The correctional client who enters the criminal justice system as a misdemeanant may well be the future felon at the state prison. Effective correctional programs designed to reform the misdemeanant at the earliest possible point are crucial. The volume of misdemeanor offenders is so great that more resources *must* be provided for upgrading the facilities, programs, and quality of personnel they encounter. As the following chapters suggest, a comprehensive community-based corrections program is necessary for every large metropolitan area.

Institutions: The Unfulfilled Promise

To comprehend current conditions and circumstances of corrections in the United States, it is useful to start with a study of the Enlightenment and the many demands for social change made by influential thinkers during that period.

As the seventeenth century drew to a close, the absolute power of the state to intervene in adjudication of criminal acts, regulation of feuds, collection of fines, and keep "the King's peace" had led to extensive use of capital and corporal punishment. England had over 200 offenses for which an offender could be executed. The English system at the time had a strong impact on American correctional philosophy, first in the colonies and later in the newly formed republic. Hanging, banishment, burning at the stake, breaking on the rack, the chopping block—all testified to the firm hold in England of the conception of retribution by the state, and many of these features were transferred, albeit somewhat modified, to the colonies across the Atlantic. Arrest and incarceration were only the prelude to the trial and gory punishment that would follow. Vengeance ruled and forgiveness was inexorably opposed.

A philosophic upheaval occurred in the Western world in the next century: the social and intellectual movement known as the Enlightenment. The essential imperfection but basic dignity of the human being were recognized in the writings of such influential figures as Baron de Montesquieu (b. 1689–d. 1755), Jean-Jacques Rousseau (b. 1712–d. 1778), Voltaire (b. 1694–d. 1779), Cesare Beccaria (b. 1738–d. 1794), Jeremy Bentham (b. 1748–d. 1832), the prison reformer John Howard (b. 1726–d. 1790), and, a century later, John Stuart Mill (b. 1806–d. 1873). Collectively, their writings and actions revolutionized the approaches of Western societies to crime and criminals, among other things. Only their major contributions as they relate specifically to penology can be noted here.

In France during the Enlightenment, Montesquieu and Voltaire were among the strongest voices expressing concern for the rights of all human beings. While Montesquieu attacked abuses of criminal law through his writing, Voltaire took action on a number of occasions, challenging earlier ideas of justice, criminal responsibility, and legalized torture. At about the same time in Italy the most influential legal reformer of all was quietly and modestly compiling a work that would ultimately have repercussions from Tsarist Russia to the newly formed United States. This was Cesare Beccaria.

In 1764 Beccaria published anonymously his famous essay *Dei delitti e delle pene* (the early translation into English appeared under the title *An Essay on Crimes and Punishments*, with a commentary by Voltaire). Almost immediately Beccaria's essay became influential in legal and penological circles. The major principles enunciated by Beccaria (see Beccaria, 1953), eventually widely accepted, include the following:

1. The basis of all social action must be the utilitarian conception of the greatest happiness for the greatest number.
2. Crime must be considered an injury to society, and the only rational measurement of crime is the extent of that injury.
3. Prevention of crime is more important than punishment for crimes; indeed, punishment is justifiable only on the supposition that it helps to prevent criminal conduct. In preventing crime it is necessary to improve and publish the laws, so that the nation can understand and support them; to reward virtue; and to improve the public's education both in regard to legislation and to life.
4. In criminal procedure secret accusations and torture should be abolished. There should be speedy trials. The accused should be treated humanely before trial and must have every right and facility to bring forward evidence in his own behalf. Turning state's evidence should be done away with, as it amounts to no more than the public authorization of treachery.
5. The purpose of punishment is to deter persons from the commission of crime and not to provide social revenge. Not severity, but certainty and swiftness in punishment best secure this result. Punishment must be sure and swift and penalties determined strictly in accordance with the social damage wrought by the crime. Crimes against property should be punished solely by fines, or by imprisonment when the person is unable to pay the fine. Banishment is an excellent punishment for crimes against the state. There should be no capital punishment. Life imprisonment is a better deterrent. Capital punishment is irreparable and hence makes no provision for possible mistakes and the desirability of later rectification.
6. Imprisonment should be more widely employed but its mode of application should be greatly improved through providing better physical quarters and by separating and classifying the prisoners as to age, sex, and degree of criminality.

From his seminal ideas, four were incorporated into the French criminal codes in 1808 and 1810, and had a strong influence on the development of criminal law in the United Kingdom and the United States:

1. An accused is innocent until proven guilty.
2. An accused should not be forced to testify against himself.
3. An accused should have the right to employ counsel and to cross-examine the state's witnesses.
4. An accused should have the right to a prompt and public trial and, in most cases, a trial by jury.

Anyone familiar with the United States Constitution will quickly perceive our legal debt to this Italian writer.

In the late eighteenth and early nineteenth centuries, Jeremy Bentham and his reformist intellectual heirs Samuel Romilly (b. 1757–d. 1818) and Robert Peel (b. 1788–d. 1850) undertook to reform the British criminal law system by strongly advancing the concept of graduated penalties designed to make the punishment fit the social harm. When the philosophy of political equality became more widespread, new penal policies were largely based upon the thought of Bentham. Thorsten Sellin states:

> Older penal law had reflected the views dominant in societies where slavery or serfdom flourished, political inequality was the rule, and sovereignty was assumed to be resting in absolute monarchs. Now the most objectionable features of that law, which had favored the upper classes and had provided often arbitrary, brutal and revolting corporal and capital punishments for the lower classes, were to be removed and equality before the law established. Judicial torture for the purpose of extracting evidence was to be abolished, other than penal measures used to control some conduct previously punished as crime, and punishments made only severe enough to outweigh the gains expected by the criminal from his crime. This meant a more humane law, no doubt, applied without discrimination to all citizens alike in harmony with the new democratic ideas. [Sellin, 1967: 20]

Arguing that human behavior can be influenced in a scientific fashion, Bentham averred that the prime objective of an intelligent person is to maximize pleasure while minimizing pain. This concept, which came to be known as the hedonistic or felicific calculus, governed much of his effort to reform the British criminal code. Like Beccaria, Bentham believed that punishment, if appropriate to the crime, could act as a deterrent.

The great name in English prison reform in the eighteenth century was John Howard, whose interest in the subject was sharpened when, as sheriff of Bedfordshire in 1773, he witnessed horrors that he never dreamed were possible. Temporary prison ships or "hulks"—converted, broken-down war vessels, stripped and anchored in waterways—were unsanitary, vermin-infested, and unventilated. These hulks were pockets of vice, immorality, and deadly disease that periodically would wipe out an entire ship's population. (In some jurisdictions of the United States, such as California and New York, prison hulks were still to be seen in the nineteenth century.) The jails (or gaols) were primarily places of detention for three types of offenders:

some waiting to be tried, others who could not pay their fines, and those condemned and awaiting execution. Disease, debauchery, extortion, and starvation were rampant. There was no segregation by age, sex, or crime committed.

Howard was sufficiently appalled to lobby for legislation to abate abuses and improve basic conditions, at least with regard to sanitation. His *State of Prisons* contributed to the passage by Parliament of the Penitentiary Act, which legislated secure and sanitary structures for imprisonment, abolished payment of fees to jailors, and established systematic inspection. In short, his work instituted a period of administration of prisons oriented toward reform.

America: William Penn and the Quakers

The influence of the Enlightenment and the prison reformers was felt in America, particularly by William Penn and the Quakers of Pennsylvania. It was Penn who brought the concept of humanitarian treatment of offenders to this side of the Atlantic. Generally, the colonies had been noted for harsh treatment of offenders, as seen in the codes established by the Duke of York in 1676 and the earlier Hampshire code of 1664. Both were similar to the English system from which they were derived: capital and corporal punishment were widespread, including hanging, branding, flogging, and use of the stocks and pillory. However, the "Great Law" of the Quakers, in effect until 1718, contrasted sharply with other colonial practices. Capital punishment was almost completely eliminated, with hard labor instituted instead, as being not only humane but more effective than death for the deterrence of serious crime. Only premeditated murder was punishable by death; all other crimes received punishments that varied according to the circumstances. Religious offenses were abolished.

Under the Great Law, a "house of corrections" was established in which confinement at hard labor was used as punishment. In 1718 the Quaker rules were replaced by the more severe Anglican Code of England, reflecting political changes in Pennsylvania. But in 1790, with the Revolution behind them and widespread public antipathy to anything British, the Quakers reasserted their concern about treatment of convicted criminals, convincing the Pennsylvania legislature to declare a section of the Walnut Street Jail an experimental site for offenders (except those sentenced to death) to reflect upon their crimes and repent. There the offender would become penitent, and thus was born the concept of a place for fostering penitence and housing the penitent—namely, the penitentiary.

The Walnut Street penitentiary was the first prison to be used exclusively for the purpose of correction—as opposed to punishment—of convicted felons. Philadelphia, home of the Declaration of Independence and birthplace of the nation, also gave the world the modern concept of the prison.

As originally conceived, the Pennsylvania penitentiary system demanded solitary confinement without work; it was assumed that such isolation would lead to quicker reformation, since offenders could reflect on their crimes all day and would soon repent. However, the psychological and physical effects of enforced isolation soon led to its abandonment. Instead, to maintain the mental and physical health of prisoners, work schedules and moral and religious instruction were provided. Ultimately, increased use of the Walnut Street Jail, overcrowding, and funding problems led to the breakdown of the program. Despite its failures, the jail was a major event in the history of punishment. After its demise, many new prisons began to spring up, some influenced by the Philadelphia experience, others often departing from it. One of the first and most important was in the State of New York.

The Auburn Prison: Penitence with Profits

In 1819, what became the dominant model for American prisons for felons was established at Auburn, New York. Here, convicts working together in prison shops during the day were housed in separate cells at night, marched in lock-step, and ate together—all in complete silence. Violators of the rule of silence were subjected to solitary confinement, corporal punishment, or limited rations.

Unlike the larger cells of the Pennsylvania system, which had work areas and private exercise yards ("outside" cell design), Auburn had cells "inside" the block, and long wings of cells stacked in tiers, thus holding literally hundreds of offenders, each in small spaces ($6' \times 9' \times 6'$). The inside cell design became the most common model in America (see Figure 23–1).

A spirited debate over the merits of the two systems arose. Both were predicated on the theme that a regimen of penitence and silence would prevent cross-infection of criminal values, inhibit the learning of further criminal behavior, and generally improve the conduct of prisoners. Those proclaiming the advantages of the Pennsylvania system claimed it was easier to control offenders, gave more consideration to individual inmate needs, prevented contamination through total separation, and gave more time for meditation and repentance. And it was held that prisoners could leave the institution with only a few fellow-warders knowing their identities.

The Auburn supporters argued that their congregate system was superior: cheaper to construct and implement, providing better vocational training, and thus producing more revenue for the state. The argument of profit prevailed. Using Auburn as a model, over one hundred similar institutions were built in the various states of the young republic during the next decades. Most were located far out in the countryside, free from both interference and inspection by "trouble-making do-gooders." Administrators were evaluated on the basis of prison productivity and frequency of escapes and disturbances, not the number of successful penitents.

In order to make prisons economically self-sustaining, prison workshops were designed like typical factories of the period. When mass production and factory efficiency were implemented in prisons, the profits were sufficient to convince legislators that the correctional ideology was the proper one. Thus, early prison industries became systems for the exploitation of free labor, for the primary purpose of making profits. In this way, a vested interest in the perpetuation of these institutions was established. However, as a result of the nationwide transformation of prisons under the Auburn

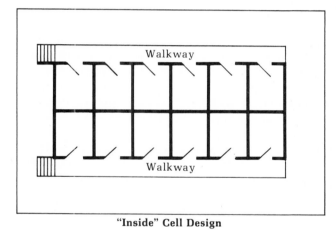

"Outside" Cell Design

"Inside" Cell Design

**FIGURE 23-1
Cell Designs**

Source: Allen and Simonsen, 1978, p. 42.

system, mechanics and cabinetmakers started very early in the nineteenth century to denounce them for unfair competition. In response to these criticisms lease and contract systems were developed, in which inmates were leased out to entrepreneurs or prisons contracted to develop products. Abuses were widespread, growing with each decade and culminating in major scandals. With the development of the labor union movement, the lease-and-contract system was effectively eliminated by the end of the nineteenth century. However, road work gangs (sometimes known as chain gangs), with prisoners working outside confinement but literally chained to one another, continued to flourish, particularly in the South, through the first quarter of the twentieth century and right into the Great Depression.

Eventually most prison labor was abolished. At this point a new problem arose, in the form of enforced idleness among prisoners. Whatever vestiges of prison labor for profit (profit for the state and sometimes prison administrators, not inmates) still existed were effectively stopped by the enactment of two federal laws, the Hawes-Cooper Act of 1929 and the Ashurst-Summers Act of 1935, essentially outlawing the interstate transportation of products manufactured in prison (resulting in prison administrators turning to the manufacture of license plates, one of the few products having no interstate sale).[1] When the Great Depression came, states quickly passed laws prohibiting the sale of prison products on the open market. Prison industries died, and with their death prison administrations and inmates were faced with a major problem of "doing time": namely, having nothing to do.

The nineteenth century also witnessed the growth of what came to be called the reformatory movement. Based on the work of an Englishman and an Irishman, Captain Alexander Maconochie (b. 1787–d. 1860) and Sir Walter Crofton (b. 1815–d. 1897) respectively, the American reformatory era commenced in 1870. In that year, leaders of American penology and prison administration met in the American Prison Congress at Cincinnati, Ohio. Concerned about overcrowding of prisons and what the future might hold, the participants at the Congress adopted a combination of concepts suggested by Maconochie and Crofton. In essence, these reformers proposed the abandonment of the fixed sentence and its replacement by the indeterminate sentence, particularly for the more tractable and younger offenders. The burden of determining the time of release from prison was placed, so to speak, on the prisoners. The indeterminate sentence, it was argued, could be used to prepare an offender for eventual return to the community. This would take place when it was clear that he was penitent and prepared for a law-abiding life, including particularly a legitimate occupation. Once these goals of repentance and training were achieved, the offender would be ready to be freed. A new prison was established in 1876 at Elmira, New York, embodying the spirit of the reformatory era, appropriately called the Elmira Reformatory. It manifested the major differences between reformatories and other previous adult prisons in its programming. Reformatories stressed reform, particularly of youthful offenders, with special emphasis on those under the age of thirty.

Elmira offered schooling, vocational training (such as mechanical drawing, wood and metal work, cabinetmaking, iron molding), the indeterminate sentence, and a system for grading inmate behavior so that authorities might know the optimal time for early release on condition of future good behavior while in the community (parole). Eventually adult prisons nationwide would adopt the indeterminate sentence, parole, and in part the training programs of the reformatories. The adult prisons of the period, however, were barren, arid soil in which the seeds of education, vocational training, and individual rehabilitation were slow to sprout. Many years and a number of prison wardens were to pass before these newer ideas were accepted.

In retrospect, it is easy to see why there was wide belief that the reformatory—working with the most amenable of offenders, new programs, en-

---

1. The Hawes-Cooper Act of 1929 defined prison products as subject to the laws of any state to which they were shipped. The Ashurst-Summers Act of 1935 in effect stopped interstate transportation of prison-made goods by mandating that all such goods shipped out of state be labeled with the prison name, and forbidding interstate shipment where state laws specifically forbid it. State legislatures, especially in jurisdictions with a strongly organized labor force, quickly acted in the "best interests of the law-abiding public."

thusiastic wardens, and exciting aspirations for penitence and reform—would succeed. Soon after the turn of the century, however, the reformatory movement went into decline, and by the advent of the First World War disillusionment was widespread. Critics have pointed to many sources of this failure, among the shortcomings noting excessively large physical plants, inadequate financial support for institutions, official and public indifference, overcrowding, substandard and untrained personnel, lack of professional leadership and programs, political interference with the prisons, political motivations of management, and questionable sentencing and parole practices.

By the mid-years of the twentieth century, all that remained of the optimism of the 1870 Congress was the word "reformatory," and even that was not heard with great frequency. The most important problem that had emerged was the need of administrators to maintain control and custody at all costs. The era of the modern prison had opened.

Prisons: The
Modern Era

From the decline of prison industry to the current situation, several major developments occurred. Parole was gradually expanded so that now about 60 percent of all felons are paroled prior to termination of sentence (not including those released after serving a full sentence less time off for good behavior). In addition, special courts for juveniles were started in 1899, and probation was widely used in them. By 1956, there was a system of adult probation in every state. (Probation is generally perceived as a sentence involving not confinement but the imposition of conditions for proper conduct for a period of time during which the sentencing court retains authority; if these conditions are violated, the court can remand the offender to prison.) Adult probation, whose history goes back to the mid–nineteenth century, varies widely among local and state jurisdictions in the extent to which it is employed.

Procedures for graduated release from prison have been developed in an effort to ease the offender's transition from the negative prison environment into the community. Some of these include work and education release and furlough, community treatment centers, halfway houses, community reintegration centers, and diversion programs. Note that these are in large part attempts to avoid the negative impact of prisons on the rehabilitation potential of many offenders during incarceration.

ADMINISTRATIVE
PROBLEMS

Three of the major current problems with institutions for offenders are associated with their size, the paucity of funding, and unionization (of both personnel and inmates).

Size. The President's Commission on Law Enforcement and Administration of Justice (1967b), appointed by President Lyndon Johnson, reported declining prison populations, both federal and state, from December 1961 to December 1967. During this period the inmate population decreased from 220,000 to 195,000. For six years afterward, the figure remained below 200,000, despite a steady rise in national population and a spectacular increase in reported crime rates. Then the inmate population began to increase; by the end of 1977 the more than 330 state prisons in the United States held a total of just over 275,000 people, a figure which rises to just under 300,000 when federal prisons are counted (this does not include jails and other detention facilities). There were about 131 Americans in federal or state prison per every 100,000 persons on any given day in 1977—a rate that rises considerably when the local jail population is included. This is the highest rate for any democratic country in the world. If present trends continue, there will be about 380,000 American prisoners in 1985. The rate mentioned above—131 per 100,000—is much higher for males, some racial and ethnic minorities, and youth.

Why this increase in the prison population? There is no single answer, but with the higher crime rates and greater population more offenders are flowing through the system. Yet growth in crime rate and population was true of the 1960s as well. Several new factors appear to be significant. First, high unemployment apparently enhances the chances of commitment by the courts for all categories of offenders. Getting a job is an important factor in successful completion of probation, and judges know that jobs are scarce. Second, the punishment ideology has been reactivated, due to widespread fear of crime. The public fears for safety of persons and property, and tends under such circumstances to become punitive and demand incarceration. Third, the effectiveness of the treatment ideology has been called into question, particularly by law enforcement, penological, and criminal justice evaluators. Fourth, some state judiciary systems have begun clearing up their massive court backlog of unheard cases. (There may have been political implications in their speed and their sentencing patterns, designed to influence elections.) Fifth, the Law Enforcement Assistance Administration has put billions of dollars into the law enforcement wing of the criminal justice system, resulting in a greater number of arrests. Finally, the average sentence has become longer during this period, and offenders with indeterminate sentences have been serving longer terms.

Public sentiment cannot be discounted. The 1970s saw massive propaganda by groups favoring punishment rather than programs that allow offenders to remain in the community on condition of good behavior. The victims of crimes—hitherto almost totally ignored by the criminal justice system, and who have often complained of being treated as second-class citizens in their role of complainant and witness—have joined the offensive to increase incarceration. Many victims prefer restitution or compensation to prosecution and incarceration of their offenders, but some insist on both. Where there is no compensation (or where it is dependent upon the victim's appearing as a witness), the likelihood of a punitive attitude may be enhanced. Although the slogan has not been articulated in these words, the attitudes of victims can be summarized by the statement, "If we can't have compensation, we will at least have a pound of flesh—but let's have both!"

As prison populations increase, administrators are forced to house two or more inmates in cells constructed for one person, construct dormitories with double- and triple-tier beds, house convicts in corridors, and in at least one state assign inmates to tent cities. This increase also means that a smaller proportion of inmates can work within prisons, idleness increases, and inmates fight among themselves. The correctional staff, in order to maintain even a semblance of control within prisons, has to compromise standards and rules of behavior for the sake of safety, and inmates perceive this and react to it. The essence of prison—at least overcrowded ones—becomes corruption of the keepers and the kept.

Funding.   While a section of the public is often willing to espouse reformatory goals for corrections, it is seldom willing to provide the financial support that would make such reforms a legislative reality. This inconsistency places the dedicated correctional administrator in an awkward position: only the most meager of programs can be implemented, and even then an overall emphasis on control and punishment must be maintained. Regardless of the approach to the problem, some aspect of prison operation will suffer. For example, if required to increase the number of security guards, the administrator must obtain the necessary funds by decreasing support for some treatment program. If treatment goals are to be stressed, it must be at the expense of the custodial staff, so the latter develop a vested interest in opposing many therapeutic and rehabilitative efforts.

Unionization of Correctional Officers.   Unionization, found in almost every sector of industry, is now widespread among state and federal employees, including those charged with police, fire, and correctional protection of the public. The personnel in police and fire departments have established collective bargaining agencies in most urban areas, and as a result have obtained improved working conditions and higher wages. However, they are prohibited by law in many states from going on strike to back up their demands, and as a result have developed a variety of slow-down strategies, such as massive outbreaks of "blue flu," mass ticketing for minor infractions usually ignored, and literal enforcement of laws originally intended for more flexible interpretation.[2]

In the correctional field, the union movement has taken root more slowly. However, it achieved a foothold, and has added a further factor in the balance of forces in corrections. The administrator must deal with the union if the institution is to function effectively, and, as a result of collective action by corrections officers through their union, the institutional balance of power has swung further in the direction of custody, as contrasted with treatment. Given the fact of union strength, a major task for correctional administrators during the last decades of the twentieth century will be the prevention of a return to outmoded procedures that are harsh and often brutal.

The great move of the late 1960s and the years immediately following had been toward more professionalism, reduction of prison populations, and

2. "Blue flu" refers to the practice by uniformed officers of taking "sick leave" en masse to back up their demands regarding salary raises, working conditions, and similar issues. This method gives them negotiating leverage without resorting to strikes, illegal in many jurisdictions.

establishment of community corrections and other programs emphasizing some of the needs not only of inmates but of the long-neglected correctional officers. Their initial efforts to organize had met with disapproval from administrators, often because of limited budgets and already overtaxed security forces in the crowded prisons. Most administrators wanted available funds to be used largely for new personnel and facilities rather than raises for officers already on the job. In some cases the correctional officers have conducted strikes, with their duties temporarily assumed by administrative and office personnel or the National Guard.

Because correctional institutions tend to be widely scattered, growth of the union movement has been slow and fragmented. The goals of these collective bargaining agencies do not necessarily coincide with the rehabilitation goals of many administrators. Organization and collective action have brought many benefits to correctional officers, but the interests of the officers are sometimes perceived as being in conflict with those of the public, and certainly of the inmates.

Unionization of Inmates.   One of the most interesting developments in recent years has been the effort to form unions of inmates. The prisoner-union movement in America began at California's Folsom Prison in 1970. The prison had just suffered internal disturbances and been through a nineteen-day inmate strike, focusing on their demand for elimination of the indeterminate sentence. The strike was punctuated by the fatal shooting of three black inmates at Soledad, another part of the California prison system. The "Soledad Brothers" became a rallying point for prisoners who sought to form a union. The three main goals of the California union were as follows:

1. abolition of the indeterminate sentence
2. establishment of the right of prisoners to organize and bargain collectively
3. restoration of civil and human rights for prisoners.

Under the second and third demands would be the rights of private correspondence, access to libraries, visitation, a system for making complaints against officers without reprisal, and having better sanitation, recreation, and food facilities.

Elsewhere, prisoner unions have had their greatest success in Scandinavia. Ronald Huff, who has studied the prisoner unionization movement in America and abroad, notes that in Sweden

> representatives of all five thousand Swedish prisoners negotiated in 1971 with the National Correctional Administration after a hunger strike. Despite the comparatively advanced conditions under which most Swedish prisoners live, they still believe that collective action is necessary to obtain those things which they do not have. [Huff, 1974]

Most correctional administrators in this country strongly oppose inmate unionization, as this comment by a state director of corrections suggests: "These men are convicted felons—convicted of breaking the laws of society.

Under no circumstances will I recognize their so-called union." The inmate union organizers are often dispersed to other institutions around the state ("bus therapy") when they begin to become "troublemakers" for administrators. Nonetheless, prisoner unions may be here to stay, and some procedure for collective bargaining seems likely to be established. There is a relationship of this union movement to violence, unrest, and protest in prison, with unionization likely to allay such violence and be a safety valve for the expression of protest (Irwin, 1980). Correctional administrators, however, are not likely to cooperate unless they can be convinced that unionization will not threaten security and control of the institution. The concerned administrator's main fear is that union power will quickly gravitate to a few particularly magnetic or authoritative inmates who will use that power to advance their own viewpoints and interests.

The movement for inmate unionization was dealt a blow by the U.S. Supreme Court in a 1977 decision, in which the Court majority upheld regulations formulated by the North Carolina Department of Correction, which had been designed to prohibit meetings, solicitation of members, and other union activities. In its decision, the majority stated that the right of association

> may be curtailed whenever the institution's officials, in the exercise of their informed discretion, reasonably conclude that such associations . . . possess the likelihood of disruption to prison order or stability, or otherwise interfere with the legitimate penological objections of the prison environment. [Jones v. North Carolina Prisoners' Labor Union, 1977: 2541]

Commenting on this decision, Ronald Huff finds that it is an anachronism that fails to take into account the true sources of violence within the prison:

> Some might argue that current prison violence occurs among inmates and therefore does not present a threat to the institution, whereas prisoners' unions, if successful in uniting inmates, may present such a threat. Two facts, however, strongly refute this reasoning. First, an examination of statistics concerning inmate assaults on staff in almost any state quickly refutes the notion that staff are in any way immune from this violence; on the contrary, such assaults seem to be increasing in most states. Furthermore, the notion that prisoners' unions could achieve such a substantial degree of organization and consensus among prisoners as to pose a significant threat is simply inconsistent with what we know about contemporary prisons and prisoners (they are divided on many issues, united on few) and inconsistent with what we know about collective inmate violence (many causes have been identified, but prisoner unionization has never been one of them). [Huff, 1980: 62]

DISENCHANTMENT WITH PRISONS

The public, correctional officials, and prisoners themselves are becoming increasingly disillusioned with a system that has so obviously failed to rehabilitate offenders. The prisons, huge and with enormous yet inadequate budgets, consume approximately seventy cents out of every dollar spent for corrections. Though prisons and jails house less than 25 percent of convicted offenders, they employ more than 75 percent of the people working in the field of corrections. Widespread disenchantment with the idea of correction has meant that new administrators must use their power and influence to bring about fundamental changes. However, this has been difficult to implement, because the old bureaucracies, with old ideologies, are firmly entrenched.

Personnel who spend many years in correctional institutions become increasingly concerned primarily with the security of their jobs and other benefits accruing from employment as well as with the problem of safety for themselves. Concern for the welfare of society is a powerful argument that they always present, but as a motivation for their actions it is no doubt secondary.

DEINSTITUTION-ALIZATION

With increasing and salient charges that penal institutions cannot rehabilitate, prisoners are not sick, incarceration does not cure, treatment is a myth, and nothing works, some critics have turned toward deinstitutionalization. It might be better, they conclude, if we face reality and devote our energies to more productive alternatives. Indeed, some states (e.g., Maine and Illinois) have abandoned the parole system, the rationale for which was a belief in rehabilitation followed by deinstitutionalization of the offender, and other states may follow.

Research Critics.   The success or failure of the medical model, based on the treatment ideology, has been widely debated. Robert Martinson, for example, examined 231 treatment projects and found that very few were significantly or consistently successful. Indeed, he called rehabilitation a myth (a view that he later renounced, just before his death), and contended:

> Except for castration, there is no startling evidence of success. There is no method for reversing the powerful tendency of offenders to persist in criminal activity. The tendency may be reduced somewhat by a given method but percentage differences are small and the costs of achieving these small reductions may be high. In the face of such facts it seems absurd to insist that the official aim of the post-adjudicatory process is to "rehabilitate" the offender. Worse, such a demand may tempt prison officials to achieve the impossible. [Martinson, 1974]

Earlier, Walter Bailey had looked at 100 projects and was similarly disappointed. "How corrective is correctional treatment?" he asked, and replied:

> Of the total sample of correctional outcomes evaluated, 10 percent described effects of the treatment as resulting in either "harm" or "no change" in behavior. Thirty-eight percent reported a statistically significant difference in the direction of improvement for the group treated. Five percent of the reported results were classified as "not relevant" to the outcome problem posed by the study.
>
> Thus, roughly one-half of the outcome reports evaluated concluded considerable improvement in the treatment group. Almost one-fourth of the reports concluded either harmful results or "no change." These results, based upon the re-

ported findings themselves, raise some serious questions regarding the efficacy of correctional treatment. [Bailey, 1966]

Martinson, Bailey, and many other criminologists were suggesting that treatment programs predicated on the notion of sickness, and hence cure through treatment of the ailment, are doomed from the start.

David Rothman (1971, 1974) calls the prison system "the failure model." He suggests that, rather than nourishing correctional myths, it would be better to admit failure and make plans analogous to those in the business world, where insurance underwriting assuages the pain of unexpected fires and catastrophes. The American penchant for coping with failure by risk control, Rothman argues, would alleviate the failure of corrections.

Finally, the American Friends Service Committee, while remarking at length on the failure of therapy in prison, has given a variety of reasons to explain why the treatment model is so firmly entrenched:

> The underlying rationale of this treatment model is deceptively simple. It rejects inherited concepts of criminal punishment as the payment of a debt owed to society, a debt proportioned to the magnitude of the offender's wrong. Instead, it would save the offender through constructive measures of reformation, protect society by keeping the offender locked up until that reformation is accomplished, and reduce the crime rate not only by using cure-or-detention to eliminate recidivism, but hopefully also by the identification of potential criminals in advance so that they can be rendered harmless by preventive treatment. Thus the dispassionate behavioral expert displaces judge and theologian.[3] [American Friends Service Committee, 1971]

Prisoners, as correctional administrators are increasingly realizing, constitute a sizable political body. Through demonstrations, hunger strikes, work stoppages, riots, and other manifestations of discontent, they have won some concessions from administrators. These include inmate councils, grievance procedures, elimination of mail censorship, and in some jurisdictions the right to bargain collectively. Inmates are increasingly perceiving that rehabilitation is a game to be played, and that, in exchange for minimal conformity to prison rules, the system can be corrupted. Their demands for concessions are, in part, an outgrowth of that recognition.

Impact of Court Cases.   Until the 1960s, the courts would not interfere with the internal affairs of prisons, particularly state institutions. This "hands off" policy, often associated with the name of Justice Felix Frankfurter, has gradually been eroded as courts have begun to express dismay and concern over correctional practices and in many instances have found that the treatment of prisoners violated constitutional guarantees. In Arkansas, Alabama, and Florida, courts have even threatened to close down the prison

---

3. It may seen paradoxical that the Quakers, who contributed so significantly to the philosophy of penitence and rehabilitation, have recently joined the antitreatment movement. It appears that abuses of treatment in the institution and during parole, or as a condition of parole, brought about this shift.

system unless changes were made, and in New York City a major facility was closed by court order. In other jurisdictions courts have forced prison administrators to institute due process and humane practices. In some cases (e.g., Sostre v. Rockefeller, 1970), courts have ruled against prison administrators. Occasionally, punitive damages have been awarded. The "jailhouse lawyer" is no longer either a rarity or a humorous expression, as courts pay increasing attention to an escalating number of inmate briefs.

In general, the U.S. Supreme Court, in its unofficial role as a regulatory agency of the criminal justice system, has begun to limit discretion by police and lower courts, and, more haltingly, has extended this limitation to correctional institutions, the third basic component of the system with which the offender comes into contact. In addition to the problem of the death penalty, the courts have concerned themselves with overcrowding, the right to unionize, demands for security from homosexual attack, and other problems that inmates must face, although not all decisions have been favorable to the protesting inmates. But perhaps the most important of all problems is that of treatment, which implies both the right to have adequate treatment and the right to refuse it without penalty such as denial of parole.

Along this line, attention has focused especially on the behavior modification technique, about which considerable controversy rages. In the case of Mackey v. Procunier (1973), the Ninth Circuit Court raised the issue of "impermissible tinkering with the mental process," and ruled in favor of Mackey, who had complained of being given a "fright drug" without his consent, which thus violated the "cruel and unusual punishment" clause of the Constitution. In the same year, in a case involving a lobotomy operation (Kaimowitz v. Michigan Department of Mental Health, 1973), the Michigan Circuit Court held not only that such "impermissible tinkering with the mental process" is a violation of the First Amendment but also that incarceration is prima facie evidence of coercion and the offender cannot give informed consent under these circumstances. Unless some treatments for criminal behavior are found that do not violate basic rights and yet are highly effective, the treatment model will receive diminishing support.

Economic Factors.   Economists, too, are currently looking upon American correctional institutions with some dismay. With state money chronically in short supply, it has become evident that criminal justice and corrections can be very expensive. Total spending nationwide at federal, state, and local levels for police, prosecution, courts, and prisons rose from $3.5 billion in 1969 to $21.5 billion in 1977, in which year the police spent $11.9 billion, the courts $4.2 billion, and the penal system $4.9 billion.

High capital construction costs have become a major consideration in criminal justice planning. Many millions of dollars worth of new prisons were either in the planning or construction stage toward the end of 1979, and their costs were certain to rise with inflation.

With initial capital costs well over $28,000 per cell, the expense of keeping a felon incarcerated for one year can reach $12,000 (a figure also constantly rising with inflation). The waste due to inmate idleness is equally staggering. Neil Singer (1973) conducted an analysis of potential inmate economic benefits and found that 208,000 convicts, if employed in prison, could earn more than a billion and a half dollars a year, with figures again constantly on the rise. Such economic realities cause legislators, business managers, and the citizenry to reappraise the whole concept of the institution. However, the problems of getting prisoners to work, especially at a time of unemployment in many industries and regions, are many.

While the exact cost figures are unknown, it is estimated that probation costs approximately three hundred dollars per year per offender. Parole is only slightly more expensive. Even though pre-parole institutional costs must be considered along with the expenses of parole, in one Canadian study it cost several times as much to keep a person in prison as to supervise him on parole (Waller, 1974). A 1974 report on costs in California gave figures of $8,000 and $1,000 for one year of imprisonment and of parole supervision, respectively. This is not to indicate that the two methods of handling convicts are equally effective, whether for control, deterrence, rehabilitation, retribution, or incapacitation, or that probation or parole could be applied to all those found guilty or who have served a part of their sentence.

The correctional administrator faces a series of challenging tasks. The inmate population, for which custody and treatment must be provided, has grown in size. Furthermore, this population has changed drastically: many inmates see themselves as victims of society, and they have been alerted to certain rights and provided with counsel to help obtain them. Citizen groups, official and unofficial, have taken an interest in corrections. Union activity among correctional staff and the prison population has spread. As treatment techniques are developed to aid in the rehabilitation of some categories of offenders, the issue is raised of an administration's right to use them and the offender's right to obtain or refuse them. However, given the failure of a plethora of individual treatment models in correctional institutions, it appears to many that the problems of crime and recidivism should be tackled by initiating changes in the political-economic structure of society.

Yet hopeful signs of progress can be observed. Public disenchantment with the prison as a means to achieve rehabilitation and reintegration of offenders has given rise to a general movement toward community-based corrections. This in turn has stimulated a general upgrading of corrections personnel, accompanied by a movement toward professionalism and collective action by both custody and treatment staffs.

Community-Based Corrections

Some prison wardens are fond of quoting a subtle reflection on the punishment ideology: "One doesn't get sent to prison for singing too loud in church"—implying that inmates are there because they have committed serious offenses. Some, of course, committed even more serious crimes than those to which they pleaded guilty during the bargaining process.

American opinion contains widely differing, sometimes contradictory attitudes toward the incarceration of offenders. Some express the sentiment that far too many are being sent to prison and that society would in no way be harmed by their release, while others demand imprisonment of large numbers of offenders and for longer periods of time. It is sometimes argued that there is an overdependence on incarceration, as a result of which America is reaping more crime and other social evils. Others lay the blame for greater crime on the "coddling" of suspects and convicted felons, and the failure to send more of them to prison.

The consequences of conviction and incarceration are many and they are complex.

Consequences of Conviction

Adjudication of guilt for an offense carries with it whatever sentence and punishment are imposed by the determination of that guilt. There are also accompanying or collateral consequences that result from conviction, and these, in the view of many, can contribute to future criminal behavior by the offender.

410

In most states, conviction on a felony charge permanently disenfranchises an offender. While many eligible voters refrain from exercising their right to cast a ballot, deprivation of that right in a nation of adult universal suffrage is a blow to a person's self-esteem. If our correctional goals include the encouragement of offenders to participate in the political process and thus identify with the values and beliefs of a free society, it might well behoove us to enhance the potential for reintegration by permitting at least the ex-offender, if not the offender, to vote.

Some of the legal rights commonly denied convicted felons (permanently, in some states) are the rights to hold public office, serve on a jury, testify, make contracts, and sue in court. Variations among the states in the specificity of disabling legislation make generalization about them impossible.

The consequences are also severe in the area of employment. A study by the American Bar Association (1973) found 1,948 different statutes in the fifty states that affect offenders in their efforts to obtain various types of licenses. Of these, 134 identify commission of a criminal act as a basis for denial of a license, and 707 impose the additional requirement that the applicant possess "good moral character." Another 410 statutes disqualify applicants on grounds of "moral turpitude," committing acts of inherent "baseness" in private, and of failure to perform social or public duties that a person owes to other citizens, to society, or to the nation and its institutions and government. These grounds are sufficiently vague to cover almost any criminal offense. Even in jobs where workers are almost always in demand, such as hairdressing, cosmetology and practical nursing, statutory disqualifications are found, designed to deny the offender an occupation and career in these fields. The job situation becomes more difficult as a result of widespread bonding and investigations by private corporations.

The person with a record of conviction is at a major disadvantage when it comes to reintegration into the community. The deprivation of rights and bars to employment are consequences of that record. In this era of computers—the "age of information"—many difficulties can arise as a result of having an arrest record. Even a record of mere contact with the criminal justice system is difficult to shed, once acquired, as is most stigma.

Many local regulations require a convicted felon to register with local law enforcement officials. This tends to single out the offender for special attention, and becomes an especially serious problem for the ex-offender who is trying to reform and may have moved from another city to avoid stigma. Many critics assert that these are obsolete practices which contribute to the reentry of the offender into the life of crime. They call for expungement of the record after a stated period of time has elapsed without further conviction. This would involve a court process by which arrest and conviction records can be erased or sealed.

Many individuals who have been successful in combatting the effects of an arrest and conviction have done so by embracing new values and new roles. Several have taken on religious roles ("dedicating a life to Christ," doing missionary work with "heathens," or becoming evangelists), and a few have dedicated themselves to prison reform or antidelinquency work among youth. For most offenders, successful handling of their past is accomplished by a combination of secrecy and change of behavior: "Putting distance between yourself and your record."

Consequences of Incarceration

As serious and even crime-producing as a conviction record may be for the offender, even more serious are the consequences of incarceration.

Both convict and taxpayer bear the burden of incarceration, although in radically different ways, of course. For the taxpayer, in addition to the cost of upkeep, there are arrest and court costs, and public aid to families of offenders in jail and prison.

The prison is geared to supervision, control, and surveillance of the inmate's every move. Depersonalization, prisonization, and routinization are reflected in daily events, for the prison is a total institution, to use the concept developed by Erving Goffman (1961), in which almost every action, need-gratification, and activity of the inmate are scheduled, supervised, and controlled by persons with whom he has hardly any reciprocal relationship. The buildings, policies, rules, regulations, and control procedures are all designed to minimize the inmate's control over self and environment.

In maximum security prisons, privacy is reduced to zero by the use of windowless open cells; even the toilet is open to view, and showers are taken under close supervision. Every consideration has been given by the designers and operators to prevent both privacy and intrusion or contact from the outside. Whereas in all prisons visits are carefully supervised, with many institutions allowing no physical contact but only conversation between visitors and inmates, in the maximum security prison a body search of the inmate, including the most intimate orifices, is routinely conducted following suspected contact with a visitor. Considerations of custody take precedence over the needs of rehabilitative programs. In short, an inmate is infantilized, allowed to make few decisions on his own, and crowded into architecturally archaic facilities full of hostile and angry persons. Underemployed or at best employed on job assignments irrelevant to life in the free world, untrained, cut off from most outside contacts, bored and idle, frequently threatened by other inmates, the offender may be exploited, sexually assaulted by another inmate or a gang—all, it has often been charged, without interference from correctional officers. Many prisoners claim to have been beaten by other prisoners or by custodial personnel.

Prisons are increasingly polarized along racial, ethnic, and gang lines; several institutions are so potentially explosive that prison administrators have the entire population under "lock and feed"—i.e., locked in cells almost twenty-four hours a day, and fed there rather than in the mess hall.

It is small wonder that entering convicts are rather quickly absorbed into the inmate culture and social system, viewing correctional officers as enemies, psychiatrists and psychologists as untrustworthy people who are to be manipulated, and other program staff as incompetent and hypocritical. The inmate's loss of self-esteem, infantilization, identification with criminal values and attitudes, and his dangerous environment do little to prepare him for even a marginal noncriminal career on the outside. The gap in work history caused by incarceration is difficult to explain to a potential employer.

While the effectiveness of prison in reducing further criminal behavior is not easily ascertained and undoubtedly varies by institution, rates as low as 15 percent have been documented for a reformatory group, and failure rates (rate of return to prison over a two-to-five-year period) of 30 to 60 percent are not considered unusual.

Alternatives to Imprisonment

Skyrocketing costs of institutional programs, high recidivism rates, the need for victims to receive restitution from the offender, relatively lower probation and parole costs as compared to confinement, an influx of large amounts of federal funds for innovation in the criminal justice system, rising involvement of citizens, disenchantment of correctional administrators with routine and failing operations, problems of prison disturbances and inmate protests, officer and inmate unionization, and an increasing public demand for accountability—all have contributed to a major emphasis on developing alternatives to imprisonment for offenders.

The major focus of these alternatives centers around what has come to be called "community corrections"—a term covering a wide variety of types of punishment imposed without incarceration and without removal of the offender from his area of residence and employment, if any. The crux of community corrections is supervision in the community. As stated in a document of the National Institute of Mental Health:

> The most rigorous research designs generally have elicited the finding that offenders eligible for supervision in the community in lieu of institutionalization do *as well* in the community as they do in prison or training school. When intervening variables are controlled, recidivism rates appear to be about the same. [National Institute of Mental Health, 1974: 33]

Even if the results are only equal, the monetary cost of community corrections is so much lower than with institutionalization that emphasis on it can be justified by economics alone. And even if the costs were the same, the community programs would be worth consideration on humanitarian grounds as a more reasonable approach to social control than are the fortress prisons.

Before prisons are abandoned, however, it is essential to recognize that the correctional utopia promised by community-based programs cannot be created with great rapidity. Crime and violence will continue to generate public fear, concern, and overreaction. Overselling community-based programs as a panacea for *all* crime misleads the public. Newspaper headlines seldom note that the ex-offender who has returned to crime may *not* have had the benefit of community-based treatment, and large parts of the public assume that community programs are worthless and that more offenders should be incarcerated.

A proper balance between small, humane, program-oriented maximum security institutions and community-based programs is recommended by supporters of deinstitutionalization for the foreseeable future. Until effective programs are developed for offenders who are so drug-dependent, violent, or disadvantaged that community programs cannot help them and they cannot help themselves, it is reasoned, society must be protected from their depredations by other means. The remaining offenders, however, should be given more opportunity for participation in community-based programs, which are generally divided into two subcategories: diversion programs, and programs designed to augment the existing correctional system.

One of the basic principles underlying community-based corrections is minimization of the offender's contact with institutional incarceration. The emphasis away from the dehumanizing and alienating effects of institutionalization mandates avoiding the use of jails, workhouses, and prisons to an extent consistent with the protection of society. To be effective, community-based programs must take advantage of every aspect of the services available to the offender in the outside world. This goal requires a whole new set of roles for all involved in the correctional process. Citizens, correctional workers, and offenders themselves must adjust to new expectations and functions. This will require extensive recruiting and retraining in order to provide the personnel with the orientation needed to make the system work.

DIVERSION: KEEPING THE OFFENDER OUT OF THE SYSTEM

Diversion involves suspension of the criminal process in favor of some noncriminal disposition. Only about 30 percent of reported offenses in America result in arrest, and only about one-third of these arrests result in a criminal conviction; preconviction diversion is one reason for this low percentage. Diversion generally occurs at three points, as identified in a National Advisory Commission report:

> There are three main points at which diversion may occur; prior to police contact, prior to official police processing, and prior to official court processing. Analysis of each of these potential points of diversion yields three basic models in terms of responsibility for diversion: community-based diversion programs, police-based diversion programs, and court-based diversion programs. While each of these models usually involves more than one agency or group, programs will be grouped according to who initiates and is primarily responsible for their operation. [National Advisory Commission, 1973: 77]

Most diversion programs now in effect constitute informal responses to the ambiguities of existing legislation. The value of such programs is difficult, if not impossible, to estimate. Their goals and procedures must be clearly articulated and integrated with the rest of the criminal justice system.

Diversion projects are most effective when integrated into a community-based correctional system with a number of levels of supervision and custody. Formalizing the currently informal options on an accountable basis must be done without rigidifying the process. If community-based programs become too restricted, they will be merely "institutions without walls." Diversion is the first threshold of the community corrections system, designed to remove as many offenders as possible from the criminal justice process before conviction and further criminalization can occur.

In Cook County, Illinois, a diversionary program was set up, aimed at elimination of stigma for the first offender in "soft drug" cases:

> The Cook County State's Attorney's Program for the Prevention of Drug Abuse depends on judicial and prosecutorial discretion rather than statute. The State's Attorney's office works with the director of the program to divert from prosecution first offenders charged with possession of small amounts of marijuana, stimulants, depressants, and hallucinogens. The Illinois Cannabis Control Act offers guidelines to determine whether the quantity of a drug in an offender's possession is for personal use or for sale.
>
> Eligible offenders must waive the right to a speedy trial, and the court continues the case for the program's two or three months' duration. Participants attend five weekly group therapy sessions and submit urine samples for up to three months. Arrest, absence from group therapy, or traces of opiates, amphetamines, or barbiturates in the urine are cause for removal from treatment and either a resumption of prosecution or enrollment in a more intensive program....
>
> The State's Attorney moves to *nolle prosequi* charges against persons who successfully complete treatment and refrain from further arrest. Failure in the program does not influence the court in cases where prosecution is resumed. The State's Attorney's Office plans to expand the process of diverting users of "soft" drugs from prosecution. Approximately 80 percent of the cases have been successful, lending credence to the argument for diversion of drug offenders. [National Advisory Commission, 1973: 88–89]

Prosecutors have immense discretion over which cases will be carried forward to trial; typically with a burdensome volume of cases and an understaffed office, the prosecutor is willing to bargain for justice to meet the caseload demand. One of the tools increasingly used is contractual nonprosecution, in which the accused agrees to accept moral (if not legal) responsibility for an act, make restitution to any victim, voluntarily enter into a community treatment program, and refrain from criminal behavior for a specified period of time (e.g., one year). If the offender abides by the contract, the prosecutor dismisses the charge. Increasing numbers of jurisdictions are adopting this procedure.

PROBATION

Probation is viewed as the bright hope for the future of corrections. It is generally conceded, however, that the full potential of this alternative to imprisonment cannot be reached without some effort to fulfill two major needs: (1) development of an effective system to determine which offenders should receive probation, and (2) provision of support and services to probationers out in the community to allow them to live independently in a socially accepted way. To achieve these goals, probation services must be organized, staffed, and funded properly. The shifting of money and resources to the efforts of community-based projects is necessary to make probation a viable alternative. The National Advisory Commission on Criminal Justice Standards and Goals has recommended the national use of probation as the most desirable disposition, preferably without adjudication of guilt. It has also recommended that probation, which started on a volunteer basis, seek out volunteers to serve in all capacities.

Probation has established itself as the new wave in corrections. It appears that such developments as the current moratorium on prison construction and the emphasis on probation as the preferred disposition will remain in the forefront of correctional reform. Successes have been claimed, but they are difficult to verify. As an alternative to imprisonment—less costly and probably as effective—probation offers great appeal, for it appears to answer the need for a sound and economical approach to corrections (Carlson and Parks, 1979).

Adjuncts to Institutionalization

The distinction between treatment methods in an institution and in a community has become blurred as increasing numbers of offenders are released under supervision. The most effective response to their differential needs is to develop a spectrum of custody and supervision modalities. The problems of bridging the gap between the institution and the community have been recognized since prisons first began to release offenders on "tickets of leave"; in the middle and later decades of the nineteenth century, Ireland's Sir Walter Crofton provided prisoners with a chance to work in the community for a period of time prior to release. The concept of work release has since become an important adjunct to institutional programs (Shichor and Allen, 1977). According to this concept, offenders are allowed to work at jobs in the community and still receive the benefit of certain programs available at an institution. Work release may often be the first phase in the establishment of some form of residential and custodial transition to the community for offenders able to function at a job but still in need of treatment under supervision. Such community-based facilities are usually referred to as "halfway houses," because residents are considered to be halfway out of the institution (Allen et al., 1978). Halfway houses are often located in depressed neighborhoods in older buildings originally designed for some other purpose.

Halfway houses are often operated by private organizations under state guidelines or standards. Funds have been made available from various sources, and halfway houses have developed with a number of different organizational and ideological orientations. Some states have begun to take a much closer look at the functions and merits of halfway house programs and to require an accounting of results.

The increasing use of diversionary and probationary alternatives to imprisonment has resulted in the development of "halfway-in" houses for those offenders who need supportive residential treatment but are not so dangerous as to be sent, even briefly, to prison. It is probable that an integrated system of the future would place halfway-out and halfway-in offenders in the same residence, with the emphasis on the kinds of treatment provided rather than the types of offender housed. These two categories may well be joined by a third: new reintegration centers will become an important part of the correctional system. The future emphasis on provision of residential care and custody will most likely center on referral to available community services and programs rather than just personal contact with the offender (as in probation and parole).

The community correctional center and treatment facility have been the most appealing developments toward community-based institutions in recent years. These centers have been organized in a variety of models, utilizing local resources for the provision of services. Centers serve a number of purposes, including detention, treatment, holding, and pre-release adjustment, and are based on a variety of facilities ranging from currently existing jails to hotels and motels. With growing support, the centers can establish a specific and integrated set of services. Instead of a *criminal* justice system at the local level, there is hope for a *social* justice system dealing with many kinds of individuals.

It appears that sufficient major alternatives for diversion and alternative community-based correctional programs exist to warrant consideration of a comprehensive state- or county-wide community-based correctional system. One such system, using a reintegration model, is described below. This particular model would not necessarily lend itself to adoption by every jurisdiction, but it is an example of a comprehensive and responsive system, some form of which can be developed that would be suitable throughout the United States.

**INTEGRATED
CORRECTIONS**

The reintegration model presented here assumes the following:
1. Relatively few offenders perpetrate crime due to medical, psychiatric, or psychological abnormalities.
2. Offenders are apt to commit crime of their own volition; they are not compelled by some irresistible impulse; criminals exercise "free will."
3. Most offenders can be handled through community-based corrections and relatively few (15–20 percent) require incapacitation or punishment.
4. Reintegration is a gradual process; there are few offenders who are able to escape an economically and socially marginal life-style in a brief period of time.
5. Sufficient community-based programs exist or can be coordinated to permit the gradual reintegration of offenders.
6. Offenders' problems arise in the community and must be handled in the community.
7. Given the option between punishment and community-based correctional programming, most offenders will not opt for punishment.
8. Some offenders are too dangerous to be handled even in a coordinated and comprehensive community-based program; prisons are necessary.
9. The courts must be an integral part of the overall reintegration of offenders.
10. The role of the defense attorney extends into the offender's decision to participate in a punishment or reintegration package.
11. Both punishment and the reintegration model programming are the domain of a state's department of corrections.

417

THE CONTRACT   In the course of processing offenders, numerous alternatives—all of which have reintegration into society as their aim—are available. Let us focus on the offender, pleading guilty or adjudged guilty of a felony. Once guilt is determined, prior to disposition of the case, the judge would formally preside over and participate in the offender's choice of either punishment or reintegration. In this initial decision and in later sentencing questions, the defense attorney would continue to provide legal advice and protect the offender's rights. Prosecution should remain a viable entity up to the point of the final contract.

Upon conviction of those offenders not opting for punishment, the state's department of corrections would then develop a comprehensive reintegration plan predicated on maximizing delivery of services, victim restitution, the least restrictive environment, and a detailed program for handling of the offender. Various options for the possible plans are shown in Figure 24–1, and include behavior modification, halfway houses, probation hostels for heavily dependent offenders, community treatment centers, community reintegration centers, and education-vocation furlough programs. The individualized plan would be presented to the court in the form of a proposed contract. Both defense and prosecutorial attorneys could consent or dissent; the court would retain authority in development of the final contract.

Once the contracts are approved and signed by all parties (which might possibly include the victim, usually excluded from criminal justice decisions), the court would then formally dispose of the offender by commitment as a probationer to the state's department of corrections, whose responsibility would include implementation of the contract, provision of services, and supervision (the levels of which could subsequently be varied in accordance with the offender's progress toward defined goals within the contractual time period). The court would retain the right to make formal revocation of the reintegration contract and to impose prison as the alternative.

There would be five categories of offenders for whom this program would not be applicable; mandatory prison terms might be required for those who have perpetrated murder in the first degree, have committed any crime in which a firearm is used, are third-time felony offenders, are convicted of forcible rape, or are convicted as large-scale drug dealers.

The philosophy of imprisonment would be one of incapacitation only, with determinate sentences ("flat" time, except for mandatory time off for good behavior). Recidivists would receive multiples of the determinate sentence. Inasmuch as parole would not exist as a mandatory requirement and sentences would be determinate, a parole agency would not be necessary. However, ex-prisoners desiring assistance would, on a voluntary basis, be eligible for all services available to probationers.

The private sector could contract with prison inmates in their factories inside the prisons (or miniature production communities); the inmates would earn prevailing wages equal to those received by noncriminal employees, produce modern products for a competitive market, pay taxes, support their dependents (and relieve welfare rolls), compensate victims, amass some savings to supplement any "gate money," obtain continuity in work history, contribute toward retirement benefits, and (assuming favorable work histories

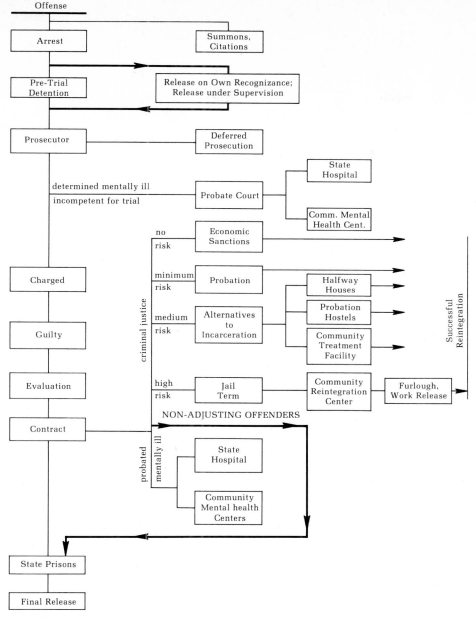

We are indebted to Richard P. Seiter for the original conception of this figure.

**FIGURE 24-1
A Reintegration Model**

within the prison) have a guaranteed job on release. Such a plan is under consideration in a number of states, such as Georgia; it has been frequently observed in the Scandinavian countries.

This model can serve as an initial statement in the dialogue on the implications of developing a comprehensive correctional system. It is from such a dialogue that deliberate, effective, and constitutional alternatives can ultimately be devised.

References for Part V

ALLEN, HARRY E., and CLIFFORD E. SIMONSEN. *Corrections in America.* Encino, Calif.: Glencoe Press, 1978.

ALLEN, HARRY E., et al. *Halfway Houses: Program Model.* Washington, D.C.: Government Printing Office, 1978.

AMERICAN BAR ASSOCIATION. *Laws, Licenses and the Offender's Right to Work.* Washington, D.C.: National Clearinghouse for Offender Employment Restrictions, 1973.

AMERICAN FRIENDS SERVICE COMMITTEE. *Struggle for Justice.* New York: Hill & Wang, 1971.

BAILEY, WALTER C. "Correctional Outcome: An Analysis of 100 Reports." *Journal of Criminal Law, Criminology and Police Science*, 1966, 57: 153–160.

BARNES, HARRY ELMER, and NEGLEY TEETERS. *New Horizons in Criminology.* Englewood Cliffs, N.J.: Prentice-Hall, 1959.

BECCARIA, CESARE. *An Essay on Crimes and Punishments.* Stanford, Calif.: Academic Reprints, 1953. (First published in 1764.)

BURNS, ROBERT. *I Am a Fugitive from a Georgia Chain Gang!* New York: Vanguard Press, 1932.

CARLSON, ERIC, and EVELYN PARKS. *Issues in Probation Management.* Washington, D.C.: Government Printing Office, 1979.

CLEMMER, DONALD. *The Prison Community.* New York: Holt, Rinehart and Winston, 1958. (First published in 1940.)

COMMUNITY RESEARCH, INC. *Evaluation of Alcoholic Rehabilitation Program.* Dayton, Ohio: Community Research, Inc., 1972.

DURKHEIM, EMILE. *The Division of Labor in Society.* New York: Free Press, 1947. (First published in 1893.)

Gardner v. Florida. 430 U.S. Reports 349, 1976.

GIBBONS, DON C. *Changing the Lawbreaker: The Treatment of Delinquents and Criminals.* Montclair, N.J.: Allanheld, Osmun, 1981. (First published in 1965.)

GOFFMAN, ERVING. *Asylums: Essays on the Social Situation of Mental Patients and Other Inmates.* New York: Doubleday, 1961.

GOLDFARB, RONALD. *Jails: The Ultimate Ghetto.* Garden City, N.Y.: Anchor/Doubleday, 1975.

HAGAN, JOHN. "The Social and Legal Construction of Criminal Justice: A Study of Presentencing Processes." *Social Problems*, 1975, 22: 620–637.

HOWARD, RICHARD. *Determinant Sentencing in California.* Lexington, Ky.: Council of State Governments, 1979.

HUFF, C. RONALD. "Unionization behind the Walls." *Criminology*, 1974, 12: 175–194.

———. "The Discovery of Prisoners' Rights: A Sociological Analysis." In Geoffrey Alpert, ed., *The Legal Rights of Prisoners*, pp. 47–65. Beverly Hills, Calif.: Sage Publications, 1980.

IRWIN, JOHN. *Prison Turmoil.* Boston: Little, Brown, 1980.

IRWIN, JOHN, and DONALD R. CRESSEY. "Thieves, Convicts and the Inmate Culture." *Social Problems*, 1962, 10: 142–155.

JOHNSON, ELMER. *Crime, Corrections and Society.* Homewood, Ill.: Dorsey Press, 1964.

Jones v. North Carolina Prisoners' Labor Union, Inc. 433 U. S. 119, 1977.

Kaimowitz v. Michigan Department of Mental Health. 42 U.S.L.W. 2063, Michigan Circuit Court, 1973.

KAPLAN, JOHN. *Criminal Justice.* Mineola, N.Y.: Foundation Press, 1973.

KITTRIE, NICHOLAS N. *The Right To Be Different: Deviance and Enforced Therapy.* Baltimore: Johns Hopkins Press, 1971.

Mackey v. Procunier. 477 F.2d, 9th Cir. Ct., 1973.

MARTINSON, ROBERT. "What Works?: Questions and Answers about Prison Reform." *Public Interest*, 1974, 12: 22–55.

Mempa v. Rhay. 389 U.S. 128, 1967.

Morrisey v. Brewer. 408 U.S. 471, 1972.

National Advisory Commission on Criminal Justice Standards and Goals. *Corrections.* Washington, D.C.: Government Printing Office, 1973.

National Conference on Corrections. *Proceedings.* Williamsburg, Va.: The Conference, 1971.

National Institute of Law Enforcement and Criminal Justice. *Community Based Corrections in Des Moines.* Washington, D.C.: Government Printing Office, 1974.

National Institute of Mental Health (prepared by Eugene Doleschal and Gilbert Geis). *Graduated Release.* Washington, D.C.: Government Printing Office, 1971.

National Institute of Mental Health. *Community-Based Corrections: Models and Practices.* Washington, D.C.: Government Printing Office, 1974, 1–73.

Packer, Herbert L. *The Limits of the Criminal Sanction.* Stanford, Calif.: Stanford University Press, 1968.

People v. Andrew. 239 N.E.2d, 314, 1968.

Petersen, David, and Paul C. Friday. "Shock of Imprisonment: Comparative Analysis of Short-Term Incarceration as a Treatment Technique." *Canadian Journal of Criminology and Corrections,* 1973, 12: 1–11.

———. "Early Release from Incarceration: Race as a Factor in 'Shock Probation.' " *Journal of Criminal Law and Criminology,* 1975, 66: 79–87.

President's Commission on Law Enforcement and Administration of Justice. *The Challenge of Crime in a Free Society.* Washington, D.C.: Government Printing Office, 1967a.

President's Commission on Law Enforcement and Administration of Justice. *Corrections.* Washington, D.C.: Government Printing Office, 1967b.

Reckless, Walter C. *The Crime Problem.* 4th ed. New York: Appleton-Century-Crofts, 1967.

Rothman, David. *The Discovery of the Asylum.* Boston: Little, Brown, 1971.

———. "Prisons: The Failure Model." *The Nation,* 1974, 219: 656–659.

Sellin, Thorsten. "A Look at Prison History." *Federal Probation,* September 1967, 31: 18–23.

———. *Slavery and the Penal System.* New York: Elsevier, 1976.

Shichor, David, and Harry Allen. "Study Release: A Correctional Alternative." *Offender Rehabilitation,* 1977, 2: 7–17.

Singer, Neil. *The Value of Inmate Manpower.* Washington, D.C.: American Bar Association Commission of Correction Facilities and Manpower, 1973.

Sostre v. Rockefeller. 312 F. Supp. 863, S.D.N.Y., 1970.

Special Conference on Determinate Sentencing. *Determinate Sentencing: Reform or Regression?* Washington, D.C.: National Institute of Law Enforcement and Criminal Justice, 1978.

Sykes, Gresham M. *The Society of Captives: A Study of a Maximum Security Prison.* Princeton, N.J.: Princeton University Press, 1958.

Szasz, Thomas S. *Psychiatric Justice.* New York: Macmillan, 1965.

United States v. Needles. 472 F.2d, 652, 1973.

United States v. Wiley. 278 F.2d, 500, 1960.

U.S. Department of Justice. *1970 National Jail Census.* Washington, D.C.: Government Printing Office, 1971.

U.S. Department of Justice. *The Nation's Jails.* Washington, D.C.: Government Printing Office, 1975.

von Hirsch, Andrew. *Doing Justice: The Choice of Punishments.* New York: Hill & Wang, 1976.

Waller, Irvin. *Men Released from Prison.* Toronto: University of Toronto Press, 1974.

Williams v. New York. 337 U.S. 241, 1949.

Wolfgang, Marvin E. "Crime and Punishment." *New York Times,* March 2, 1980.

PART VI

Directions
and Outlook

The Future of Crime, Criminals, and Criminology

It has often been said that science is predictive but not prophetic (Merton, 1960). On the basis of observation, experiment, and experience in a limited, typical number of cases, science draws generalizations which can then be applied to an entire category or class of phenomena—including those cases not observed—and thus predicts what will occur when the hitherto unstudied comes into view. But even this tentative foresight is seldom given to social scientists, who deal with an almost infinite number of variables and factors that affect any given social situation.

Crime: Its Past and Future

To speak of the future of crime in America is to invite a cynical response: "Crime has a great future! It is a fast-growing industry!" Or one might be met with a mélange of patriotism and optimism: "American morality, ingenuity, free enterprise, democracy, and all the other features that have made this a powerful nation will triumph over crime, as they have triumphed over slavery, the lawlessness of the frontier, the vigilantism and anti-black terror in the South, the excesses of Al Capone and Murder, Inc. in the Prohibition era and immediately thereafter, and many other evils, problems, and difficulties."

There are no crystal balls, although there are many gazers. Instead, one can find a few trends and isolate a few factors that are most likely to influence the decades ahead. The only clear-cut prediction that has been made in criminological circles is the demographic one: by the mid-1980s—this argument goes—the percentage of Americans in the most crime-prone age groups will have declined and street crime will decline with it, perhaps to return in a cyclical fashion when the vulnerable ages again become more heavily populated (around the turn of the century or shortly thereafter). In addition, some criminologists are predicting that the gap between male and female criminality will narrow if not entirely disappear (see Adler, 1975; Simon, 1975). It has been noted that people are increasingly being socialized with the idea that there are no tasks, activities, occupations, and roles that are sex-specific except those centering on reproduction and the nursing of the infant. Hence, there will be smaller differences between men and women in the proportion that becomes doctors, lawyers, detectives, police officers, and criminals.

Neither of these two predictions seems to us beyond dispute as a blueprint for the future. The demographic one gambles on a single factor. While the large percentage of American youths in their teens and twenties from 1963 to 1979 did coincide with a considerable increase in crime—the "war babies" had come of age—this is by no means the sole explanation of the greater amount of crime. Furthermore, these optimistic demographers overlook the salient fact that the birth rate has not seriously diminished in the lower socioeconomic classes and in those ethnic and racial groups that have made a disproportionate contribution to the total American crime rate.

The argument on female criminality is an interesting one. While women have increased their criminal activity (or so it would appear from official statistics) in many respects far out of proportion to the increases perpetrated by men, it is likely that many major crimes will remain male-dominated. Women have thus far played only a minuscule part in organized crime, and continue to constitute a small percentage of those responsible for armed robbery, street mugging, burglary, automobile theft, spouse battering, and all important sex crimes (although there is some increase in female pimping). There is no reason to believe that women will be more greatly represented in the future than now in criminal child abuse. In contrast, with white-collar crime—dominated by men because males have had the opportunities as a result of their monopoly of powerful positions in politics, corporate life, and such professions as medicine and law—women may come to be more equally represented in criminal activity as they obtain statuses that give them more nearly equal opportunity to perform illegal acts.

Looking at these two predictions, however, one is struck by their mutually cancelling effects on crime in America. The demographic one gives us a rosy outlook, because crime-committing cohorts will diminish in size. The female-criminal prediction tells us that we had better not rest easy and look forward to a less crime-prone population, for a new group will come to replace the diminishing ranks of male youths.

Criminologists have frequently emphasized the multiplicity of factors (as distinguished from causes) that result in a single incident of crime. On a national scale, so many factors beyond the predictive range of the social scientist will be influencing the crime scene that it would perhaps be more helpful simply to enumerate a few of them than to attempt to extend the graphs of violent crime, property crime, and other types of criminal activity into the future. The nature, scope, intensity, and volume of crime, it seems to us, will be strongly influenced by perceived social morality, perceived social inequality, economic conditions, the tendency of America to move toward greater social cohesion or greater social dissensus, the forces either bringing more intergroup amity or exacerbating intergroup tensions, and the diminution or aggrandizement of the culture or subculture of violence. Finally, notwithstanding the never-ending debates on the efficacy of deterrence, crime will surely be influenced by the perception among impressionable would-be offenders of the likelihood of apprehension and the certainty and severity of anticipated punishment.

Most of the factors outlined above, and others that could be added, are themselves difficult to discuss with any degree of confidence in the accuracy of prediction for the near or far-off future. Specialists know little of the impact of changed economic conditions on crime, for example, and even less about the economic conditions that will prevail in the United States in the final years of the century. Similar uncertainties govern developments in intergroup relations, perceived inequality, family relationships, and the mass media.

Crime as Continuity

Despite these uncertainties, we will venture to make one generalization about the future, based on the concept of the dynamic nature of crime. Crime, like almost all other phenomena in society, has both a dynamism of its own and a built-in process for slowing down its own acceleration. The dynamism works by suggestion and imitation as well as by differential association. One hears, "Everybody has his hustle," and whether or not this is true becomes less important than the fact that large numbers of people believe it. And if everybody else is being lawless, more and more people feel they are denying themselves the advantages they could obtain through one form or another of lawlessness, and so are tempted to do what "everybody" allegedly is doing. People learn about crime through the media, through their friends, or by being victimized. Some people (it takes only a minority) are impressionable, and when they learn that a type of crime exists and how it is carried out, when they receive what may be a distortion of its frequency through the media, they may begin to be drawn into a circle consisting of those who will, when opportunity arises, put into practice what they have learned. Or if the opportunity does not arise it can be created or discovered.

The inequalities, real or putative, of the criminal justice system become common knowledge and folk wisdom. Upperworld crimes become publicized through the media, which report the leniency if not actual deference shown the offenders while the small percentage of perpetrators of street crimes who are caught and convicted are often given lengthy sentences. The leniency shown to the white-collar criminal may result not only in more upper-class persons committing similar acts when they have or can create the opportunities but also in many lower-class people reacting with anger, hostility, and envy when they hear about welfare programs for the rich and rip-offs perpetrated by the powerful and the affluent.

The poor have been victimized in the past, often criminally, by storekeepers, landlords, and corporations. Such direct victimization has in recent years been more thoroughly exposed and publicized, and to a small degree opposed by courts, legislatures, and regulatory agencies. The poor, like other victims, react with anger, frustration and sometimes despair, and out of such reactions a few turn to crime. They may justify and rationalize their criminal activity as a struggle for survival. That their victims are themselves most often poor and of the same race and ethnic group as the offenders does not seem to stay the hand of those drawn by this logic into the world of crime.

There are patterns and careers in crime, as we have shown earlier in this book. People go in and out of criminal activity, but while in it they often recruit new accomplices and assistants. These new recruits remain in the crime scene after the recruiters have retired or been incarcerated—if not killed.

Crime has its reciprocal role relationships: there are corrupt politicians working hand-in-hand with bribing industrial executives, corrupt policemen and organized crime figures. Each lives off the other and needs the other. They are locked into each other's criminal activities, and hence it is difficult for either to step out. In short, there is crime today because there was crime yesterday; it is not an activity that can be expected to disappear like a plague that has spent itself.

But dynamism does not work that simply; if it did, whatever is would continue or increase and seldom diminish or change course. Crime not only can be influenced by technology, demography, social movements, economic conditions, and various cultural phenomena: it can also bring into existence the forces that will contain or diminish it. When crime, or any specific form of it, reaches a level beyond the point of tolerability in a society, the society reacts to contain it or in some way reinstitute conditions so that ongoing social life may continue uninterrupted. This is a dialectic process, along almost classic Hegelian-Marxist lines: thesis (crime-ridden society) creates antithesis (forces to suppress, contain, legitimate, or in other ways rid society of enough crime so that social institutions can function), and the clash of thesis and antithesis bringing about a new emergent form, the synthesis (a changed society in which crime is reduced to a tolerable level). This is not a sudden process but a subtle and continuing one, and some of its manifestations are already seen in the United States.

It is seductively easy to envision this process in terms of progress, with new reforms coming about because old methods are inadequate for the protection of people and property. The theft of a bicycle from a rider, for example, can result in a ruling that bicyclists must use special paths during special hours, and the aggregation of cyclists reduces the thefts. An increase in forcible rape might result in watchdog groups demanding greater police patrols, more vigorous investigations, and greater certainty of apprehension and prosecution of the accused, in turn resulting in the diminution of this form of crime. However, the dialectic process can also result in the formation, for example, of dangerous vigilante groups in neighborhoods where there is dissatisfaction with police protection, and these groups can direct their anger against the innocent as well as the guilty, and against entire racial, religious, and ethnic peoples. On an official level, a large amount of crime can foster repressive acts, including an attack on freedom of citizens from search and seizure, freedom from intrusions on one's privacy, and many other rights held to be important in America.

One can therefore make few predictions with regard to the future of crime, but some trends seem to be apparent. A few of these trends, as they relate to criminological theory, criminal justice, corrections, and criminology as a discipline, have been highlighted earlier in this text, and some of the remarks that follow constitute a summary and recapitulation.

Trends in Criminological Theory

In the period that might approximately be fixed as starting after the First World War and continuing until the mid-1960s—a span of almost half a century—criminology was particularly fertile, in America and abroad, for the development of new theory. Culture conflict, ecology and social disorganization, anomie, differential association, learning, imitation, psychoanalysis, biology, the subculture of violence: all were the basis of many theories during this period. Theories competed with one another; each had its vigorous supporters and detractors. Then came the great increase in crime in the United States generally believed to have started between 1963 and 1965, but explanations of the new crime, and new explanations of the old, were not forthcoming. It is striking that the era in America which appears to have seen the greatest rise in street crime, organized crime, and white-collar crime, among other forms of lawlessness, should have been theoretically so sterile. Only the demographic explanation (the war-baby bulge in the population profile) has been seriously put forth to account for the changing crime situation, and only labeling theory, which has focused almost exclusively on victimless crimes and on noncriminal deviance, has had a serious following during this period of heightened criminality. The labeling concept, with its considerable support among sociologists, was never taken seriously by more than a few people as an explanation of adult crime (see Tittle, 1980). Thus one is faced with the irony that the theoretical orientation that has attracted the most attention during the time of the greatest crime increase is one that has not addressed the issue.

Nevertheless, this apparent lack of criminological response in the form of productive new theory during a critical period of increased criminality may be largely an illusion. Relatively few years have passed since the precipitate increase in crime, and it is still too early to have assimilated the events, adequately studied them, and reacted to them with well-considered explanations. A few have been forthcoming: in addition to the demographic factor, one can note the anger and disillusionment among blacks and Hispanics that set in with the failures of the civil rights movement, the decline nationwide in social cohesion and moral unity with the war in Vietnam, and the rising tide of discontent among oppressed but formerly more passive parts of the population.

What appears to be occurring in theoretical criminology today is a resurgence of old theory in new and usually more sophisticated format, combined with a highly successful effort to integrate not only various disciplines but theoretical approaches (see Wolfgang and Ferracuti, 1967).

In the resurgence of old theory in new garb, there are two major, and many minor, thrusts. Of the major ones, the most notable has been the new and in some respects unexpected reappearance of the biological theory of criminal predilection. From the days of the early phrenologists who examined bumps on the head, through the work of Cesare Lombroso, William Sheldon, and many others, the biological approach to crime had seemingly been disposed of many times, but it is an idea that has never died. Almost no one talks of criminal destiny today, as did Hooton (1939). Rather, many have suggested—and Sarnoff Mednick and Karl Christiansen (1977) seem to have offered the most convincing evidence—that people are born with different constitutional givens that make it more or less likely that some persons rather than others will be violent, commit predatory crime, be unable to exercise self-control, show signs of extreme irritability, have short-range and not long-range hedonistic goals, and be self-destructive ("a born loser" or "his own worst enemy," in words frequently spoken by and about prisoners).

Biological arguments can of course be misused by powerful groups in a society; they can be manipulated for racist viewpoints in a way that overlooks the actual social, economic, and cultural reasons for disproportionate distribution of various types of crime among different ethnic groups. Those who use the biological thrust in this manner pay little or no attention to the racial identities of members of the dominant groups in society who commit crimes. They ignore the fact that Nixon is a Quaker, and that upperworld crime is not only white collar but white. Biological theory may also be used as an excuse to avoid serious economic reform, justify a return to Social Darwinism, or abandon rehabilitation programs because the subjects of such efforts are deemed literally incorrigible.

As a field of study, criminology has had its fashions and trends, and its taboos as well. Like the behavioral sciences generally, particularly sociology, it has looked with some skepticism at those who have suggested biological sources of human behavior. If some of the biologically oriented people were simplistic and their work vulnerable—the story is retold countless times of Lombroso performing an autopsy on a criminal and seeing criminality in the brain formation—the antibiologists in criminology have stood on no firmer ground. They raise a cry about biological determinism, ignoring the fact that predisposition or predilection is not determinism. Furthermore, an argument is not scientifically weakened by pinning on it a negative label, such as "racist," and pointing out how horrible it would be if it is found to be true.

Counterposed to biology—but even more drastically to many other theories having psychological, psychiatric, and sometimes sociocultural implications—is so-called labeling theory (discussed above in Part II of this volume). Many people using this approach argue that there are no discernible and significant differences between the criminal and noncriminal populations except that the former have been caught and apprehended. It is not the individual offender who should be examined to reveal what characteristics distinguish him from others, for such traits either are not to be found or are the result of his being apprehended and labeled criminal. In this orientation, it is asserted that there is a power group in society that, through legislative, judicial, and other activities, makes a distinction that separates criminals from all others; in short, the criminal population is simply the group that has been declared criminal by its oppressors.

Sometimes such sweeping statements can be made to work out by a neat selectivity, as when Bruce Franklin (1978) shows how the black American victim, first in the form of slave and then of newly freed but still oppressed person of color, was defined as criminal and treated as such by the slaveholders and their successors. The definition of an entire group as criminal, or the criminalization of their behavior by oppressive legislators and judges, conflicts sharply with study of the relatively small proportion of the population that commits violent and predatory acts. As recognized also by biological and psychoanalytic approaches, the offenders may well differ in constitution, genetic traits, temperament, family backgrounds, and numerous other respects from the larger number of people who do not commit such acts.

Thus labeling orientation turned criminologists away from their centuries-old activity of looking at the offender, only to encounter a return to that approach with the resurgence of the biological approach. It is often noted that those who focus on the offender show an almost exclusive interest in street crime and lower-class crime, and seldom in upperworld or even organized crime. Few people seriously inquire into the biological backgrounds, Oedipal complexes, or unresolved sibling rivalries of Nixon and his colleagues of Watergate notoriety, or of the perpetrators of corporate frauds involving millions of dollars. Rorschach and MMPI tests may be given to those who loot from a store during a disaster, but the storekeepers who routinely loot from customers—in violation of criminal codes that cover price gouging—are not subject to analysis to discover their peculiarities of biology and psychology.

To these very righteous objections to focusing on some categories of offenders and not on others, two counterarguments can be set forth. First, it is entirely possible that biological and constitutional predilections (and other distinctions separating the criminal from the noncriminal population) can be found in some types of offenders but not others. Rapists and other violent persons, burglars and other predators, may show distinctions that are not less real because they are not found as well in perjurers, obstructors of justice, donors and recipients of bribes, perpetrators of fraud, or those who commit war crimes. Second, and perhaps more significant, it is possible that white-collar and upperworld criminals do not differ from noncriminals in that they are acting out the mandates of their culture, which has socialized them to prey on others as long as this is accomplished in nonviolent ways.

Whether or not biology survives as a partial explanation of criminality, it hardly seems likely to us that criminology can or will turn away from studying the characteristics and traits of offenders and how, by implication, the offenders significantly differ from other portions of the population. Criminology, in the pursuit of studies of offenders, will have to produce better methods of obtaining samples than relying on the incarcerated, or even the accused; while the biological and psychological schools will have to produce more reliable methods for measuring differences or similarities between groups of persons than those found in current projective tests.

After biology and the dispute over labeling and the study of offenders, a major orientation is found in the revival, with many modifications, of conflict theory. Some have called conflict theory, or at least their own special version of it, the "new criminology" (Taylor, Walton, and Young, 1974), while others have insisted that there is nothing new in it, and that it is all found in the theories that were abundant in the 1930s and later decades (see Meier, 1976). Conflict theory has bifurcations and pathways not always reconcilable with one another; along this line, Vold (1979) contrasts the approaches in the work of Richard Quinney (1970), Austin Turk (1969), and the self-labeled new criminologists. Conflict theory is traceable to the Marxists (see Bonger, 1967), to Sellin (1938), to the first theoretical synthesis of Vold (1958, 1979), to anomie theory as developed by Merton (1957), to subculture-of-violence theory (Wolfgang and Ferracuti, 1967), and to the ecologists (especially of Chicago). Nonetheless, there is a great deal in conflict theory that seems to be emerging as a dominant emphasis in criminology. There is a new stress on who holds the power to legislate and enforce laws, who is responsible for the differential labeling of some (but not all) antisocial behavior as criminal, the discretionary power of police and prosecutors, and against whom this power is directed. Conflict theory may be inchoate and its diverse strands contradictory, but its stress on conflict between social groups—particularly the relatively powerless and the comparatively more powerful—emerges as a theme that is likely to be widely espoused in criminology during the years ahead. That it has potential for social action of an ameliorative nature, to assist in the struggle against class, race, and other types of inequality, should make it appealing to criminologists and sociologists.

Trends in Criminological Research

During the 1970s, probably as a result of the apparent increase in street and ordinary crime and the consequent rise in public fear of victimization, the federal government started to finance more heavily than previously various programs in criminological research, experimental work on crime prevention, studies of alternative modes of rehabilitation, and related work. Much of this was done through the Law Enforcement Assistance Administration, to a lesser extent the National Institute of Mental Health, and a variety of other agencies.

This work has come under criticism from different perspectives. Some have claimed that the bulk of the funds has gone to purchase hardware that was sometimes not needed and often used for ostentatious display, the personal aggrandizement of local police leaders and sheriffs, or, more frequently, in order to make law enforcement agencies more effective as repressive bodies against protesters, untried but accused defendants, and convicted offenders. Although the charge that LEAA funds have been transforming American police systems into protofascist organizations is an exaggeration, it cannot be denied that much of the funds have been ineffective in crime reduction and have served mainly to beef up local police units already heavily overstocked with military equipment.[1] The more effective use of po-

1. Not to be denied, also, is that these funds have given lucrative jobs to criminological researchers (see Nicolaus, 1969).

lice for prevention of crime and apprehension of offenders, critics claim, will not be enhanced by the purchase of helicopters, machine guns, and more sophisticated instruments of destruction.

From an entirely different perspective, the highly funded work of LEAA has been criticized for its failure to bring about reduction in crime or recidivism. Such results, even if they did come, could hardly emerge immediately from research, for the latter is conducted slowly and its effects felt gradually. But the public, political leaders, and governmental agencies are not in a mood to display patience. They cannot readily embrace a program that spends tens of millions of dollars on something called criminological research that, whether or not it adds to accumulated knowledge (hardly of interest except to social scientists), does not become transformed into policy and does not bring the longed-for results.

One can add to these a third criticism, this one from the viewpoint of the criminologist: namely, that so many LEAA studies have been highly quantitative exercises in statistical sophistication directed toward minute areas that are unlikely to add significant knowledge or make contributions to the formation of sound public policy. Much of the grant-sponsored work, taken singly, appears to be trivial. One hopes that there can be an accumulation of these small studies and their findings, a synthesis that builds upon them and can then be used to validate empirically old or newly emergent theoretical perspectives—or to invalidate them, which is equally if not more important. Minute, even minuscule studies on the role of the public defender, sentencing differentials for people of different social backgrounds convicted of the same crime, comparative performances of lawyers for indigent and other defendants: it is entirely possible that numerous such studies could add up to a significant total image of courtroom performance and the criminal justice system. But funded research has not focused on the major issues of criminology; it has brought forth only a disappointingly small amount of work that can be considered a contribution to the body of knowledge that comprises the discipline.

For purposes of immediate prognosis, it appears that this research may have had a not entirely anticipated, stimulating effect on the future of criminology. Criminal justice centers have arisen in abundance, and large numbers of specialists in sociology, political science, public administration, and psychology, among other areas of study, have been trained in criminology. The field has had an influx of people of a variety of specializations and diverse trainings and outlooks, and it is likely to be enriched by it. There is now on the horizon, more than ever, an intellectually sharp and well-trained group of young criminologists who may make their influence felt in the coming generation.

It is today generally recognized that the prevention of crime and the apprehension of offenders are complementary processes. Social and political leaders can work simultaneously toward reduction of crime—which we should remember can never be totally obliterated—and arrest and prosecution of violators of law. Street crime can be reduced by many techniques.

*Crime
Prevention
and the Police*

Among these, what has come to be known as environmental defense appears to offer the greatest promise (Jeffery, 1977; Newman, 1972; Reppetto, 1974).

The primary trend in the field of police has been toward greater professionalization. Police nowadays are more frequently college trained, and on the police staffs of larger cities there are psychologists, attorneys, and other specialists. The American police have become extremely sensitive to problems of an ethnic and racial character, and where once it was rare to find members of racial minority groups on police staffs, it has become relatively rare to find large staffs on which they are unrepresented (although they are still frequently underrepresented). A continuing debate rages as to whether police in largely ghettoized cities should be of the same ethnic and racial origin as those dominant in the areas in which they work. Individual instances of police corruption and brutality continue to be exposed and highly publicized, but as an institutionalized practice, both racial hostility and brutality are not condoned, and are in fact condemned.

Some have raised the point that the police are now "handcuffed," their investigations are hindered, and handling of hardened criminals with deference is hardly in the best interests of community and society. Whatever merit these arguments may have in defense of harsh treatment in prison (and we do not believe they have much), it must be remembered that a suspect is only that—an accused—when in the hands of the police, and should be accorded all courtesies and rights of anyone presumed to be innocent. It may be that he was caught red-handed, that the presumption is thus only a technicality for courtroom purposes, and that if roughness is required in order to discover the whereabouts of confederates or other such information, the protection of society seems to justify its use. However, history, worldwide and specifically American, attests to the unfortunate repercussions of such a policy: brutality cannot be effectively contained, and discretion cannot be given to an interrogator to use improper methods when he is certain the suspect is guilty without finding the courts deluged with confessions that will later be denied and that sometimes are indubitably false.

Police-community relations were strained during the 1960s, when many young people with alternate life-styles, blacks and their allies in the civil rights movement, antiwar demonstrators, and others identified the police as enemies and used the term "pig" to describe the police officer. Community relations with police, which sometimes were set back by a single instance of unprovoked killing by a police officer, have nevertheless become progressively better. However, police probably will continue to be a target of criticism and hostility in the years ahead; the major reason for this may be the continued high crime rate. While more police—and better deployment of them—can assist in preventing and deterring crime and making arrests, police cannot solve problems of unemployment, disaffection with society, lesser adherence to a code of morality, or even better intergroup relations.

The current shift in attention to technological crime prevention is hardly likely to bring startling results. Only rarely is there developed, in order to overcome a type of crime, improved technology that cannot be matched by criminals. One of the exceptions occurred when the large cities of the United States were faced with an outbreak of rifling of public telephones; engineers were able to design and install new types of phones extremely resistant to such criminal endeavor. It is unlikely that our homes and streets could be given similar protection to make them virtually crimeproof, although some reduction in crime can be effected by lighting, sophisticated locks, and other prudent devices.

In short, more and better police and crime-prevention measures may save some lives and avert some illegal activity, but can hardly be the panacea the public is seeking.

Trends in Criminal Justice

The United States seems to be moving in the direction of national uniformity in its penal codes and procedures for administration of justice. Greater geographic mobility and ease of transportation and communication have reduced regional variations, although this does not mean that there is a homogenized national culture, for huge differences exist between urban and rural regions, ethnic-racial groups, and social classes.

While it is extremely unlikely that state penal codes will disappear to be replaced by federal criminal law, it is very likely that the state codes will come to resemble one another more and more in the years ahead. This is occurring not only through the influence of the American Law Institute and its Model Penal Code (1962) and through many decisions of the U.S. Supreme Court involving rights of the accused; it occurs even more significantly in the subtle, undramatic, often unnoticed ways in which a law becomes obsolete or is declared unconstitutional in a state appellate court and the issue is not further appealed. The forces calling for change in sentencing procedures, for example, are national in character, and in all likelihood the pressures for such change will be felt in every state (although not all fifty states will fall into exactly the same line). With halting steps and occasional setbacks, criminal justice has been proceeding toward national homogenization, and although it is improbable that it will ever reach the stage of complete uniformity throughout the United States—perhaps many would oppose such an eventuality—there will doubtless be an approach to national unity close enough for the formerly great disparities of definition, sentencing, and courtroom procedure to be noticeably diminished.

The U.S. Supreme Court, during the period from 1953 to 1969 when Earl Warren was chief justice, saw a revolution in the administration of criminal justice, although the roots of that revolution can be seen as early as the 1930s. With the almost complete nationalization of the Bill of Rights and the disappearance of effective opposition to federal "interference" in state criminal matters, the developments in criminal justice associated with the Warren Court have probably run their course. In a high-crime period, the public is not in a mood for further steps to be taken toward the protection of the accused; on the contrary, the emphasis has shifted to the rights of the victim. Still the decisions of the Supreme Court since the retirements of Earl Warren, Hugo Black, William Douglas, and other stalwarts who advanced the protection of suspects and defendants, while generally leaning in the direction of a conservative interpretation of the Constitution, have not reverted to the status of criminal justice of a generation or two before, nor is that likely to occur.

The Future of Corrections

In the area of corrections, much debate has raged, little has been resolved. Some proclaim that rehabilitation almost always fails, and point to the high recidivism rates as evidence, if not proof. Others challenge the data and the conclusions, claiming that rehabilitation has never been tried in the United States, and hence all the evaluation studies are spurious. However, even if one concedes that rehabilitation has been a notorious failure and that the word "corrections" is a mockery, it is not entirely clear what policy conclusions should be drawn. Some argue that society should knock down the prison walls because they are useless; others proclaim the opposite, that we should throw away the keys because the inmates, if released, will return to their predatory acts. Neither position appears to be justified. Nor do they exhaust the suggestions. There are calls for greater employment and other opportunities for ex-convicts; for more parole supervision; in the opposite direction, for the complete abolition of parole, so that once the gates are opened the inmate goes out a free man.

A few directions seem to be making themselves felt in corrections, ideas around which there has assembled a considerable consensus of scholars and practitioners otherwise often in disagreement. These strands, which we believe will be the center of interest and will be effectuated (or at least experimented with) during the next decades, include the following:

1. A greatly diminished use of indeterminate sentences, if not their complete elimination, is a likely trend. The indeterminate sentence—for example, "one to five years" or even, as occurred until recently in California, "one day to life"—is largely discredited. It is now widely agreed that in effect it gave the true sentencing ability to a parole board, usually consisting of people ill equipped to handle this job. The poor training of parole board members and the political nature of their appointment, without regard to ability, can of course be corrected, although not as easily as the replacement of ill-trained or prejudiced judges. The members of a parole board can usually have little knowledge of an individual case, although they might have a voluminous file on it, for they do not have sufficient time to give to each case, as the judge did when the original trial took place. It has sometimes been charged that parole boards have systematically discriminated against racial and ethnic minorities, sex offenders, and others, in addition to more subtle discriminatory practices favoring convicts with jobs and families awaiting them. The indeterminate sentence was supposedly based upon the concept of rehabilitation: to keep a person in prison until he showed signs that he was no longer "a menace to society." In practice, it did not mean rehabilitation or even any effort in that direction but rather taught the prisoner to assume an obsequious and sycophantic stance before corrections personnel, to give the answers that such personnel want to hear, and to become a master at pretending to be "corrected."

2. There may be an increased number of people sent to prison upon being found guilty (or pleading guilty), and less use of probation and suspended

sentence. This may include white-collar offenders, women, middle- and upper-class white offenders, youthful offenders—in fact, almost all categories except the older. All of these groups have received favored treatment in the past, except for whites from privileged backgrounds who were war resisters during the Vietnamese conflict and a few who were treated severely as a result of "drug busts."

3. Despite the above, it appears that there will not be large increases in the prison population during the coming decades. This is because of the generally shorter sentences being handed down (with some highly publicized extremely long sentences as well). Experiments with work release, shock sentences, shock probation, school release, sentences served only on weekends so that the prisoner can retain a job, or only during the week so that he can be at home on Saturday and Sunday with his family, will continue to be made. However, these are usually isolated instances and seldom have an impact on the corrections system as a whole.

4. The movement toward humanization of prisons—with establishment of sanitary conditions, protection of the young and weak from the more powerful, protection from sexual assault, and changes in prison architecture so that maximum security can be achieved without maximum grimness—will continue, despite cynical remarks from critics and politicians about prisons being country clubs and inmates being treated better than their victims.[2]

5. The most important single movement in the field of corrections will probably be the involvement of the community, but it is hardly likely that this will embrace anything but juvenile offenses of a less than heinous nature and extremely minor adult offenses.

Victimology: The New Subdiscipline

Study of the victim has emerged as one of the most important developments in criminology during the past decade, and it is likely to continue to be the center of much attention in research, conferences, books, journals, and investigations. Actually, there are two approaches to the victim: some argue that there are many types of victims—victims of war, natural disasters, maiming illnesses, political harassment by government, and crime, so that criminal victims are only one sector of a much broader phenomenon that might be called "victimity." Others see little logic in putting such disparate groups into a single category, and see victims of crime as a special area of study within the larger field of criminology. Whatever may be the merits of the first approach, it is the second that interests criminologists.

Victimology has often been attacked by laymen on the ground that a focus on traits, characteristics, and activities of victims tends to shift attention and even blame from the perpetrator to the entirely innocent. While this was probably never the intention of the pioneers in victimology, it is inherent in some of the work that has emanated from this field.

Study of victims can make essentially three contributions to an understanding of crime:

1. It can assist in the correction of statistical errors, particularly those derived from the dark figure of unreported crime (see Chapter 2). This does

---

2. U.S. Code 42, Section 1983, will be used increasingly to force correctional administrators to ensure constitutionally adequate prison conditions and practices.

not mean that statistical corrections from victimization surveys allow us to believe that the new figures are extremely accurate, for there are still pitfalls—victims can overreport in order to please the interviewer, misunderstand the nature of the offense, lie in order to collect insurance or compensation, or fail to place an event in the proper time period (a crucial error for statistical purposes). Nor do these failings exhaust the problems with victims' reports on the incidence and frequency of crime. Nevertheless, the contribution that these reports make to the statistics of law-breaking is valuable and will no doubt continue to be pursued in the future.

2. Victimology can uncover information that will enable people to be more prudent because of increased knowledge about the likely targets of criminals. Police and other protective resources can be better deployed to protect the most probable victims. This does not assume that the victims are responsible for being female or elderly, for example, but only if more is known about them, they can be better protected. In that sense, victimology may be one of the most useful criminological tools for the development of social policy.

3. Victimology can focus on certain crimes (of which homicide and assault are probably the major examples) in which the victim makes a contribution to the crime itself. For this, Marvin Wolfgang (1958) has coined the expression "victim-precipitated crime." Precipitation is quite different from proneness. In precipitation all parties in the event are culpable, although not necessarily to an equal degree; in proneness there is vulnerability, without necessarily implying contributory responsibility.

Criminology: Two Perspectives

One of the bifurcations among criminologists that has occurred during our high-crime era has manifested itself in the emergence of the so-called "hardliners" and of the "fight-back" movement of their opponents. James Q. Wilson (1975) is probably the foremost spokesman in the world of scholarship for the concept that the answer to the crime problem is more and stricter police enforcement, greater vigilance in the apprehension of offenders, more vigorous prosecution, and unsentimental willingness to imprison. He is joined in this approach by Ernest van den Haag (1975). Others, including but not limited to scholars with a generally critical and radical view toward society, believe that the hard line has been tried before and has failed, that the answer is not more prisons and prisoners but rather a frontal attack on the criminogenic factors in society.

The two views are not irreconcilable, although the primary emphasis obviously cannot be placed on both at the same time. Certainly Wilson does not deny that ameliorative social change toward the diminution of inequality and toward offering greater job training, more job opportunities, and better housing and schooling, are desirable, although how much they would contribute toward diminishing crime is disputable and speculative. At the same time, Edwin Schur (1967), Richard Quinney (1970), and others who place great emphasis on the social origins of crime do not deny that some defense of potential victims is necessary, and that when all else fails, this must include such measures as incarceration of convicted offenders.

The difference between the two schools of thought is delineated by the emphasis of the hard liners on prevention of crime and control of criminals, and of the liberal-radical wing on prevention of crime and justice for the suspect. There can, of course, be a strong effort to control and punish criminals while at the same time fiercely defending the rights of all suspects (some of whom no doubt are criminals). This position, which seems to be embraced by Marvin Wolfgang (1979) among others, is not a straddling one but rather is grounded in the belief that the two efforts can be complementary.

It is possible that criminology—which in its purest form is involved with the accumulation of scientific knowledge and not the formation of policy—will nonetheless be drawn into policy-making to a greater extent in the future, for policy implications are present in the theoretical orientations. The hard-line versus social-amelioration dispute will no doubt continue to rage, but it is likely that criminology will see an interweaving of these two strands —that indeed the twain shall meet.

A Task To Be Performed

The student who pursues a field of specialization in criminology has an exciting career ahead. It is unfortunate for society that such a career will not prove needless because of the disappearance of crime as a grave problem. We find it axiomatic that, where problems exist, knowledge rather than ignorance can serve as a guide for action. It is the accumulation of such knowledge that criminology pursues. Those engaged in this study in the decades ahead will, in adding to our knowledge, be faced with great challenges, and in meeting them may contribute to the alleviation of some severe social ills and personal suffering.

References for Part VI

ADLER, FREDA. *Sisters in Crime: The Rise of the New Female Criminal.* New York: McGraw-Hill, 1975.

AMERICAN LAW INSTITUTE. *Model Penal Code.* Philadelphia: American Law Institute, 1962.

BONGER, WILLEM A. *Criminality and Economic Conditions.* New York: Agathon Press, 1967.

FRANKLIN, H. BRUCE. *The Victim as Criminal and Artist: Literature from the American Prison.* New York: Oxford University Press, 1978.

HOOTON, EARNEST A. *Crime and the Man.* Cambridge, Mass.: Harvard University Press, 1939.

JEFFERY, C. RAY. *Crime Prevention through Environmental Design.* Beverly Hills, Calif.: Sage Publications, 1977.

MEDNICK, SARNOFF, and KARL O. CHRISTIANSEN, eds. *Biosocial Bases of Criminal Behavior.* New York: Gardner Press, 1977.

MEIER, ROBERT F. "The New Criminology: Continuity in Criminological Theory." *Journal of Criminal Law and Criminology,* 1976, 67: 461–469.

MERTON, ROBERT K. "Social Structure and Anomie." *American Sociological Review,* 1938, 3: 672–682. Republished in Merton, *Social Theory and Social Structure,* rev. ed., New York: Free Press, 1957.

_____. "The Ambivalences of Le Bon's *The Crowd*." In Gustave Le Bon, *The Crowd: A Study of the Popular Mind*, p. v–xxxix. New York: Viking, 1960.

NEWMAN, OSCAR. *Defensible Space*. New York: Macmillan, 1972.

NICOLAUS, MARTIN. "The Professional Organization of Sociology: A View from Below." *Antioch Review*, 1969, 29: 375–387.

QUINNEY, RICHARD. *The Social Reality of Crime*. Boston: Little, Brown, 1970.

REPPETTO, THOMAS A. *Residential Crime*. Cambridge, Mass.: Ballinger, 1974.

SCHUR, EDWIN M. *Our Criminal Society: The Social and Legal Sources of Crime in America*. Englewood Cliffs, N.J.: Prentice-Hall, 1967.

SELLIN, THORSTEN. *Culture Conflict and Crime*. Bulletin No. 41. Social Science Research Council, 1938.

SIMON, RITA JAMES. *Women and Crime*. Lexington, Mass.: Lexington Books, 1975.

TAYLOR, IAN, PAUL WALTON, and JOCK YOUNG. *The New Criminology: For a Social Theory of Deviance*. New York: Harper & Row, 1974.

TITTLE, CHARLES R., "Labelling and Crime: An Empirical Evaluation." In Walter Gove, ed., *The Labelling of Deviance: Evaluating a Perspective*, pp. 241–270. 2d ed., Beverly Hills, Calif.: Sage Publications, 1980.

TURK, AUSTIN T. *Criminality and Legal Order*. Chicago: Rand McNally, 1969.

VAN DEN HAAG, ERNEST. *Punishing Criminals*. New York: Basic Books, 1975.

VOLD, GEORGE B. *Theoretical Criminology*. New York: Oxford University Press, 1958. Rev. ed., revised by Thomas J. Bernard, 1979.

WILSON, JAMES Q. *Thinking About Crime*. New York: Basic Books, 1975.

WOLFGANG, MARVIN E. *Patterns in Criminal Homicide*. Philadelphia: University of Pennsylvania Press, 1958.

_____. "Change and Stability in Criminal Justice." In Edward Sagarin, ed., *Criminology: New Concerns—Essays in Honor of Hans Mattick*, pp. 61–72. Beverly Hills, Calif.: Sage Publications, 1979.

WOLFGANG, MARVIN E., and FRANCO FERRACUTI. *The Subculture of Violence: Towards an Integrated Theory in Criminology*. London: Tavistock, 1967.

Name Index

441

Subject Index